FROMMER'S
EasyGuide
TO
TOKYO, KYOTO & WESTERN HONSHU

By
Beth Reiber

Easy Guides are ✦ **Quick To Read** ✦ **Light To Carry**
✦ **For Expert Advice** ✦ **In All Price Ranges**

Frommer~~Media~~ LC

Published by
FROMMER MEDIA LLC

Copyright © 2015 by Frommer Media LLC. All rights reserved. No part of this publication may be repro-
duced, stored in a retrieval system, or transmitted in any form or by any means, electronic, mechanical,
photocopying, recording, scanning or otherwise, except as permitted under Sections 107 or 108 of the
1976 United States Copyright Act, without the prior written permission of the Publisher. Requests to the
Publisher for permission should be addressed to the support@frommermedia.com.

Frommer's is a registered trademark of Arthur Frommer. Frommer Media LLC is not associated with any
product or vendor mentioned in this book.

ISBN 978-1-62887-166-1 (paper), 978-1-62887-167-8 (e-book)

Editorial Director: Pauline Frommer
Editor: Arthur Frommer
Production Editor: Heather Wilcox
Cartographer: Roberta Stockwell
Cover Design: Howard Grossman

For information on our other products or services, see www.frommers.com.

Frommer Media LLC also publishes its books in a variety of electronic formats. Some content that
appears in print may not be available in electronic formats.

Manufactured in the United States of America

5 4 3 2

FROMMER'S STAR RATINGS SYSTEM

Every hotel, restaurant, and attraction listed in this guide has been ranked for quality and value. Here's
what the stars mean:

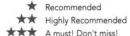

★ Recommended
★★ Highly Recommended
★★★ A must! Don't miss!

AN IMPORTANT NOTE

The world is a dynamic place. Hotels change ownership, restaurants hike their prices, museums
alter their opening hours, and busses and trains change their routings. And all of this can occur
in the several months after our authors have visited, inspected, and written about, these hotels,
restaurants, museums and transportation services. Though we have made valiant efforts to keep
all our information fresh and up-to-date, some few changes can inevitably occur in the periods
before a revised edition of this guidebook is published. So please bear with us if a tiny number
of the details in this book have changed. Please also note that we have no responsibility or liabil-
ity for any inaccuracy or errors or omissions, or for inconvenience, loss, damage, or expenses suffered by anyone as a result of assertions in this guide.

CONTENTS

ABOUT THE AUTHOR

Beth Reiber's career as a full-time travel writer has spanned more than three decades and has included 4 years living in Germany and 3 years in Japan. The author of eight guidebooks, she has been writing Frommer's guides to Japan and Tokyo for more than 30 years. Since 2009, she has been a "Visit Japan Ambassador," an honorary title awarded by the Japanese government for her contributions in promoting travel in Japan.

ABOUT THE FROMMER'S TRAVEL GUIDES

For most of the past 50 years, Frommer's has been the leading series of travel guides in North America, accounting for as many as 24% of all guidebooks sold. I think I know why.

Although we hope our books are entertaining, we nevertheless deal with travel in a serious fashion. Our guidebooks have never looked on such journeys as a mere recreation, but as a far more important human function, a time of learning and introspection, an essential part of a civilized life. We stress the culture, lifestyle, history, and beliefs of the destinations we cover and urge our readers to seek out people and new ideas as the chief rewards of travel.

We have never shied from controversy. We have, from the beginning, encouraged our authors to be intensely judgmental, critical—both pro and con—in their comments, and wholly independent. Our only clients are our readers, and we have triggered the ire of countless prominent sorts, from a tourist newspaper we called "practically worthless" (it unsuccessfully sued us) to the many rip-offs we've condemned.

And because we believe that travel should be available to everyone regardless of their incomes, we have always been cost-conscious at every level of expenditure. Although we have broadened our recommendations beyond the budget category, we insist that every lodging we include be sensibly priced. We use every form of media to assist our readers and are particularly proud of our feisty daily website, the award-winning Frommers.com.

I have high hopes for the future of Frommer's. May these guidebooks, in all the years ahead, continue to reflect the joy of travel and the freedom that travel represents. May they always pursue a cost-conscious path, so that people of all incomes can enjoy the rewards of travel. And may they create, for both the traveler and the persons among whom we travel, a community of friends, where all human beings live in harmony and peace.

Arthur Frommer

THE BEST OF TOKYO, KYOTO & WESTERN HONSHU

Japan is a stunning travel experience, a nation modern and dynamic and yet historic and deeply cultural. It fascinates every kind of visitor, from digital engineers to theater buffs engrossed in *kabuki,* from naturalists enchanted by the country's awesome mountain scenery to lovers of sushi and sashimi, or Japanese gardens and hot-spring spas. And it provides the greatest number of its rewards on its largest and most heavily populated island, Honshu, whose western half includes Tokyo, Kyoto, Hiroshima, and many other captivating and trend-setting towns. In this book, I supplement descriptions of Tokyo and Kyoto with other highlights of western Honshu. And to begin our journey, I've compiled a list of what I consider the best Japan has to offer, based on years of traveling through the country. From the weird to the wonderful, the profound to the profane, the obvious to the obscure, these recommendations should fire your imagination and launch you toward discoveries of your own.

THE best AUTHENTIC EXPERIENCES

- **Feeling the Adrenalin Rush of Tokyo:** Tokyo is Japan's showcase for all that's high tech, sophisticated, zany, and avant-garde, making this a must-see for just about everyone. Seeing main sights, such as the Tokyo National Museum and Sensoji Temple, tops the list, but wandering the metropolis's many neighborhoods adds a totally new dimension to the Tokyo experience. See chapters 4 and 5.
- **Living the Past in Kyoto:** If you see only one city in Japan, Kyoto should be it. Japan's capital from 794 to 1868, Kyoto boasts some of the country's best temples, imperial villas,

Japanese-style inns, traditional restaurants, shops, and gardens. It's also one of the country's most beautiful cities. See chapter 8.

o **Making a Pilgrimage to a Temple or Shrine:** From mountaintop Buddhist temples to neighborhood Shinto shrines, Japan's religious structures rank among the nation's most popular attractions. They're often visited for specific reasons: Couples wishing for a happy marriage, for example, head to Kyoto's **Jishu Shrine** (p. 244), devoted to the deity of love.

o **Taking a Communal Hot-Spring Bath:** No other people on earth bathe as enthusiastically, as frequently, and for such duration as the Japanese. Their many hot-spring baths—thought to cure all sorts of ailments as well as simply make you feel good—range from elegant, Zen-like affairs to rustic outdoor baths with views of the countryside. See "Bathing," in chapter 2.

o **Riding the Shinkansen Bullet Train:** One of the world's fastest trains whips you across the countryside at up to 300km (187 miles) an hour as you relax, see Japan's rural countryside, and dine on boxed meals filled with local specialties. See "Getting Around Japan," in chapter 12.

o **Strolling Through a Japanese Garden:** Most of Japan's famous gardens are relics of the Edo Period, when the shogun, *daimyo* (feudal lords), imperial family, and even samurai and Buddhist priests developed private gardens for their own viewing pleasure. The garden at **Katsura Imperial Villa** (p. 249) in Kyoto is, in my view, Japan's most beautiful, but other personal favorites are **Rikugien** in Tokyo (p. 128), **Kenrokuen** in Kanazawa (p. 185), and several in Kyoto, including Ryoanji Temple's rock garden and those at the Golden and Silver Pavilions (see chapter 8).

o **Watching the Fat Guys Wrestle:** There's nothing quite like watching two monstrous sumo wrestlers square off, bluff, and grapple as they attempt to throw each other on the ground or out of the ring. Both Tokyo and Osaka have annual 15-day tournaments, but even if you can't attend one, you can watch them on TV. For more information, see "Sumo," in chapter 2, and "Spectator Sports," in chapter 5.

o **Staying in a Ryokan:** Japan's legendary service reigns supreme in a top-class *ryokan,* a traditional Japanese inn. You'll bathe in a Japanese tub or hot-spring bath, feast your eyes on lovely views past *shoji* screens, dine like a king in your *tatami* room, and sleep on a futon. See "Tips on Accommodations," in chapter 2.

o **Attending a Kabuki Play:** Based on universal themes and designed to appeal to the masses, *kabuki* plays are extravaganzas of theatrical displays, costumes, and scenes—but mostly they're just plain fun. See "Japanese Arts in a Nutshell," in chapter 2, and the *kabuki* section of "Tokyo After Dark," in chapter 5.

o **Shopping in a Department Store:** Japanese department stores are microcosms of practically everything Japan produces, from the food halls in the basement to the many floors selling clothing, accessories, office supplies, souvenirs, pottery, household goods, and even rooftop garden centers.

What's more, service is great, and purchases are beautifully wrapped. If you arrive when the store opens, staff will be lined up at the front door to bow as you enter. You'll be spoiled for life.

THE best HOTELS & INNS

- **Most Famous Setting: Park Hyatt Tokyo** (Tokyo): Occupying the 39th to 52nd floors of a skyscraper designed by Kenzo Tange, this gorgeous property offers stunning views of the city, one of Tokyo's hottest restaurants, rooms you could live in, and legendary service. No wonder it has many imitators and was featured in *Lost in Translation.* See p. 80.

- **Best Views Without Spending a Fortune: Park Hotel Tokyo** (Tokyo): With a great location near the Ginza, a light-filled lobby filled with art, and rooms with outstanding views (including some designed by Japanese artists), this contemporary high-rise hotel delivers plenty but doesn't break the bank. See p. 75.

- **Best Historic Hotel: The Fujiya Hotel** (Hakone): Established in 1878 and nestled on a wooded hillside, the Fujiya is one of Japan's oldest, grandest, and most majestic Western-style hotels. Resembling a Japanese *ryokan* from the outside, it boasts a comfortable interior of detailed woodwork; old-fashioned, antiques-filled guest rooms; a delightful 1930s dining hall; hot-spring baths; and extensive landscaping. A stay here makes you feel as though you've traveled not just to Hakone but to another century. See p. 176.

- **Best Japanese Inn Experience: Hiiragiya Ryokan** (Kyoto): If ever there was an example of the quintessential *ryokan,* Hiiragiya is it. Located in the heart of old Kyoto, it's the ultimate in *tatami* luxury: a dignified enclave of polished wood and rooms with antique furnishings overlooking private gardens. Six generations of the same family have provided impeccable service here since 1861. See p. 216.

- **Best Inexpensive Japanese Inn: Homeikan** (Tokyo): This is my top pick for an affordable, authentic Japanese inn in the capital. Rooms do not have private bathrooms, but pluses include a Japanese garden, nice public baths, and detailed *tatami* rooms with traditional architectural features. See p. 79.

- **Best Youth Hostel: Kyoto Utano Youth Hostel** (Kyoto): With a lovely lodgelike atmosphere, free nightly events, and rooms ranging from twins to dorms, this is certainly Japan's most attractive youth hostel. See p. 224.

- **Best Contemporary Digs: Osaka Marriott Miyako Hotel** (Osaka): Opened in 2014 in Japan's tallest building, this is the most unhotel-like hotel I've seen in Japan, where the emphasis is clearly on the views and the experience, whether it's gazing at the horizon or celebrating at the 57th-floor restaurant. See p. 273.

- **Best Rural Experience: Staying at a Minshuku in Shirakawa-go:** Nestled in the Japan Alps, Shirakawa-go is a narrow valley of paddies, irrigation canals, and 200-year-old thatched farmhouses, several of which offer simple *tatami* accommodations and meals featuring local cuisine. This is a great, inexpensive escape. See chapter 7.

o **Best Temple Stay: Mount Koya:** If your vision of Japan includes temples, towering cypress trees, shaven-headed monks, and religious chanting at the crack of dawn, head for the religious sanctuary atop Mount Koya, where some 50 Buddhist temples offer *tatami* accommodations and two vegetarian meals a day. See chapter 10.

o **Best Backpacker Hostel: Cuore Kurashiki** (Kurashiki): Virtually nonexistent a decade ago, inexpensive guesthouses can now be found virtually everywhere. This one, opened in 2014, proves just how far hostels have come, offering a hip lounge/restaurant complete with hammocks and private rooms in addition to dormitory rooms (including two just for women). See p. 302.

THE best FOOD & DRINK EXPERIENCES

o **Experiencing a Kaiseki Feast:** The ultimate in Japanese cuisine, *kaiseki* is a feast for the senses and spirit. Consisting of a variety of exquisitely prepared and arranged dishes, a *kaiseki* is a multicourse meal consisting of seasonal ingredients served on complementing tableware. There are hundreds of exceptional *kaiseki* restaurants in Japan, from old-world traditional to sleek modern. Traditional *ryokan* also serve *kaiseki*. See "Eating & Drinking in Japan," in chapter 2.

o **Rubbing Elbows in an Izakaya:** *Izakaya* are pubs in Japan—usually tiny affairs with just a counter, serving up skewered grilled chicken, fish, and other fare. They're good places to meet the natives and are inexpensive as well. You'll find them in every nightlife district in the country.

o **Dining on Western Food in a Memorable Setting:** The **New York Grill** (p. 93) epitomizes the best of the West with its sophisticated setting, spectacular Tokyo views, and great food. In Kyoto, personal favorites include **Misoguigawa** (p. 228), serving French *kaiseki* in a former teahouse and with an open-air pavilion in summer, and the **Sodoh** (p. 235), an Italian restaurant in a 1929 villa.

o **Listening to the Shamisen at Waentei-Kikko** (Tokyo): Just steps away from bustling Sensoji Temple, this charming restaurant in a rustic farmhouse offers *kaiseki* and bento meals and live shamisen performances. See p. 90.

o **Getting Healthy with Buddhist Vegetarian Cuisine:** Mount Koya's temple lodgings (see chapter 10) are among the most memorable places to dine like a monk, but I also like **Kotobuki-Ya** (p. 184), which occupies a 170-year-old merchant's house in Kanazawa, and **Kakusho** (p. 199), offering *kaiseki shojin-ryori* in a historic setting with views of a garden.

o **Slurping Noodles in a Noodle Shop:** You're supposed to slurp when eating Japanese noodles, which are prepared in almost as many different ways as there are regions. Noodle shops range from stand-up counters to traditional restaurants.

o **Making a Meal of Tofu:** You may have had tofu before, but you've never had it like this. **Tokyo Shiba Toufuya Ukai** (p. 101) specializes in tofu prepared many different ways, in a restaurant surrounded by a garden. Elsewhere, Nikko is famous for *yuba,* delicate layers formed by boiling soymilk (see chapter 6), while Kyoto restaurants offer *yudofu,* a one-pot stew with tofu and vegetables (see chapter 8).

o **Feeling Adventuresome in the Hinterlands:** Virtually every region in Japan has its own local specialties, from oysters in Hiroshima to mountain vegetables in Takayama to Kobe's famous beef. You can even enjoy local specialties by ordering regional box lunches on the Shinkansen bullet train. See individual chapters.

THE best FREE THINGS TO DO

o **Sitting Pretty Above Tokyo:** On the 45th floor of the Tokyo Metropolitan Government Office (TMG), designed by well-known architect Kenzo Tange, this observatory offers a bird's-eye view of the never-ending metropolis and, on fine winter days, Mount Fuji. See p. 122.

o **Joining a Free Guided Tour:** English-speaking volunteers lead free tours at many of Japan's iconic landmarks, including the Asakusa and Ueno areas in Tokyo, Nara Park, Kanazawa Castle Park, and Himeji Castle. See individual chapters.

o **Browsing the Electronics & Anime Shops of Akihabara:** Even if you don't buy anything, it's great fun—and very educational—to see the latest in electronic gadgetry in Japan's largest electronics district. In recent years, shops specializing in *manga* (Japanese comic books and graphic novels) and *anime* (Japanese animation) have also opened, along with so-called maid cafes. See p. 133 and 138.

o **Joining the Crowds at a Festival:** With Shintoism and Buddhism as its major religions, and temples and shrines virtually everywhere, Japan abounds in festivals. Celebrations range from those featuring horseback archery to parades of huge fake phalluses; you may want to plan your trip around one (and book early for a hotel). See "Calendar of Events," in chapter 2.

o **Walking to Kobo Daishi's Mausoleum on Mount Koya:** Since the 9th century, when Buddhist leader Kobo Daishi was laid to rest at Okunoin on Mount Koya, his faithful followers have followed him to their graves—and now tomb after tomb lines a 1.5km (1-mile) pathway to Daishi's mausoleum. Cypress trees, moss-covered stone lanterns, and thousands upon thousands of tombs make this the most impressive graveyard stroll in Japan, especially at night. See chapter 10.

- **Visiting a Local Market:** Tokyo's Tsukiji Fish Market is Japan's largest, but there are local seafood and produce markets virtually everywhere. Those in Kyoto, Kanazawa, and Takayama are among my favorites. See p. 259, 189, and 200.
- **Viewing the Cherry Blossoms:** Nothing symbolizes the approach of spring so vividly to Japanese as the appearance of the cherry blossoms—and nothing so amazes visitors as the way Japanese gather under the blossoms to celebrate the season with food, drink, and dance. See "Calendar of Events," in chapter 2, for cherry-blossom details.

THE best FOR FAMILIES

- **Joining the Throngs at Sensoji Temple:** Tokyo's oldest temple is also its liveliest, with throngs of visitors and stalls selling both traditional and kitschy items, giving it a festival-like atmosphere every day of the year. There's enough excitement to keep everyone entertained, but top it off with a stop at nearby **Hanayashiki amusement park** for its old-fashioned kiddie rides. See p. 115.
- **Learning History at the Edo-Tokyo Museum:** Housed in a high-tech modern building, this ambitious museum chronicles the fascinating and somewhat tumultuous history of Tokyo (known as Edo during the Feudal Era) with models, replicas, artifacts, and dioramas. Not only can children climb into a palanquin and a rickshaw, but volunteers stand ready to give free guided tours in English. See p. 127.
- **Traveling in Hakone:** With its mountain railway, cable car, ropeway, and sightseeing boat outfitted like a pirate ship, this circuitous route through scenic Hakone is a great excursion for families. The best place to stay? The historic **Fujiya Hotel,** hands down my favorite hotel in Japan. See p. 176.
- **Spending a Sunday in a Local Park:** Parks are popular Sunday destinations for families with kids and young couples on dates, making for great people-watching and a restorative afternoon. Among my favorites: **Ueno Park** and **Yoyogi Park** in Tokyo and the extensive park surrounding **Osaka Castle.** See p. 115 and 277.
- **Seeing Fish Eye-to-Eye in an Aquarium:** Because Japan is surrounded by sea, it's no surprise that it has more than its share of aquariums, many with innovative displays that put you eye-to-eye with the creatures of the deep. Among the best is the **Osaka Aquarium** (p. 279).
- **Hanging Out in Harajuku:** If you have teenagers, nothing beats a day in teenybopper heaven with its many clothing and accessory stores lining narrow streets packed with a never-ending flow of humanity. Lots of restaurants are geared to the younger generation, too, in this vibrant Tokyo neighborhood, but for a bit of culture (and quietude), head to nearby **Meiji Shrine,** enveloped in woods.
- **Exploring a Japanese Castle:** The past comes alive when you tromp the many wooden stairs in a Japanese castle, gaze upon samurai helmets and

gear (and even try them on), and pretend you're the feudal lord viewing his domain from the keep's top floor. **Himeji Castle** (p. 296) is Japan's most famous, but even **Osaka Castle** (p. 277) and **Hiroshima Castle** (p. 316), both resurrected after being destroyed during World War II, are impressive and contain good museums.

o **Cycling Through History in the Kibiji District:** Just a short train ride from Kurashiki is the ancient Kibiji District, where you can rent bicycles and cycle your way past ancient burial mounds, temples, and paddies on a marked trail. See p. 305.

o **Feeding the Deer:** Deer, considered divine messengers, roam freely in Nara Park and on the island of Miyajima. But they're just the bonus to seeing World Heritage Sites at both of these destinations. See chapters 9 and 10.

THE best NEIGHBORHOODS

o **Asakusa** (Tokyo): Asakusa is the best place to experience Tokyo's old downtown, with its popular Sensoji Temple, Nakamise shopping lane with crafts and kitsch, and casual traditional restaurants. As in days of yore, arrive by boat on the Sumida River. See chapters 4 and 5.

o **Ni-Chome** (Tokyo): With its 300 bars, dance clubs, shops, and other establishments, Ni-Chome is Japan's largest gay nightlife district and boasts the country's liveliest street scene. Many bars are accepting to people of all persuasions. See chapter 5.

o **Higashiyama-ku District:** Kyoto's eastern sector is a lovely combination of wooded hills, temples, shrines, museums, shops, and traditional restaurants, making it one of the best neighborhoods in Japan for a stroll. See "A Stroll Through Higashiyama-ku," in chapter 8.

o **Sanmachi District in Takayama:** Nicknamed "Little Kyoto" of the **Hida Mountains,** Takayama has a downtown lined with traditional wooden buildings and shops, a morning market, Japanese inns, and a wealth of museums. For a more rural setting, Takayama's Higashiyama Walking Course is a hiking path that leads past temples and shrines and provides a different perspective on the city. See chapter 7.

o **Bikan Historic Quarter** (Kurashiki): With its willow-fringed canal and black-and-white old granaries, the historic district of this former merchant town is a photographer's dream. See chapter 11.

JAPAN IN CONTEXT

2

Hardly a day goes by that you don't hear something about Japan, whether the subject is travel, traditional Japanese cuisine (placed on UNESCO's Intangible Cultural Heritage list in 2013), the arts, *anime,* the upcoming 2020 Olympics in Tokyo, or on-going clean-up efforts of the 2011 Great East Japan Earthquake. Yet Japan remains something of an enigma to people in the Western world. What best describes this Asian nation? Is it the giant producer of cars and robots? Or is it still the land of geisha and bonsai, the punctilious tea ceremony, and the delicate art of flower arrangement? Has it become, in its outlook and popular culture, a country more Western than Asian? Or has it retained its unique ancient traditions while forging a central place in the contemporary post-industrialized world?

In fact, Japan has long adopted the best of the West (and the East, for that matter) and then adapted it to its own needs. Its cities may look Westernized—often disappointingly so—but beyond first impressions, there's very little about this Asian nation that could lull you into thinking you're in the West. Japan also differs greatly from its Asian neighbors, mostly because the island remained steadfastly isolated from the rest of the world throughout much of its history, usually deliberately so.

Thus, that modern high-rise may look Western, but it may contain a rustic-looking restaurant with open charcoal grills, corporate offices, a pachinko parlor, a high-tech bar with surreal city views, a McDonald's, an acupuncture clinic, a computer showroom, and a rooftop shrine. Because of this unique synthesis of East and West into a culture that is distinctly Japanese, Japan eludes easy definition. Discovering it is like peeling an onion—you uncover one layer only to discover more layers underneath. Thus, no matter how long you stay in Japan, you never stop learning something new about it—and to me that constant discovery is one of the most fascinating aspects of being here. Although there's plenty in Tokyo and Kyoto to keep visitors fully occupied, this guide also introduces a treasure trove of easily reached destinations throughout western Honshu, from mountain-top temples and exquisite inns to hip restaurants and vibrant neighborhoods.

JAPAN TODAY

You can't talk about Japan today without mentioning its biggest earthquake in recorded history, known as the Great East Japan Earthquake, which struck off the Tohoku coast on March 11, 2011. While all the consequences of the triple whammy—earthquake, tsunami, and meltdown of the Fukushima nuclear power plant—may not be entirely evident for years to come, it seems safe to say that for Japan, 3/11 will remain a defining moment in its history and its future.

Although much of Japan, including western Honshu, was not directly affected by the Great East Japan Earthquake, tourism to Japan plummeted following the disaster, dropping from 8.6 million in 2010 to 6.2 in 2011. Since then, however, international tourism to Japan has dramatically increased, with more than 13 million people touring Japan in 2014, the most ever recorded. Almost 8 million of those visitors hailed from China, Taiwan, and South Korea, a figure that has dramatically changed the face of tourism in Japan. Whereas just a decade ago I used to see other Asians (mostly South Koreans) primarily on the southern island of Kyushu, I now see busloads of Asian tourists everywhere, from the narrow streets of Kyoto (sometimes decked out for the day in rented kimonos) to designer shops in Tokyo's fashionable Ginza, plus everywhere in between. North Americans, who are also visiting Japan in record numbers, make up the largest number of long-haul visitors. At least part of the driving force could be the recent fall of the Yen, giving overseas visitors a favorable exchange rate and making Japan more affordable than it's been in years.

The upside of increased tourism to Japan is more information in English and other foreign languages than ever before, from bus schedules to signage, as well as better services and infrastructure to lure and accommodate more visitors, including more frequent runs of rural buses that used to be few and far between, the increase of inexpensive guesthouses, and the expansion of Japan's duty-free allowances to include consumables like alcohol and cosmetics. The downside, of course, is that transportation and accommodations are more crowded than I've ever seen them, especially during peak seasons like spring for cherry blossom viewing and autumn for leaf viewing, which have always been huge draws for Japanese admirers. I expect tourism only to grow in the years ahead, especially since the Japanese government has set a goal of attracting 20 million annual overseas visitors by 2020, when Tokyo will host the summer Olympics.

THE HISTORY OF JAPAN

ANCIENT HISTORY (CA. 30,000 B.C.–A.D. 710) Although the exact origin of Japanese people is unknown, we know the territory of Japan was occupied as early as 30,000 B.C. According to mythology, however, Japan's history began when the sun goddess, Amaterasu, sent one of her descendants down to the island of Kyushu to unify the people of Japan. Unification, however, was not realized until a few generations later when Jimmu, the great-grandson of the goddess's emissary, succeeded in bringing all of the country under his rule. Because of his divine descent, Jimmu became emperor in 660 B.C. (the date is mythical), thus establishing the line from which all of Japan's emperors are said to derive. However mysterious the origin of this imperial dynasty, it is acknowledged as the longest reigning such family in the world.

Legend begins to give way to fact only in the A.D. 4th century, when a family by the name of Yamato succeeded in expanding its kingdom throughout much of the country and set up court in what is now Nara Prefecture. At the core of unification was the Shinto religion. Indigenous to Japan, Shintoism is marked by the worship of natural things (like rivers and foxes) and of the spirits of ancestors, a well as the belief in the emperor's divinity.

Eventually, Yamato (present-day Japan) also began pointing cultural feelers toward its great neighbor to the west, China. In the 6th century, Buddhism, which originated in India, was brought to Japan via China and Korea, followed by the importation of Chinese cultural and scholarly knowledge—including art, architecture, and the use of Chinese written characters. In 604, the prince regent Shotoku, greatly influenced by the teachings of Buddhism and Confucianism and still a beloved figure today, drafted a document calling for political reforms and a constitutional government. By 607, he was sending Japanese scholars to China to study Buddhism, and he started building Buddhist temples, including Shitennoji Temple in what is now Osaka and Horyuji Temple near Nara, the latter said to be the oldest existing wooden structure in the world. Even today, both Buddhism and Shintoism are driving influences in Japanese life.

THE NARA PERIOD (710–84)   Before the 700s, the site of Japan's capital changed every time a new emperor came to the throne. In 710, however, a permanent capital was established at Nara. Although it remained the capital for only 74 years, seven successive emperors ruled from Nara. The period was graced with the expansion of Buddhism and flourishing temple construction throughout the country. Buddhism also inspired the arts, including Buddhist sculpture, metal casting, painting, and lacquerware. It was during this time that Emperor Shomu, the most devout Buddhist among the Nara emperors, ordered the casting of a huge bronze statue of Buddha to be erected in Nara. Known as the Daibutsu, it remains Nara's biggest attraction.

THE HEIAN PERIOD (794–1192)   In 794, the capital was moved to Heiankyo (present-day Kyoto), and, following the example of cities in China, Kyoto was laid out in a grid pattern with broad roads and canals. Heiankyo means "capital of peace and tranquillity," and the Heian Period was a glorious time for aristocratic families, a period of prosperous luxury during which court life reached new artistic heights. Moon viewing became popular. Chinese characters were blended with a new Japanese writing system, allowing

SHRINES & TEMPLES: religion IN JAPAN

The main religions in Japan are Shintoism and Buddhism, and many Japanese consider themselves believers in both. Most Japanese, for example, will marry in a Shinto ceremony, but when they die, they'll have a Buddhist funeral.

A native religion of Japan, **Shintoism** is the worship of ancestors and national heroes, as well as of all natural things–mountains, trees, stars, seas, fire, animals, even vegetables–as the embodiment of *kami* (gods). There are no scriptures in Shintoism, nor any ordained code of morals or ethics. The place of worship in Shintoism is called a *jinja*, or shrine. The most obvious sign of a shrine is its *torii,* an entrance gate, usually of wood, consisting of two tall poles topped with either one or two crossbeams. Another feature common to shrines is a water trough with communal cups, where the Japanese will wash their hands and sometimes rinse out their mouths. Purification and cleanliness are important in Shintoism because they show respect to the gods. At the shrine, worshipers will throw a few coins into a money box, clap their hands twice to get the gods' attention, and then bow their heads and pray for whatever they wish—good health, the safe delivery of a child, or a prosperous year.

Founded in India in the 6th to 5th centuries B.C., **Buddhism** came to Japan in the A.D. 6th century, bringing with it the concept of eternal life. Whereas Shintoists have shrines, Buddhists have temples, called *otera*. Instead of *torii,* temples will often have an entrance gate with a raised doorsill and heavy doors. Temples may also have a cemetery on their grounds (which Shinto shrines never have) as well as a pagoda.

for the first time the flowering of Japanese literature and poetry. The life of the times was captured in works by two women: Sei Shonagon, who wrote a collection of impressions of her life at court known as the *Pillow Book;* and Murasaki Shikibu, who wrote the world's first major novel, *The Tale of Genji.*

Because the nobles were completely engrossed in their luxurious lifestyles, however, they failed to notice the growth of military clans in the provinces. The two most powerful warrior clans were the Taira (also called Heike) and the Minamoto (also called Genji), whose fierce civil wars tore the nation apart until a young warrior, Minamoto Yoritomo, established supremacy.

THE KAMAKURA PERIOD (1192–1333) Wishing to set up rule far away from Kyoto, Minamoto Yoritomo established his capital in a remote and easily defended fishing village called Kamakura, not far from today's Tokyo. In becoming the nation's first shogun, or military dictator, Minamoto Yoritomo laid the groundwork for 700 years of military governments—in which the power of the country passed from the aristocratic court into the hands of the warrior class—until the imperial court was restored in 1868.

The Kamakura Period is perhaps best known for the unrivaled ascendancy of the warrior caste, or **samurai.** Ruled by a rigid honor code, samurai were bound in loyalty to their feudal lord *(daimyo),* and they became the only caste allowed to carry two swords. They were expected to give up their lives for their lord without hesitation, and if they failed in their duty, they could regain their honor only by committing ritualistic suicide, or *seppuku.* Spurning the soft life led by court nobles, samurai embraced a spartan lifestyle. When **Zen Buddhism,** with its tenets of mental and physical discipline, was introduced into Japan from China in the 1190s, it appealed greatly to the samurai. Weapons and armor achieved new heights in artistry, while *Bushido,* the way of the warrior, contributed to the spirit of national unity.

In 1274, Mongolian forces under Kublai Khan made an unsuccessful attempt to invade Japan. They returned in 1281 with a larger fleet, but a typhoon destroyed it. Regarding the cyclone as a gift from the gods, Japanese called it *kamikaze,* meaning "divine wind," which took on a different significance at the end of World War II when Japanese pilots flew suicide missions in an attempt to turn the tide of war.

THE AGE OF THE WARRING STATES (1336–1603) After the fall of the Kamakura shogunate, a new feudal government was set up at Muromachi in Kyoto. The next 200 years, however, were marred by bloody civil wars as *daimyo* staked out their fiefdoms. Similar to the barons of Europe, the *daimyo* owned tracts of land, had complete rule over the people who lived on them, and had an army of retainers, the samurai, who fought his enemies. This period of civil wars is called Sengoku-Jidai, or Age of the Warring States. Yet these centuries of strife also saw a blossoming of art and culture. Kyoto witnessed the construction of the extravagant Golden and Silver pavilions as well as the artistic arrangement of Ryoanji Temple's famous rock garden. *Noh* drama, the tea ceremony, flower arranging, and landscape gardening became passions of the upper class. At the end of the 16th century, many mountaintop castles were built to demonstrate the strength of the *daimyo,* guard their fiefdoms, and defend themselves against the firearms introduced by the Portuguese.

THE EDO PERIOD (1603–1867) In 1600, power was seized by Tokugawa Ieyasu, a statesman so shrewd and skillful in eliminating enemies that his heirs would continue to rule Japan for the next 250 years. After defeating his greatest rival in the famous battle of Sekigahara, Tokugawa set up a shogunate government in 1603 in Edo (present-day Tokyo), leaving the emperor intact but virtually powerless in Kyoto.

In 1639, fearing the expansionist policies of European nations and the spread of Christianity, the Tokugawa shogunate adopted a policy of total isolation. Thus began an amazing 215-year period in Japanese history during which Japan was closed to the rest of the world. It was a time of political stability at the expense of personal freedom, as all aspects of life were strictly controlled by the Tokugawa government. Japanese society was divided into four distinct classes: samurai, farmers, craftspeople, and merchants. Class determined everything in daily life, from where a person could live to what he was allowed to wear or eat. Samurai led the most exalted social position, and it was probably during the Tokugawa Period that the samurai class reached the zenith of its glory. At the bottom of the social ladder were the merchants, but as they prospered under the peaceful regime, new forms of entertainment arose to occupy their time. *Kabuki* drama and woodblock prints became the rage, while stoneware and porcelain, silk brocade for kimono, and lacquer-ware improved in quality. In fact, it was probably the shogunate's rigid policies that actually fostered the arts. Because anything new was considered dangerous and quickly suppressed, Japanese were forced to retreat inward, focusing their energies on the arts and perfecting handicrafts down to the minutest detail whether it was swords, kimonos, or lacquered boxes. Only Japan's many festivals and pilgrimages to designated religious sites offered relief from harsh and restrictive social mores.

To ensure that no *daimyo* in the distant provinces would become too powerful and a threat to the shogun's power, the Tokugawa government ordered each *daimyo* to maintain a second mansion in Edo, leave his family there as permanent residents (effectively as hostages), and spend a prescribed number of months in Edo every year or two. Inns and townships sprang up along Japan's major highways to accommodate the elaborate processions of palanquins, samurai, and footmen traveling back and forth between Edo and the provinces. In expending so much time and money traveling back and forth and maintaining elaborate residences both in the provinces and in Edo, the *daimyo* had no resources left with which to wage a rebellion.

Yet even though the Tokugawa government took such extreme measures to ensure its supremacy, by the mid–19th century it was clear that the feudal system was outdated and economic power had shifted into the hands of the merchants. Many samurai families were impoverished, and discontent with the shogunate became widespread. In 1853, American Commodore Matthew C. Perry sailed to Japan, seeking to gain trading rights. He left unsuccessful, but returning a year later he forced the Shogun to sign an agreement despite the disapproval of the emperor, thus ending Japan's 2 centuries of isolation. In 1867, powerful families toppled the Tokugawa regime and restored the emperor as ruler, thus bringing the Feudal Era to a close.

MEIJI PERIOD THROUGH WORLD WAR II (1868–1945)

In 1868, Emperor Meiji moved his imperial government from Kyoto to Edo, renamed it Tokyo (Eastern Capital), and designated it the official national capital. During the next few decades, known as the Meiji Restoration, Japan rapidly progressed from a feudal agricultural society of samurai and peasants to an industrial nation. The samurai were stripped of their power and no longer allowed to carry swords, thus ending a privileged way of life begun almost 700 years earlier in Kamakura. A prime minister and a cabinet were appointed, a constitution was drafted, and a parliament (called the Diet) was elected. With the enthusiastic support of Emperor Meiji, the latest in Western technological know-how was imported, including railway and postal systems, along with specialists and advisers: Between 1881 and 1898, about 10,000 Westerners were retained by the Japanese government to help modernize the country.

Meanwhile, Japan made incursions into neighboring lands. In 1894 to 1895, it fought and won a war against China; in 1904 to 1905, it attacked and defeated Russia; and in 1910, it annexed Korea. After militarists gained control of the government in the 1930s, these expansionist policies continued;

Manchuria was annexed, and Japan went to war with China again in 1937. On December 7, 1941, Japan bombed Pearl Harbor, entering World War II against the United States. Although Japan went on to conquer Hong Kong, Singapore, Burma, Malaysia, the Philippines, the Dutch East Indies, and Guam, the tide eventually turned, and American bombers reduced every major Japanese city to rubble with the exception of historic Kyoto. On August 6, 1945, the United States dropped the world's first atomic bomb over Hiroshima, followed on August 9 by a second over Nagasaki. Japan submitted to unconditional surrender on August 14, with Emperor Hirohito's radio broadcast telling his people the time had come for "enduring the unendurable and suffering what is insufferable." American and other Allied occupation forces arrived and remained until 1952. For the first time in history, Japan had suffered defeat by a foreign power; the country had never before been invaded or occupied by a foreign nation.

POSTWAR JAPAN (1946–89)   The experience of World War II had a profound effect on the Japanese, yet they emerged from their defeat and began to rebuild. In 1946, under the guidance of the Allied military authority headed by U.S. Gen. Douglas MacArthur, they adopted a democratic constitution renouncing war and the use of force to settle international disputes and divesting the emperor of divinity. A parliamentary system of government was set up, and 1947 witnessed the first general elections for the National Diet, the government's legislative body.

Avoiding involvement in foreign conflicts as outlined by its constitution, Japanese concentrated on economic recovery. Through a series of policies favoring domestic industries and shielding Japan from foreign competition, they achieved rapid economic growth. In 1964, Tokyo hosted the Summer Olympic Games, showing the world that not only had Japan recovered from the war's destruction but had also transformed into a formidable industrialized power. By the 1980s, Japan was by far the richest industrialized nation in Asia and the envy of its neighbors, who strove to emulate Japan's success. Sony was a household word around the globe; books flooded the international market touting the economic secrets of Japan, Inc. After all, Japan seemed to have it all: a good economy, political stability, safe streets, and great schools. As the yen soared, Japanese traveled abroad as never before, and Japanese companies gained international attention as they gobbled up real estate in foreign lands and purchased works of art at unheard-of prices.

In 1989, Emperor Hirohito died of cancer at age 87, bringing the 63-year Showa Era to an end and ushering in the **Heisei Period** under Akihito, the 125th emperor, who proclaimed the new "Era of Peace" (Heisei).

AFTER THE BUBBLE BURST (1990–PRESENT)   In the early 1990s, shadows of financial doubt began to spread over the Land of the Rising Sun, with alarming reports of bad bank loans, inflated stock prices, and overextended corporate investment abroad. In 1992, recession hit Japan, bursting the economic bubble and plunging the country into its worst recession since World War II.

Although Japan, whose foremost trading partner had shifted from the United States to China, seemed to be on the economic mend by the mid-2000s, the 2008 global financial meltdown (referred to in Japan as the "Lehman Shock"), hijacked its recovery by causing a downward spiral in foreign trade as demand for Japanese cars, electronics, and other exports dropped dramatically around the world. For Japan's young generation, economic stagnation was all they'd known. Instead of being envied as an Asian superpower, Japan had become an example of an economy other nations wished to avoid. Furthermore, Japan continued to suffer a declining birthrate, coupled with one of the most rapidly aging populations in the world.

On the international front, Japan's most immediate worry has long been its neighbor, North Korea, which lobbed its first missile over Japan in 1988 and launched its first satellite rocket over Japan in 2008. Relations with other neighboring countries are strained too, due to territorial disputes over several islands and Japan's revisionist views of its wartime aggression and war crimes, including its denial of so-called "comfort women" forced to work in brothels established by Japanese military. Even Japan's Prime Minister Shinzo Abe has questioned whether comfort women were coerced and has angered the rest of Asia with visits to Tokyo's Yasukuni Shrine, dedicated to war dead.

But all of Japan's woes paled to what happened on March 11, 2011, when Japan's strongest quake in recorded history struck off the Tohoku coast with a magnitude of 9.0, unleashing a massive tsunami up to three stories high that raced up to 10km (6 miles) inland. More than 19,000 people died or vanished, entire towns and villages along the Tohoku coast (in eastern Honshu) were obliterated, and the Fukushima nuclear power plant was severely crippled.

Meanwhile, cleanup and decontamination in Tohoku continues. Experts say it could take 40 years to fully decommission the Fukushima power plant; 110,000 houses were contaminated in Fukushima Prefecture alone. Japan's 50 nuclear power plants, which provided 30% of Japan's energy before March 2011, were all shut down after the disaster, pending new safety standards. As we go to press, they remain offline.

Just as 9/11 remains seared in American minds, 3/11 is the day that for most Japanese changed their nation forever.

TRADITIONAL ARTS

KABUKI Japan's best-known traditional theater art, *kabuki* is also one of the country's most popular forms of entertainment. Visit a performance and it's easy to see why—*kabuki* is fun! The plays are dramatic, the costumes are gorgeous, the stage settings are often fantastic, and the themes are universal—love, revenge, and the conflict between duty and personal feelings. Plots are easy to follow, though some theaters have English-language programs and earphones that describe everything in minute detail. Probably one of the reasons *kabuki* is so popular even today is that it developed centuries ago as a form of entertainment for the common people in feudal Japan, particularly the merchants. And one of *kabuki*'s interesting aspects is that all roles—even those depicting women—are played by men.

Altogether there are more than 300 *kabuki* plays, dating mostly from the 18th century. *Kabuki* stages almost always revolve and have an aisle that extends from the stage to the back of the spectator theater. For a Westerner, one of the more arresting things about a *kabuki* performance is the audience itself. Because this has always been entertainment for the masses, the audience can get quite lively with yells, guffaws, shouts of approval, and laughter. The best place to enjoy *kabuki* is Tokyo, where performances are held throughout much of the year.

NOH Whereas *kabuki* developed as a form of entertainment for the masses, *Noh* was a much more traditional and aristocratic form of theater. Most of Japan's shogun were patrons of *Noh;* during the Edo Period, it became the exclusive entertainment of the samurai class. In contrast to *kabuki*'s extroverted liveliness, *Noh* is very calculated, slow, and restrained. The oldest form of theater in Japan, it has changed very little in the past 600 years, making it the oldest theater art in the world. The language is so archaic that Japanese cannot understand it at all, which explains in part why *Noh* does not have the popularity that kabuki does.

As in *kabuki,* all *Noh* performers are men, with the principal characters consisting mostly of ghosts or spirits, who illuminate foibles of human nature or tragic-heroic events. Performers often wear masks. Spoken parts are chanted by a chorus of about eight; music is provided by a *Noh* orchestra that consists of several drums and a flute. In between *Noh* plays, short comic reliefs, called *kyogen,* usually make fun of life in the 1600s, depicting the lives of lazy husbands, conniving servants, and other characters with universal appeal.

BUNRAKU *Bunraku* is traditional Japanese puppet theater. But contrary to what you might expect, *bunraku* is for adults, and themes center on love and revenge, sacrifice and suicide. Many dramas now adapted for *kabuki* were first written for the *bunraku* stage. Popular in Japan since the 17th century, *bunraku* is fascinating to watch because the puppeteers are right onstage with their puppets, dressed in black and wonderfully skilled in making puppets seem like living beings. Usually, there are three puppeteers for each puppet, which is about three-fourths human size: One puppeteer is responsible for movement of the puppet's head, the expression on its face, and for the movement of the right arm and hand; another puppeteer operates the puppet's left arm and hand; while the third moves the legs. Although at first the puppeteers are somewhat distracting, after a while you forget they're there as the puppets assume personalities of their own. The narrator, who tells the story and speaks the various parts, is accompanied by a *shamisen,* a three-stringed Japanese instrument. The most famous *bunraku* presentations are at the Osaka Bunraku Theater, but there are performances in Tokyo and other major cities, too.

THE TEA CEREMONY Tea was brought to Japan from China about 1,200 years ago. It first became popular among Buddhist priests as a means of

sumo

The Japanese form of wrestling known as **sumo** was first mentioned in written records in the 6th century but was probably popular long before that. Today it's still popular, with the best wrestlers revered as national heroes, much as baseball or basketball players are in North America. Often taller than 1.8m (6 ft.) and weighing well over 136kg (300 lb.), sumo wrestlers follow a rigorous training period, which usually begins when they're in their teens and includes eating special foods to gain weight. Unmarried wrestlers even live together at their training schools, called sumo stables. Many sumo wrestlers nowadays are non-Japanese, with the majority from Mongolia.

A sumo match takes place on a sandy-floored ring less than 4.5m (15 ft.) in diameter. Wrestlers dress much as they did during the Edo Period—their hair in a samurai-style topknot, an ornamental belt/loincloth around their huge girths. Before each bout, the two contestants scatter salt in the ring to purify it

from the last bout's loss; they also squat and then raise each leg, stamping it into the ground to crush, symbolically, any evil spirits. They then squat down and face each other, glaring to intimidate their opponent. Once they rush each other, each wrestler's object is to either eject his opponent from the ring or cause him to touch the ground with any part of his body other than his feet. This is accomplished by shoving, slapping, tripping, throwing, and even carrying the opponent, but punching with a closed fist and kicking are not allowed. Altogether there are 48 holds and throws, and sumo fans know all of them.

There are six 15-day sumo tournaments in Japan every year: Three are held in Tokyo (Jan, May, and Sept); the others are held in Osaka (Mar), Nagoya (July), and Fukuoka (Nov). Each wrestler in the tournament faces a new opponent every day; the winner of the tournament is the wrestler who maintains the best overall record. Tournament matches are also widely covered on television.

staying awake during long hours of meditation; gradually, its use filtered down among the upper classes, and in the 16th century, the tea ceremony was perfected by a merchant named Sen-no-Rikyu. Using the principles of Zen and the spiritual discipline of the samurai, the tea ceremony became a highly stylized ritual, with detailed rules on how tea should be prepared, served, and drunk. The simplicity of movement and tranquility of setting are meant to free the mind from the banality of everyday life and to allow the spirit to enjoy peace. In a way, it is a form of spiritual therapy.

The tea ceremony, *cha-no-yu*, is still practiced in Japan today and is regarded as a form of disciplinary training for mental composure and for etiquette and manners. In Kyoto, I once met a fellow guest in an inexpensive Japanese inn who asked whether she could serve me Japanese tea and a sweet after breakfast. She apologized for her ineptitude, saying she was only a mere apprentice of tea. When I asked how long she'd been studying *cha-no-yu*, she replied 7 years. That may seem like a long time, but the study of the tea ceremony includes related subjects like the craftsmanship of tea vessels and implements, the design and construction of the teahouse, the landscaping of gardens, and literature related to the tea ceremony.

Several of Japan's more famous landscape gardens have teahouses on their grounds where you can sit on *tatami,* drink the frothy green tea (called *maccha*), eat sweets (meant to counteract the bitter taste of the tea), and contemplate the view. Tea pottery changes with the seasons and are often valuable art objects.

IKEBANA   Whereas a Westerner is likely to put a bunch of flowers into a vase and be done with it, the Japanese consider the arrangement of flowers an art in itself. Most young girls have at least some training in flower arranging, known as *ikebana.* First popularized among aristocrats during the Heian Period (A.D. 794–1192) and spreading to the common people in the 14th to 16th centuries, traditional *ikebana,* in its simplest form, is supposed to represent heaven, man, and earth; it's considered a truly Japanese art without outside influences. As important as the arrangement itself is the vase chosen to display it. Department store galleries sometimes have *ikebana* exhibitions, as do shrines; otherwise, check with the local tourist office.

GARDENS   Nothing is left to chance in a Japanese landscape garden: The shapes of hills and trees, the placement of rocks and waterfalls—everything is skillfully arranged in a faithful reproduction of nature. To Westerners, it may seem a bit strange to arrange nature to look like nature; but to Japanese, even nature can be improved upon to make it more pleasing through the best possible use of limited space. Japanese are masters at this, as a visit to any of their famous gardens will testify.

Japanese have been sculpting gardens for more than 1,000 years. At first, gardens were designed for walking and boating, with ponds, artificial islands, and pavilions. As with almost everything else in Japanese life, however, Zen Buddhism exerted an influence, making gardens simpler and attempting to create the illusion of boundless space within a small area. To the Buddhist, a garden was not for merriment but for contemplation—an uncluttered and simple landscape on which to rest the eyes. Japanese gardens often use the principle of "borrowed landscape"—that is, the incorporation of surrounding mountains and landscape into the overall design and impact of the garden.

ETIQUETTE

Much of Japan's system of etiquette and manners stems from its feudal days, when the social hierarchy dictated how a person spoke, sat, bowed, ate, walked, and lived. Failure to comply with the rules would bring severe punishment, even death. Many Japanese have literally lost their heads for committing social blunders.

Today, Japanese still attach much importance to proper behavior, though as a foreigner you can get away with a lot. There are two cardinal sins, however, you should never commit: Never wear your shoes into a Japanese home, traditional inn, temple, or any room with *tatami,* and never wash with soap inside a communal Japanese bathtub or pull the plug. Except for these two horrors, you will probably be forgiven any other social blunders (such as standing with your arms folded or your hands in your pockets).

If you're invited to a Japanese home, you should know that it's both a rarity and an honor. Most Japanese consider their homes too small and humble for entertaining guests, which is why there are so many restaurants, coffee shops, and bars. If you're invited to a home, don't show up empty-handed. Bring a small gift such as candy, fruit, flowers, alcohol, or perhaps a souvenir from your hometown. And if someone extends you a favor or plays host, be sure to thank him again the next time you see him—even if it's a year later.

BOWING   The main form of greeting in Japan is the bow rather than the handshake. Although at first glance it may seem simple enough, the bow—together with its implications—is actually quite complicated. The depth of the bow and the number of seconds devoted to performing it, as well as the total number of bows, depend on who you are, to whom you're bowing, and how he's bowing back. In addition to bowing in greeting, Japanese also bow upon departing and to express gratitude. The proper form for a bow is to bend from the waist with a straight back and to keep your arms at your sides if you're a man or clasped in front of you if you're a woman, but if you're a foreigner, a simple nod of the head is enough. Knowing foreigners shake hands, a Japanese may extend his hand, although he probably won't be able to stop himself from giving a little bow as well. (I've even seen Japanese bow when talking on the telephone.) Although I've occasionally witnessed Japanese businessmen shaking hands among themselves, the practice is still quite rare. Kimono-clad hostesses of a high-end traditional Japanese inn will often kneel on *tatami* and bow to the ground as they send you off on your journey.

VISITING CARD   You're a nonentity in Japan if you don't have a visiting card, called a ***meishi.*** Everyone—from housewives to bank presidents—carries *meishi* to give out during introductions. If you're trying to conduct business in Japan, you'll be regarded suspiciously—even as a phony—if you don't have business cards. *Meishi* are very useful business tools for Japanese. Likewise, a *meishi* can be used as an introduction to a third party—a Japanese may give you his *meishi,* scribble something on it, and tell you to present it to his cousin who owns a restaurant in Fukuoka. *Voilà*—the cousin will treat you like a royal guest. As a tourist, you don't have to have business cards, but it certainly doesn't hurt. The card should have your address and occupation on it; you might even consider having your *meishi* made in Japan, with *katakana* (Japanese syllabic script) written on the reverse side. Needless to say, there's a proper way to present a *meishi.* Turn it so that the other person can read it (that is, upside-down to you) and present it with both hands and a slight bow.

SHOES   Nothing is so distasteful to Japanese as the soles of shoes. Therefore, you should take off your shoes before entering a home, a Japanese-style inn, temple or shrine, and even some museums and restaurants. Usually there are plastic slippers at the entryway for you to slip on, but whenever you encounter *tatami,* you should take off even these slippers—only bare feet or socks are allowed to tread upon *tatami.*

Restrooms present another set of slippers. If you're in a home, Japanese inn, or restaurant where you've removed your shoes, you'll notice another pair of slippers sitting right inside the restroom door. Slip out of the hallway plastic shoes and into the bathroom slippers, and wear these the entire time you're in the restroom. When you're finished, change back into the hallway slippers. If you forget this last changeover, you'll regret it—nothing is as embarrassing as walking into a room wearing toilet slippers and not realizing what you've done until you see the mixed looks of horror and mirth on the faces of Japanese people.

BATHING On my very first trip to Japan, I was certain I would never enter a Japanese bath. I was under the misconception that men and women bathed together, and I couldn't imagine getting into a tub with a group of smiling and bowing Japanese men. I needn't have worried—in almost all circumstances, bathing is gender segregated. There are some exceptions, primarily at outdoor hot-spring spas in the countryside, but the women who go to these are usually grandmothers who couldn't care less. Young Japanese women wouldn't dream of jumping into a tub with a group of male strangers.

Japanese baths are delightful—I'm addicted to them. You'll find them at Japanese-style inns, at *onsen* (hot-spring spas), and at *sento* (neighborhood baths). Sometimes they're elaborate affairs with indoor and outdoor tubs, and sometimes they're nothing more than a tiny tub. Public baths have long been regarded as social centers for Japanese—friends and co-workers will visit hot-spring resorts together; neighbors exchange gossip at the neighborhood bath. Sadly, neighborhood baths have been in great decline over the past decades, as most Japanese now have private baths in their homes. Hot-spring spas, however, remain hugely popular.

In any case, whether large or small, the procedure at all Japanese baths is the same. After completely disrobing in the changing room and putting your clothes in either a locker or a basket, hold a washcloth (provided free or available for sale at the bathhouse) in front of you so that it covers your vital parts and walk into the bathing area. There you'll find plastic or wood basins and stools and faucets along the wall. Sit on the stool in front of a faucet and use the basin (or hand-held faucet if available) to splash water all over you. If there's no hot water from the faucet, it's acceptable to dip your basin into the hot bath, but your washcloth should never touch the tub water. Rinsing yourself thoroughly is not only proper *onsen* manners; it also acclimatizes your body to the bath's hot temperature so you don't suffer a heart attack. Only when all traces of soap are removed and you feel squeaky-clean should you enter the tub.

As in a Jacuzzi, everyone uses the same bath water. For that reason, you should never wash yourself in the tub, never put your washcloth into the bath (place it on your head or lay it beside the bath), and never pull the plug when you're done. After your bath is when you scrub your body and wash your hair. I have never seen a group of people wash themselves so thoroughly as the Japanese, from their ears to their toes. All *sento* provide shampoo and body soap, along with interesting products provided free by companies hoping to rope in new customers, but in small public baths you might have to provide your own.

The Japanese are so fond of baths that many take them nightly, especially in winter when a hot bath keeps them toasty warm for hours. At an *onsen,* where hot-spring waters are considered curative, Japanese will bathe both at night and again in the morning, often making several trips between the faucet and the tubs and being careful not to rinse off the curative waters when they're done. With time, you'll probably become addicted, too. ***Note:*** Because tattoos in Japan have long been associated with *yakuza* (Japanese mafia), most public baths do not admit people with tattoos. However, if your tattoo is discreet and you're at, say, a small Japanese inn, you probably won't have any problems.

THE JAPANESE LANGUAGE

No one knows the exact origins of the Japanese language, but we do know it existed only in spoken form until the 6th century. That's when the Japanese borrowed the Chinese pictorial characters, called *kanji*, and used them to develop their own form of written language. Later, two phonetic alphabet systems, *hiragana* and *katakana*, were added to kanji to form the existing Japanese writing system. Thus, Chinese and Japanese use some of the same pictographs, but otherwise there's no similarity between the languages.

As for the spoken language, there are many levels of speech and forms of expression relating to a person's social status and sex. Even nonverbal communication is a vital part of understanding Japanese, because what isn't said is often more important than what is. It's little wonder that St. Francis Xavier, a Jesuit missionary who came to Japan in the 16th century, wrote that Japanese was an invention of the devil designed to thwart the spread of Christianity. And yet, astoundingly, adult literacy in Japan is estimated to be 99%.

It's worth noting that Japanese nouns do not have plural forms; thus, for example, *ryokan,* a Japanese-style inn, can be both singular and plural, as can

JAPANESE english

English-language words are often misspelled, sometimes with wonderful results. Menus can be entertaining, listing dishes like "lice" (instead of rice) or "sandwitches." English is also fashionable in Japanese advertising, appearing on shop signs, posters, shopping bags, and T-shirts. Sometimes, however, you can only guess at the original intent. What, for example, can possibly be the meaning behind TODAY BIRDS, TOMORROW MEN, which appeared below a picture of birds on a shopping bag? I have treasured ashtrays that read THE YOUNG BOY GRASPED HER HEART FIRMLY and LET'S TRIP IN HOKKAIDO. In Okayama, I saw a shop whose name was a stern admonition to customers to GROW UP, while in Gifu you can only surmise at the pleasures to be had at HOTEL JOYBOX. A staff member of the Hokkaido Tourist Association whose business card identified him working for the PROPAGANDA SECTION was probably more truthful than most. And imagine my consternation upon stepping onto a bathroom scale that called itself the BEAUTY-CHECKER. But the best sign I've seen was at Narita Airport years ago, where each check-in counter displayed a notice about checking in FOR YOUR FRIGHT. I explained the cause of my amusement to the person behind the counter, and when I came back through 2 weeks later, I was almost disappointed to find that all signs had been corrected. That's Japanese efficiency.

kimono. Plural sense is indicated by context. In addition, the Japanese custom is to list the family name first followed by the given name, though nowadays Japanese working with international companies increasingly follow the Western custom of listing the family name last. In this guide, I've listed family names first for Japanese born before the Meiji Period (1868) and given names first for people born after that.

Finally, you may find yourself confused because of suffixes attached to Japanese place names. For example, *dori* can mean street, avenue, or road; sometimes it's attached to a street name with a hyphen, while at other times it stands alone. Thus, you may see Chuo-dori, Chuo Dori, or even Chuo-dori Avenue on English-language maps and street signs, but they're all the same street. Likewise, *dera* means "temple" and is often included at the end of the name, as in Kiyomizudera, which may be translated into English as Kiyomizu Temple. *Jo* means "castle," while *ji* at the end of a word means "shrine."

EATING & DRINKING IN JAPAN

Whenever I leave Japan, it's the food I miss the most. Sure, there are sushi bars and other Japanese specialty restaurants in many major cities around the world, but they don't offer nearly the variety available in Japan and often they aren't nearly as good. For just as America has more to offer than hamburgers and steaks and England more than fish and chips, Japan has more than just sushi and *teppanyaki*. For both the gourmet and the uninitiated, Japan is a treasure-trove of culinary surprises and a foodie's delight.

Japanese Cuisine

There are more than a dozen different and distinct types of Japanese cuisine, plus countless regional specialties. A good deal of what you eat may be completely new to you as well as completely unidentifiable. Don't worry; often even Japanese don't know what they're eating, so varied and so wide is the range of available edibles. The rule is simply to enjoy, and enjoyment begins even before you raise your chopsticks to your mouth.

To the Japanese, **presentation** of food is as important as the food itself, and dishes are designed to appeal to the palate and to the eye. In contrast to the American way of piling as much food as possible onto a single plate, Japanese traditionally use lots of small plates, each arranged artfully with bite-size morsels of food. After you've seen what can be done with maple leaves, flowers, bits of bamboo, and even pebbles to enhance the appearance of food, your relationship with what you eat may change forever. If there's such a thing as designer cuisine, Japan is its home. No wonder traditional Japanese cuisine is on UNESCO's Intangible Cultural Heritage list.

Below are explanations of some of the most common types of Japanese cuisine. Generally, only one type of cuisine is served in a given restaurant—for example, raw seafood is the specialty in a sushi bar, whereas tempura is featured at a tempura counter. There are exceptions to this, especially in regards to raw fish, which is served as an appetizer in many restaurants, and set meals, which contain a variety of dishes. Hotel restaurants may also offer a great variety, and some Japanese drinking establishments (called *izakaya* or *nomiya*) offer a wide range of foods from soups to sushi to skewered pieces of chicken known as *yakitori*.

KAISEKI   The king of Japanese cuisine, *kaiseki* is the epitome of delicately and exquisitely arranged food, the ultimate in Japanese aesthetic appeal. It's also among the most expensive meals you can eat, though some restaurants do offer more affordable mini-*kaiseki* courses. In addition, the better Japanese inns serve *kaiseki,* a reason for their high cost. *Kaiseki,* which is not a specific dish but rather a complete meal, is expensive because much time and skill are involved in preparing each of the many dishes, with the ingredients cooked to preserve natural flavors. Even the plates are chosen with great care to enhance the color, texture, and shape of each piece of food.

Kaiseki cuisine is based on the four seasons, with the selection of ingredients and their presentation dependent on the time of the year. In fact, so strongly does a *kaiseki* preparation convey the mood of a particular season, the *kaiseki* gourmet can tell what season it is just by looking at a meal. A *kaiseki* meal is usually a lengthy affair with various dishes appearing in set order. Although meals vary greatly depending upon the region and what's fresh, common dishes include some type of sashimi, tempura, cooked seasonal fish, and bite-size pieces of various vegetables. Because *kaiseki* is always a set meal, there's no problem in ordering. Let your budget be your guide.

KUSHIAGE/KUSHIKATSU   *Kushiage* foods (also called *kushikatsu*) are breaded and deep-fried on skewers and include chicken, beef, seafood, and lots of seasonal vegetables like snow peas, green pepper, gingko nuts and lotus root. Their morsels are served with a slice of lemon and usually a specialty sauce. Ordering the set meal is easiest, and what you get is often determined by both the chef and the season.

OKONOMIYAKI   *Okonomiyaki,* which originated in Osaka after World War II and literally means "as you like it," is often referred to as Japanese pizza or pancake, to which meat or seafood, shredded cabbage, and vegetables are added, topped with Worcestershire sauce. At some places the cook makes it for you, but at other places it's do-it-yourself at your table. *Yakisoba* (fried Chinese noodles with cabbage) is also usually offered at *okonomiyaki* restaurants, which are always very reasonably priced.

RICE   As in other Asian countries, rice has been a Japanese staple for about 2,000 years. In fact, rice is so important to the Japanese diet that *gohan* means both "rice" and "meal." There are no problems here—everyone is familiar with rice. The difference, however, is that in Japan it's quite sticky, making it easier to pick up with chopsticks. Traditionally it was eaten plain, though nowadays trendy restaurants sprinkle rice with black sesame seeds, plum powder, or other seasoning. In the old days, not everyone could afford the expensive white kind, which was grown primarily to pay taxes or rent to the feudal lord; peasants had to make do with a mixture of brown rice, millet, and greens. Restaurants offering organic foods often offer *genmai* (unpolished brown rice).

ROBATAYAKI *Robatayaki* refers to restaurants in which seafood and vegetables are cooked over an open charcoal grill. In days of yore, a *robata* (open fireplace) in the middle of an old Japanese house was the center of activity for cooking, eating, socializing, and keeping warm. Today's *robatayaki* restaurants are therefore like nostalgia trips back into Japan's past and are often decorated in rustic farmhouse style with staff dressed in traditional clothing. There's no special menu in a *robatayaki* restaurant; rather, it includes just about everything eaten in Japan, with the difference being that most of the foods are grilled. Favorites of mine include *ginnan* (gingko nuts), asparagus wrapped in bacon, *piman* (a type of green pepper), mushrooms (various kinds), grilled skewers of beef and chicken, and just about any kind of fish. Because ordering is often a la carte, you'll just have to look and point.

SASHIMI & SUSHI Like rice, seafood is a staple of the Japanese diet. Although it may be served in any number of ways from grilled to boiled, a great deal of it is eaten raw. Sashimi is simply raw seafood, usually served as an appetizer and eaten with soy sauce. If you've never tried it, you might start out with *maguro,* or lean tuna, which doesn't taste fishy at all and is so delicate in texture that it almost melts in your mouth. Sushi, which is raw fish with vinegared rice, comes in many varieties. The best known is *nigiri-zushi:* raw fish, seafood, or vegetables placed on top of vinegared rice with just a touch of wasabi. It's also dipped in soy sauce. Use chopsticks or your fingers to eat sushi; remember you're supposed to eat each piece in one bite—quite a mouthful, but about the only way to keep it from falling apart. Another trick is to turn it upside down when you dip it in the sauce, to keep the rice from crumbling.

Also popular is *maki-zushi,* which consists of seafood, vegetables, or pickles rolled with rice inside a sheet of *nori* seaweed. *Inari-zushi* is vinegared rice and chopped vegetables inside a pouch of fried tofu bean curd.

Typical sushi includes *maguro* (tuna), *hirame* (flounder), *tai* (sea bream), *ika* (squid), *tako* (octopus), *ebi* (shrimp), *anago* (sea eel), and *tamago* (omelet). Ordering is easy because you usually sit at a counter where you can watch the sushi chefs at work and see all the food in a refrigerated glass case in front of you, with the typical meal starting with sashimi and followed by sushi. If you don't want to order separately, there are always various *seto* (set meals or courses). Pickled ginger is part of any sushi meal.

One way to enjoy sushi without spending a fortune is at a *kaiten* sushi shop, in which plates of sushi circulate on a conveyor belt on the counter—customers reach for the dishes they want and pay for the number of dishes they take.

SHABU-SHABU & SUKIYAKI Until the Meiji Restoration beginning in 1868, which brought foreigners to Japan, Japanese could think of nothing as disgusting as eating the flesh of animals (fish was okay). Meat was considered unclean by Buddhists, and consuming it was banned by the emperor way back in the 7th century. It wasn't until Emperor Meiji himself announced his intention to eat meat that Japanese accepted the idea. Today, Japanese are quite skilled in preparing beef dishes.

Sukiyaki is among Japan's best-known dishes. Like fondue, it's cooked at the table and consists of thinly sliced beef cooked in a broth of soy sauce, stock, and sake along with scallions, spinach, mushrooms, tofu, bamboo shoots, and other vegetables. All diners serve themselves from the simmering pot and then dip their morsels into their own bowl of raw egg. You can skip the raw egg if you want (most Westerners do), but it adds to the taste and also cools the food down enough so that it doesn't burn.

Shabu-shabu is also prepared at your table and consists of thinly sliced beef cooked in a broth with vegetables in a kind of Japanese fondue. (It's named for the swishing sound the beef supposedly makes when cooking.) For dipping, there's typically either sesame sauce with diced green onions or a more bitter fish stock sauce.

The main difference between the two dishes is the broth: Whereas in suki-yaki it consists of stock flavored with soy sauce and sake and is slightly sweet, in *shabu-shabu* it's relatively clear and has little taste of its own. The pots used are also different. Restaurants serving sukiyaki usually serve *shabu-shabu* as well, and they're usually happy to show you the right way to prepare and eat it.

SHOJIN RYORI   *Shojin Ryori* is the ultimate vegetarian meal, created centuries ago to serve the needs of Zen Buddhist priests and pilgrims. Dishes may include *yudofu* (simmered tofu) and an array of local vegetables. Kyoto is the best place to experience this type of cuisine.

SOBA, UDON & RAMEN   Japanese love eating noodles, but I suspect at least part of the fascination stems from the way they eat them—they slurp, sucking in the noodles with gravity-defying speed. What's more, slurping noodles is considered proper etiquette; it also helps cool the noodles when they're piping hot. In any case, noodles are among the least expensive dishes in Japan.

There are many different kinds of noodles, with seemingly every region proud of its own special style or kind—some are eaten plain, some in combination with other foods such as shrimp tempura, some served hot, some served cold. *Soba,* made from unbleached buckwheat flour and enjoyed for its nutty flavor and high nutritional value, is eaten hot *(kake-soba)* or cold *(zaru-soba).* *Udon* is a thick white wheat noodle originally from Osaka, usually served hot. *Somen* is a fine white noodle eaten cold in the summer and dunked in a cold sauce. Establishments serving noodles range from stand-up eateries to more refined noodle restaurants with *tatami* seating.

Although technically considered Chinese fast food, **ramen** is very popular in Japan and is a thousand times tastier than packaged products sold in stores, with noodles served in a broth that may have simmered for hours. Ramen shops can be found everywhere. In addition to ramen, you can also usually order *yakisoba* (fried noodles) or—my favorite—*gyoza* (fried pork dumplings).

What these places lack in atmosphere is made up for in price; they're some of the cheapest places in Japan for a meal.

TEMPURA Today a well-known Japanese food, tempura was actually introduced by the Portuguese in the 16th century. Tempura is fish and vegetables coated in a batter of egg, water, and wheat flour, delicately deep-fried, and served piping hot. To eat it, dip it in a sauce of soy, fish stock, *daikon* (radish), and grated ginger; in some restaurants, only some salt, powdered green tea, or a lemon wedge is provided as an accompaniment. Various tempura specialties may include *nasu* (eggplant), *shiitake* (mushroom), *satsumaimo* (sweet potato), *shishito* (small green pepper), *renkon* (sliced lotus root), *ebi* (shrimp), *ika* (squid), *shisho* (lemon-mint leaf), and various fish. Again, the easiest thing to do is to order the *teishoku* (set meal).

TEPPANYAKI A *teppanyaki* restaurant is a Japanese steakhouse. The chef slices, dices, and cooks your meal of tenderloin or sirloin steak and vegetables on a smooth, hot grill right in front of you—though with much less fanfare than most Japanese restaurants in the U.S. *Teppanyaki* restaurants tend to be expensive, simply because of the price of beef in Japan, with Kobe beef the most prized.

TOFU Originally from China, tofu, or bean curd, is made from soy milk. It has little flavor of its own and is served cold in summer and *yudofu* (boiled) in winter. A byproduct of tofu is *yuba,* thin sheets rich in protein.

TONKATSU *Tonkatsu* is Japanese comfort food, made by dredging pork in wheat flour, moistening it with egg and water, dipping it in bread crumbs, and deep-frying it in vegetable oil. Because *tonkatsu* restaurants are inexpensive, they're popular with office workers and families. It's easiest to order the *teishoku,* which usually features either the *hirekatsu* (pork filet) or the *rosukatsu* (pork loin). In any case, *tonkatsu* is served on a bed of shredded cabbage, and one or two different sauces will be at your table, a Worcestershire sauce and perhaps a specialty sauce. If you order the *teishoku,* it will come with rice, miso soup, and pickled vegetables. Pork cutlet served on a bowl of rice is *katsudon.*

UNAGI I'll bet that if you eat *unagi* without knowing what it is, you'll find it very tasty—and you'll probably be very surprised to find out you've just eaten eel. Popular as a health food because of its rich protein and high vitamin A content, eel is supposed to help you fight fatigue during hot summer months but is eaten year-round. *Kabayaki* (broiled eel) is prepared by grilling filet strips over a charcoal fire; the eel is repeatedly dipped in a sweetened barbecue soy sauce while cooking. A favorite way to eat broiled eel is on top of rice, in which case it's called *unaju* or *unagi donburi.*

YAKITORI *Yakitori* is chunks of chicken or chicken parts basted in a sweet soy sauce and grilled over a charcoal fire on thin skewers. The cheapest way to dine on yakitori is to order a set course, which will often include various parts of the chicken including the skin, heart, and liver. If this isn't to your taste, you may wish to order a la carte, which is more expensive but gets you exactly what you want. In addition to chicken, other skewered, charcoaled delicacies are usually offered (called *kushi-yaki*). If you're ordering by the stick, you might want to try *sasami* (chicken breast), *tsukune* (chicken meatballs), *piman* (green peppers), *negima* (chicken and leeks), *shiitake* (mushrooms), or *ginnan* (gingko nuts). Places that specialize in yakitori (*yakitori-ya,* often identifiable by a red paper lantern outside the front door) are technically not restaurants but drinking establishments; they usually don't open until 5 or 6pm.

OTHER CUISINES   During your travels you might also run into these types of Japanese cuisine: *Kamameshi* is a rice casserole served in individual-size cast-iron pots with different toppings that might include seafood, meat, or vegetables. *Donburi* is also a rice dish, topped with tempura, eggs, and meat such as chicken or pork. *Nabe,* a stew cooked in an earthenware pot at your table, consists of chicken, sliced beef, pork, or seafood; noodles; and vegetables. *Oden* is a broth with fish cakes, tofu, eggs, and vegetables, served with hot mustard. If a restaurant advertises that it specializes in *Kyodo-Ryori,* it serves local specialties for which the region is famous and is often very rustic in decor. See individual city lists for more on regional cuisine.

Drinks

All Japanese restaurants serve complimentary green tea with meals. You might also want to order sake (also known as *nihonshu*), an alcoholic beverage made from rice and served hot or cold. Produced since about the 3rd century, sake varies by region, production method, alcoholic content, color, aroma, and taste. There are more than 1,800 sake brewers in Japan producing about 10,000 varieties. Miyabi is a prized classic sake; other brands are Gekkeikan, Koshinokanbai, Hakutsuru (meaning White Crane), and Ozeki.

Japanese beer is also very popular. The biggest sellers are Kirin, Sapporo, Asahi, and Suntory, with each brand offering a bewildering variety of brews. Microbreweries are also found everywhere in Japan. Businessmen are fond of whiskey, which they usually drink with ice and water. *Shochu,* a clear, distilled spirit usually made from rice but sometimes from wheat, sweet potatoes, barley, or sugar cane, can be consumed straight but is often combined with soda water in a drink called *chuhai.* My personal favorite is *ume-shu,* a plum-flavored *shochu.* But watch out—the stuff can be deadly. Wine, usually available only at restaurants serving Western food, has become popular in recent years, with both domestic and imported brands available. Although cocktails are available in dance clubs, hotel lounges, and fancier bars at rather inflated prices, most Japanese stick with beer, wine, sake, *shochu,* or whiskey.

Tips on Dining in Japan

UPON ARRIVAL   As soon as you're seated in a Japanese restaurant (that is, a restaurant serving Japanese food), you'll be given a wet towel, which will be steaming hot in winter or pleasantly cool in summer. Called an *oshibori,* it's for wiping your hands. In all but the fancy restaurants, men can get away with wiping their faces as well, but women are not supposed to (although some ignore this if it's hot and humid outside). Sadly, cheaper Japanese restaurants now resort to a paper towel wrapped in plastic, which isn't nearly the same. *Oshibori* are not provided in Western restaurants.

ORDERING   The biggest problem facing the hungry foreigner in Japan is ordering a meal in a restaurant without an English-language menu. This book alleviates the problem to some extent by recommending sample dishes and giving price ranges; I've also noted which restaurants offer English-language menus.

One aid to simplified ordering is the use of plastic food models in glass display cases either outside or just inside the front door of many restaurants, especially those in tourist areas and department stores. Sushi, tempura, daily specials, spaghetti—they're all there in mouthwatering plastic replicas along with corresponding prices. Simply decide what you want and point it out to staff.

Not all restaurants, however, have plastic display cases, especially the more exclusive or traditional ones. In fact, you'd be missing a lot of Japan's best cuisine if you restrict yourself to eating only at places with displays. If there's no display, English menu or photographs in the Japanese menu, a simple solution is to order the *teishoku,* or daily special meal (also called "seto," "set course" or simply "course," especially in restaurants serving Western food); these fixed-price meals consist of a main dish and several side dishes, including soup, rice, and Japanese pickles. Although most restaurants have set courses for dinner as well, lunch is the usual time for the *teishoku,* generally from 11 or 11:30am to 1:30 or 2pm.

In any case, once you've decided what you want to eat, flag down a waiter or waitress; they will not hover around your table waiting for you to order but come only when summoned. In most restaurants there are no assigned servers to certain tables; rather, servers are multitaskers, so don't be shy about stopping any who pass by.

EATING & DRINKING ETIQUETTE   The first thing you'll be confronted with in a Japanese restaurant is chopsticks (in restaurants serving Western food, knives and forks are provided instead). Chopstick etiquette says that if you're taking something from a communal bowl or tray, you're supposed to turn your chopsticks upside down and use the part that hasn't been in your mouth; after transferring the food to your plate, you turn the chopsticks back to their proper position. The exception is *shabu-shabu* and *sukiyaki.*

You don't use a spoon with Japanese soup. Rather, you'll pick up the bowl and drink from it, using your chopsticks to fish out larger pieces of food. You should also pick up a bowl of rice to eat it. It's considered good taste to slurp with

---

Eating on the Move

It's considered bad manners to walk down the street eating or drinking (except at a festival). You'll notice that if a Japanese buys a drink from a vending machine, he'll stand there, gulp it down, and throw away the container before going on. To the chagrin of their elders, young Japanese sometimes ignore this rule.

gusto, especially if you're eating hot noodles. Noodle shops in Japan are always well orchestrated with slurps and smacks.

As for drinking etiquette, women should hold their glass or cup with both hands, but men do not. The main thing to remember if you're with a group is that you never pour your own glass (bottles of beer are so large that people often share one). The rule is that in turn, one person pours for everyone else in the group, so be sure to hold up your glass when someone is pouring for you. As the night progresses Japanese get sloppy about this rule. If someone wants to pour you a drink and your glass is full, the proper thing to do is to take a few gulps so that he or she can fill your glass. Because each person is continually filling everyone else's glass, you never know exactly how much you've had to drink, which (depending on how you look at it) is either very good or very bad. If you really don't want more to drink, leave your glass full and refuse refills.

PAYING THE BILL If you go out with a group of friends (not as a visiting guest of honor and not with business associates), it's customary to split the dinner bill equally, even if you all ordered different things. Even foreigners living in Japan adopt the practice of splitting the bill; it certainly makes figuring everyone's share easier, especially since there's no tipping in Japan. But it can be hard on frugal diners on a budget. If you're with friends who do wish to pay for only what they ate, tell the cashier you want to pay *"betsu, betsu."*

EXTRA CHARGES & TAXES Japan's consumption tax imposed on goods and services, including restaurant meals, is 8% (it's scheduled to rise to 10% in Apr 2017). Some restaurants include the tax in their menu prices, while others do not (it's usually stated on the menu whether taxes are included). In finer restaurants and nightlife establishments, a 10% to 15% service charge may also be levied (there is no tipping in Japan). You should also be aware of the "table charge" imposed on customers by some bars (especially *nomiya*), many cocktail lounges, and, only rarely, restaurants. Included in the table charge is usually a small appetizer—maybe nuts, chips, or a vegetable; for this reason, some locales call it an *otsumami,* or snack charge. At any rate, the charge is usually between ¥300 and ¥500 per person.

HOURS In larger cities, most restaurants are open from about 11am to 9pm and later. Many close for a few hours in the afternoon (2–5pm), though inexpensive ones are open all day. In big cities like Tokyo or Osaka, try to avoid the lunchtime rush from noon to 1pm. In rural areas, restaurants tend to close early, often by 7:30 or 8pm. Traditional Japanese restaurants hang a *noren* (split curtain) over the front door to signify they're open. Keep in mind that the closing time posted for most restaurants is exactly that—everyone is expected to pay his or her bill and leave. A general rule of thumb is that the last order is taken at least a half-hour before closing time, sometimes an hour or more for *kaiseki* restaurants (staff members will usually alert you they're taking last orders). To be on the safe side, try to arrive at least an hour before closing time so you have time to relax and enjoy your meal.

How to Eat without Spending a Fortune

During your first few days in Japan—particularly if you're in Tokyo—money will seem to flow from your pockets like water. In fact, money has a tendency to disappear so quickly that many people become convinced they must have lost some of it somehow. Here are some tips for getting the most for your yen.

BREAKFAST Buffet breakfasts are popular at Japanese hotels and can be an inexpensive way to eat your fill. Otherwise, coffee shops offer what's called "morning service" until 10 or 11am; it generally consists of a cup of coffee, a small salad, a boiled egg, and toast. There are also many coffee-shop chains, including Doutour, Pronto, and the ever-expanding Starbucks (1,034 in Japan at last count). Except at most hotel breakfast buffets, there's no such thing as the bottomless cup in Japan.

SET LUNCHES Eat your biggest meal at lunch. Many restaurants serving Japanese food offer a daily set lunch, or *teishoku,* at a fraction of what their set dinners might be, from about 11am to around 2pm. A Japanese *teishoku* will include the main course (such as tempura, grilled fish, or the specialty of the house), soup, pickled vegetables, rice, and tea, while the set menu in a Western-style restaurant (often called a "seto" or *coursu*) usually consists of a main dish, salad, bread, and coffee.

CHEAP EATS Inexpensive restaurants can be found in department stores (often one whole floor will be devoted to many restaurants, most with plastic-food displays), underground shopping arcades, nightlife districts, and in and around train and subway stations. Hotel restaurants can also be good bargains for inexpensive set lunches or buffets (called *viking* in Japanese; buffets always give price breaks for children).

Some of the cheapest establishments for a night out on the town are *yakitori-ya, izakaya* (Japanese pubs), noodle and ramen shops, coffee shops (which often offer inexpensive pastries and sandwiches), and conveyor-belt sushi restaurants. Restaurants serving *gyudon* (beef bowl) are also cheap, with Yoshinoya the largest chain, while CoCo Curry House serves Japanese-style curry rice. Japan also has American fast-food chains, such as McDonald's and KFC, as well as Japanese chains—Freshness Burger, MOS Burger, and First Kitchen, among them. Ethnic restaurants, particularly those serving Indian, Korean, Chinese, Italian, and other cuisines, are plentiful and usually inexpensive.

Street-side stalls, called *yatai,* are also good sources of inexpensive meals. These restaurants-on-wheels sell a variety of foods, including *oden* (fish cakes), *yakitori* (skewered barbecued chicken), and *yakisoba* (fried noodles), as well as sake and beer. They appear mostly at night, lighted by a single lantern or a string of lights, and most have a counter with stools as well, protected in winter by a wall of tarp. Sadly, traditional pushcarts are being replaced by motorized vans, which are not nearly as romantic and do not offer seating.

PREPARED FOODS You can save even more money by avoiding restaurants altogether. There are all kinds of prepared foods you can buy; some are even complete meals, perfect for picnics in a park or right in your hotel room.

Perhaps the best known is the *bento,* or box lunch, commonly sold at train-stations, in food sections of department stores, and at counter windows of tiny shops throughout Japan. In fact, the bento served by vendors on some Shinkansen trains and at train stations are an inexpensive way to sample regional cuisine since they often include food typical of the region you're passing through. The basic bento contains a piece of meat (generally fish or chicken), various side dishes, rice, and pickled vegetables. Sushi boxed lunches are also readily available.

My favorite place to shop for prepared foods is department stores. Located in basements, these enormous food and produce sections harken back to Japanese markets of yore, with vendors yelling out their wares and crowds of housewives deciding on the evening's dinner. Different counters specialize in different items—tempura, yakitori, Japanese pickles, cooked fish, sushi (sometimes made by robots!), salads, vegetables, and desserts. Almost the entire spectrum of Japanese cuisine is available, as are numerous samples. There are also counters selling bento box meals. In any case, there's nothing like milling with Japanese housewives to make you feel like one of the locals. Though not as colorful, 24-hour convenience stores and grocery stores also sell packaged foods like sandwiches, cooked foods, and bento.

TIPS ON ACCOMMODATIONS

Accommodations available in Japan range from Japanese-style inns *(ryokan)* to large Western-style hotels, in all price categories. Although you can travel throughout Japan without making reservations beforehand, it's essential to book in advance if you're traveling during peak travel seasons and is recommended at other times (see "When to Go," p. 37, for peak travel times). If you arrive in a town without reservations, most local tourist offices—generally located in or near the main train station—will find accommodations for you at no extra charge. Note that many accommodations, especially in popular destinations, raise their rates in peak season and on weekends.

All accommodations levy an 8% consumption tax (10% starting in Apr 2017). Upper-end and some moderately priced hotels also add a 10% to 15% service charge, while expensive *ryokan* will add a 10% to 20% service charge. No service charge is levied at business hotels and inexpensive lodgings for the simple reason that no services are provided. In hot-spring resort areas, an *onsen* (spa) tax of ¥150 is added per night. Tokyo levies its own local hotel tax (¥100–¥200 per person per night, depending on the room rate). Unless otherwise stated, prices in this guide include all consumption taxes and service charge, but not *onsen* or local hotel tax.

Japanese-Style Inns

Although an overnight stay in a *ryokan* can be astoundingly expensive, it's worth the splurge at least once during your stay. Nothing quite conveys the simplicity and beauty—indeed the very atmosphere—of old Japan more than these inns with their gleaming polished wood, *tatami* floors, rice-paper sliding doors, and meticulously pruned gardens. Personalized service by kimono-clad hostesses and exquisitely prepared *kaiseki* meals are the trademarks of such inns, some of which are of ancient vintage. Indeed, staying in one is like taking a trip back in time.

If you want to experience a Japanese-style inn but can't afford the prices of a full-service *ryokan,* a number of alternatives are described below. Although they don't offer the same personalized service, beautiful setting, or memorable cuisine, they do offer the chance to sleep on a futon in a simple *tatami* room and, in some cases, eat Japanese meals.

RYOKAN *Ryokan* developed during the Edo Period, when *daimyo* (feudal lords) were required to travel to and from Edo (present-day Tokyo) every 2 years. They always traveled with a full entourage including members of their family, retainers, and servants. The best *ryokan,* of course, were reserved for the *daimyo* and members of the imperial family. Some of these exist today, passed down from generation to generation.

Traditionally, *ryokan* are small, only one or two stories high, contain about 10 to 30 rooms, and are made of wood with a tile roof. Most guests arrive at their *ryokan* around 3 or 4pm. The entrance is often through a gate and small courtyard garden; upon entering, you're met by a bowing woman in a kimono. Take off your shoes, slide on the proffered plastic slippers, and follow your hostess down the long wooden corridors until you reach the sliding door of your room. After taking off your slippers, step into your *tatami* room, almost void of furniture except for a low table in the middle of the room, floor cushions, an antique scroll hanging in a *tokonoma* (alcove), and a simple flower arrangement. Best of all is the view past rice-paper sliding screens of a Japanese landscaped garden with bonsai, stone lanterns, and a meandering pond filled with carp. Notice there's no bed in the room.

Almost immediately, your hostess serves you welcoming hot tea and a sweet at your low table so you can sit there for a while, recuperate from your travels, and appreciate the view, the peace, and the solitude. Next comes your hot bath, either in your own room or in the communal bath. Because many *ryokan* are clustered around *onsen,* many offer the additional luxury of bathing in thermal baths, including outdoor baths. (For bathing, be sure to follow the procedure outlined above under "Etiquette"— soaping and rinsing *before* getting into the tub.) After bathing and soaking away all travel fatigue, aches, and pains, change into your *yukata,* a cotton kimono provided by the *ryokan.* You can wear your *yukata* throughout the *ryokan,* even to its restaurant if there is one (in Western-style hotels, however, never wear a *yukata* outside your room unless you're going to its public bath, or it's located in a resort *onsen* setting; take your cue from other guests).

> ### How to Wear Your Yukata
>
> The proper way to wear a *yukata* is to first fold the right side over your body and then wrap over it with the left side on the outside; the opposite is done only when a person has died.

When you return to your room from your bath, you'll find the maid ready to serve your *kaiseki* dinner, an elaborate spread that is the highlight of a *ryokan* stay. It generally consists of locally grown vegetables, sashimi (raw fish), grilled or baked fish, tempura, and various regional specialties, all spread out on many tiny plates; the menu is determined by the chef. Admire how each dish is in itself a delicate piece of artwork; it all looks too wonderful to eat, but finally hunger takes over. If you want, you can order sake or beer to accompany your meal (you'll pay extra for drinks).

After your meal, your maid will return to clear away the dishes and to lay out your futon, a two-layered mattress with quilts, on the *tatami* floor. The next morning, the maid will wake you, put away the futon, and serve a breakfast of fish, pickled vegetables, soup, dried seaweed, rice, and other dishes. Feeling rested, well fed, and pampered, you're then ready to pack your bags and pay your bill. Your hostess sees you off at the front gate, smiling and bowing as you set off for the rest of your travels.

Such is life at a good *ryokan.* Sadly, the number of upper-class *ryokan* diminishes each year. Unable to compete with more profitable high-rise hotels, many *ryokan* in Japan have closed down, especially in large cities; very few remain in such cities as Tokyo and Osaka. If you want to stay in a Japanese inn, it's best to do so in Kyoto, smaller towns like Takayama, or at a hot-spring spa like Hakone.

In addition, although ideally a *ryokan* is an old wooden structure that once served traveling *daimyo* or was perhaps the home of a wealthy merchant, many today—especially those in hot-spring resort areas—are actually modern concrete affairs with as many as 100 or more rooms, with meals served in communal dining rooms. What they lack in intimacy and personal service, however, is made up for with cheaper prices and such amenities as modern bathing facilities and perhaps outdoor recreational facilities.

Although I heartily recommend you try spending at least 1 night in a *ryokan,* there are a number of disadvantages to this style of accommodations. The most obvious problem is that you may find it uncomfortable sitting on the floor. And because the futon is put away during the day, there's no place to lie down for an afternoon nap or rest, except on the hard, *tatami*-covered floor. In addition, some of the older *ryokan,* though quaint, can be cold in the winter and—though increasingly rare—may have only Japanese-style toilets (see "Toilets," on p. 340). As for breakfast, you might find it difficult to swallow raw egg, rice, and seaweed in the morning. Some *ryokan,* however, offer a Western-style breakfast if you order it the night before, but more often than not the fried or scrambled eggs will arrive cold, leading you to suspect they were cooked right after you ordered them. Resort *ryokan* with dining halls almost always offer breakfast buffets, however, with both Western and Japanese dishes.

Roller Bag Etiquette

I love my roller bag, but under no circumstances should you roll a bag on *tatami* or on old wooden floors of Japanese inns.

A traditional *ryokan* is also quite rigid in its schedule. You're expected to arrive sometime between 3 and 5pm, take your bath, and then eat at around 6 or 7pm. Breakfast is served early, usually by 8am, and checkout is by 10am. That means you can't sleep in, and because the maid is continually coming in and out, you have a lot less privacy than you would in a hotel.

RATES & RESERVATIONS Rates in a *ryokan* are always per person rather than per room and include breakfast, dinner, and often service and tax. Thus, while rates may seem high, they're actually competitively priced compared to what you'd pay for a hotel room and comparable meals in a restaurant. Although rates can vary from ¥9,000 to an astonishing ¥150,000 per person, the average cost is generally ¥12,000 to ¥25,000. Even within a single *ryokan* the rates can vary greatly, depending on the room you choose, the dinner courses you select, and the number of people in your room. If you're paying the highest rate, you can be certain you're getting the best room with the best view and maybe even a more elaborate meal than lower-paying guests. All the rates for *ryokan* in this book are based on double occupancy; if there are more than two of you in one room, you can generally count on a slightly lower per-person rate; small children who sleep in the same bed as their parents often receive a discount as well. Although most Japanese would never dream of checking into an exclusive *ryokan* solo, lone travelers may be able to secure a room if it's not peak season.

You should always make a **reservation** if you want to stay in a first-class *ryokan* (and even in most medium-priced ones unless it offers buffet meals), because the chef has to shop for and prepare your meals. For more information on *ryokan,* including destinations not covered in this guide, check the websites of the **Japan Ryokan & Hotel Association** (www.ryokan.or.jp), which lists some 1,200 inns and hotels, and **Japanese Guest Houses** (www.japaneseguesthouses.com), with more than 600 member high-end and moderately priced Japanese inns.

MINSHUKU Technically, a *minshuku* is inexpensive Japanese-style lodging in a private home—the Japanese version of a bed-and-breakfast. Usually located in tourist areas, rural settings, or small towns, *minshuku* can range from thatched farmhouses and rickety old wooden buildings to modern concrete structures. Because *minshuku* are family-run affairs, there's no personal service, which means you may be expected to lay out your own futon at night, stow it away in the morning, and tidy up your room. Most also do not supply a towel or *yukata,* nor do they have rooms with a private bathroom. There is, however, a public bathroom, and meals, usually included in the rates, are served in a communal dining room. Many *minshuku* owners have day jobs, so it's important for guests to be punctual for meals and checkout.

Officially, what differentiates a *ryokan* from a *minshuku* is the level of service and corresponding price, but the differences in each category are sometimes large. I've stayed in cheap *ryokan* providing almost no service and in *minshuku* too large to be considered private homes. The average per-person cost for 1 night in a *minshuku,* including two meals, is generally ¥7,000 to

¥10,000 with two meals; most do not accept credit cards. Reservations for *minshuku* should be made directly with the establishment.

SHUKUBO These are lodgings in a Buddhist temple, similar to inexpensive *ryokan,* except they're attached to temples and serve vegetarian food. There's usually an early morning service at 6am, which you're welcome—in some *shukubo,* required—to join. Probably the best place to experience life in a temple is at Mount Koya (see chapter 10) or in Kyoto. Prices at shukubo generally range from about ¥5,000 to ¥16,000 per person, including two meals.

Western-Style Accommodations

Western-style lodgings range from luxurious first-class hotels to inexpensive ones catering primarily to Japanese business travelers.

HOTELS Both first-class and mid-priced hotels in Japan are known for excellent service and cleanliness. Japan's first-class hotels can compete with the best in the world, offering exceptional service and wide-ranging facilities, including health clubs and spas, top-class restaurants, and shopping arcades. Unfortunately, health clubs and swimming pools usually cost extra—anywhere from ¥1,050 to an outrageous ¥5,000 per single use. In addition, outdoor pools are open only from about mid-July through August (the school holiday season); many of these also charge a fee.

Almost all hotels in Japan offer a spectrum of rooms at various prices, with room size the overwhelming factor in pricing, though other factors can include bed size, floor height (higher floors are more expensive), and in-room amenities. Rooms with views—whether of the sea or a castle or even of cityscapes—are usually pricier.

Rooms come with such standard features as a minibar or empty fridge you stock yourself, TV, high-speed Internet or Wi-Fi, *yukata* or pajamas, a hot-water pot and tea (and occasionally coffee, although you usually have to pay extra for it), a hair dryer, and a private bathroom with a tub/shower combination. (Because Japanese are used to soaping down and rinsing off before bathing, it would be rare to find tubs without showers; similarly, showers without tubs are practically nonexistent in this nation of bathers.) Virtually all hotels also have "Washlet" toilets, which are combination toilets and spray bidets with a controllable range of speeds and temperatures.

> ### A Double or a Twin?
>
> In Japan, a **twin room** refers to a room with twin beds, and a **double room** refers to one with a double (or larger) bed; most hotels charge more for a twin room, but others charge more for doubles. Because Japanese couples generally prefer twin beds, doubles are often in short supply, especially in business hotels. A **Hollywood twin** means two twin beds pushed together side by side. *Note:* For the sake of convenience, the "double" rates for hotels listed in this book refer to two people in one room and include both twin and double beds.

Be sure to give your approximate time of arrival, especially if it's after 6pm, or they might give your room away. Check-in ranges from about 1 or 2pm in first-class hotels to 3 or 4pm for business hotels. Checkout is generally 10am for business hotels and 11am or noon for upper-range hotels. In any case, it's perfectly acceptable to leave luggage with the front desk or bell captain if you arrive early or want to sightsee after checking out.

BUSINESS HOTELS   Catering traditionally to Japanese business travelers, a "business hotel" is a no-frills establishment with tiny, sparsely furnished rooms, most of them singles but usually with some twin and maybe double rooms also available. Primarily just places to crash for the night, these rooms usually have everything you need, but in miniature form—minuscule bathroom, tiny bathtub/shower, small bed (or beds), TV, telephone, radio, clock, *yukata* or pajamas, Wi-Fi or Internet connections, empty fridge, and barely enough space to unpack your bags. There are no bellhops, no room service, and sometimes not even a lobby or coffee shop, although usually there are vending machines selling beer, soda, cigarettes, and snacks. The advantages of staying in business hotels are price—starting as low as ¥6,000 or ¥7,000 for a single—and location—usually near major train and subway stations. Check-in is usually not until 3 or 4pm, and checkout is usually at 10am; you can leave your bags at the front desk.

As for business-hotel chains, I'm partial to Toyoko Inn (www.toyoko-inn. com), which boasts more than 240 locations around Japan and almost always employs female managers. Other budget and medium-priced chains are Tokyu Inns, most with specially designed Ladies Rooms with female-oriented toiletries and amenities (www.tokyuhotels.com); Washington Hotels (www.wh-rsv. com); the Sunroute Hotel Chain (www.sunroute.jp); Mitsui Garden Hotels (www.gardenhotels.co.jp); APA Hotels & Resorts (www.apahotel.com); and Super Hotel (www.superhoteljapan.com/en), with the lowest rates around.

GUESTHOUSES   Virtually nonexistent more than a decade ago, low-cost guesthouses have opened in cities around the country, catering primarily to backpackers and travelers who don't mind close quarters. Although they often have a few tiny private rooms with *tatami* or beds for one or two people, the majority are known primarily for their dormitory rooms, with shared bathrooms down the hall. Many have communal kitchens and lounging areas as well. Some are better than others; I've included those that rise above the rest in some of the more expensive cities.

YOUTH HOSTELS   There are some 230 youth hostels in Japan, most of them privately run and operating in locations ranging from temples to concrete blocks. There's no age limit (although children 3 and younger may not be accepted), and although most require a youth hostel membership card, some let foreigners stay without one at no extra charge or for ¥600 extra per night (after 6 nights, you automatically become a YH member). Or, buy an International Hostel Card for ¥2,800. Youth hostels average about ¥3,360 per day without meals, and can be reserved in advance. However, there are usually quite a few restrictions, such as a 9 or 10pm curfew, a lights-out policy shortly thereafter, an early breakfast time, and closed times through the day, generally from about 10am to 3pm. In addition, rooms are generally dormitory-style with bunk beds or futons, though some have rooms for two or more persons. Because youth hostels are often inconveniently located, I have included only two (in Tokyo and Kyoto), but if you plan on staying almost exclusively in hostels, pick up a pamphlet called "Youth Hostel Map of Japan," available at the Tourist Information Centers in Japan, or check www.jyh.or.jp.

CAPSULE HOTELS   Capsule hotels, which became popular in the 1980s, are used primarily by Japanese businessmen who have spent an evening out drinking and missed the last train home—costing about ¥3,000 to ¥5,000 per person, a capsule hotel is sometimes cheaper than a taxi to the suburbs. Units are small—no larger than a coffin—and are usually stacked two deep in rows down a corridor; the only thing separating you from your probably inebriated neighbor is a curtain. A cotton kimono and a locker are provided, and bathrooms and toilets are communal. Most capsule hotels don't accept women, but those that do have separate facilities.

LOVE HOTELS   Finally, a word about Japan's so-called "love hotels." Usually found close to entertainment districts and along major highways, such hotels do not provide sexual services themselves; rather, they offer rooms for rent by the hour to couples. You'll know that you've wandered into a love-hotel district when you notice hourly rates posted near the front door, though gaudy structures shaped like ocean liners or castles are also a dead giveaway. Because many of them have reasonable overnight rates as well, I have friends who, finding themselves out too late and too far from home, have checked into love hotels, solo.

WHEN TO GO

The best times to visit western Honshu are spring (Apr to mid-June) and autumn (Sept–Nov). Most of the area lies in a temperate seasonal wind zone similar to that of the East Coast of the United States, which means there are four distinct seasons. Japanese are very proud of their seasons and place much more emphasis on them than people do in the West. Kimono, dishes and bowls used for *kaiseki,* and even *Noh* plays change with the season. Almost all haiku have seasonal references. The cherry blossom signals the beginning of spring, and most festivals are tied to seasonal rites. Even urban dwellers note the seasons; almost as though on cue, businessmen will change virtually overnight from their winter to summer attire.

Summer, which begins in June, is heralded by the rainy season, which lasts from about mid-June to mid-July. Although it doesn't rain every day, it does rain a lot, sometimes quite heavily, making umbrellas imperative. After the rain stops, it turns unbearably hot and uncomfortably humid throughout the country, with the exception of mountaintop resorts such as Hakone and the Japan Alps. You'll be more comfortable in light cottons, though you should bring a light jacket for unexpected cool evenings or air-conditioned rooms. You should also pack sunscreen and a hat (Japanese women are also fond of parasols).

The period from the end of August to September is **typhoon season,** although the majority of storms stay out at sea and generally vent their fury on land only in thunderstorms.

Autumn, lasting through November, is one of the best times to visit Japan, but it's also one of the most crowded seasons. The days are pleasant and slightly cool, and the changing red and scarlet of leaves contrast brilliantly with the deep blue skies. There are many chrysanthemum shows in Japan at this time, popular maple-viewing spots, and many autumn festivals. Bring a warm jacket.

Winter, lasting from December to March, is marked by snow in much of Japan, especially in the mountain ranges. Many tourists also flock to hot-spring resorts during this time. The climate is generally dry, and on the Pacific coast the skies are often blue. Tokyo doesn't get much snow, though it can be crisp, cold, and wet. Wherever you are, you'd be wise to bring warm clothing throughout the winter months.

Spring arrives with a magnificent fanfare of plum and cherry blossoms in March and April, an exquisite time when all of Japan is ablaze in whites and pinks. The blossoms themselves last only a few days, symbolizing to Japanese the fragile nature of beauty and of life itself. Other flowers blooming through May or June include azaleas and irises. Numerous festivals throughout Japan celebrate the rebirth of nature.

Tokyo's Average Daytime Temperatures & Rainfall

	JAN	FEB	MAR	APR	MAY	JUNE	JULY	AUG	SEPT	OCT	NOV	DEC
TEMP. (°F)	42	45	50	61	69	71	78	81	76	68	57	48
TEMP. (°C)	5	7	10	16	21	22	26	27	24	20	14	9
DAYS OF RAIN	4.3	6.1	8.9	10	9.6	12.1	10	8.2	10.9	8.9	6.4	3.8

BUSY SEASONS Japanese have a passion for travel, and they generally travel at the same time, resulting in jam-packed trains and hotels. The worst times to travel are around New Year's, from the end of December to January 4; Golden Week, from April 29 to May 5; and during the Obon Festival, about a week in mid-August. Avoid traveling on these dates at all costs, since all long-distance trains and most accommodations are booked solid and prices are higher. The weekends before and after these holidays are also likely to be crowded or booked.

Other busy times are during the school summer vacation, from around July 19 or 20 through August, cherry blossom season, and when leaves change in autumn. In addition, you can expect destinations to be packed during major festivals, so if one of these is high on your list, make plans well in advance.

HOLIDAYS National holidays are January 1 (New Year's Day), second Monday in January (Coming-of-Age Day), February 11 (National Foundation Day), March 20 (Vernal Equinox Day), April 29 (Showa Day, after the late Emperor Showa), May 3 (Constitution Memorial Day), May 4 (Greenery Day), May 5 (Children's Day), third Monday in July (Maritime Day), August 11 (Mountain Day, a new holiday beginning in 2016); third Monday in September (Respect-for-the-Aged Day), September 23 (Autumn Equinox Day), second Monday in October (Health Sports Day), November 3 (Culture Day;

many municipal museums are free), November 23 (Labor Thanksgiving Day), and December 23 (Emperor's Birthday).

When a national holiday falls on a Sunday, the following Monday becomes a holiday. Although government offices and some businesses are closed on public holidays, most stores and restaurants remain open. The exception is during the New Year's celebration, January 1 through January 3 or 4, when virtually all restaurants, public and private offices, stores, and even ATMs close; during that time, you'll have to dine in hotels.

All museums close for New Year's for 1 to 4 days, but most major museums remain open for the other holidays. If a public holiday falls on a Monday (when most museums are closed), many museums will remain open but will close instead the following day, Tuesday. Note, however, that privately owned museums, such as art museums or special-interest museums, generally close on public holidays. To avoid disappointment, be sure to phone ahead if you plan to visit a museum on a holiday or the day following it.

Western Honshu Calendar of Events

JANUARY

New Year's Day is the most important national holiday in Japan. Because this is a time when Japanese are with their families and virtually all businesses, restaurants, museums, and shops close down, it's not a particularly rewarding time for visitors. Best bets are shrines and temples, where Japanese come in their best kimono or dress to pray for health and happiness. January 1.

Dezomeshiki (New Year's Parade of Firemen), Tokyo Big Sight, Odaiba, Tokyo. Agile firemen dressed in Edo-Era costumes prove their worth with acrobatic stunts atop tall bamboo ladders in this parade, with fire trucks, helicopters, and emergency drills adding to the excitement. January 6.

Coming-of-Age Day, a national holiday. This day honors young people who have reached the age of 20, when they can vote, drink alcohol, and assume other responsibilities. On this day, they visit shrines throughout the country to pray for their future, with many women dressed in kimono. In Tokyo, the most popular shrine is Meiji Shrine near Hara-juku Station. Second Monday in January.

Toka Ebisu Festival, Imamiya Ebisu Shrine, Osaka. Ebisu is considered the patron saint of business and good fortune, so this is the time when businesspeople pray for a successful year. The highlight of the festival is a parade of women dressed in colorful kimono and carried through the streets in palanquins (covered litters). Stalls sell good-luck charms. January 9 to January 11.

Toh-shiya, Kyoto. This traditional Japanese archery contest is held in the back corridor of Japan's longest wooden structure, Sanjusan-gendo Hall. Sunday closest to January 15.

Yamayaki (Grass Fire Ceremony), Nara. As evening approaches, Wakakusayama Hill is set ablaze and fireworks are displayed. The celebration marks a time more than 1,000 years ago when a dispute over the boundary of two major temples in Nara was settled peacefully. Fourth Saturday in January.

FEBRUARY

Setsubun Mantoro (Lantern Festival), Kasuga Shrine, Nara. A beautiful sight in which more than 3,000 stone and bronze lanterns are lit from 6:30 to 9pm. February 3 and August 14 and 15.

MARCH

Omizutori (Water-Drawing Festival), Todaiji Temple, Nara. This festival includes a solemn evening rite in which young ascetics brandish large burning torches and draw circles of fire. The biggest event takes place on March 13, when is drawn and offered to Buddhist deities to the accompaniment of ancient Japanese music. March 1 to March 14.

Hinamatsuri (Doll Festival), observed throughout Japan. It's held in honor of young girls to wish them a future of happiness. In homes where there are girls, dolls dressed in ancient costumes representing the emperor, empress, and dignitaries are set up on a tier of shelves along with miniature household articles. Many hotels also display dolls in their lobbies. March 3.

AnimeJapan, Tokyo Big Sight, Odaiba (www.anime-japan.jp). One of the world's largest Japanese animation events draws more than 100 production companies, film agencies, toy and game software companies, publishers, and other *anime*-related companies. Usually third weekend in March.

APRIL

Kanamara Matsuri, Kanayama Shrine, Kawasaki (just outside Tokyo). This festival extols the joys of sex and fertility (and, more recently, raises awareness about AIDS), featuring a parade of giant phalluses, some carried by transvestites. You'll definitely get some unusual photographs here. First Sunday in April.

Buddha's Birthday (also called Hana Matsuri, or Floral Festival), observed nationwide. Ceremonies are held at all Buddhist temples. April 8.

Kamakura Matsuri, Tsurugaoka Hachimangu Shrine, Kamakura. This festival honors heroes from the past, including Minamoto Yoritomo, who made Kamakura his shogunate capital back in 1192. Highlights include horseback archery (truly spectacular to watch, although fewer and fewer men have the skill), a parade of portable shrines, and sacred dances. Second to third Sunday of April.

Takayama Spring Festival, Takayama. Supposedly dating from the 15th century, this festival is one of Japan's grandest with a dozen huge, gorgeous floats that are wheeled through the village streets. April 14 and 15.

Gumonji-do (Firewalking Ceremonies), Miyajima. Walking on live coals is meant to show devotion and to pray for purification and protection from illness and disaster. Daishoin Temple. April 15 and November 15.

Yayoi Matsuri, Futarasan Shrine, Nikko. Yayoi Matsuri features parades of portable shrines and dance, with the biggest a parade of floats embellished with artificial cherry blossoms and paper lanterns on April 17. April 13 to April 17.

MAY

Children's Day is a national holiday honoring all children, especially boys. The most common sight throughout Japan is colorful streamers of carp—which symbolize perseverance and strength—flying from poles. May 5.

Takigi Noh Performances, Kofukuji Temple, Nara. These *Noh* plays are presented outdoors after dark under the blaze of torches. Third Friday and Saturday in May.

Kanda Festival, Kanda Myojin Shrine, Tokyo. This festival, which commemorates Tokugawa Ieyasu's famous victory at Sekigahara in 1600, began during the Feudal Period as the only time townspeople could enter the shogun's castle and parade before him. Today this major Tokyo festival features a parade of dozens of portable shrines carried through the district, plus geisha dances and a tea ceremony. Held in odd-numbered years (with a smaller festival held in even years) on the Saturday and Sunday closest to May 15.

Aoi Matsuri (Hollyhock Festival), Shimogamo and Kamigamo Shrines, Kyoto. This is one of Kyoto's biggest events, a colorful parade with 500 participants wearing ancient costumes to commemorate the days when the imperial procession visited the city's shrines. May 15.

Shunki Reitaisai (Grand Spring Festival), Nikko. Commemorating the day in 1617 when Tokugawa Ieyasu's remains were brought to his mausoleum in Nikko, this festival re-creates that drama with more than 1,000 armor-clad people escorting three palanquins through the streets. May 17 and 18.

Sanja Matsuri, Asakusa Shrine, Tokyo. Tokyo's most celebrated festival features about 100 portable shrines carried through the district on the shoulders of men and women in traditional garb. Third Sunday and preceding Friday and Saturday of May.

JUNE

Takigi Noh Performances, Kyoto. Evening performances of *Noh* are presented on an open-air stage at the Heian Shrine. June 1 and 2.

Hyakumangoku Matsuri (One Million Goku Festival), Kanazawa. Celebrating Kanazawa's production of one million *goku* of rice (1 goku is about 150kg/330 lb.), this extravaganza features folk songs and traditional dancing in the streets, illuminated paper lanterns floating downriver, public tea ceremonies, geisha performances, and—the highlight—a parade that winds through the city in reenactment of Lord Maeda Toshiie's triumphant arrival in Kanazawa on June 14, 1583, with lion dances, ladder-top acrobatics by firemen, and a torch-lit outdoor *Noh* performance. Three days centered on first Saturday in June.

Sanno Festival, Hie Shrine, Tokyo. This Edo Period festival, one of Tokyo's largest, features the usual portable shrines, transported through the busy streets of the Akasaka District. June 6 to June 17.

Otaue Rice-Planting Festival, Sumiyoshi Taisha Shrine, Osaka. In hopes of a successful harvest, young girls in traditional farmers' costumes transplant rice seedlings in the shrine's rice paddy to the sound of traditional music and songs. June 14.

JULY

Tanabata Matsuri (Star Festival), celebrated throughout Japan. According to myth, the two stars Vega and Altair, representing a weaver and a shepherd, are allowed to meet once a year on this day. If the skies are cloudy, however, the celestial pair cannot meet and must wait another year. Celebrations differ from town to town, but in addition to parades and food/souvenir stalls, look for bamboo branches with colorful strips of paper bearing children's wishes. July 7.

Gion Matsuri, Kyoto. One of the most famous festivals in Japan, this dates back to the 9th century, when the head priest at Yasaka Shrine organized a procession to ask the gods' assistance in a plague raging in the city. Although celebrations continue throughout the month, the highlight is on the 17th, when more than 30 spectacular wheeled floats wind their way through the city streets to the accompaniment of music and dances. Many visitors plan their trip to Japan around this event. July 17.

Obon Festival, nationwide. This festival commemorates the dead who, according to Buddhist belief, revisit the world during this period. Many Japanese return to their hometowns for religious rites, especially if a family member has died recently. As one Japanese whose grandmother had died a few months before told me, "I have to go back to my hometown—it's my grandmother's first Obon." Mid-July or mid-August, depending on the region.

Tenjin Matsuri, Temmangu Shrine, Osaka. One of Japan's biggest festivals, this dates from the 10th century when the people of Osaka visited Temmangu Shrine to pray for protection against diseases prevalent during the long, hot summer. They would take pieces of paper cut in the form of human beings and, while the Shinto priest said prayers, would rub the paper over themselves in ritual cleansing. Afterward, the pieces of paper were taken by boat to the mouth of the river and disposed of. Today, events are reenacted with a procession of more than 100 sacred boats making their way downriver, followed by a fireworks display. There's also a parade of some 3,000 people in traditional costume. July 24 and 25.

Kangensai Music Festival, Itsukushima Shrine, Miyajima. There are classical court music and *Bugaku* dancing, and three barges carry portable shrines, priests, and musicians across the bay along with a flotilla of other boats. Because this festival takes place according to the lunar calendar, the actual date changes each year. Late July or early August.

Hanabi Taikai (Fireworks Display), Tokyo. This is Tokyo's largest summer celebration, and everyone sits on blankets along the banks of the Sumida River near Asakusa to see the show. It's great fun! Last Saturday of July.

AUGUST

Oshiro Matsuri, Himeji. This celebration is famous for its *Noh* dramas lit by bonfire and performed on a special stage on the Himeji Castle grounds, as well as a procession from the castle to the city center with participants dressed as feudal lords and ladies in traditional costume. First Friday and Saturday of August.

Peace Ceremony, Peace Memorial Park, Hiroshima. This ceremony is held annually at 8:15am in memory of those who died in the atomic bomb blast of August 6, 1945. In the evening, thousands of lit lanterns are set adrift on the Ota River in a plea for world peace. August 6.

Daimonji Bonfire, Mount Nyoigadake, Kyoto. A huge bonfire in the shape of the Chinese character *dai*, which means "large," and other motifs are lit near mountain peaks; it's the highlight of the Obon Festival (see July, above). August 16.

SEPTEMBER

Reitaisai (Yabusame), Tsurugaoka Hachimangu Shrine, Kamakura. Archery performed on horseback recalls the days of the samurai, along with classical Japanese dance and a parade of portable shrines. September 16.

OCTOBER

Takayama Matsuri (Autumn Festival), Takayama. As in the festival held here in April, huge floats are paraded through the streets. October 9 and 10.

Nada no Kenka Matsuri (Nada Fighting Festival), Matsubara Hachiman Shrine, Himeji. Men shouldering portable shrines jostle each other as they attempt to show their skill in balancing their heavy burdens. October 14 and 15.

Doburoku Matsuri, Ogimachi, Shirakawago. This village festival honors unrefined sake, said to represent the spirit of God, with a parade, an evening lion dance, and plenty of eating and drinking. October 14 to October 19.

Nikko Toshogu Shrine Festival, Nikko. A parade of warriors in early-17th-century dress are accompanied by spear-carriers, gun-carriers, flag-bearers, Shinto priests, pages, court musicians, and dancers as they escort a sacred portable shrine. October 17.

Jidai Matsuri (Festival of the Ages), Kyoto. Another of Kyoto's grand festivals, this one began in 1894 to commemorate the founding of the city in 794. It features a procession of more than 2,000 people dressed in ancient costumes representing different epochs of Kyoto's 1,200-year history, who march from the Imperial Palace to Heian Shrine. October 22.

NOVEMBER

Daimyo Gyoretsu (Feudal Lord Procession), Yumoto Onsen, Hakone. The old Tokaido Highway that used to link Kyoto and Tokyo comes alive again with a faithful reproduction of a feudal lord's procession in the olden days. November 3.

Shichi-go-san (Children's Shrine-Visiting Day), held throughout Japan. Shichi-go-san literally means "seven-five-three" and refers to children of these ages who are dressed in their kimono best and taken to shrines by their elders to express thanks and pray for their future. November 15.

Tori-no-Ichi (Rake Fair), Otori Shrine, Tokyo. This fair in Asakusa (and other Otori shrines throughout Japan) features stalls selling rakes lavishly decorated with paper and cloth, which are thought to bring good luck and fortune. Based on the lunar calendar, the date changes each year. Mid-November.

DECEMBER

Kasuga Wakamiya On-Matsuri, Kasuga Shrine, Nara. This festival features court music with traditional dance and a parade of people dressed as courtiers, retainers, and wrestlers of long ago. December 15 to December 18.

Hagoita-Ichi (Battledore Fair), Sensoji Temple, Tokyo. Popular since Japan's feudal days, this Asakusa festival features decorated paddles of all types and sizes. Most have designs of *kabuki* actors—images made by pasting together padded silk and brocade—and make great souvenirs and gifts. December 17 to December 19.

New Year's Eve. At midnight, many temples ring huge bells 108 times to signal the end of the old year and the beginning of the new. Families visit temples and shrines throughout Japan to pray for the coming year. December 31.

SUGGESTED ITINERARIES

With its rich culture and stunning scenery, the western half of Honshu has much to offer the curious visitor, not only in and around the major cities like Tokyo and Osaka but in outlying rural regions and villages as well. As the largest of Japan's four major islands and home to most of the country's population, Honshu is where the majority of the country's important historical events took place; you'll find castles, gardens, temples, shrines, and other attractions linked to the past here, many of them World Heritage Sites. Throw in museums displaying everything from avant-garde art to folk art, shops selling everything from lacquerware to designer wear, and scenery ranging from the rugged Japan Alps to the coast of the Seto Inland Sea, and it's little wonder that many travelers to Japan never make it off this central island.

3

If you want to see *everything* outlined in this book, you should plan on spending a minimum of 2 months in Japan. More likely, your time will be limited to a week or two, so you'll have to be selective. This chapter will help you decide on an itinerary and whether you're better off buying one of several options for rail passes or even traveling by bus (see chapter 12). If you're lucky enough to be in Japan for several weeks, you can fashion a personalized tour by combining several of these suggested itineraries and adding a town or more from the chapters that follow. But regardless of what itinerary you plan, *Kyoto is a must for first-time visitors.* It served as the nation's capital for more than 1,000 years and has more temples, shrines, and historic sights than any other Japanese city.

THE REGIONS IN BRIEF

Separated from China and Korea by the Sea of Japan, Japan stretches in an arc about 2,900km (1,800 miles) long from northeast to southwest, yet it is only 403km (250 miles) wide at its broadest point. Japan consists primarily of four main islands—**Honshu, Hokkaido, Shikoku,** and **Kyushu,** surrounded by more than 6,000 smaller, mostly uninhabited islands and islets. If you were to superimpose Japan's four main islands onto a map of the United States, they would stretch all the way from Boston to Atlanta.

Yet Japan's total landmass is slightly smaller than California in area, with as much as 70% of it mountainous and uninhabitable and another 20% devoted to agriculture. That means that Japan's 127 million people are concentrated primarily in only 10% of the country's landmass, mostly along Honshu's vast plains surrounding Tokyo and Osaka. In other words, imagine 40% of the U.S. population living in California—primarily in San Diego County—and you get an idea of how crowded Japan is.

Because many of Japan's mountains are volcanic in origin, earthquakes have plagued the country throughout history. In the 20th century, the two most destructive earthquakes were the 1923 Great Kanto Earthquake, which killed more than 100,000 people in the Tokyo area, and the 1995 Great Hanshin Earthquake, which claimed more than 6,000 lives in Kobe. They were followed in 2011 by Japan's largest earthquake in recorded history, the Great East Japan Earthquake, which struck off the northeast Honshu coast and triggered a massive tsunami that contributed to the loss of more than 19,000 lives.

For this island nation—isolated physically from the rest of the world, struck repeatedly through the centuries by earthquakes, tsunamis, fires, and typhoons, and possessed of only limited space for harmonious living—geography and topography have played major roles both in determining its development and in shaping its culture, customs, and arts.

As Japan's largest island, Honshu might be considered the Japanese mainland (its name translates as "Main Province"). It has 80% of Japan's population, Japan's tallest mountain (Mount Fuji), and 34 of Japan's 47 **prefectures,** which are comparable to the U.S. state or the British county and each with its own capital. The western half of Honshu can be divided into four regions, namely Kanto (where the Tokyo metropolitan area is located), Chubu (central Honshu), Kansai (home to Kyoto and Osaka), and Chugoku (the westernmost end of Honshu).

TOKYO & THE KANTO DISTRICT   Located in east-central Honshu, this district is characterized by the vast Kanto Plain, the largest flatland in Japan. Although development of the area didn't begin in earnest until the establishment of the shogunate government in Edo (present-day Tokyo) in 1603, Tokyo and surrounding mega-cities like Yokohama comprise the most densely populated region in Japan, if not the world, home to more than 35 million people. There are seven prefectures in Kanto, including Tokyo, the name of both the city (with 9 million inhabitants) and the larger prefecture (with 13 million inhabitants). Although Tokyo is the main tourist draw, worthwhile side trips include Nikko, Kamakura, and Hakone.

KANSAI DISTRICT   Also called the Kinki District and encompassing seven prefectures, this is Japan's most historic region. **Nara** and **Kyoto**—two of Japan's ancient capitals—are here, as are two of Japan's most important port cities, **Kobe** and **Osaka.** Since the 1994 opening of Kansai International Airport outside Osaka, many foreign visitors opt to bypass Tokyo altogether in favor of Kansai's many historic spots, including **Mount Koya** with its many temples, **Himeji** with what I consider to be Japan's most beautiful castle, Nara with its Great Buddha and temples, and, of course, Kyoto, the former capital for more than 1,000 years, with so many temples, imperial villas, and gardens that it ranks as Japan's foremost tourist destination.

CHUBU DISTRICT The Chubu, or central, District lies between the Kanto and Kansai plains and straddles central Honshu from the Pacific Ocean to the Japan Sea, encompassing nine prefectures. The district features mountain ranges, including the **Japan Alps,** host of the 1998 XVIII Winter Olympics, volcanoes (including **Mount Fuji**), large rivers, and coastal regions on both sides of the island. The quaint mountain villages of **Takayama** and **Shirakawa-go** are rewarding respites from city life. In 2015, Japan's newest bullet train, the Hokuriku Shinkansen, made **Kanazawa** with its spectacular garden and Edo-era attractions easily accessible from Tokyo.

CHUGOKU DISTRICT Honshu's southwestern district has five prefectures and is divided by the Chugoku Mountain Range. Industrial giant **Hiroshima** is one of the region's biggest cities and draws many tourists to its Memorial Peak Park, dedicated to victims of the world's first atomic bomb. En route to Hiroshima is **Kurashiki,** a must-see for its photogenic warehouse district, while **Miyajima,** part of the Seto-Naikai (Inland Sea) National Park, is considered one of Japan's most beautiful islands.

WESTERN HONSHU HIGHLIGHTS

This trip, designed for first-timers, takes you to Japan's highlights, from fast-paced Tokyo to the quiet temples of Kyoto, along with a couple of other worthwhile destinations like Hiroshima. Plan on about a week, but if time permits, add destinations from the other two itineraries outlined below or one of the recommended side trips in chapters 6 or 10.

Days 1 & 2: Tokyo ★★★

No one should miss this adrenaline-rush of a metropolis; you'll need at least 2 full days to do it justice. Hit the highlights like the **Tsukiji Fish Market,** the 45th-floor **observatory** in Shinjuku for its eye-popping views, and the **Tokyo National Museum** with the world's largest collection of Japanese art. Be sure to allow time wandering its diverse neighborhoods, including **Asakusa** with its famous temple and old downtown atmosphere, electrifying **Akihabara** with stores selling everything from cameras to anime figurines, and **Harajuku** with its vibrant teeny-bopper scene and Oriental Bazaar souvenir shop. Top it off with a stroll through **Kabuki-cho,** Japan's most notorious and crazy nightlife district. See chapters 4 and 5.

Day 3: Hakone ★★★

Take an early train to Hakone Yumoto, gateway to the wonderful **Fuji-Hakone-Izu National Park.** Here you can see some of Japan's most

Western Honshu Highlights

scenic countryside via a circuitous route that includes a three-car mountain train, a cable car, ropeway, and a boat, while seeing such sights as the wonderful **Hakone Open-Air Museum** and, if you're lucky, the elusive **Mount Fuji.** Be sure to schedule some time for a dip in a hot-spring bath, and spend the night in the historic **Fujiya Hotel** or a Japanese inn. See chapter 6.

Days 4, 5 & 6: Kyoto ★★★

Capital for more than 1,000 years, Kyoto is Japan's number-one must see. Top historic sites include **Nijo Castle,** former home of the shogun; **Ryoanji Temple** with its famous Zen rock garden; and the **Golden Pavilion.** Take a self-guided walk through eastern Kyoto, seeing **Sanjusangendo Hall** with its 1,001 wooden statues and **Kiyomizu Temple,** shopping for crafts along the way. Be sure to sample Kyoto's legendary Buddhist vegetarian cuisine, stroll through its famous geisha quarters, and spend at least 1 night in a Japanese-style inn. See chapter 8.

Day 7: Hiroshima ★★

The top destination in Hiroshima is **Peace Memorial Park** with its memorials and museum that detail events surrounding the explosion of the atomic bomb. Within walking distance of the park is also a castle, garden, and art museum, but if you have another day, be sure to include a trip to the nearby island of **Miyajima,** home of a famous shrine and considered one of Japan's most scenic places. See chapter 11.

HIGHLIGHTS OF CHUBU

The completion of the Hokuriku Shinkansen in March 2015 made Kanazawa easily accessible from Tokyo for the first time, cutting the trip between the two cities from 4 hours to about 1½. The destinations I outline here—a former castle town, a mountain village, and an attractive former merchants' town— are a fun alternative to the usual tourist agenda. The circuitous route can begin and end in Tokyo, or it can be added to a trip that continues onward to Kyoto. For more on these towns, see chapter 7.

Days 1 & 2: Kanazawa ★★

A former castle town, Kanazawa is famous for its **Kenrokuen Garden,** considered one of Japan's best landscape gardens and the one I recommend the most. Because of its lofty position, there are no skyscrapers to detract from its gorgeous setting of ponds, streams, and strategically placed trees and rocks. It once served as the outer garden of **Kanazawa Castle,** of which the original Ishikawa Gate remains along with reconstructed fortifications built using traditional methods. While in Kanazawa be sure to visit other sights related to Japan's feudal era, including its well-preserved former geisha and samurai districts and **Myoryuji Temple** (known as the Ninja Temple).

Day 3: Shirakawa-go ★★

It's a 90-minute bus ride onward to Shirakawa-go, where you'll find the village of **Ogimachi,** part of a World Heritage Site due to its thatch-roofed houses. Several farmhouses are open to the public as museums, but your reason for coming here is to actually spend the night in one so you can explore this unique place after day-trippers have gone. For further relaxation, you might even consider taking a dip in the public hot-spring bath.

Days 4 & 5: Takayama ★★★

An hour's bus ride from Shirakawa-go, Takayama is nestled in the Japan Alps and is often nicknamed "Little Kyoto" because of the picturesque, narrow streets of this old castle town. It's the perfect place to experience *tatami* living, with accommodations available at various price ranges. A must-see is **Takayama Jinya,** the only regional administrative building

Highlights of Chubu

1 Kanazawa
2 Shirakawa-go
3 Takayama

from the shogun era still in existence, but I also wouldn't miss the two **merchant homes** open to the public. Other highlights include the **Hirata Folk Art Museum** filled with everyday items used during the feudal age and the quirky **Takayama Showa Museum** that provides fascinating insights into life in Japan from the 1920s to 1980s. On your second day, the **Miyagawa Morning Market** is a great way to start the morning, followed by explorations through the historic district and a hike along the Higashiyama Walking Course on a ridge above the town that leads past a dozen temples and shrines. From Takayama you can take a bus back to Tokyo or board a train for Osaka or Kyoto.

WEST HONSHU'S WORLD HERITAGE SITES

Japan has 18 cultural and natural properties inscribed on the World Heritage List, 12 of them in west Honshu. It should be noted, however, that many listed sites actually consist of numerous properties, such as the 17 temples, shrines, and castle that make up the "Historic Monuments of Ancient Kyoto." For that reason, you'd have to be pretty dedicated to visit all the World Heritage Sites contained in this book. This tour takes in the highlights, excluding Shirakawa-go already mentioned above; if time is limited, you could also skip Nikko and fly directly into KIX airport and then head to Kyoto. But don't forget to schedule time for kicking back and enjoying the Japan of today, including that most satisfying of experiences, dining on Japanese cuisine. But even that could be considered part of this tour, since *washoku,* traditional Japanese cuisine, was added to UNESCO's Intangible Cultural Heritage list in 2013.

Day 1: Nikko ★★★

About 2 hours north of Tokyo, **Nikko** is famous for its sumptuous mausoleum of Tokugawa Ieyasu, Japan's most famous shogun, set in a forest of majestic cedars. It's part of the "Shrines and Temples of Nikko," which became a World Heritage Site in 1999 and were constructed mostly in the 17th century. To get the most out of your stay, spend the night in the old Nikko Kanaya Hotel or in a Japanese inn with hot-spring baths. See chapter 6.

Days 3, 4 & 5: Kyoto ★★★

En route to Kyoto on the Shinkansen, keep a lookout as you near Shizuoka Station for views of **Mount Fuji,** declared a World Heritage Site in 2013 as a sacred place and the source of artistic inspiration. Otherwise, **Kyoto,** Japan's capital and center of Japanese culture for more than 1,000 years, could be considered the epitome of World Heritage Sites in Japan. Its 16 religious structures and **Nijo Castle,** most built or designed from the 10th to the 17th centuries, include an astounding 189 buildings and 12 gardens. Among the must-sees are Nijo Castle (where the shogun stayed whenever he came to Kyoto), **Ryoanji** with its Zen rock garden, **Kiyomizu Temple, Ginkakuji** (Temple of the Silver Pavilion), and **Kinkakuji** (Temple of the Golden Pavilion). See chapter 8.

Days 6 & 7: Nara ★★★ & Horyuji ★★★

Less than an hour's train ride from Kyoto, **Nara** is even older than Kyoto and served as the nation's capital for 74 years. Although it can be visited in a day's outing, you'll need to spend the night to see all that make up the "Historic Monuments of Ancient Nara" and the "Buddhist Monuments in the Horyuji Area." On the way, stop in Uji to see **Byodoin Temple,** part of Kyoto's heritage sites and considered one of the best examples of temple architecture from the Heian Period (795–1192); it's famous for its Phoenix Hall, which graces the back of ¥10 coins. Most of Nara's impressive sights are within expansive **Nara Park,** where deer (considered divine messengers) roam free; foremost here is the **Great**

West Honshu's World Heritage Sites

Legend:
1. Nikko
2. Kyoto
3. Nara
4. Mt. Koya
5. Himeji Castle
6. Hiroshima's Peace Memorial Park
7. Miyajima

Buddha, housed inside the largest wooden structure in the world (p. 287). In Horyuji are Japan's earliest Buddhist monuments, some of them dating from the 7th century and considered the oldest surviving wooden buildings in the world (p. 288).

Day 8: Mount Koya ★★★

Accessible from Osaka via train and cable car, **Mount Koya** (p. 292) is Japan's most sacred religious site, achingly beautiful with more than 115 Buddhist temples spread through the dense forests of the Kii Mountain Range. Be sure to take both a day and a nighttime stroll past towering cypress trees and countless tombs and memorial tablets to **Okunoin,** the burial ground of Kobo Daishi, one of Japan's most revered Buddhist priests. Spend the night in a temple, dining on vegetarian food.

Day 9: Himeji Castle ★★★

If you see only one castle in town, **Himeji Castle** (p. 296) is the one. Said to resemble a white heron poised in flight over the plains, it is quite simply Japan's finest example of early-17th-century Japanese castle architecture and in 1993 became Japan's first World Heritage Site along with Horyuji. You'll want to spend at least 2 hours exploring the extensive grounds with their ingenious defense mechanisms, including a five-story keep, gates, moats, turrets, and maze of passageways that have survived virtually intact since feudal times. Then hop back on the Shinkansen for Hiroshima.

Day 10: Hiroshima's Peace Memorial Park ★★★

Hiroshima is most famous for its **Peace Memorial Park** (p. 314), which contains some 50 statues and memorials and the Peace Memorial Museum dedicated to those who lost their lives because of the atomic bomb. While you'll certainly want to see it all, the most eye-catching structure here is the **Genbaku Dome,** the only structure left standing from the World War II destruction and declared a World Heritage Site in 1996.

Day 11: Miyajima ★★★

Most visitors see **Miyajima** on a day trip from Hiroshima, but you'll get more out of this gem of an island, a holy Shinto site since early times, by spending the night. Ikutsukushima Shrine, built over the sea and with Mount Misen rising in the background, does an outstanding job of combining traditional Shinto architecture with nature. Although reconstructed twice, the shrine meticulously preserves its original styles from the late 12th and early 13th centuries. Be sure to see the shrine at night when it's illuminated. And if time permits, you should also hike or take the cable car up to Mount Misen, where you'll be rewarded with great views of the Inland Sea and hiking paths to religious sites. If it's summer, you might also want to hit Miyajima's beaches. After this treasure-laden itinerary, you deserve it.

TOKYO ESSENTIALS

To the uninitiated, **Tokyo** ★★★ may seem like a whirlwind of traffic and people, so dense and confusing that visitors might think they have landed on another planet. More than 13 million people reside in Greater Tokyo's 2,188 sq. km (845 sq. miles); no matter where you go, you're never alone. After you've been here for a while, Paris, London, and even New York will seem deserted. Perhaps that's why some visitors are disappointed with Tokyo: It has almost nothing of historical importance to match, say, Kyoto. Yet crowds and urban sprawl are what you'll see only if you don't bother to look beneath the surface. So put your notions of quaint Japan out of your mind and plunge headfirst into the 21st century, because that's what Tokyo is all about.

But even though the city has a fast-paced, somewhat zany side, it also has a quieter and often overlooked side that makes the city both lovable and livable. Although formidable at first glance, Tokyo is nothing more than a series of small towns and neighborhoods clustered together, each with its own atmosphere and history. What's more, beneath Tokyo's concrete shell is a thriving cultural life left very much intact. In fact, if you're interested in Japan's performing arts like Kabuki as well as such diverse activities as sumo, Tokyo is your best bet for offering the most at any one time. It is rich in museums and claims the largest repository of Japanese art in the world. It also gets my vote as the pop-art capital of the world, so if you're into kitsch or *anime* (Japanese animation), you'll be in high heaven. And if you're into style, you'll find Tokyo a mecca for cutting-edge fashion and innovative design.

I love Tokyo. I can't imagine being bored here, even for a minute.

ESSENTIALS

Arriving

BY PLANE

Tokyo has two international airports. **Narita International Airport (NRT;** www.narita-airport.jp; © **0476/34-8000**), located in Narita about 66km (41 miles) east of Tokyo, is by far the largest and serves the most flights. Closer at just 14km (8.6 miles) is **Haneda Airport**

A LOOK AT THE past

Though today the nation's capital, Tokyo is a relative newcomer to the pages of Japanese history. For centuries it was nothing more than a rather unimportant village called Edo, which means simply "mouth of the estuary." In 1603, Edo was catapulted into the limelight when the new shogun, Tokugawa Ieyasu, made the sleepy village the seat of his government. He expanded Edo Castle, making it the largest and most impressive castle in the land, and surrounded it with an ingenious system of moats that radiated from the castle in a great swirl, giving him easy access to the sea and an upper hand in thwarting enemy attack.

The town developed quickly, due largely to the shogun's decree requiring all *daimyo* (feudal lords) to permanently leave their families in Edo, a shrewd move to thwart insurrection in the provinces. There were as many as 270 *daimyo* in Japan in the 17th century, all of whom maintained several mansions in Edo, complete with elaborate compounds and expansive gardens. The *daimyo*'s trusted samurai soon accounted for more than half of Edo's population, and the merchant class expanded as well. By 1787 the population had grown to 1.3 million, making Edo—even then—one of the largest cities in the world.

When the Tokugawas were overthrown in 1868, the Japanese emperor was restored to power and moved the capital from Kyoto to Edo, now renamed Tokyo (Eastern Capital). Japan's Feudal Era—and its isolation from the rest of the world—was over. As the capital city, Tokyo was the hardest hit in this new era of modernization, with fashion, architecture, food, and even people imported from the West. West was best, and things Japanese were forgotten or ignored.

It didn't help that Tokyo was almost totally destroyed twice in the first half of the 20th century: In 1923, a massive earthquake measuring 7.9 on the Richter scale destroyed more than a third of the city and claimed more than 140,000 lives in Tokyo and Yokohama; disaster struck again in 1945, toward the end of World War II when Allied incendiary bombs laid more than half the city to waste and killed another 100,000 people.

But under Allied occupation, which lasted until 1952, Tokyo quickly rebuilt. By 1964 it showcased as one of Asia's most progressive cities when it hosted the Summer Olympics. Although the 6-minute 2011 Great East Japan Earthquake was the most terrifying most Tokyoites had ever experienced, there was virtually no damage to the city itself. It is now gearing up for another big moment in its history, the 2020 Olympics.

(**HND;** www.haneda-airport.jp; © **03/6428-0888**), which operates as Tokyo's domestic airport but is increasingly serving international flights.

NARITA AIRPORT   There are two terminals (1 and 2), both with ATMs and counters for money exchange and open daily 6:30am to 11pm; change enough money here to last several days, as the exchange rate is about the same as in town, the process is speedy, and facilities in town are somewhat limited. There are also **Tourist Information Centers (TIC)** in the arrival lobbies of both terminals open daily 8am to 8pm and offering free maps and pamphlets; staff here can make budget hotel reservations until 7:30pm. If you've purchased a Japan Rail Pass, you can turn in your voucher at the **Japan Railways (JR) Travel Service Center,** located in both terminals and open daily 6:30am to 9:45pm. Other facilities and services at both terminals include post offices, medical clinics, shower rooms, day rooms for napping, children's playrooms, luggage storage and lockers, cellphone rentals, coin-operated Internet terminals (¥100 for 10 min.), and free Wi-Fi. You can also have your suitcase delivered to your place of lodging; it costs about ¥2,000 per bag in the Tokyo area.

By Train   The quickest way to reach Tokyo is by train, with several options available. Trains depart directly from the airport's two underground stations, called Narita Airport Terminal (Terminal 1) and Airport Terminal 2. The JR **Narita Express (N'EX**; www.jreast.co.jp; ⌀ **050/2016-1603**) is the fastest way to reach Tokyo Station, Shinagawa, Shibuya, Shinjuku, or Ikebukuro, with departures approximately twice an hour. The 56-minute trip to Tokyo Station costs ¥3,020 one-way. At Tokyo Station, the train splits, with the front cars going to Shibuya, Shinjuku, and, less frequently, to Ikebukuro, and rear cars going to Shinagawa (cost to these stations: ¥3,190). At the time of going to press, however, a special **N'EX Tokyo Direct Ticket** was being offered to foreign visitors for only ¥1,500. Sold only at Narita Airport, it even allows you to transfer to another JR train line to reach your Tokyo destination; check the website for more information.

Otherwise, if you've validated your JR Rail Pass as mentioned above, you can ride the N'EX free. If the N'EX is sold out and you're still determined to use your rail pass (or you simply wish to save money), you can take the slower **JR Airport Liner,** which will get you to Tokyo Station in 90 minutes. Without a rail pass, this costs ¥1,320.

Another train option, especially if your destination is Ueno, is the privately owned **Keisei Skyliner** (www.keisei.co.jp; ⌀ **03/3831-0131**), which departs directly from both terminals and travels to Ueno Station in Tokyo in as little as 41 minutes. Trains depart Narita approximately one to three times an hour between 8:17am and 10:18pm. The fare between Narita Airport and Ueno Station is ¥2,470 one-way. Travelers on a budget can take one of Keisei's slower limited express trains to Ueno Station, with fares starting at ¥1,240 for the 80-minute trip. Or, if your destination is Asakusa, Nihombashi, Higashi-Ginza, Shimbashi, or Shinagawa, you can also travel on the Narita Sky Access Line or Keisei Main Line, with fares to Asakusa starting at ¥1,100 and to Shimbashi at ¥1,140. You'll find Keisei ticket counters in the arrival lobbies of both terminals.

By Bus   The most popular and stress-free way to get from Narita to Tokyo is via the **Airport Limousine Bus** (www.limousinebus.co.jp; ⌀ **03/3665-7220**), which picks up passengers and their luggage from just outside the arrival lobbies of Terminals 1 and 2 and delivers them to downtown hotels. This is the best mode of transportation if you have heavy baggage or are staying at one of the 40 or so major hotels served by the bus. Buses depart for the various hotels generally once an hour, and it can take almost 2 hours to reach a hotel in Shinjuku. Buses also travel to both Tokyo and Shinjuku stations, Haneda Airport, and the **Tokyo City Air Terminal (TCAT)** in downtown Tokyo, with more frequent departures (up to four times an hour in peak times); all are served by public transportation. Even if your hotel is not served

If you're going to be traveling around Tokyo by public transportation (and who doesn't?), you can save money by purchasing a combination Keisei Skyliner and Tokyo subway ticket, available only at Narita Airport. One-, 2-, and 3-day tickets offering unlimited subway rides are ¥2,800, ¥3,200, and ¥3,500, respectively, and are good for up to 6 months. Tickets that include roundtrip Skyliner passes are also available. Likewise, there's an Airport Limousine & Subway Pass combination ticket that includes one Airport Limousine trip plus 1 day of unlimited rides on all subways (it doesn't have to be the same day of arrival) for ¥3,400. This ticket, which I consider very good value, is available at Airport Limousine counters at the airport, TCAT, and Shinjuku Station West Exit in front of Keio Department Store. There are also combination tickets for visitors arriving at Haneda airport. Check websites for more information.

by limousine bus, you can still take it to the hotel or station nearest your destination. Check with the staff at the Airport Limousine Bus counter in the arrival lobbies to inquire which bus stops nearest your hotel and its departure time. The fare to most destinations is ¥3,100. Children 6 to 12 are charged half fare; those 5 and under ride free.

A cheaper bus, called **The Access Narita** (www.accessnarita.jp), travels from Narita to Tokyo and Ginza for only ¥1,000 one-way (children pay half fare). Travel time is approximately 95 to 105 minutes, with departures up to three times an hour during peak times. Pay in cash upon boarding.

By Taxi   Jumping into a **taxi** is the easiest way to get to Tokyo, but it's also prohibitively expensive—and may not even be the quickest if you happen to hit rush hour. Expect to spend around ¥21,000 to ¥25,000 for a 1½- to 2-hour taxi ride to central Tokyo. If you plan ahead, however, **KM Taxi** (www.km-group.co.jp; © **03/5530-6001**) provides fixed-fare service between Narita and Tokyo for ¥16,000 to ¥21,000, depending on the destination (highway toll charges and rides 10pm–5am cost more). Reservations must be made 72 hours in advance.

HANEDA AIRPORT   **Haneda Airport** has both domestic and international terminals (the latter is officially named Tokyo International Airport, but everyone calls it Haneda). The international terminal has a **Tokyo Tourist Information Center** (on the second floor of the arrival lobby, open daily 9am–11pm), currency exchange, free Wi-Fi, luggage storage and delivery, and cell phone rental. But the overriding benefit to Haneda is its central location compared to Narita. Taxi fares from Haneda are more reasonable than from Narita, but you can still expect to spend about ¥7,000 to reach downtown Tokyo.

Like Narita, Haneda Airport is served by the **Airport Limousine Bus,** with service to Shinjuku Station, Tokyo Station, the Tokyo City Air Terminal (TCAT) in downtown Tokyo, and selected hotels in Ginza, Hibiya, Shinjuku, Ikebukuro, Shibuya, Roppongi, and Akasaka. Fares run ¥820 to ¥1,230 for most destinations.

Locals, however, are more likely to take the **monorail** from Haneda 16 minutes to Hamamatsucho Station (fare: ¥490), or the **Keikyu Line** 11 minutes to Shinagawa (fare: ¥410). Both Hamamatsucho and Shinagawa connect to the very useful Yamanote Line, which travels to major stations like Tokyo and Shinjuku.

BY TRAIN

If you're traveling to Tokyo from elsewhere in Japan, you'll most likely arrive via Shinkansen bullet train at Tokyo, Ueno, or Shinagawa stations (avoid Tokyo Station if you can; it's very big and confusing). All are well served by trains (including the useful JR Yamanote Line), subways, and taxis.

BY BUS

Long-distance bus service from Hiroshima, Osaka, Kyoto, and other major cities delivers passengers mostly to Tokyo and Shinjuku stations, both of which are connected to the rest of the city via subway and commuter train, including the JR Yamanote Line, which loops around the city. For more information on long-distance bus service, check websites www.bus.or.jp, www.jrbuskanto.co.jp, and http://travel.willer.co.jp/endex.php, as well as individual city descriptions in this guide.

Visitor Information

In addition to those located at both airports (see above), there's another **Tourist Information Center (TIC)** in the heart of Tokyo in the Shin-Tokyo Building, 3–3–1 Marunouchi (www.japantravelinfo.com; ⓒ **03/3201-3331;** station: Yurakucho), within walking distance of the Ginza. The TIC staff is courteous and efficient; I cannot recommend them highly enough. In addition to city maps and sightseeing materials, the office has more information on the rest of Japan than any other tourist office, including pamphlets and brochures on major cities and attractions such as Nikko and Kamakura. Hours are daily 9am to 5pm.

Another great source of information is the **Tokyo Tourist Information Center,** operated by the Tokyo Metropolitan Government and located on the first floor of the Tokyo Metropolitan Government (TMG) Building no. 1, 2–8–1 Nishi-Shinjuku (www.gotokyo.org; ⓒ **03/5321-3077;** station: Tochomae or Shinjuku). You'll probably want to come here anyway for the great views from TMG's free observation floor. The center dispenses pamphlets, its own city map (which is a great complement to the one issued by TIC), and handy one-page detailed maps of various city districts, from Ueno to Roppongi. It's open daily 9:30am to 6:30pm. Other city-run information counters are located at Keisei Ueno Station (ⓒ **03/3836-3471**), open daily 9:30am to 6:30pm, and at Haneda Airport's International Terminal (ⓒ **03/6428-0653**), open daily 9am to 11pm.

Near Tokyo Station, there's the **TIC TOKYO,** facing the Nihombashi exit of Tokyo Station's north end at 1–8–1 Marunouchi (www.tictokyo.jp; ⓒ **03/5220-7055**). Open daily 10am to 7pm, it dispenses information on traveling in Tokyo and Japan. There are also an increasing number of neighborhood tourist offices, including the **Asakusa Culture Tourist Information Center,**

2–18–9 Kaminarimon (© **03/6280-6710;** daily 9:30am–8pm); the hard-to-find **Shibuya Station Tourist Information Desk** (daily 10am–7pm); and **Tokyo City i,** in JP Tower next to the Central Post Office, 2–7–2 Marunouchi (http://tokyocity-i.jp; daily 8am–8pm), which provides support and information to both international tourists and foreigners conducting business in Japan.

Tourist Publications: Of the many free giveaways available at tourist information centers, restaurants, bars, bookstores, hotels, and other establishments visitors and expats are likely to frequent, the best are the weekly *Metropolis* (www.metropolisjapan.com), with features on Tokyo, club listings, and restaurant and movie reviews, and the quarterly *TimeOut Tokyo* (www.timeout.jp) which covers so much information, including offbeat destinations, that it's useful also for expats living in Tokyo. Look also for the free *att.Japan* (www.att-japan.net). Local English-language newspapers the *Japan Times* and the *Japan News* also carry entertainment sections and articles.

City Layout

Your most frustrating moments in Tokyo will probably occur when you find that you're totally lost. Maybe it will be in a subway or train station, when all you see are signs in Japanese, or on a street somewhere as you search for a museum, restaurant, or bar. At any rate, accept it here and now: You *will* get lost if you are at all adventurous and strike out on your own. It's inevitable. But take comfort in the fact that Japanese get lost, too. And don't forget that most of the hotel and restaurant listings in this book have the number of minutes (in parentheses) it takes to walk there from the nearest station; if you take note, you'll at least know the radius from the station to your destination. It's wise, too, to always allow extra time to find your way around.

Tokyo, situated at one end of Tokyo Bay and spreading across the Kanto Plain, still retains some of its Edo Period features. If you look at a map, you'll find a large green oasis in the middle of the city, site of the Imperial Palace and its grounds. Surrounding it is the castle moat; a bit farther out are remnants of another circular moat built by the Tokugawa shogun. The JR Yamanote Line forms another loop around the inner city; most of Tokyo's major hotels, nightlife districts, and attractions are near or inside this oblong loop.

For administrative purposes, Tokyo is broken down into **23 wards,** known as *ku.* Its business districts of Marunouchi and Hibiya, for example, are in Chiyoda-ku, while Ginza is part of Chuo-ku (Central Ward). These two ku are the historic hearts of Tokyo, for it was here that the city had its humble beginnings. Greater Tokyo is also a prefecture (similar to a state or province), with a population of more than 13 million, and includes 26 cities, five towns, and eight villages in addition to its 23 wards, as well as Pacific islands. For most purposes, however, references to Tokyo in this guide pertain mostly to central Tokyo's 23 wards, home to 9 million residents.

MAIN STREETS & ARTERIES One difficulty in finding your way around Tokyo is that hardly any streets are named. Think about what that means: 9 million people living in a huge metropolis of nameless streets. Granted, major

Tokyo at a Glance

Amuse Museum **12**
Asakura Choso Museum **2**
East Garden **18**
Edo-Tokyo Museum **14**
Fukugawa Edo Museum **15**
Hama Rikyu Garden **30**
Hanayashiki **10**
Imperial Palace **19**
Kokugikan
   (Sumo Stadium) **13**
Meiji Jingu Shrine **22**
Mori Art Museum **29**
The National Art Center,
   Tokyo **25**
National Children's
   Castle **24**
National Museum of
   Modern Art **17**
National Museum of
   Nature and Science **4**
National Museum of
   Western Art **8**
Oedo-Onsen Monogatari **31**
Rikugien Garden **1**
Sensoji Temple **11**
Shinjuku Gyoen **21**
Suntory Museum of Art **26**

Key continues below

To Disneyland → Tokyo

KEIYO LINE

Shinkiba

Shiomi

Port of Tokyo

WAKASU GOLF CLUB →

Toyosu

Kiyosumi

Harumi

Harumi Wharf

Ferry Terminal

ODAIBA

Rainbow Bridge

HAMA RIKYU GARDEN

30

31

Tokyo Bay

Central Wholesale Market

Hamamatsucho

Tamachi

Shinagawa

Daiichi-keihin Dori

Hara Museum of Contemporary Art

SHINAGAWA-KU

Omachi

Shimoshinmei

Omori

To Tokyo International Airport ↗

TOKAIDO LINE

ROPPONGI HILLS

29

MINATO-KU

Roppongi Dori

See Roppongi map

NATIONAL PARK FOR NATURE STUDY

Sakurada-Dori

Shibuya

Ebisu

Meguro

Gotanda

Osaki

MEGURO-KU

Daini-keihin Doro

Kannana-Dori

SHINKANSEN LINE

YOKOSUKA LINE

JAPAN

Tokyo ✳

TMG Observation Platform **20**
Tokyo National Museum **3**
Tokyo Sky Tree **9**
Tokyo Tower **27**
Toshogu Shrine **6**
Tsukiji Fish Market **28**
Ueno Zoo **5**
Ukiyo-e Ota Memorial Museum **23**
Yasukuni Shrine **16**
Yushukan **16**

ⓘ Tourist Info
Expressway
Monorail
Railway

thoroughfares received names after World War II at the insistence of American occupation forces, and more have been labeled or given nicknames since then, but for the most part, Tokyo's address system is based on a complicated number scheme that must make the postal worker's job here a nightmare. To make matters worse, most streets in Tokyo zigzag—an arrangement apparently left over from olden days, to confuse potential attacking enemies. Now they confuse Tokyoites and visitors alike.

Among Tokyo's most important named streets are **Meiji Dori,** which follows the loop of the Yamanote Line and runs from Minato-ku in the south through Ebisu, Shibuya, Harajuku, Shinjuku, and Ikebukuro in the north; **Yasukuni Dori** and **Shinjuku Dori,** which cut across the heart of the city from Shinjuku to Chiyoda-ku; and **Sotobori Dori, Chuo Dori, Harumi Dori,** and **Showa Dori,** which pass through Ginza. Other major thoroughfares are named after the districts they're in, such as **Roppongi Dori** in Roppongi and **Aoyama Dori** in Aoyama (*dori* means avenue or street, as does *michi*).

Intersections in Tokyo are called a crossing (and more recently a scramble); it seems every district has a famous crossing. **Ginza 4-chome Crossing** is the intersection of Chuo Dori and Harumi Dori. **Roppongi Crossing** is the intersection of Roppongi Dori and Gaien-Higashi Dori. The Shibuya Scramble became famous after being featured in the movie *Lost in Translation.*

ADDRESSES Because streets did not have names when Japan's postal system was established, the Tokyo has a unique address system. A typical address might read 7–10–1 Ginza, Chuo-ku, which is the address of Hotel Gracery. Chuo-ku is the name of the ward. Wards are further divided into named districts, in this case Ginza. Ginza itself is broken down into *chome* (numbered subsections), the first number in the series, here 7. The second number (10 in the example) refers to a smaller area within the *chome*—usually an entire block, sometimes larger. Thus, houses on one side of the street will usually have a different middle number from houses on the other side. The last number, in this case 1, refers to the actual building.

Addresses are usually, but not always, posted on buildings beside doors, on telephone poles, and at major intersection traffic lights, but sometimes they are written in kanji only. One frustrating trend is that newer buildings omit posting any address whatsoever on their facades, perhaps in the belief that no one understands the address system anyway.

FINDING YOUR WAY AROUND If you're traveling by subway or JR train, the first thing you should do upon exiting your compartment is to look for **yellow signs** posted on every platform that tell you which exit to take for particular buildings, attractions, and *chome*. At Roppongi Station, for example, you'll find yellow signboards that tell you the exit to take for Roppongi Hills, which will at least get you pointed in the right direction once you emerge from the station. Stations also have maps of the areas either inside the station or at the exit; these are your best plan of attack when trying to find a particular address.

As you walk around Tokyo, you will also notice **map boards** posted beside sidewalks (look for a white circle with an "i" in the middle) giving a breakdown of the postal number system for that particular neighborhood. The first time I tried to use one, I stopped one Japanese, then another, and asked them to locate a specific address on the map. They both studied the map and pointed out the direction. Both turned out to be wrong. Not very encouraging, but if you learn how to read these maps, they're invaluable. Nowadays, many of them include landmarks translated in English.

Another invaluable source of information is the numerous **police boxes,** called *koban,* located in major neighborhoods and beside major train and subway stations throughout the city. Police officers have area maps and are very helpful (helping lost souls seems to occupy much of their time). You should also never hesitate to ask a Japanese the way, but be sure to ask more than one. You'll be amazed at the conflicting directions you'll receive. Apparently, Japanese would rather hazard a guess than impolitely shrug their shoulders and leave you standing there. The best thing to do is ask directions of several Japanese and then follow the majority opinion. You can also duck into a shop and ask someone where a nearby address is, although in my experience employees do not even know the address of their own store. However, they may have a map of the area.

MAPS Before setting out on your own, arm yourself with maps. Maps are so much a part of life in Tokyo that they're often included in shop or restaurant advertisements or brochures, on business cards, and even in private party invitations. Even though I've spent years in Tokyo, I rarely venture forth without a map. You can pick up free maps at Tokyo's many tourist information centers (see p. 56 for locations), many of which include a subway map. Tokyo Tourist Information Centers, run by the Tokyo Metropolitan Government, also have detailed leaflets of Tokyo's many districts, including Shinjuku, Roppongi, Ueno, and other areas you'll probably visit. Hotels sometimes distribute their own maps. Major Metro subway stations, like Tokyo and Roppongi stations, also have area maps of surrounding neighborhoods, so don't be shy about asking the attendant. Armed with these maps, you should be able to locate at least the general vicinity of every place mentioned in this book. In short, never pass up a free map.

Tokyo's Neighborhoods in Brief

Taken as a whole, Tokyo seems formidable and unconquerable. It's best, therefore, to think of it as nothing more than a series of villages scrunched together, much like the pieces of a jigsaw puzzle. Holding the pieces together, so to speak, is the **Yamanote Line,** a commuter train loop around central Tokyo that passes through such important stations as Yurakucho, Tokyo, Akihabara, Ueno, Ikebukuro, Shinjuku, Harajuku, Shibuya, and Shinagawa.

Marunouchi Bounded by the Imperial Palace to the west and Tokyo Station (used by about 500,000 people daily) to the east, Marunouchi is one of Tokyo's oldest business districts. On the site of the Imperial Palace is where the Tokugawa shogun built his magnificent castle and was the center of old Edo; many samurai had mansions here. Remnants of the castle can be seen in the wonderful **East Garden,** open free to the public. Marunouchi has undergone a massive revival since the turn of this century. It's home to the Tourist Information Center, office buildings, swanky hotels, and wide avenues like the fashionable, tree-lined **Marunouchi Naka Dori,** with international boutiques from Armani to Tiffany and famous for its winter illuminations.

Ginza Across the train tracks and to the south of Marunouchi is the Ginza, the swankiest and most expensive **shopping area** in all Japan. When the country opened to foreign trade in the 1860s, following 2 centuries of self-imposed seclusion, it was here that Western imports and adopted Western architecture were first displayed. Today, it's where you'll find many department stores, international name-brand boutiques, exclusive restaurants, hotels, art galleries, and drinking establishments.

Tsukiji Located only two subway stops from Ginza, Tsukiji was born from reclaimed land during the Tokugawa shogunate; its name, in fact, means "reclaimed land." Today it's famous for the **Tsukiji Fish Market,** one of the largest wholesale fish markets in the world, which in 2016 is slated to move 2.5km (1½ miles) away to larger quarters in Toyosu, thus freeing up valuable land for the 2020 Olympics. Near Tsukiji is **Hama Rikyu Garden,** one of Tokyo's most famous gardens.

Akihabara Two stops north of Tokyo Station on the Yamanote Line, Akihabara has long been Japan's foremost shopping destination for electronic and electrical appliances, with hundreds of shops offering a look at the latest in gadgets, including Yodobashi Camera, Japan's largest appliance store. More recently, Akihabara has also become a mecca for *otaku* (geek) culture, home of *anime* and *manga* stores and maid cafes. This is a fascinating area for a stroll, even if you don't buy anything.

Asakusa Northeast of central Tokyo, Asakusa and areas to its north served as the pleasure quarters for old Edo. Today it's known throughout Japan as the site of the famous **Sensoji Temple,** one of Tokyo's top and oldest attractions. It also has a wealth of tiny shops selling traditional Japanese crafts. When Tokyoites talk about old *shitamachi* (downtown), they are referring to the traditional homes and tiny narrow streets of the

Asakusa and Ueno areas. Every visitor should spend at least half a day here.

Ueno Located just west of Asakusa, on the northern edge of the JR Yamanote Line loop, Ueno is also part of the city's old downtown. Ueno boasts **Ueno Park,** a huge green space comprising a zoo and several acclaimed museums, including the **Tokyo National Museum,** which houses the largest collection of Japanese art and antiquities in the world. Under the train tracks of the JR Yamanote Line loop is the spirited **Ameya Yokocho,** a thriving market for food, clothing, and accessories.

Shinjuku Originating as a post town in 1698 to serve the needs of feudal lords and their retainers traveling between Edo and the provinces, Shinjuku was hardly touched by the 1923 Great Kanto Earthquake, making it an attractive alternative for businesses wishing to relocate following the destruction. Today dozens of skyscrapers, including several hotels, dot the Shinjuku skyline, and with the 1991 opening of the **Tokyo Metropolitan Government Office (TMG,** with a tourist office and a great free observation floor), Shinjuku's transformation into the capital's upstart business district was complete. Separating eastern and western Shinjuku is **Shinjuku Station,** the nation's busiest commuter station, located on the western end of the Yamanote Line loop. Shinjuku is also known for its nightlife, especially in **Kabuki-cho,** one of Japan's most famous—and naughtiest—amusement centers; and in **Shinjuku 2–chome,** Tokyo's premier gay nightlife district. An oasis in the middle of Shinjuku madness is **Shinjuku Gyoen Park,** with a tranquil Japanese garden at its center.

Harajuku The mecca of Tokyo's younger generation, Harajuku swarms throughout the week with teenagers in search of fashion and fun. **Takeshita Dori** is a narrow pedestrian lane packed elbow to elbow with young people looking for the latest in inexpensive clothing; at its center is the ¥100 discount shop Daiso. Harajuku is also home to one of Japan's major attractions, the **Meiji Jingu Shrine,** built in 1920 to deify Emperor and Empress Meiji; and to the small but delightful **Ukiyo-e Ota Memorial Museum of Art,**

with its woodblock prints. Another draw is the **Oriental Bazaar,** Tokyo's best shop for souvenir hunting. Linking Harajuku with Aoyama (below) is **Omotesando Dori,** a fashionable tree-lined avenue flanked by trendy shops, restaurants, and sidewalk cafes, making it a premier promenade for people-watching. The upscale **Omotesando Hills** shopping center on Omotesando Dori stretches from Harajuku to Aoyama.

Aoyama   While Harajuku is for Tokyo's teeny-boppers, nearby chic Aoyama is its playground for trendsetting yuppies, boasting sophisticated restaurants, pricey boutiques, and more cutting-edge designer-fashion outlets than anywhere else in the city. It's located on the eastern end of **Omotesando Dori** (and an easy walk from Harajuku), centered on Aoyama Dori. Its cultural highlight is Nezu Museum, devoted to items related to the tea ceremony, Chinese bronzes and more. The **Japan Traditional Crafts Aoyama Square** sells beautifully crafted items made by artisans from around Japan.

Shibuya   Located on the southwestern edge of the Yamanote Line loop, Shibuya serves as a vibrant nightlife and shopping area for the young. More subdued than Shinjuku, more down-to-earth than Harajuku, and less cosmopolitan than Roppongi, it's home to more than a dozen department stores specializing in everything from designer clothing to housewares and CDs and to **Hikarie,** a 34-story complex with shops, a theater, restaurants, and a gallery for artists and artisans from around Japan. Don't miss the light change at **Shibuya Scramble,** reportedly Japan's busiest intersection, with its hordes of pedestrians, neon, and five video billboards that have earned it the nickname "Times Square of Tokyo" (and a spot in the movie *Lost in Translation*).

Roppongi   Tokyo's best-known nightlife district for young Japanese and foreigners, Roppongi has more bars and nightclubs than any other district outside Shinjuku, as well as a multitude of restaurants serving international cuisines. It's anchored by two sprawling developments: the eye-popping, 11-hectare (28-acre) **Roppongi Hills,** Tokyo's largest urban development housing 230 shops and restaurants, a first-class hotel, a garden, apartments, offices, a cinema complex, and Tokyo's highest art museum, on the 53rd floor of Mori Tower; and the smaller **Tokyo Midtown,** which boasts Tokyo's tallest building, a luxury hotel, medical center, 130 restaurants and fashion boutiques, apartments, offices, a garden, and the Suntory Museum of Art. Also in Roppongi is **The National Art Center, Tokyo,** focusing on changing exhibitions of modern and contemporary art.

Shinagawa   Once an important post station on the old Tokaido Highway, Shinagawa remains an important crossroads due to **Shinagawa Station,** a stop on the Shinkansen bullet train route and on the southern end of the Yamanote Line loop. It's home to office buildings and hotels but otherwise has little to attract sightseers.

Odaiba   Tokyo's newest district was constructed from reclaimed land in Tokyo Bay. Connected to the mainland by the **Rainbow Bridge** (famous for its chameleon colors after nightfall), the Yurikamome Line monorail, the Rinkai Line, and a vehicular harbor tunnel, it's home to hotels, Japan's largest convention space, shopping and amusement complexes, museums, the **Ooedo-Onsen Monogatari** hot-spring baths, and **Megaweb,** a car amusement and exhibition center sponsored by Toyota. It's also one of Tokyo's hottest date spots and offers great views of Tokyo's skyline.

Getting Around Town

The first rule of getting around Tokyo: It will always take longer than you think. For short-term visitors, calculating travel times in Tokyo is tricky business. Taking a taxi is expensive and involves the probability of getting stuck interminably in traffic, with the meter ticking away. Taking the subway is usually more efficient, even though it's more complicated and harder on your feet: Choosing which route to take isn't always clear, and transfers between lines are sometimes quite a hike in themselves. If I'm going from one end of Tokyo to the other by subway, I usually allow anywhere from 30 to 60 minutes, depending on the number of transfers and the walking distance to my final destination. If you don't have to change trains, you can travel from one end of central Tokyo to the other (say, from Shibuya to Ueno) in about 30 minutes or less. In any case, travel times to destinations within each line are posted on platform pillars, along with diagrams showing which train compartments are best for making quick transfers between lines.

Your best bet for getting around Tokyo is to take the subway or a Japan Railways (JR) commuter train such as the Yamanote Line to the station nearest your destination. From there you can either walk, using a map and asking directions along the way, or take a taxi. For all hotels, *ryokan,* restaurants, sights, shops, and nightlife venues listed in this chapter and the next, I've included both the nearest station and, in parentheses, the approximate number of minutes' walk to get from the station to the destination.

TIPS ON TRAVELING BY PUBLIC TRANSPORTATION Each mode of transportation in Tokyo—subway (with two different companies), JR train (such as the Yamanote Line), private rail companies, and bus—has its own fare system and therefore requires a new ticket each time you transfer from one mode of transport to another. If you're going to be in Tokyo for a few days, therefore, it's much more convenient to purchase a **Suica,** a contactless pre-paid card issued by JR East that automatically deducts fares and can be used on virtually all modes of transportation, including JR trains (excluding the Shinkansen), private railways (such as the Rinkai Line to Odaiba), subways, and buses in the greater Tokyo area (including trips to Kamakura). It can even be used for purchases at designated vending machines, convenience stores, and fast-food outlets that display the Suica sign. First-time buyers must purchase the Suica from vending machines or JR ticket offices for a minimum of ¥1,000, which includes a ¥500 deposit. The Suica is rechargeable, at amounts ranging from ¥1,000 to ¥10,000. Note, however, that when you return your Suica to get your deposit back, you must be sure that the card is depleted, or you'll be charged a ¥220 handling fee for any remaining stored balance on the card. A similar card to the Suica is the **Pasmo** (www.pasmo. co.jp), also available from vending machines and which can also be used on various modes of transportation throughout Tokyo and even other parts of Japan. Although there are other options available, including 1-day cards and metro-only cards, the Suica and the Pasmo are by far my favorites. They even give a slight discount on fares, and there's a movement underway to make them valid for traveling in other cities throughout Japan as well.

That being said, if you think you're going to be traveling a lot by public transportation on any given day, consider purchasing a **Tokyo Tour Ticket (Furii Kippu)** for ¥1,590, which allows unlimited travel for 1 day on all subways, JR trains, and Toei buses within Tokyo's 23 wards. It's available at almost all JR and subway stations. There are also 1-day tickets that can be used only on Metro subway lines for ¥710, on all subway lines of both companies for ¥1,000, or only on JR trains for ¥750. Children 6 to 11 pay half fare on public transportation in Japan; children 5 and under ride free.

Avoid taking the subway or JR train during the weekday morning **rush hour,** from 8 to 9am—the stories you've heard about commuters packed into trains like sardines are all true. There are even "platform pushers," men who push people into compartments so that the doors can close. If you want to witness Tokyo at its craziest, go to Shinjuku Station at 8:30am—but go by taxi unless you want to experience the crowding firsthand. Most lines provide women-only compartments at the end of the train weekdays until 9am.

Finally, please note that all cellphones should be switched to silent mode (called "manner mode" in Japanese) on public conveyances.

BY SUBWAY

To get around Tokyo on your own, it's imperative to learn how to ride its subways. Fortunately, the subway system is efficient, modern, clean, and easy to use; in fact, I think it's one of the most user-friendly systems on the planet. Most Tokyo subway stations even provide free Wi-Fi.

Altogether, there are 13 underground subway lines crisscrossing the city, operated by two companies: Tokyo Metro (the bigger of the two, which uses a symbol "M" vaguely reminiscent of McDonald's famous arches) and Toei (which operates four lines). All station names are written in English, and each subway line is color-coded and assigned a letter (usually the subway's initial). The Ginza Line, for example, is orange, which means that all its trains and signs are orange, and it's identified by the letter "G." Additionally, each station along each line is assigned a number in chronological order beginning with the first station (Shibuya Station, for example, is G1 because it's the first station on the Ginza Line, while Asakusa Station is G19). Before boarding, however, make sure the train is going in the right direction—signs at each station show both the previous and the next stop, so you can double-check you're heading in the right direction. Tokyo's newest line, Toei's Oedo Line, makes a zigzag loop around the city and is useful for traveling between Roppongi and Shinjuku; be aware, however, that it's buried deep underground and that platforms take a while to reach, despite escalators.

Whereas it used to be a matter of skill to know exactly which train compartment to board if making transfers down the line, diagrams at each station (usually on a pillar at the entrance to each platform) show which end of the train and compartment is most useful for connections. There are also signs that show exactly how many minutes it takes to reach every destination on that line. Once on your way, trains display the next station in English on digital signs above their doors and announce stops in English.

Remember, once you reach your destination, look for the yellow signs on station platforms designating which exit to take for major buildings, museums, and addresses. If you're confused about which exit to take, ask an attendant near the ticket gate. Taking the right exit can make a world of difference, especially in Shinjuku, where there are some 60 station exits.

Vending machines at all subway stations sell tickets; fares begin at ¥170 for the shortest distance and increase according to how far you're traveling. Vending machines give change, even for a ¥10,000 note. **To purchase your ticket,** insert money into the vending machine until the fare buttons light up, and then push the amount for the ticket you want.

Before purchasing your ticket, you first have to figure out your **fare.** Fares are posted on a large subway map above the vending machines, but they're often in Japanese only; major stations also post a smaller map listing fares in English, but you may have to search for it (this will certainly have to change before the 2020 Olympics). An alternative is to look at the subway map contained in the "Tokyo Handy Map" issued by the Tokyo Metropolitan Government—it lists most stations in both Japanese and English. When you know what the Japanese characters look like, you may be able to locate your station and the corresponding fare. If you still don't know the fare, just buy the cheapest ticket for ¥170. When you reach your destination, look for the **fare adjustment machine;** insert your ticket to find out how much more you owe, or look for a subway employee at the ticket window to tell you how much extra you owe. In any case, be sure to hang onto your ticket, as you must give it up at the end of your journey. Since buying individual tickets is a hassle (and vending machines are unfortunately not as user-friendly as the subway system is), I suggest buying either a Suica or Pasmo card (see above).

Most subways run from about 5am to midnight, although the times of the first and last trains depend on the line, the station, and whether it's a weekday or a weekend. Schedules are posted in the stations, and throughout most of the day, trains run every 3 to 5 minutes.

For more information on tickets, passes, and lines for the subway, as well as a detailed subway map, stop by **Metro Information desks** located at Ginza, Shinjuku, Omotesando, and other major stations in Tokyo. Or check the website **www.tokyometro.jp.** Information on **Toei Subway** is available at **www.kotsu.metro.tokyo.jp.**

BY TRAIN

In addition to subway lines, commuter trains operated by the **East Japan Railway Company (JR)** run aboveground throughout greater Tokyo. These are also color-coded, with fares beginning at ¥140. Buy your ticket from vending machines just as you would for the subway, but more convenient is the Suica. Otherwise, if you think you'll be traveling a lot by JR lines on any given day, consider purchasing a **1-Day Metropolitan District Pass (Tokunai Pass),** which allows unlimited travel within Tokyo's 23 wards for ¥750. If you have a validated Japan Rail Pass, you can travel on JR trains for free.

The **Yamanote Line** (green-colored coaches) is the best-known and most convenient JR line. It makes an oblong loop around the city in about an hour, stopping at 29 stations along the way, all of them announced in English and with digital signboards in each compartment. Another convenient JR line is the orange-colored **Chuo Line;** it cuts across Tokyo between Shinjuku and Tokyo stations, with both express (which doesn't make as many stops) and local trains available. The yellow-colored **Sobu Line** runs between Shinjuku and Akihabara and beyond to Chiba. Other JR lines serve outlying districts for the metropolis's commuting public, including Yokohama and Kamakura. Because the Yamanote, Chuo, and Sobu lines are rarely identified by their specific names at major stations, look for signs that say JR LINES.

For more information on JR trains, as well as train travel throughout Japan, stop by the **JR East Travel Service Center** at Tokyo Station's Marunouchi North Exit. Open daily 7:30am to 8:30pm, it also offers free Wi-Fi, hotel reservations, tourist information, currency exchange, and luggage storage. You can also exchange vouchers here for the Japan Rail Pass. Otherwise, for information about traveling in Tokyo, stop by a **JR Information Center** at Ueno, Shinjuku, Shibuya, Akihabara or Shinagawa stations, call the English-language **JR East Infoline** at ✆ **050/2016-1603** daily from 10am to 6pm, or visit the website **www.jreast.co.jp/e.**

In addition to JR, there are private train companies that provide service from Tokyo to outlying areas. **Tobu Railway,** for example, operates trains to Nikko, while **Odakyu Electric Railway** covers the Hakone area. Both offer discount travel passes. For more information, see individual destinations in chapter 6.

BY BUS

Buses are not as easy to use as trains or subways unless you know their route, because only the end destination is written on the bus, bus stops might list routes only in Japanese, and many bus drivers don't speak English. Buses are sometimes convenient for short distances, however (such as traveling between Roppongi and Shibuya). If you're feeling adventurous, board the bus at the front and drop the exact fare (usually ¥210) into the box. If you don't have the exact amount, fare boxes accept coins or bills; your change minus the fare will come out below. Better yet, use a Suica or Pasmo. A signboard at the front of the bus displays the next stop, usually in English. When you wish to get off, press one of the purple buttons on the railing near the door or the seats. You can pick up an excellent Toei bus map showing all major routes at one of the Tokyo Tourist Information Centers operated by the Tokyo Metropolitan Government (see "Visitor Information," p. 56). Or check the Toei website at **www. kotsu.metro.tokyo.jp.**

An exception to the city buses above is Toei's **Tokyo Shitamachi Bus,** a user-friendly sightseeing bus that follows a fixed route to nine sightseeing spots, including Ueno Park, Kappabashi-dougugai Dori with its many kitchen stores, Asakusa, and Tokyo SkyTree. On weekends and holidays, the route extends to Tokyo Station. Buses travel in both directions at 20-minute intervals daily from about 9:30am and 6pm. The fare is ¥210 each time you board (you can use a Suica or Pasmo card); or purchase a 1-day Toei bus pass for ¥500. For information about the Tokyo Shitamachi Bus, including a schedule and map, stop by the Tokyo Tourist Information Center in Shinjuku or Ueno or see the Toei website above.

There's also the **Sky Bus** (www.skybus.jp; ✆ **03/3215-0008**), which offers double-decker open-top bus tours around the Imperial Palace (¥1,600) and other tourist sites, as well as hop-on, hop-off buses that travel three routes—Asakusa/Tokyo SkyTree, Odaiba, and Roppongi. These begin and end in Marunouchi and cost ¥2,500 for a 1-day pass or ¥3,500 for 2 days. Frankly, taking public transportation is much cheaper.

BY TAXI

Taxis are shamefully expensive in Tokyo. **Fares** start at ¥730 for the first 2km (1¼ miles) and increase ¥90 for each additional 280m (924 ft.) or 90 seconds of waiting time. There are also smaller, more compact taxis for a maximum of four persons that charge slightly less, but they are fewer in number. Fares are posted on the back of the front passenger seat. If you're like me, you probably won't shop around—you'll gratefully jump into the first taxi that stops. Note that from 10pm to 5am, an extra 20% is added to your fare. Perhaps as an admission of how expensive taxis are, fares can also be paid by credit card in many taxis, though some companies require a minimum fare of ¥5,000.

With the exception of some major thoroughfares in the downtown area, you can hail a taxi from any street or go to a taxi stand or a major hotel. A red light above the dashboard shows if a taxi is free to pick up a passenger; a yellow light indicates that the taxi is occupied. *Note:* Be sure to stand clear of the back left door—it swings open automatically. Likewise, it shuts automatically once you're in. Taxi drivers are quite perturbed if you try to maneuver the door yourself. The law requires that back-seat passengers wear seat belts.

Many taxis have a Point-and-Speak Foreign Language Sheet, which allows you to point to some major destinations and communicate about expected fare and other basics. Still, unless you're going to a well-known landmark or hotel, it's best to have your destination written out in Japanese, since most taxi drivers don't speak English. But even that may not help. Tokyo is so complicated that taxi drivers may not know a certain area, although many now have navigation systems or will call their central office to inquire about a specific address.

There are so many taxis cruising Tokyo (about 50,000) that you can hail one easily on most thoroughfares—except when you need it most: When it's raining, or just after 1am on weekends when subways and trains have stopped. To call a taxi for a pickup (which carries a ¥410 surcharge), try **Nihon Kotsu** (www.nihon-kotsu.co.jp; © **03/5755-2336**) for an English-speaking operator. I have rarely telephoned for a taxi—as in the movies, one usually cruises by just when I raise my hand.

Like in many cities around the world, **Uber Taxi** (www.uber.com/cities/tokyo) has also come to Tokyo, but its use isn't as widely spread as in other locations.

[FastFACTS] TOKYO

If you can't find answers to your questions here, check "Fast Facts: Japan," in chapter 12. If you still can't find an answer, call one of the tourist information offices listed above under "Visitor Information." Another good source is the free **Foreign Residents'** **Advisory Center** (© **03/5320-7744**), which can answer questions on a wide range of topics concerning daily life in Japan, including legal matters, taxes, traffic accidents, emergency numbers and even Japanese social customs; it's open Monday to Friday from 9:30am to noon and 1 to 5pm. Finally, if you're staying in a first-class hotel, another valuable resource is the concierge or guest-relations desk, where the staff can tell you how to reach your destination, answer general questions, and even make restaurant reservations.

ATMs/Banks **Narita Airport** and **Haneda Airport** have exchange counters for all incoming international flights that offer better exchange rates than what you'd get abroad, as well as ATMs. Change enough money to last several days, since the exchange rate is the same as in town. Otherwise, all banks displaying an AUTHORIZED FOREIGN EXCHANGE sign can exchange currency and traveler's checks, with exchange rates usually displayed at the appropriate foreign-exchange counter. More convenient—and quicker—are **Travelex** foreign-exchange kiosks (www.travelex.co.jp), with more than a dozen locations across town, including Tokyo Station (℗ **03/5220-4311**), next to the JR East Travel Service Center and open daily 7:30am to 8:30pm; 3rd floor of Tokyo Midtown Tower, 9–7–1 Akasaka (℗ **03/3408-2280;** station: Roppongi), open daily 11am to 7pm; and Keisei Ueno Station (℗ **03/5708-0832**), open daily 6:15am to 7pm. Other locations are in Shinjuku, Shibuya, Shinagawa,

and Akihabara, among others. **WORLD CURR€nc¥ $HOP** (℗ **03/5275-7610**) is a Japanese company offering similar money-exchange services, with counters in the Ginza Core Building, 5–8–20 Ginza (℗ **03/6254-6851;** station: Ginza), open daily 11am to 8pm; in Roppongi Hills, 6–19–1 Roppongi (℗ **03/5413-9722;** station: Roppongi), open Monday to Friday 11am to 7pm and Saturday, Sunday and holidays from noon to 5pm; and in Shinjuku, Shibuya, Ikebukuro, Ueno, Nihombashi and other locations. For ATMs that accept foreign credit cards, head to any post office or 7-Eleven. For more information on changing money, see "Money & Costs," in chapter 12.

Dentists The **Tokyo Clinic Dental Office,** 3–4–30 Shiba-koen, Minato-ku (www.tcdo.jp; ℗ **03/3431-4225**), is near Kamiyacho, Onarimon, Akabanebashi or Daimon stations and across from Tokyo Tower. Just a 3-minute walk away is the **United Dental Office,** 2–3–8 Azabudai, Minato-ku (http://uniteddentaloffice.com; ℗ **03/5570-4334**). Tokyo Midtown Medical Center (see "Doctors & Hospitals," below) also has a **Dental Clinic;** call ℗ **03/5413-7912** for an appointment. All have English-speaking staff.

Doctors & Hospitals Many first-class hotels offer medical facilities or an in-house doctor. The **Tokyo Metropolitan Medical Institution Information;**

(www.himawari.metro.tokyo.jp/qq/qq13enmnlt.asp; ℗ **03/5285-8181;** daily 9am–8pm) can refer you to medical professionals who speak English and has staff who can also explain the health insurance system in Japan; its emergency translation services at ℗ **03/5285-8185** is staffed with translators who can act as go-betweens during treatment if problems arise, available Monday to Friday 5 to 8pm and weekends and holidays from 9am to 8pm. Providing similar services is the **AMDA International Medical Information Center** (http://amda-imic.com/lng_eng; ℗ **03/5285-8088**), open Monday to Friday 9am to 5pm. Embassies (see chapter 12) also have lists of English-speaking health professionals.

Otherwise, clinics with English-speaking staff and popular with foreigners living in Tokyo include **Tokyo Midtown Medical Center,** an affiliate of Johns Hopkins and offering an International Clinic Service on the sixth floor of Midtown Tower, 9–7–1 Akasaka, Minato-ku, near Roppongi Station (www.tokyomidtown-mc.jp; ℗ **03/5413-7911**), and **Tokyo Medical & Surgical Clinic** (www.tmsc.jp; ℗ **03/3436-3028**), in the same building as Tokyo Clinic Dental Office, above.

Large hospitals in Japan are open only a limited number of hours (designated hospitals remain open for emergencies, however, and an ambulance will automatically take you there).

Otherwise, hospitals with English-speaking staff (you can also make appointments to see a doctor) include the **Seibo International Catholic Hospital,** 2–5–1 Naka-Ochiai, Shinjuku-ku, near Mejiro Station on the Yamanote Line (www.seibokai.or.jp; ✆ **03/3951-1111**); **St. Luke's International Hospital (Seiroka Byoin),** 9–1 Akashi-cho, Chuo-ku, near Tsukiji Station on the Hibiya Line (www.luke.or.jp; ✆ **03/3541-5151**); and **Japanese Red Cross Medical Center (Nihon Sekijujisha Iryo Center),** 4–1–22 Hiroo, Shibuya-ku (www.med.jrc.or.jp; ✆ **03/3400-1311**), whose closest subway stations are Roppongi, Hiroo, and Shibuya—from there, you should take a taxi.

Emergencies See "Fast Facts" in chapter 12, p. 332. Otherwise, The Metropolitan Police Department also maintains a telephone counseling service for foreigners at ✆ **03/3501-0110** Monday through Friday from 8:30am to 5:15pm.

Internet & Wi-Fi Access
Most accommodations in Tokyo provide computers for travelers without a laptop, usually in the lobby or business center and either for free or for a fee, as well as free Wi-Fi. Otherwise, a good place to set up a temporary office is at the sophisticated **Gran Cyber Café Bagus,** on the 12th floor of the Roi Building, 5–5–1 Roppongi (✆ **03/5786-2280**; station: Roppongi). Open 24 hours, it offers individual cubicles with prices that depend on the chair you select: For a seat that reclines, it's ¥290 for 30 minutes. Three- and 4-hour packages are also available, and, unsurprisingly given Tokyo's high taxi and accommodation prices, it even offers a 24-hour package for ¥4,770, as well as—brace yourself—booths for couples. You have to wonder how many people actually work. For free access, try the laid-back **Café Salvador,** located on the tree-lined Marunouchi Naka Dori avenue in the Shin Fuji Building, 3–2–3 Marunouchi (✆ **03/5220-6466;** stations: Marunouchi or Tokyo). It offers computers and free Wi-Fi and is open Monday to Friday 7am to 11pm, Saturday 10am to 11pm, and Sunday 10am to 8pm.

As for free Wi-Fi, lots of restaurants, bars and coffee shops offer it to paying customers, but you might need to ask for the password. Free Wi-Fi is also available at more than half of the subway stations used most frequently by foreign visitors. Several neighborhoods offer their own free Wi-Fi, like Marunouchi and Shibuya. In addition, foreign visitors to Tokyo and the surrounding area (including Hakone and Nikko) can get free Wi-Fi for up to 2 weeks by showing their passport at designated places, including Narita Airport, Tokyo Tourist Information Center (see "Visitor Information," p. 56), tax refund counters of department stores Isetan in Shinjuku and Mitsukoshi in Ginza and Nihombashi, and other places around town. After logging in with a provided ID and password, participants can get free service at thousands of hotspots throughout the metropolitan area wherever the Wi-Fi logo is shown. For more information, go to http://flets.com/freewifi.

Mail & Postage
Although all post offices (called a *yubinkyoku*) are open Monday to Friday from 9am to 5pm, major post offices located in every ward remain open to 7pm (to mail a package, you'll need to go to one of these). Tokyo's **Central Post Office,** 2–7–2 Marunouchi, Chiyoda-ku (✆ **03/3217-5231;** station: Tokyo or Marunouchi) is open Monday to Friday 9am to 9pm and Saturday and Sunday 9am to 6pm, but it also has a counter open 24 hours for mail and packages. For information on domestic and international postage, see "Fast Facts" in chapter 12 or go to www.post.japanpost.jp.

Newspapers & Magazines In addition to two English-language newspapers published daily in Japan—the **Japan Times** (www.japantimes.co.jp), which comes distributed also with the *International New York Times*, and the **Japan News** (www.the-japan-news.com)—**Metropolis** (www.metropolisjapan.com) is a free weekly with features on Tokyo, club listings, and restaurant and movie reviews, while quarterly **TimeOut Tokyo** (www.timeout.jp)

offers more in-depth coverage of the city.

Pharmacies There are no 24-hour drugstores (kusuri-ya) in Tokyo, but ubiquitous 24-hour convenience stores such as 7-Eleven, Lawson, and FamilyMart carry things like aspirin. If you're looking for specific pharmaceuticals, a good bet is the **American Pharmacy,** in the basement of the Marunouchi Building, 2-4-1 Marunouchi, Chiyoda-ku (📞 **03/5220-7716;** station: Tokyo or Marunouchi; Mon–Fri 9am–9pm, Sat 10am–9pm, Sun and holidays 10am–9pm), which has many of the same over-the-counter drugs you can find at home (many of them imported from the United States) and can fill American prescriptions—but note that you *must first visit a doctor in Japan* before foreign prescriptions can be filled, so it's best to bring an ample supply of any prescription medication with you.

Safety According to a 2015 study by *The Economist,* Tokyo is the safest major urban destination in the world. There are, however, precautions you should always take when traveling: Stay alert and be aware of your immediate surroundings. Be especially careful with cameras, purses, and wallets, particularly in crowded subways, department stores, or tourist attractions (such as the retail district around Tsukiji Fish Market), especially because pickpocketing has been on the rise. Some Japanese also caution women against walking through parks alone at night.

WHERE TO STAY

Tokyo has no old, grand hotels in the tradition of Hong Kong's Peninsula or Bangkok's Oriental; it has hardly any old hotels, period. But what the city's hotels may lack in quaintness or old grandeur is more than made up for by excellent service—for which Japanese are legendary—as well as cleanliness and efficiency. Be prepared, however, for small rooms. Space is at a premium in Tokyo, so with the exception of Tokyo's expensive hotels, rooms seem to come in only three sizes: small, minuscule, and barely adequate.

Unfortunately, Tokyo also doesn't have many first-class *ryokan,* or Japanese-style inns. I suggest, therefore, that you wait for your travels around the country to experience a first-rate *ryokan.* Otherwise, there are moderate and inexpensive Japanese-style inns in Tokyo. In fact, if you're traveling on a tight budget, a simple Japanese-style inn is often the cheapest way to go, though don't expect

> ### Mapping out Tokyo's Hotels
>
> Once you've chosen a hotel or inn that appeals to you, you can locate it using the following neighborhood maps:
>

much in the way of service or amenities. In addition, most upper-bracket hotels offer at least a few Japanese-style rooms, with *tatami* mats, a Japanese bathtub (deeper and narrower than the Western version), and a futon. Although these rooms tend to be expensive, they're usually large enough for four people.

price CATEGORIES

Expensive	¥35,000 and up
Moderate	¥15,000–¥35,000
Inexpensive	Under ¥15,000

The hotel recommendations below are arranged by geographical location. However, because Tokyo's attractions, restaurants, and nightlife are widely scattered, and because the public transportation system is fast and efficient (I've provided the nearest subway or train stations for each listing), there's no one location in Tokyo that's more convenient than another—and because this is one of the most expensive hotel cities in the world, the overriding factor in selecting accommodations will likely be cost. Note that the prices provided below reflect low and high seasons (with the exception of New Year's, when they will be even higher), though inexpensive accommodations tend to charge the same rate year-round.

Unless otherwise indicated, units have private bathrooms. Note, too, that in Japan, a **twin room** refers to a room with two twin beds, while a **double room** refers to a room with one double bed. For convenience's sake, however, the "double" rates for hotels listed in this book refer to two people in one room and include both twin and double beds.

For more on available types of accommodations, see "Tips on Accommodations" in chapter 2.

TAXES & SERVICE CHARGES All hotel rates below include an 8% government tax unless stated otherwise. An additional local hotel tax will be added to bills that cost more than ¥10,000 per person per night. ¥100 is levied per person per night for rates between ¥10,000 and ¥14,999; rates of ¥15,000 and up are taxed at ¥200. Furthermore, all upper-class hotels and most medium-range hotels add a **service charge** of 10% to 15% (cheaper establishments do not add a service charge, because no service is provided). Unless otherwise stated, prices for accommodations include taxes (but not the local hotel tax) and service charge.

Hotels In & Around Ginza
EXPENSIVE

Conrad Tokyo ★★★ There are many attributes of this fine, contemporary hotel that win me over, starting with the large *sumi-e* (Japanese brush painting) in the lobby by one of my favorite Japanese artists, Toko Shinoda, just one of 23 leading Japanese craftsmen with artwork gracing the hotel. It also has one of the city's largest spa and fitness centers, occupying the entire 29th floor with 10 treatment rooms, a 25-meter pool (with a *sumi-e* design on the bottom, naturally), and a gym with aerobics, yoga, and other classes. But it's what's outside the hotel that makes this property special: fantastic views over Hama Riku Garden of Tokyo Bay and Odaiba. Because the cheapest rooms, which are a very respectable 48 sq. m (516 sq. ft.), face the city, I think it's worth splurging for bayside rooms, which take full advantage of those panoramic views with couches that extend the entire length of the wall-to-wall

WHY THE big range IN HOTEL PRICES?

In Tokyo, Kyoto and other major Japanese cities, nearly all high-end and medium-range hotels offer various categories of rooms at varying rates, with names such as premium, superior, etc., that are based on a variety of factors that may or may not include room size, decor, view, and what floor they're on.

Because of those many different levels of quality at the top-rated hotels, the wide range of rates for hotels are generally not only because of seasonal demand but also because of room types. For a hotel with a price range of 30,000 to 60,000 yen, you can expect to pay about 30,000 for the cheapest room (such as a small one on a low floor facing another building) in low season and about 60,000 in high season for a deluxe bigger room with views of Mt. Fuji or a castle. Sometimes, rooms can even be fairly identical but still vary in price because of the floor they're on and the views. Often, therefore, you can specifically request a room priced at a mid-level between the lowest and highest rates listed.

window and are great places to relax with the morning newspaper or evening drink. There are several options for fine dining, but most impressive is China Blue for its contemporary Cantonese cuisine and sweeping views over the bay. Located a short walk from Ginza and Shiodome, it's surrounded by office buildings housing mostly TV and advertising conglomerates, which perhaps explains why half of Conrad's guests are international travelers, the majority of them American.

1–9–1 Higashi-Shinbashi, Minato-ku. www.conradhotels.com. 𝒞 **03/6388-8000.** 290 units. ¥42,000–¥81,000 single or double; ¥57,000–¥88,000 executive room; from ¥101,000 suite. Rates exclude tax and service charge. Station: Shiodome (1 min.) or Shimbashi (7 min.). **Amenities:** 4 restaurants, lounge/bar, concierge; executive-level rooms; free entrance to health club and 25m indoor pool (classes cost ¥3,000); room service; spa; free Wi-Fi.

Imperial Hotel ★★★ This is one of Tokyo's oldest and most-respected hotels, with a prime location near subway stations, Ginza, Hibiya Park, and Imperial Palace. First opened in 1890 at the request of the Imperial family to house foreigners visiting Japan, it was rebuilt in 1922 by Frank Lloyd Wright and survived the horrific 1923 earthquake, only to succumb in 1970 to developers in a complete makeover. Wright's legacy lives on in the hotel's Art Deco Old Imperial bar and Wright-inspired designs and furniture in public spaces. Rooms are spread in the main building, popular with Japanese because of showers located outside of tubs (which allows them to bathe in traditional fashion), and in a 31-story tower added in 1983. Although access to the tower is a bit cumbersome, via a second-floor passageway, and rooms are smaller, foreign guests tend to like rooms here because views are better (with a choice of either the Ginza with its sparkling neon or Hibiya Park and Imperial Palace) and it's near the pool and gym. *Tip:* Join Imperial Club International—membership is free—and you can use the pool and gym for free and get other hotel discounts.

1–1–1 Uchisaiwaicho, Chiyoda-ku. www.imperialhotel.co.jp/e/tokyo. $\mathcal{C}$ **03/3504-1111.** 1,019 units. ¥38,880—¥64,800 single; ¥44,280–¥70,200 double; from ¥54,000 Imperial Floor double; from ¥97,200 suite. Rates exclude service charge. Station: Hibiya (1 min.). **Amenities:** 13 restaurants; 2 bars; lounge; babysitting; children's day-care center for ages 2 weeks to 6 years (fee: ¥5,400 for 2 hr.); concierge; executive-level rooms; exercise room (fee: ¥1,080; free for Imperial Club International members); 20th-floor indoor pool and sauna (fee: ¥1,080; free for Imperial Club International members); room service; tea-ceremony room; post office, free Wi-Fi.

MODERATE

Ginza Grand Hotel (formerly Hotel Com's Ginza) ★ Because of its great location in Ginza, this attractive hotel caters to business and leisure travelers alike. Although the building is about 40 years old, the hotel was recently updated to make it more hip, sporting splashes of Marimekko Finnish fabric artwork against a minimalist design, as well as more safe (a spiderlike steel construction was anchored to the back facade as a safeguard against earthquakes). Rooms, from the 3rd to 11th floors, are tiny but pleasant, including single rooms painted a pale yellow and with large beds and desks. Note, however, that standard rooms do not have closets or space to unpack. In any case, I suggest asking for a room away from the highway overpass beside the hotel, in which case you'll probably get a view of that spider contraption noted above.

8–6–15 Ginza, Chuo-ku. www.ginzagrand.com. $\mathcal{C}$ **03/3572-4131.** 266 units. ¥14,000–¥22,500 single; ¥17,000–¥46,800 double. Station: Shimbashi (3 min.). **Amenities:** 3 restaurants; bar; lounge; free Wi-Fi.

A Double or a Twin?

For the sake of convenience, the price for two people in a room is listed as a "double" in this book. Japanese hotels, however, differentiate between rooms with a double bed or two twin beds, usually with different prices. Although most hotels charge more for a twin room, sometimes the opposite is true; so be sure to inquire about prices for both. Note, too, that hotels usually have more twin rooms than doubles, for the simple reason that Japanese couples, used to their own futon, traditionally prefer twin beds.

Hotel Gracery ★★ Rooms here may be tiny, but high-powered Ginza is literally just outside the door. Targeting business travelers by offering convenient locations in city centers across the country, this business chain stays ahead of the pack with accommodations that are updated and minimally chic, with duvet-covered beds and colorful bed runners and pillows. There are rooms geared just toward women, some with wood floors (thought to foster a feeling of well-being when trod upon barefoot), and offering female toiletries and the Takarazuka Sky Stage cable channel (with programs centering on this all-female troupe), as well as doubles and executive-level rooms with massage chairs.

7–10–1 Ginza, Chuo-ku. www.ginza.gracery.com. $\mathcal{C}$ **03/6686-1000.** 270 units. ¥9,500–¥18,500 single; ¥15,000–¥25,000 double. Station: Ginza (3 min.) or Shimbashi (7 min.). 1 block east of Chuo Dori, behind Ginza Sapporo Lion. **Amenities:** Restaurant; bar; free Wi-Fi.

Mitsui Garden Hotel Ginza Premier ★★★   Mitsui Garden is a chain of business hotels that generally rises above the others in terms of decor and facilities, but this one ranks as one of Mitsui Garden's top properties. Its location is superb for business and leisure travelers alike, on the southern edge of Ginza near Shimbashi. Occupying the upper floors of an office building, it has a 16th-floor lobby that welcomes guests with lots of sofas, a comfy computer corner for travelers without laptops, and floor-to-ceiling windows revealing great views of Tokyo Bay, Hama Rikyu Garden, and Tokyo Tower. Rooms are compact though thoughtfully designed, but their best feature is their panoramic views of Tokyo Tower (the most requested), the Ginza (most beautiful at night), or the bay (note that a new building now obstructs bay views from some rooms, so be sure to request an unobstructed view). Views are even afforded from bathrooms, either through windows that look out past the bedroom toward the city in the cheaper rooms or, in View Bath and Premier rooms, from windows right beside the tub that let you take in the views as you soak. Although this hotel has lots going for it (unfortunately, in-room Wi-Fi is not one of them, though it does have LAN cable), the views in this price range really set it apart.

8–13–1 Ginza, Chuo-ku. www.gardenhotels.co.jp/eng/ginza-premier. ✆ **03/3543-1131.** 361 units. ¥16,400–¥27,200 single; ¥19,000–¥47,920 double. Station: Shimbasi (5 min.) or Ginza (7 min.). **Amenities:** Restaurant; bar; free Internet.

Park Hotel Tokyo ★★★   Occupying the top 10 floors of a building it shares with international media organizations (like Kyodo News), this hotel is well located within walking distance of the Ginza, Tsukiji Fish Market, and Hama Rikyu Garden. Its lobby, on the 25th floor and decorated with large trees and dark woods in a theme of "nature and health," is bathed in the natural sunlight afforded by its 10-story atrium topped with an opaque ceiling, making its ART Lounge a great place for breakfast. The front desk is one of the most dramatic I've seen, backed by nothing but great views of Tokyo Tower and the city. Rooms, simply decorated with original art, also provide views, the best of which can be found on the 30th floor and above facing Hama Rikyu Garden and Tokyo Bay or facing Tokyo Tower (and Mount Fuji on clear winter days). One of the things I like most about this hotel is its dedication to art, with changing exhibits on lobby walls and with 10 rooms painted by Japanese artists, like the Bamboo Room with wall murals of greenery.

Shiodome Media Tower, 1–7–1 Higashi Shimbashi, Minato-ku. www.parkhoteltokyo. com. ✆ **03/6252-1111.** 273 units. ¥15,500–¥20,000 single; ¥16,999–¥36,000 double. Rates exclude service charge and hotel tax. Station: Shiodome (1 min.) or Shimbashi (8 min.). **Amenities:** 2 restaurants; bar; lounge; concierge; personal-size gym (free, on a reservation basis); room service; spa; free Wi-Fi.

remm Hibiya ★   This low-key business hotel slips under the radar of most passersby, despite its prime location across from the Imperial Hotel and just steps away from the Ginza. Its second-floor reception shares space with a branch of Muji Café & Meal, known for its inexpensive salads and healthy dishes and open from 6:30am for breakfast. Rooms are tiny, but all have the surprising addition of massage chairs and some single and double rooms facing west even have views of Hibiya Park or palace grounds between buildings; note that single/double rooms, with showers instead of tubs, are actually the same room and are cramped for two people. Glass walls separating bathrooms from living space give the illusion of space (thank goodness there's a blind you can pull down). Although a business hotel, this place also caters to women with a devoted Ladies Floor and the Takarazuka Sky Stage cable channel free of charge, but the extremely popular Takarazuka Kagekidan theater just down the street, with its all-female cast performing musical revues, is what draws in devoted fans, who are overwhelmingly women. There's another branch in Akihabara.

1–2–1 Yurakucho, Chiyoda-ku. www.hankyu-hotel.com/english/sitemap.html. © **03/3507-0606.** 225 units. ¥14,000–¥17,480 single; ¥16,000–¥29,360 double. Station: Hibiya (2 min.) or Yurakucho (5 min.). **Amenities:** 1 restaurant; free Wi-Fi.

Near Tokyo Station
MODERATE

Tokyo Station Hotel ★★   Tokyo Station was built in 1914 in the tradition of Europe's great train stations; the Tokyo Station Hotel opened a year later. After a 6-year massive renovation that restored the brick Marunouchi facade and century-old domed station to its former glory, the Station Hotel reopened in 2012 as Japan Railways' flagship hotel. Luckily, the Marunouchi side is just a small part of sprawling Tokyo Station, so the hotel itself receives little foot traffic and has its own dedicated entrance (as well as direct access to subway and train stations, handy in inclement weather). Much of the old hotel remains, including the high-ceilinged lobby lounge, which once served as the first-class waiting lounge, and the original 330-m.-long (1,082-ft.) corridor leading to rooms. Even Hisashi Sugimoto, at the hotel since 1958, is back at the historic Bar Oak concocting his signature cocktails. Six different styles of rooms, all with high-vaulted ceilings and expansive windows, are available, from Classic Queens, which are fairly standard but are also dark since they face another building, to Dome Side Rooms that face a concourse with the spectacularly restored reliefs of the copula domed ceiling. With its fine and casual dining and Old World ambiance, not to mention easy access to one of the busiest train stations in the world, this is a unique property in Tokyo. Train buffs won't want to stay anywhere else.

Tokyo Station, 1–9–1 Marunouchi, Chiyoda-ku. www.thetokyostationhotel.jp. © **03/5220-1111.** ¥24,455–¥32,540 single; ¥30,230–¥67,390 double. Slight discount for holders of Japan Rail Pass. Station: Tokyo (1 min.). **Amenities:** 7 restaurants; 2 bars; lounge; concierge; small gym (fee: ¥1,000); room service; spa; free Wi-Fi.

INEXPENSIVE

Super Hotel Lohas Tokyo-eki Yaesu Chuo-guchi (スーパーホテル Lohas東京駅八重洲中央口) ★   It's a mouthful, but what its name really means is that it's super cheap (by central Tokyo standards) and has a super location only a block east of Tokyo Station. Part of a growing hotel chain that edges competitors out with low prices, it offers small rooms with all the basics, plus pull-down window shades for total darkness, wall-mounted TVs (there's nowhere else to really put them), and humidifier/air purifiers. There's also a ladies' floor that offers the additions of face steamers, makeup mirrors and other amenities in rooms done up in feminine colors. However, with the rest of Tokyo within such easy reach, I'm betting you won't want to spend much quality time in your room, though you might want to take a dip in the large public baths.

2–2–7 Yaesu, Chuo-ku. www.superhoteljapan.com/en/s-hotels/yaesu. ✆ **03/3241-9000.** 325 units. ¥11,000–¥11,500 single; ¥14,000–¥18,500 double. Station: Tokyo (Yaesu Central exit, 3 min.) or Kyobashi (4 min.). **Amenities:** Restaurant; free Wi-Fi.

Asakusa

MODERATE

Sadachiyo Sukeroku-no-yado ★★★   This 67-year-old *ryokan* is a rarity in Tokyo and a great find in Asakusa's traditional neighborhood. It has lots of Edo-era touches, from the rickshaw outside its front door to stone and paper lanterns, bamboo screens, and antiques that fill public places. Even the staff wears traditional clothing, and the lounge is typically Japanese with floor seating. Rooms are all *tatami* and have woodblock prints, shoji screens, and other traditional features, with some large enough for a family of six. The cypress-and-granite public baths are a perk, and to really feel like you're living in old Edo (present-day Tokyo), sign up for the Japanese dinner, featuring dishes typical of the times and beginning at ¥7,000 for a 12-dish meal (make dinner reservations when you reserve your room). Note that there's a 2am curfew.

2–20–1 Asakusa, Taito-ku. www.sadachiyo.co.jp. ✆ **03/3842-6431.** 20 units. ¥14,100 single; ¥19,600 double. ¥1,000 extra Fri, Sat, and night before holidays. Station: Tawaramachi (8 min.), Asakusa (15 min.), or Tsukuba Express Asakusa (3 min.). **Amenities:** Restaurant; free Wi-Fi.

Ryokan Asakusa Shigetsu ★★   Whenever a foreigner living in Tokyo, soon to host first-time visitors to Japan, asks me to recommend a moderately priced Japanese-style inn in Tokyo, this is the one I often suggest due to its great location near Sensoji Temple in Asakusa, an area that gives you a feel for the older Japan. It represents the best of modern yet traditional Japanese design—simple yet elegant, with shoji, unadorned wood, and artwork throughout. Two public Japanese baths have views of the nearby five-story pagoda and SkyTree in the distance (a jarring contrast). While there are six Western-style single rooms, I prefer the 15 slightly more expensive Japanese-style *tatami* rooms, which include Japanese-style mirrors and comfortable chairs for those who don't like relaxing on the floor. This *ryokan* costs no more than a regular business hotel but has much more class.

1–31–11 Asakusa, Taito-ku. www.shigetsu.com. ✆ **03/3843-2345.** 21 units. ¥7,000–¥11,160 single; ¥15,150–¥19,900 double. Rates higher on Sat., nights before holidays and consecutive holidays. Station: Asakusa (4 min.). **Amenities:** Restaurant; free Wi-Fi.

INEXPENSIVE

Khaosan Kabuki ★   One of seven no-frills Khaosan guesthouses in Tokyo catering to international backpackers, this one has a great location just a couple minutes' walk from Nakamise Dori, a colorful shop-lined pedestrian street leading to the famous Sensoji Temple. Formerly a love hotel (p. 37), it offers a communal room with a kitchen, TV, free coffee and tea, computers you can use for free, and a laundry room with free detergent. Most of its rooms are for four people (you can either rent the whole room or, for slightly less, stay dormitory-style with others, although you might be sharing a room with the opposite sex). There's also a double, a twin, and a *tatami* room that sleeps three people. Check the website for the other guesthouses, most of them also in Asakusa, including Khaosan Laboratory, done up in such bright colors it reminds me of an elementary school, and Khaosan World, which also has women-only dorm rooms. Only Khaosan Kabuki's rooms, however, are all with private bathrooms.

1–17–2 Asakusa, Taito-ku. www.khaosan-tokyo.com. © **03/5830-3673.** 11 units. ¥3,400 per person. **Amenities:** Free Wi-Fi.

Ryokan Kamogawa ★★ Established in 1948 by the present owner's parents and located just off Nakamise Dori, this inn is small and personable, with a coffee shop and a Japanese-style bath you can lock and use privately (reserve in advance). Its *tatami* rooms, with shoji screens and other traditional touches, sleep up to five persons, making them a good choice for families. Note that only one room (the size of four-and-a-half *tatami* mats; a single *tatami* measures 1m×1.8m), is available at the cheapest rates below. In any case, the inn is usually fully booked in April, October, December, and February, so if you hope to stay here then, book far ahead. Note, too, that the front door is locked at 11:30pm; if you wish to stay out later be sure to ask for the back-door key. Dinners, served in the coffee shop, start at ¥2,400, but must be ordered in advance.

1–30–10 Asakusa, Taito-ku. www.f-kamogawa.jp. © **03/3843-2681.** 10 units. ¥7,600–¥15,000 single; ¥13,800–¥22,000 double; ¥27,000 triple. Station: Asakusa (3 min.). **Amenities:** Coffee shop; free Wi-Fi.

Ueno

MODERATE

Hotel Coco Grand ★★★ This hotel is located in the *shitamachi* (old downtown) area of Ueno where commoners once lived, but guests aren't sacrificing style or comfort to stay here. Across the street from the south end of Shinobazu Pond and an easy walk from Ueno Park and Ueno's Keisei Station with direct service from Narita airport, it has an upbeat, boutiquelike atmosphere, with a welcoming gas fireplace in the lobby, a cake shop that draws in Japanese women, public baths, and small but chic rooms, many with views of the pond and decorated with splashes of bright colors. Rooms are mostly small singles, but even the cheapest are snazzy and perfectly fine. There are also doubles and twins, including two Park View Doubles with views of the pond and Zen Twins, which impart an air of traditional Japan with their raised beds on *tatami* and shoji-like window coverings. The best room in the house is the Villa Suite Twin, which seems like an exotic getaway with its private outdoor terrace outfitted with Jacuzzi, sofa, and TV, plus a steam room and bathroom tub big enough for two. The website is only in Japanese, but it does have photos of rooms. Unfortunately, prices have risen since its 2010 opening, but I still consider this a good deal.

2–12–14 Ueno, Taito-ku. www.cocogrand.co.jp/uenoshinobazu. $\mathcal{C}$ **03/5812-1155.** 58 units. ¥9,800–¥14,300 single; ¥16,800–¥28,300 double. Rates include breakfast. Station: Ueno (4 min.). **Amenities:** Sauna; spa; free Wi-Fi.

INEXPENSIVE

Annex Katsutaro ★★   Old-fashioned Yanaka neighborhood, home to many temples and the Yanaka Ginza shopping street, is part of what makes a stay here special. It's also within a 20-minute walk from Ueno Park with its many museums, and the Keisei Skyliner from Narita Airport stops at nearby Nippori Station. Though the inn itself is a three-story concrete building, it manages to convey a sense of place with its spotless Japanese-style *tatami* rooms and a complimentary map that introduces the area and how to navigate it. There's free coffee in the lobby, as well as two computers guests can use for free and rental bikes. It's the sister inn of nearby Katsutaro Ryokan, which is older and slightly cheaper but isn't nearly as nice.

3–8–4 Yanaka, Taito-ku. www.katsutaro.com. $\mathcal{C}$ **03/3828-2500.** 17 units. ¥6,500–¥6,800 single; ¥10,800–¥13,600 double; ¥15,300–¥17,700 triple. Station: Sendagi (2 min.) or Nippori (7 min.). **Amenities:** Rental bikes (¥300/day); free Internet.

Homeikan ★★★   You won't find many places like this in Tokyo any more. In fact, "places" is the key word here, since Homeikan actually consists of three historic buildings, purchased long ago by the present owner's grandfather and clustered in a very traditional residential neighborhood. The Honkan (the main building) is the oldest, acquired by the family more than a century ago and listed as a "Tangible Cultural Property" since 2000. The Morikawa annex, a 5-minute walk away, isn't quite as old but has all the traditional elements of a classic inn. Across the street from the Honkan is my favorite, the Daima-chi annex, which was built as the family home after World War II and has striking architectural details, from hallways inlaid with pebbles to *tatami* rooms that incorporate gnarled wood trim, bamboo lattice, or other natural features in their design. Daimachi also has a Japanese garden with a pond and a communal mineral bath, along with simple *tatami* rooms for travelers on a budget. English-speaking owner Koike-san says travelers who expect modern conveniences (like private bathrooms or Wi-Fi) will be happier elsewhere; those seeking a traditional *ryokan* experience, however, will not be disappointed. It's hard to find, so be sure to print out the map on Homeikan's website or come by taxi. And note that it's a bit of a hike from Ueno Park, about 30 minutes.

5–10–5 Hongo, Bunkyo-ku. www.homeikan.com. $\mathcal{C}$ **03/3811-1187.** 89 units (none with private bathroom). ¥8,100–¥11,340 single; ¥14,040–¥20,520 double. Station: Hongo Sanchome (8 min.) or Kasuga (5 min.). **Amenities:** Free Internet.

Ryokan Sawanoya ★★★   I stayed here on one of my earliest trips to Japan; I'm happy to report that it has only gotten better over the years and remains one of my favorites. A family-run affair since 1949, the smoke-free inn is now in the capable hands of the original proprietress' grandson, though the elder Sawa-san still pours his heart and soul into the business and even wrote a book about the history of Sawanoya and his experiences as an inn-keeper. Located about a 15-minute walk from Ueno Park and 5 minutes from Nezu Shrine, it's nestled in a residential area known for its *shitamachi* (old downtown) atmosphere and traditional architecture. Upon arrival, guests are given a short tour of the establishment, which includes two baths with views of a garden (which can be locked for privacy), before being led upstairs to their *tatami* room on the second or third floor (there's no elevator). Guests also receive a hand-drawn map outlining restaurants and other nearby facilities. The large lobby offers free coffee and tea, a communal computer, and a huge selection of brochures from throughout Japan. A traditional Japanese lion dance is staged free of charge several times a month, and the inn even donates ¥100 of every room charge towards the Tohoku Earthquake Relief Fund. It's also LGBT friendly. In short, Sawanoya has a long history of making travelers feel welcome in Tokyo and thus comes highly recommended.

2–3–11 Yanaka, Taito-ku. www.sawanoya.com. © **03/3822-2251.** 12 units (2 with bathroom). ¥5,184–¥5,508 single without bathroom; ¥9,720 double without bathroom, ¥11,016 double with bathroom; ¥13,284 triple without bathroom, ¥15,876 triple with bathroom. Closed Dec 29–Jan 3. Station: Nezu (exit 1, 7 min.). **Amenities:** 2 rental bikes (¥300/day); free Wi-Fi.

Shinjuku

EXPENSIVE

Park Hyatt Tokyo ★★★ When the Park Hyatt opened in 1994 as Tokyo's first skyscraper hotel, I knew it was bound for glory the moment I stepped out of the elevator onto the light-drenched 41st floor. No hotel yet offered views as surreal as this; and with its gorgeous layout, high-tech rooms, and polished service (check-in is at one of three sit-down desks), it seemed light-years ahead of the competition. No wonder it starred in the 2003 hit, "Lost in Translation" and has inspired many competitors. Rooms, measuring a minimum of 45 sq. m (480 sq. ft.), have walk-in closets, deep soaking tubs (and separate showers), original pieces of artwork, Japanese-style paper lamps, paneling made from 2,000-year-old wood from Hokkaido, and great views (although east views of Shinjuku's nightlife and the greenery of several parks are the most popular, the west side sometimes has glimpses of Mount Fuji). I also like the hotel's 2000-book library, the New York Grill with outstanding views and cuisine, the free bikes for exploration of nearby Yoyogi, Chuo, and Shinjuku parks (complete with helmets, bottled water, and more), and the 47th-floor fitness facilities overlooking the city, with free use of a sky-lit lap pool, gym, and studio offering complimentary yoga, aerobics, Pilates, and a relaxing "Good Night Sleep Stretch." I'm ready to move in.

3–7–1–2 Nishi-Shinjuku, Shinjuku-ku. www.tokyo.park.hyatt.com. © **03/5322-1234.** 177 units. ¥60,200–¥95,191 single or double; from ¥180,619 suite. Station: Shinjuku (a 13-min. walk or 5-min. free shuttle ride); Hatsudai, on the Keio Line (7 min.); or Tocho-mae (8 min.). **Amenities:** 3 restaurants; 2 bars; lounge; babysitting; concierge; free entrance to gym and dramatic 20m indoor pool w/great views; room service; free shuttle service to Shinjuku Station up to 3 times an hour; spa; free Wi-Fi.

MODERATE

Hotel Century Southern Tower ★★★
Conveniently located amidst the skyscrapers of Shinjuku and connected to Takashimaya Shinjuku shopping complex via a footbridge, this superb choice offers smallish rooms with a view, at a fraction of the price of nearby competitors. Luggage carts instead of bellhops and vending machines in place of room service seem like no sacrifice at all when rewarded with mesmerizing panoramas from the 20th-floor lobby lounge, the small exercise room, Tribecks restaurant (I like their Continental lunches), and rooms, occupying the 22nd to 35th floors and recently renovated in shades of brown and with good reading lights at the desk and bedside (ask for a room on a higher floor). The best—and most expensive—rooms face east or south, where views over central Tokyo take on a neon glow at night. Rooms on the west side take in Yoyogi Park, high-rises, and, from higher floors, Mt. Fuji in fine weather. Maps placed in each room help identify landmarks, while TVs have keyboards for Internet access free of charge. Couples might note, however, that doubles are much smaller than twins.

2–2–1 Yoyogi, Shibuya-ku. www.southerntower.co.jp. ℗ **03/5354-0111.** 375 units. ¥16,000–¥19,000 single; ¥25,000–¥31,000 double. Rates exclude tax. Station: Shinjuku (south exit, 3 min.). **Amenities:** 3 restaurants; lounge; exercise room; free Wi-Fi.

INEXPENSIVE

Tokyo Central Youth Hostel ★
This spotless hostel is definitely the best place to stay in its price range—situated on the 18th and 19th floors of a highrise, it offers fantastic Tokyo views. Otherwise, couples can pay less at business hotel chains like Toyoko Inn and even have more privacy, as this location is prime real estate and no private rooms are offered. Rather, all beds are dormitory style, with four or more bunk beds to a room. Rooms are very pleasant, with big windows, and each bed has its own curtain for privacy and comes with a locker. There are also two *tatami* rooms sleeping four to six people. There's a tiny communal kitchen; Wi-Fi is available only in public areas. In summer, it's a good idea to reserve about 2 months in advance (reservations can be made up to 3 months in advance). Check in is from 3pm, the front door is locked at 11pm (lights out at midnight), and check out is by 10am.

Central Plaza Building, 18th floor, 1–1 Kagura-kashi, Shinjuku-ku. www.jyh.gr.jp/tcyh. ℗ **03/3235-1107.** 158 beds. ¥4,050 adult (¥600 less for youth hostel members), ¥2,910 child. Breakfast ¥600. Station: Iidabashi (take the west exit from the JR station or the B2b subway exit, 2 min.).

Aoyama & Akasaka

EXPENSIVE

Hotel New Otani ★★
This hotel's most splendid feature is its garden, the best of any Tokyo hotel: more than 400 years old and once the private estate of a feudal lord. Spreading over 4 hectares (10 acres), it contains ponds filled with koi, waterfalls, arched bridges, manicured bushes (the many

azaleas are especially striking in spring), stone lanterns, bamboo groves, and a stone garden; it's not unusual to see Japanese in their kimono finest gathered here for family photographs. The large outdoor pool, shrouded by greenery, provides more privacy than most hotel pools and is free for members of Otani Club International (membership is free). That's about it, however, when it comes to communing with nature, as this is one of Tokyo's largest hotels (be sure to pick up hotel and garden maps at the concierge, because you're going to need them). Its 31 restaurants and 6 bars draw huge crowds of locals, especially its very popular Garden Lounge offering the best views of the garden. Rooms are spread among the main building, built for the 1964 Olympics and offering the best up-close views of the garden, and the 40-story Garden Tower with views over the glittering city. Because rates are the same regardless of view, ask for a room facing the garden. Hotel facilities are so exhaustive this is like a city within a city; folks who shun crowds will be happier elsewhere.

4–1 Kioi-cho, Chiyoda-ku. www.newotani.co.jp. © **03/3265-1111.** 1,479 units. ¥23,000– ¥34,650 single; ¥23,000–¥52,500 double; from ¥50,400 Executive House Zen; from ¥89,250 suite. Rates exclude service charge and hotel tax. Station: Akasaka-mitsuke or Nagatacho (3 min.). **Amenities:** 31 restaurants and cafes; 6 bars and lounges; children's day-care center for ages 2 months to 5 years old (fee: ¥6,480 for 2 hr.); concierge; executive-level rooms; small exercise room; health club w/indoor pool and spa (fee: ¥5,400; ¥3,240 before 10am); outdoor pool (fee: ¥2,000 weekdays, ¥3,000 weekends and holidays; free for Club International members); room service; lighted outdoor tennis courts; medical and dental clinics; art museum (free for hotel guests); post office; tea-ceremony room; free Wi-Fi.

MODERATE

Tokyu Stay Aoyama Premier ★★★ Tokyu Stay hotels are designed for business travelers who intend to stay put for a while and want the comforts of home. That also means picking up after yourself, as rooms are not cleaned as often as in hotels (daily for stays of 6 days or less, twice a week for stays of 7 nights or more). Rooms come with extra storage space, kitchenettes (including cooking utensils and tableware; the cheapest have microwaves but no stovetop) and even combination washers/dryers. Of the 15 Tokyu Stay hotels in the Tokyo, the Aoyama Premier is the chain's star property, with a great location near Roppongi and Aoyama, rooms just for ladies, and good city views from its perch atop an office building. On the first two floors are high-end shops and restaurants (think confectionaries, cosmetics, and a tofu restaurant). Cheaper locations include those in Ikebukuro, Nishi-Shinjuku, Suidobashi, Gotanda, Shibuya, Nihombashi, and Higashi-Ginza. Check the website for details.

2–27–18 Minami-Aoyama, Minato-ku. www.tokyustay.co.jp. © **03/3497-0109.** 170 units. ¥10,800–¥21,000 single; ¥16,600–¥32,400 double. Rates include breakfast. Discounts for stays longer than 6 nights. Station: Gaienmae (exit 1a, 2 min.). **Amenities:** Restaurant; free Wi-Fi.

INEXPENSIVE

Hotel Asia Center of Japan (Asia Kaikan) ★★ A great location in central Tokyo, a decent cafeteria complete with outdoor terrace that's popular with area office workers, and reasonable rates for Western-style rooms have made this a favorite domicile for everyone from business travelers and educators to students and youth groups for decades. Established in 1957, it has the atmosphere of a college dormitory, with mostly single tiny rooms equipped with just the basics. For Wi-Fi you have to go to the lobby (which also dispenses free bottled water and other items, such as razors and toothbrushes), though after renovations are complete in October 2015 it will be extended to all rooms; until then, expect daytime construction noise. There are only 20 double and 20 twin rooms, as well as 65 so-called semi-double rooms that have a bed larger than a twin-size mattress but narrower than a full. These are great for one person, but they're also sold for two people, oddly at the same price as a true double. Unless you're fond of cramped quarters, therefore, make reservations far in advance. It's also a good idea to avoid rooms on the ground floor, since windows can be opened (a rarity in many hotels) and in Japan there are no screens. Probably my favorite feature of the hotel is that it's only a 15-minute walk to Roppongi or Akasaka, or one station away by subway. Aoyama Dori, lined with shops and restaurants on its way to Omotesando, is just a 5-minute walk away.

8–10–32 Akasaka, Minato-ku. www.asiacenter.or.jp. ✆ **03/3402-6111.** 173 units. ¥8,850–¥10,580 single; ¥12,740–¥19,220 double. Station: Aoyama-Itchome (exit 4, 5 min.) or Nogizaka (exit 3, 5 min.). **Amenities:** Restaurant; free Internet.

Roppongi
INEXPENSIVE

Arca Torre ★ This 10-story business hotel has a great location on Roppongi Dori near Roppongi Crossing, making it popular with business types and tourists on a budget. Its mostly single rooms are small but cheerful, with complimentary bottled water in the otherwise empty fridge; two people can opt to stay in one but they'll be happier in a double room. Rooms facing the back are quiet but face another building with glazed windows and are rather dark. If you opt for a room facing the front, spring for more expensive rooms on higher floors above the freeway; otherwise, from the cheaper rooms on lower floors your view will be of cars and, at certain times of the day, traffic jams.

6–1–23 Roppongi, Minato-ku. www.arktower.co.jp/arcatorre.✆ **03/3404-5111.** 77 units. ¥9,420–¥10,900 single; ¥10,500–¥18,360 double. Station: Roppongi (1 min.). **Amenities:** Free Wi-Fi.

the b roppongi ★★ The b roppongi opened in 2004 as the first of 10 business hotels under the "b" brand. Its quirky name is based on four concepts: a comfortable **b**ed, a good **b**reakfast (which nonetheless costs extra), a **b**alanced life, and a contemporary and relaxed atmosphere for conducting **b**usiness. What this boils down to is a boutique business hotel that is more stylish than most of its genre, with beds that are indeed comfortable and have focused reading lamps. Otherwise, standard and superior rooms are your typical business-hotel tiny size, so travelers yearning for a bit more space might want to splurge on a deluxe, which offers the advantage of more windows in addition to more space. Facilities are practically nonexistent, unless you count the free coffee in the lobby, but in any case Roppongi's nightlife is just outside the door. Other b hotels in Tokyo are in Ochanomizu, Akasaka, Ikebukuro, and other locations; check the website.

3–9–8 Roppongi, Minato-ku. www.itheb-hotels.com. ℂ **03/5412-0451.** 76 units. ¥7,800–¥18,000 single; ¥12,600–¥27,000 double. Station: Roppongi (1 min.). **Amenities:** Restaurant; free Wi-Fi.

Shibuya
MODERATE
Shibuya Excel Hotel Tokyu ★★   If you saw the movie *Lost in Translation*, you might remember a scene of an intersection that's crazy busy with pedestrians walking in all directions when the light turns red. That's Shibuya Scramble, and it's just a stone's throw from this hotel, located across from bustling Shibuya Station and connected by underground passage and a footbridge (*Tip:* The footbridge is a good place to photograph Shibuya Scramble). Located above Mark City shopping mall, with reception on the fifth floor, it's a business hotel that appeals also to women with its women-only floor accessed by a special key and offering the extras of makeup remover, face cream, jewelry boxes, face steamer, and other amenities. Rooms are on the 7th to 24th floors, with those higher up facing Shinjuku providing great night views; the 25th-floor French restaurant also offers great views along with reasonable prices. There are many dining options near the hotel, including the Center Gai nightlife district, a pedestrian lane lined with restaurants and bars, and the Hikarie complex.

1–12–2 Dogenzaka, Shibuya-ku. www.tokyuhotelsjapan.com. ℂ **03/5457-0109.** 408 units. ¥24,948–¥28,512 single; ¥33,264–¥57,024 double. Station: Shibuya (1 min. by footbridge). **Amenities:** 3 restaurants; room service; free Wi-Fi.

Other Neighborhoods
MODERATE
Shiba Park Hotel ★★   This is a well-respected older hotel, tucked away in a quiet residential area near Shiba Park, Zozoji Temple and Tokyo Tower (and a sobering 25-min. walk from Roppongi nightlife). Friendly staff and the hotel's low-key atmosphere make it more intimate than the beehive activity of Tokyo's larger hotels, though all bets are off in winter, when it serves as a popular way station for Australians headed for the slopes. Although the hotel consists of two buildings, a main building and an annex across the street in back, rooms in the main building have been closed since 2011 but are expected to reopen in 2016 after a complete renovation. Until then, various rooms are available in the annex, from fairly standard twins and doubles to Stylish Twins that exude a bit more class. There are also rooms that sleep four people, as well as Business Class Single rooms geared toward productivity with larger desks and ergonomic chairs.

1–5–10 Shiba-koen, Minato-ku. www.shibaparkhotel.com. ℂ **03/3433-4141.** 212 units. ¥12,999–¥19,000 single; ¥13,999–¥29,000 double. Rates exclude service charge and hotel tax. Station: Onarimon (2 min.), Daimon (4 min.), or Hamamatsucho (8 min.). **Amenities:** 4 restaurants; bar; room service; free Wi-Fi.

The Hilltop Hotel (Yama-no-Ue Hotel) ★★ This delightfully old-fashioned, unpretentious (some might say dowdy) relic qualifies as historic in contemporary Tokyo. Built in 1937 and serving as a research institute and then as living quarters for US occupation forces before becoming a hotel in 1954, it remains true to its past, not much different from when it was a favorite retreat of writers like novelist Yukio Mishima (its annex across the street closed in 2014). With a distinctive Art Deco facade, most of its rooms have such endearing, homey touches as fringed lampshades, doilies and cherrywood furniture. Some twins even combine a *tatami* area and shoji with beds; the most expensive twin overlooks its own Japanese garden. While not as conveniently located as other tourist hotels, this is a nostalgia-invoking place (don't be surprised if reception staffers remember you by name), hidden on a hill near Meiji University and near restaurants, bookshops, and other student hangouts, which bring lots of young people and liveliness to the area. And though small by Tokyo standards, this hotel has an impressive number of restaurants and bars, due, no doubt, to its popularity among steadfast local fans.

1–1 Surugadai, Kanda, Chiyoda-ku. www.yamanoue-hotel.co.jp. © **03/3293-2311.** 74 units. ¥17,000–¥20,000 single; ¥24,000–¥32,000 double. Rates exclude service charge and taxes. Station: Ochanomizu or Shin-Ochanomizu (8 min.) or Jimbocho (5 min.). **Amenities:** 5 restaurants; 2 bars; room service; free Internet.

INEXPENSIVE

Kimi Ryokan ★★★ This inexpensive Japanese-style inn has long been on the international radar as one of the best in Tokyo for its traditional details and up-to-date conveniences. Flower arrangements (created by English-speaking owner Minato Kisaburo), shoji screens, scrolls of calligraphy and other artwork, a public bath made of cypress, and polished wood-floor corridors where traditional Japanese music plays faintly in the background are complemented by a lounge with cable TV (a good place to meet fellow travelers, who are mostly in their twenties), a kitchen, an inviting rooftop terrace, and a bulletin board and newsletter providing information on rental apartments and jobs, mostly as English teachers. Guest rooms are all Japanese style and rather small, with the cheapest room (for one or two persons) measuring four-and-a-half *tatami* mats, and the larger room (for two or three guests) six mats. Be sure to download the area map on Kimi's website, as this place is a bit difficult to find, and note that there's a 2am curfew.

2–36–8 Ikebukuro, Toshima-ku, Tokyo 171-0014. www.kimi-ryokan.jp. © **03/3971-3766.** 38 units (none with private bathroom). ¥4,500 single; ¥6,500–¥7,500 double; ¥9,500–¥12,000 triple. Station: Ikebukuro (west exit; 7 min.). **Amenities:** Free Wi-Fi.

Toyoko Inn Shinagawa-Eki Takanawaguchi ★ Business hotels were often dingy and dismal before this chain raised the bar a couple decades back, offering clean and inexpensive rooms and a slew of freebies that have since become standard, including Internet connection, lobby computers guests can use for free, and even free breakfast. Now with more than 200 locations throughout Japan, usually within easy walking distance of stations and noted for having managers that are mostly women, it offers very tiny rooms that are nonetheless equipped with everything guests need. This one is convenient for connections to Narita airport or via Shinkansen bullet train to the rest of Japan, but other Tokyo locations include those in Shinjuku, Ikebukuro, Asakusa, Ueno, Nihombashi, and Akihabara.

4–23–2 Takanawa, Minato-ku, Tokyo 108-0074. www.toyoko-inn.com. © **03/3280-1045.** 180 units. ¥7,884–¥8,424 single; ¥8,964–¥11,880 double. Rates include continental breakfast. Station: Shinagawa (3 min.). From JR station's Takanawa (west) exit, cross the street and turn left. **Amenities:** Free Wi-Fi.

WHERE TO EAT

From stand-up noodle shops and pizzerias to exclusive *kaiseki* restaurants and sushi bars, there are more than 80,000 restaurants in Tokyo—which gives you some idea of how fond Japanese are of eating out. In a city where apartments are so small and cramped that entertaining at home is almost unheard of, restaurants serve as places for socializing, meeting friends, and wooing business associates—as well as great excuses for drinking a lot of beer, sake, and whiskey.

One of the best deals is the **fixed-price lunch,** usually available from 11am to 2pm. Called a *teishoku* in a Japanese restaurant and a "seto coursu" (or simply "seto" or *coursu*) in restaurants serving Western food, the set lunch you to dine in style at reasonable prices. If possible, avoid the noon-to-1pm weekday crush when Tokyo's army of office workers flood area restaurants. Because Japanese tend to order fixed-price meals rather than a la carte, set dinners are also usually available (although they're not as cheap as set lunches). All-you-can-eat buffets (called *viking* in Japanese, probably because Japan's first buffet was in a restaurant called Viking in Tokyo's Imperial Hotel), offered by many hotel restaurants, are also bargains for hearty appetites. See p. 30 in chapter 2 for more recommendations on saving money.

Mapping Out Tokyo's Restaurants

You can locate the restaurants reviewed below using the following neighborhood maps:

- To locate restaurants in and around **Ginza,** p. 108.
- To locate restaurants in **Asakusa,** p. 114.
- To locate restaurants in **Ueno,** p. 117.
- To locate restaurants in **Shinjuku,** p. 120.
- To locate restaurants in **Harajuku** and **Aoyama,** p. 123.
- To locate restaurants in **Roppongi,** p. 126.

Otherwise, so many of Tokyo's good restaurants fall into the moderate category that it's tempting to simply eat your way through the city—and the range of cuisines is so great you could eat something different at each meal. Bargain hunters should note that many of the most colorful, noisy, and popular restaurants fall into the inexpensive category, where many offer meals for less than ¥2,000 and lunches for ¥1,000 or less. The city's huge working population heads to these places to catch a quick lunch or to socialize with friends after hours. There are also many excellent yet inexpensive French bistros, Italian trattorie, and ethnic restaurants, particularly those serving Indian, Chinese, and other Asian cuisines. Finally, see "Entertainment & Nightlife," in chapter 5, for suggestions on inexpensive drinking places that serve food. And because I can cover only a limited number of cheap restaurants in each neighborhood, I also suggest you ask your concierge or hotel manager for recommendations; there's probably a great little place just around the corner.

Note that an 8% consumption tax is added to meals in restaurants. Some restaurants include the tax in their prices; others do not. In any case, menus usually state whether prices include taxes. The prices listed in this book are those taken directly from menus, so be prepared for tax to be added to your meal. In addition, first-class restaurants, as well as hotel restaurants, also add a 10% to 15% service charge to the bill. For information on Japanese food, see "Eating & Drinking in Japan," in chapter 2.

Finally, keep in mind that the **last order** is taken at least 30 minutes before the restaurant's actual closing time, sometimes even an hour before closing at the more exclusive restaurants. I've included some websites only in Japanese, either because they have photos of dishes or maps that will help you locate them.

In & Near Ginza
EXPENSIVE

Ten-ichi ★★ TEMPURA Founded in 1930, this may well be the most famous tempura restaurant in the world, with many foreign dignitaries among its customers over the years. With branches all over Japan, its main shop is here on Namiki Dori, a street blazing with neon in Ginza's nightlife district, but indoors it's spartan and spare, decorated only with blond wood trim, sliding doors, and flower arrangements. Tempura counters on each floor seat no more than 10 customers, providing an intimate view of master chefs going about their work (reservations are recommended for lunch, required for dinner). Ten-ichi is famous for its delicately fried food, with a batter so refined and an oil so light, the flavor of fish, shrimp, scallop, eggplant, sweet potato, and other ingredients is enhanced rather than overwhelmed. The piping hot morsels can be dipped into a variety of sauces, from the restaurant's own secret recipe to a simple lemon juice with a pinch of salt. Although it's not on the menu, a ¥4,320 lighter lunch of tempura over rice is also usually available. Ten-ichi branches include those in the Imperial Hotel's Tower basement and the Sony Building, as well as several located in department stores, including Seibu in Ikebukuro, Tokyu in Shibuya, Takashimaya in Nihombashi, and Isetan and Odakyu in Shinjuku.

6-6-5 Ginza. www.tenichi.co.jp. © **03/3571-1949.** Set lunches ¥8,400–¥12,960; set dinners ¥10,800–¥19,440. Daily 11:30am–9:30pm. Station: Ginza (3 min.). On Namiki Dori.

The Imperial Viking Sal ★★ INTERNATIONAL All over Japan, the all-you-can-eat buffet is called "Viking" because that's how the Imperial Hotel introduced the concept with the country's very first spread back in 1953, calling it a Viking smorgasbord. Today, of course, many hotels offer buffets fit for a true Viking, but this remains one of the most famous and luckily bears no resemblance to what passed as Western food back in the 1950s. In fact, this might well be the priciest buffet in Japan (as with all buffets, there are discounted prices for children). More than 40 mostly European dishes make their debut with offerings that change monthly, from roast beef with horse radish to salmon, desserts, and more, with seasonal promotions adding ethnic cuisine from around the world. Live jazz serenades in the evenings, but if you opt for the more economical lunch, make a reservation and ask for a table overlooking the Ginza or Hibiya Park.

Imperial Hotel, 17th floor, 1–1–1 Uchisaiwai-cho. www.imperialhotel.co.jp. ℂ **03/3504-1111.** Buffet lunch Mon–Fri ¥5,500, Sat–Sun and holidays ¥6,000; buffet dinner Mon–Fri ¥8,200, Sat–Sun and holidays ¥8,700. Daily 11:30am–2:30pm; Mon–Fri 5:30–9:30pm; Sat–Sun and holidays 5–9:30pm (last order). Station: Hibiya (1 min.).

MODERATE

Also worth seeking out is **Maru** (p. 96), offering modern interpretations of Japanese food, at 6–12–15 Ginza (ℂ **03/5537-7420**).

Rangetsu (らん月) ★ SUKIYAKI/SHABU-SHABU/KAISEKI/BENTO
"Orchid moon" is the English translation of Rangetsu, a Ginza restaurant founded in 1947 and still under the same family ownership. It specializes in sukiyaki and shabu-shabu, made with A5-grade Japanese Wagyu beef and cooked at your table. The English-language menu with photos lists many other dishes, too, from yaki shabu-shabu cooked on a grill at your table and crab dishes (like the crab shabu-shabu set meal for ¥9,990) to bento, *kaiseki,* and more. Lunch sets, served until 4pm, are especially good deals, offering steaks, shabu-shabu, and many other combinations. A sake bar in the basement stocks more than 80 varieties from all over Japan, all of which you can also order with your meal no matter which floor you dine on.

3–5–8 Ginza. ℂ **03/3567-1021.** Beef sukiyaki or shabu-shabu set meals from ¥7,650 for dinner, ¥2,600 for lunch; *kaiseki* ¥5,500–¥9,600; bento meals and mini-*kaiseki* ¥2,400–¥5,800. Daily 11:30am–10pm. Station: Ginza (3 min.). On Chuo Dori, across from the Matsuya department store.

INEXPENSIVE

In addition to the restaurants here, check out **Meal Muji,** 3–8–3 Marunouchi (ℂ **03/5208-8241**), a cafeteria on the second floor of the popular minimalist Muji clothing and housewares store, where you can load up on mostly salads and veggies daily from 10am to 9pm. There are also a number of restaurants on the eighth floor of **Matsuya Ginza department store** serving everything from French and Chinese food to sushi, tempura, noodles, and more. For Chinese dumplings, there's a **Din Tai Fung** at 1–8–19 Ginza (ℂ **03/5159-4141**); see p. 95 for a review.

For atmospheric dining, head to an arch underneath the elevated Yamanote railway tracks located about halfway between Harumi

---

A Note on Establishments with Japanese Signs

Many establishments and attractions in Japan do not have signs in Roman (English-language) letters. Those that don't are provided with the Japanese equivalent to help you locate them.

Dori and the Imperial Hotel Tower; it has a handful of tiny *yakitori* **stands,** each with a few tables and chairs. They cater to a rather boisterous working-class clientele, mainly men. The atmosphere, unsophisticated and dingy, harks back to prewar Japan, somewhat of an anomaly in otherwise chic Ginza. Stalls are open from about 5pm to midnight Monday through Saturday.

Andy's Shin Hinomoto ★ VARIED JAPANESE This hole-in-the-wall underneath the Yamanote train tracks looks like it's been here since the rubble of post–World War II . . . because it has. Founded in 1945 when there were cubbyholes like this under raised train tracks throughout a bombed-out Tokyo, it is owned by the founder's son-in-law, a Brit named Andy. As tiny as it is, it has an upstairs with an arched ceiling that is only marginally better than the downstairs with the charm of a fall-out shelter. Yet this place is packed elbow to elbow every night with office workers, and the only way you might get your foot in the door without a reservation is by coming right when it opens. The food, made with seafood and vegetables bought fresh daily at Tsukiji Market, includes tempura, a fish of the day, deep-fried chicken, chili prawns, salads (usually sold out by 8pm), and its signature stuffed *gyoza* chicken wings. Even with its fluorescent lighting, soot-blackened walls, and no-credit-card policy, this throwback is, in the words of Andy, always "insanely busy," and all from word of mouth.
2–4–4 Yurakucho. www.andysfish.com/Shin-Hinomoto. ✆ **03/3214-8021.** Main dishes ¥500–¥1,000. Mon–Sat 5pm–midnight. Station: Yurakucho or Ginza (1 min.). Underneath the Yamanote elevated tracks, across from the Yurakucho Denki Building.

Genkatsu (ゲンカツ) ★ TONKATSU *Tonkatsu* is Japanese comfort food, breaded and then deep-fried and served with cabbage and a thick sauce reminiscent of Worcestershire. Although usually associated with fast, cheap meals for office workers and the older generation, this restaurant attracts a younger crowd with an enthusiastic staff, top Billboard music at night, and a totally new way of preparing this national favorite. Ditching the usual pork cutlet, the *tonkatsu* here consists of razor-thin slices of pork, filled with a choice of cheese, black pepper, green onion, garlic, or sour plum and miso and then deep fried and served with three dipping sauces. I have to say that a cheese-filled *tonkatsu* seems like sacrilege (and isn't as tasty as I imagined), but ones with black pepper or green onion are definitely worth a try. Purists won't go wrong ordering plain *tonkatsu* either. And like most *tonkatsu* restaurants, your meal comes with rice, cabbage, miso soup, and pickles plus free refills, which should be satisfying for most appetites. There's no English menu, but the young staff is helpful.
Ginza Act Building, 3rd floor, 4–6–18 Ginza. ✆ **03/3567-1129.** Set lunches ¥1,350–¥1,980; set dinners ¥1,980–¥2,160. Mon–Fri 11:30am–2pm and 6–10pm; Sat–Sun 11:30am–10pm (last order). Station: Ginza (1 min.). On Chuo Dori, between Mitsukoshi and Matsuya department stores.

La Boheme ★ ITALIAN The food is passable, but what sets La Boheme apart is that it's open every day until 5am, making it a good bet for a late-night meal. In addition to pizza (like the one topped with shrimp, bacon, mushrooms, bell peppers, and cheese) and pasta (like the one served with a salmon and spinach cream sauce), it also offers a few meat dishes like roasted chicken. This restaurant is actually one of four restaurants under the same ownership and ensconced under a freeway in a winding dining complex called **G-Zone,** with Southeast Asian fare offered at **Monsoon** (www.monsoon-cafe. jp); burritos, shrimp enchiladas, tacos, and other Tex-Mex food served at **Zest Cantina** (www.zest-cantina.jp); and Japanese food dished out in **Gonpachi** (p. 103). English-language menus, cheap prices, friendly staff, and late open hours make these restaurants winners.

1–2–3 Ginza. www.boheme.jp. ☎ **03/5524-3616.** Pizza and pasta ¥780–¥1,580; set lunches ¥1,000–¥1,100. Daily 11:30am–5am. Station: Kyobashi (exit 3, 2 min.) or Ginza-Itchome (exit 7, 1 min.). On Chuo Dori, at the northern edge of Ginza.

Shabusen (しゃぶせん) ★★ SHABU-SHABU Ginza Core is a fashion department store near the Ginza 4–chome Crossing (the Harumi Dori–Chuo Dori intersection) and is the improbable home to not one, but two very reasonably priced Shabusen restaurants. Although shabu-shabu is usually shared between two or more diners since you cook it yourself in a communal boiling pot at your own table, Shabusen caters also to individuals with one-person portions. The second-floor Shabusen is a bit nicer (and surprisingly, also slightly cheaper), with round counters good for lone diners and tables that are perfect for groups, while the second-basement restaurant features U-shaped counters that are a great choice if dining alone or with one other person. I personally love the experience of dining at the counter, because you can watch chefs preparing orders and, with other customers seated in close quarters, it doesn't really feel like you're eating alone. The English-language menu lists both pork and beef shabu-shabu sets, which you cook along with vegetables and eat with either a ponzu or sesame dipping sauce.

Core Building, 5–8–20 Ginza. ☎ **03/3572-3806** (2nd basement) or 03/3571-1717 (2nd floor). Set lunches ¥1,296–¥3,132 on 2nd floor, ¥1,697–¥3,304 basement; set dinners ¥2,366–¥4,428 2nd floor, ¥2,880–¥4,423 basement. Daily 11am–9pm (last order). Station: Ginza (1 min.). On the east side of Chuo Dori just south of Harumi Dori.

Tsukiji Sushi Sen (築地すし鮮) ★ SUSHI Recently renovated to provide more privacy between tables and with dimmer lights than its interrogation-room-like predecessor, this second-floor Ginza branch offers fresh sushi at bargain prices, served at a counter or at tables overlooking busy Harumi Dori. Other dishes are also available on the English-language menu, including salads, grilled seafood, and tempura. If you find yourself hungry in Ginza in the dead of night, this all-nighter is a good choice.

5–9–1 Ginza. ☎ **03/5537-2878.** Sushi a la carte ¥98–¥398; set lunches ¥999–¥1,980; *nigiri* sets ¥1,980–¥4,800. 24 hr. Station: Higashi Ginza or Ginza (2 min.). From Ginza 4-chome Crossing, on the right side of Harumi Dori heading toward Showa Dori.

Asakusa

EXPENSIVE

Waentei-Kikko (和えん亭 吉幸) ★★★ KAISEKI/BENTO I can't imagine a better place to cap off a visit to Asakusa than this. Located in a tiny house just a stone's throw from Sensoji Temple, it evokes the atmosphere of a farm-house with its flagstone entry, wooden rafters, rustic furnishings, and *tatami* seating (with leg wells recently added for those errant appendages). But what sets this place apart are the engaging couple who manage it and the live per-formances of traditional Japanese music five times daily (at 12:15, 1:30, 3, 6:30, and 8pm), including concerts by Fukui Kodai, the husband of the man-aging duo and one of Japan's most accomplished Tsugaru shamisen musi-cians, who plays with the fervor of a rock star. Ordering is easy, as only seasonal set meals that change every month or so are served. Lunch features bento boxes, while *kaiseki* is served for dinner, including *fugu* (blowfish) *kaiseki* if you order it in advance. In short, dining here provides nourishment for both the soul and the stomach and is an experience you're likely to remem-ber long after your trip has ended.

2–2-13 Asakusa. www.waentei-kikko.com. ℭ **03/5828-8833.** Bento lunches ¥2,500 and ¥3,500; *kaiseki* dinners ¥6,800–¥13,800. Thurs–Tues 11:30am–1:30pm and 5–9pm (last order). Station: Asakusa (5 min.). Walk on Nakamise Dori toward Sensoji Temple, turn-ing right after the last shop; go past the 2 stone Buddhas, and then turn right again at the tiny Benten-do Temple with the large bell. The restaurant is on the right side of the street across from the playground.

MODERATE

Chinya (ちんや) ★★ SHABU-SHABU/SUKIYAKI   Established in 1880 but now ensconced in a seven-story building just steps away from Sensoji Temple, this well-known restaurant has been welcoming foreigners with an English-language menu for many decades. Its foyer entrance, next to its own butcher shop (always a good sign), gives no hint as to what lies beyond, but soon there's a man taking your shoes and a kimono-clad hostess leading you upstairs to one of the *tatami*-floored rooms. It has various options for sukiyaki and shabu-shabu set meals and even provides instruction for how to cook them at your table, making it a good bet for the sukiyaki/shabu-shabu novice. The set lunch is the best deal, served until 3:30pm and including an appetizer, pickles, miso soup, rice, dessert, and shabu-shabu or sukiyaki, while dinners require reservations and are much more extensive. These are not quick meals (and at this price you wouldn't expect them to be), so come prepared to relax and enjoy the occasion.

1–3-4 Asakusa. www.chinya.co.jp. ℭ **03/3841-0010.** Set lunches ¥3,800–¥4,300; set dinners ¥4,300–¥13,000. Table charge ¥400 extra per person for lunch, ¥500 for dinner. Mon and Wed–Fri noon–3:30pm and 4:30–9:30pm; Sat–Sun and holidays 11:30am–9pm (guests should arrive 2 hr. before closing time). Station: Asakusa (1 min.). On Kaminarimon Dori; located to the left of the Kaminarimon Gate if you stand facing Asakusa Kannon Temple (look for the SUKIYAKI sign).

INEXPENSIVE

Kamiya Bar ★ VARIED JAPANESE/WESTERN   I'm including this all-purpose restaurant not because it serves great food, but because it's been an Asakusa institution since 1880 and, attracting a largely working-class and elderly Japanese crowd, has a down-home atmosphere that has all but died out in sophisticated Tokyo. Plus, ordering is easy due to plastic-food display cases and it gives a choice of both Japanese and Western food (the Japanese food is better). For the full immersion, there's a bar on the first floor that's famous for its Denki Bran, a concoction of brandy, gin, wine, vermouth, Curacao, and herbs (¥270 for a glass). The second floor serves *yoshoku* (the Japanese interpretation of Western food), like hamburger steak, crab croquette, spaghetti, fried shrimp, and fried chicken, while the third floor is the place to go for everything from sashimi and *udon* noodles to *yakitori* and tempura, as well as *kaiseki* lunches and, with advance reservations, dinners. Credit cards are accepted only on the second and third floors.

1–1–1 Asakusa. www.kamiya-bar.com. © **03/3841-5400.** Main dishes ¥530–¥1,540; set lunches ¥700–¥1,000; Japanese set meals ¥1,500–¥3,600; *kaiseki* ¥5,000–¥7,000. Wed-Mon 11:30am–9:30pm (last order; 1st and 3rd floors closed 2–4pm). Station: Asakusa (1 min.). Located on Kaminarimon Dori in a plain, brown-tiled building btw. Kaminarimon Gate and the Sumida River.

Sansada (三定) ★★ TEMPURA   Established in 1837 and located right beside Kaminarimon Gate, next to the Kurodaya paper shop, this simple tempura restaurant specializes in Edo-style tempura, fried in a light sesame oil. On the first floor seating is either at tables or on *tatami*, while the upstairs is more traditional with *tatami* seating; one room overlooks the temple gate. Run by an army of very able grandmotherly types, the restaurant has an English-language menu with photos of various options, including *don* (tempura on rice), noodles with tempura, bento boxes, and full-course meals.

1–2–2 Asakusa. www.tempura-sansada.co.jp. © **03/3841-3400.** *Don* ¥1,460–¥2,700; set meals ¥1,700–¥6,080. Daily 11:30am–9:30pm (last order). Station: Asakusa (1 min.). East of Kaminarimon Gate, with entrances beside Kurodaya paper shop and also on Kaminarimon Dori.

Sometaro (染太郎) ★ OKONOMIYAKI   This very atmospheric neighborhood restaurant specializes in *okonomiyaki*, a working-class meal that is basically a Japanese pancake filled with beef, pork, and vegetables, and prepared by the diners themselves as they sit on *tatami* at low tables inset with griddles. Realizing that some foreigners may be intimidated by having to cook an unfamiliar meal, this restaurant makes the process easier with an English-language menu complete with instructions. The busy but friendly staff can help you get started. In addition to *okonomiyaki, yakisoba* (fried noodles) with meat or vegetables and other do-it-yourself dishes are available, and help yourself to glasses of water. This is a fun, convivial way to enjoy a meal, but note that no credit cards are accepted. Before entering the restaurant, be sure to deposit your shoes in the proffered plastic sacks by the door.

2–2–2 Nishi-Asakusa. www.sometaro.com. © **03/3844-9502.** Main dishes ¥680–¥1,180. Daily noon–10pm (last order). Station: Tawaramachi (2 min.) or Asakusa (5 min.). At the west end of Kaminarimon Dori, past Kokusai Dori with the corner police station, in the 2nd block on the right.

Ueno

MODERATE

In addition to the choices here, **Kohmen,** 4–8–8 Ueno (© **03/5807-4535**), offers tasty ramen and *gyoza*. See p. 103 for a review.

Innsyoutei (韻松亭) ★★★ KAISEKI/BENTO   I love the museums and other attractions in Ueno Park, but a meal at this traditional restaurant makes the outing even more special. A Tokyo landmark since 1875, it has a simple tearoom with snacks on the ground floor and a restaurant upstairs, where meals are served in private *tatami* rooms or a small dining room overlooking greenery. There's an English-language menu, but let your budget be your guide in choosing a vegetarian, bento, or *kaiseki* set lunch, all of which change with the seasons. Dinner offers more expensive *kaiseki* and chicken sukiyaki. This restaurant is extremely popular with older Japanese women, but reservations are accepted only for four or more so be prepared to wait in line. During the cherry blossom season, when Ueno Park swarms with sightseers, Innsyoutei limits its menu to only a few set meals complete with flowers to honor the season, but you'll be lucky to get your foot in the door then. Note that credit cards are not accepted.

In Ueno Park. www.innsyoutei.jp. © **03/3821-8126.** Set lunches ¥1,680–¥6,800; set dinners ¥5,500–¥12,000. Daily 11am–3pm; Mon–Sat 5–9:30pm; Sun 5–8:30pm (last order). Station: JR Ueno (6 min.). Btw. Grill Fukushima and the row of orange *torii* leading downhill.

Unagi Kappo Izu'ei Honten (鰻割烹伊豆栄本店) ★★ EEL   This restaurant's history goes back a mere 265 years to the middle of the Edo Period, but you'd never know that from the modern multistoried building that stands here today. The dining rooms are pleasant and overlook Shinobazu Pond, but the star of the show here is grilled eel. The quality of charcoal used to grill the eel is considered paramount, so this restaurant is justly proud of its very own furnace in the mountains of Wakayama Prefecture, said to produce the best charcoal in Japan. An English-language menu with photos will help you select from about 15 different set meals featuring eel, but there's also tempura, bento, and, with advance reservations, *kaiseki*. Not all eel restaurants go to the lengths this one does to assure the quality of its food, so I consider this place a real treat.

2–12–22 Ueno. www.izuei.co.jp. © **03/3831-0954.** Set meals ¥1,620–¥4,860; *kaiseki* ¥6,480–¥16,200. Daily 11am–9:30pm (last order). Station: JR Ueno (3 min.). On Shinobazu Dori, across the street from Shinobazu Pond and the Shitamachi Museum, next to KFC.

Shinjuku

EXPENSIVE

New York Grill ★★★ AMERICAN   Stunning views, great steaks and seafood, an artsy vibe, and live jazz wafting in from the adjoining bar all contribute in making a meal at this 52nd-floor venue an experience to remember. Even the short walkway to the dining area is singular, with an all-white open kitchen on the left side and a glass wall on the right that gives the illusion of a sheer drop-off. Definitely not for the vertigo-challenged. The restaurant backs up its dramatic setting with a menu that offers a variety of grilled and baked dishes using ingredients from around the world, including steaks from various regions of Japan, Australian rack of lamb with a grain-mustard crust, and Hokkaido scallops with sun-dried tomato and wasabi salsa. Although its 1,600-bottle cellar has long featured almost exclusively Californian wines, it has recently added boutique vintages you won't find anywhere else in Japan. For less formal dining (and where I like to sit when eating solo), there are counter seats along the open kitchen where you can watch the chefs in action. Both the set lunch and the weekend and holiday brunches are among the city's best and most sumptuous—and are great options for those who don't want to pawn their belongings to eat dinner here. No matter when you come, reservations are a must. I wouldn't miss it.

Park Hyatt Tokyo, 3–7–1–2 Nishi-Shinjuku. www.tokyo.park.hyatt.com. ℭ **03/5323-3458.** Main dishes ¥4,600–¥12,400; set lunch ¥5,000; set dinners ¥11,000–¥20,000; Sat–Sun and holiday brunch ¥6,900. Daily 11:30am–2:30pm and 5:30–10pm. Station: Shinjuku (west exit, 13-min. walk or 5-min. free shuttle ride), Hatsudai on the Keio Line (7 min.), or Tochomae on the Oedo Line (8 min.).

Kakiden (柿伝) ★★ KAISEKI Although it's located on the eighth floor of a rather uninspiring building, Kakiden has a relaxing teahouse atmosphere, with shoji screens providing privacy between tables and soothing traditional Japanese music playing softly in the background. Sibling restaurant to one in Kyoto founded more than 270 years ago as a catering service for practitioners of the tea ceremony, this *kaiseki* restaurant serves set meals that change with the seasons, according to what's fresh and available. An English-language menu lists the set meals, but it's probably best to simply pick a meal to fit your budget. Set lunches are available until 3pm. Set dinners include box *kaiseki* starting at ¥5,940, mini-*kaiseki* for ¥9,504, and *kaiseki* courses starting at ¥8,316. Some of the more common dishes here include fish, seasonal vegetables, sashimi, shrimp, and mushrooms, but don't worry if you can't identify everything—I've found that even the Japanese don't always know what they're eating.

Yasuo Building 8F, 3–37–11 Shinjuku, 8th floor. www.kakiden.com. ℭ **03/3352-5121.** Set lunches ¥4,752–¥5,940; set dinners ¥5,940–¥17,800. Daily 11am–9pm (last order). Station: Shinjuku (east exit, 1 min.). Next to Shinjuku Station's east side.

MODERATE

Ban-Thai (バンタイ) ★ THAI One of Tokyo's longest-running Thai restaurants and credited with introducing authentic Thai food to the Japanese, Ban-Thai prepares excellent Thai fare, with 90-some mouthwatering items on the menu. My favorites are the spicy minced chicken salad, the chicken soup with coconut and lemon grass, the deep-fried flatfish with sweet and spicy topping, and the pad Thai. Note that portions are not large, so if you order several portions and add beer, your tab can really climb. Also, the service is indifferent. Yet this place is packed every time I come here; there's a row of chairs where you can queue and wait, but the line moves fairly quickly.

1–23–14 Kabuki-cho, 3rd floor. www.ban-thai.jp. ℭ **03/3207-0068.** Main dishes ¥1,200–¥1,800; set lunches ¥730–¥1,300 (Mon–Fri only). Mon–Fri 11:30am–3pm and 5–11:30pm; Sat–Sun and holidays 11:30am–11:45pm. Station: Shinjuku (east exit, 7 min.). In the seediest part of Kabuki-cho (don't worry, the interior is nicer than the exterior). From

Yasukuni Dori, take the pedestrian street beside 7-Eleven with a red neon archway; it's on the left side, above St. James Bar.

INEXPENSIVE

Din Tai Fung ★ CHINESE   Tokyo's first branch of Taiwan's most popular dim sum (dumpling) restaurant is so popular, you'll probably have to join the long line of people waiting to get in. Luckily, the line moves fast and soon you'll find yourself either dining inside the noisy restaurant or outside on the spacious terrace (unfortunately, there are no views). The English-language menu lists various dim sum priced from ¥210 to¥1,000, including the signature steamed pork dumplings served in piping hot bamboo steamers, along with various soups and other dishes such as mashed black sesame seeds and fried pork spareribs. By the way, Din Tai Fung started out in 1958 as a retailer selling cooking oil in Taiwan and has been a smashing success across Asia. The Japanese are among its most avid customers, with seven locations in Tokyo alone, including the newest one at 1–8–19 Ginza.

Takashimaya Shinjuku, 12th floor, 5–24–2 Sendagaya. www.dintaifung.com.tw/en. ℭ **03/5361-1381.** Main dishes ¥1,050–¥1,260; set meals ¥1,470–¥1,785. Daily 11am–11pm. Station: Shinjuku (New South Exit, 1 min.). Next to Uniqlo.

Green House ★ VARIED JAPANESE   This is probably the cheapest place in town for a meal with a view. Located on the 32nd floor in the north tower of the Tokyo Metropolitan Government Office (TMG), which offers a free observation room on its 45th floor, this cafeteria serves public employees but is open to everyone. Choose your meal—which can include pork cutlet, fried fish, sushi, tempura, curry rice, or noodles—from the cart laden with displays of daily set meals or the display case, where every item is identified by a number. You then purchase your selections from a vending machine (no credit cards accepted) and take your tickets to the cafeteria window. My last set meal consisted of fish tempura, rice, soup and salad. The cafeteria lacks charm, but if you can get a table by the window, you'll have a good view of Tokyo. Although it's open throughout the weekday, only snacks like ramen are available from 2 to 4pm. For dinner, only three set meals are available, along with a limited offering of curry rice and other fast foods. There's another staff restaurant, Seiyo Food, on the 32nd floor of the South Tower with the same system and hours; note, however, that on Wednesday and Friday evenings, only one of the two is open.

TMG, 32nd floor of North Tower (take the office elevator, not the elevator to the observatory), 2–8–1 Nishi-Shinjukuku. ℭ **03/5320-7513.** Set lunches ¥600–¥680; set dinners ¥570. Mon–Fri 11:30am–6:45pm. Closed holidays. Station: Tochomae (1 min.), Shinjuku (10 min.), or Nishi-Shinjuku (5 min.).

Tsunahachi (つな八) ★★ TEMPURA   Tsunahachi has been serving tempura since 1923, with this location opened the same year as the Tokyo Olympics, in 1964. Occupying a modest, old-fashioned building east of Shinjuku Station, it's nevertheless Tsunahachi's largest outlet, with both tables and—more fun—counter seating along the open kitchen. Unfortunately, during busy times foreigners tend to be shunted to the second-floor counter, so try to avoid the meal-time rush for a seat on the more atmospheric ground floor. There's an English-language menu, but probably the easiest thing to do is to order one of three set meals, with the cheapest including six pieces of tempura deep-fried in sesame oil, including shrimp, conger eel, seasonal fish, shrimp balls, and vegetables, plus rice, miso soup, and Japanese pickles; if you're still hungry, you can always order a la carte. Branches are located in department stores around town, including Keio in Shinjuku, Matsuya in Ginza, Lumine in Ikebukuro, and Daimaru on the Yaesu side of Tokyo Station.

3–31–8 Shinjuku. www.tunahachi.co.jp. © **03/3352-1012.** Set lunches ¥1,260–¥3,990; tempura set meals ¥2,100–¥5,200. Daily 11am–10pm (last order). Station: Shinjuku Sanchome (2 min.) or Shinjuku (east exit, 5 min.). Off Shinjuku Dori on the side street that runs along the east side of the combination Bic Camera/Uniqlo store.

Harajuku & Aoyama

EXPENSIVE

Two Rooms Grill/Bar ★★★ CONTINENTAL Dress smartly to fit in with the fashion-conscious 40-somethings who gather here for high-powered business lunches and after-work cocktails. The sleek dining room looks like a setting in a black-and-white movie with its white walls and table cloths, waiters decked out in black with crisp white aprons, and liberal use of steel and glass architectural details. Bringing the scene to life are warm woods (including 50,000-year-old swamp kauri timber from New Zealand used for some of the tables), jazz playing softly in the background, and an open kitchen briskly turning out orders. But what I love most about this place is the bar, separated from the restaurant by an open-air catwalk suspended over an infinity pool and offering poster-perfect views of the city's skyline from its outdoor terrace with comfy sofas. As for the menu, Wagyu beef reigns supreme, though there are plenty of other yummy choices like the lamb chops or the slow-cooked Aomori duck breast. Weekday lunches and weekend brunches also come highly recommended (make reservations), but even if you don't dine here, a drink on the outdoor terrace will make Tokyo seem like the most relaxing place in the world. The bar is open until 2am (Sun until 10pm).

AO Building, 5th floor, 3–11–7 Kita-Aoyama. www.tworooms.jp. © **03/3498-0002.** Main dishes ¥3,700–¥9,500; set lunches ¥1,850–¥5,800; set dinners ¥8,000–¥10,000. Daily 11:30am–2:30pm; Mon–Sat 6–10pm; Sun 6–9pm (last order). Station: Omotesando (exit B2, 1 min.). It's on the right side of Aoyama Dori in the direction of Shibuya, in the striking, trapezoidal AO Building.

MODERATE

Maru (圓) ★★ MODERN JAPANESE Reservations are a must at this tiny, smoke-free hideaway off Aoyama Dori, where seating is confined to only a few wooden tables and a long counter stretching along the open kitchen. The English-language menu, which changes often to reflect what's in season, offers a tempting roster of choices ranging from classic Kyoto-style *kaiseki* to creative dishes with a contemporary twist. The friendly and hip staff is happy to help narrow down selections based on individual preferences, but one dish you shouldn't pass up is the restaurant's signature *donabe,* rice simmered in a clay pot and served with a choice of toppings. Other main dishes may include free-range chicken with salt and yuzu pepper, beef preserved in Kyoto miso, or a seasonal vegetable tempura. But for those who still can't make up their mind, there's also a monthly set meal that always includes *donabe.* Drinks range from wine to sake and *shochu,* including *awamori,* an Okinawan *shochu* made from Thai rice. There's a branch in Ginza, serving only two set meals for dinner and also open for lunch; check the website for its location.

5–50–8 Jingumae. www.maru-mayfont.jp. ⓒ **03/6418-5572.** Main dishes ¥1,050–¥2,800; set meal ¥5,000. Mon–Fri 6–11:30pm; Sat, Sun, and holidays 5–11:30pm. Station: Omotesando (3 min.). Walk toward Shibuya on Aoyama Dori and turn right at Muji; it's almost immediately on the right, in a basement.

Yasaiya Mei (やさい家めい) ★★ VARIED JAPANESE/VEGETARIAN

If you like veggies, this restaurant specializing in fresh, seasonal vegetables is a must (as are reservations). For starters you might choose the green papaya kimchi or the Mei Special bagna cauda from the English-language menu, which comes with a variety of veggies—such as eggplant, radish and asparagus—plus a dipping sauce. Not to be missed is the wild plant tempura, which changes with the seasons; spring might feature young bamboo shoots, while autumn may include eggplant and water chestnuts. Although the emphasis here is clearly on things that grow in the ground, supplied directly from contract farms and mostly organic, a few meat dishes are also available, such as grilled pork with mashed potatoes. Set lunches many feature a vegetable curry or fish. Seating is either at the U-shaped open kitchen or a table (try to snag one beside the large windows overlooking the trees of Omotesando Dori). There's a branch in Roppongi Hills, on the fifth floor of Mori Tower in an area called West Walk.

Omotesando Hills, 3rd floor, 4–12–10 Jingumae. http://www.eat-walk.com/mei. ⓒ **03/5785-0606.** Main dishes ¥1,100–¥1,800; set lunches ¥1,490–¥2,090; set dinners ¥3,690–¥5,550. Mon–Sat 11am–10:30pm; Sun 11am–9:30pm (last order). Station: Meiji-Jingumae or Omotesando (4 min.). On Omotesando Dori.

INEXPENSIVE

In addition to the choices below, consider **La Boheme** (p. 89), serving pizza and pasta, with two locations at 3–6–25 Kita-Aoyama (ⓒ **03/5766-1666**), and on Omotesando Dori at 5–8–5 Jingumae (ⓒ **03/5467-5666**). **Kohmen** (p. 103), 6–2–8 Jingumae (ⓒ **03/5468-6344**), serves tasty ramen and *gyoza.*

Harajuku Gyoza Lou (原宿餃子樓) ★ GYOZA

If you like *gyoza* (pork dumplings), you owe yourself a meal here. Unlike most greasy spoons that specialize in fast-food Chinese (and tend to be on the dingy side), this restaurant in the heart of Harajuku is hip yet unpretentious and draws a young crowd with its straightforward menu posted on the wall (an English-language menu is also available). Only one type of *gyoza* is offered, which you can order steamed *(sui-gyoza)* or fried *(yaki-gyoza),* and with or without garlic *(nin-niku).* A few side dishes, such as cucumber, boiled cabbage with vinegar, sprouts with a spicy meat sauce, and rice, are available, as are beer and sake.

A U-shaped counter encloses the open kitchen, which diners can watch as they chow down on the very good *gyoza*. There's sometimes a queue out the door, but this isn't the kind of place where people linger so it's worth the wait. No credit cards accepted.

6–2–4 Jingumae. (℃) **03/3406-4743.** Gyoza ¥290 for a plate of 6. Mon–Sat 11:30am–4:30am; Sun and holidays 11:30am–10:30pm (last order). Station: Meiji-Jingumae (3 min.) or Harajuku (5 min.). From the Meiji/Omotesando Dori intersection, walk on Omotesando Dori toward Aoyama and take the 3rd right (just before Kiddy Land); it's at the end of this alley, on the right.

Heirokuzushi (平禄寿司) ★ SUSHI   Bright (a bit too bright), clean, and modern, this is one of those fast-food sushi bars where plates of food are conducted along a conveyor belt on the counter. Customers help themselves to whatever strikes their fancy, from the usual tuna to more unusual avocado (a reflection, perhaps, of the tourists that swarm here). To figure your bill, the cashier counts the number of plates you took from the conveyor belt: Green plates cost ¥130, for example, blue ones ¥160, and so on; no credit cards are accepted. You can also order takeout, which you might want to eat in nearby Yoyogi Park.

5–8–5 Jingumae. (℃) **03/3498-3968.** Plates of sushi ¥130–¥490. Daily 11am–9pm. Station: Meiji-Jingumae (2 min.) or Omotesando (5 min.). On Omotesando Dori close to Oriental Bazaar.

Hiroba ★★ VARIED JAPANESE/VEGETARIAN   Located in the basement of the Crayon House, which specializes in Japanese children's books, this natural-food restaurant offers lunch and dinner buffets of organic veggies, fish, brown rice, and other health foods. From 2:40 to 5:30pm, during so-called tea time, it also offers three curry set meals (including a vegetarian option) and desserts. The dining hall, next to an organic food store, is very simple (its atmosphere reminds me of a potluck supper in a church basement), but it also offers outdoor seating in a sunken courtyard surrounded by plants. And because of the upstairs bookstore, there are likely to be families here.

Crayon House, 3–8–15 Kita-Aoyama. (℃) **03/3406-6409.** Lunch buffet ¥1,296; dinner buffet ¥2,160. Mon–Fri 11am–2pm; Sat–Sun 10:30am–2pm; daily 5:30–10pm (last order). Station: Omotesando (2 min.). From the Omotesando/Aoyama Dori intersection, walk on Omotesando Dori toward Harajuku and take the first left (between Coach and Hugo Boss).

Maisen (まい泉) ★★ TONKATSU   Plenty of Tokyoites consider this the best *tonkatsu* (deep-fried breaded pork cutlet) restaurant in Tokyo. In business since 1965, it now has several locations around town, including the basement of Daimaru department store next to Tokyo Station. But this is the main store and the most atmospheric, with a main dining hall ensconced in what was once the dressing room of a pre-World War II public bathhouse, with a tall ceiling and other original architectural details that hint at its former life. The English-language menu lists various dishes and set meals, the most famous of which features *tonkatsu* made from black pig from Kagoshima, which has a sweet, more intense flavor than regular pork. *Tonkatsu* comes with finely shredded cabbage and Maisen's own sauce. Lunch specials, available until 4pm, are listed only in Japanese, but there are photos. There's also a takeout window offering various bento boxes and Maisen products, including its own curry sauce.

4–8–5 Jingumae. www.mai-sen.com. ✆ **03/3470-0071.** Set meals ¥1,480–¥3,960; set lunches ¥890–¥1,260. Daily 11am–10pm (last order). Station: Omotesando A2 exit (4 min.). Heading toward Harajuku on Omotesando Dori, take the first right (there's an archway here with FITNESS CLUB GOLD'S GYM written on it), then the 1st left and an immediate right. It will be in the next block on the left.

Toriyoshi (鳥良) ★ VARIED JAPANESE/INTERNATIONAL   This hip, upscale bar is a popular dining spot as well, especially for its chicken specialties such as fried chicken wings and half a fried chicken. The English menu isn't up to date, but it has photos and is a good starting point for ordering ramen, skewered meats, salads, kimchi, and other Japanese and Asian pub fare. You'll want to order several dishes tapas style and then share. A good place for a convivial evening.

4–28–21 Jingumae. ✆ **03/3470-3901.** Main dishes ¥480–¥880. Mon–Fri 5–11pm; Sat–Sun 4–11pm (last order). Station: Meiji-Jingumae (3 min.). From the Meiji Dori/Omotesando intersection, walk on Omotesando Dori toward Aoyama and take the 1st left; it's down this street on the right side, beside a willow tree.

Venire Venire ★ ITALIAN   You'll have to see for yourself how inexpensive doesn't necessarily mean drab. This tall-ceilinged trattoria is light and airy, with a large outdoor terrace (open from the end of Apr to Oct) affording sweeping views over the surrounding rooftops. It offers mostly pizzas and pastas, such as fettuccini with sliced duck, porcini and Bolognese sauce or pizza topped with sliced bacon, shimeji mushroom and ricotta, as well as a handful of main dishes like lamb chop with red wine and a green herb sauce. There's a large selection of Italian wines. Because this is a popular wedding venue, call ahead to avoid disappointment, or have an alternative plan.

Y.M. Square, 5th floor; 4–31–10 Jingumae. ✆ **03/5775-5333.** Pizza and pasta ¥1,200–¥2,200; main dishes ¥1,500–¥2,800; set lunches ¥2,000–¥3,500. Mon–Fri 11:30am–3pm and 5–11pm; Sat–Sun and holidays 11:30am–3:30pm and 5–10:30pm. Station: Harajuku (1 min.). On Meiji Dori, just north of Gap and across from La Foret.

Yai Yai (やいやい) ★ OKONOMIYAKI   Instead of having to cook your own *okonomiyaki*, all you have to do here is order, whereupon the young staff sets to work cooking your meal on a griddle in front of you. You choose your toppings—such as pork and leek, seafood mix, and kimchi—which are then added to the pancakelike base, cabbage, and egg. Fried noodles and *negi-yaki* (flat dough with leeks, also cooked with a choice of toppings) are also available. The interior is dark and homey, a good escape from the crowds of Harajuku.

6–8–7 Jingumae. ✆ **03/3406-8181.** *Okonomiyaki* or fried noodles ¥950–¥2,700. Mon–Fri 5pm–3am; Sat–Sun and holidays noon–11pm. Station: Meiji-Jingumae (3 min.) or Harajuku (7 min.). From the Meiji Dori/Omotesando intersection, walk on Omotesando Dori toward Aoyama and take the 2nd right; it will be on the left, past TGI Friday's.

Roppongi

Because Roppongi is such a popular nighttime hangout for young Tokyoites and foreigners, it boasts a large number of both Japanese and Western restaurants. To find the location of any of the Roppongi addresses below, stop by the tiny police station on Roppongi Crossing (Roppongi's main intersection of Roppongi Dori and Gaien-Higashi Dori) to study a map of the area or ask a policeman for directions. Opposite the police station, on the other side of the overhead expressway, is the number-one meeting spot in Roppongi, in front of Almond coffee shop with its pink sign and facade. If you are asked to meet someone in Roppongi, this will likely be the spot.

About a 10-minute walk west of Roppongi (via Roppongi Dori in the direction of Shibuya) is **Nishi Azabu** with more restaurants and bars. Between Roppongi Crossing and Nishi Azabu is **Roppongi Hills,** a sprawling urban development with many choices in dining. **Tokyo Midtown** also has many restaurants.

EXPENSIVE

Fukuzushi (福鮨) ★★ SUSHI   Tokyo has thousands of sushi restaurants in all price ranges, but this classy restaurant has proven the test of time with its superb fresh fish and devoted following. Founded in 1917 and located in Roppongi since 1968, it has a courtyard entrance that beckons with lit lanterns and the sound of water, but inside it's all contemporary Tokyo, with pop-out reds contrasted against black furnishings. Featuring fresh fish from Hokkaido, its dishes change with the seasons. Lunch offers four set meals, from a *nigiri-zushi* course to *anago-jyu* (sea eel on rice), all with side dishes like steamed egg custard and miso soup, as well as dessert. Set dinners feature many more dishes, with the ¥9,000 meal including an appetizer, various sashimi and sushi, egg custard, the day's dish (like grilled fish), miso soup, dessert, and coffee. Unfortunately, set dinners require a minimum of two people, but you can also tell the chef your budget and preferences and he'll take it from there.
5–7–8 Roppongi. www.roppongifukuzushi.com. © **03/3402-4116.** Set lunches ¥2,500–¥3,500; set dinners ¥7,000–¥15,000. Mon–Sat 11:30am–1:30pm and 5:30–10pm (last order). Closed holidays. Station: Roppongi (4 min.). From Roppongi Crossing, walk toward Tokyo Tower on Gaien-Higashi Dori, turning right at McDonald's, left in front of Hard Rock Cafe, and then right.

Inakaya (田舎屋) ★★ ROBATAYAKI   Although tourist-oriented and over-priced, this restaurant is still great fun; the drama of the place alone is worth it. Customers sit at a long, U-shaped counter, on the other side of which are mountains of fresh vegetables, beef, and seafood. And in the middle of all that food, seated in front of a grill, are male chefs—ready to cook whatever you point to in the style of *robatayaki*. Orders are yelled out by your waiter and are repeated in unison by all the other waiters, resulting in ongoing, excited yelling. Sounds strange, I know, but actually it's a lot of fun. Food offerings may include yellowtail, red snapper, scallops, king crab legs, giant shrimp, steak, meatballs, gingko nuts, potatoes, eggplant, and asparagus, all piled high in wicker baskets and ready for the grill. My main gripe is that there is no menu (although there is one online you can study beforehand for prices), and individual dishes quickly add up, with most meals averaging around ¥15,000 to ¥20,000. Come expecting to spend money, and you won't be disappointed. There's another branch nearby, at 5–3–4 Roppongi (✆ **03/3408-5040**).

4–10–11 Roppongi. www.roppongiinakaya.jp. ✆ **03/5775-1012.** Grilled vegetables ¥702–¥2,160; grilled seafood and meats ¥1,134–¥10,800. Table charge ¥864 per person. Daily 5–10:30pm (last order). Station: Roppongi (2 min.). Off Gaien-Higashi Dori on a side street; from Roppongi Crossing, walk on Gaien-Higashi Dori in the direction of Midtown and take the 2nd right.

Ruby Jack's Steakhouse & Bar ★★★ STEAK   These people really know their steak. If you wish, they'll give you a primer on the differences among Japanese Wagyu (aged 45 days in the restaurant and the fattiest and, to my mind, most tender), U.S. prime cuts, and Australian grain-fed black Angus. If you really want to go all out, be sure to order the teppan-grilled foie gras to go with that grilled steak. There are other char-grilled choices on the menu, including free-range chicken and tuna, but really, why bother? The ciabatta is housemade and oysters make a great starter, but you may also want to add the yummy mashed potatoes with garlic chips and the creamed spinach. And what would be a good steak without red wine? This is a very corporate type of place, with tall ceilings and a glass facade overlooking a terrace where you can enjoy drinks and dessert. Lunches add sandwiches and lighter fare, while weekend brunches add breakfast choices on top of that. There's also a bar, open until 1am (midnight on Sun).

Ark Hills South Tower, 1–4–5 Roppongi. www.rubyjacks.jp. ✆ **03/5544-8222.** Main dishes ¥3,300–¥12,500. Mon–Fri 11am–2:30pm; Sat–Sun and holidays 11am–3pm; Mon–Sat 6–10pm; Sun and holidays 6–9pm (last order). Station: Roppongi (8 min.), Roppongi-Itchome (3 min.), or Tameike-Sanno (5 min.). At the bottom of Roppongi Dori, near ANA InterContinental Tokyo.

Tokyo Shiba Toufuya Ukai ★★★ TOFU   This restaurant is practically in the shadows of Tokyo Tower, but it has such a serene setting and lush gardens that it instantly transports customers to another time and place. Specializing in classic tofu cuisine, the restaurant is spread over several structures that are remakes of traditional architecture, from the *kura* (warehouse) with its thick, white walls and vaulted door to the main building with its heavy beams and foot-thick lacquered pillars that were once part of an old farmhouse in Takayama. Surrounding the buildings are exquisite gardens, tended to by three fulltime gardeners and boasting ponds, streams, gnarled pines, stone lanterns, arched bridges, and strolling paths (be sure to walk through the back garden after your meal). The main dining hall overlooks the back garden, but most guests opt for one of the private *tatami* rooms, many also with garden views. It offers only set meals, which change with the seasons and are explained on an English-language menu. The least expensive lunch (available only weekdays) may start with a lotus root cake with sea urchin and deep-fried tofu coated with miso sauce, followed by assorted sashimi, deep-fried simmered tofu with crab, a main dish, tofu boiled in a seasoned soy milk, rice with sweet potato, and dessert. Reservations are a must.

4–4–13 Shibakoen. www.ukai.co.jp. ✆ **03/3436-1028.** Set lunches ¥5,670–¥6,970; set dinners ¥8,960–¥13,280. Daily 11am–10pm (last order 8pm). Station: Akabanebashi (5 min.). On the slope behind Tokyo Tower.

MODERATE

Yasaiya (p. 97), specializing in fresh veggies, has a branch in Roppongi Hills, on the fifth floor of Mori Tower in an area called West Walk (✆ **03/5775-2960**).

Roti Roppongi ★★ AMERICAN   A casual brasserie with both indoor (nonsmoking) and outdoor seating, Roti counts many expats among its loyal customers, due in part to its quiet, tucked-away location just a minute's walk from Roppongi Hills. It offers a fresh take on modern American fare, which includes imported oysters, free-range rotisserie chicken (available with garlic, mushroom, or the superdelicious peri peri spicy sauce), grilled steaks, lobster (Thurs–Fri nights only), a variety of burgers, serious Caesar salads, and many other delectable dishes too numerous to mention. More than 90 bottles of New World, Australian, and New Zealand wines, as well as American craft beers and Belgian microbrews, round out the menu. It's also a great place for the weekend brunch, served until a decent 5pm.

6–6–9 Roppongi. www.roti.jp. ✆ **03/5785-3671.** Main dishes ¥1,600–¥3,200; set lunches (Mon–Fri only) ¥1,400–¥1,600. Daily 11:30am–5pm and 6–11pm. Station: Roppongi (A1 exit, 1 min.). On a side street that parallels Roppongi Dori (behind a police station), a stone's throw from Roppongi Hills and beside Frijoles.

INEXPENSIVE

Frijoles ★ MEXICAN   Next to Roti (above), this casual eatery serves only a few dishes—burritos, tacos, and salads—but it does it extremely well, making this a very popular choice for lunch and takeout. Head to the counter and choose your medium (taco, burrito, or burrito salad bowl), your meat (chicken, steak, or seasoned pork; vegetarian also available), toppings (black beans, pinto beans, cheese, etc.), and salsa (from mild to fiery hot), and then head to the small dining counter or one of the outdoor tables. Most of the food is prepared on-site, and it shows. Frijoles will remind you of Chipotle, except that here you can also order a margarita.

6–6–9 Roppongi. www.frijoles.jp. ✆ **03/6447-1433.** Main dishes ¥980–¥1,216. Daily 11am–10pm (to 3pm 2nd Sun of every month). Station: Roppongi (A1 exit, 1 min.). On a side street that parallels Roppongi Dori, a stone's throw from Roppongi Hills, beside Roti.

Ganchan (がんちゃん) ★ YAKITORI   This is one of my favorite *yakitori-ya*. Small and intimate, with seating along a single counter with room for only a dozen or so people, it has a young and fun-loving staff. Though there's an English-language menu, it's easiest to order the *yakitori seto,* a delicious set course that comes with salad and soup and eight skewers of such items as chicken, beef, meatballs, green peppers, and asparagus rolled with bacon. There's a table charge of ¥630 per person, but it includes an appetizer.

6–8–23 Roppongi. © **03/3478-0092.** *Yakitori* skewers ¥320–¥750; *yakitori* set course ¥2,700. Mon–Fri 5pm–1:30am; Sat–Sun and holidays 5–11:30pm. Station: Roppongi (7 min.). From Roppongi Crossing, take the small street going downhill to the left of the Almond coffee shop; Ganchan is at the bottom of the hill on the right, just before the stoplight.

Gonpachi ★★ VARIED JAPANESE/YAKITORI   Housed in a re-created *kura* (traditional Japanese warehouse) with a high ceiling, three-tiered seating, and a central, open kitchen, this is one of Tokyo's most imaginative inexpensive Japanese restaurants (it's said to have served as the inspiration for the animated restaurant scene in the movie *Kill Bill*). It offers a wide variety of dishes, including *yakitori* (such as duck breast with wasabi), fish (such as miso-glazed black cod), sushi (on the third floor), noodles, and more. From the outside, you'd expect this place to be much more exclusive than it is—and you probably will be excluded if you fail to make reservations for dinner. Branches of Gonpachi in the G-Zone, 1–2–3 Ginza, and in Shibuya on the 14th floor of E-Space Tower, 3–6 Maruyama-cho. However, they don't match the Nishi Azabu location's atmosphere.

1–13–11 Nishi Azabu. www.gonpachi.jp. © **03/5771-0170.** *Yakitori* ¥300–¥1,500; main dishes ¥1,200–¥3,200; set lunches ¥1,000–¥3,000; set dinners ¥4,500–¥6,000. Daily 11:30am–3:30am. Station: Roppongi (12 min.). From Roppongi Crossing, walk toward Shibuya on Roppongi Dori. It will be on your right, at the corner of Gaien-Nishi Dori.

Kohmen (光麺) ★ RAMEN   I like popping in here when it's mid-afternoon and I missed lunch, but it's also a lifesaver for those very late almost-to-dawn revelries (make sure you have cash, as no credit cards are accepted). There are branches across the city, including Shinjuku, Ikebukuro, Ueno, Akihabara, Harajuku, and Ebisu, each with its own decor and opening hours. This one is dark, with decorations that might confuse the inebriated (like fish swimming in a repurposed birdcage) and with a black-clad staff moving around like ninja to swiftly deliver steaming bowls of ramen. The English-language menu lists options like thick or thin noodles, various broths (the basic soup is made from stewing pig and chicken bones for up to 12 hr.), and extra toppings like grilled pork. I like the *kagashi-tantanmen* (a creamy sesame soup with noodles, hot chili, and char-grilled marinated pork) so much that I've never tried anything else, which is highly unusual for me. I also can't resist an order of *gyoza*. At your table is minced garlic and spices in case you want to add them to your ramen.

7–14–3 Roppongi. www.kohmen.com/en. © **03/6406-4565.** Ramen ¥780–¥1,100. Daily 11am–7am. Station: Roppongi (1 min.). From Roppongi Crossing, head away from Tokyo Tower on Gaien-Higashi Dori; it will be on the left, just past the construction site.

Shibuya
MODERATE
Legato ★★★ ITALIAN/FUSION   With its dramatic setting and innovative cuisine, you'd expect this restaurant to be much more expensive than it is. After the elevator delivers you to the 15th floor, you might be tempted to stop

or come back later for a drink at the tear-shaped bar, where the view takes in the shimmering lights of Shibuya. Then you'll make your entrance down the short flight of steps to the sunken restaurant below, bathed in the warm glow of lanterns hanging from the ceiling and candles on each table, which are spaced widely enough to make this an intimate romantic splurge. The open kitchen turns out a handful of main dishes like steak and a daily fish, plus a few choices in pasta and pizza, and the knowledgeable staff is happy to make recommendations. The wine list travels the world with bottles in all price ranges, but there's also plenty of the bubbly stuff to help celebrate the occasion. You can also come on weekdays for lunch, with the cheapest set meal featuring pasta.

E-Space Tower, 15th floor, 3–6 Maruyama-cho. www.legato-tokyo.jp. © **03/5784-2121.** Main dishes ¥2,500–¥5,500; set lunches ¥1,200–¥3,500; set dinners ¥3,800–¥5,800. Mon–Fri 11:30am–2pm; daily 5:30–10:30pm (last order). Station: Shibuya (Hachiko, 8 min.). From the station, walk straight up Dogenzaka; it will be on the right, just past the *koban* police box.

INEXPENSIVE

In addition to the recommendation here, there's a branch of **Maisen** (p. 98), offering *tonkatsu*, on the sixth floor of Hikarie (© **03/3486-2365**). **Gonpachi** (p. 103), on the 14th floor of E-Space Tower, 3–6 Maruyama-cho (© **03/5784-2011**), offers Japanese fare at inexpensive prices.

d47 Shokudo ★★ VARIED JAPANESE   Since I've traveled to most of Japan's 47 prefectures and grown fond of many regional dishes, I'm excited that now I don't have any farther to go than Shibuya. The menu can't offer all prefectural dishes at once, of course, but the staff travels around Japan and continually brings back new recipes for the kitchen. You might, therefore, get to sample Oita Prefecture's famous chicken, *natto* (fermented soybean) with Japanese plum sauce and ginger from Nagano, or Okinawan specialties that are foreign even to Japanese. Beer (like stout beer from Shizuoka) and sake (¥1,400 for a sampler of four kinds) from around Japan are also a treat. If you can, get a seat facing bustling Shibuya Station.

Hikarie, 8th floor, 2–21–1 Shibuya. © **03/6427-2303.** Main dishes ¥500–¥1,000; set meals ¥1,200–¥1,650. Daily 11am–11pm. Station: Shibuya (east gate, 1 min.).

Uobei ★ SUSHI   Genki Sushi is a wildly successful chain of conveyor-belt sushi restaurants, with branches throughout Japan, China (I first encountered them in Hong Kong) and the U.S. West Coast, but this one takes it up a notch by taking humans out of the equation. Not exactly, I guess, as the hostess takes you to your assigned counter seat and there must be an army back in the kitchen making your order. But then it's just you and your touch screen, available in English and other languages, making this a super-easy place to dine if you don't speak Japanese. Simply place your order of sushi, add side dishes like miso soup or French fries, help yourself to the hot water spigot and powdered tea, and voila! Your meal comes racing down the conveyor belt and stops right in front of you, with almost all plates costing just ¥108. It's a bit eerie, and you have to wonder, is this the restaurant of the future?

2–29–11 Dogenzaka. ℂ **03/3462-0241.** Main dishes ¥108. Daily 11am–midnight. Station: Shibuya (Hachiko exit, 6 min.). From the station, walk straight up Dogenzaka until you get to Dubliner's (on your right) and then turn right.

Akasaka
EXPENSIVE

Ninja ★ VARIED JAPANESE   At this themed restaurant, diners enter the secret world of the ninja as soon as they step inside the darkened entrance, where costumed waiters appear out of nowhere to lead the hungry through a labyrinth of twisting passageways to private dining nooks. The English-menu language, written on a scroll, offers a la carte dishes like sweet-and-sour pork, salmon grilled with saikyo miso, roast lamb with Korean flavoring, and various sushi, soups, and salads, but most people go with one of the set dinners like the shabu-shabu course. As the meal winds down, on most nights a roaming ninja will drop by to entertain with a variety of magic acts that are darn near impossible to figure out (tipping is up to you). Although I admit Ninja may be corny, the food is good, the intimate dining venues are great for couples and groups, and the staff is beyond reproach. For families with kids, this place is tough to beat. Reservations are a must.

Akasaka Tokyu Plaza, 1st floor, 2–14–3 Nagata-cho. ℂ **03/5157-3936.** Main dishes ¥1,500–¥6,800; set dinners ¥5,500–¥20,000. Mon–Sat 5–10:30pm (last entry); Sun and holidays 5–9:45pm. Station: Akasaka-mitsuke (1 min.). In the candy cane–striped building, below the Akasaka Excel Tokyu Hotel.

EXPLORING TOKYO

Tokyo hasn't fared very well over the centuries. Fires and earthquakes have taken their toll, old buildings have been torn down in the zeal of modernization, and World War II left most of the city in ruins. Save your historical sightseeing, therefore, for places such as Kyoto or Takayama, and consider Tokyo your introduction to the newest of the new in Japan and the showcase of the nation's accomplishments in the arts, technology, fashion, pop art, and design. Tokyo also has more museums than any other city in Japan, as well as a wide range of other attractions, including parks, temples, and shrines. In Tokyo you can explore mammoth department stores, sample unlimited cuisines, walk around unique neighborhoods, revel in kitsch, and take advantage of glittering nightlife.

When planning your sightseeing itinerary, keep in mind that the city is huge and it takes time to get from one end to the other. It's best, therefore, to cover Tokyo neighborhood by neighborhood, coordinating sightseeing with dinner and evening plans. Most museums in Tokyo are closed 1 day of the week (usually Mon) and for New Year's (generally the last day or two in Dec and the first 1 to 3 days of Jan). If Monday happens to be a national holiday, most national and municipal museums will remain open but will close Tuesday instead. Some of the privately owned museums, however, are closed on national holidays, as well as for exhibition changes. Call beforehand or check websites to avoid disappointment. Remember, too, that you must enter museums at least 30 minutes before closing time. For a listing of current exhibitions, including those being held at major department stores, consult *Metropolis,* an English-language weekly available in hotels, restaurants, and bars around town as well as online at www.metropolisjapan.com.

3 Kitanomaru Koen Park, Chiyoda-ku. www.momat.go.jp. © **03/3214-2561.** Admission ¥420 adults, ¥130 college students, free for children and seniors; special exhibits cost more. Tues–Sun 10am–5pm (Fri to 8pm). Station: Takebashi (exit 1b, 3 min.).

Yasukuni Shrine ★ SHRINE/MUSEUM   Built in 1869 to commemorate Japanese war dead, Yasukuni Shrine is constructed in classic Shinto style, with a huge steel *torii* gate at its entrance. During times of war, soldiers were told that if they died fighting for their country, their spirits would find glory here; even today, it's believed that the spirits of some 2.4 million Japanese war dead are at home here, where they are worshipped as deities. Every August 15, the shrine is thrust into the national spotlight when World War II memorials are held. Visits by prime ministers and other officials have caused national outrage among Japan's Asian neighbors, who think it improper to visit—and thereby condone—a shrine so closely tied to Japan's nationalistic and militaristic past.

If you can, come on a Sunday, when a flea market for antiques and curios is held at the entrance to the shrine from about 6am to 3pm. But the most important thing to see is the **Yushukan,** a war memorial museum outlining Japan's military history. It chronicles the rise and fall of the samurai, the colonization of Asia by Western powers by the late 1800s, the Sino-Japanese War, the Russo-Japanese War, and World Wars I and II, though explanations in English are rather vague and Japan's military aggression in Asia is barely touched. Still, a fascinating 90 minutes can be spent here gazing on samurai armor, swords, uniforms, tanks, guns, a Mitsubishi Zero fighter plane, and artillery, as well as such thought-provoking displays as a human torpedo (a tiny submarine guided by one occupant and loaded with explosives) and a suicide attack plane. But the most chilling displays are the seemingly endless photographs of war dead, some of them very young teenagers. In stark contrast to the somberness of the museum, temporary exhibits of beautiful *ikebana* (Japanese flower arrangements) and bonsai are often held on the shrine grounds in rows of glass cases. Yasukuni Shrine is also famous for its cherry blossoms.

Yasukuni Shrine, 3–1–1 Kudan-kita, Chiyoda-ku. www.yasukuni.or.jp. © **03/3261-8326.** Free admission to shrine; Yushukan ¥800 adults, ¥500 students, ¥300 junior-high and high-school students, ¥100 children. Shrine daily 24 hr.; Yushukan daily 9am–5pm. Station: Kudanshita (5 min.) or Ichigaya or Iidabashi (10 min.). On Yasukuni Dori, northwest of Imperial Palace grounds.

TSUKIJI & SHIODOME

Hama Rikyu Garden PARK/GARDEN   Considered by some to be the best garden in Tokyo (but marred, in my opinion, by skyscrapers in Shiodome that detract from its charm; there ought to be a law), this urban oasis has origins stretching back 300 years, when it served as a retreat for a former feudal lord and as duck-hunting and falconry grounds for the Tokugawa shogun. In 1871, possession of the garden passed to the imperial family, which used it to entertain such visiting dignitaries as Gen. Ulysses S. Grant. Come here to see how the upper classes enjoyed themselves during the Edo Period; to gain a better understanding, pick up the park's free audio guide. The garden contains an inner tidal pool, spanned by three bridges draped with wisteria (views from the south end of the garden are the most picturesque). There are also other ponds; a refuge for ducks, herons, and migratory birds; a promenade along the bay lined with pine trees; a 300-year-old pine; moon-viewing pavilions; and teahouses (powdered green tea and a sweet will cost you ¥500). Plan on at least an hour's stroll to see everything, but the best reason for coming here is to board a ferry from the garden's pier bound for Asakusa, with departures every hour or so between 10:30am and 4:15pm; the fare is ¥740 one-way.

1–1 Hamarikyuteien, Chuo-ku. www.tokyo-park.or.jp. © **03/3541-0200.** Admission ¥300 adults, ¥150 seniors, free for children 12 and under. Daily 9am–5pm. Station: Shiodome (exit 5, 5 min.) or Tsukiji-shjjo (7 min.).

Tsukiji Market ★★★ MARKET   This huge wholesale fish market—the largest in Japan and one of the largest in the world—is a must for anyone who has never seen such a market in action. The action here starts early: Throughout the night, boats and trucks arrive with seafood from the seas around Japan, from Africa, and even from America, with enough fish to satisfy the demands of a nation where seafood reigns supreme. To give you some idea of its enormity, this market handles almost all the seafood—about 450 kinds of seafood amounting to about 2,000 tons daily—consumed in and around Tokyo. The king is tuna, huge and frozen, unloaded around 3am, laid out on the ground, and numbered. Wholesalers walk up and down the rows, jotting down the numbers of the best-looking tuna, and by 5:30am, the tuna auctions are well underway. Other auctions of seafood and vegetables are also held. The wholesalers then transfer what they've bought to their own stalls in the market, subsequently selling fish and produce to their regular customers, usually retail stores and restaurants.

Although I used to be able to arrive before dawn and visit the entire market freely, an increasing number of tourists over the years has prompted authorities to close tuna auctions to visitors except for a small viewing area open to the first 120 visitors on a first-come first-serve basis starting at 5am (apply at the Fish Information Center, located on Harumi Dori near the Kochidoki-bashi Bridge, well before 5am and expect to wait in line). Otherwise, I think it's just as fun to arrive after 9am to visit the wholesale market area, held in a cavernous, hangarlike building, which means you can visit it even on a dismal rainy morning. There's a lot going on—men in black rubber boots rushing wheelbarrows and forklifts through the aisles, hawkers shouting, knives chopping and slicing. Wander the aisles and you'll see things you never dreamed were edible. This is a good place to bring your camera, but note that no flash photography of auctions or the market is allowed. Also, the floors are wet, so leave your fancy shoes at the hotel. Finally, be mindful of the many forklifts and carts, and please don't touch the fish. The overlooked produce market is located toward the back, past the seafood.

Tsukiji is also a good place to come if you want sushi for breakfast. Alongside the covered market are rows of barracklike buildings divided into sushi restaurants and shops related to the fish trade. In addition, in between the market and Tsukiji Station is the Outer Market (*Jogai*), a delightful district of tiny retail shops and stalls where you can buy the freshest seafood in town, plus dried fish and fish products, seaweed, vegetables, knives, rubber boots, and cooking utensils, with many open to 2pm. *Warning:* While walking through the Outer Market, my Japanese friend and I were warned several times by local shopkeepers to watch our purses, advice we didn't take lightly. Apparently, pickpockets have been at work here on unsuspecting tourists.

Note: Tsukiji Market, established in 1935, will move to much larger grounds in Toyosu in November 2016, with the current grounds being eyed for development ahead of the 2020 Olympics.

5–2–1 Tsukiji, Chuo-ku. www.tsukiji-market.or.jp. © **03/3542-1111.** Free admission. Mon–Sat 9–11am. Closed some Wed, holidays, several days around New Year's, and 3 days in mid-Aug. Station: Tsukijishijo (exit A2, 2 min.) or Tsukiji (Honganji Temple exit, 10 min.).

ASAKUSA

On the corner of Kaminarimon Dori and Asakusa Dori (across from the entry gate to Sensoji Temple) is the Asakusa Culture Tourist Information Center, open daily 9:30am to 8pm, where you can get a map of the area and take in views of the temple from the 8th-floor observation room. On Saturdays and Sundays, volunteers give free 1-hour tours of Asakusa, departing here at 11am and 1:15pm.

Amuse Museum ★★★ MUSEUM   This is one of my favorite museums in Tokyo, and while you certainly can amuse yourself here, it's not in a way you may think. Rather, this museum with the curious name has a very serious purpose: to preserve and display items and traditions of Japan's past that might otherwise slip from public view. The perfect example of this is the museum's fascinating collection of *boro,* which is patchwork clothing originating in Japan's cold and snowy north, lovingly mended through the years with additional stitching and pieces of cloth, and passed down from generation to generation. Although they were made solely for practical reasons—such as sheets used in childbirth or blankets so large and heavy that the entire family would huddle naked under one as they slept—today they are celebrated as textile art. The fact that they have survived at all is due to the diligence of Chuzaburo Tanaka, a private collector who scoured the hinterlands for *boro,* folk art, and antiques. Japanese director Akira Kurosawa was so impressed with Tanaka's rare *boro* collection that he used some of them in his movie "Dreams"; one room is dedicated to the movie. In addition to temporary exhibitions, other displays feature antique clocks, teapots, and other everyday household objects. At the Ukiyo-e Theater, an educational 28-minute film teaches us how to see woodblock prints as windows to the past, from clothing worn by fishermen to hairstyles of the Edo Period. On the roof is a viewing deck offering great vistas of Sensoji Temple, while on the sixth floor is Bar Six, open from 6pm to 2am and offering night views of the illuminated temple. The ground-floor museum shop is also worth browsing for its arts and crafts from all over Japan.

2–34–3 Asakusa, Taito-ku. www.amusemuseum.com. © **03/5806-1181.** Admission ¥1,080 adults, ¥864 university and high-school students, ¥540 children. Tues–Sun 10am–6pm. Station: Asakusa (5 min.). Just east of Sensoji Temple, past Nitemmon Gate.

Asakusa

ASAKUSA 3-CHOME

1

ASAKUSA 6-CHOME

Kototoi Dori

NISHI-ASAKUSA 3-CHOME

Hisago Dori

Hanayashiki Amusement Park

Asakusa Shrine

HANAKAWADO 2-CHOME

Sensoji Temple

ASAKUSA 2-CHOME

Roku Broadway

Umamichi Dori

Five-storied Pagoda

Hozomon Gate

Benten-do Temple

HANAKAWADO 1-CHOME

Edo Dori

NISHI-ASAKUSA 2-CHOME

Kokusai Dori

Dempoin Temple

7

Dempoin Dori

JR TOBU ASAKUSA LINE

Sushiya Dori

Dori

Chinyoko Dori

Nakamise Dori

Kannon Dori

Asakusa Station

Sumida Park

Drum Museum

2

ASAKUSA 1-CHOME

3

4

5

Matsuya Dept. Store

Sumida River

Orange

Kaminarimon Gate

NISHI-ASAKUSA 1-CHOME

Kaminarimon Dori

6

8

9

Asakusa

Ferry Pier

Tarawamachi

Asakusa Information Center

i

Azuma

KAMINARIMON 1-CHOME

Asahi Beer Tower

KAMINARIMON 2-CHOME

Asahi Beer Hall

Asakusa Dori

TOKYO METRO GINZA LINE

TOEI ASAKUSA LINE

Bridge

KOTOBUKI 4-CHOME

Asakusa

Komagata

Shuto (Metropolitan) Expwy. No. 6

KOMOGATA 1-CHOME

Bridge

Kiyosumi Dori

Edo Dori

i Information

Tokyo Metro station

Toei station

Shinto shrine

0   100 y
0   100 m

10

HOTELS ■

Khaosan Kabuki **5**

Ryokan Kamogawa **4**

Ryokan Asakusa Shigetsu **3**

Sadachiyo Sukeroku-no-Yado **1**

Toyoko Inn Asakusa Kuramae
  Kaminarimon **10**

RESTAURANTS ◆

Chinya **6**

Kamiya Bar **9**

Sansada **8**

Sometaro **2**

Waentei-Kikko **7**

Hanayashiki ★ AMUSEMENT PARK   Opened in 1853 while the shogun still reigned, this small and rather corny amusement park is Japan's oldest. It offers a small roller coaster, a kiddie Ferris wheel, a carousel, a haunted house, a 3-D theater, samurai and ninja shows, and other diversions that appeal to younger children. Note, however, that after paying admission, you must still buy tickets for each ride; tickets are ¥100 each, and most rides require two to four tickets.

2–28–1 Asakusa (northwest of Sensoji Temple), Taito-ku. www.hanayashiki.net. ℂ **03/3842-8780.** Admission ¥1,000 adults, ¥500 children 7–12 and seniors, free for children 6 and under. Daily 10am–6pm (to 5pm in winter). Station: Asakusa (5 min.).

Sensoji Temple ★★★ TEMPLE   Also popularly known as Asakusa Kannon, this is Tokyo's oldest and most popular temple, with a history dating back to A.D. 628. That was when, according to popular lore, two brothers fishing in the nearby Sumida River netted the catch of their lives: a tiny golden statue of Kannon, the Buddhist goddess of mercy and happiness who is empowered with the ability to release humans from all suffering. Sensoji Temple was erected in her honor, and although the statue is housed here, it's never shown to the public. Still, through the centuries, worshipers have flocked here seeking favors of Kannon; and when Sensoji Temple burned down during a 1945 bombing raid, the present structure was rebuilt with donations from the Japanese people. After sunset, the temple and pagoda are illuminated until 11pm.

Entrance to the temple is via colorful Kaminarimon Gate onto lively **Nakamise Dori,** a pedestrian lane leading to the shrine that is lined with more than 80 stalls selling souvenirs and traditional Japanese goods. In fact, the whole Asakusa area is one of my favorite neighborhoods, and you can easily spend half a day here. Or, if you're here on a Saturday or Sunday, free 1-hour tours of Sensoji and the neighborhood are led by volunteers at 11am and 1:15pm; the meeting place is at the Asakusa Culture Tourist Information Center, across the street from Kaminarimon Gate.

2–3–1 Asakusa, Taito-ku. www.senso-ji.jp/about/index_e.html. ℂ **03/3842-0181.** Free admission. Daily 6:30am–5pm. Station: Asakusa (2 min.).

UENO & VICINITY

Ueno is a hugely popular family destination, making this a priority for those traveling with kids. Among the must-sees are the National Museum of Nature and Science, Shitamachi Museum, and Ueno Park.

Asakura Choso Museum ★★★ HISTORIC HOME   This museum is actually a very unique home that once belonged to a famous artist, making it a must if you've never had the opportunity to visit a traditional Japanese house. Of course, this isn't just any house. Designed by sculptor Fumio Asakura (1883–1964) to serve as his residence, studio, and Asakura Sculpture School, it's a delightful combination of both modern and traditional architecture, recently restored to reflect how it would have looked in 1955. Probably the most enviable feature is the inner courtyard pond, fed by a natural spring and visible from many rooms in the house. There's a library, his airy studio, and tatami rooms, including one for visitors where they could enjoy the rising sun. On the roof is a garden, where Asakura's students tended vegetables to sharpen their senses. And throughout the house are furniture, antiques, hundreds of orchids, and statues of statesmen, women, and cats (Asakura loved cats; he once had as many as 10). An audio guide, available for ¥200 extra, is worth it for the additional information it gives on everything from the books in his library to his statue "Grave-Keeper." Visitors are asked to take off their shoes and wear socks through the museum.

7–18–10 Yanaka, Taito-ku. www.taitocity.net/taito/asakura/english. © **03/3821-4549.** Tues–Thurs and Sat–Sun 9:30am–4:30pm. Station: Nippori (northwest exit, 5 min.).

National Museum of Nature and Science (Kokuritsu Kagaku Hakubutsukan) ★★ MUSEUM

Of all of Tokyo's museums, this is the one that would probably delight both kids and parents the most. Even better, as Japan's largest science museum, it has an informative section that concentrates just on Japan, making it a good learning tool as well, and has lots of imaginative displays and exhibits geared toward youngsters. It contains two sections, a Global Gallery covering earth, space, the diversity of life, and the evolution of humans, dinosaurs, and other life forms, and the Japan Gallery that focuses on the natural history of Japan. One of my favorite sections is the hallway filled with an incredible 100-some taxidermic animals from around the world, including a polar bear, camel, gorilla, tiger, bear, and more; some of the animals are those that died at nearby Ueno Zoo. Other highlights include dinosaur exhibits; a hands-on discovery room where children can learn about sound, light, magnetism, and other scientific phenomena; a Japanese mummy from the Edo Period still curled up in a burial jar; Hachiko (stuffed and so famous there's a statue of the dog at Shibuya Station); a detailed explanation of rice cultivation in Japan; and recreated wood and marine habitats. Expect to spend a minimum of 2 hours here, though you'll stay longer if you rent the audio guide for ¥200, recommended since English-language descriptions are limited.

Ueno Park, Taito-ku. www.kahaku.go.jp. © **03/5777-8600.** Admission ¥620 adults, free for children and seniors. Tues–Sun 9am–5pm. Station: Ueno (5 min.).

Shitamachi Museum (Shitamachi Fuzoku Shiryokan) ★

One of the things I like about this museum is the spirit it conveys of Tokyo's *shitamachi* (old downtown), both in its folksy, down-to-earth presentation and in the friendliness of the people who work there, including volunteers eager to give free tours. *Shitamachi* is where commoners used to live, mainly in the north part of Tokyo around Ueno and Asakusa, but after the 1923 Great Kanto Earthquake and air raids of World War II, precious little remains. Much of what you see here was donated by people living in the area. The ground floor contains a reconstructed *shitamachi* street as it might have looked around 1920, with a life-size merchant's house, a candy shop, and a small tenement shared by two families. These row tenements were long and narrow, with thin wooden walls separating one from the next and with narrow alleyways serving as communal living rooms. On the second floor are displays of cooking utensils, tools, toys, and games, most of which you can pick up and try out yourself, as well as a

Ueno

HOTELS ■
Annex Katsutaro **1**
Homeikan **3**
Hotel Coco Grand **5**
Ryokan Sawanoya **2**

RESTAURANTS ◆
Innsyoutei **4**
Kohmen **7**
Unagi Kappo Izu'ei Honten **6**

━━━ Railway
- - - - - Railway (tunnel)
━━━ Subway
ⓘ Tourist Information

reconstruction of what was once the entrance to a public bath. A new display describes the 1923 earthquake, which hit at lunchtime when housewives were busy cooking over fires and which destroyed nearly half of Tokyo and killed more than 105,000 people (after the earthquake, up to 500,000 people sought refuge in Ueno Park alone). Since the museum is small, you can tour it in about 20 minutes, but I suggest the free tour as well, since volunteers can explain things you might not notice on your own, like the old-fashioned fly-catcher.

Ueno Park, Taito-ku. www.taitocity.net/taito/shitamachi/index.html ℂ **03/3823-7451.** Admission ¥300 adults, ¥100 children. Tues–Sun 9:30am–4:30pm. Station: Ueno (3 min.). On the southwest edge of Shinobazu Pond, north of Shinobazu Dori avenue.

The National Museum of Western Art (Kokuritsu Seiyo Bijut-sukan) ★★ MUSEUM   This is Japan's only national museum of Western art, and how it came to be is just as notable as its collection of sculpture and art from the end of the Middle Ages through the 20th century. Kojiro Matsukata was a wealthy shipbuilder who made frequent trips to Europe to buy art, eventually acquiring about 10,000 works that he intended to show in a Tokyo museum. The Great Depression interrupted those plans and forced him to sell off much of his collection, while those that had been left in a London warehouse perished in a 1939 fire. About 400 works remained, in Paris, but those were sequestrated by the French government during World War II and only returned to Japan in 1951, a year after Matsukata had died. Those works form the basis of this museum, opened in 1959 in a building designed by Le Corbusier and now including works by Old Masters like Lucas Cranach the Elder, Rubens, El Greco, Murillo, Tintoretto, and Tiepolo, and by 19th- and 20th-century French painters like Delacroix, Monet (an entire room is devoted to his works alone), Manet, Renoir, Pissarro, Sisley, Courbet, Cézanne, Van Gogh, and Gauguin. The museum's 20th-century works, by Picasso, Max Erst, Miró, Dubuffet, Pollock, and others round out the collection, but the museum is also noted for possessing one of the largest Rodin collections in the world, with 50-some sculptures that include "The Kiss," "The Thinker," and, outside the museum's front entrance, "The Gates of Hell." Plan on at least an hour here, unless you also take advantage of one of the special exhibitions—often from prestigious overseas collections—that almost always draw large crowds.

Ueno Park, Taito-ku. www.nmwa.go.jp. ℂ **03/3828-5131.** Admission ¥430 adults, ¥130 college students, free for children 17 and under and seniors; special exhibits require separate admission fee. Free admission to permanent collection 2nd and 4th Sat of the month. Tues–Sun: 9:30am–5:30pm in summer, 9:30–5pm in winter (to 8pm Fri year-round). Station: Ueno (4 min.).

Tokyo National Museum (Tokyo Kokuritsu Hakubutsukan) ★★★
MUSEUM   Quite simply, this is Tokyo's top museum, if not all of Japan's. It has the largest collection of Japanese art in the world, making it the single best place to see a vast variety of Japanese antiques and art, including lacquerware, metalwork, pottery, old kimono, samurai armor, swords, scrolls, screens, *ukiyo-e* (woodblock prints), calligraphy, textiles, ceramics, and more. And that's just the main building (Japanese Gallery), with other galleries displaying Japanese

archaeological finds, art from other Asian countries, priceless treasures from Nara, and frequent special exhibitions. As Japan's oldest museum, founded in 1872 and moving to Ueno Park in 1882, it has amassed an inventory of more than 113,000 objects, with about 3,000 items on display at any one time, which means that there's always something new to see every time you visit. Schedule a morning or afternoon to see everything. Barring that, concentrate on the Japanese Gallery with its 24 exhibition rooms, which you can see in 1 or 2 hours, depending on your interest. I also recommend browsing the newly renovated museum shop, moved from its former basement location to the first floor, with its reproductions of museum masterpieces and traditional crafts by contemporary artist, including jewelry, miniature screens, fans, and more.

If time allows, I also highly recommend a tour of the **Gallery of Horyuji Treasures (Horyuji Homotsukan),** which displays priceless Buddhist treasures from the Horyuji Temple in Nara, founded by Prince Shotoku in A.D. 607. Although it seems incongruous that antiquities should find a home in a building as starkly modern as this, low lighting and spacious displays allow the bronze Buddhist statues, ceremonial Gigaku masks used in ritual dances, lacquerware, textiles, and paintings to shine.

The **Asian Gallery (Toyokan)** is the place to go to see art and archaeological artifacts from surrounding Asian regions, including China, Korea, Southeast and Central Asia, India, and Egypt. Chinese art—including jade, paintings, calligraphy, and ceramics—makes up the largest part of the collection, a reflection of China's tremendous influence on Japanese art, architecture, and religion. Although exhibitions change, items on display might include Buddhas from China and Gandhara, embroidered wall hangings and cloth from India, Iranian and Turkish carpets, Thai and Vietnamese ceramics, and Egyptian relics.

The **Heiseikan Gallery** houses archaeological finds of ancient Japan, including pottery and Haniwa clay burial figurines of the Jomon Period (10,000 B.C.–1000 B.C.) and ornamental, keyhole-shaped tombs from the Yayoi Period (400 B.C.–A.D. 200). The Hyokeikan, built in 1909 to honor the wedding of Emperor Taisho, has occasional special exhibitions.

Ueno Park, Taito-ku. www.tnm.jp. ⓒ **03/3822-1111.** Admission ¥620 adults, ¥410 college students, free for seniors and children. Special exhibits cost more. Tues–Sun 9:30am–5pm; Apr–Dec open to 8pm Fri during special exhibitions and to 6pm weekends and holidays). Station: Ueno (10 min.).

Toshogu Shrine ★ Come here to pay respects to the man who made Edo (present-day Tokyo) the seat of his government and thus elevated the small village to the most important city in the country. Erected in 1651, it's dedicated to Tokugawa Ieyasu, founder of the Tokugawa shogunate. Like Toshogu Shrine in Nikko, it was built by Ieyasu's grandson, Iemitsu, and boasts some of the same richly carved, ornate design favored by the Tokugawas, especially the Chinese-style main gate, erected in 1651. Remarkably, it survived the civil war of 1868, the Great Kanto Earthquake of 1923, and even World War II. The pathway to the shrine is lined with massive stone lanterns, as well as 50 copper lanterns donated by *daimyo* from all over Japan, while the grounds themselves

Shinjuku

Shinjuku West

NISHI-SHINJUKU 6-CHOME

Ohme Kaido

Shinjuku Nomura Bldg.

Yasuda Kasai Kaijo Bldg.

L Tower Bldg.

Shinjuku Dai-ichi Seimei Bldg.

Sumitomo Bldg.

Shinjuku Mitsui Bldg.

Odakyu HALC

Shinjuku Center Bldg.

Chuo Dori

NISHI-SHINJUKU 2-CHOME

Bus Terminal

Kogakuin Univ.

Shinjuku Post Office

Odakyu Dept. Store

Keio Dept. Store

i Tokyo Metropolitan Government Building

No. 10 Street

No. 9 Street

NISHI-SHINJUKU 1-CHOME

Shinjuku Station

No. 11 Street

N.S. Bldg.

KDD Bldg.

ODAKYU LINE

Koshu-Kaido Dori

KEIO LINE

YOYOGI

0 ——— 1/4 mi
0 ——— 0.25 km

Railway
Subway
i Tourist Information

is shrouded by a 600-year-old camphor tree. Paying admission allows a closer look at the shrine's magnificent carvings. At the counter to the left you can buy good-luck charms that will supposedly bring you fortune, happiness, and other earthly desires. On a more somber note, a flame on shrine grounds, lit from flames burning in both Hiroshima and Nagasaki, appeals for world peace.

Ueno Park, Taito-ku. ✆ **03/3822-3455.** Free admission to shrine grounds; admission to inner compound ¥500 adults, ¥200 children. Daily 9am–4:30pm. Station: Ueno (4 min.).

Ueno Zoo ★ ZOO   Founded in 1882, Japan's oldest zoo is small by today's standards but remains one of the most well-known zoos in Japan, with about 2,600 animals in residence. Its most celebrated residents are Ri-Ri and Shin-Shin, two pandas on loan from a wildlife sanctuary in China's Sichuan province. A vivarium houses amphibians, fish, and reptiles, including snakes and crocodiles. Also of note is the five-story pagoda dating from the Edo era, along with a teahouse built 350 years ago to receive the shogun when visiting nearby Toshogu Shrine. Shinobazu Pond, on the southwest end of the zoo, serves as a sanctuary for wild cormorants and other birds. Personally, I can't help but feel sorry for some of the animals in their small spaces, but children

Shinjuku East

HOTELS ■
Hotel Century
  Southern Tower **5**
Park Hyatt **1**
Toyoko Inn Shinjuku
  Kabuki-cho **9**

RESTAURANTS ◆
Ban-Thai **6**
Din Tai Fung **10**
Green House **2**
Kakiden **11**
New York Grill **1**
Ten-ichi **3**, **14**
Tsunahachi **4**, **13**

NIGHTLIFE ◆
Advocates **18**
Albatross **8**
Arty Farty **15**
Bar Goldfinger **17**
Dubliners **12**
Robot Restaurant **7**
Shinjuku Pit Inn **16**

5

EXPLORING TOKYO   Shinjuku

will enjoy the Japanese macaques, polar and Hokkaido brown bears, California sea lions, penguins, gorillas, giraffes, zebras, elephants, hippos, deer, and tigers. Expect to spend a minimum of 2 hours here.

Ueno Park, Taito-ku. www.tokyo-zoo.net/english. ℂ **03/3828-5171.** Admission ¥600 adults, ¥300 seniors, ¥200 children 13–15, free for children 12 and under. Tues–Sun 9:30am–5pm (enter by 4pm). Closed some holidays. Station: Ueno (4 min.).

SHINJUKU

Shinjuku Gyoen ★★ PARK/GARDEN   Formerly the private estate of a feudal lord and then of the imperial family, this is considered one of the most important parks of the Meiji Era. It's wonderful for strolling because of the variety of its planted gardens; styles range from French and English to Japanese traditional. The park's 58 hectares (143 acres) make it one of the city's largest, and each bend in the pathway brings something completely different: Ponds and sculpted bushes give way to a promenade lined with sycamores that opens onto a rose garden. This place amazes me every time I come here. Cherry blossoms, azaleas, chrysanthemums, and other flowers provide splashes of color from spring through autumn. The Japanese garden, buried in the center, is exquisite; if you have time only for a quick look at traditional landscaping, you won't be disappointed here. There are also wide grassy expanses, popular for picnics and playing, and a greenhouse filled with tropical plants. You could easily spend a half-day of leisure here, but it's also good for a quick fix of rejuvenation.

11 Naitocho, Shinjuku-ku. www.env.go.jp/garden/shinjukugyoen/english/index.html. © **03/3350-0151.** Admission ¥200 adults, ¥50 children. Tues–Sun 9am–4:30pm. Station: Shinjuku Gyoen-mae (3 min.) or Sendagaya (5 min.).

Tokyo Metropolitan Government Office (TMG) ★★★ OBSERVATION DECK   Tokyo's city hall—designed by one of Japan's best-known architects, Kenzo Tange—comprises three buildings—TMG no. 1, TMG no. 2, and the Metropolitan Assembly Building—and together they contain everything from Tokyo's Disaster Prevention Center to the governor's office. Most important for visitors is TMG no. 1, the tall building to the north that offers the best free view of Tokyo. This 48-story, 240m (787-ft.) structure, among the tallest building in Shinjuku, boasts two observatories located on the 45th floors of both its north and south towers. Both observatories offer the same spectacular views—on clear winter days you can even see Mount Fuji—as well as a small souvenir shop and coffee shop (the North Tower also has a Hakuhinkan Toy Park, with fun souvenirs, but a large restaurant annoyingly takes up the entire east side of the observatory). In expensive Tokyo, this is one of the city's best bargains, and kids love it. On the first floor is a Tokyo Tourist Information Center, open daily 9:30m to 6:30pm, as well as a shop open Monday to Friday from 10am to 6:30pm selling products made in Tokyo Prefecture, including sake, food items, glassware, and other traditional crafts.

2–8–1 Nishi-Shinjuku. www.metro.tokyo.jp/ENGLISH/TMG/observat.htm © **03/5321-1111.** Free admission. Daily 9:30am–10:30pm. Closed Dec 29–Jan 3. Station: Tochomae (1 min.), Shinjuku (10 min.), or Nishi-Shinjuku (5 min.).

HARAJUKU & AOYAMA

Meiji Jingu Shrine ★★ SHRINE   This is Tokyo's most venerable Shinto shrine, opened in 1920 in honor of Emperor and Empress Meiji, who were instrumental in opening Japan to the outside world more than 140 years ago. Japan's two largest *torii* (the traditional entry gate of a shrine), built of cypress more than 1,700 years old, give dramatic entrance to the grounds, once the estate of a *daimyo*. The shaded pathway is lined with trees, shrubs, and dense woods, making it an incredible sanctuary in the middle of the city. In late May/June, the **Iris Garden** is in spectacular bloom (admission fee charged). About a 10-minute walk from the first *torii*, the shrine is a fine example of dignified and refined Shinto architecture. It's made of plain Japanese cypress and topped with green-copper roofs. Meiji Jingu Shrine is the place to be on New Year's Eve, when more than two million people crowd onto the grounds to usher in the new year.

Meiji Shrine Inner Garden, 1–1 Kamizono-cho, Yoyogi, Shibuya-ku. www.meijijingu. or.jp. © **03/3379-5511.** Free admission. Daily sunrise to sunset (about 6:40am–4pm in Dec, 5am–6:30pm in June). Station: Harajuku or Meiji-Jingumae (1 min.).

Harajuku & Aoyama

HOTELS ■
Hotel Asia Center of Japan **5**
Tokyu Stay Aoyama
Premier **5**

RESTAURANTS ◆
Casita **16**
Harajuku Gyoza Lou **9**
Heirokuzushi **11**
Hiroba **12**
Kohmen **8**
La Boheme **10, 13**
Maisen **4**
Maru **15**
Toriyoshi **2**
Two Rooms Grill/Bar **14**
Venire Venire **1**
Yai Yai **7**
Yasaiya Mei **3**

NIGHTLIFE ◆
Crocodile **6**

5 EXPLORING TOKYO | Harajuku & Aoyama

123

National Children's Castle (Kodomo-no-Shiro) ★ MUSEUM   Conceived by the Ministry of Health and Welfare to commemorate the International Year of the Child in 1979 and recognized by the colorful, multi-armed statue by Taro Okamoto out front, the Children's Castle holds various activity rooms for children of all ages (although most are geared to elementary-age kids and younger). The third floor, designed for spontaneous and unstructured play, features a large climbing gym, building blocks, a playhouse, dolls, books, and a preteen corner with billiards, Foosball, and other age-appropriate games; there's also an art room staffed with instructors to help children with projects suitable for their ages. On the fourth floor is a music room with instruments the kids are invited to play, as well as a video room with private cubicles where visitors can make selections from a library of English-language and Japanese DVDs, including Disney films. On the roof is an outdoor playground complete with a wading pool (open summer only; ¥200 extra admission) and tricycles. Various programs are offered throughout the week, including puppet shows, fairy tales, live music performances, and origami presentations.

5–53–1 Jingumae, Shibuya-ku. www.kodomono-shiro.com/english/index.shtml. ℰ **03/3797-5666.** Admission ¥500 adults, ¥400 children 3–17, free for children 2 and under. Tues–Fri 12:30–5:30pm; Sat–Sun and holidays (including school holidays) 10am–5:30pm. Station: Omotesando (exit B2, 8 min.) or Shibuya (10 min.). On Aoyama Dori btw. Omotesando and Shibuya stations.

Ukiyo-e Ota Memorial Museum of Art (Ota Kinen Bijutsukan) ★ MUSEUM   Harajuku is teenybopper heaven, so it comes as something of a surprise to find this small but delightful museum tucked away on a side street. It specializes in *ukiyo-e* (woodblock prints), collected by the late Seizo Ota over a period of more than 50 years in an attempt preserve this uniquely Japanese art form. Although the collection contains 12,000 prints, fewer than 100 are displayed at any one time, in thematic exhibitions that change monthly. You can tour it in about 30 minutes, and be sure to pop in to the small basement shop with its *furoshiki* (traditional wrapping cloth), handkerchiefs, and other items (there's a separate basement entrance for those not visiting the museum).

1–10–10 Jingumae, Shibuya-ku. www.ukiyoe-ota-muse.jp. ℰ **03/3403-0880.** Admission ¥700–¥1,000 adults, ¥500–¥700 high-school and college students, free–¥200 children; price depends on the exhibit. Tues–Sun 10:30am–5:30pm (enter by 5pm). Closed from about the 27th to end of each month for exhibition changes. Station: Harajuku (2 min.) or Meiji-Jingumae (exit 5, 1 min.). Near the Omotesando Dori and Meiji Dori intersection, behind La Forêt.

ROPPONGI

Mori Art Museum (Mori Bijutsukan) ★★★ MUSEUM/OBSERVATION DECK   This is one of Tokyo's top museums, not only because its exhibits are always topnotch, but also because it's the highest museum in the city. Fifty-three stories high, in fact, giving unparalleled panoramas in virtually all directions, but if that's not high enough you have the option of going all the way to the top, to the open-air rooftop Sky Deck for ¥500 extra. As for the art, exhibits change four times a year for innovative shows from both new and established artists, with past shows covering everything from contemporary African art to the largest Warhol exhibition ever presented in Japan. The art space is gorgeous, too, with 6m-tall (20-ft.) ceilings and controlled natural lighting. Most shows give access to a free audio guide. You'll want to spend at least 90 minutes here.

Roppongi Hills Mori Tower, 6–10–1 Roppongi, Minato-ku. www.mori.art.museum/eng/index.html. © **03/5777-8600.** Admission varies according to the exhibit but averages ¥1,500 adults, ¥1,000 high-school and college students, and ¥500 children. Wed–Mon 10am–10pm; Tues 10am–5pm. Station: Roppongi (Roppongi Hills exit, 1 min.) or Azabu Juban (5 min.).

The National Art Center, Tokyo ★★ MUSEUM   This museum boasts one of Japan's largest exhibition spaces, yet it doesn't even have a permanent collection of its own. Rather, it serves as the canvas for Japanese artists' associations, shows organized by its own curators, and joint exhibitions in cooperation with other art institutions and even mass media corporations. As such, its shows are both eclectic and impressive, with past exhibitions including a retrospective of Japanese government-sponsored art exhibitions from the past century; a powerful display of masks, religious idols, and other objects from around the world from Japan's National Museum of Ethnology; a study of California design from 1930 to 1965, with everything from fashion and film to architecture; and Impressionist works from Paris's Musée d'Orsay. In other words, you never know what you might see, and in addition to large shows are smaller galleries showing the works of regional and national artists. Many people drop by just to dine in the museum's Brasserie Paul Bocuse Le Musée or browse the expansive museum shop in the basement (you can enter both without paying admission). Of the three museums in the Art Triangle Roppongi, which includes the nearby Mori Art Museum and Suntory Museum of Art, this is by far the sexiest, with a seductive undulating facade that would make me want to go there even without knowing what's inside.

7–22–2 Roppongi, Minato-ku. www.nact.jp. © **03/5777-8600.** Admission varies, but top shows are ¥1,000–¥1,600 adults, ¥500–¥1,200 college students, free–¥800 high-school students, free for children. Wed–Mon 10am–6pm (Fri to 8pm). Station: Nogizakai (exit 6, 1 min.) or Roppongi (exit 4A or 7, 5 min.).

Suntory Museum of Art (Suntory Bijutsukan) ★★ ART MUSEUM This private museum (part of the same corporation that brews beer and other alcoholic beverages) boasts a collection of 3,000 Japanese antiques and arts and crafts, including lacquerware, ceramics, paintings, glassware, *Noh* costumes, kimono, ornamental hairpins, scrolls, teaware, and other items, which it displays in themed exhibitions, along with visiting collections. An audio guide, when available, costs ¥500 extra. Although modern in design, the museum incorporates such traditional Japanese materials as wood and paper in darkened rooms to create a soothing, inviting atmosphere. That's in keeping with its basic philosophy and mission: to make us see ancient art in a renewed way, to bridge the differences of time, place and culture.

Roppongi

HOTELS ■
Arca Torre **13**
Asia Center **7**
the b roppongi **14**

RESTAURANTS ◆
Frijoles **5**
Fukuzushi **18**
Ganchan **6**
Gonpachi **1**
Inakaya **10, 17**
Kohmen **9**
Roti Roppongi **4**
Ruby Jack's
  Steakhouse
  & Bar **8**
Tokyo Shiba Toufaya **21**
Ukai **21**
Yasaiya Mei **3**

NIGHTLIFE ◆
Ant 'n Bee **15**
Geronimo **12**
Kingyo **16**
Lex Tokyo Red
  Carpet **19**
Parabola Wine
  + Bar **2**
R2 Supper Club **11**
Red Area Club **20**
Rigoletto Bar & Grill **3**
The Pink Cow **19**

Tokyo Midtown, 9–7–4 Akasaka, Minato-ku. www.suntory.com/sma. ℂ **03/3479-8600.** Admission varies, averaging ¥1,300 adults, ¥1,000 high-school and college students, free for children. Sun–Mon and Wed–Thurs 10am–6pm; Fri–Sat 10am–8pm. Station: Roppongi (2 min.) or Nogizaka (exit 3, 3 min.).

Tokyo Tower ★ OBSERVATION DECK   Japan's most famous observation tower was built in 1958 and was modeled after the slightly smaller Eiffel Tower in Paris. Lit up at night, this 330m (1,083-ft.) tower, a relay station for TV and radio stations, is a familiar and beloved landmark in the city's landscape; but with the construction of skyscrapers over the past few decades (including the TMG Observatory and Sky Tree), it has lost some of its appeal as an observation platform and seems more like a relic from the 1950s. With its tacky souvenir shops selling everything from T-shirts to key chains and small aquarium, this place is about as kitsch as kitsch can be. The tower has two observatories: the main one at 149m (489 ft.) and the top observatory at 250m (825 ft.). The best time of year for viewing is said to be during Golden Week at the beginning of May. With many Tokyoites gone from the city and most factories and businesses closed down, the air at this time is thought to be the cleanest and clearest.

4–2 Shiba Koen, Minato-ku. www.tokyotower.co.jp. ℂ **03/3433-5111.** Admission to both observatories ¥1,600 adults, ¥1,000 primary and junior-high students, ¥800 children. Daily 9am–10pm. Station: Onarimon or Kamiyacho (6 min.).

ODAIBA

Ooedo-Onsen Monogatari ★★ SPA   For a unique bathing experience, nothing beats a 3- or 4-hour respite at this re-created Edo-Era bathhouse village, which tapped mineral-rich hot-spring waters 1,380m (4,528 ft.) below ground to supply its various baths. After changing into a *yukata* (cotton kimono, with a choice of nine patterns) and depositing your belongings in a locker (your key is bar-coded, so there's no need to carry any money), you'll stroll past souvenir shops and restaurants on your way to massage rooms, sand baths (extra fee charged), and *onsen* (hot-spring baths) complete with outdoor baths, Jacuzzi, steam baths, foot baths, and saunas. Because it can be quite crowded on weekends, try to come on a weekday. Also, signs in English are virtually nonexistent, so observe gender before entering bathing areas (a hint: Women's baths usually have pink or red curtains, men's blue), though there is an English pamphlet with a map and instructions for proper bathing etiquette. Finally, because tattoos are associated with the Japanese mafia, people with tattoos are prohibited here, as they are in virtually all public baths in Japan.

2–57 Aomi, Odaiba. www.ooedoonsen.jp. ℂ **03/5500-1126.** Admission ¥2,600 adults, ¥1,600 children 4 to 12; reduced prices weekdays and after 6pm (for adults only). Daily 11am–9am the next day. Station: Telecom Center Station (2 min.).

OTHER NEIGHBORHOODS

Edo-Tokyo Museum (Edo-Tokyo Hakubutsukan) ★★★ MUSEUM
Tokyo's history is riveting, making this museum's job easy as it vividly portrays

the history, art, culture, architecture, and disasters of Tokyo from its founding in 1590—when the first shogun, Tokugawa Ieyasu, chose it as the seat of his government—to the 1964 Tokyo Olympics. Displays begin on the sixth floor, where you'll start your journey through the centuries with a walk over a replica Nihombashi Bridge, once the starting point for all roads leading out of Edo (old Tokyo). Displays of the Edo Period (1603–1868) center on the lives of the shogun, merchants, craftsmen, and townspeople, and though descriptions are mostly in Japanese, no explanations are necessary for the replica *kabuki* theater, models of Edo and a feudal lord's mansion, maps, photographs, portable festival floats, and a life-size replica row-house tenement, measuring only 10 sq. m (108 sq. ft.), where most of Edo's commoners lived. Other displays relay the events of the Meiji Restoration and Japan's opening to the rest of the world, the Great Kanto Earthquake of 1923 that killed more than 100,000 people, and the bombing raids of World War II that destroyed much of the city (although I must add that Japan's role as aggressor is disappointingly glossed over). It takes a good 2 hours to see the museum, but you can also enhance your visit with a free museum tour offered by volunteers daily from 10am to 3pm (last tour). Tours last from 1 to 2 hours, depending on your interest, and are good for gaining an understanding for displays that are only in Japanese, but you'll probably still want to take time seeing the museum on your own.

1–4–1 Yokoami, Sumida-ku. www.edo-tokyo-museum.or.jp. ✆ **03/3626-9974.** Admission ¥600 adults, ¥480 college students, ¥300 seniors and junior-high/high-school students, free for younger children. Tues–Sun 9:30am–5:30pm (Sat to 7:30pm). Station: Ryogoku on the JR Sobu Line (west exit, 3 min.) and Oedo Line (exit A4, 1 min.).

Fukagawa Edo Museum (Fukagawa Edo Shiryokan) ★ MUSEUM There's no better place than this to ignite children's imagination of what old Edo might have looked like in the 19th century. Even for adults without children, this museum is fun. Ensconced in the museum's hangarlike building is a life-size reproduction of a prosperous Fukugawa neighborhood, with 11 full-scale replicas of Japanese homes, inns, a watchtower, and shops selling vegetables, rice, and fish, most of them open so you can explore and actually touch the items inside. There's delightful attention to details, like the dog relieving itself on a pole, the cat sleeping on a roof, and the voice of a vendor selling his wares. And like a real village, it even changes with the seasons, with the clap of thunder during summer storms and cherry blossoms in spring. Finally, every 45 minutes or so, the village goes through a day's cycle, beginning with the rising of the sun and roosters crowing in the morning to sunset at night. Just don't confuse this museum with the Edo-Tokyo Museum, which covers the history of the city.

1–3–28 Shirakawa, Koto-ku. www.kcf.or.jp/fukagawa/english.html. ✆ **03/3630-8625.** Admission ¥300 adults, ¥50 children. Daily 9:30am–5pm. Station: Kiyosumi-Shirakawa (3 min.).

Rikugien Garden ★★★ GARDEN Though not as centrally located nor as easy to reach as Tokyo's other famous gardens, this one is a must for fans of traditional Japanese gardens and is probably my favorite. It was created in 1702 by a trusted confidante of the shogun, who began as a page and rose to

SPECTATOR sports

Baseball Japanese are so crazy about baseball, you'd think they invented the game. Actually, it was introduced to Japan by the United States way back in 1873. Today, it's as popular among Japanese as it is among Americans. Even the annual high-school playoffs keep everyone glued to the TV set. As with other imports, the Japanese have added their modifications, including cheerleaders. Several American players have proven very popular with local fans; more recently, there's been a reverse exodus of top Japanese players defecting to American teams.

There are two professional leagues, the Central and the Pacific, which play from April to October and meet in the Japan Series. In Tokyo, the home teams are the **Yomiuri Giants,** who play at Tokyo Dome (www.tokyo-dome.co.jp; ☎ **03/5800-9999;** station: Korakuen or Suidobashi), and the **Yakult Swallows,** who play at Jingu Stadium (www.yakult-swallows.co.jp; ☎ **03/3404-8999;** station: Gaienmae). Good English-language websites that follow Japanese baseball are http://japanesebaseball.com and www.japanball.com.

Except for the Giants, who often sell out, you can usually get tickets at the ballpark before the game. Otherwise, advance tickets can be purchased through each team's website, at convenience stores like Lawson, or at **Ticket Pia** locations around town (ask your hotel for the one nearest you). But probably the easiest method for obtaining tickets is through the website www.japanballtickets.com; tickets must be ordered at least 4 days in advance and can even be delivered to your hotel. Prices for Tokyo Dome, all for reserved seating, range from ¥1,700 in the outfield to ¥5,900 for seats behind home plate. The Giants are so popular, however, that tickets are sometimes hard to come by. Tickets for Jingu Stadium range from ¥1,600 for an unreserved seat in the outfield to ¥4,600 for seats behind home plate.

Sumo Sumo matches are held in Tokyo at the **Kokugikan,** 1–3–28 Yokoami, Sumida-ku (www.sumo.or.jp; ☎ **03/3622-1100;** station: Ryogoku, then a 1-min. walk). Matches are held in January, May, and September for 15 consecutive days, beginning at around 9:30am and lasting until 6pm; the top wrestlers compete after 3:30pm. The best seats are ringside box seats, but they're snapped up by companies or the friends and families of sumo wrestlers. Usually available are balcony arena seats, which can be purchased at Ticket Pia locations around town or through the websites www.sumo.pia.jp/en or www.japanballtickets.com. You can also purchase tickets directly at the Kokugikan ticket office beginning at 9am every morning of the tournament. Prices range from about ¥2,200 for an unreserved seat (sold only on the day of the event at the stadium, with about 400 seats available); reserved seats start at ¥3,800.

If you can't make it to a match, watching on TV is almost as good. Tournaments in Tokyo, as well as those that take place annually in Osaka, Nagoya, and Fukuoka, are broadcast on the NHK channel from 4 to 6pm daily while tournaments are taking place. For more information on sumo, see p. 17.

see p. 17.

the highest rank as a feudal lord. During the Meiji Era, the founder of Mitsubishi took it over for his second residence and later donated it to the city. What I like most about the garden is that it's dominated by a pond in its center, complete with islands and islets, viewing hills, and strolling paths around its perimeter, providing enchanting views. The garden is especially famous for its changing maple leaves in autumn. Since it takes some effort to reach, you'll probably want to enjoy at least an hour here.

6–16–3 Hon-Komagome, Bunkyo-ku. www.tokyo-park.or.jp. © **03/3941-2222.** Admission ¥300 adults, ¥150 seniors, free for children 12 and under. Daily 9am–5pm. Station: Komagome (8 min.) or Sengoku (10 min.).

Tokyo Disneyland & Tokyo DisneySea ★★★ THEME PARK   Virtually a carbon copy of Disneyland in California, this one also boasts the Jungle Cruise, Pirates of the Caribbean, the Haunted Mansion, and Space Mountain. Other hot attractions include Toontown, a wacky theme park where Mickey and other Disney characters work and play, and Star Tours, a thrill adventure created by Disney and George Lucas.

Adjacent to Disneyland is **DisneySea,** a theme park based on ocean legends and myths. It offers seven distinct "ports of call," including the futuristic Port Discovery marina with its StormRider that flies straight into the eye of a storm; the Lost River Delta with its Indiana Jones Adventure; Mermaid Lagoon based on the film *The Little Mermaid;* the Arabian Coast, with its Sinbad's Seven Voyages boat ride; and the American Waterfront with its Tower of Terror. Because DisneySea is unique to Tokyo, I personally think this is the one to see; its installations are a class act.

1–1 Maihama, Urayasu-shi, Chiba. www.tokyodisneyresort.co.jp. © **047/310-0733.** 1-day passport to either Disneyland or DisneySea, including entrance to and use of all attractions, ¥6,900 adults, ¥6,200 seniors, ¥6,000 children 12–17, ¥4,500 children 4–11, free for children 3 and under. Daily 8 or 9am to 10pm, with slightly shorter hours in winter. Station: Maihama, on the JR Keiyo Line from Tokyo Station (1 min.).

Tokyo SkyTree ★★ OBSERVATION DECK   I used to think Tokyo Tower was expensive (p. 127), but then the world's tallest free-standing telecommunications tower (documented by Guinness World Records) took over as Japan's tallest structure, with sky-high admissions to boot. Opened in 2012 to handle digital broadcasting and cellphone transmission, the 634m (2,080-ft.) tower contains two observatories, one at 350m (1,150 ft.) and the highest at 450m (1,476 ft.). Yet despite the steep price and potentially long queues (try to go on a weekday before noon), I have to say I found identifying Tokyo's landmarks from such a lofty vantage challengingly fun, and there are plenty of 360-degree viewing areas that make the hour or so you'll spend here go quickly. For visitors less familiar with the capital's iconic buildings, high-tech touch panels let you explore the cityscape and zoom in on what you're seeing. Other diversions include a cafe in the first observatory and restaurant 634 Musashi (http://restaurant.tokyo-skytree.jp/english; reservations required) at the top, offering fusion Japanese/French cuisine and what is certainly Tokyo's most expansive views. At the tower's base is Solamachi, a complex with 300 more shops and restaurants. If you're in Tokyo only a couple days, I'd spend my time elsewhere. But for people who have been here, done that, this makes for an entertaining new destination. In any case, visible from many areas of Tokyo, SkyTree makes Tokyo Tower seem downright diminutive.

1–32–3 Mukojima, Sumida-ku. www.tokyo-skytree.jp. © **0570/55-0634.** Admission to lower observatory ¥2,060 adults, ¥1,540 children 12–17, ¥930 children 6-11, ¥620 children

4-5; to top observatory an extra ¥1,030, ¥820, ¥510, and ¥310, respectively. Daily 8am–10pm. Station: Oshiage (exit B3, 2 min.), Tokyo SkyTree (2 min.), or Asakusa (15 min.).

ORGANIZED TOURS

With the help of this book and a good map, you should be able to visit Tokyo's major attractions easily on your own. Should you be pressed for time, however, you might consider taking a group tour of Tokyo and its environs offered by the **Japan Travel Bureau** (**JTB;** www.jtb-sunrisetours.jp; ☎ **03/5796-5454**). Day tours may include Tokyo Tower, the Imperial Palace and Ginza districts, Asakusa Sensoji Temple, Meiji Jingu Shrine, and a harbor or river cruise. There are also specialized tours that take in Tsukiji Fish Market or neighborhoods like Akihabara, as well as cultural-themed tours that allow participants to experience such activities as the tea ceremony, making sushi, or dressing up in a kimono. Be warned, however, that tours are very tourist-oriented, do not allow much time for exploration, and are more expensive than touring Tokyo on your own. Prices range from about ¥4,500 for a half-day tour to ¥12,000 or more for a full-day tour (children pay half fare). Tours are easily booked through most hotels and travel agencies like JTB. Although its offerings are not nearly as extensive, **Japan Gray Line** (www.jgl.co.jp/inbound/index.htm; (☎ **03/3595-5939**) also offers a morning, afternoon and full-day tour.

Although they cover less ground, 10 tours offered by the **Tokyo Metropolitan Government** concentrate on specific areas or themes, such as Japanese gardens, Asakusa, or Harajuku. What I like most about these tours is that they are more personable than those above, with a maximum tour group size of only 5 persons. Lasting 2 to 3½ hours, they are conducted mostly on foot or utilize public transportation and vary in price from free (a walking tour of Shinjuku and the food floor of Isetan department store) to ¥3,640 (a tour taking in the Ginza, Hama Rikyu Garden, and Odaiba), plus admission costs of the volunteer guides. Prices may be cheaper for some tours if there's more than one participant. Tours depart from the Tokyo Tourist Information Center in the TMG Building No. 1 in Shinjuku (the same building as the free observatory; see p. 56) at 1pm Monday to Friday (excluding public holidays; some tours depart also at 10am). Preregistration 3 days in advance of the tour is required, and a minimum of one participant must be at least 20 years old. For more information, contact the tourist office (see p. 56, earlier in this chapter) or go to www.gotokyo.org/en/tourists/guideservice/guideservice/index.html.

Volunteer guides are also on hand at the Ueno Green Salon in Ueno Park every Wednesday, Friday, and Sunday for free 90-minute walking tours departing at 10:30am and 1:30pm; and at the Asakusa Culture Tourist Information Center every Saturday and Sunday for 1-hour tours departing at 11am and 1:15pm. No registration is required, but you should arrive 10 minutes beforehand. For more information, call ☎ **03/6280-6710.**

Free guided tours are also offered through www.tokyofreeguide.com, staffed by volunteers ranging from students and housewives to retirees and businesspeople. You're expected to pay for the guide's entrance to museums, meals, and transportation fees if applicable, but you get to choose what you'd like to see; because many of these volunteers work, weekends are the best days to book a tour.

One tour I especially like is a **boat trip on the Sumida River** between Hama Rikyu Garden and Asakusa. Commentary on the 45-minute trip is in both Japanese and English (be sure to pick up the English-language leaflet, too). You'll get descriptions of the 12 bridges you pass along the way and views of Tokyo you'd otherwise miss. Boats depart Hama Rikyu Garden hourly or more frequently between 10:30am and 4:15pm, with the fare to Asakusa costing ¥740 one-way. There are also other cruise routes, including those between Hinode Pier (closest station: Hinode, about a 1-min. walk) and Asakusa (fare: ¥780), Asakusa and Odaiba (fare: ¥1,560), and Hinode Pier and Odaiba (fare: ¥410). For more information, contact the **Tokyo Cruise Ship Co.** (℅ **0120-977311;** www.suijobus.co.jp).

You can also see Tokyo by bike by joining one of four guided **Tokyo Bicycle Tours** (www.tokyobicycletours.com; ℅ **080/3209-9666**). The 4-hour ride, costing ¥5,000 per person, takes in Shibuya, Yoyogi Park, Meiji Jingu Shrine, Harajuku, and Aoyama. See the website for more information.

Finally, for personalized, one-on-one tours of Tokyo, contact **Jun's Tokyo Discovery Tours,** managed by Tokyoite Junko Matsuda, which offers tailored sightseeing trips to Tsukiji, Asakusa, Imperial Palace, Harajuku, Aoyama, Shibuya, Shinjuku, and Yanaka, as well as shopping and personalized trips designed to fit your interests. Tours utilize public transportation and are especially useful if you wish to communicate with shopkeepers and the locals, want to learn more about what you're seeing, or are timid about finding your way on public transportation (if you wish, you'll be met at your hotel). The cost is ¥20,000 for a half day (4 hr.) for up to four adults or a family. Reserve tours at least 3 days in advance (1 week preferred) by e-mail (me2@gb3.so-net.ne.jp), stating the desired tour date and what you'd like to see; messages can also be left at ℅ **090/7734-0079** (if you're calling from abroad, drop the initial 0).

SHOPPING

It won't take you long to become convinced that shopping is the number-one pastime in Tokyo. Women, men, couples, and even entire families go on buying expeditions in their free time, making Sunday the most crowded shopping day of the week—though with today's economic climate, many of them may just be window-shopping. But even those on a budget can shop; 100-Yen discount stores are virtually everywhere.

The Shopping Scene

BEST BUYS   Tokyo is the country's showcase for everything from the latest in camera, computer, or music equipment to original woodblock prints, anime products, and designer fashions. Traditional Japanese crafts and souvenirs that make good buys include toys (both traditional and the latest in technical wizardry), kites, Japanese dolls, carp banners, swords, lacquerware, bamboo baskets, *ikebana* (flower-arranging) accessories, ceramics, pottery, iron tea-kettles, chopsticks, fans, masks, knives, scissors, sake, incense, and silk and cotton kimono. And you don't have to spend a fortune: You can pick up hand-made Japanese paper *(washi)* products, such as lanterns, boxes, stationery, and other souvenirs, for a fraction of what they would cost in import shops in the United States. In Harajuku, stores sell the latest fashion craze at cheap prices, and I can't even count the number of pairs of fun, casual shoes I've bought for a song. Reproductions of famous woodblock prints make great inexpensive gifts, and most items—from pearls to electronic video and audio equipment and even food—can be bought tax-free if you spend over a certain amount in one store (see "Taxes," below).

GREAT SHOPPING AREAS   Another enjoyable aspect of shopping in Tokyo is that specific areas are often devoted to certain goods. **Akihabara** is packed with shops selling the latest in electronics, as well as anime-related items. **Ginza** (station: Ginza) is the chic address for high-end international designer brands and art galleries. **Aoyama** (station: Omotesando) boasts the city's largest concentration of Japanese designer-clothing stores and an ever-increasing number of international names, while nearby **Harajuku** (stations: Harajuku, Meiji-Jingu-mae, or Omotesando) and **Shibuya** (station: Shibuya) are the places to go for youthful, fun, and inexpensive fashions.

The best place to shop for items related to cooking and serving is **Kappabashi-dougugai Dori** (station: Tawaramachi), popularly known as Kappabashi; this is Japan's largest wholesale area for cookware, but most stores sell to individual shoppers as well. There are approximately 150 specialty stores here selling everything a restaurant needs, including sukiyaki pots, woks, lunch boxes, pots and pans, aprons, knives, china, lacquerware, rice cookers, plastic food (the kind you see in restaurant display cases), *noren* (Japanese curtains), and disposable wooden chopsticks in bulk. Stores are closed on Sunday.

TAXES   An 8% consumption tax is included in the price of marked goods, but all major department stores and tourist shops will refund the tax to foreign visitors if the total purchases in 1 day in any one store amount to more than ¥10,001 (excluding tax) for general items like household goods, clothing, and accessories. Consumables—including foods, beverages, and cosmetics—totaling more than ¥5,001 are also eligible for the tax refund. Note, however, that stores generally charge a service fee equivalent to 1.1% of your total tax-free purchases, and you must present your passport. For more information, see "Fast Facts" in chapter 12.

Shopping from A to Z
ANIME & MANGA
Although **Akihabara** has long boasted Japan's largest concentration of electronics shops, in the past decade it has also gained a reputation as *the* place to shop for manga (Japanese comic books and graphic novels) and items related

to anime (Japanese animation) and cosplay (costume play). One of the best anime/manga chain stores in Japan is **Mandarake,** which first opened in 1987 as a second-hand shop for manga. It's shop in Akihabara, about 4 minutes from JR Akihabara Station at 3–11–2 Soto-Kanda (www.mandarake.co.jp; ✆ **03/3252-7007**), offers eight floors of both new and second-hand goods, including pop and vintage figurines, video games, manga, and posters (some products are definitely X-rated; even the website is an eye-opener). There's also a branch in Shibuya, deep underground beneath Shibuya BEAM on Inokashira Dori, 31–2 Udagawacho (✆ **03/3477-0777;** station: Shibuya). Serious shoppers, however, will want to make a pilgrimage to **Nakano Broadway Mall** at 5–52–15 Nakano (✆ **03/3388-7004**), a 5-minute walk from the north exit of Nakano Station and known throughout the country as *otaku* (geek) heaven for its slew of shops dedicated to both new and retro pop goods from Japan and overseas, including software, games, manga, figures, and anima and cosplay fare. Mandarake (✆ **03/3228-0007**) is the biggest player here, and the biggest in the world, with 16 different departments spread throughout the mall, each specializing in particular products, from manga and cosplay clothing to CDs of anima songs and figurines. All Mandarake stores are open daily from noon to 8pm.

Back in Akihabara, **Radio Kaikan,** just outside the Denkigai exit of JR Akihabara Station at 1–15–16 Soto-Kanda (www.akihabara-radiokaikan. co.jp) offers 10 floors of anime-related goods, including figurines, trading cards, manga, capsule toys, dolls and doll clothing (for adults, not kids), posters, DVDs, and other items from 10am to 8pm daily. It's also worth popping into **Don Quijote** (p. 142), on the main drag of Chuo Dori. It has to be seen to appreciate its jumble of everyday goods too numerous to mention, including maid costumes and even an @home maid cafe (I don't even want to get into why these are so popular) on the fifth floor. If maid cafes are why you're here, however, there are more **@home Cafés** in the nearby Mitsuwa Building, 1–11–4 Soto-Kanda (www.cafe-athome.com; ✆ **03/3255-2808**), with maid cafes on the 4th, 6th and 7th floors and open Monday to Friday 11:30am to 10pm and Saturday and Sunday 10:30am to 10pm.

ANTIQUES & CURIOS

In recent years, it has become a buyer-beware market in Japan, with fake antiques produced in China infiltrating the Japanese market. You shouldn't have any problems with the reputable dealers listed here, but if you're buying an expensive piece, be sure to ask whether there are any papers of authenticity.

In addition to the listings here, Tokyo's outdoor **flea markets** (see later in this section) are also good places to browse.

Antique Mall Ginza ★★★ Japanese, European, and some American antiques, collectibles, and odds and ends crowd two floors of Tokyo's largest antiques mall, where you could spend hours browsing among furniture, jewelry, watches, porcelain, pottery, dolls, *netsuke,* fans, scrolls, glassware, kimono, folk art, and more. Around the corner is an annex, but it's only one tiny room. Open Thursday to Tuesday 11am to 7pm. 1–13–1 Ginza, Chuo-ku. www.antiques-jp.

com. $\copyright$ **03/3535-2115.** Station: Ginza-Itchome, Kyobashi, or Takaracho (3 min.). Btw. Chuo Dori and Showa Dori.

Ginza Antiques ★   While not nearly as extensive as the Antique Mall Ginza (see above), the dozen or so stalls here on the second floor of the Ginza 5 Building (located under an expressway) offer a variety of high-end antiques, including porcelain, furniture, dolls, swords, kimono, and other treasures from Japan and Europe, interspersed with stalls selling crafts, clothing, and jewelry. Open daily 10 or 11am to 7 or 8pm (some stalls are closed on Sun). 5–1 Ginza, Chuo-ku. $\copyright$ **03/5572-5559.** Station: Ginza (exit C1, 1 min.) or JR Yurakucho (2 min.). On Harumi Dori, across from the Hankyu Men's Tokyo department store.

CRAFTS & TRADITIONAL JAPANESE PRODUCTS

If you want to shop for traditional Japanese folk crafts in a festival-like atmosphere, nothing beats **Nakamise Dori** (station: Asakusa), a pedestrian lane leading to Sensoji Temple in Asakusa. It's lined with stall after stall selling souvenirs galore, from hairpins worn by geisha to T-shirts, fans, umbrellas, toy swords, and dolls. Most are open daily from 10am to 6pm; some may close 1 day a week. The side streets surrounding Nakamise Dori, including Demboin Dori and a covered pedestrian lane stretching from both sides of Nakamise Dori, are also good bets.

Another good place to search for traditional crafts are **flea markets,** as well as **department stores,** which usually have sections devoted to ceramics, pottery, bambooware, flower-arranging accessories, and kimono.

Japan Traditional Crafts Aoyama Square (Zenkoku Dentoteki Kogeihina) ★★★   Established to promote the country's artisans, this beautiful shop is a great introduction to both traditional and contemporary Japanese design, with explanations in English about the products and where they're from. It sells various top-quality crafts from all over Japan on a rotating basis, so there are always new items on hand. Crafts for sale may include woodblock prints, pottery, lacquerware, ceramics, textiles, paper products, calligraphy brushes, fans, metalwork, knives, furniture, and sometimes even stone lanterns or Buddhist family altars. Be sure to look in the sliding drawers along the wall, as these also hold prints and other works of art. Prices are high, but rightfully so. Craftsmen are sometimes on hand, demonstrating their techniques. Open daily 11am to 7pm. 8–1–22 Akasaka. www.kougeihin.jp. $\copyright$ **03/5787-1301.** Station: Aoyama-Itchome (exit 4 north, 5 min.). On Aoyama Dori, between the Akasaka Post Office and the Canadian embassy.

Oriental Bazaar ★★   If you have time for only one souvenir shop in Tokyo, this should be it. This is the city's best-known and largest souvenir/crafts store, selling products at reasonable prices and offering three floors of souvenir and gift items, including cotton *yukata,* kimono (new and used), woodblock prints, jewelry boxes, fans, chopsticks, Imari chinaware, sake sets, Japanese dolls, pearls, books on Japan, and antique furniture. This store will also send purchases home for you (via airmail, although it also works with a shipping company should you purchase furniture) and even accepts U.S.

dollars and euro. Open Friday to Wednesday 10am to 7pm. 5–9–13 Jingumae, Shibuya-ku. www.orientalbazaar.co.jp. ✆ **03/3400-3933.** Station: Meiji-Jingumae (3 min.), Harajuku (4 min.), or Omotesando (5 min.). On Omotesando Dori in Harajuku; look for its shrinelike facade of orange and green.

Wa Space ★ The space is modest but the mission is big: to showcase the best in Japanese design and thereby promote the arts. With an inventory that changes constantly and with special exhibitions highlighting particular artists, it offers a variety of housewares, decorative art, and other objects that are as wonderful to look at as they are to use, with items for sale that may include glassware, sake cups, pottery, lacquerware, incense, handmade candles, cloth covers for iPads, trivets, and pillows. It's a big difficult to find, so check out directions on the website. Open Tuesday to Saturday 11am to 6pm. 4–3–27 Akasaka, Minato-ku. www.the-wa-group.com/space. ✆ **03/4520-9335.** Station: Akasaka (exit 1, 3 min.) or Akasaka-mitsuke (exit 10, 6 min.). On a small side street beside Tomod's drugstore, on the left side down a bamboo-lined pathway.

DEPARTMENT STORES

Japanese department stores are institutions in themselves. Usually enormous, well designed, and chock-full of merchandise, they have about everything you can imagine, including museums and art galleries, travel agencies, restaurants, grocery markets, and, on the rooftop, playgrounds, greenhouses or even shrines. You could easily spend an entire day in a department store—eating, attending cultural exhibitions, planning your next vacation, exchanging money, and, well, shopping.

One of the most wonderful aspects of the Japanese department store is the **courteous service.** If you arrive at a store as its doors open at 10 or 10:30am, you'll witness a daily rite: Lined up at the entrance are staff members who bow in welcome. Some Japanese shoppers arrive just before opening time so as not to miss this favorite ritual. Sales clerks are everywhere, ready to help you. In some stores, you don't even have to go to the cash register once you've made your choice; just hand over the product, along with your money, to the sales clerk, who will return with your change, your purchase neatly wrapped, and an *"Arigato gozaimashita"* ("Thank you very much"). Many department stores will also ship your purchases home for you, send them to your hotel, or hold them until you're ready to leave the store. A day spent in a Japanese department store could spoil you for the rest of your life.

Most department stores include **boutiques** by famous Japanese and international fashion designers, like Issey Mkiiyake, Rei Kawakubo (creator of Comme des Garçons), Tsumori Chisato, Yohji Yamamoto, Takeo Kikuchi, Vivienne Westwood, Armani, and Paul Smith, as well as a department devoted to the kimono. Near the **kimono department** may also be the section devoted to **traditional crafts,** including *ikebana* vases, pottery, and lacquerware. Many famous **restaurants** maintain branches in department stores, but not to be missed is the basement (nicknamed a *depachika*, which is a combination of *depa*—from department store—and *chika,* meaning basement), where you'll find one or two levels devoted to **foodstuffs:** fresh fish, produce, green tea, sake, prepared snacks and dinners, and delectable pastries. There are often free samples of food; if you're hungry, walking through the food department could do nicely for a snack.

To find out what's where, stop by the store's information booth located on the ground floor near the front entrance and ask for the floor-by-floor English-language pamphlet. Be sure, too, to ask about **sales** on the promotional floor—you never know what bargains you may chance upon. Department stores also have **tax-free counters** where you can get an immediate cash refund on taxes paid for items totaling more than a specific amount (see p. 338, in chapter 12), so make sure you bring your passport.

Isetan ★★★   With a history stretching 130 years, Isetan is a favorite among foreigners living in Tokyo. Part of the Isetan-Mitsukoshi conglomerate, it has a good line of conservative work clothes, as well as contemporary and fashionable styles, including designer goods by Issey Miyake, Yohji Yamamoto, Comme des Garçons, Marc Jacobs, Junya Watanabe, and Tsumori Chisato, as well as great kimono section along with all the traditional accessories (*obi*, shoes, purses). The tax-free counter is on the 6th floor, but since both the 5th and 6th floors were undergoing renovation at the time of going to press, ask the information counter for an update. On the seventh floor are branches of well-known restaurants offering grilled eel, tonkatsu, sushi, and Western food, including **Ten-ichi,** specializing in tempura (p. 87). Its basement food hall is legendary, with its dessert and massive chocolate sections an especially illuminating commentary on Japan's obsession with food. Following a recent trend wooing male shoppers, a nine-floor annex behind the main building caters entirely to men (there's even a golf school on its roof). Open daily 10:30am to 8pm. http://isetan.mistore.jp/store/shinjuku/foreign_customer_service/index.html. 3–14–1 Shinjuku, Shinjuku-ku. © **03/3352-1111.** Station: Shinjuku San-chome (1 min.) or Shinjuku (east exit, 6 min.). On Shinjuku Dori, east of Shinjuku Station.

Matsuya Ginza ★★★   This is one of my favorite department stores in Tokyo; if I were buying a wedding gift, Matsuya, in business 145 years, is one of the first places I'd look. It has a good selection of Japanese folk crafts items, kitchenware, kimono, and beautifully designed contemporary household goods, in addition to the usual designer clothes and accessories ("queen" sizes are on the sixth floor). I always make a point of stopping by the seventh floor's Design Collection, which displays items from around the world selected by the Japan Design Committee as examples of fine design, from the Alessi teapot to Braun razors. Two basement floors are devoted to food. Also in the basement is the tax-free counter (Isetan refunds the entire 8% and does not charge a service fee), where there's also free Wi-Fi and currency-exchange machines. Open daily 10am to 8pm. There's a branch in Asakusa at 1–41–1 Hanakawado (© **03/3842-1111;** daily 10am–7:30pm). 3–6–1 Ginza, Chuo-ku. www.matsuya.com. © **03/3567-1211.** Station: Ginza (2 min.). On Chuo Dori, just a long block north of Ginza 4–chome Crossing.

Mitsukoshi ★★★   This Nihombashi department store is one of Japan's oldest and grandest, founded in 1673 by the Mitsui family as a kimono store.

In 1683, it became the first store in the world to deal only in cash sales; it was also one of the first stores in Japan to display goods on shelves rather than have merchants fetch bolts of cloth for each customer, as was the custom of the time. Today, housed in a building dating from 1935, it remains one of Tokyo's loveliest department stores, with a beautiful and stately Renaissance-style facade and an entrance guarded by two bronze lions, replicas of the lions in Trafalgar Square. The store carries many name-brand boutiques, from Chanel to Salvatore Ferragamo. Its kimono, by the way, are still hot items. The tax-free counter is in the annex. Open daily 10am to 7pm (basement food floors and the first three floors open until 8pm). A branch, located at Ginza 4–chome Crossing (✆ **03/3562-1111;** open daily 10am–8pm), is popular with young shoppers. 1–4–1 Nihombashi Muromachi, Chuo-ku. http://mitsukoshi.mistore.jp/store/nihombashi/fcs/english/index.html. ✆ **03/3241-3311.** Station: Mitsukoshimae (1 min.).

Takashimaya ★★★ This department store has always provided stiff competition for Mitsukoshi, with a history just as long. It was founded as a kimono shop in Kyoto during the Edo Period and opened in Tokyo in 1933. Today it's one of the city's most attractive department stores, with a Renaissance-style building and gloved elevator operators whisking customers to eight floors of shopping and dining. Naturally, it features boutiques by such famous designers as Chanel, Louis Vuitton, Gucci, Issey Miyake, and more. Its sale of used kimono draws huge crowds. Its tax-refund counter, formerly in the basement, has moved to the second floor. Open daily 10am to 8pm. A branch, **Takashimaya Shinjuku,** 5–24–2 Sendaygaya, Shinjuku (✆ **03/53610111;** open daily 10am–8pm; station: Shinjuku), boasts 14 floors of clothing and restaurants (lower floors target affluent seniors, while upper floors appeal to younger shoppers and families; petite and "queen-size" clothing are on the sixth floor); here, too, is **Tokyu Hands,** with everything imaginable for the home hobbyist (p. 143), and Kinokuniya bookstore with English-language books on the sixth floor. 2–4–1 Nihombashi (on Chuo Dori Ave.), Chuo-ku. www.takashimaya.co.jp/tokyo/store_information/index.html. ✆ **03/3211-4111.** Station: Nihombashi (1 min.).

ELECTRONICS

There are several areas around town known for their electronics stores, especially just west of **Shinjuku Station,** where Yodobashi dominates with several stores devoted to electronics. The largest concentration of electronics and electrical-appliance shops in Japan, however, is in an area of Tokyo called **Akihabara,** also known simply as Akiba and centered on Chuo Dori (station: Akihabara). This is a must-see simply for its sheer size, with hundreds of multilevel stores, shops, and stalls. Even if you don't buy anything, it's great fun walking around. Most stores and stalls are open-fronted and painted in eye-catching colors. Salespeople yell out their wares, trying to get customers to look at cellular phones, computers, digital cameras, TVs, calculators, watches, and rice cookers. This is the best place to see the latest models of everything electronic; it's an educational experience in itself.

If you intend to buy, however, it pays to do some comparison shopping before you leave home so that you can spot a deal when you see one, as you can probably find these products just as cheaply, or even more cheaply, there. On the other hand, you may be able to pick up something that's unavailable back home. Make sure, too, that whatever you purchase is made for export—that is, with instructions in English, an international warranty, and the proper electrical connectors. All the larger stores have duty-free floors where products are made for export. Most shops are open daily from about 10am to 8pm or later.

Bic Camera ★★ This chain electronics store has about 40 shops in Japan, including its main shop in Ikebukuro, several locations in Shinjuku, and Shibuya. But this eight-floor store in Yurakucho is the largest, offering not only single-lens reflex, large and medium format, and digital cameras (plus all the accessories, including that all-important selfie extender), but also computers, cellphones, camcorders, watches, eyeglasses, toys, home appliances, sporting goods, and much more. Note, however, that it caters primarily to Japanese; English-speaking sales clerks are scarce, and export models are limited (duty-free overseas models are in the second basement). Ask for the English-language brochure and, if you're buying sensitive equipment, make sure it will work outside Japan and comes with English-language instructions. Open daily 10am to 10pm. 1–11–1 Yurakucho, Chiyoda-ku. www.biccamera.co.jp ✆ **03/5221-1112.** Station: Yurakucho (1 min.), Hibiya (exit D4, 3 min.), Ginza (6 min.).

Yodobashi Akiba ★★★ This is Akihabara's largest store, offering a staggering number of electronic-related goods such as phones, cameras, computers, printers, TVs, microwaves, vacuum cleaners, hairdryers, and more. But it also offers a slew of other leisure-related items as well, including bicycles, games, luggage, and watches, plus two dozen restaurants on the eighth floor. Yodobashi is found also in west Shinjuku, with a main shop and many branches specializing in various goods like watches or games. Open daily 9:30am to 10pm. 1–1 Hanaoka-cho, Chiyoda-ku. ✆ **03/5209-1010.** Station: Akihabara (1 min.). Just east of JR Akihabara Station.

FASHION

The **department stores** listed earlier are good places to check out the latest trends. For international designers, chic boutiques abound in **Ginza** and neighboring **Marunouchi.** Otherwise, **Harajuku** and **Shibuya** are the places to go for hundreds of small shops selling inexpensive designer knockoffs, as well as fashion department stores—multistoried buildings filled with concessions of various designers and labels, like Shibuya 109 selling clothing and accessories and packed with teenagers.

La Forêt ★★★ This is not only the largest store in Harajuku but also one of the most fashionable, appealing mostly to teenage and 20-something shoppers. Young and upcoming Japanese designers are here as well as established names, in boutiques spread on several floors. In addition to men's and women's fashions there are also shops selling jewelry, shoes, handbags, and other accessories. There's so much to see—from pink frilly dresses to Goth—you can easily kill a few hours here. Note, however, that not all shops offer tax-free shopping, and since each shop is its own entity, you can't combine purchases to qualify for the tax refund. Open daily 11am to 9pm. 1–11–6 Jingumae, Shibuya-ku.

www.laforet.ne.jp. © **03/3475-0411.** Station: Meiji-Jingumae (1 min.) or Harajuku (3 min.). On Meiji Dori, just off Harajuku's main intersection of Omotesando Dori and Meiji Dori.

Uniqlo ★★   Having seemingly taken the world by storm, with stores in the US, UK, Australia, Germany, Russia and throughout Asia, this store specializes in inexpensive, basic clothing (think: Japanese version of Gap) and has 40-some outlets in Tokyo alone. This is its flagship, with 12 stories offering T-shirts, jeans, socks, shirts, and other clothing for the whole family. Its T-shirts on the ground floor are arranged according to color in an eye-catching display that covers a whole palette of choices. Connected to Uniqlo in the back is Dover Street Market, with six small floors offering men's and women's fashions by Comme des Garçons, A Bathing Ape, Junya Watanabe, and other designers. Open daily 11am to 9pm. 6–9–5 Ginza, Chuo-ku. © **03/6252-5161.** Station: Ginza (2 min.). On Chuo Dori.

Designer Boutiques

Ginza is home to international designer names, including Prada, Bally, Cartier, Chanel, Christian Dior, and Louis Vuitton. Nearby, on Marunouchi Naka Dori, there are outlets for Hermes, TOD's, Tiffany & Co., Armani, and Issey Miyake, among others.

For top Japanese designers, the blocks between Omotesando Crossing and the Nezu Museum in **Aoyama** (station: Omotesando, 2 min.) are the Rodeo Drive of Japan. Even if you can't buy here (steep prices for most pocketbooks), a stroll is de rigueur for clothes hounds and those interested in design. Most shops are open daily from 11am to 8pm. **Issey Miyake** (www.issey miyake.com; © **03/3423-1408**), on the left side as you walk from Aoyama Dori, offers two floors of cool, spacious displays of Miyake's interestingly structured and colorful designs for men and women. His very popular Pleats Please line is next door (© **03/5772-7750**). Across the street is **Comme des Garçons** (www.comme-des-garcons.com; (© **03/3406-3951**), Rei Kawakubo's showcase for her daring—and constantly evolving—men's and women's designs (even her shop is constantly evolving). The goddess of Japanese fashion and one of the few females in the business when she started, Kawakubo has remained on the cutting edge of design for more than 3 decades. Farther down the street on the right is **Yohji Yamamoto** (www.yohjiyamamoto.co.jp; © **03/3409-6006**), where Yamamoto's unique, classically wearable clothes are sparingly hung, flaunting the avant-garde interior space. Of the many non-Japanese designers to have invaded this trendy neighborhood, none stands out as much as **Prada** (© **03/6418-0400**), a bubble of convex/concave windows on the right side of the street. Most shops are open daily 11am to 8pm.

Kimono

Chicago, on Omotesando Dori in Harajuku (© **03/3409-5017;** station: Meiji-Jingumae or Harajuku), is a good place for used kimono. It stocks hundreds of affordable used kimono, cotton *yukata* (casual kimono), and *obi* (sashes) back in the far left corner of the basement shop, past the used American clothes. It's open daily from 11am to 8pm. The nearby **Oriental Bazaar** (p. 135) also has a decent selection of new and used kimono at affordable prices, including elaborate wedding kimono.

In addition, department stores sell new kimono, notably **Takashimaya** and **Mitsukoshi** in Nihombashi and **Isetan** in Shinjuku. They also hold sales for rental wedding kimono. **Flea markets** are also good for used kimono and *yukata*.

MARKETS

Flea markets are good places to shop for antiques as well as for delightful junk. You can pick up secondhand kimono at very reasonable prices, as well as kitchenware, vases, cast-iron teapots, small chests, woodblock prints, dolls, household items, and odds and ends. (Don't expect to find any good buys in furniture.) The markets usually begin as early as dawn or 6am and last until 3 or 4pm or so, but go early if you want to pick up bargains. Bargaining is expected. Note that since most markets are outdoors, they tend to be canceled if it rains.

Hanazono Shrine ★, 5–17–3 Shinjuku (✆ **03/3200-3093**), near the Yasukuni Dori/Meiji Dori intersection east of Shinjuku Station (Shinjuku Sanchome Station, 4 min.), has a flea market every Sunday from about 8am to 2pm (except in May and Nov, due to festivals).

Nogi Shrine ★, a 1-minute walk from Nogizaka Station at 8–11–27 Akasaka (✆ **03/3478-3001**), has an antiques flea market from dawn to about 3pm the fourth Sunday of each month except January and February. It has a lovely setting; the shrine commemorates General Nogi and his wife, both of whom committed suicide on September 13, 1912, to follow the Meiji emperor into the afterlife. Their simple home and stable are on shrine grounds.

Yasukuni Shrine ★★, a 4-minute walk from Kudanshita Station at 3–1–1 Kudanshita (✆ **03/3261-8326**), holds a flea market every Sunday from 6am to about 3pm on the long walkway to this very famous shrine (see p. 111 for information on the shrine and its military museum).

Oedo Antique Market ★★★, beside Yurakucho Station in the courtyard of the Tokyo International Forum, 3–5–1 Marunouchi (www.antique-market.jp; ✆ **03/6407-6011**), claims to be the largest outdoor antiques market in Japan, with about 250 vendors (it has also taken away vendors from Tokyo's other flea markets). Held the first and third Sunday of the month (check the website, as dates can change) from 9am to 4pm, it features Western antiques (at highly inflated prices), as well as Japanese glassware, furniture, ceramics, furniture, kimono, woodblock prints, and odds and ends. If you hit only one flea market, this should be it. Once a month on irregular dates, it stages a flea market also in Yoyogi Park, with about 180 vendors selling antiques and crafts.

Ameya Yokocho ★★ (also referred to as Ameyoko, Ameyokocho or Ameyacho) is the closest thing Tokyo has to a permanent flea market. Occupying a long but narrow area near Ueno Park that runs along and underneath the elevated tracks of the JR Yamanote Line between Ueno and Okachimachi stations, it has stall after stall selling vegetables and discounted items ranging from cosmetics and handbags to tennis shoes, watches, and casual clothes. The scene retains something of the *shitamachi* spirit of old Tokyo. Although housewives have been coming here for years, young Japanese have also discovered it a good bargain spot for youthful fashions and accessories like baseball caps. Some shops close on Wednesdays, but hours are usually daily from 10am to 7pm; early evening is the most crowded time. Don't even think of coming here on a holiday—it's a standstill pedestrian traffic jam.

VARIETY STORES

The **department stores** listed earlier also sell home furnishings, including bedding, kitchenware, lighting, and decor.

Daiso ★★   The largest chain of 100-Yen shops in Japan (comparable to dollar stores in the U.S.), with more than 2,500 locations in the country as well as 700 stores abroad, this four-story shop is also one of the better discount stores, offering mostly its own brand goods, purchased directly from manufacturers (many of which are in China). Items, priced mostly at ¥100 or multiples thereof, include kitchenware, tableware, cosmetics, office supplies, candy, and other household goods and daily necessities, making it a good place to shop for cheap souvenirs such as chopsticks, plastic lunchboxes, and *ikebana* (flower-arranging) accessories. This place is so popular, there's usually a long queue at checkout. Open daily 10am to 9pm. 1–19–24 Jingumae, Shibuya-ku. www.daisoglobal.com. ✆ **03/5775-9641.** Station: Harajuku (north exit, 3 min.) or Meiji-Jingumae (4 min.). On Takeshita Dori, about midway down.

Don Quijote (ドン・キホーテ) ★   Teenagers don't seem to mind the jumble of everyday goods offered here, but I find it so packed along its narrow aisles that it makes me feel claustrophobic. It offers household goods and gadgets, kitchen appliances, sporting goods, electronics, clothing, cosmetics, toiletries, party items, food, alcohol, and much, much more, including cosplay fare such as maid costumes (a perennial favorite). It's hard to come up with anything Don Quijote *doesn't* sell, but strangely, I never find anything I'm compelled to buy. You might, however, want to check out the @home Maid Café on the 5th floor, games arcade on the 7th floor, or Color Yellow nail salon on the ground floor, where staff decorate your nails with anime characters or any design of your choosing. It's open daily from 10am to 5am. Known for its discounted prices and late hours, Don Quijote has almost 40 branches in the Tokyo area, including ones on Yasukuni Dori at 1–16–5 Kabuki-cho (✆ **03/5291-9211;** station: Shinjuku) and in Roppongi, on the left side of Gaien-Higashi Dori if walking from Roppongi Crossing toward Tokyo Tower, at 3–14–10 Roppongi (✆ **03/5786-0811;** station: Roppongi), both open a mind-boggling 24 hours. 4–3–3 Soto-Kanda, Chiyoka-ku. www.donki.com. ✆ **03/5298-5411.** Station: Akihabara (3 min.). On Chuo Dori.

Loft   Loft is Seibu's store for the young homeowner, including tableware (chopsticks, *bento* boxes, sake cups, and so forth, on the third floor), cookware, glassware, bathroom accessories, bed linens, office supplies, mobile phone accessories, watches, cosmetics (the choice in face masks alone is bewildering), stationery, games, and more. Don't miss the fifth-floor variety goods department with character items, wind-up toys, party goods, including some weird costumes and small plastic female figurines designed to hang from the side of a glass, and gag gifts. Open daily 10am to 9pm. 21–1 Udagawa-cho, Shibuya-ku. ✆ **03/3462-3807.** Station: Shibuya (Hachiko exit, 4 min.). Behind Seibu B.

Muji ★★★ Muji was founded in 1980 as a backlash to conspicuous consumption prevalent in bubble-era Japan. Today, with shops around the world, it's known for its minimalist yet hip cotton clothing in basic colors, as well as well-designed housewares at affordable prices, many of them made from recycled materials at affordable prices. Futon, bed linens, kitchen appliances, tableware, storage units, furniture (think rattan and unbleached woods), clothing, cosmetics, and other practical goods are offered at more than 280 locations in Japan, but this is its head store. It has a Muji Meal upstairs offering inexpensive and healthy meals; there's a Loft (see above) in the same building. Open Monday to Saturday 10:30am to 9:30pm and Sunday and holidays 10:30am to 9pm. 3–8–3 Marunouchi, Chiyoda-ku. www.muji.com. ✆ **03/5208-8241.** Station: Yurakucho (2 min.) or Ginza (4 min.).

Tokyu Hands ★★★ Billing itself the "Creative Life Store," Tokyu Hands, part of the Tokyu chain, is a huge department store for the serious homeowner and hobbyist, with everything from travel accessories (like padded eye masks), *noren* (doorway curtains), beauty products (including wigs), chopsticks, suitcases, miniature Shinkansen models, pet accessories, and kitchen knives, to equipment and materials for do-it-yourselfers and hobbyists, like paper for repairing shoji. If there's a practical Japanese product you've decided you can't live without (lunchbox? bathroom slippers? hanging laundry rack?), this is a good place to look. Open daily 10am to 8:30pm. You'll also find Tokyu Hands at 1–28–10 Higashi Ikebukuro beside the Sunshine City Building (✆ **03/3980-6111;** station: Higashi Ikebukuro or Ikebukuro) and in the Takashimaya Shinjuku complex (✆ **03/5361-3111;** station: Shinjuku). 12–18 Udagawacho, Shibuya-ku. www.tokyu-hands.co.jp/en/index.html. ✆ **03/5489-5111.** Station: Shibuya (Hachiko exit, 6 min.). At the top of Inokashira Dori.

ENTERTAINMENT & NIGHTLIFE

By day, Tokyo's sprawl can make it seem monotonous and colorless. Come dusk, however, Tokyo comes into its own. The drabness fades, the city blossoms into a profusion of giant neon lights and billboards, and its streets fill with millions of overworked Japanese out to have a good time. If you ask me, Tokyo at night is one of the craziest cities in the world, a city that never gives up and never sleeps. Entertainment districts are as crowded at 3am as they are at 10pm, with many establishments open until the first subways start running after 5am. Whether it's jazz, gay bars, dance clubs, or mania that you're searching for, Tokyo has them all.

GETTING TO KNOW THE SCENE Tokyo has several nightlife districts spread throughout the city, each with its own atmosphere, price range, and clientele. Most famous are probably **Ginza, Kabuki-cho** in Shinjuku, and **Roppongi.** Before visiting any of the locales suggested below, be sure to just walk around one of these neighborhoods and absorb the atmosphere. The streets will be crowded, the neon lights will be overwhelming, and you never know what you might discover on your own.

The most popular nightlife spots are **drinking establishments,** where the vast majority of Japan's office workers, college students, and expatriates go for an evening out. These places include Western-style bars as well as Japanese-style watering holes, called *nomi-ya* (literally "drinking place") or *izakaya*, a Japanese-style pub also serving food. *Yakitori-ya,* restaurant-bars that serve *yakitori* and other snacks, are included in this group. Dancing and live-music venues are also popular with young Tokyoites. At the low end of the spectrum are Tokyo's topless bars, strip shows, massage parlors, and porn shops, with the largest concentration of such places in Shinjuku's **Kabuki-cho District.**

A chic and expensive shopping area by day, **Ginza** transforms itself into a dazzling entertainment district of restaurants, bars, and first-grade hostess bars at night. It's the most sophisticated of Tokyo's nightlife districts and can also be one of the most expensive. However, because Ginza has great restaurants and several hotels, I've included some reasonably priced recommendations for a drink if you happen to find yourself here after dinner. The cheapest way to absorb the atmosphere in Ginza is simply to wander about, particularly around **Namiki Dori** and its side streets.

In **Shinjuku,** northeast of Shinjuku Station, is **Kabuki-cho,** which undoubtedly has the craziest nightlife in all of Tokyo, with block after block of strip joints, massage parlors, pornography shops, peep shows, love hotels, bars, restaurants, and, as the night wears on, lots of drunk revelers. A world of its own, it's sleazy, chaotic, crowded, vibrant, and fairly safe. Despite its name, Shinjuku's primary night hot spot has nothing to do with *kabuki,* though at one time, there was a plan to bring some culture to the area by introducing a *kabuki* theater. The plan never materialized but the name stuck. Although Kabuki-cho used to be the domain of businessmen out on the town, nowadays young Japanese, including college-age men and women, have claimed parts of it as their own, adding inexpensive eating and drinking venues to the mix.

The best thing to do in Shinjuku is to simply walk about. In the glow of neon light, you'll pass everything from smoke-filled restaurants to hawkers trying to get you to step inside so they can part you from your money. If you're looking for strip joints, topless or bottomless coffee shops, peep shows, or porn, I leave you to your own devices, but you certainly won't have any problems finding them. Just be sure you know what you're getting into; your bill may end up much higher than you bargained for.

A word of **warning** for women traveling alone: Forgo the experience of strolling around Kabuki-cho. The streets are crowded and therefore relatively safe, but you may not feel comfortable with so many inebriated men stumbling around. If there are two of you, however, go for it. I took my mother to Kabuki-cho for a spin around the neon, and we escaped relatively unscathed. You're also fine walking alone to any of my recommended restaurants.

About a 5-minute walk east of Kabuki-cho, just west of Hanazono Shrine, is a smaller district called **Goruden Gai,** which is "Golden Guy" mispronounced. It's a warren of tiny alleyways leading past even tinier bars, each consisting of just a counter and a few chairs. Although many thought Goruden Gai would succumb to land-hungry developers in the 1980s, the economic recession brought a stay of execution and now Goruden Gai has experienced a revival, with more than 200 tiny drinking dens lining the tiny streets. Still, it occupies such expensive land that I still fear for the life of this tiny enclave, one of Tokyo's most fascinating.

A 5-minute walk farther east is **Shinjuku Ni-chome** (pronounced "knee-chomay"). With 300-some bars, lounges, dance clubs, and shops, it's the largest gay-bar district in Japan, if not all of Asia. Its lively street scene of mostly gays and some straights of all ages (but mostly young) make this one of Tokyo's most vibrant nightlife districts. It's here that I was once taken to a host bar featuring young men in crotchless pants. The clientele included both gay men and groups of young, giggling office girls. That place has since closed down, but Shinjuku is riddled with other spots bordering on the absurd.

To Tokyo's younger crowd, **Roppongi** is one of the city's most fashionable places to hang out. It's also a favorite with the foreign community, including models, business types, English-language teachers, and tourists staying in Roppongi's posh hotels. Some Tokyoites complain that Roppongi is too crowded, too crass, and too commercialized (and has too many foreigners). However, for the casual visitor, Roppongi offers an excellent opportunity to see what's new and hot in the capital city and is easy to navigate because nightlife activity is so concentrated. There is one huge **caveat,** however: Roppongi's concentration of foreigners has also attracted the unscrupulous, with reports of spiked drinks causing patrons to pass out, only to awaken hours later to find their credit cards missing or fraudulently charged for huge amounts. In other words, never leave your drinks unattended, and you're best off following the buddy system.

The center of Roppongi is **Roppongi Crossing** (the intersection of Roppongi Dori and Gaien-Higashi Dori), at the corner of which sits the Almond Coffee Shop with its pink flags and decor. The shop has mediocre coffee and desserts at inflated prices, but the sidewalk in front is the number-one meeting spot in Roppongi.

If you need directions, there's a conveniently located *koban* (police box) catty-corner from the Almond Coffee Shop and next to a bank. It has a big map of the Roppongi area showing the address system, and someone is always there to help.

EXTRA CHARGES & TAXES One more thing you should be aware of is the **"table charge"** imposed on customers by some bars (especially *nomiya*) and many cocktail lounges. Included in the table charge is usually a small snack—maybe nuts, chips, or a vegetable; for this reason, some locales call it an *otsumami,* or snack charge. At any rate, the charge is usually between ¥300 and ¥500 per person. Some establishments levy a table charge only after a certain time in the evening; others may add it only if you don't order food from the menu. If you're not sure and it matters to you, be sure to ask before you order anything. Remember, too, that there's an 8% consumption tax, though some menus already include it in their prices. Some higher-end establishments, especially nightclubs, hostess bars, and dance clubs, will also add a service charge ranging anywhere from 10% to 20%.

Keep an eye out for *Metropolis* (www.
metropolisjapan.com), a free weekly that
carries a nightlife section covering concerts, theaters, and events and is available
at bars, restaurants, and other venues
around town. The *Japan Times* and *Daily
Yomiuri* also have entertainment sections. For an online rundown of what's
happening at Tokyo's hundreds of venues, live houses and clubs every week,
check out www.tokyogigguide.com.

GETTING TICKETS If you're staying in a higher-end hotel, the concierge or guest-relations manager can usually get tickets for you. Otherwise, you can head to the theater or hall itself. An easier way is to go through one of many ticket services available such as **Ticket PIA;** ask your hotel concierge for the one nearest you. Lawson and Family-Mart convenience stores also sell tickets to many events from kiosks, but instructions are in Japanese only.

The Performing Arts

For descriptions of Japanese traditional performance arts such as *kabuki* and *Noh*, see "Japanese Arts in a Nutshell," in chapter 2. In addition to the performance art listings below, Tokyo also has occasional shows of more avant-garde or lesser-known performance art productions, including highly stylized Butoh dance performances and percussion demonstrations by Kodo drummers and other Japanese drum groups. See publications listed above for complete listings.

Kabukiza Theatre ★★★ Kabukiza Theatre, an easy walk from Ginza, is one of Japan's most famous *kabuki* theaters. It has been rebuilt several times since making its debut in 1889, with the most recent version, completed in 2013 and adding a 29-story tower, thankfully preserving its eye-catching Momoyama-style facade influenced by 16th-century castle architecture. Like all *kabuki* theaters, its stage includes a revolving circle in its center, a platform that can be lowered below the floor level so that actors can magically appear and disappear to dramatic effect, and a runway that extends into the audience. In the lobby, stalls sell *bento* lunch boxes and souvenirs (you're welcome to eat at your seat during intermission), while up on the fifth floor is a roof garden and the Kabukiza Gallery, where you can get a close look at *kabuki* costumes, stage props, old posters and other related items daily from 10am to 6pm; admission here is ¥600 for adults, ¥500 for children.

There are eight or nine *kabuki* productions a year, with each production running from about the first or third of each month for 25 days (note that there are no shows in Aug). Generally, each production consists of two shows, with matinees staged from about 11 or 11:30am to 4pm and evening shows starting at around 4:30. Of course, you won't be able to understand what the actors are saying, but *kabuki* plays, all written before the 20th century, have plots that are easy to follow, with love, duty, and revenge popular themes. Furthermore, because *kabuki* developed as a form of entertainment for commoners in feudal Japan, it doesn't have any of the highbrow seriousness attached to, say, *Noh*, which was popular among the aristocracy. In fact, one of the things I most love

5

EXPLORING TOKYO | Entertainment & Nightlife

about *kabuki* is the level of spectator engagement, with fans shouting out approval during particularly good performances. And of course, one of the most interesting things about *kabuki* is that all roles are played by men, even the female ones.

Luckily, there are English-language earphones for ¥700 (plus a ¥1,000 refundable deposit) that provide information about the plot, music, actors, and other aspects of *kabuki* so you can follow what's going on. Tickets can be purchased at the Box Office in Basement Level 2 from 10am to 6pm and from automatic ticket dispensers. You can also make advance reservations by phone at 03/6745-0888 or online.

Because programs are long, you might wish to buy tickets for only part of a production. Or, if you think one act *(makumi)* is enough and you don't mind being up in the balcony (on the fourth floor, a bit far from the stage), you can save money by taking advantage of single-act tickets. A single act usually lasts about 1 or 1½ hours. These tickets, sold to the left of the main entrance (no credit cards are accepted), go on sale just before each act and are available on a first-come, first-served basis. Everyone in your party must be present and stand in line (that is, no substitutions and no one holding your place). Note that there are only 96 seats available, with another 60 spaces for standing room only. You'll be assigned a number and allowed into the auditorium accordingly. There are no assigned seats, but by your place in line they'll be able to tell you whether you're standing or sitting. If you wish, you can buy tickets for consecutive acts as well. English-language earphones for one act cost ¥500 and are available on the fourth-floor lobby. 4–12–15 Ginza, Chuo-ku. www.kabuki-bito.jp/eng/top.html. 🕿 **03/3545-6800;** 🕿 03 6745-0888 for reservations Regular tickets ¥4,000–¥20,000, depending on the program and seat location; single-act tickets ¥1,000–¥1,400, depending on time of day and length of show. Station: Higashi-Ginza (1 min.).

Kingyo ★★ For unique, casual entertainment, nothing beats an evening at an entertainment nightclub, featuring fast-paced dancing in intimate venues. Although the emcee may speak Japanese only, no translation is necessary for the stage productions, which center on easy-to-understand themes or include humorous antics. Kingyo is one of Tokyo's oldest show nightclubs (since 1994, with management recently passed down to the second generation). It stages one of the most high-energy, visually charged 1-hour shows I've seen—nonstop action of ascending and receding stages and stairs, fast-paced choreography, elaborate costumes, and loud music. In addition to female dancers, there are also male dancers assuming female parts, just like in *kabuki* (and I swear, it's difficult to tell the difference). Some of the acts center on

---

Mapping Out Tokyo's Nightlife

Once you've chosen a nightlife spot that appeals to you, you can locate it using the following neighborhood maps:

○ To locate bars and clubs in **Ginza,** p. 108.

○ To locate bars and clubs in **Shinjuku,** p. 120.

○ To locate bars and clubs in **Roppongi,** p. 126.

traditional Japanese themes with traditional dress and kimono (a perennial favorite is a well-known song from Okinawa), but there are also satires and social commentaries. It's great fun, and you'll admire the cast not only for their talent but for their quick costume changes. Shows are Tuesday to Sunday at 7:30 (doors open at 6pm) and 10pm (doors open at 9pm). Reservations are recommended. 3–14–17 Roppongi, Minato-ku. www.kingyo.co.jp. ✆ **03/3478-3000.** Cover ¥3,500, plus a minimum of 1 drink and 1 food item; or admission packages including set meal and drinks starting at ¥4,800. Station: Roppongi (4 min.). From Roppongi Crossing, walk toward Tokyo Tower on Gaien-Higashi Dori and take the second left; it's on the right.

National Noh Theatre (Kokuritsu Nogakudo) ★★ *Noh* is performed at a number of locations in Tokyo, but this is the most famous stage. Opened in 1983, it's dedicated to presenting classical *Noh* and *kyogen,* with about three to five performances monthly, many of which have English subtitles. Tickets are often sold out in advance, but about 30 tickets are held back to be sold on the day of the performance. In addition, privately sponsored *Noh* performances are also held here, for which the admission varies. See www. theatrenohgaku.org for information on *Noh* performances being staged throughout Japan. 4–18–1 Sendagaya, Shibuya-ku. www.ntj.jac.go.jp. ✆ **03/3432-1331** or 3230-3000 for reservations. Tickets ¥2,700–¥4,900. Station: Sendagaya (5 min.).

Robot Restaurant ★★ I can hardly think about this bizarre place without cracking up; it's definitely one of those only-in-Japan experiences. Although it calls itself a restaurant, you are not coming here for the rather ordinary and optional *bento* box. You're here for the 1-hour show that includes larger-than-life-sized robots (controlled mostly by remote control), loud music, flashing lights, and scantily clad women in a fast-paced revue that will have you laughing at the absurdity of it all and in awe of the robots. Is it cheesy? Yes, and delightfully so. But this sensory-overload experience is also expensive, so while I am thoroughly glad I've seen it, I probably wouldn't go twice—unless, of course, I just had to bring a friend new to Japan. Shows are staged three or four times nightly, and reservations are recommended. 1–7–1 Kabuki-cho, Shinjuku-ku. www.robot-restaurant.com. ✆ **03/3200-5500.** Cover ¥6,000; bento meal ¥1,000 extra. Station: Shinjuku (5 min.). From Yasukuni Dori, take the street with the blue archway and a FamilyMart on the corner.

Tokyo Takarazuka Theater (Tokyo Takarazuka Kagekidan) ★★ This world-famous, all-female troupe stages elaborate musical revues with dancing, singing, and gorgeous costumes. Performances range from Japanese versions of Broadway hits to original Japanese works based on local legends. The first Takarazuka troupe, formed in 1912 at a resort near Osaka, gained instant notoriety because all its performers were women, in contrast to the all-male *kabuki.* When I went to see this troupe perform, I was surprised to find that the audience also consisted almost exclusively of women; indeed, the troupe has an almost cultlike following. Posters outside the box office show current and upcoming shows. Performances, with story synopses available in English, are generally held in March, April, July, August, November, December, and sometimes in June. Tickets are available at the box office or through **Ticket Pia.** Tokyo

Takarazuka Gekkjo, 1–1–3 Yurakucho, Chiyoda-ku. www.kageki.hankyu.co.jp/english. © **03/5251-2001.** Cover ¥3,500–¥11,000. Station: Hibiya (1 min.). Down the street from the Imperial Hotel.

Live Music Clubs

The live-music scene exploded in the 1990s and is now located throughout the metropolis. In addition to the dedicated venues below, which represent only the tip of the iceberg, be sure to check out http://metropolis.co.jp and www.tokyogigguide.com for more suggestions.

Crocodile ★★ Crocodile has spoken to generations of young Japanese with its casual rock-n-roll vibe and eclectic schedule of live bands offering everything from rock and blues to jazz-fusion, reggae, soul, experimental, salsa, and country. It's a good place to check out what people are listening to and to mingle with a mostly Japanese crowd, except on the last Friday of every month, when the Tokyo Comedy Store (www.tokyocomedy.com) provides more than 2 hours of comedy and improv in English starting at 8pm for ¥1,500. The club has a good, laid-back atmosphere; although it's a not a dance club per se, no one will mind if you just can't help yourself. Open daily 6pm to 2am; performances start around 8pm. 6–18–8 Jingumae, Shibuya-ku. www.crocodile-live.jp. © **03/3499-5205.** Cover generally ¥2,500–¥3,500, more for big acts. Station: Meiji-Jingumae or Shibuya (10 min.). On Meiji Dori halfway btw. Harajuku and Shibuya.

Liquidroom ★★★ Once a scruffy place in Shinjuku, this venue shot to stardom after relocating to this cavernous space with a fantastic sound system in Ebisu. It's well known for its concerts (bands often use it as a launching pad for world tours), DJs, and other stage events most nights of the week. Otherwise, if you just want to chill, there's a Time Out Café & Diner on the second floor, open from 11:30am Monday to Friday and from 1pm on weekends, offering free Wi-Fi and a menu that includes pastrami sandwiches and burgers. Liquidroom opens around 6 or 7pm, with performances 1 hour later. 3–16–6 Higashi, Shibuya-ku. www.liquidroom.net. © **03/5464-0800.** Cover generally ¥3,000–¥6,000, depending on the event. Station: Ebisu (3 min.). Take the west exit, cross Komazawa Dori and turn right, and then turn left at Meiji Dori; it will be almost immediately on your left.

The Ruby Room ★★★ I've seen living rooms larger than this second-floor venue, home to local acts, open-mic Tuesdays, house and techno DJs, and other events. The crowd depends on the music, but because there's no room to move, people dance where they are. The band is close, close, close—any closer and you'd be in the drummer's lap. In any case, the energy in this place is great, making it one of my favorite live-music venues. Open daily from 7pm or later, depending on the event (some concerts get underway at midnight), until 5am. 2–25–17 Dogenzaka, Shibuya-ku. www.rubyroomtokyo.com. © **03/3780-3022.** Cover ¥1,000–¥2,000 Fri–Sat only, including 1 drink; Tues open mike free, with a 2-drink minimum. Station: Shibuya (Hachiko exit, 4 min.). Walk on Dogenzaka past the round 109 building and take the 1st right at Mos Burger; keep to the left at the Y intersection.

Shinjuku Pit Inn ★★★ Musicians from Japan and abroad have been playing their hearts out at this famous institution since 2001. It's still one of the best clubs in town for jazz, fusion, or blues, nothing fancy but dedicated to the music (there's even a recording studio here). There are two programs daily, with up-and-coming bands performing at 2:30pm and more established groups taking the stage in the evening, around 7:30 or 8pm, making it a great place to stop for a bit of music in the middle of the day. In any case, this is *the* place for serious jazz fans interested in seeing firsthand the level of talent in Japan. 2–12–4 Shinjuku, Shinjuku-ku. www.pit-inn.com. ℂ **03/3354-2024.** Cover, including 1 drink, ¥1,300 for the 2:30pm show (¥2,500 Sat–Sun and holidays); ¥3,000 for the evening shows. Station: Shinjuku Sanchome (3 min.). Northeast of the Shinjuku Dori/Meiji Dori intersection.

What the Dickens! ★★   This laid-back expat bar is kind of a dive, but it's been much-loved for almost 20 years as a great place to kick back and hear free live music nightly. Bands play everything from rock and pop to reggae, jazz, blues, folk, and even Dixieland jazz, with live music from about 8:30 to 11:30pm. It has British beer on tap, as well as a menu offering steak pie, fish and chips, and other pub fare, with happy hour Monday to Saturday from 5 to 7pm. Hours are Tuesday to Thursday 5pm to 1am, Friday and Saturday 5pm to 2am, and Sunday 5pm to midnight. 1–13–3 Ebisu Nishi, Shibuya-ku. 4th floor of the Roob Building. www.whatthedickens.jp. ℂ **03/3780-2099.** Station: Ebisu (west exit, 3 min.). On the other side of Komazawa Dori street, take the small street beside St. Marc Café; it's at the end of the 2nd block on the left, on the corner.

Bars & Dance Clubs

GINZA

Ginza Sapporo Lion ★   Yebisu and Sapporo beer are the draw at this large beer hall, a Ginza institution since 1934 and popular with older Japanese for its mock Gothic ceiling, wall murals, colored mosaic tiles, and German decor. It's also a big hit with Chinese tourists, probably because it's located next to the recently opened Laox duty-free store. A large display of plastic foods and an English-language menu offer snacks ranging from *yakitori* and tempura to sausage and spaghetti. Hours are Monday to Saturday from 11:30am to 11pm, Sunday and holidays from 11:30am to 10:30pm. 7–9–20 Ginza. ℂ **03/3571-2590.** Station: Ginza (3 min.). On Chuo Dori, next to Laox.

Nelson's Bar Gabbiano ★   You could spend a fortune in the Ginza, or you could come here and pay only ¥500 for a glass of beer, wine or mixed drink. Decorated like an old sailor's bar with its rustic decor, hurricane lamp, wooden parrot, and other memorabilia, the two-level yet tiny bar is small and usually crowded, a favorite haunt of Japanese and expats alike. If you want to make a night of it, there's a limited menu of snacks, like a chicken wrap, olives, French fries, and that Japanese snack favorite, raisin butter. It's open Monday to Friday from 5pm to 1am and Saturday and Sunday from 4pm to midnight. 2–5–16 Ginza. www.nelsons-bar.jp/gabbiano.html. ℂ **03/3564-8600.** Station: Ginza (4 min.). From Ginza 4-chome Crossing, walk north on Chuo Dori past Apple, turn left at Chanel, take the first right, and then turn left at the Yebisu bar; it will be on the right of this small alleyway among the row of cubbyhole restaurants, up on the second floor.

Old Imperial Bar ★★   This clubby bar is a Tokyo institution, the only place in the Imperial Hotel that Frank Lloyd Wright's legacy as architect of the former 1923 Imperial lives on. It has a subdued atmosphere, with dim lighting, comfortable chairs and tables that are remakes of Wright furniture, as well as Wright originals like the small desk at the entrance, standing lamp in the corner, the mural, and the Art Deco terracotta wall behind the bar. To pay tribute to Wright, consider ordering the bar's own Mount Fuji, a cocktail with dry gin, lemon juice, pineapple juice, egg white, and maraschino cherry, first served in 1924. This is a quiet escape from busy Tokyo, but it's also recommended for a lunchtime sandwich if you're in the neighborhood. Hours are daily 11:30am to midnight. Imperial Hotel, 1–1–1 Uchisaiwai-cho. www.imperialhotel.co.jp. ✆ **03/3539-8088.** Station: Hibiya (1 min.).

300 Bar ★ You don't want to come here when you're drop-dead tired, because there are no seats in this standing bar. But you do come because it's cheap, with all food and drink items priced at only ¥300 plus tax, the same price as when it opened 20-some years ago. I find it a good place for a quick drink or a place to meet up with friends in the Ginza, as by 10pm there can be a line of mostly young Japanese lined up at the door. It's self-service, and upon entry you're required to purchase a minimum of two tickets (at ¥324 each) if you're a woman, three if you're male, which can be redeemed for any drink or food item from the 100-plus menu listing everything from the excellent mojito made with the bar's own herbs to the Genova Burger with basil, thyme, and sage. In addition to this one, there's another location at 8–3–12 Ginza, with the same hours. Open daily 5pm to 2am. 5–9–11 Ginza. www.300bar.com. ✆ **03/3572-6300.** Station: Ginza (2 min.). On a side street southeast of the Ginza 4–chome Crossing called Ginza Mihara Dori.

SHINJUKU

Albatross ★★ I've been a *Goruden Gai* (Japanese pronunciation for "Golden Guy") regular for almost 30 years and have seen its metamorphosis from a mysterious hidden enclave accessible only to Japanese customers to a boarded up place that seemed on the brink of extinction to the thriving hotspot it is today. The 200 or so miniature establishments packed into Goruden Gai attract a healthy mix of both Japanese and foreigners, young and old, straight and gay, and it's fun to just walk around and see where the night takes you. For a recommendation, however, Albatross has been around for a while, with a mostly young clientele and an eclectic decor that ranges from chandeliers to a deer head. You'll have to squeeze in to find a seat, either at the counter or up the narrow stairs to one of two Lilliputian levels above. Once settled, you'll find it has a very welcoming vibe. There's a ¥500 snack charge per person. Open daily 7pm to 5am. 1–1–7 Kabuki-cho. www.alba-s.com ✆ **03/3203-3699.** Station: Shinjuku Sanchome (7 min.). In Goruden Gai, on 5th St. (Gobangai).

Dubliners' Irish Pub ★ Attracting expats and locals alike—mostly in their 30s and 40s—is this chain Irish bar, especially for its weekday happy hour from 3 to 7pm. A menu lists such perennial favorites as fish and chips and minced lamb shepherd's pie, as well as pizza. Free live Irish music is staged twice a month. Check the website for a schedule and for addresses of other Dubliners' in Ikebukuro, Akasaka, Shibuya, and Shinagawa. Open Monday to Thursday 3 to 11:30pm, Friday 3pm to 1am, Saturday noon to 1am, Sunday noon to 11pm. 3–28–9 Shinjuku. www.dubliners.jp ✆ **03/3352-6606.** Station: Shinjuku (east exit, 3 min.). In east Shinjuku, behind the Bic Camera/Uniqlo complex to the southwest, above Sapporo Lion.

ROPPONGI

Ant 'n Bee ★★   Not sure what ants and bees have to do with beer, but this secret hideaway offers a cozy, laidback vibe and about 20 Japanese craft beers on tap, making it a great place to sample national brews. Decent food (like buffalo wings, pasta, and pizza), a friendly staff, and free Wi-Fi make this a good place to hang out in Roppongi, away from all the hype. Open daily 5pm to 6am. 5–1–5 Roppongi. ✆ **03/3478-1250.** Station: Roppongi (1 min.). From Roppongi Crossing, on the right side of Gaien-Higashi Dori in the direction of Tokyo Tower (look for the sign, as this basement bar is easy to miss).

Geronimo Shot Bar ★   This is such a tiny place, it is darn near impossible to elbow your way up to the bar and avoid conversation with the people around you. That's because it's a party scene most nights of the week, fueled, no doubt, by the 40 or so different shots available. If you hear the gong sound it means someone has bought a shot for you and everyone else in the bar (it happens more than you'd think). If you're up to the challenge (or so far gone), drink 15 shots in 1 night and you'll get a free T-shirt and your name immortalized on the Shot Hall of Fame. If I even tried, management would probably see fit to establish a secondary Wall of Shame. Maybe that's why people seem to either love or hate this place. But there must be more of the former than the latter, because this shot bar has been in business for more than 20 years and attracts many regulars. Happy hour is daily until 9pm. Open Monday to Friday 6pm to 5am, Saturday and Sunday 7pm to 5am. 7–14–10 Roppongi. www.geronimo shotbar.com. ✆ **03/3478-7449.** Station: Roppongi (1 min.). On Roppongi Crossing, across from Almond Coffee Shop.

Lex Tokyo Red Carpet ★   This dance club is older than most of its patrons. A Roppongi mainstay since 1980 and counting Green Day, Marilyn Manson, Stephen Dorff, and Denzel Washington among its celeb guests, it moved here in 2014 until its home at 3–13–14 Roppongi has completed renovation, some time in 2016. Its DJs appeal to a wide range of tastes by spinning many genres, from pop and rock to R&B. In today's world of cavernous clubs, this place seems like the throwback that it is, with a small dance floor and cubby-hole seating, though all bets are off on what the new digs will look like. This is the best place to be on Halloween and New Year's, if you can stand the crowds. Open daily 8pm to 5am. Roi Building basement, 5–5–1 Roppongi. www.newlex tokyo.com. ✆ **03/3479-7477.** Cover ¥3,000, including 3 free drinks; women free including 2 drinks until midnight. Roppongi (3 min.). On Gaien-Higashi Dori, on the right as you walk from Roppongi Crossing toward Tokyo Tower.

Parabola Wine + Bar ★★★   It took a while, but wine bars have finally made their mark in Tokyo, including this one in Nishi Azabu. It's owned by

Richard Dawson, who has lectured at the Academie du Vin in Tokyo and can usually be found working behind the bar, ready to impart his knowledge and recommendations. Parabola buys directly from the source as much as possible and offers a large selection of both unknown and big-name vintages from around the world, including a good and ever-changing lineup of wines by the glass (a sampler of six costs ¥3,000). Craft beers, single malt whisky, and a limited selection of dishes that complement the wines are also available, like the cheese plate served with homemade bread and the very tender homemade coq au vin. Its walls serve as an art gallery, with a winding staircase leading up to the small upstairs. It's located in a very cool-looking brick building, on the top two floors of space originally constructed as an art gallery. Open Sunday to Thursday from 6pm until the last train, Friday and Saturday from 6pm to the last customer is standing. Art Silo Building, 7th floor, 4–2–5 Nishi Azabu. www.parabola7. com. ✆ **03/6805-1926.** Station: Hiro (8 min.) or Roppongi (12 min.). On Gaien-Nishi Dori.

Red Area Club ★   DJs, a dance floor and cheap prices draw in the young crowd, especially on Thursdays when all drinks are only ¥300 (on other days, drinks cost ¥300 until 11pm). There's no cover charge, but patrons are asked to never leave their drinks unattended and to order another one when finished. This place can get rowdy, probably because everyone is required to keep drinking. Open daily 8pm to 5am. 3–14–11 Roppongi. http://redareaclub.jp. Station: Roppongi (3 min.). On Gaien-Higashi Dori, on the left just before Don Quijote as you walk from Roppongi Crossing toward Tokyo Tower.

Rigoletto Bar & Grill ★★   It's standing room only for the young professionals who crowd the bar of this swanky yet reasonably priced establishment in Roppongi Hills, especially on Friday nights when it's buzzing with disco music. The bar overlooks the restaurant, which offers upscale bar food like pizza, pasta, and main dishes like shrimp paella. Note, however, that smoke from the bar wafts over the restaurant, which can be a real turnoff for some. Open Monday to Saturday 11am to 5am, Sunday and holidays 11am to 11pm. Roppongi Hills, 5th floor of West Walk, 6–10–1 Roppongi. www.rigoletto.jp. ✆ **03/6438-0071.** Station: Roppongi (Roppongi Hills exit, 3 min.).

R2 Supper Club ★★★   The owners of this lounge decided that Roppongi needed a sophisticated hangout for expats with money, and it must be working, because R2 can be crazy full from 10pm onward, with the targeted corporate types packing the place. With a dark interior centering on a huge bar in the middle of the room, it offers a large selection of mojitos (like yuzu mojito) and fruit-driven cocktails (like the Açai Caipirinha made with cachaça and fresh lime, strawberries and raspberries, plus brown sugar and apple juice); according to staff, drinks seem healthy so customers drink more. It gets kudos for promoting mostly local up-and-coming Japanese (and some international) DJs Wednesday to Saturday nights, who combine electronic jazz with live trumpets on weekends. Open daily 4pm to 4am (to midnight on Sun). 7–14–23 Roppongi. www.r2sc.jp. ✆ **03/6447-0002.** Station: Roppongi (2 min.). From Roppongi Crossing, walk on Gaien-Higashi Dori toward Tokyo Midtown and take the first left.

The Pink Cow ★★ This neighborhood bar is a great place to hang out, whether solo with a good book or socializing with friends. It's a comfy place, more like a living room than a bar, with artwork, mismatched furniture, and a slightly feminine and funky vibe that reflects the personality of California transplant, artist, and owner Traci. In an effort to serve as a cultural center, it offers events every month, including a twice-monthly Cow Jam with live music and a dinner buffet, for which there's a ¥2,000 cover. The food, too, is reason enough to come, with a menu that includes burritos, burgers, pasta of the day, and more, with about half of the offerings vegetarian-friendly. But don't mistake this as some touchy-feely Bohemian place—it was the first restaurant in Japan to accept Bitcoins and also has a Bitcoin ATM. Open Sunday to Thursday 6 to 11pm, Friday and Saturday 6pm to 5am. Roi Building basement, 5-5-1 Roppongi. www.thepinkcow.com. © **03/6434-5773.** Station: Roppongi (3 min.). On Gaien-Higashi Dori, on the right as you walk from Roppongi Crossing toward Tokyo Tower.

Gay & Lesbian Bars

Shinjuku Ni-chome (pronounced "knee-chomay"), southeast of the Yasukuni-Gyoen Dori intersection (station: Shinjuku Sanchome), is Tokyo's gay and lesbian quarter, with a lively street scene and countless establishments catering to a variety of age groups and preferences. The following are good starting points, but you'll find a lot more in the immediate area by exploring on your own.

Advocates Café ★★ Where to start in Ni-chome? This is a good bet, right on Ni-chome's main drag, Naka-dori, and with an open facade that overflows with both gays and straights (but mostly gays) extending past the sidewalk to the street most nights. Open since 2000, it's a good place to gain bearings, check out the people parading past, and network with the friendly crowd. A few drinks here, and you'll probably have a list of several places you want to hit next. Open Monday to Saturday 6pm to 3am, Sunday 6pm to midnight. 2-18-1 Shinjuku. www.advocates-cafe.com. © **03/3358-3988.** Station: Shinjuku Sanchome (4 min.). On the street behind Bygs, to the right.

Arty Farty ★★★ One of Ni-chome's larger gay bars is also one of the best places to dance, due to a good sound system and music ranging from house to hip hop. On the first Saturday of the month, the nightly party turns into a major event; the ¥1,500 cover for this includes two drinks. Although Arty Farty used to be strictly males only, it threw open its doors to all when it moved to this location across from the legendary **Pit Inn** jazz house (p. 149). A fun climax to a pub crawl in Shinjuku. Open 6pm to 1am daily. 2-11-7 Shinjuku. www.arty-farty.net. © **03/5362-9720.** Station: Shinjuku Sanchome (3 min.). Northeast of the Shinjuku Dori/Meiji Dori intersection.

Bar Goldfinger ★ This small women-only bar offers free popcorn and karaoke, though it does let in a mixed LGBT crowd Mondays and Fridays. Happy hour is from 6 to 9pm. Open Sunday, Monday, Wednesday and Thursday from 6pm to 2am, Friday and Saturday 6pm to 4am. 2-12-11 Shinjuku. www.goldfingerparty.com. © **03/6383-4649.** Station: Shinjuku Sanchome (4 min.).

SIDE TRIPS FROM TOKYO

I f your stay in Tokyo is long enough, consider taking an excursion or two. **Kamakura** and **Nikko** rank as two of the most important historical sites in Japan, renowned for temples and shrines that relate to former shogun (military dictators). For an overnight stay, I heartily recommend **Hakone,** famous for its hot-spring spas, spectacular scenery, and unique modes of transportation that include travel by ropeway and boat; you might even see Mt. Fuji on the way.

Your main problem will be deciding where to go. If you take only one day-trip, I would probably choose Kamakura, especially if you're unable to include the ancient capitals of Kyoto and Nara in your travels. If you're going to Kyoto and Nara, however, I would probably go to Nikko, but note that it's a much longer journey and that the main gate is undergoing renovation until 2018. As for Hakone, it can be enjoyed as a side trip from Tokyo or seen en route to other destinations like Kyoto.

KAMAKURA, ANCIENT CAPITAL ★★★

51km (32 miles) S of Tokyo

Kamakura is a delightful hamlet with no fewer than 65 Buddhist temples and 19 Shinto shrines spread throughout the town and surrounding wooded hills. Most of these were built centuries ago, when a warrior named Minamoto Yoritomo seized political power and established his shogunate government in Kamakura back in 1192. Wanting to set up his seat of government as far away as possible from what he considered to be the corrupt imperial court in Kyoto, Yoritomo selected Kamakura because it was easy to defend. The town is enclosed on three sides by wooded hills and on the fourth by the sea—a setting that lends a dramatic background to its many temples and shrines.

Although Kamakura remained the military and political center of the nation for a century and a half, the Minamoto clan was in power only a short time. After Yoritomo's death, both of his sons were assassinated, one after the other, after taking up military rule. Power then passed to the family of Yoritomo's widow, the Hojo clan,

ATTRACTIONS ●
Great Buddha (Daibutsu) **4**
Hase Kannon Temple **6**
Tsurugaoka Hachimangu Shrine **1**

RESTAURANTS ◆
Kaisen Misakikou **2**
Raitei **3**
Sometaro **5**

Information
Post Office
Rail Station
Shinto Shrine

0   1/4 mi
0   0.25 km

JAPAN

Tokyo
Kamakura

To Tokyo

Engakuji Temple

Kita-Kamakura

Tokeiji Temple

Meigetsuin Temple

Jochiji Temple

Kenchoji Temple

JR YOKOSUKA LINE

Kamakura Kaido

Museum of Modern Art, Kamakura Annex

Kamakura Municipal Museum

Zeniarai Benten Shrine

Genjiyama Park

Museum of Modern Art, Kamakura

3rd Torii

Gempei Pond

OGIGAYATSU

YUKINOSHITA

Shiyakusho Dori

Komachi Dori

Wakamiya Oji

Nameri River

KOMACHI

2nd Torii

To Fujisawa

Kamakura

Kotokuin Temple

ENODEN LINE

Wakamiya Oji

O-MACHI

Yuigahama Dori

Yuigahama

Wadazuka

1st Torii

JR YOKOSUKA LINE

YUIGAHAMA

Hase

HASE

ZAIMOKUZA

To Zushi

134

Yuigahama Beach

Zaimokuza Beach

Sagami Bay

134

which ruled until 1333, when the emperor in Kyoto sent troops to crush the shogunate government. Unable to stop the invaders, 800 soldiers retired to the Hojo family temple at Toshoji, where they disemboweled themselves in ritualistic suicide known as *seppuku.*

Today Kamakura is a thriving seaside resort (pop. 174,400), with old wooden homes, temples, shrines, and wooded hills—a pleasant 1-day trip from Tokyo. (There's also a beach in Kamakura called Yuigahama Beach, but I find it unappealing; it's often strewn with litter and unbelievably crowded in summer. Skip it.)

Essentials

GETTING THERE   Take the **JR Yokosuka Line** bound for Zushi, Kurihama, or Yokosuka; it departs every 10 to 15 minutes from Shinagawa, Shimbashi, and Tokyo JR stations. The trip takes almost 1 hour from Tokyo Station and costs ¥920 to Kamakura Station. From Shinjuku, Ebisu, Shibuya or Ikebukuro, there's the JR Shonan-Shinjuku Line for the same price. Suica (see "Getting Around" in chapter 4) and Japan Rail Passes can be used for both lines.

VISITOR INFORMATION   In Kamakura, there's a **tourist information center** (www.city.kamakura.kanagawa.jp; ✆ **0467/22-3350**) inside Kamakura Station to the right of the east (main) exit. Pick up a map here and get directions to the village's most important sights and restaurants. It's open daily 9am to 5pm.

ORIENTATION & GETTING AROUND   Kamakura's major sights are clustered in two areas: **Kamakura Station,** the town's downtown with souvenir shops and restaurants spread along Komachi Dori and Wakamiya Oji on the way to Tsurugaoka Hachimangu Shrine; and **Hase,** with the Great Buddha and Hase Kannon Temple. You can travel between Kamakura Station and Hase Station in 5 minutes via the **Enoden Line,** a wonderful small train, or you can walk the distance in about 20 minutes. Destinations are also easily reached by buses from Kamakura Station.

Exploring Kamakura

AROUND KAMAKURA STATION   About a 12-minute walk from Kamakura Station, **Tsurugaoka Hachimangu Shrine ★★★** (www.tsurugaoka-hachimangu.jp; ✆ **0467/22-0315**) is the spiritual heart of Kamakura and one of its most popular attractions. It was built by Yoritomo and dedicated to Hachiman, the Shinto god of war who served as a protector of the warrior class and the clan deity of the Minamoto family. The pathway to the shrine is along Wakamiya Oji, a cherry tree–lined pedestrian lane that was constructed by Yoritomo in the 1190s so that his oldest son's first visit to the family shrine could be accomplished in style with an elaborate procession. The lane stretches from the shrine all the way to Yuigahama Beach, with three massive *torii* gates set at intervals along the route to signal the approach to the shrine. On both sides of the pathway are souvenir and antiques shops selling lacquerware, pottery, and folk art. (I suggest returning to Kamakura Station via Komachi Dori, a pedestrian shopping lane that parallels Wakamiya Oji to the west.)

At the bottom of the 62 stairs to the vermilion-colored shrine is the massive trunk of a 1,000-year-old gingko tree that was sadly uprooted during a 2010 storm, but it appears some offshoots are making a comeback. It was at this site that Yoritomo's second son was ambushed and murdered in 1219; his head was never found. Such stories of murder and betrayal were common in feudal Japan. Fearful that his charismatic brother had designs on the shogunate, Yoritomo banished him and ordered him killed. Rather than face capture, the brother committed *seppuku*. When the brother's mistress gave birth to a boy, the baby was promptly killed. Today, the lotus ponds, arched bridge, and bright vermillion sheen of the shrine give little clue to such violent history.

At the top of the stairs is the shrine with its small museum (admission here is ¥200). You can also get your fortune in English for ¥100 by shaking out a bamboo stick with a number on it and giving it to the attendant, or buy a charm to assure good luck in health, driving a car, business, or other ventures. Shrine grounds, free to the public, are open daily 5am to 8:30pm (from 6am Oct–Mar).

AROUND HASE STATION   To get to these next attractions, you can take any bus departing from platform no. 1 or 6 from in front of Kamakura Station and getting off at the Daibutsuen-mae stop). Or, for a more romantic adventure, you can go by the **JR Enoden Line,** a tiny train that putt-putts its way seemingly through backyards on its way from Kamakura Station to Hase and beyond. Since it's mostly only one track, trains have to take turns going in either direction. I suggest that you take the bus from Kamakura Station directly to the Great Buddha, walk to Hase Shrine, and then take the Enoden train back to Kamakura Station.

Probably Kamakura's most famous attraction is the **Great Buddha ★★★** (www.kotoku-in.jp; ✆ **0467/22-0703**), called the Daibutsu in Japanese and located at **Kotokuin Temple.** Eleven meters (36 ft.) high and weighing 93 tons, it's the third-largest bronze image in Japan. The second-largest Buddha is in Nara and the largest (erected in the 1990s) is near Ushiku Station outside Tokyo, but in my opinion the Kamakura Daibutsu is much more impressive. For one thing, the Kamakura Buddha sits outside against a dramatic backdrop of wooded hills. Cast in 1252, the Kamakura Buddha was indeed once housed in a temple like the Nara Buddha, but a huge tidal wave destroyed the wooden structure—and the statue has sat under sun, snow, and stars ever since. I also prefer the face of the Kamakura Buddha; I find it more inspiring and divine, as though with its half-closed eyes and calm, serene face it's above the worries of the world. It seems to represent the plane above human suffering, the point at which birth and death, joy and sadness merge and become one. Open daily from 8am to 5:30pm (to 5pm Oct–Mar). Admission is ¥200 for adults and ¥150 for children. If you want, you can pay an extra ¥20 to go inside the statue—it's hollow—but there's usually a line and I find it claustrophobic.

About a 10-minute walk from the Daibutsu is **Hase Kannon Temple (Hasedera)** ★★★ (www.hasedera.jp; ✆ **0467/22-6300**), located on a hill with sweeping views of the sea. This is the home of an 11-headed gilt statue of Kannon, the goddess of mercy, housed in the Kannon-do (Kannon Hall). More than 9m (30 ft.) high and the tallest wooden image in Japan, it was made in the 8th century from a single piece of camphor wood. The legend surrounding this Kannon is quite remarkable. Supposedly, two wooden images were made from the wood of a huge camphor tree. One of the images was kept in Hase, not far from Nara, while the second was given a short ceremony and then tossed into the sea to find a home of its own. The image drifted about 483km (300 miles) eastward and washed up on shore but was thrown back in again when all who touched it became ill or incurred bad luck. Finally, the image reached Kamakura, where it gave the people no trouble. This was interpreted as a sign that the image was content with its surroundings, and Hase Kannon Temple was erected at its present site. Note how each face has a different expression, representing the Kannon's compassion for various kinds of human suffering. Also in the Kannon-do is a museum with religious treasures from the Kamakura, Heian, Muromachi, and Edo periods.

Another golden statue housed here is of **Amida,** a Buddha who promised rebirth in the Pure Land to the West to all who chanted his name. It was created by order of Yoritomo Minamoto upon his 42nd birthday, considered an unlucky year for men. You'll find it housed in the Amida-do (Amida Hall) beside the Kannon-do to the right. **Benten-kutsu Cave** contains many stone images, including one of Benzaiten (seated, with a lute and a money box in front). A sea goddess and patroness of music, art, and good fortune, she is the only female of Japan's Seven Lucky Gods. **Prospect Road** is a 10-minute hiking path featuring flowers in bloom and panoramic views.

As you climb the steps to the Kannon-do, you'll encounter statues of a different sort. All around you will be likenesses of **Jizo,** the guardian deity of children. Although parents originally came to Hase Temple to set up statues to represent their children in hopes the deity would protect and watch over them, through the years the purpose of the Jizo statues changed. Now they represent miscarried, stillborn, or aborted infants. The hundreds or so you see here will remain only a year before being burned or buried to make way for others. Some of the statues are fitted with hand-knitted caps, bibs, and sweaters; the effect is quite chilling.

Hase Temple is open daily 8am to 5:30pm (to 5pm Oct–Feb); admission is ¥300 for adults, ¥100 for children.

Where to Eat

Kaisen Misakikou (海鮮三崎港) ★ SUSHI   Located just past the red *torii* gate that marks the entrance to the Komachi Dori pedestrian lane (cattycorner from Kamakura Station to the left), this is a simple kaiten (conveyor belt) sushi restaurant. The color of the plates indicate the price, with red plates priced at ¥110, bright blue ones at ¥180, white ones at ¥240 and dark blue ones at ¥300. It's fine, however, to order from the menu with photos of each dish (many people do just to assure freshness); help yourself to the tea dispensed at the counter.

1–7–1 Komachi. ℂ **0467/22-6228.** Plates of 2 pieces of sushi ¥110–¥300. Daily 11am–9:30pm (last order). Station: Kamakura (2 min.). On Komachi Dori, almost immediately to the right after passing under the red *torii;* look for its red sign and pictures of sushi.

Raitei (擂亭) ★★★ NOODLES/BENTO   Though it's a bit inconveniently located, this is the absolute winner for a meal in Kamakura. Visiting Raitei is as much fun as visiting the city's temples and shrines. The restaurant is situated in the hills on the edge of Kamakura, surrounded by verdant countryside, and the wonder is that it serves inexpensive *soba* (Japanese noodles) and *bento* lunch boxes, as well as priestly *kaiseki* feasts. After paying an entry fee of ¥500, which counts toward the price of your meal, follow the stone steps to the right of the traditional house to the back entry, where you'll be given an English-language menu with such offerings as noodles with chicken and *bento* lunchboxes. If you make a reservation for *kaiseki* (which requires a minimum of two people and starts at ¥6,500 per person), you'll dine upstairs in your own private room in a refined traditional setting with great views. The house, once owned by a wealthy landowner, was moved to this site in 1929. Be sure to take the 20-minute looping path through the garden, past a bamboo grove, Buddhist stone images, and a miniature shrine; in fine weather you can even see Mt. Fuji.

Takasago. www.raitei.com. ℂ **0467/32-5656.** Noodles ¥950–¥1,650; *bento* ¥3,780; *soba* set meal ¥2,700; *kaiseki* from ¥6,500. Daily 11am–sundown (about 7pm in summer). Closed last week of July. Bus: 4 from platform no. 6 at Kamakura Station or Daibutsuen-mae to Takasago stop, then straight ahead on the left (or a 15-min. taxi ride).

Sometaro (染太郎) ★ OKONOMIYAKI   Located near the approach to Hase Temple, this small, second-floor restaurant offers do-it-yourself *okonomiyaki* (a kind of Japanese pancake; cooking instructions are available in English) stuffed with cabbage, bean sprouts, and a choice of a main ingredient like beef, pork, or shrimp. It also serves *yakisoba* (fried noodles) and *teppanyaki* (grilled steak, seafood, or vegetables), all from an English-language menu. No credit cards are accepted.

3–12–11 Hase. ℂ **0467/22-8694.** Main dishes ¥900. Thurs–Tues 11:30am–9pm (last order). Station: Hase (2 min.). On the slope leading to the entrance of Hase Temple, at the beginning on the left side.

SHOGUN COUNTRY: NIKKO ★★★

150km (93 miles) N of Tokyo

James Clavell's novel *Shogun* was fictional, but it was based on the life and times of Tokugawa Ieyasu, the powerful shogun of the 1600s who quashed all rebellions and unified Japan under his leadership. Tokugawa established such a military stronghold that his heirs continued to rule Japan for the next 250 years without serious challenge, making him one of the most important figures in Japanese history.

HOTELS ■
Annex Turtle Hotori-An **8**
Nikko Kanaya Hotel **13**
Turtle Inn **9**

RESTAURANTS ◆
Gyoshin-Tei **11**
Hippari Dako **14**
Kouzushi **15**
Main Dining Hall **13**

🚌 Bus stop
ⓘ Information
⊠ Post Office

ATTRACTIONS ●
Futarasan Shrine **2**
Ieyasu's Mausoleum **3**
Nikko Tamozawa Imperial Villa **7**
Nikko Tamozawa Treasure Museum **6**
Rinnoji Temple **10**

Sacred Bridge (Shinkyo) **12**
Statue of Shodo **10**
Taiyuin Mausoleum **1**
Toshogu Shrine **4**
Yomeimon Gate **5**

TOSHUGU SHRINE AREA

Tamozawa Bus Stop
← To Lake Chuzenji

Nishi-sando Bus Stop

Ticket Office

Hotel Seikoen-mae Bus Stop

Rinnoji Office

Ticket Office

Shinkyo Bus Stop

Shinkyo (Sacred) Bridge

Ashikaga Bank

Post Office

City Hall

Stadium

Kirifuri Bridge

Nikko Police Station

Tobu-Nikko Sta.

JR-Nikko Sta.

JAPAN
Nikko
Tokyo

1/10 mi
100 m

If you'd like to join the millions of Japanese who through the centuries have paid homage to this great leader, head north of Tokyo to Nikko, where **Toshogu Shrine ★★★** was constructed in his honor in the 17th century and where Tokugawa's remains were entombed in a mausoleum. Nikko means "sunlight"—an apt description of the way the sun's rays play upon this sumptuous shrine of wood and gold leaf. In fact, nothing else in Japan matches Toshogu Shrine for its opulence. Nearby is another mausoleum containing Tokugawa's grandson, as well as a temple, a shrine, and a garden. Surrounding the sacred grounds, known collectively as Nikko Sannai and designated a World Heritage Site by UNESCO in 1999, are thousands of majestic cedar trees in the 80,000-hectare (200,000-acre) **Nikko National Park ★★**. Another worthwhile sight is the **Nikko Tamozawa Imperial Villa ★★**, built in 1899.

I've included a few recommendations for an overnight stay. Otherwise, you can see Nikko in a very full day. Plan on 4 to 5 hours for round-trip transportation, 2½ hours to see Toshogu Shrine and vicinity, and 1 hour to see the imperial villa.

Essentials

GETTING THERE   The fastest and most luxurious way to get to Nikko is on the Tobu Line's Limited Express **Spacia,** which departs every hour or more frequently from Tobu's Asakusa Station. The cost is ¥2,700 one-way for the 1-hour-and-50-minute trip on weekdays and ¥2,800 on weekends and holidays. All seats are reserved, which means you are guaranteed a seat; if you're traveling on a holiday or a summer weekend, you may wish to purchase and reserve your ticket in advance. Otherwise, you can also reach Nikko on Tobu's slower **rapid train** from Asakusa, which costs ¥1,360 one-way and takes 2 hours and 10 minutes to 2½ hours depending on the train, with departures every hour or so until 10:40am and every 2 hours after that. There are no reserved seats, which means you might have to stand if trains are crowded. Make sure to board cars 5 and 6 at the back of the train, as train cars are separated at Shimo-Imaichi Station.

To save yourself the hassle of buying individual tickets, consider purchasing Tobu's 2-Day Nikko Pass, which provides round-trip train travel between Asakusa and Nikko via rapid train, unlimited bus travel in Nikko, and other discounts listed on its website. Cost of the pass, valid for 2 days, is ¥2,600 for adults and ¥1,340 for children; you can upgrade to the Limited Express Spacia for an extra charge. You can purchase the pass online at www.tobu.co.jp/foreign if you buy it at least 4 days before your trip, or at the Tobu Sightseeing Service Center at Tobu Asakusa Station (*©* **03/3841-2871**), open daily 7:45am to 5pm.

If you have a Japan Rail Pass, take the Tohoku Shinkansen bullet train from Tokyo Station to Utsunomiya (there are departures every 20–40 min., and the trip takes about 50 min.), where you then change for the JR train to Nikko (45 min., with departures every hour or less).

VISITOR INFORMATION   The **Tobu Sightseeing Service Center** (see above) stocks pamphlets on train schedules and sightseeing. In Nikko, you'll find the Tobu and JR stations located almost side by side in the village's downtown area. Inside Tobu Station is the **Nikko Tobu Station tourist information counter** (www.nikko-kankou.org; ⟨ **0288/53-4511;** daily 8:30am–5pm), with staff who can give you a map, answer basic questions, and point you in the right direction. If you arrive before noon, you can also leave your luggage here for delivery by 3pm to a limited list of area hotels and *ryokan* for ¥500 per bag. Next to the tourist office is in Tobu Station is the **accommodations-reservation counter** (⟨ **0288/54-0864;** daily 9am–5pm), where you can make reservations at some 50 member hotels and *ryokan* for ¥540 per room.

Another tourist office, the **Nikko Information Center** (⟨ **0288/54-2496**), is located on the left side of the main road leading from the train station to Toshogu Shrine. It has English-speaking staff and lots of information in English, including information on public hot springs and hiking trails. Open daily from 9am to 5pm.

GETTING AROUND Nikko Sannai with its Toshogu Shrine and other sights is on the edge of town, but you can walk there from the JR or Tobu train stations in about half an hour, passing souvenir shops and restaurants along the way. Head straight out the main exit, pass the bus stands, and then turn right. English-language signs point the way throughout town. Keep walking on this main road (you'll pass the Nikko Information Center about halfway down on the left side) until you come to a T-intersection with a vermilion-colored bridge spanning a river to the left (about a 15-min. walk from the train stations). The stone steps opposite lead up the hill into the woods and to Toshogu Shrine in 15 minutes.

You can also travel to Nikko's attractions by bus. The World Heritage Bus travels from both the JR station (platform 1A) and Tobu station (platform 2C) to Nikko Sannai for about ¥290. There are also regular buses that you can take to Shinkyo (a 7-min. ride; fare: ¥290), Omotesando (a 9-min. ride; fare: ¥290) and Tamozawa Imperial Villa (a 12-min. ride; fare: ¥300). Roundtrip tickets are available for ¥500 but are sold only at the train stations (not on the bus). Digital signboards at the front of buses announce stops in English. Still, I almost always walk.

Exploring Nikko

The first indication that you're nearing Nikko Sainnai is the vermilion-painted **Sacred Bridge (Shinkyo)** arching over the rushing Daiyagawa River. It was built in 1636 for visiting shogun and their emissaries. Across the road from the Sacred Bridge, steps lead uphill into a forest of cedar where, after a 5-minute walk, you'll see a statue of **Shodo** (also spelled Shoto), a priest who founded Nikko 1,200 years ago when mountains were revered as gods. In the centuries that followed, Nikko became one of Japan's greatest mountain Buddhist retreats, with 500 subtemples spread through the area. Behind Shodo is the first major temple, Rinnoji Temple, with the other shrines and mausoleums spread past it underneath the verdant canopy of trees. It's worth noting that Toshogu Shrine celebrates its 400-year anniversary in 2015.

Toshogu Shrine and the other sights in Nikko Sannai are open daily from 8am to 5pm April through October (to 4pm the rest of the year); you must enter at least 30 minutes before closing time.

RINNOJI TEMPLE ★   This temple (*℗* **0288/54-0531**) was founded by the priest Shodo in the 8th century, long before the Toshogu clan came onto the scene. Here you can visit **Sanbutsudo Hall,** a large building that enshrines three 8.4m-high (28-ft.) gold-plated wooden images of Buddha, considered the "gods of Nikko"; today people pray here for world peace. Admission is ¥400 for adults, ¥200 for children (*note:* Sanbutsudo Temple is undergoing restoration until 2019, but you can still go inside). A combination ticket for both Rinnoji and Taiyuin Mausoleum (see below) is ¥900 and ¥400, respectively. Perhaps the best thing to see at Rinnoji Temple is **Shoyo-en Garden** (opposite Sanbutsudo Hall), which costs ¥300 extra for adults and ¥100 for children. Completed in 1815 and typical of Japanese landscaped gardens of the Edo Period, this small strolling garden provides a different vista with each turn of the path, making it seem much larger than it is. Your ticket to the garden also gains entrance to a small treasure house, where relics are displayed on a rotating basis. The nearest bus stop is Shodo Shoninzo-mae.

TOSHOGU SHRINE ★★★   The most important and famous structure in Nikko is Toshogu Shrine (*℗* **0288/54-0560**). When Ieyasu died in 1616 at the age of 75, his wish was to be enshrined in Nikko so that he could serve as a guardian from evil demons, who were thought to come from the north, and thereby ensure the safety and long reign of the Tokugawa regime. Although Ieyasu requested a small shrine, Tokugawa's grandson (and third Tokugawa shogun), Tokugawa Iemitsu, replaced the modest 1616 shrine with this grand complex as an act of devotion. It seems that no expense was too great in creating the monument: It took some 4.5 million artisans and other workers 1½ years to erect a group of buildings more elaborate and gorgeous than any other Japanese temple or shrine. Rich in colors and carvings, Toshogu Shrine is gilded with 2.4 million sheets of gold leaf (they could cover an area of almost 2.4 ha/6 acres). The mausoleum was completed in 1636, almost 20 years after Ieyasu's death, and was most certainly meant to impress anyone who saw it as a demonstration of the Tokugawa shogunate's wealth and power. The shrine is set in a grove of magnificent ancient **Japanese cedars** planted over a 20-year period during the 1600s by a feudal lord named Matsudaira Masatsuna. Some 13,000 of the original trees still stand, adding a sense of dignity to the mausoleum and shrine.

You enter Toshogu Shrine via a flight of stairs that passes under a huge stone *torii* gateway, one of the largest in Japan. On your left is a five-story, 35m-high (115-ft.) **pagoda.** Although normally pagodas are found only at temples, this pagoda is just one example of how Buddhism and Shintoism are combined at Toshogu Shrine. After climbing a second flight of stairs, turn left and you'll see the **Sacred Stable,** which houses a sacred white horse. Horses have long been dedicated to Shinto gods and are kept at shrines. Shrines also kept monkeys as well, since they were thought to protect horses from disease; look for the three monkeys carved above the stable door, fixed in the poses of "see no evil, hear no evil, speak no evil." Across from the stable is **Kami-Jinko,** famous for its carving by Kano Tanyu, who painted the images of the two elephants (under the eaves) after reading about them but without seeing what they actually looked like.

The central showpiece of Nikko is **Yomeimon Gate,** popularly known as the Twilight Gate, implying that it could take you all day (until twilight) to see everything carved on it. Painted in red, blue, and green, and gilded and lacquered, this gate is carved with more than 500 flowers, dragons, birds, and other animals. It's almost too much to take in at once and is very un-Japanese in its opulence, having more in common with Chinese architecture than with the usual austerity of most Japanese shrines. Unfortunately, due to renovation it is under wraps until 2018, but the grandeur of the shrine's other buildings give an inkling of how magnificent this gate is.

Be sure to enter the shrine's main sanctuary, **Hai-den,** comprising three halls: One was reserved for the Imperial family, one for the shogun, and one (the central hall) for conducting ceremonies. You can buy good-luck charms here that will guard against such misfortunes as traffic accidents, or that will ensure good health, success in business, easy childbirth, or other achievements in daily life. To the right of the main hall is the entrance to **Tokugawa Ieyasu's mausoleum,** where there's a carving of a sleeping cat above the door, dating from the Edo Period and famous today as a symbol of Nikko (you'll find many reproductions in area souvenir shops). Beyond that are 200 stone steps leading past cedars to Tokugawa's tomb. After the riotous colors of the shrine, the tomb seems surprisingly simple.

On the way out you'll pass **Yakushido,** famous for its dragon painting on the ceiling. A monk gives a brief explanation (in Japanese) and demonstrates how two sticks struck together produce an echo that supposedly resonates like a bell. Twelve statues here represent the Chinese zodiac calendar.

Admission to Toshogu Shrine is ¥1,300 for adults and ¥450 for children.

FUTARASAN SHRINE ★   Directly to the west of Toshogu Shrine is Futarasan Shrine (📞 **0288/54-0535**), one of the oldest buildings in the district (ca. 1617), which has a pleasant garden and is dedicated to the gods of mountains surrounding Nikko. You'll find miniature shrines dedicated to the god of fortune, god of happiness, god of trees, god of water, and god of good marriages. On the shrine's grounds is the so-called **ghost lantern,** enclosed in a small vermilion-colored wooden structure. According to legend, it used to come alive at night and sweep around Nikko in the form of a ghost. It apparently scared one guard so much that he struck it with his sword 70 times; the marks are still visible on the lamp's rim. Entrance is ¥200 for adults, ¥100 for children.

TAIYUIN MAUSOLEUM ★★   Past Futarasan Shrine is **Taiyuin Mausoleum** (📞 **0288/53-1567**), the final resting place of Iemitsu, the third Tokugawa shogun (look for his statue). Completed in 1653, it's not nearly as large as Toshogu Shrine, but it's ornate and serenely elegant nevertheless. To show respect for the first shogun, Taiyuin's buildings face Toshogu Shrine. Tourists usually bypass this shrine, making it a pleasant last stop on your tour of Nikko Sannai. If you didn't buy a combination ticket with Rinnoji Temple, admission here is ¥550 for adults, ¥250 for children. The nearest bus stop is Taiyun Temple-Futarasan Shrine.

NIKKO TAMOZAWA IMPERIAL VILLA (TAMOZAWA GOYOUTEI KINEN KOEN) ★★★ If you haven't seen the Imperial villas of Kyoto (which require advance planning), this villa, at 8–27 Honcho (© **0288/53-6767**), is a great alternative. It's not as old, having been built in 1899 for Prince Yoshihito (who later became the Taisho emperor), and painstakingly restored so that it looks brand-new. It has the distinction of being the largest wooden Imperial villa of its era, with 106 rooms, 37 of which are open to the public. In addition, the central core of the villa is actually much older, constructed in 1632 by a feudal lord and brought to Nikko from Edo (present-day Tokyo). Altogether, three emperors and three princes used the villa between 1899 and 1947. A self-guided tour of the villa provides insight into traditional Japanese architectural methods—from its 11 layers of paper-plastered walls to its nail-less wood framing—as well as the lifestyle of Japan's aristocracy. If you have time, there's an audio guide for ¥200 which covers 20 stops along the way in about an hour. Be sure to also see the small outdoor garden. Admission is ¥510 for adults, ¥250 for children. Open Wednesday to Monday 9am to 5pm (to 4:30pm Nov–Mar). You must enter by 4pm. It's about a 20-minute walk from Nikko Sannai, or take the bus to Tamozawa stop.

Where to Eat

In addition to rainbow trout, Nikko is famous for *yuba,* a high-protein byproduct formed by boiling soymilk, which causes a thin film to rise to the liquid's surface. Thought to have originated in Kyoto, it was popular among monks training at Rinnoji Temple for its nutrition, meatlike protein, and light weight for carrying on mountain retreats. Only priests and members of the Imperial family were allowed to consume it until the Meiji Period. Now you can enjoy it, too, at many restaurants in Nikko. Another popular dish is *Mizu-yokan,* a traditional sweet made from the Azuki bean.

Gyoshin-Tei (堯心亭) ★★★ VEGETARIAN/KAISEKI This lovely Japanese restaurant, with a simple tatami room and a view of pines, moss, and bonsai, serves two kinds of set meals—*kaiseki* and Buddhist vegetarian cuisine (Shojin Ryori)—both of which change monthly and include the local specialty, *yuba.* Another restaurant in the parklike setting under the same management (and with the same open hours and phone number) is Meiji-no-Yakata. Occupying a stone house built more than 110 years ago as the private retreat of an American businessman and little changed since then, it serves Western food such as grilled rainbow trout, veal cutlet, and steak, as well as set meals ranging from ¥4,000 to ¥10,800. The drawback: This place is harder to find than my other recommendations, but it's only a 4-minute walk northeast of Rinnoji Temple, on the other side of a parking lot.

2339–1 Sannai. © **0288/53-3751.** Vegetarian/*kaiseki* meals ¥3,800–¥5,500; set lunches ¥2,800–¥3,000. Fri–Wed 11am–7pm (from 11:30am in winter). A 25-min. walk from Nikko Tobu Station, or the World Heritage Bus to the Hotel Seikoen stop.

Hippari Dako (ひっぱり凧) ★ VARIED JAPANESE This tiny, three-table establishment offers a limited selection of noodle dishes, including ramen and stir-fried noodles with vegetables, as well as *yakitori* (skewered barbecued chicken), *gyoza* (dumplings), and vegetarian dishes that include *yuba*. There's an English-language menu complete with photos, and the walls and ceiling are covered with business cards and messages left by travelers from around the world. Cash only at this place.

1011 Kami-Hatsuishi. ℂ **0288/53-2933.** Main dishes ¥550–¥950. Daily 11am–7:30pm (last order). A 15-min. walk from the station, on the left side of the main street leading to Nikko Sannai, 1 min. before the Sacred Bridge; or by bus to the Shinkyo stop.

Kouzushi (晃寿司) ★★ SUSHI/YUBA Although it looks so new it might have opened yesterday, this restaurant has actually been serving its own secret recipe for *yuba* for generations, with ordering made easy by an English menu complete with pictures. Although you can order a dish of delicious yuba for just ¥650 or any number of sushi and sashimi combination platters, I recommend the special set for ¥2,900 that includes yuba, sushi, sashimi, soup, and seasonal dishes. The restaurant is easy to find, on Nikko's main street not far from the station.

9–1 Matsubara-cho. ℂ **0288/54-0752.** Set meals ¥1,296–¥2,900. Daily 11am–9pm (last order). Closed occasionally Wed or Thurs. A 3-min. walk from the station, on the right side of the main street.

Main Dining Hall ★★★ CONTINENTAL Even if you don't spend the night here, the Kanaya Hotel's quaint dining hall with its colorful wood-carved pillars is a great place for lunch. I suggest Nikko's specialty: locally caught rainbow trout available three different ways. I always order mine cooked Kanaya style—covered with soy sauce, sugar, and sake; grilled; and served whole. The best bargain is the set lunch, available until 3pm, which comes with soup, salad, a main dish such as veal cutlet cordon bleu, bread or rice, and dessert. Steak, lobster, salmon, chicken, and other Western fare are also listed on the English-language menu. At the restaurant's entrance is a table where original tableware, silver tea and coffee pots and other items from long ago are displayed; in any other country, they'd surely be locked behind glass. In another nod to the past, a chime announces when the restaurant opens for dinner.

Nikko Kanaya Hotel, 1300 Kami-Hatsuishi. ℂ **0288/54-0001.** Main dishes ¥2,970–¥9,500; set lunches ¥3,600–¥10,800; set dinner ¥10,800. Daily 11:30am–2:30pm and 6–8pm (last order). A 20-min. walk from Nikko Tobu Station; or by bus to the Shinkyo stop.

Where to Stay

If it's peak season (Golden Week, Aug, Oct–Nov.) or a weekend, it's best to reserve a room in advance.

Annex Turtle Hotori-An ★★ Owned by the friendly family that runs Turtle Inn (below), this is one of my favorite places to stay in Nikko. One dip in the hot-spring bath overlooking the Daiyagawa River (which you can lock for privacy) will tell you why; at night, you're lulled to sleep by the sound of the rushing waters. A simple but spotless modern structure (all nonsmoking), it's located in a nice rural setting on a quiet street with a few other houses; an adjoining park and playground make it an excellent choice also for families. All rooms except one are Japanese style. A plentiful Western-style breakfast costs ¥1,000 in the pleasant living area/dining room. For dinner, you can go to the nearby Turtle Inn (available only Sat; reservations should be made the day before). There's also a communal refrigerator where you can store food.

8–28 Takumi-cho. www.turtle-nikko.com. ✆ **0288/53-3663.** 11 units. ¥6,700–¥6,800 single; ¥13,100 double. Bus: From Nikko Station to the Sogo Kaikan-mae stop, a 7-min. ride; then a 9-min. walk. **Amenities:** Free Wi-Fi.

Nikko Kanaya Hotel ★★★ Founded in 1873 as Nikko's first hotel (until then, visitors stayed in area temples), this distinguished-looking place on a hill above the Sacred Bridge combines the rustic heartiness of a European country lodge with elements of old Japan. The present complex, built in spurts over the past 140-some years, has a rambling, delightfully old-fashioned atmosphere that fuses Western architecture with Japanese craftsmanship. Through the decades it has played host to a number of VIPs, from Charles Lindbergh to Indira Gandhi to Shirley MacLaine; Frank Lloyd Wright left a sketch for the bar fireplace, which was later built to his design. Even if you don't stay here, you might want to drop by for lunch and to gaze at the old photographs lining the hallways. Pathways lead to the Daiyagawa River and several short hiking trails. All rooms are Western-style twins, with the differences in price based on room size, view (river view is best), and facilities. Some 10 rooms have been updated, but I prefer the older, simpler rooms because they have more character; some have antiques and claw-foot tubs. The best (and priciest) room is the annex corner room in the 80-year-old wing where the emperor once stayed.

1300 Kami-Hatsuishi. www.kanayahotel.co.jp. ✆ **0288/54-0001.** 70 units. ¥17,820–¥53,460 single or double. ¥3,564–¥4,752 extra on Fri, Sat, and eve before national holidays; ¥5,940–¥7,128 extra in peak season. Bus: From Nikko Tobu Station to the Shinkyo stop, a 5-min. ride. On foot: 17 min. from Nikko Tobu Station. **Amenities:** 3 restaurants, including the Main Dining Hall (see review); bar; small outdoor heated pool (mid-July to Aug only); outdoor skating rink (Dec–Feb, free for guests, including shoes); shuttle bus from Tobu Nikko Station 2–4 times a day.

Turtle Inn ★ This excellent, nonsmoking pension is within walking distance of Nikko Sannai in a newer two-story house (recently painted a bright orange) on a quiet side street beside the Daiyagawa River. The friendly owner, Mr. Fukuda, speaks English and is helpful in planning a sightseeing itinerary. Rooms are bright and cheerful in both Japanese and Western styles; the five tatami rooms are without private bathroom, but there are hot-spring baths. Excellent Japanese dinners, served on local Mashiko pottery are available for ¥2,000 if you order a day in advance (available only Sat), as are Western breakfasts for ¥1,000.

2–16 Takumi-cho. www.turtle-nikko.com. ✆ **0288/53-3168.** 10 units (3 with bathroom). ¥4,950–¥5,500 single without bathroom, ¥6,000 single with bathroom; ¥9,600 double without bathroom, ¥10,300–¥11,300 double with bathroom. Bus: From Nikko Station to the Sogo Kaikan-mae stop, a 7-min. ride; then a 5-min. walk. **Amenities:** Free Wi-Fi.

HAKONE ★★★

97km (60 miles) SW of Tokyo

Part of **Fuji-Hakone-Izu National Park,** Hakone is one of the closest and most popular weekend destinations for residents of Tokyo. Beautiful Hakone has about everything a vacationer could wish for—hot-spring resorts, mountains, lakes, breathtaking views of Mount Fuji when the weather is clear (visible mostly in cooler months), and interesting historical sites. You can tour Hakone as a day trip if you leave very early in the morning and limit your sightseeing to a few key attractions, but adding an overnight stay or two—complete with a soak in a hot-spring tub—is much more rewarding. If you can, travel on a weekday, when modes of transportation are less crowded and some hotels offer cheaper weekday rates.

Essentials

GETTING THERE & GETTING AROUND Getting to and around Hakone is half the fun! An easy loop tour you can follow through Hakone includes various forms of unique transportation: Starting out by train from Tokyo, you switch to a three-car mountain railway that zigzags up the mountain, then change to a cable car, and then to a smaller ropeway, and end your trip with a boat ride across Lake Ashi, stopping to see major attractions along the way. From Lake Ashi (that is, from the villages of Togendai, Hakone-machi, or Moto-Hakone), you can then take a bus to Odawara Station (an hour's ride), where you board the train back to Tokyo. Buses also connect all the recommendations listed below, which is useful if you wish to complete part of your sightseeing the first day before going to your hotel for the evening. A bus also runs directly between Togendai and Shinjuku in about 2¼ hours.

Odakyu operates the most convenient network of trains, buses, trams, cable cars, and boats to and around Hakone. The most economical and by far easiest way to travel is Odakyu's **Hakone Free Pass,** which, despite its name, isn't free but does give you a round-trip ticket on the express train from Shinjuku Station to Odawara or Hakone-Yumoto and includes all modes of transportation in Hakone listed above and described below. The pass lets you avoid the hassle of buying individual tickets and gives nominal discounts on most Hakone attractions. A 2-day pass costs ¥5,140 and a 3-day pass is ¥5,640. Children pay ¥1,500 and ¥1,750 respectively.

The trip from Shinjuku to Odawara via Odakyu Express takes 100 minutes, with departures two to four times an hour. In Odawara, you then transfer to another train for a 15-minute trip to Hakone-Yumoto. If time is of the essence or if you want to ensure a seat during peak season, reserve a seat on the faster and more luxurious **Odakyu Romance Car,** which travels from Shinjuku all the way to Hakone-Yumoto in 1½ hours and costs an extra ¥890 one-way with a Hakone Pass.

Hakone

HOTELS ■

Khaosan Kabuki **5**

Ryokan Kamogawa **4**

Ryokan Asakusa Shigetsu **3**

Sadachiyo Sukeroku-no-Yado **1**

Toyoko Inn Asakusa Kuramae
  Kaminarimon **10**

RESTAURANTS ◆

Chinya **6**

Kamiya Bar **9**

Sansada **8**

Sometaro **2**

Waentei-Kikko **7**

If you have a **Japan Rail Pass,** you should take the Shinkansen bullet train first to Odawara (not all bullet trains stop here, so make sure yours does). From there, you can buy a 2-day Hakone Free Pass for ¥4,000 or a 3-day Pass for ¥4,500. Children pay ¥1,000 and ¥1,250 respectively.

All passes described above can be purchased at any station of the Odakyu Railway, including Shinjuku, Odawara, and Hakone-Yumoto. In Tokyo, the best place to purchase Hakone Free Pass tickets is at the **Odakyu Sightseeing Service Center,** located on the ground floor near the west exit of Odakyu Shinjuku Station (www.odakyu.jp/english; (ⓒ 03/5321-7887; daily 8am–6pm), where you can obtain sightseeing information and maps in English in addition to purchasing tickets. Next to the Service Center is a Travelex counter for changing money.

In addition to the different modes of transportation described below, Hakone has a very efficient bus network (included in the Free Pass), with lines conveniently identified by a letter that is also on the front of the bus. The Togendai (T) Line is the most useful, traveling between Togendai and Odawara and making stops near the three accommodations recommended below. Pick up a route map for **Hakone Tozan Bus** (www.hakone-tozanbus.co.jp; ⓒ **0465-35-1271**) at the Yumoto Tourist Office.

VISITOR INFORMATION   In addition to the Odakyu Sightseeing Service Center, in Hakone-Yumoto there's the **Yumoto Tourist Office** (ⓒ **0460/85-8911;** daily 9am–5:45pm), across the street from Hakone-Yumoto Station. You can also make hotel and *ryokan* reservations here. Information on Hakone is also available at www.hakone.or.jp.

LUGGAGE   If you plan to return to Tokyo, I suggest leaving your luggage in storage at your Tokyo hotel or at Shinjuku Station and traveling to Hakone with only an overnight bag. If you're heading onward to, say, Kyoto, you can leave your bags at the **Left Luggage** check-in counter at Hakone-Yumoto Station, located just outside the ticket gate to the right and open daily 8am to 10pm (a large bag costs ¥510 per day). Or, if you deliver your bags to the **Hakone Baggage Service** (ⓒ **0460/86-4140**) located just ahead after getting off the train at Hakone-Yumoto Station, between 8:30am and 12:30pm, it will transport your bags to your Hakone accommodations by 3pm. The next day, it will also pick up your bags at your hotel by 10am and deliver them to Hakone-Yumoto Station by 1pm, where they will keep them until 7pm. The service costs ¥800 to ¥1,100 per bag, depending on size and weight; a ¥100 discount is provided for holders of the Hakone Free Pass.

Exploring Hakone

If you plan on spending only a day in Hakone, you should leave Tokyo very early in the morning and plan on visiting only a few key attractions—I recommend the **Hakone Open-Air Museum** and **Owakudani.** Keep in mind that most forms of transportation (like the ropeway and sightseeing boat) as well as museums close around 5pm.

If you're spending the night—and I strongly urge that you do—you can arrange your itinerary in a more leisurely fashion and devote more time to Hakone's attractions. You may wish to travel only as far as your hotel the first day, stopping at sights along the way and in the vicinity. The next day you could continue with the rest of the circuit through Hakone. Or, you could head straight to your accommodation in the afternoon and then do your sightseeing the next day. Finally, if it's a clear day and there's a chance Mt. Fuji is visible, you might want to do this tour in reverse from what's given below to make sure you get to Hakone-machi in the morning, as clouds sometimes cloak the mountain by afternoon.

SCENIC RAILWAY TO GORA   Regardless of whether you travel via the Odakyu Romance Car or the ordinary Odakyu express, you'll end up at Hakone-Yumoto Station. Here you'll transfer to the **Hakone Tozan Railway,** in operation since 1919. This delightful, mountain-climbing, three-car electric train winds its way through forests and over streams and ravines as it travels upward to Gora, making several switchbacks along the way. The entire trip from Hakone Yumoto Station to Gora takes only 40 minutes, but the ride through the mountains is beautiful and this is my favorite part of the whole journey. The railway, which runs every 15 to 20 minutes, makes about a half-dozen stops before reaching Gora, including **Tonosawa** and **Miyanoshita,** two hot-spring spa resorts with a number of old *ryokan* and hotels. Some of the *ryokan* date back several centuries, to the days when they were on the main thoroughfare to Edo, called the old Tokaido Highway. Miyanoshita is the best place for lunch. See "Where to Eat" and "Where to Stay," later.

For relaxing hot-springs bathing en route, visit the thoroughly modern, sophisticated public bath called **Hakone Kowaki-en Yunessun ★★** (www. yunessun.com/english; ✆ **0460/82-4126**). To reach it, disembark from the Hakone Tozan Railway at Kowakudani, and then take a 15-minute taxi or bus ride (bus stop: Kowaki-en). This self-described "Hot Springs Amusement Park" offers a variety of both indoor and outdoor family baths, which means you wear your bathing suit. In addition to indoor Turkish, Roman, and salt baths, there's also a children's play area with slides and a large outdoor area with a variety of small baths, including those mixed with healthy minerals and—I am not making this up—coffee, green tea, sake, or wine. For more traditional bathing, there's the Mori No Yu, with both indoor and outdoor baths separated for men and women (you don't wear your suit here). Most people who come stay 2 to 3 hours. As with most public bathhouses, people with tattoos are not allowed. Admission to Yunessun is ¥2,900 for adults and ¥1,600 for children. Admission to Mori No Yu is ¥1,900 and ¥1,200 respectively. Admission to both is ¥4100 and ¥2,100. If you have a Hakone Free Pass, you'll receive a slight discount. Upon admission, you'll be given a towel, robe, and wristband to pay for drinks and extras (rental suits are available), so you can leave all valuables in your assigned locker. Yunessun is open daily 9am to 7pm March to October, 9am to 6pm in November to February; Mori No Yu is open daily 11am to 9pm year-round.

The most important stop on the Hakone Tozan Railway is the next-to-the-last stop, Chokoku-no-Mori, where you'll find the famous **Hakone Open-Air Museum (Chokoku-no-Mori Bijutsukan)** ★★★ (www.hakone-oam.or.jp; © 0460/82-1161), a minute's walk from the station. With the possible exception of views of Mount Fuji, this museum is, in my opinion, Hakone's number-one attraction. Using nature as a dramatic backdrop, it showcases sculpture primarily of the 20th century in a spectacular setting of glens, formal gardens, ponds, streams, and meadows. There are 400 sculptures on display, both outdoors and in several buildings, with works by Carl Milles, Manzu Giacomo, Jean Dubuffet, Willem de Kooning, Barbara Hepworth, Taro Okamoto, and Joan Miró, as well as more than 25 pieces by Henry Moore, shown on a rotating basis. Several installations geared toward children allow them to climb and play. The Picasso Pavilion contains works by Picasso from pastels to ceramics, one of the world's largest collections. I could spend all day here; barring that, count on staying at least 2 hours. Be sure to stop off at the "foot *onsen*," where you can immerse your tired feet in soothing, hot-spring water. The museum is open daily 9am to 5pm; admission is ¥1,600 adults, ¥1,200 university and high-school students, and ¥800 children (children are free on Sat). Your Hakone Free Pass gives you a ¥200 discount.

BY CABLECAR TO SOUNZAN & ROPEWAY TO TOGENDAI Hakone Tozan Cablecars leave Gora every 20 minutes or so and arrive 10 minutes later at the end station of Sounzan, making several stops along the way as they travel steeply uphill. From Sounzan, you board the Hakone Ropeway with gondolas for an 8-minute ride to **Owakudani** ★, the ropeway's highest point. You have to change gondolas here for the final stretch into Togendai, so you might as well stay for the views and the 10-minute hike to the Tamago-Chaya Teahouse. Owakudani means "Great Boiling Valley," and you'll soon understand how it got its name when you see (and smell) the sulfurous steam escaping from fissures in the rock, testimony to the volcanic activity still present here. Most Japanese commemorate their trip by buying boiled eggs cooked here in the boiling waters, available at the small teahouse. The ropeway continues another 16 minutes to Togendai, which lies beside Lake Ashi, known as Ashinoko in Japanese. Note that the ropeway stops running at around 5:15pm in summer and 4:15pm in winter.

ACROSS LAKE ASHI BY BOAT From Togendai you can take a pleasure boat across Lake Ashi, which was formed by a volcanic eruption some 3,000 years ago. Believe it or not, a couple of the boats plying the waters are replicas of a man-of-war pirate ship. It takes about half an hour to cross the lake to Hakone-machi (also called Hakonemachi-ko; *machi* means city and *ko* means lake) and Moto-Hakone, two resort towns right next to each other on the southern edge of the lake. This end of the lake affords the best view of Mount Fuji, one often depicted in tourist publications (mornings in cooler months offer the best chance to see this elusive beauty). Boats are in operation year-round, though they run less frequently in winter and not at all in stormy weather; the last boat departs around 5:15pm from the end of March to the end of November. If you miss it, buses connect Togendai with Odawara and Shinjuku.

After the boat ride, if you're heading back to Tokyo, buses depart for Hakone-Yumoto and Odawara near the boat piers in both Hakone-machi and Moto-Hakone. Otherwise, for more sightseeing, get off the boat in Hakone-machi, turn left, and walk about 5 minutes along the town's main road, following the signs and turning left to **Hakone Check Point (Hakone Sekisho)** ★★ (http://hakonesekisyo.jp; 🕾 **0460/83-6635**), on a road lined with souvenir shops. This is a reconstructed guardhouse originally built in 1619 to serve as a checkpoint along the famous Tokaido Highway, which connected Edo (present-day Tokyo) with Kyoto. In feudal days, local lords, called *daimyo,* were required to spend alternate years in Edo; their wives were kept in Edo as virtual hostages to discourage the lords from planning rebellions while in their homelands. This was one of 53 check points in Japan that guarded against the transport of guns, spies, and female travelers trying to flee Edo. Passes were necessary for travel, and although it was possible to sneak around it, male violators who were caught were promptly executed, while women suffered the indignity of having their heads shaven and then being given away to anyone who wanted them. Inside the reconstructed guardhouse, which was rebuilt on the site of the original checkpoint using traditional carpenter tools and architectural techniques of the Edo Period, you'll see life-size models reenacting scenes inside a checkpoint. Other reconstructions include soldiers' quarters, gates, and a hilltop lookout. A small museum has displays relating to the Edo Period, including woodblock prints and photos of the old checkpoint and items used for travel, including a tiny abacus and an even smaller case holding grooming supplies. Open daily from 9am to 5pm (to 4:30pm Dec–Feb); admission is ¥500 for adults and ¥250 for children. Your Hakone Free Pass gives a ¥100 discount. It shouldn't take more than 20 minutes to see everything.

Just beyond the Hakone Check Point, at the big parking lot with the traditional gate, is the **Hakone Detached Palace Garden (Onshi-Hakone-Koen)** ★, which lies on a small promontory on Lake Ashi and has spectacular views of the lake and, in clear weather, Mount Fuji. Originally part of an Imperial summer villa built in 1886, the well-kept garden is free and open to the public and is a great place for wandering. Be sure to stop by the **Lakeside Observation Building** (closed Tues and daily at 4:30pm), with a cafe offering tea and sweets and with free displays relating to Hakone Palace, destroyed by earthquakes.

Just a 5-minute walk away is the neighboring resort town, **Moto-Hakone,** but you'll want to get there by crossing the highway for a shaded footpath lined with ancient and mighty cedars, once part of the old **Tokaido Highway.** During the Edo Period, more than 400 cedars were planted along this important road, which today stretches 2.5km (1½ miles) along the curve of Lake Ashi. Upon entering Moto-Hakone, up the hill to the right when you reach the orange *torii* gate, **Narukawa Art Museum** ★★ (www.narukawamuseum.co.jp; 🕾 **0460/83-6828**) offers both art and sweeping scenic views (look for the series of escalators to help you reach it). It specializes in modern works of the *Nihonga* style of painting, developed during the Heian Period (794–1185) and sparser than Western paintings (which tend to fill in backgrounds and every inch of canvas). Large paintings and screens by contemporary *Nihonga* artists are on display, including works by Kyujin Yamamoto, Susumu Maki, Ikuo Hirayama, and Fumiko Hori. Changing exhibitions on two floors feature younger up-and-coming artists, as well as some glassware. I wouldn't miss it; views of Lake Ashi and Mount Fuji, especially from its tea lounge, are a bonus. Open daily 9am to 5pm; admission is ¥1,300 for adults, ¥1,000 for high-school and university students, and ¥700 for children. The Hakone Free Pass gives a ¥200 discount.

WHEN YOU'RE DONE SIGHTSEEING FOR THE DAY Buses depart for Hakone-Yumoto and Odawara from both Hakone-machi and Moto-Hakone two to four times an hour. Be sure to check the time of the last departure; generally it's around 8pm, but this can change with the season and the day of the week. The trip from Moto-Hakone takes approximately 30 minutes to Hakone Yumoto and 50 minutes to Odawara, where you can catch the Odakyu train back to Shinjuku or the Shinkansen bullet train onward toward Kyoto.

Where to Stay & Eat

Most accommodations cost more during peak travel times like Golden Week, school holidays, New Year's, weekends and national holidays, and during cherry blossom season in spring and the changing of the leaves in autumn.

For casual dining, the Hakone Open-Air Museum has a pleasant restaurant, **Bella Foresta ★**, overlooking the park's fantastic scenery and offering a buffet lunch of mostly Western fare daily from 11am to 3pm for ¥1,980. There are also informal restaurants at the **Owakudani** Ropeway Station and **Togendai** boat cruise building, both serving curry rice and other fare for less than ¥1,400.

But my favorite place for a meal is the **Fujiya ★★★**, located in Hakone's grandest, oldest hotel (see "The Fujiya Hotel," below), serving French food and offering impressive views of the Hakone hills. This main dining hall, dating from 1930, is very bright and cheerful, with a high and intricately detailed ceiling, large windows with Japanese screens, a wooden floor, and white tablecloths. For lunch, served daily from 11:30am to 2pm, you can have such dishes as curry, beef stew, rainbow trout, and sirloin steak, or opt for one of the set lunches starting at ¥4,390. A cheaper option is the **Orchid Lounge ★★**, which provides a limited selection of sandwiches and other dishes until 5pm in an old-fashioned tearoom overlooking a small waterfall and pond filled with koi. Afterward, be sure to tour the landscaped garden, because that's one of the reasons you're here.

Otherwise, just a minutes' walk from Miyanoshita Station is the cute **Naraya Café ★** (© **0460/82-1259**), offering coffee, tea, beer, desserts, and a limited selection of pizzas, hot dogs, and soups, but my favorite part is the outdoor terrace complete with a table over a footbath so you can soak your feet while you eat. It's open from 10:30am to 6pm, closed Wednesday and the fourth Thursday of every month.

Fuji-Hakone Guest House ★★ It's not on the circuitous route detailed above, but this family-owned Japanese inn has been welcoming foreign guests since 1984 and offers inexpensive, spotlessly clean lodging in tatami rooms, all nonsmoking, in two buildings located side by side. Situated in tranquil surroundings set back from a tree-shaded road, it's run by a couple who speak good English and go out of their way to provide sightseeing information, bus schedules, and a map of the area marked with area restaurants and attractions, including many art museums. In fact, if you stay here, you may well be tempted to stay 2 nights. There four hot-spring baths that can be reserved for private use, including an outdoor bath (for which there's an extra ¥500 charge). The best rooms are in the annex, with room no. 6 facing woods and a stream and room no. 7 big enough for three or four people. But if this inn is full, the Takahashi family also owns the Moto-Hakone Guest House, across Lake Ashi.

912 Sengokuhara, Hakone. www.fujihakone.com. ℰ **0460/84-6577.** 15 units (none with private bathroom). ¥5,000–¥6,000 single; ¥10,000–¥12,000 double; ¥15,000–¥18,000 triple. Rates exclude taxes. Peak season and Sat–Sun ¥1,000–¥2,000 extra. Minimum 2-night stay preferred. Western buffet breakfast ¥810 extra. Bus: Hakone Tozan T (included in the Hakone Free Pass) from Togendai (10 min.) or from Odawara Station (50 min.) to the Senkyoro-mae stop (announced in English), and then a 1-min. walk (there are also direct buses from Shinjuku and Haneda airport). **Amenities:** Hot-spring bath; free Wi-Fi.

The Fujiya Hotel ★★★ The Fujiya, established in 1878 but recently spruced up with a new paint job, is quite simply the grandest, most majestic old hotel in Hakone; indeed, it might be the loveliest historic hotel in Japan. I love this hotel for its comfortably old-fashioned atmosphere, including such Asian touches as a Japanese-style roof and long wooden corridors with photographs of famous guests, from Einstein to Eisenhower. A landscaped garden out back, with a waterfall, pond, greenhouse, outdoor pool, and stunning views over the valley is great for strolls and meditation. There's also an indoor thermal pool and public hot-spring baths (hot-spring water is also piped in to each guest's bathroom). Even if you don't stay here, come for a meal or tea.

There are five separate buildings, all different and added on at various times in the hotel's long history, but management has been meticulous in retaining its historic traditions. Rooms are old-fashioned and spacious with high ceilings and antique furnishings. The most expensive rooms are the largest, but my favorites are those in the Flower Palace, which has an architectural style reminiscent of a Japanese temple and seems unchanged since its 1936 construction. There are also three Japanese-style rooms. Be sure to ask the front desk for the hotel's map of the surrounding village and leaflets describing how to reach sightseeing spots in Hakone from the hotel.

359 Miyanoshita, Hakone. www.fujiyahotel.jp. ℰ **0460/82-2211.** 146 units. ¥20,680–¥34,650 single or double. ¥36,850–¥50,820 Sat, night before holiday, and peak season. Rates include service charge but exclude taxes. Station: Miyanoshita (Hakone Tozan Railway; 5 min.). Bus: From Odawara, Hakone-Yumoto, Moto-Hakone, Hakone-Machi or Togendai to Miyanoshita Onsen stop (1 min.). **Amenities:** 3 restaurants; lounge; bar; hot-spring baths; Jacuzzi; indoor/outdoor pools; room service; sauna; free Wi-Fi.

HIGHLIGHTS OF CHUBU

The Chubu (central) region of Honshu varies dramatically, from rugged coastline to volcanic mountain ranges, including the **Japan Alps National Park (Chubu Sangaku Kokuritsu Koen).** With the exception of Japan's tallest mountain, Mount Fuji, all of Japan's loftiest mountains are in Chubu. Because some of the villages nestled in these mountains retain much of their traditional architecture, the Japan Alps provide a unique look at mountain life both past and present, especially in **Takayama** and **Shirakawa-go.** In addition, the opening of the Hokuriku Shinkansen in early 2015 from Tokyo to **Kanazawa** has made this former castle town with its spectacular garden and Edo-era attractions more accessible than ever before.

KANAZAWA, RENOWNED FOR ITS GARDEN & CRAFTS ★★

622km (386 miles) W of Tokyo; 224km (140 miles) NE of Kyoto

Near the northwest coast of Honshu on the Sea of Japan, Kanazawa is the gateway to the rugged, sea-swept Noto Peninsula. It was the second-largest city (after Kyoto) to escape bombing during World War II, and some of the old city has been left intact, including a district of former samurai mansions, old geisha quarters, Edo-Era canals, and tiny narrow streets that run crookedly without rhyme or reason (apparently to confuse any enemies foolish enough to attack). Kanazawa is most famous for its **Kenrokuen Garden,** one of the most celebrated gardens in all of Japan (and one of my favorites). It's the main reason people come here, though several fine museums are also worth the visit. Kanazawa is also renowned for its crafts dating from the shogun era.

Kanazawa first gained notoriety about 500 years ago, when a militant Buddhist sect joined with peasant rebels to overthrow the feudal lord and establish its own autonomous government, an event unprecedented in Japanese history. The independent republic

Kanazawa

Kanazawa Loop Bus
← Right Loop
← Left Loop

ACCOMMODATIONS ■
APA Hotel Kanazawa-Ekimae 4
APA Hotel Kanazawa-Chuo 25
Hotel Nikko Kanazawa 5
Kanazawa Manten 1
Kanazawa Tokyu Hotel 16
Murataya Ryokan 24
Toyoko Inn Kanazawa-eki
　Higashi-guchi 6
Toyoko Inn Kanazawa
　Kenrokuen Korinbo 15
Via Inn Kanazawa 3

RESTAURANTS ◆
Bimisaizen 17
Bistro Kanazawa
　Todoroki-Tei 8
Budoonoki 23
Jugatsu 10
Kotobuki-Ya 7
Mori Mori Zushi 2
Miyoshian 19

ATTRACTIONS ●
21st Century Museum
　of Contemporary
　Art, Kanazawa 18
Ashigaru Kinenkan 12
Ishikawa Prefectural Museum
　for Traditional Products
　and Crafts 21
Kanazawa Castle Park 11
Kenrokuen Garden 20
Myoryuji Temple 26
Nomura Samurai House 13
Seisonkaku Villa 22
Shima Geisha House 10
Shinise Kinenkan 14

survived almost 100 years before it was attacked by an army commanded by Oda Nobunaga, who was trying to unite Japan at a time when civil wars wracked the nation. Kanazawa was subsequently granted to one of Nobunaga's retainers, Maeda Toshiie, who constructed a castle and transformed the small community into a thriving castle town. The Maeda clan continued to rule over Kanazawa for the next 300 years, amassing wealth in the form of land and rice and encouraging development of the arts. Throughout the Tokugawa shogunate, the Maedas, remained the second-most powerful family in Japan and controlled the largest domain in the country. The arts of Kutani ware, Yuzen silk dyeing, lacquerware, and *Noh* theater flourished—and enjoy popularity in Kanazawa even today. Japan's fourth-largest city at the end of the Feudal Era, Kanazawa with a population today of 462,000 is capital of Ishikawa Prefecture. With about 160 rainy days a year, it has a local proverb you'd be wise to heed: "Even if you forget your packed lunch, don't forget your umbrella."

Essentials

GETTING THERE By Train The **Hokuriku Shinkansen** from Tokyo takes about 2½ hours and costs ¥14,120 for an unreserved seat. From Osaka (via Kyoto), direct **JR trains** depart once or twice an hour; the ride takes about 2 hours and 45 minutes and costs ¥7,130 for an unreserved seat.

By Bus JR Highway buses (www.jrbuskanto.co.jp; ✆ **03/3844-1950**) depart six times daily from Shinjuku Station's New South Exit in Tokyo (with a stop also at Ikebukuro Station's east exit), arrive at Kanazawa Station about 8 hours later, and cost ¥8,050. There are also two night buses, departing from Tokyo Station's Yaesu South Exit and arriving the next morning for the same price. Buses also depart eight times a day from Osaka's Umeda Station (¥4,600, with trips taking 4 hr., 40 min.). Nohi buses (www.nouhibus.co.jp; ✆ **0577/32-1688**) connect Kanazawa with Takayama (with a stop in Shirakawa-go) six times a day; reservations are required and the fare is ¥3,390 for the 2¼-hour trip.

VISITOR INFORMATION In Kanazawa Station near the east gate exit, the **Tourist Information Center** (www.kanazawa-tourism.com; ✆ **076/232-3993**), open daily 9am to 7pm, can book hotel rooms and distributes maps, bus schedules, brochures, and the useful *Eye on Kanazawa* with tips on sightseeing.

GETTING AROUND Kanazawa's attractions spread south and southeast from the station's East Gate exit. Katamachi and adjacent Korinbo, 3km (2 miles) southeast of the station, is Kanazawa's downtown. Sights are too far-flung to see everything on foot, so the easiest way to get around Kanazawa is by **bus.** Although there are many city buses departing from Kanazawa Station, dedicated tourist buses service major attractions, with departures every 15 to 20 minutes from about 8:30am to 6pm. A single ride costs ¥200 and a 1-day pass, which also allows rides on city buses, costs ¥500. The **Kanazawa Loop Bus,** departing from platform 3 at Kanazawa Station's east exit, makes a circular route to all the tourist sights (stops are announced in English). The **Kenrokuen Shuttle,** departing from platform 6, makes a shorter run to sights around Kenrokuen Garden. Pick up a map and schedule at the tourist office.

[FastFACTS] KANAZAWA

ATM/Mail The **Kanazawa Central Post Office,** 1–1 Sanja (☏ **076/224-3822**), is Monday to Friday 9am to 9pm, but a counter remains open 24 hours for mail. It's ATMs are open 12:05am to 11:55pm Monday through Saturday and 12:05am to 9pm on Sunday.

Internet & Wi-Fi Access Kanazawa offers free Wi-Fi in Kanazawa Station, with plans to introduce service to more areas of the city; ask the tourist office for details. Travelers who don't have computers or smart phones should head to the **Ishikawa Foundation for International Exchange,** a 5-minute walk from the east exit of Kanazawa Station (on the road running btw. the Miyako and Nikko hotels). In its library on the third floor of the Rifare building, 1–5–3 Honmachi (☏ **076/262-5931**), there are four computers you can use free of charge for 30 minutes daily from 9am to 6pm (to 5pm Sat–Sun).

Where to Stay

Keep in mind that some accommodations charge higher rates on Saturday and nights before public holidays. Many also add a surcharge during peak season—New Year's, Golden Week (Apr 29–May 5), and mid-July through mid-November.

Directions are from Kanazawa Station; minutes in parentheses indicate the walking time required from the bus stop.

EXPENSIVE

Hotel Nikko Kanazawa ★★★ Kanazawa's tallest building (30 stories) was designed by a Japanese-French team, who succeeded in giving it a boutique-hotel ambience despite its size. Its lobby exudes a French-colonial drawing room atmosphere, adorned with a bubbling fountain, rattan chairs stuffed with pillows, fake trees, antiques, and Asian decorative art ranging from ginger jars to Japanese lacquered boxes. The English-speaking concierge staff receives high marks, and its location in front of Kanazawa Station can't be beat for convenience. Spacious rooms, from the 17th to 28th floors, have been recently renovated to reflect Kanazawa's craft heritage, with accents of Yuzen cloth, ceramics, and artwork trimmed with gold leaf created by local artisans. Twin rooms, which are larger, cost more than rooms with a double bed. On the highest floors are Luxe Rooms, which offer great views of either mountains or the Japan Sea in the distance.

2–15–1 Hon-machi. www.hnkanazawa.jp. ☏ **076/234-1111.** 254 units. ¥26,730–¥48,114 single or double. Station: Kanazawa (east exit, 1 min.). **Amenities:** 5 restaurants; bar; 2 lounges; concierge; access to next-door health club and spa w/indoor pool (fee: ¥2,100); room service; free Wi-Fi.

Kanazawa Tokyu Hotel ★★ This has been one of Kanazawa's most respected hotels for more than 30 years, but it recently underwent a complete upgrade that also elevated it to one of Kanazawa's best. It has a convenient downtown location surrounded by shops and restaurants, just minutes from the Naga-machi Samurai district and within walking distance of Kenrokuen Garden and Myoryuji Temple. Its design is contemporary Japanese, reflected in its lobby simply decorated in gold and black with splashes of red. Rooms are comfortably spacious, with local touches like Kutani pottery coffee cups or with pine silhouettes stenciled on the walls.

2–1–1 Korinbo. www.kanazawa-h.tokyuhotels.co.jp. ℂ **076/231-2411.** 236 units. ¥14,850–¥18,057 single; ¥26,017–¥45,144 double. Loop Bus: Korinbo (1 min.). **Amenities:** 2 restaurants; bar; lounge; concierge; room service; free Wi-Fi.

MODERATE

APA Hotel Kanazawa-Ekimae ★ Although a business hotel, this place does have a special feature that sets it apart: large public baths complete with sauna and open-air bath, free to hotel guests. Other pluses include a convenient location just steps away from Kanazawa Station (but on the opposite side from where buses depart); bold use of bright colors that are a welcome relief from the usual bland white of most business hotels; and a Seattle's Best Coffee. If you're not a fan of public baths, however, you might choose to stay elsewhere; rooms are so minuscule that if you open your luggage you may have to leap to reach your bed (there are no closets). Double rooms, which have only one reading light beside the bed, are about right for one person, and twins provide barely enough room for two people to move about.

If you'd rather be in the heart of the city, there are three downtown APA hotels, including **APA Hotel Kanazawa-Chuo,** 1–5–24 Katamachi (ℂ **076/ 235-2111**), which offers similar-size rooms at similar rates and a Seattle's Best Coffee, but the water tapped for its indoor and outdoor baths is from hot springs.

1–9–28 Hirooka. www.apahotel.com. ℂ **076/231-8111.** 456 units. ¥8,000–¥11,000 single; ¥12,500–¥18,000 double. Prices exclude tax. Station: Kanazawa (west exit, 1 min.). **Amenities:** 3 restaurants; bar; sauna; free Wi-Fi.

Kanazawa Manten ★ A small fountain outside the entrance, a front desk backed by trees, jazz playing in the hotel restaurant, indoor/outdoor baths, and attentive service all conspire to make this business hotel (located on the opposite side of the station from where the buses depart) seem like it's more expensive than it is. Alas, the mostly single rooms (there are 141 twin rooms and 42 doubles) are no different or larger than those of any other business hotel, though window panels can be closed for complete darkness. Also, there are ladies' rooms with face steamers and women's toiletries, and couples might want to opt for twin rooms, as they are larger than doubles but also more expensive. Ask for a room on a higher floor; those facing the station give views of trains coming and going. In short, cramped quarters reinforce the business-hotel status, but at least in the lobby and the baths you can feel grand.

1–6–1 Kita-yasue. www.manten-hotel.com. ℂ **076/265-0100.** 509 units. ¥6,800–¥8,900 single; ¥11,800–¥15,000 double. Prices exclude tax. Station: Kanazawa (west exit, 4 min.). Turn right out of the station and continue walking alongside the station, past the car park. **Amenities:** Restaurant; lounge; public baths w/Jacuzzi, sauna (men only), and steam room (women only); free Wi-Fi.

INEXPENSIVE

In addition to the recommendations here, there are two **Toyoko Inns** in Kanazawa, **Toyoko Inn Kanazawa-eki Higashi-guchi** just a 4-minute walk from the east exit of Kanazawa Station and **Toyoko Inn Kanazawa Kenrokuen Korinbo** in the heart of the city. Go to www.toyoko-inn.com for more information on this chain.

Murataya Ryokan ★★ This friendly Japanese-style inn, owned by the Murata family for 65 years, is in the heart of Kanazawa, just off the Katamachi and Tatemachi shopping streets and within walking distance of Kenrokuen and Naga-machi Samurai district. Although the two-story structure is rather uninteresting from the outside, inside it's comfortable and pleasant, with a tiny courtyard moss garden containing a stone lantern; note the old-fashioned 60-some-year-old telephone in the reception used to connect Murataya with the outside world. All rooms are clean and are Japanese style with *tatami,* with extra-long futon for tall foreigners. Note that there's no elevator, but there is a room on the ground floor with a view of the garden. In addition to laundry facilities, a plus is the inn's own map of the Katamachi area, showing the locations of banks, post offices, stores, and restaurants.

1–5–2 Katamachi. www.murataya-ryokan.com/e. *☎* **076/263-0455.** 11 units (none with private bathroom). ¥4,900–¥5,700 single; ¥9,400–¥11,400 double. Loop Bus: Katamachi (3 min.). Take the small pedestrian lane on the left side of the APA Hotel (*not* the APA Villa) and then turn right. **Amenities:** Free Wi-Fi.

Via Inn Kanazawa ★ This business hotel, located inside Kanazawa Station with reception on the third floor, offers all of life's basic necessities, including decent-size rooms and a microwave on each floor (there's a grocery store below the hotel). Free Wi-Fi, however, is available only in the lobby. There are only eight twin rooms and no doubles, but two people can stay in a single room for the lowest price below if they don't mind forced togetherness.

Kanazawa Station. http://kanazawa.viainn.com. *☎* **076/222-5489.** 206 units. ¥7,000 single; ¥8,300–¥13,400 double. Station: Kanazawa (inside the station, toward the west gate). **Amenities:** Free Internet.

Where to Eat

Kanazawa's local specialties, known collectively as ***Kaga Ryori,*** consist of seafood, such as tiny shrimp and winter crabs, as well as freshwater fish, duck, and mountain vegetables. Popular in winter is *jibuni,* a duck-and-vegetable stew.

All directions are from Kanazawa Station.

AROUND KANAZAWA STATION

Forus, a shopping center located next to Kanazawa Station (look for *Aeon* on its facade), has a slew of restaurants on its sixth floor, including Mori Mori Zushi and Budoonoki (see reviews below), as well as those serving noodles, *tonkatsu, okonomiyaki,* and Indian and Chinese fare. Most are open daily from 11am to 11pm.

Mori Mori Zushi (もりもり寿し) ★ SUSHI   This conveyor-belt sushi restaurant has colored plates, each signifying a specific price, but there's also a touch panel at each seat with photos so you can order what you want if it doesn't float past. There are spigots for hot water at the counter; serve yourself and add powdered tea. There's a more colorful branch at Omi-cho Market (① **076/262-7477**), open daily from 10am to 9pm.

Forus, 6th floor, 3–1 Horikawashinmachi. ① **076/265-3510.** Sushi platters ¥120–¥470. Daily 11am–9:30pm (last order). Station: Kanazawa (east exit, 1 min.). Turn left out of the station.

AROUND KENROKUEN GARDEN

Miyoshian (三芳庵) ★★ KAGA KAISEKI   A great place to try the local *Kaga* cuisine right in Kenrokuen Garden, this 100-year-old restaurant consists of two separate wooden buildings, the best of which is a traditional room extending over a large pond. This is where you'll probably dine, seated on *tatami* with a view of a waterfall and an ancient pond with giant carp swimming in the murky waters. Only set meals of *Kaga* cuisine are served, all featuring *jibuni*. The more expensive the meal, the more dishes it adds. The ¥1,500 *yugao* meal includes soup, *jibuni*, sashimi, a seasonal dish such as eel on rice, and pickles. The ¥3,000 *chakaisekifu* meal adds such dishes as salmon, crab, tofu, and various small delicacies. Lunch is served from 11am to 2:30pm, but you can also come just for green tea and sweets for ¥700. By the way, there's another hut called Uchihashitei that extends over Kasumigaike Pond that also sells a set meal with *jibuni* for ¥2800.

Kenrokuen Garden, 1–11 Kenrokumachi. ① **076/221-0127.** *Kaga teishoku* ¥1,500–¥3,000. Thurs–Tues 9am–4pm. Loop Bus or Kenrokuen Shuttle: Kenrokuen Garden (5 min.). In front of the park's Renchimon Gate.

KATAMACHI

Radiating around the downtown Katamachi and Korinbo shopping areas are lots of restaurants and drinking establishments.

Bimisaizen (美味彩膳) ★ TONKATSU/UDON NOODLES   Easy to find in Daiwa department store and also convenient for people who wish to dine in the middle in the afternoon, this casual eatery combines cuisine from two restaurants–*udon* noodles from Tsuruhan and *tonkatsu* from Tazamura. In addition to a display case showing options, it also has an English menu. I opted for a set meal that included pork, shrimp and cheese *tonkatsu*, which arrived crispy and flakey. But the best thing about dining here is its view over Central Park, with the woods of Castle Park rising beyond (avoid the noon rush, however).

Daiwa department store, 8th floor. 1–1–1 Korinbo. ① **076/222-0236.** Set meals ¥1,263–¥1,728. Daily 11am–10pm. Loop Bus or Kenrokuen Shuttle: Korinbo (1 min.). In front of the bus stop.

Budoonoki ★ ITALIAN   An informal eatery with a high ceiling and an open facade with a few outdoor tables facing a courtyard, this pleasant restaurant offers salads, pizzas, and pastas, including versions you've probably never thought of, like a soy milk cream pasta with cod roe and sweet potato. During lunch there's a weekly set that gives a choice of pasta along with soup and a little salad, as well as weekly specials, a ladies lunch and omelet rice sets (omelets filled with rice are popular in Japan). Dinner adds more choices, liked smoked duck breast, spicy grilled shrimp, and ratatouille. There's a branch on the sixth floor of Forus next to Kanazawa Station (℃ 076/265-3521), open daily 11am to 11pm.

1–3–21 Katamachi. ℃ **076/232-7878.** Main dishes ¥864–¥1,491; set lunches ¥840–¥1,113. Daily 11am–9:30pm (last order). Closed irregularly. Loop Bus: Katamachi (2 min.). In a small alley off Katamachi St. called Prego.

HIGASHI CHAYA DISTRICT

Bistro Kanazawa Todoroki-Tei ★ FRENCH   This former bank dating from the Taisho Period (1912–26) has been turned into an attractive restaurant boasting tall ceilings, gleaming dark wood, and period light fixtures. Big-band jazz and swing music playing in the background add to its nostalgic atmosphere. For dinner you might opt for the Caesar salad, prepared tableside and large enough for two to share, followed by roast lamb, fish wrapped in paper and grilled or seafood paella. Lunch sets might give a choice of hamburger steak, pulled pork from Noto Peninsula, roasted fish or beef stew.

1–2–1 Higashiyama. ℃ **076/252-5755.** Main courses ¥1,300–¥3,500; set lunches ¥1,300–¥1,800; set dinners ¥3,500–¥7,000. Daily 11:30am–2:30pm (to 3:30pm Sat–Sun and holidays) and 6–10:30pm. Loop Bus: Hashiba-cho (1 min.). Beside the bus stop and *koban* (police box).

ELSEWHERE

Kotobuki-Ya (壽屋) ★★★ VEGETARIAN   Specializing in *shojin ryori kaiseki* meals (Buddhist vegetarian cooking), Kotobuki-ya occupies a beautiful 170-year-old merchant's house with a two-story airy entryway, with various rooms added in the Taisho (1912–26) and Showa (1926–89) eras. Dining here, on beautiful lacquer and pottery tableware while seated at tables or on *tatami* in your own private room, is a wonderful experience—not surprisingly, they have had many fine reviews. Although the *kaiseki* served is generally vegetarian, meals with fish are also available. For lunch, you can also dine in a communal room for ¥2,800 on a *donburi teishoku* featuring a rice dish topped with fish and fish eggs, plus sashimi and dessert, or splurge on vegetarian or fish *kaiseki* starting at ¥4,500. Reservations should be made by 4:30pm for dinner, 1 day in advance on weekends.

2–4–13 Owari-cho. ℃ **076/231-6245.** Set lunches ¥2,800–¥5,500; *kaiseki* dinners ¥8,000–¥15,000. Daily 11:30am–1:30pm and 5:30–7pm (last order). Loop Bus or Kenrokuen Shuttle: Musashigatsuji (3 min.). North of Hyakumangoku Dori, on a side street with a small parking lot.

Exploring Kanazawa

Much of Kanazawa's charm lies in the atmosphere of its old neighborhoods. Be sure to wear your good walking shoes, as the best way to explore various parts of the city is via your own two feet. One suggested itinerary for tackling the city's sights is to take the Loop Bus to the Higashi Chaya district, then another Loop bus onward to Kenrokuen and the sights in its vicinity, and then walk the 15 minutes to the Naga-machi Samurai district, stopping at Seisonkaku villa, the 21st Century Museum of Contemporary Art, and other sights along the way. Directional English-language signs to major sights are posted throughout the city. Or, if you wish, call the Tourist Information Center (see above) at least 2 weeks in advance of your visit to request a Goodwill Guide to show you the city; the service is free, but you're expected to pay for the guide's entrance fees, transportation, and lunch.

AROUND KENROKUEN GARDEN

The sights here are listed in the order you'll reach them on foot from Kenrokuen. Kanazawa Castle Park should be seen *before* entering Kenrokuen.

Kanazawa Castle Park ★ PARK/GARDEN At one time, Kanazawa possessed an impressive castle belonging to the powerful Maeda clan for 14 generations, but it was destroyed by fire several times, the last time in 1881. Ishikawamon Gate, visible from the northwest corner of Kenrokuen and reached via bridge over a busy thoroughfare, served as the south entrance to the castle and is the castle's only remaining original structure. Observing how big and grand the gate is, you can appreciate the magnitude of the original Maeda castle. Remarkably, its roof tiles are actually lead, in case emergency dictated they be melted down for musket balls. The area just beyond the gate is Kanazawa Castle Park, where several castle fortifications have been reconstructed using traditional Japanese construction techniques, including Kahokumon Gate, the Hishi Yagura and Hashizume-mon Tsuzuki Yagura watchtowers, and, linking them, the Gojikken Nagaya storehouse. You can skip these empty buildings if time is of the essence. What impresses me most is the expansiveness of the grounds, including a forested area. If you want to get away from it all, this is the place. Otherwise, good to know is the information booth near Ishikawamon, where volunteer guides offer free guided tours from 9:30am to 3:30pm.

Kenroku-machi. ℭ **076/234-3800.** Free admission to Castle Park and Kahokumon; watchtowers/storehouse ¥310 adults, ¥100 children. Park Mar to mid-Oct daily 7am–6pm, mid-Oct to Feb daily 8am–5pm; watchtowers/storehouse daily 9am–4:30pm. Loop Bus or Kenrokuen Shuttle: Kenrokuen Garden (5 min.).

Kenrokuen Garden ★★★ PARK/GARDEN Kanazawa's main attraction, the 10-hectare (25-acre) **Kenrokuen Garden,** once served as Kanazawa Castle's outer garden. The largest of what are considered to be the three best landscape gardens in Japan—the other two are Kairakuen Garden in Mito and Korakuen Garden in Okayama—it's considered by some to be the grandest. Its name can be translated as "a refined garden incorporating six attributes"— spaciousness, careful arrangement, seclusion, antiquity, elaborate use of water, and scenic charm. Ponds, trees, winding streams, rocks, mounds, and footpaths have all been combined so aesthetically that the effect is spellbinding. Best of all, unlike most other gardens in Japan, there are no surrounding skyscrapers to detract from splendid views, making this one of my personal favorites.

Altogether, it took about 150 years to complete the garden. The fifth Maeda lord started construction in the 1670s, and successive lords added to it according to their individual tastes. The garden as you now see it was finished by the 13th Maeda lord in 1837; only after the Meiji Restoration was it opened to the public, in 1874. In addition to pines, cherry trees, irises, ponds, and other elements of natural beauty, there are several historic structures, including the Yugaotei tea-ceremony house dating from 1774 and, most important, Seisonkaku Villa (see below). Plan on 1½ hours of blissful wanderings. *Tip:* You may want to arrive early in the morning or near the end of the day, as Kenrokuen Garden is a favorite destination of Japanese tour groups, led by flag-carrying guides who explain everything in detail—through loudspeakers.

1–4 Kenroku-machi. www.pref.ishikawa.jp/siro-niwa/kenrokuen. ✆ **076/234-3800.** Admission ¥310 adults, free for seniors, ¥100 children. Mar to mid-Oct daily 7am–6pm; mid-Oct to Feb daily 8am–5pm. Loop Bus or Kenrokuen Shuttle: Kenrokuen Garden (3 min.).

Ishikawa Prefectural Museum for Traditional Products and Crafts (Ishikawa Kenritsu Dento Sangyo Kogeikan) ★★ MUSEUM If I had time to visit only one museum in Kanazawa, this would be my choice. It's the best place in town to view 36 different handcrafted items for which Ishikawa Prefecture has long been famous (the Maeda lords promoted crafts over warfare). With the help of a detailed English-language pamphlet, you'll learn about the famous Kutani pottery, first produced under the patronage of the Maeda clan in the 1600s and known for its hues of green, red, purple, navy blue, and yellow, as well as Kaga Yuzen dyeing and hand-painting on silk, Kanazawa lacquerware (which uses raised lacquer painting), paulownia woodcrafts, metalwork, family Buddhist altars, Kanazawa gold leaf, *taiko* drums, *koto* and *shamisen* stringed instruments, lion masks, fishing lures (using feathers of wild birds), folk toys, *washi* (Japanese paper), umbrellas, and even fireworks. Plan on 1 hour to appreciate everything.

1–1 Kenroku-machi. www.ishikawa-densankan.jp. ✆ **076/262-2020.** Admission ¥260 adults, ¥200 seniors, ¥100 children. Daily 9am–5pm (closed 3rd Thurs of every month Apr–Nov and every Thurs Dec–Mar). Loop Bus: Hirosaka (6 min.); Kenrokuen Shuttle: Seisonkaku-mae (1 min.). Next to Seisonkaku Villa; you can also enter the museum directly from Kenrokuen.

Seisonkaku Villa (成巽閣) ★★★ HISTORIC HOME   Just outside the Kodatsuno (southeast) exit of Kenrokuen Garden is this must-see villa, built in 1863 by the 13th Maeda lord as a retirement home for his widowed mother. Elegant and graceful, it has a distinctly feminine atmosphere with delicately carved, brightly painted wood transoms and painted *shoji* screens decorated with seashells, butterflies, flowers, and other motifs. The first-floor bedroom is decorated with tortoises painted on the *shoji* wainscoting; tortoises were associated with long life, and it must have worked—the mother lived to be 84. Upstairs, rooms are painted in brilliant colors of blue, red and purple. Expect to linger about 20 minutes here, but unfortunately you can only photograph the inner garden.

1–2 Kenroku-machi. www.seisonkaku.com. ℭ **076/221-0580.** Admission ¥700 adults, ¥300 junior-high and high-school students, ¥250 children. Thurs–Tues 9am–5pm. Loop Bus: Hirosaka (5 min.); Kenrokuen Shuttle: Seisonkaku-mae (1 min.). Next to the Ishikawa Prefectural Museum for Traditional Products and Crafts.

21st Century Museum of Contemporary Art, Kanazawa ★★

MUSEUM   In a word, this museum is fun! Centrally located between Kenrokuen and the Katamachi shopping district, Kanazawa's newest museum, with the aim of revitalizing the arts in Kanazawa and attracting young visitors, is ensconced in a striking circular building that has no front or back, allowing visitors to explore it from all directions (and, from time to time, lose themselves in it). Galleries, which range from bright spaces with sunlight pouring through glass ceilings to darkened rooms with no natural light, display a collection that concentrates on works of the past 30 years, particularly of Japanese artists born after 1965, along with contemporary works from around the world shown in changing exhibitions. My favorite: Leandro Erlich's outdoor "swimming pool" topped with a roof of glass and shallow water; look in, and you might see people who, having entered through a subterranean tunnel, look like they're walking underwater. James Turrell's *Blue Planet Sky Room* is a white courtyard open to the sky, making heaven appear like a work of art.

1–2–1 Hirosaka. www.kanazawa21.jp. ℭ **076/220-2800.** Admission ¥360 adults, ¥280 seniors and university students, free for children 17 and under. Special exhibits (which sometimes take over most of the museum) ¥1,000, ¥800, and ¥400 respectively. Sun and Tues–Thurs 10am–6pm; Fri–Sat 10am–8pm. Loop Bus and Kenrokuen Shuttle: Hirosaka (2 min.).

THE NAGA-MACHI SAMURAI (BUKE YASHIKI) DISTRICT

About a 15-minute walk west of Kenrokuen Garden and just a couple minutes' walk west of Katamachi/Korinbo (Kanazawa's main shopping district), the Naga-machi Samurai District is basically a few streets lined with beautiful wooden homes hidden behind gold-colored mud walls (higher-ranked samurai had higher walls; the lowest rank had only hedges) and bordered by canals left over from the Edo Period. An unhurried stroll in the neighborhood will give you an idea of what a feudal castle town might have looked like, though on a much reduced scale. Lord Maeda had as many as 8,000 samurai retainers, who in turn had their own retainers, making the samurai population here very large indeed. To see how those in the lowest military class lived, stop by the **Kanazawa Ashigaru Kinenkan** (金沢市足軽資料館), consisting of two modest homes–the Shimizu house and the Takanishi house, both occupied until the 1990s and open free to the public daily 9:30am to 5pm. In addition, the **Kanazawa Shinise Kinenkan** (ℭ **076/220-2524;** daily 9:30am–5pm), a former Chinese pharmacy established in 1579, displays the old store and family residence and, upstairs, Kanazawa crafts and products from some 60 local stores; admission here is ¥100.

To reach the Naga-machi Samurai District from Katamachi, take the side street to the right of the Tokyu Hotel.

Nomura Samurai House (Buke Yashiki Ato Nomura Ke; 武家屋敷跡野村家) ★ HISTORIC HOME

Stop 20 minutes here to see how higher-ranking samurai lived back in the Edo Period. Occupied by 11 generations of the Nomura family for 400 years, this traditional Japanese home boasts a drawing room made of Japanese cypress, with elaborate designs in rosewood and *shoji* screens painted with landscapes, and a tea-ceremony room upstairs (tea costs ¥300 extra). Rooms overlook a small, charming garden with a miniature waterfall, a winding stream, huge carp, and stone lanterns (many people come just for the garden). Personal effects of the Nomura family and objects from the Edo Period are on display, including a samurai outfit, swords, lacquerware, the family altar, and a box for bush warblers (deliberately dark so the birds would sing).

1–3–32 Naga-machi. © **076/221-3553.** Admission ¥550 adults, ¥400 high-school students, ¥250 children. Apr–Sept daily 8:30am–5:30pm; Oct–Mar daily 8:30am–4:30pm. Loop Bus: Korinbo (5 min.). Take the side street to the right of the Excel Hotel Tokyu, turn right at the T, and then turn left.

OTHER SIGHTS

Higashi Chaya District   There are approximately 50 geisha practicing their trade in three old entertainment quarters in Kanazawa, including this one. A walk here reveals rather solemn-looking, wood-slatted facades of geisha houses dating from the 1820s, where men of means have long come to be entertained with music, dancing, songs, the tea ceremony, poem recitals, and other pleasurable pursuits. Geisha still perform at seven houses in the Higashi Chaya District, but most of the other former geisha homes have been turned into shops, inns, and restaurants. For an inside peek at the geisha world, visit the 200-year-old **Shima Geisha House** (志摩) ★, 1–13–21 Higashiyama (© **076/252-5675;** daily 9am–6pm), a former tearoom where geisha performed. Inside, you'll find rooms that were allotted to personal use, as well as to performing, along with displays of ordinary artifacts from hair ornaments, pipes, and game boards to cooking utensils. Architectural details worth noting include several stairways (so that customers could come and go without being seen); a small Shinto shrine at the entrance to the home; a more elaborate family Buddhist altar in a place of honor in a front room; the gleaming wood-lacquered surfaces of furniture; and cloisonné door pulls on sliding doors. Admission is ¥400 for adults, ¥300 for children; you can also enjoy tea in the peaceful new addition facing a garden, which, depending on the accompanying sweet, costs ¥500 to ¥700. Plan on 15 minutes to tour the house. To reach it, take the Loop Bus to the Hashiba-cho stop.

Myoryuji Temple (妙立寺) ★★ TEMPLE   Myoryuji Temple (1–2–12 Nomachi; www.myoryuji.jp; © **076/241-0888**) is popularly known as Ninja-dera (Temple of the Secret Agents) because of its secret chambers, hidden stairways, and trick doors. Built by the Maeda clan for family prayer in 1643, it looks small from the outside, just two stories high to comply with height restrictions during the Edo Period. Inside, four stories are evident, but even this is false: Three more levels are concealed. The fortresslike structure contains an amazing 29 stairways and a labyrinth of corridors, along with such trick devices as pitfalls to trap unsuspecting intruders, slatted stairs where lances could stab at passing legs, escape hatches, secret stairways, and rooms that could be opened only from the outside—just one more example of how deep paranoia ran during the Edo Period. Although rumor has it that a tunnel once connected the temple to the castle to serve as an escape route for the feudal lord in case of attack, a river running between them makes it unlikely. Unfortunately, photography is not allowed.

You must phone ahead for a reservation; chances are good that you'll be able to see it the same day you call. To ensure that you don't get lost (which would be quite easy because of all the trick doors), you must join a guided tour. Unfortunately, tours are in Japanese only, but there's an English-language booklet with photos that lets you follow along, and demonstrations of the various trick devices are fairly self-explanatory. Tours, given daily from 9am to 4:30pm (to 4pm in winter), last 30 to 40 minutes and cost ¥800 for adults, ¥600 for children (however, the temple does not recommend tours for children of any age, due to their tendency to talk and make noise, and children 5 and younger are not admitted). To reach it, take the Loop Bus to Hirokoji, and arrive at least 10 minutes before the start of your tour.

Shopping

Kanazawa's most famous products are its **Kutani pottery,** with its bright five-color overglaze patterns, and its hand-painted **Yuzen silk.** Kanazawa also produces *maki-e* lacquerware, sweets, toys, wooden products, and almost all of Japan's gold leaf. For convenient shopping for these and other souvenirs, including food products, there's the **100 bangai shopping arcade** right in Kanazawa Station, open daily 8:30am to 7pm.

For department stores like Daiwa, boutiques, and contemporary shops, visit downtown **Katamachi** and the pedestrian **Tatemachi shopping street. Omi-cho Market,** just off Hyakumangoku Dori between Kanazawa Station and downtown, was established 280 years ago as the "kitchen of Kanazawa" and today is a vibrant city market with more than 170 stalls selling seafood, vegetables, fruit, and more. It's open Monday to Saturday from 10am to 6pm (some shops open also on Sunday).

Ishikawa Prefectural Products Center (Kanko Bussankan) ★
Located just north of Kenrokuen Garden, this is the place to come for one-stop shopping of all the products Ishikawa Prefecture is famous for. The ground floor sells crafts ranging from lacquerware and pottery to glassware, food-stuff, and toys, while the second floor houses more crafts and a sushi restaurant. Open daily 10am to 6pm (upstairs closes at 4pm; closed some Tues Nov–Mar). 2–20 Kenroku-machi. ℂ **076/222-7788.** Loop Bus or Kenrokuen Shuttle: Kenrokuen Garden. On Hyakumangoku Dori.

Sakuda (さくだ) ★ Thinking about wallpapering a room in gold leaf? Then you'll want to pay a visit to Sakuda, located in a modern building in the Higashi Chaya District. (As much as 98% of Japan's entire national output of gold leaf is produced in Kanazawa.) You can watch artisans at work, pounding the gold leaf and spreading it until it's paper-thin and translucent; it's the equivalent of pounding a ¥10 coin into the size of a *tatami* mat. But most people come here to shop for gold-leafed vases, boxes, chopsticks, bowls, trays, screens, furniture, and—this being Japan—golf balls and iPhone covers. You can even buy gold flakes to add to your coffee or sake or gold-laden cosmetics. Don't miss the second-floor bathrooms; the women's is done entirely in gold leaf, the men's in platinum. The staff serves complimentary tea spiked with gold leaf to visitors. Open daily 9am to 6pm. 1–3–27 Higashiyama. www.goldleaf-sakuda.jp. ℂ **076/251-6777.** Loop Bus: Hashiba-cho (4 min.).

RURAL SHIRAKAWA-GO & OGIMACHI ★★

555km (347 miles) NW of Tokyo; 77km (48 miles) S of Kanazawa; 47km (29 miles) NE of Takayama

With its thatched-roof farmhouses, paddies trimmed with flowerbeds, roaring river, and pine-covered mountains rising on all sides, **Shirakawa-go** is one of the most picturesque regions in Japan. Unfortunately, it also has more than its fair share of tour buses (especially in May, Aug, and Oct). Still, because of its rather remote location, accessible only by car or bus, Shirakawa-go remains off the beaten path for many foreign tourists. A visit to this rural region in Gifu Prefecture could well be the highlight of your trip.

Although Shirakawa-go stretches about 39km (24 miles) beside the Sho-kawa River and covers 229 sq. km (88 sq. miles), mountains and forest account for 95% of the region, and Shirakawa-go's 1,700 residents and cultivated land are squeezed into a valley averaging less than 3km (2 miles) in width. Thus, land in Shirakawa-go for growing rice and other crops has always been scarce and valuable. As a result, farmhouses were built large enough to hold extended families, with as many as several dozen family members living under one roof. Because there wasn't enough land available for young couples to marry and build houses of their own, only the eldest son was allowed to marry; the other children were required to spend their lives living with their parents and helping with the farming. But even though younger children weren't allowed to marry, a man was allowed to choose a young woman, visit her in her par-ents' home, and father her children. The children then remained with the mother's family, becoming valuable members of the labor force.

Before the roads came to Shirakawa-go, winter always meant complete isola-tion as snow 2m (6 ft.) deep blanketed the entire region. *Irori* (open-hearth fire-places) in the middle of a communal room were used for cooking, warmth, and light during the long winter months. The family lived, therefore, on the ground floor, while upper floors were used for silk cultivation and storage of utensils. Because of the heavy snowfall, thatched roofs were constructed at steep angles, known as *gassho-zukuri* in reference to the fact that the tops of the roofs look like hands joined in prayer. The steep angle also allowed rain to run off quickly, and the thatch (Japanese pampas grass) dried quickly in the sun, preventing decay. Remarkably, the massive homes were constructed without nails; rather, sturdy ropes held the framework together and helped withstand earthquakes. Because there were no chimneys, smoke from the *irori* simply rose into the levels above, helping to ward off insects in the thatch and to keep the ropes taut.

Today, there are about 114 thatched farmhouses, barns, and sheds in Shirakawa-go, most of them built about 200 to 300 years ago. The thatched roofs are about .6m (2 ft.) thick and last some 40 years. The old roofs are replaced in Shirakawa-go every April, when one to four roofs are changed on successive weekends. The entire process involves about 200 or more people, who can replace one roof in a couple of days.

Shirakawa-go's inhabitants live in several small villages. Of these, **Ogimachi ★★★**, declared a UNESCO World Cultural and Natural Heritage site in 1995 and often referred to as Shirakawa, boasts the greatest concentration of thatched-roof buildings. With just 600 residents, it's a delightful hamlet of narrow lanes winding past thatched-roof farmhouses, which stand like island sentinels surrounded by paddies. Many of the farmhouses have been turned into *minshuku,* souvenir shops, restaurants, and museums, including an **open-air museum** that depicts life in the region before roads opened it to the rest of the world.

Essentials

GETTING THERE The most common way to reach Ojimachi is by **Nohi Bus** (www.nouhibus.co.jp; ✆ **0577/32-1688**) from Takayama or Kanazawa. From Takayama Station, it takes about 1 hour and costs ¥2,470, with about 11 departures daily. From Kanazawa Station, you have to make a reservation for one of the six buses daily, which you can do right before departure if there's room; the fare is ¥1,850 for the 1½-hour trip. In any case, buses arrive at a parking lot next to the Gassho Zukuri Minka-en open-air museum (see below); *minshuku* are located in the village on the other side of the river, reached via pedestrian suspension bridge.

VISITOR INFORMATION There's a **tourist office** (www.shirakawa-go.org; ✆ **05769/6-1013;** daily 8:30am–5pm) located next to the bus parking lot. You can pick up an English-language map, reserve a room in a *minshuku* if you have not already done so, and store luggage here for ¥600 if it won't fit in any of the adjacent lockers.

GETTING AROUND Your own two feet can do it best. You can **walk** from one end of the village to the other in about 15 minutes; English-language signs direct you to the various attractions.

Seeing the Sights in & Around Ogimachi

In addition to an open-air museum, several old farmhouses in Ogimachi are open to the public. *Note:* Because Ogimachi is so small, no addresses are given in this section. This is a very small village, basically just one main street and some side streets.

A View of Ogimachi

For an overview (and the best vantage point for photographs) of the entire village, walk along the gently sloping road that leads from the north side of Ogimachi to the **Shiroyama Viewing Point ★★**. There's a souvenir shop/restaurant here, but the best thing to do is to turn left at the crest of the hill and walk to the hill's westernmost point (toward the river), where there are some secluded benches. From here, you'll have a marvelous view of the entire valley, made even more picturesque because all the thatched houses face north and south so that sun hitting the thatched roofs melt snow more quickly. If you're thirsty or hungry, go to the restaurant (also with an outdoor viewing point) to buy a drink or a snack and then take it with you to the lookout.

Gassho Zukuri Minka-en ★★★ MUSEUM   To see how rural people lived in centuries past, visit Shirakawa-go's top attraction, an open-air museum with 25 *gassho-zukuri* houses and sheds that were relocated mostly from Kazura village and restored here. Filled with the tools of everyday life and displays ranging from silk production to straw clothing, the buildings are picturesquely situated around ponds, paddies, flowerbeds, and streams, a photographer's dream. Occasionally, there are artisans making traditional handicrafts. A couple of the structures show DVDs, including one that depicts rural life almost 50 years ago in Kazura, abandoned in 1967; another shows *gassho-zukuri* construction and re-thatching. Plan on 1½ hours.

ⓒ **05769/6-1231.** Admission ¥500 adults, ¥300 children 7–15. Mar–Nov daily 8:40am–5pm; Dec–Feb 9am–4pm (closed Thurs Dec–Mar; if Thurs is a holiday, it remains open but closes Wed instead). Beside the bus parking lot and tourist office.

Nagase Ke (長瀬家) ★★   Of several homes open to the public, this is my favorite. Built in 1890 using 150- to 200-year-old cypress and 300- to 400-year-old chestnut and other wood, the Nagase house is the largest home here, once housing 44 people (three generations of the Nagase family still live here). The enormous cross beam is 18m (59 ft.) long and the height of the five-story house is more than 17m (55 ft.) high. A 15-minute video shows the 2001 re-thatching in which 500 people took part, including 40 women involved just in cooking meals for the workers. Because Nagase ancestors were personal doctors of the powerful Maeda lords from the Kanazawa region, the house displays gifts from the Maedas as well as medical tools. Like other homes, it contains a family altar, this one 500 years old and adjoined to the house so it could be quickly removed in case of fire. Upstairs is a mezzanine where 17 laborers lived, while the next level displays tools used for everything from threshing rice and making rope to weaving cloth; in this remote area, almost everything people used was handmade. The fourth floor, where silk production once took place, contains tools related to the business, including flat trays where the silk worms were bred.

ⓒ **05769/6-1047.** Admission ¥300 adults, ¥150 children. Daily 9am–5pm. Occasionally closed. Just north of the main street.

Where to Stay & Eat

Because huge extended families living under one roof are a thing of the past, some residents of Ogimachi have turned their *gassho-zukuri* homes into *minshuku*. Staying in one gives you the unique chance to lodge in a thatched farmhouse with a family that might consist of grandparents, parents, and children. English is often limited to the basics of "bath," "breakfast," and "dinner," but smiles go a long way. Most likely, the family will drag out their family album with its pictures of winter snowfall and the momentous occasion when their thatched roof was repaired. What I like best about staying overnight is that most tourists are day-trippers, which means you have the village pretty much to yourself by late afternoon. Be sure to take both an evening and early morning stroll.

Most *minshuku* are fairly small, with about four to nine *tatami* rooms open to guests. Rooms are basic without bathroom or toilet, and you may be expected to roll out your own futon. Privacy may be limited, as only a flimsy sliding partition may separate you from the guest next door. All recommended *minshuku* below are in thatch-roofed homes; rates include breakfast and dinner (add ¥400 in winter—about Nov–Apr—for heating charges), and none accept credit cards or have private bathrooms. Check-in is at 3pm; checkout is 9am. The tourist office can make a reservation for you at these or any of the others around town.

Although all *minshuku* have public baths, I like soaking in the town's only hot-spring indoor and outdoor baths, at **Shirakawa-go no Yu** (白川郷の温泉; ✆ **05769/6-0026**), a 12-minute walk from the bus stop. Open daily from 7am to 9:30pm, it charges ¥700 for adults and ¥300 for children, but ask your *minshuku* for a ¥200 discount coupon.

Juemon (十右ヱ門) ★★   Juemon is a favorite among foreigners traveling in Japan. This attractive *minshuku*, in a 300-year-old farmhouse, features a stone-ringed pond with flowering shrubs and a couple of benches where you can relax and enjoy the view. In addition, there's an *irori* in the dining room; don't be surprised if the outgoing 70-something Mrs. Sakai, who runs this place along with her son, serenades you during dinner with a *shamisen* and folk songs. Visitors will be happy to know that toilets were recently upgraded to Washlets.

1653 Ogimachi, Shirakawa Mura. ✆ **05769/6-1053.** 4 units (none with bathroom). ¥9,000 per person. A 15-min. walk from the bus stop, on the south edge of Ogimachi past Doburoku Festival Hall.

Koemon (幸ヱ門) ★★★   This is my top choice for accommodations. It's now run and managed by fifth- and sixth-generation innkeepers of this 200-year-old farmhouse, which became a *minshuku* 45 years ago but has been modernized with a heated floor, automatic sensor lights, communal Washlet toilets, and even dim switches to enhance the mood around his *irori* fireplace, where you'll have your meals and watch a video during dinner showing the re-thatching of the farmhouse. Rooms are spotless, with the best one facing a pond. If you have heavy luggage, you'll be happy to know that this one is closest to the bus terminal. The best way to reserve is by phone (✆ **05769/6-1748**).

456 Ogimachi, Shirakawa Mura. ✆ **05769/6-1446.** 4 units (none with bathroom). ¥9,000 per person. A 3-min. walk from the bus stop, just over the footbridge.

Ochudo (落人)   Because *minshuku* provide dinner and breakfast, all you'll probably need is lunch. With its small front porch overlooking a paddy and welcoming old-fashioned interior in a thatched house, this tea and coffee shop with soothing music makes for a relaxing place for a snack or light meal. It's owned by charming Miyako-san (whose husband is from the Nagase family; see above), who lets you choose your own cup for tea or coffee and offers a yummy daily beef curry that strays from the usual (with, for example, asparagus). No credit cards are accepted.

✆ **090/5458-0418.** Set meal ¥1,000. Daily 10am–5pm (to 6pm in summer if there are customers). In the middle of Shirakawa Mura, near the Kanda House.

Shimizu (志みづ)   On the edge of town, mercifully far from the tourist crowds and souvenir shops, this small *minshuku* in a 200-year-old thatched house surrounded by a pastoral setting is a good choice for travelers who desire more privacy than that afforded living with a family, as the owner, who speaks some English, lives in the house next door. There's a communal room with an *irori,* where you can serve yourself coffee and tea and where meals are served. Although you can stay here without opting for meals, note that dinner options in the village are minimal.

2613 Ogimachi, Shirakawa Mura. www.shimizuinn.com. ✆ **05769/6-1914.** 3 units (none with bathroom). ¥8,800 per person with meals; ¥5,900 per person without meals. A 15-min. walk from the bus stop, on the south edge of Ogimachi past Doburoku Festival Hall.

HIDA TAKAYAMA, LITTLE KYOTO OF THE MOUNTAINS ★★★

533km (331 miles) NW of Tokyo; 165km (103 miles) NE of Nagoya

Located in the Hida Mountains (part of the Japan Alps National Park) in Gifu Prefecture, **Hida Takayama** is surrounded by 3,000m (10,000-ft.) peaks, making the train or bus ride here breathtaking. The town, situated along a river on a wide plateau with a population of 93,000, was founded in the 16th century by Lord Kanamori, who selected the site because of the impregnable position afforded by the surrounding mountains. Modeled after Kyoto but also with strong ties to Edo (Tokyo), Takayama borrowed from both cultural centers in developing its own architecture, food, and crafts, all well preserved today thanks to centuries of isolation. With a rich supply of timber provided by surrounding forests, its carpenters were legendary, creating not only beautifully crafted traditional merchants' homes in Takayama but also the Imperial Palace and temples in Kyoto.

Takayama

To Castle Ruins ↗

Sanmachi Traditional Buildings Preservation Area

ⓘ Walking Course

Visitor Information

ACCOMMODATIONS ■
Antique Inn Sumiyoshi **7**
K's House Takayama **14**
Rickshaw Inn **12**
Yamakyu **1**

RESTAURANTS ◆
Agura **8**
Kakusho **2**
Le Midi **9**
Okahsan **10**
Suzuya **13**

ATTRACTIONS ●
Hirata Folk Art Museum **4**
Kusakabe Heritage House **6**
Takayama Jinya **11**
Takayama Showa Museum **3**
Yoshijima Heritage House **5**

Today, Takayama boasts a delightful and elegant historic district, called **Sanmachi,** with homes of classical design typical of 18th-century Hida. The streets are narrow and clean and are flanked on both sides by tiny canals of running water, which in centuries past were useful for fire prevention, washing clothes, and dumping winter snow, but which now give the town its distinct character. Rising from the canals are one- and two-story homes and shops of gleaming dark wood with overhanging roofs; latticed windows and slats of wood play games of light and shadow in the white of the sunshine. In the doorways of many shops, curtains flutter in the breeze.

With its quaint old character, great shopping (including a lively city market), and museums, Takayama is a town that invites exploration. As you walk down the streets, you'll also notice huge cedar balls hanging from the eaves in front of several shops, indicating one of Takayama's six sake breweries, most of them small affairs. Go inside, sample the sake, and watch the men stirring rice in large vats. There are also a surprising number of museums, most housed in traditional homes and filled with historical relics and antiques of Takayama's past.

Essentials

GETTING THERE By Train The easiest way to reach Takayama is by direct train from Nagoya (which is on the Shinkansen line), with about 10 departures daily for the 2½-hour trip that costs ¥6,030 for an unreserved seat. There's also one early-morning train that departs Osaka and Kyoto directly for Takayama.

By Bus Nohi buses (www.nouhibus.co.jp; ✆ **03/5376-2222**) depart Tokyo's Shinjuku Station six to seven times daily, arriving in Takayama 5½ hours later and costing ¥6,690. Nohi buses also travel between Kanazawa Station (✆ **076/ 234-0123**) and Takayama (✆ **0577/32-1688**) six times a day, passing through Shirakawa-go on the way and costing ¥3,390 for the 2¼-hour trip. Note that reservations are required for these buses, as all seats are assigned, but you can do so before boarding if there's room.

VISITOR INFORMATION The **Takayama Tourist Office** (www.hida.jp; ✆ **0577/32-5328;** daily 8:30am–6:30pm, to 5pm Nov–Mar) is housed in a wooden booth just outside the main (east) exit of Takayama Station. You can pick up an English-language map of the town showing the location of all museums and attractions. A small **tourist counter** on Sanno-machi street is open daily 10am to 4pm.

GETTING AROUND Takayama is one of Japan's easiest towns to navigate. Most of its attractions lie east of the train station in an area called Sanmachi and are easily reached from the station in about 10 to 15 minutes **on foot.** Throughout the town are English-language signs pointing directions to the many attractions; they're even embedded in sidewalks and streets. There is a tourist shuttle, called **Machinami Bus,** that makes a loop through the old town, but it travels only once an hour; you're better off exploring by foot.

That being said, you'll need to take the other shuttle, the **Takayama City Sarubobo Bus,** to reach Hida Folk Village and Hida Takayama Museum of Art. It departs from in front of the train station twice an hour daily from 9am to 4pm and costs ¥210 per ride. Pick up the schedule and route at the tourist office.

Alternatively, lots of shops and hotels rent **bicycles,** with most charging ¥1,200 for the day. Closest to the station is **Ikehata Shouten,** located just past the Nohi Bus Station (✆ **0577/32-0847**); they'll also store your luggage here if lockers are full, at ¥500 per bag per day. As for bike riding, note that Takayama's old town has narrow streets and it's straight up a very long hill to Hida Folk Village and Hida Takayama Museum of Art.

INTERNET & WI-FI ACCESS   You can use the tourist office's one laptop computer for free Internet access, but you have to stand. Otherwise, free Wi-Fi is available through much of the old town; select Free Wi-Fi Takayama.

Where to Stay

There are as many *minshuku* and *ryokan* in Takayama as hotels, making it the perfect place to stay in a traditional inn. In fact, staying in a *tatami* room and sleeping on a futon is the best way to immerse yourself in the life of this small community.

You should be aware that in peak season—Golden Week (Apr 29–May 5), August (especially during mid-Aug Obon), and New Year's—prices will be about 10% to 20% higher than those given below. During spring and autumn festivals, it's likely to be even higher than that.

MODERATE

Antique Inn Sumiyoshi (寿美よし) ★★★   This calls itself a *ryokan,* but its size, homey atmosphere, and the family that runs it make it seem more like a *minshuku.* Built more than 100 years ago by a well-known local carpenter to house a silkworm industry and then operating as a pawnshop, it opened in 1950 as a *ryokan* and hasn't changed much since then. An open-hearth fireplace, samurai armor, and antiques and folk toys fill the reception area, where you are invited to have tea or coffee. On the second floor is my favorite feature: an outdoor deck facing the river, across which is the morning market. *Tatami* rooms are comfortable and old-fashioned, many with painted screens and antiques; request one facing the river. Minami-san, the man running the *ryokan,* is a fifth-generation innkeeper and speaks English. In addition to Japanese and vegetarian dinners (order when making reservations), both Japanese and Western breakfasts are available. No credit cards are accepted.

21–4 Honmachi. www.sumiyoshi-ryokan.com. ✆ **0577/32-0228.** 8 units (1 with bathroom; 2 with sink/toilet). ¥6,000–¥9,000 per person. Rates exclude tax. Dinner ¥3,000 extra; breakfast ¥1,050 extra. Station: Takayama (10 min. northeast). Across from historic Sanmachi on the Miyagawa River, near the Yayoibashi Bridge. **Amenities:** Free Wi-Fi (most rooms).

Yamakyu ★★   This spotless *minshuku,* open since 1972, has a reputation of offering the best meals in town in its price range, served in a communal dining room. Although it's a bit far from the station—about a 20-minute walk or a 5-minute taxi ride—it's located in a quiet residential area adjacent to the Higashiyama Walking Course that takes in Takayama's many temples and shrines and is only a 10-minute walk or short bike ride to the historic district. Its hallways boast a good collection of folk art, antique clocks, glassware, and lamps; eaves above all guest-room doors give it a "village" atmosphere. In the mornings, free coffee is available from the small lobby lounge, where you have a view of a small courtyard garden. As with most *minshuku*, the Japanese-style rooms—nicely done with natural woods and artwork—are without private bathrooms, but the communal baths are large and include tiny outdoor tubs, one ceramic and one wood. A private shower room you can lock was recently added.

58 Tenshoji-machi. www.takayama-yamakyu.com ✆ **0577/32-3756.** 20 units (all with toilet and sink only). ¥8,640 per person. Rates include 2 meals. Station: Takayama (20 min.). **Amenities:** Rental bikes (¥500 per day or ¥300 per half-day, free for longer-staying guests); free Wi-Fi.

INEXPENSIVE

K's House Takayama ★★
This is a backpacker's guesthouse with class. The inviting lobby lounge, exuding a Zen-like peacefulness with its comfy sofas and beanbag chairs, fosters camaraderie among its mostly international guests, as does the fully equipped spotless kitchen. Information on local sights and activities is posted everywhere. In addition to dormitory rooms (for women-only or mixed sexes), it also offers very tiny singles, as well as twins (all with bunk beds) and doubles that also include deluxe rooms with one-*tatami* sitting areas, all with *shoji*-like screens. Rare for guesthouses, all rooms have private bathroom.

4–51–1 Tenmancho. http://kshouse.jp. ✆ **0577/34-4110.** 26 units. ¥4,800–¥5,800 single; ¥7,500–¥9,200 double; ¥2,900–¥3,200 dormitory. Station: Takayama (3 min.). Walk straight out of the station, cross the road, turn right and then left (next to Spa Hotel Alpina). **Amenities:** Rental bikes (¥700 per day for hostel guests ¥1,500 for public use), Free Wi-Fi.

Rickshaw Inn ★★★
In a modern house in a central location, Rickshaw Inn (entirely nonsmoking) is welcoming, due in no small part to the friendly owner Eiko-san, a Takayama native who lived in the United States and speaks flawless English. A spacious communal living room—with sofas, TV, and newspapers—is a good place to relax with fellow guests. No dinner is served, but Eiko-san can recommend restaurants (ask for her map) and is knowledge-able about museums, crafts, and Takayama's history. There's also a closet-size communal kitchen. Japanese- and Western-style rooms, with sinks or bath-rooms, feature Asian artwork and batik shades to block out light. Some Japanese rooms are big enough for three or four people, but best for families or longer stays is the Sakura suite with a large living area complete with two sofas, tables and chairs, and *tatami* areas that sleep up to six people.

54 Suehiro-cho. www.rickshawinn.com. ✆ **0577/32-2890.** 10 units (7 with bathroom). ¥4,200 single without bathroom; ¥8,900–¥10,200 double without bathroom, ¥11,900

double with bathroom. Suite from ¥19,500 triple; ¥22,000 quad. Rates exclude tax. Western breakfast ¥800 extra. Station: Takayama (6 min. east), just off Kokubunji St to the right (look for the archway over the street with a clock). **Amenities:** Free Internet.

Where to Eat

Takayama has some local specialties you should try while you're here (they may well be served at your *ryokan* or *minshuku*). The best known is *hoba miso,* which is soybean paste mixed with dried scallions, ginger, and mushrooms and cooked on a dry magnolia leaf at your table above a small clay burner. *Sansai* are mountain vegetables, including edible ferns and other wild plants; and *ayu* is a small river fish, grilled with soy sauce or salt. Other dishes include Takayama's own style of *soba* (buckwheat noodles), *mitarashi-dango* (grilled rice balls with soy sauce), and Hida beef.

EXPENSIVE

Kakusho (角正) ★★★ VEGETARIAN For a big splurge, dine at Kakusho, established 250 years ago and offering local vegetarian fare called *shojin ryori,* typically served at Buddhist temples. Situated on the slope of a hill in the eastern part of the city, a 5-minute walk from Sanmachi, this delightful restaurant serves meals either in small, private *tatami* rooms dating from the Edo Period or in a larger room from the Meiji Period that can be opened to the elements on three sides, all of which overlook a dreamy, mossy garden enclosed by a clay wall. The least expensive meals consist of various mountain vegetables, mushrooms, nuts, tofu, and other dishes, with more dishes added for more expensive meals (tax and service charge will be added to prices below). The gracious owner speaks some English. Reservations are required.

2–98 Babacho. *(C)* **0577/32-0174.** *Kaiseki shojin ryori* ¥10,000–¥20,000; set lunches ¥5,500–¥10,000. Daily 11:30am–2pm and 5–8pm (last order). Irregular closing days. Station: Takayama (15 min.). To the left of Sanmachi St., past the Takayama Museum of History and Art.

MODERATE

Le Midi ★★ FRENCH This tiny, two-level restaurant with red-and-white checkered curtains and black wood trim imparts a European flair and delivers delicious food. The owner-chef worked in France after training at a Japanese culinary school. Its specialty is Hida beef, available as sirloin, filet, or beef cheek simmered 6 hours in red wine. Even the humble hamburger steak, served on potatoes and with green beans, is quite a presentation. Other dishes include Hida pork, fish of the day, and duck breast. This restaurant is so successful, it has expanded across the street at Le Midi-i, which also serves Hida beef along with Italian food.

2–2 Honmachi. www.le-midi.jp. *(C)* **0577/36-6386.** Main courses ¥2,400–¥5,800; set lunches ¥1,800–¥4,800; set dinners ¥4,800–¥12,000. Mon–Wed and Fri 11:30am–3pm and 6–9:30pm; Sat–Sun and holidays 11:30am–3:30pm and 5–9:30pm. Station: Takayama (9 min.). On Honmachi near Ikadabashi Bridge.

Suzuya (寿々や) ★ LOCAL SPECIALTIES Darkly lit with traditional Takayama country decor, this restaurant specializing in Takayama cuisine has been a mainstay for decades. There's an English-language menu complete with photographs and explanations of each dish, including such local specialties as mountain vegetables, *hoba miso,* and Hida beef, as well as *shabu-shabu* and *sukiyaki.* Recent additions to the menu include both beef and vegetarian *hoba miso* and deep-fried breaded shrimp and pork. But Hida beef is what the restaurant is known for.

24 Hanakawa-cho. ✆ **0577/32-2484.** Set meals ¥1,186–¥6,152. Daily 11am–3pm and 5–8pm (last order). Station: Takayama (6 min.). Just off Kokubunji St. to the right, halfway btw. the station and the Miyagawa River.

INEXPENSIVE

Agura ★ VARIED INTERNATIONAL   A converted rice *kura,* with a high-beamed ceiling, wooden floors, and private nooks containing slabs of wood for tables and locally crafted bentwood chairs makes for a lovely setting, heightened by friendly waiters (there's a buzzer at each table to summon them) and jazz. A Japanese-style pub, it offers a range of inexpensive dishes from its English-language menu, including salads (I especially like the "Agura Original Salad," which changes but is always tasty), six kinds of pizzas fired in a wood-burning stove, and food that goes down well with beer (try the local Hida Korikori Beer), including *edamame,* deep-fried chicken marinated in miso, spring rolls with sweet chili sauce, and Hida beef and miso cooked on a "dead" (I think they mean "dried") *Hoba* leaf.

4–7 Shinmeicho. ✆ **0577/37-2666.** Main dishes ¥680–¥1,500. Tues–Sun 6–11:30pm (last order). Station: Takayama (12 min.). Just south of Takayama City Memorial Hall; look for the green sign with the yellow seated Buddha.

Okahsan (おかあさん) ★★ VEGETARIAN   This tiny shop sells health foods and has room for only a half-dozen customers for its simple macrobiotic set meals, free of animals products, preservatives, sweeteners, pesticides and artificial or chemical additives. It offers three lunches, with the cheapest consisting of salad, brown rice, miso soup, two vegetable dishes and pickled vegetables, which was plentiful enough for me; the more expensive meals add more dishes. Breakfast is a shortened version of lunch, while macrobiotic dinners are by reservation only, for a minimum of two people. Drinks range from organic tea to beer. No credit cards are accepted.

4–6 Yurakucho. www.okahsan.com/english. ✆ **0577/351057.** Set lunches ¥1,000–¥2,000; set breakfast ¥700; set dinners from ¥3,000. Mon–Sat 8–2pm. Walk straight out of the station on Ekimae Chuo Street; it will be on the right, before the Miyagawa River.

Exploring Takayama

Takayama's main attraction is its historic center of traditional homes and businesses in a district called **Sanmachi.** Be sure to allow time to wander around. In addition to the district's many museums, there are also shops selling antiques, souvenirs, and Takayama's specialties, including sake, yew woodcarvings, beautiful cypress furniture, and a unique lacquerware called *shunkei-nuri.*

Be sure, too, to visit the **Miyagawa Morning Market** ★★, which stretches on the east bank of the Miyagawa River between Kajibashi and Yayoibashi bridges. Held every morning from 7am (6am in summer) to noon, it's very picturesque, with cloth-covered stalls selling fresh produce, flowers, pickled vegetables, and locally made crafts. A smaller morning market is held in front of Takayama Jinya.

If you have more free time still, consider the **Higashiyama Walking Course** ★★, which leads past a string of 12 temples and a couple shrines nestled on a wooded hill on the east edge of town in an area called Higashiyama Teramachi. It also leads to Shiroyama Park, site of the Kanamori clan castle until it was torn down in 1695 by order of the Tokugawa shogunate. Parts of its stone foundations still remain. The hiking course stretches 5.5km (3 miles) end to end; there are English-language signs, but be sure to get the map provided by the tourist office. If you get lost, consider it part of the fun.

Hida Folk Village (Hida no Sato) ★★ MUSEUM This is an open-air museum of more than 30 old thatched and shingled farmhouses, sheds, and buildings, many of which were brought here from other parts of the region to illustrate how farmers and artisans used to live in the Hida Mountain range. The entire village is picturesque, with swans swimming in the central pond, green moss growing on the thatched roofs, and flowers blooming in season. Some of the houses have *gassho-zukuri*-style roofs, built steeply to withstand the region's heavy snowfalls; the tops of the roofs are said to resemble hands joined in prayer. All the structures, which range from 100 to 500 years old, are open to the public and are filled with furniture, old spindles and looms, utensils for cooking and dining, instruments used in the silk industry, farm tools, sleds, and straw boots and snow capes for winter. Some even have smoldering fires in the *irori* fire pits. Be sure to ask for the free 20-minute English-language audio guide at the entrance, which describes the social life and architecture of the region. Workshops set up in one corner of the village grounds demonstrate Takayama's well-known woodcarving, weaving, and other cottage industries; some of the artisans even live here. You'll want to spend about 1½ hours at the village, but if you're heading to Shirakawa-go, skip it; there's a similar, more accessible open-air museum there, as well as inhabited thatched houses open to the public.

1-590 Kamiokamoto-choi. www.hidanosato-tpo.jp. © **0577/34-4711.** Admission ¥700 adults, ¥200 children. Daily 8:30am–5pm. Bus: Sarubobo Bus to Hida-no-Sato. Station: Takayama (30-min. walk southwest).

Hirata Folk Art Museum (Hirata Kinen-kan) ★★ MUSEUM Takayama's most varied and extensive collection of folk art vividly conveys what life was like during the Edo Period by displaying household utensils, crafts, and fine arts found in a typical middle-class home; the house itself, built in 1897 in traditional style with a sunken hearth and both living and working quarters, belonged to a candle-maker. Storerooms *(kura)* in the back date to 1780. Items are identified in English, though detailed explanations are unfortunately lacking. On display are folk toys, coin boxes, mirrors, toiletry sets, *geta* sandals, spectacles, hair adornments, *shunkei* lacquerware, and paper and kerosene lamps; my favorite is the room outfitted with items used for travel, including guide maps, portable abacuses, compasses, a traveling pillow, a folding lantern, and even a folding hat. You'll probably spend 20 minutes here.

Ichino-machi St., 39 Kaminino-machi. © **0577/33-1354.** Admission ¥300 adults, ¥150 junior-high age and younger. Daily 9am–5pm. Station: Takayama (10 min.).

Merchants' Houses ★★★ HISTORIC HOME   In contrast to other castle towns during the Edo Period, Takayama was under the direct control of the Tokugawa government rather than a feudal lord, which meant its homes were built and owned by merchants and commoners rather than the samurai class that dominated other Japanese cities. Located side by side in the historic center and both toured easily in less than 30 minutes, **Yoshijima-ke** or Yoshijima Heritage House (© **0577/32-0038**) and **Kusakabe Heritage House** (© **0577/32-0072**) are merchants' mansions that once belonged to two of the richest families in Takayama. With its exposed attic, heavy crossbeams, sunken open-hearth fireplace, and sliding doors, Yoshijima House is a masterpiece of geometric design. It was built in 1907 as both the home and factory of the Yoshijima family, well-to-do brewers of sake. Notice how the beams and details of the home gleam, a state attained through decades of polishing as each generation of women did their share in bringing the wood to a luster. Yoshijima-ke is also famous for its lattices, typical of Takayama yet showing an elegance influenced by Kyoto. Its walls serve as an art gallery for the lithographs of female artist Shinoda Toko, one of my favorite Japanese artists (and a distant relative of present owner Yoshijima Tadao, who also uses the house for his other passion, jazz, heard softly in the back gallery).

Kusakabe Mingei-kan, built in 1879 for a merchant dealing in silk, lamp oil, and finance, is more refined and imposing. Its architectural style is considered unique to Hida but has many characteristics common during the Edo Period, including a two-story warehouse at the back of the house with open beams and an earthen floor, now filled with folk art and other items. On display, too, are personal items such as lacquerware and chests from Japan and imports from other countries, handed down through the generations and arranged just as they would have been in the 18th and 19th centuries. If you have time for only one house, this one has more to see; free green tea is served in the courtyard.

North end of Nino-machi St., Oshinmachi. Admission to either house ¥500 for adults, ¥300 for junior high and younger. Mar–Nov daily 9am–5pm, Dec–Feb Wed–Mon 9am–4:30pm (Kusakabe House closes 30 min. earlier). Station: Takayama (20 min.).

Takayama Jinya ★★★ GOVERNMENT BUILDING   I highly recommend a visit to this historical government house to anyone interested in Japanese history. The building served as the Tokugawa government's administrative building for 177 years (1692–1868). Of some 60 local government offices that were once spread throughout Japan, this is the only one still in existence. Resembling a miniature palace with its outer wall and an imposing entrance gate, the sprawling complex consists of both original buildings and reconstructions. In addition to administrative offices, chambers, and courts, the complex contained living quarters, a huge kitchen, an interrogation room for criminals with torture devices, tea room, and a 400-year-old rice granary, the oldest and biggest in Japan, where rice collected from farmers as a form of taxation was stored. Making visits here especially educational are free guided tours in English, which last about 30 to 40 minutes and provide fascinating insight into administrative life of yore.

1–5 Hachi-ken-machi. ℂ **0577/32-0643.** Admission ¥430 for adults, free for high-school age and younger. Mar–Oct daily 8:45am–5pm (to 6pm Aug); Nov–Feb daily 8:45am–4:30pm. Station: Takayama (10 min.).

Takayama Showa Museum (昭和館) ★★★ MUSEUM   If you're a history or a kitsch buff, check out this eclectic museum packed to the rafters with items used in daily life during the Showa era (Showa refers to the reign of Emperor Hirohito, 1926–89), including tiny family cars from the 1960s, posters, shop signs, bikes, washing machines, rice cookers, clocks, TVs, cameras, and much more, most of it arranged in themed rooms. You can step inside a toyshop, photo studio, doctor's office, barbershop, appliance store (it's fun to see what was considered high-tech back then), schoolroom, beauty salon, a typical living room, and even a movie theater showing news and movies from the 1960s and 1970s, all providing a unique perspective on how much Japan has changed in just a few short decades (you'll probably find yourself wishing more from the Showa era remained). After spending about 30 minutes in what is clearly a labor of love for the owner, be sure to take a look at the small museum shop selling replica tin toys and candies of yesteryear. You'll recognize the museum by the old vehicles and gas pump in the entranceway.

6 Shimoichino-machi. ℂ **0577/33-7836.** Admission ¥500 adults, ¥300 children. Daily 9am–5pm. Station: Takayama (10 min.); just off Kokunbunji Dori.

KYOTO

I f you go to only one place in all of Japan, **Kyoto ★★★** should be it. Not only is it the most historically significant town in the nation, this former capital was also the only major Japanese city spared from the bombs of World War II. It's filled with temples, shrines, imperial palaces, gardens, and *machiya* (traditional wooden houses). But what makes it exceptional are the scenes from daily life. Spend a few days exploring the city's back streets and neighborhoods, and you'll probably agree that Kyoto is Japan's most romantic city.

8

Home to the Imperial court for 1,000 years, Kyoto boasts the nation's greatest concentration of craft artisans, whose works are displayed in museums and shops dealing in textiles, dyed fabrics, pottery, bambooware, cutlery, fans, metalwork, umbrellas, and other goods. Kyoto is also famous for its own style of *kaiseki*, which blends ceremonial court cuisine with Zen vegetarian food. No fewer than 17 UNESCO World Heritage Sites are located in Kyoto Prefecture, including Kiyomizu Temple, Kinkakuji, Ginkakuji, Ryoanji Temple, and Nijo Castle, but it also has some offbeat attractions like the Kyoto International Manga Museum and a small but vibrant nightlife. And as explore the back streets, especially in Gion, you might even catch a glimpse of a geisha, decked out in all her finery.

ESSENTIALS

Getting There
BY PLANE
Kyoto is served by two airports, Kansai International Airport outside Osaka for international and domestic flights and Itami Airport for domestic flights.

KANSAI INTERNATIONAL AIRPORT **By Train** The **JR Haruka Limited Express train** has direct service every 30 to 60 minutes to Kyoto Station. The trip takes approximately 80 minutes and costs ¥3,370 for a reserved seat (recommended during busy departure times or peak season) and ¥2,850 for a nonreserved seat, or you can ride free with your JR Rail Pass. A cheaper, though slower and less convenient, alternative is the JR Kanku Kaisoku, which departs every 30 minutes or so from Kansai Airport and arrives in Kyoto 1 hour and 50 minutes later, with a change at Osaka Station. It costs ¥1,880.

By Bus If you have lots of luggage, consider taking the **Kansai Airport Limousine Bus** (www.kate.co.jp; ℂ **075/682-4400**) from Kansai Airport; buses depart every hour or less for the 1¾-hour trip to Kyoto Station and cost ¥2,550. More convenient but costlier are **shared-ride vans,** operated by local taxi companies **MK** (www.mktaxi-japan.com; ℂ **075/778-5489**) and **Yasaka** (www.yasaka.jp; ℂ **075/803-4800**), which deliver passengers to any hotel or home in Kyoto for ¥3,600, including one suitcase (a second suitcase costs ¥1,000); make reservations 2 days in advance.

BY TRAIN

Kyoto is a major stop on the Shinkansen bullet train; trip time from **Tokyo** is about 2½ hours, with the fare for a nonreserved seat ¥13,080 one-way. Kyoto is only 15 minutes from Shin-Osaka, but you may find it more convenient to take the JR Tokaido Line that connects Kyoto directly with Osaka Station in 30 minutes. From **Kobe,** you can reach Kyoto from Sannomiya and Motomachi stations on the Tokaido Line in 50 minutes. The strikingly modern **Kyoto Station,** which is like a city in itself with tourist offices, restaurants, a hotel, a department store, a shopping arcade, a theater, and stage events, is connected to the rest of the city by subway and bus.

BY BUS

Lots of long-distance buses travel between Tokyo and Kyoto; reservations are necessary. **JR Highway buses** (www.jrbuskanto.co.jp; ℂ **03/3844-1950**) depart day and night from Tokyo Station's Yaesu South Exit (some make a stop also in Shinjuku), arriving at Kyoto Station about 8 hours later and costing ¥6,200 to ¥9,600 depending on the bus and time of day. Tickets can be purchased at any major JR station or a travel agency like JTB. **Willer Express buses** (http://willerexpress.com; ℂ **050/5805-0383**) depart Tokyo, Shinjuku, and Ikebukuro stations nightly, arriving at Kyoto Station the next morning. Fares range from ¥3,900 to ¥9,800, depending on the date and type of seat selected.

Visitor Information

The **Kyoto Tourist Information Center** (www.kyoto.travel; ℂ **075/343-0548;** daily 8:30am–7pm), in the central passageway on the second floor of Kyoto Station near Isetan department store, has city and bus maps, as well as many brochures. You can find free English-language maps of Kyoto at hotels, 7-Eleven or Starbucks. For information on Kyoto Prefecture, check the website www.pref.kyoto.jp/visitkyoto/en.

PUBLICATIONS A monthly tabloid distributed free at hotels and restaurants is the *Kyoto Visitor's Guide* (www.kyotoguide.com), with maps, a calendar of events, and information on sightseeing and shopping (it's available at the Kyoto Tourist Information Center, too, but you have to ask for it). *Kansai Scene* (www.kansaiscene.com) is a monthly giveaway with information on nightlife, festivals, and other events in Osaka, Kobe, Kyoto and Nara.

City Layout

Most of Kyoto's attractions and hotels are north of Kyoto Station (take the Central exit), spreading like a fan toward the northeast and northwest. The **northern and eastern edges** of the city contain the most famous temples. The heart of the city is in **central Kyoto (Nakagyo-ku ward),** which boasts the largest concentration of restaurants, shops, and bars and which radiates outward from the intersection of Kawaramachi Dori and Shijo Dori. It includes a narrow street called Pontocho, a nightlife mecca that runs along the western bank of the Kamo River. Across the Kamo River to the east is the ancient geisha district of Gion.

FINDING AN ADDRESS Kyoto's streets are laid out in a grid pattern with named streets (a rarity in Japan) and an unofficial address system used by locals that's actually quite easy to understand once you get to know the directional terms (official postal addresses are less useful and not even used by some establishment, although some use both). The major streets north of Kyoto Station that run east-west are numbered; for example, *shi* means four and *dori* means avenue, so Shijo Dori means "Fourth Avenue." *Agaru* equates to "to the north," *sagaru* to "to the south," *nishi-iru* means "to the west," and *higashi-iru* means "to the east." Thus, an address that reads Shijo-agaru, Teramachi Higashi-iru means "north of Fourth Avenue, east of Teramachi."

On non-numbered streets, addresses generally indicate cross streets. Take the restaurant Kushi Kura, for example: Its address is Takakura Dori, Oike-agaru, which tells you it's just north of Oike Dori on Takakura Dori. Complete addresses include the ward, or *ku,* such as Higashiyama-ku.

Kyoto's Neighborhoods in Brief

The following are Kyoto's main tourist areas; to locate them, see the "Kyoto" maps on p. 212, 217, and 238.

Around Kyoto Station The southern ward of **Shimogyo-ku,** which stretches from Kyoto Station north to Shijo Dori Avenue, caters to tourists with its cluster of hotels and to commuters with its shops and restaurants. Kyoto Station, which caused quite a controversy when built because of its size, height, and futuristic appearance, is now this area's top attraction. One of Japan's largest (and to me most beautiful) station buildings, it's very futuristic looking, with soaring glass atriums, space-age chimes, loads of shops and restaurants, and dramatic public spaces, including a series of escalators and stairs leading to a rooftop plaza. I see more tourists photographing Kyoto Station than any other modern building in town.

Central Kyoto Nakagyo-ku, the central part of Kyoto west of the Kamo River and north of Shimogyo-ku, is home to city hall and embraces Kyoto's main shopping and nightlife districts, with most of the action on **Kawaramachi Dori** and **Shijo Dori** and **Teramachi** and **Shin-kyogoku** covered shopping arcades. Most of Kyoto's legendary craft stores are located here, along with numerous hotels, restaurants and bars. Home also to **Nijo Castle,** Nakagyo-ku has a number of exclusive *ryokan* tucked away in delightful neighborhoods typical of old Kyoto. But downtown is changing fast, as Kyoto's younger generation lays claim to new shopping and entertainment complexes, such as **Kyoto International Manga Museum,** housed in a former elementary school. Nakagyo-ku is one of the most desirable places to stay in terms of convenience and atmosphere.

Pontocho, a narrow lane that parallels the Kamo River's western bank just a stone's throw from the Kawaramachi-Shijo Dori intersection, is Kyoto's most famous street for nightlife. It's lined with bars and restaurants that boast outdoor verandas extending over the Kamo River in summer. Paralleling Ponto-cho to the east is **Kiyamachi,** a narrow lane beside a canal lined with bars and restaurants and bustling with nighttime revelers.

Eastern Kyoto Eastern Kyoto is a great area for walking, shopping, and sightseeing. East of the Kamo River, the wards of **Higashiyama-ku** and **Sakyo-ku** boast a number of the city's most famous temples and shrines, as well as restaurants specializing in Kyoto cuisine and Buddhist vegetarian dishes, and shops selling local pottery and other crafts. **Gion,** Kyoto's most famous geisha entertainment district, is part of Higashiyama-ku. Customers are entertained in traditional wooden geisha houses that are not open to the public (you can only gain entry through introductions provided by someone who is already a customer)—but the area makes for a fascinating stroll.

Northern Kyoto Embracing the **Kita-ku, Kamigyo-ku,** and **Ukyo-ku** wards, northern Kyoto is primarily residential but contains a number of Kyoto's top sights, including the Kyoto Imperial Palace, Kinkakuji (Temple of the Golden Pavilion), and Ryoanji Temple, site of Kyoto's most famous Zen rock garden.

GETTING AROUND

Kyoto is Japan's most visitor-friendly city, with lots of English-language signs and an easy-to-navigate transportation system. Kyoto's subway and bus networks are especially efficient and quite easy to use. For more information, stop by the **Bus and Subway Information kiosk** in front of Kyoto Station to the right of the bus platforms (☎ **075/371-4474;** daily 7:30am–7:30pm) or check schedules and routes online at www.arukumachikyoto.jp.

BY SUBWAY Kyoto has two subway lines, with stops announced in English. The older **Karasuma Line** runs north and south, from Takeda in the south to Kokusai Kaikan in the north, with stops at Kyoto Station, central Kyoto, and Imadegawa Station (convenient for visiting the Imperial Palace). The **Tozai Line** runs in a curve from east to west and is convenient for visiting Nijo Castle and Higashiyama-ku. The two lines intersect in central Kyoto at Karasuma Oike Station (if you find station names cumbersome, go by their numbers; Karasuma Oike, for example, is both K08 on the Karasuma Line and T13 on the Tozai Line). Fares start at ¥210 (children pay half fare) and service runs from about 5:30am to 11:30pm. In addition to subways, the private Keihan Railway runs north-south along the Kamo River on the east side of town and is convenient to Gion and some hotels. Although buses usually get you closer to where you want to go, in central Kyoto I sometimes opt for the subway even if I have to walk a bit, simply to avoid hassling with buses and their unknown stops.

BY BUS The most direct way to get to most of Kyoto's attractions in eastern or northern Kyoto is by bus. Buses depart from Kyoto Station's Central (north/Karasuma) Exit, with platforms clearly marked in English listing destinations. Both the Kyoto Tourist Information Center (see "Visitor Information," above) and the Bus and Subway Information counter give out excellent maps showing major bus routes. Some of the buses loop around the city, while others go back and forth between two destinations. Most convenient for sightseeing is Raku bus no. 100, which makes a run every 10 minutes from Kyoto

Station to major attractions in east Kyoto, including the Kyoto National Museum, Gojo-zaka (the approach to Kiyomizu Temple), Gion, Heian Shrine, Nanzenji, and Ginkakuji. Raku bus no. 101 departs Kyoto Station for Nijo Castle and Kinkakuji. Unfortunately, at Kyoto Station there are sometimes long queues of foreigners waiting to board these two buses. Hello, people! There are many other city buses traveling similar routes, so consult your bus map and see if there's an alternative way to reach your destination.

The fare for traveling in central Kyoto is ¥230 for a single ride (¥120 for children). Board the bus at the rear entrance and pay when you get off (the fare box can make change for coins and ¥1,000 notes). If the bus is traveling a **long distance** out to the suburbs, there will be a ticket machine right beside the back door—take the ticket and hold onto it. It has a number on it and will tell the bus driver when you got on and how much you owe. You can see for yourself how much you owe by looking for your number on a lighted panel at the front of the bus; the longer you stay on the bus, the higher the fare. Digital signboards on buses announce every stop in English.

DISCOUNT PASSES   If you think you'll be doing a lot of sightseeing in 1 or 2 days, it may pay to buy a pass. A **city bus all-day pass** costs ¥500. **Passes for both buses and subways** cost ¥1,200 for 1 day or ¥2,000 for 2 days and are available at subway stations or the Bus and Subway Information counter at Kyoto Station. Alternatively, the prepaid Traffica Kyoto Card gives a 10% discount off fares, can be used for city buses and subways, and is available in values of ¥1,000 and ¥3,000; because there's no time limit, it's convenient if you're staying in Kyoto for several days and don't want to fumble for change each ride.

For journeys farther afield, there are regional passes available only to foreign tourists that provide travel throughout the Kansai area (including Osaka, Kyoto, Kobe, Nara, Himeji, and Mount Koya) and some even as far away as Hiroshima. For more information, see p. 328 in chapter 12.

BY TAXI   Taxis in Kyoto come in two different sizes with only slightly different fares. Small ones are ¥590 for the first 1.7km (a little more than 1 mile), and large ones are ¥610. Taxis can be waved down or, in the city center, boarded at marked taxi stands or at hotels. **MK Taxi** (www.mktaxi-japan.com; ℂ 075/778-4141) also offers individualized English-language guided tours.

BY BICYCLE   A popular way to get around Kyoto is by bike, made easy because there are few hills and because most streets are named (the ride along the Kamo River is especially wonderful). During peak season, you might even be faster on a bike than a bus. However, you do have to be on guard for vehicular and pedestrian traffic, and in central Kyoto it's illegal to leave your bike parked on the street (ask the rental company for a map of bike parking lots). **Kyoto Cycling Tour Project,** a 3-minute walk from the Central (north) Exit of Kyoto Station (turn left upon exiting the station and walk past the post office and APA Hotel; www.kctp.net; ℂ 075/354-3636), open daily 9am to 7pm, rents bikes beginning at ¥1,000 a day, including a cycling map of the city. It has additional rental terminals at Nijo Castle and Kinkakuji Temple and offers guided cycling tours as well.

[Fast FACTS] KYOTO

In addition to the information here, see "Fast Facts: Japan" in chapter 12. You can also make inquiries at the Kyoto Tourist Information Center (see "Visitor Information," above).

ATMS/Banks   In addition to banks all over town, places to exchange money after banks close are large department stores like Isetan (which also has a currency-exchange machine on the second floor), Takashimaya, and Daimaru. You can also exchange money in Kyoto Station at one of two **Travelex** counters: one at the Central Exit (✆ 075/354-9181; daily 10:30am–7pm) and the other in the central pedestrian passage across from the tourist office, in the Nippon Travel Agency (✆ 075/351-5613; Mon–Fri 10am–3pm and 4–8pm; Sat–Sun and holidays 10am–2pm and 3–6pm). When changing money, be sure to bring your passport. The most convenient ATMs accepting foreign credit cards are at Kyoto Central Post Office next to Kyoto Station (see "Mail," below) or at one of many 7-Eleven convenience stores in Kyoto.

Climate   Kyoto is generally hotter and more humid than Tokyo in summer and colder than Tokyo in winter. For more information, see "When to Go," in chapter 2.

Dentists, Doctors & Hospitals   Most hospitals are not equipped to handle emergencies 24 hours a day, but a system has been set up in which hospitals handle emergencies on a rotating basis. **Kyoto University Hospital (Kyoto Daigaku Byoin),** Shogoin Kawahara-cho, Sakyo-ku (www.kuhp.kyoto-u.ac.jp/english; ✆ 075/751-3111) has English-speaking doctors. For less urgent care, **Sakabe International Clinic,** Gokomachi, Nijo-sagaru, Nakagyo-ku (www.sakabeclinic.com; ✆ 075/231-1624), also has English-speaking staff, as does **Nakai Dental Office,** 724-1 Yohoji-mae-cho, Teramachi Nijo-agaru, Nakagyo-ku (www.ndo-kyoto.jp; ✆ 075/252-1020).

Electricity   In both Kyoto and Nara it's 100 volts, 60 cycles, almost the same as in the United States (110 volts, 60 cycles); your two-pronged appliances should work, but they'll run a little slowly (there are no three-pronged plugs in Japan, so if you brought your laptop, you'll need a plug adapter; many hotels will let you use one for free).

Internet & Wi-Fi Access
Kyoto City offers 3 hours of free Wi-Fi, with hotspots located all over town, including bus stops and subway stations; for more information go to http://kanko.city.kyoto.lg.jp/wifi/en. Many restaurants and stores also offer free Wi-Fi, while most hotels offer both Wi-Fi and guest computers, often for free. Otherwise, **Media Café Popeye** has two locations in central Kyoto: next to the Kyoto Royal Hotel & Spa at Sanjo Kawaramachi (✆ 075/253-5300) and just north of Shijo Dori and east

of Teramachi. Both are open 24 hours and charge ¥420 for 1 hour, with discounts for additional hours. The Kyoto Tourist Information Center also has a couple of coin-operated computers costing ¥100 for 10 minutes.

Luggage Storage & Lockers   Kyoto Station has lockers for storing luggage beginning at ¥300 for 24 hours, including lockers large enough for big suitcases (¥600) on its south (Shinkansen) side. However, these can fill up during peak season, in which case head to the basement's check-in baggage room (open daily 8am–8pm), where you can keep luggage for ¥420 per bag. You can also drop off bags here by 2pm for delivery to most hotels in town; this service costs ¥750 per bag and is great if you want to sightsee before check in.

Mail   The **Kyoto Central Post Office,** located just west of Kyoto Station's Central (north) Exit (✆ 075/365-2471), is open Monday to Friday 9am to 9pm, Saturday 9am to 7pm, and Sunday and holidays 9am to 7pm. You can mail packages bound for international destinations here. To the south of the Central Post Office's main entrance is a counter offering 24-hour postal service. There are also ATMs here, where you can obtain currency Monday to Saturday from 5 minutes past midnight to 11:55pm, Sundays and holidays 5 minutes past midnight to 9pm.

WHERE TO STAY

Kyoto has a wide variety of accommodations, from luxurious, high-end hotels with full facilities to cookie-cutter business hotels and backpacker guesthouses. But if you've never stayed in a *ryokan,* Kyoto is one of the best places to do so. With the exception of hot-spring resorts, Kyoto has more choices of *ryokan* in all price categories than any other city in Japan. Small, usually made of wood, and often situated in delightfully quaint neighborhoods, these *ryokan* can enrich your stay in Kyoto by putting you in direct touch with the city's traditional past. Although the prices at upper- and mid-priced *ryokan* may see prohibitive at first glance, the per-person charge includes two meals and usually tax and service charge. These meals are feasts, not unlike *kaiseki* meals you'd receive at a top restaurant where they could easily cost ¥10,000. *Ryokan* in the budget category, on the other hand, usually don't serve meals unless stated otherwise and often charge per room rather than per person, but they do provide the futon experience.

Accommodations are expensive in Kyoto, about on par with Tokyo. Be sure to make reservations in advance, particularly in spring when flowers bloom, in autumn (Oct–Nov) for the changing of the leaves, during summer vacation from mid-July through August, and during major festivals (see "Calendar of Events," in chapter 2). With the exception of inexpensive lodgings, most accommodations raise their rates during these times, sometimes shockingly so: a hotel that may charge ¥30,000 to ¥40,000 for a double during most of the year, for example, may charge ¥60,000 in high season; in the off season a double might go for as little as ¥18,000. I've arranged the accommodations recommended below, therefore, based on what their average rates are for a double, with "Expensive" costing more than ¥30,000, "Moderate ranging from ¥12,000 to ¥30,000), and "Inexpensive" priced at less than ¥12,000), but keep in mind that a modestly priced hotel could very well be in the expensive category in peak season and in the inexpensive category in February. Although I've tried to provide the wide range of prices for each accommodation to reflect the seasons (singling them out if they vary greatly, especially for expensive hotels, or providing the wide low- to high-season spectrum for medium-priced hotels), they should be used only as a rough guide. Inexpensive accommodations, on the other hand, tend to have the same rates all year.

> ### A Note on Directions
>
> For all hotel and restaurant listings in this chapter, directions provided are from Kyoto Station unless otherwise indicated. Numbers in parentheses after stations and bus stops refer to the time it takes to reach your destination **on foot** after alighting from public conveyance.

Because Kyoto is relatively small and has such good bus and subway systems, no matter where you stay you won't be too far away from the heart of the city. Most lodgings are concentrated around Kyoto Station (Shimogyo-ku Ward), in central Kyoto not far from the Kawaramachi-Shijo Dori intersection (Nakagyo-ku Ward), and east of the Kamo River (in the Higashiyama-ku and Sakyo-ku wards).

Some properties have shuttle buses to Kyoto Station's south entrance, convenient for train service but not for city buses, which depart from the north side.

TAXES & SERVICE CHARGES   All accommodations levy an 8% tax on room rates, while mid- and upper-range ones also add a 10% to 15% service fee; in *ryokan,* the service charge can be as high as 20%. Unless noted otherwise, all rates below include tax and service charge.

Around Kyoto Station

EXPENSIVE

Hotel Kanra Kyoto ★★★   The Kanra's unassuming facade and discrete entrance around the side give little clue that you are about to enter one of Kyoto's coolest properties, artfully designed and with a decidedly hip vibe. Reception is low key and relaxing, with sit-down desks for check-in and little moss-garden containers gracing coffee tables. Rooms are behind lattice doors in a modern rendition of a *machiya* (merchant house), with even the smallest rooms have plenty of space and oodles of design sense, including wood or black granite floors, raised platform beds, *hinoki* (cedar) soaking tubs (and separate showers), and Japanese-style areas with *tatami* and modular furniture. Kitchen Kanra restaurant, on the ground floor, utilizes lots of local vegetables in its dishes, even for breakfast and desserts, and provides the hotel's room service.

> ### Why the Big Range in Hotel Rates?
>
> Upper- and medium-range hotels in Tokyo, Kyoto, and many other Japanese cities usually charge rates that can vary widely depending on the season and the type of room selected. The hotel prices provided in this guide, therefore, range from what you might expect to pay for the cheapest room in low season to a deluxe room in high season.

185 Kitamachi, Karasuma Dori Rokujo-sagaru, Shimogyo-ku. www.hotelkanra.jp. ✆ **075/344-3815.** 29 units. ¥30,000–¥40,000 double (as low as ¥18,000 in the off season, ¥60,000 and up in peak season). Subway: Gojo (exit 8, 1 min.); Kyoto Station (Karasuma exit, 8 min.). On Karasuma Dori, with its entrance around to the right. **Amenities:** Restaurant; room service; free Wi-Fi.

MODERATE

Citadines Karasuma-Gojo Kyoto ★★   The Kyoto branch of this Singapore-owned "apart-hotel" (apartment hotel) chain is a great choice, evident the moment you enter the stone pathway lined with hanging *washi* paper leading to the mood-lit lobby. Contemporary rooms are actually mini-apartments, complete with small galley kitchens (including range, sink, toaster, microwave, tableware, and more), and available in various configurations, from studios with double or twin beds to premier studios with king-size beds (some premiers even have balconies). Some studio doubles have sofas that can double as beds, along with a sliding door that can make each sleeping area more private. Studios don't have much storage space, however, so for longer stays you might opt for the apartment with a separate bedroom.

Around Kyoto Station

**Map labels (streets, landmarks, lines):**

0 — 1/4 mi
0 — 0.25 km

Railway
Subway

KARASUMA LINE
KEIHAN MAIN LINE
JR NARA LINE
KINTETSU KYOTO LINE

Shijo **5**
Bukkoji Temple
Bukkoji Dori **6**
Takatsuji Dori
Matsubara Dori
Manjuji Dori
Gojo Dori
Kiyomizu-gojo **8**
Gojo **9**
Costume Museum **1**
Gojo Dori
Nishi-Hongan-ji Temple
Higashi-Hongan-ji Temple **2**
11
Shosei-en Garden
10
12
13
Shichijo Dori
14
Shichijo
15 →
16
Shiokoji Dori
JR Kyoto Isetan Dept. Store
Kyoto
Kyoto
18 **17**
19
Hachijo Dori
Toji Temple
Toji
Tofukuji
Kujo Dori
Kujo
Jujo Dori
Jujo

Kamo River

Streets (vertical/labeled): Omiya Dori, Horikawa Dori, Aburanokoji Dori, Nishinotoin Dori, Wakamiya Dori, Shinmachi Dori, Muromachi Dori, Karasuma Dori, Higashinotoin Dori, Takakura Dori, Tominokoji Dori, Kawaramachi, Hinomoto Dori, Kiyamachi Dori, Honmachi Dori

RESTAURANTS ◆
Donguri **14**
Ichiba Coji **18**
Katsukura **18**
The Kitchen Salvatore Cuomo **18**
Musashi **19**
Ramen Koji **18**

ACCOMMODATIONS ■
Budget Inn **4**
Capsule Ryokan Kyoto **3**
Citadines Karasuma-Gojo Kyoto **7**
First Cabin **5**
Hana Hostel **13**
Hiraiwa Ryokan and Annex **10**
Hotel Granvia Kyoto **17**
Hotel Hokke Club Kyoto **16**
Hotel Kanra Kyoto **9**
Hyatt Regency Kyoto **15**
Irori Machiya Stay **6**
Kyoraku Ryokan **12**
Matsubaya Ryokan **11**
Ryokan Sakura **1**
Seikoro Inn **8**
Tour Club **2**

432 Matsuya-cho, Gojo Dori Karasuma Higashi-iru, Shimogyo-ku. www.citadines.com. *€* **075/352-8900.** 124 units. ¥23,760–¥30,240 double (from ¥10,000 off season). Prices exclude service charge. Monthly rates available. Subway: Gojo (exit 1, 1 min.). On Gojo Dori, 1½ blocks east of Karasuma Dori. **Amenities:** Free Wi-Fi.

Hotel Granvia Kyoto ★★★   You can't beat this hotel for convenience, since it's located in Kyoto Station and is only a minute's walk to buses and subways serving the rest of the city. Luckily, the lobby is on the second floor, away from the station's foot traffic, though it can still hum with the hotel's many guests. As part of the hotel's inclusive policy, it is LGBT friendly and also offers amenities geared toward Muslims, including Halal menus available without reservations and, on request, a prayer mat and Qibla direction sign in guest rooms. The hotel also has a list of privately guided tour options, from shopping for antiques to walking and cycling tours; it even offers a gay wedding package, with a ceremony at a temple. Standard rooms are small, have unexciting views of the station's glass roof, and are rather dark. Because Granvia is owned by the West Japan Railway Company, if you have a valid Japan Rail pass you can get a 20% to 35% discount off superior twin rooms, which face over the tracks toward the south, but note that these are on lower floors and soundproof windows don't block all of the noise. The best rooms are deluxe rooms facing north with great views of Kyoto. In any case, if you're in Kyoto only a night or two, this is a convenient choice, but it can't compete with the ambience of hotels in central Kyoto.

> ### A Double or a Twin?
>
> For the sake of convenience, the price for two people in a room is listed as a "double" in this book. Japanese hotels, however, differentiate between rooms with a double bed or two twin beds, usually with different prices. Most hotels charge more for a twin room, but sometimes the opposite is true; if you're looking for a bargain, therefore, be sure to inquire about prices for both. Note, too, that hotels usually have more twin rooms than doubles, for the simple reason that Japanese couples, used to their own futon, traditionally prefer twin beds.

JR Kyoto Station, Central Exit, Karasuma Dori Shiokoji-sagaru, Shimogyo-ku. www.granviakyoto.com. *€* **075/344-8888.** 535 units. ¥29,700–¥51,084 single or double (from ¥18,570 off season). Granvia Executive Floor from ¥45,144 single or double. 20%–35% discount off Superior Twins for holders of Japan Rail Pass (check website for blackout dates). **Amenities:** 8 restaurants; bar; 2 lounges; concierge; executive-level rooms; health club w/indoor pool, fitness gym, and sauna (fee: ¥1,080; only guests 21 and older allowed); room service; free Wi-Fi.

Hotel Hokke Club Kyoto ★   Popular with tourists thanks to its great location just opposite Kyoto Station, this chain hotel with a friendly staff first opened about 100 years ago and provides clean and pleasantly decorated Western-style rooms. You'll find reception up on the second floor, where a rack displays many English-language brochures for sightseeing in Kyoto. Singles are tiny with no closets, while doubles are larger with bigger desks and closets, but these all have glazed windows because they face another building. Twins seem downright roomy in comparison, with sofas that can served as extra sleepers and windows facing the back. The best room in the house is a corner twin facing the front, with views of Kyoto Station (although light sleepers may be distracted by train noise) and Japanese-style bathrooms with separate shower and tub areas.

Kyoto Eki-mae, Shomen Chuoguchi, Karasuma, Shimogyo-ku. www.hokke.co.jp. © **075/ 361-1251.** 187 units. ¥8,640–¥11,880 single; ¥12,520–¥22,680 double. Across from Kyoto Station's Central exit. **Amenities:** 2 restaurants; free Wi-Fi.

Ryokan Sakura (さくら) ★★ Opened in 2009, the smoke-free Sakura has a traditional facade of a *machiya* (merchant's house), but has a comfortably contemporary style inside, including a long slab of wood in the lobby that serves as a table, where guests can gather for breakfast or conversation. There's a communal kitchen, low-key jazz plays in the lobby, and stone corridors lead to Western-style rooms with twin beds and Japanese decor, Japanese-style *tatami* rooms (there are instructions for laying out your own futon), and combination rooms with both. The best room opens onto a garden with its own wooden verandah, and there's also a guest room in the style of a tea ceremony room. It's located in an interesting neighborhood of shops selling Buddhist prayer articles; the friendly staff hands out a great bilingual map of local sights and restaurants.

228 Butsuguyacho, Aburanokoji Hanayacho-sagaru, Shimogyo-ku. www.kyoto-ryokan-sakura.com. © **075/343-3500.** 30 units. ¥12,000–¥18,500 double. Prices exclude service charge. A 12-min. walk from Kyoto Station's Central (north) exit; turn left on Shiokoji Dori and right after passing the small parking lot onto Aburanokoji Dori (1 block before Horikawa Dori). **Amenities:** Free Wi-Fi.

INEXPENSIVE

Capsule Ryokan Kyoto ★ After backpacking through more than 30 countries as a university student, Keiji-san recognized a lack of inexpensive guesthouses in Kyoto and so opened Tour Club (www.kyotojp.com) in 2000 with 13 rooms for two to four people plus dormitory beds, followed in 2003 with Budget Inn (www.budgetinnjp.com) in a converted apartment building offering six *tatami* rooms for three to five persons. His latest project is this *tatami* capsule hotel, with tiny compartments complete with futon, TV, Wi-Fi, and—thank goodness—earplugs, because there are only screens for privacy. Be forewarned, also, that there's no separation of the sexes. Travelers with a bit more yen might spring for the "*ryokan* en suite" rooms, which are slightly larger than a closet and have futuristic-looking shower cylinders in a corner plus sink and toilet. In any case, all three facilities, within walking distance of each other, ensure guests get the most out of their stay by dispensing sightseeing and dining recommendations, maps showing locations of nearby restaurants and supermarkets, and free coffee and tea (and free Wi-Fi) in the lounge/communal kitchen.

204 Tsuchihashicho, Shimogyo-ku. www.capsule-ryokan-kyoto.com. © **075/344-1510.** 32 units (capsules do not have bathrooms). Capsule *tatami* beds ¥3,500–¥4,980; *ryokan* en suite rooms ¥5,980–¥11,960 single, ¥7,980–¥15,960 double. Station: Kyoto (7 min.). On Shichijo Dori just east of Horikawa Dori.

Hana Hostel ★★ This is a hostel but with a difference. In addition to four dormitory-style rooms (including one just for women), there are also Japanese-style rooms sleeping one to three people, most with their own bathrooms. This place is spotless, with a large and comfy communal kitchen for cooking and socializing and offering free coffee and tea. And it has a good location near Kyoto Station.

Shichijo-agaru, Akezu-dori, Shimogyo-ku. http://hanahostel.com. ℂ **075/371-3577.** 22 units (11 with bathroom). ¥3,900 single with or without bathroom; ¥6,000 double without bathroom, ¥7,800 double with bathroom; ¥2,500 dormitory bed. ¥300 more per person in high season. A 7-min. walk north of Kyoto Station's Central exit; walk north on Karasuma Dori, turn right on Shichijo Dori, and then left. **Amenities:** Rental bikes (¥500 per day); free Wi-Fi.

Hiraiwa Ryokan and Annex ★ The family running this *ryokan*, halfway between Kyoto Station and downtown, has been welcoming foreigners from all over the world since opening their doors in 1973, even though their English is limited. The *tatami* guest rooms, spread through the century-old traditional main building and a newer annex, are spotless. On the downside, you might have to wait to use the shower and bath facilities (which can be used privately, but there's also a neighborhood public bath and sauna just around the corner) and toilet stalls are unisex, affording little privacy for the shy. And because there's no lounge, there's no chance to meet other guests unless you pass them shuffling down the hall to the bathroom. If you're traveling with a group of friends and would like to hang out in a communal room, stay elsewhere.

314 Hayao-cho, Kaminoguchi-agaru, Ninomiyacho Dori, Shimogyo-ku. www2.odn.ne. jp/hiraiwa. ℂ **075/351-6748.** 17 units (none with private bathroom). ¥4,200–¥5,250 single; ¥8,400–¥9,450 double. Bus: 17 or 205 (don't take the express 205) to Kawaramachi-Shomen (3rd stop) and then a 4-min. walk (take the side street beside Tony Lama and continue straight, over the little stream), or a 15-min. walk from Kyoto Station. **Amenities:** Free Wi-Fi (main building only).

Kyoraku Ryokan ★★ Near the Matsubaya (see below), this pleasant and spotlessly clean property offers nicely decorated rooms, some of which look over an inner courtyard garden. Though the English-speaking son is a fourth-generation innkeeper, the building housing this *ryokan* was rebuilt in 2007 and has the bonus of an elevator and coin-op laundry machines. Guests can help themselves to free coffee and tea in the dining room. Rooms, all non-smoking and including one Western-style room with private bathroom, are simple, with screened windows that open. Note that the women's public bath can be used privately but the men's is communal (there are also private showers). In addition, rooms must be vacated during cleaning time (10am–3pm) and the *ryokan* locks its doors at 11pm.

231 Kogawa-cho, Shichijo-agaru, Akezu-dori, Shimogyo-ku. www.ryokankyoraku.jp. ℂ **075/371-1260.** 16 units (9 with bathroom). ¥6,200 single without bathroom, ¥6,800 single with bathroom; ¥10,600 double without bathroom, ¥12,700 double with bathroom. A 7-min. walk north of Kyoto Station's Central exit; walk north on Karasuma Dori, turn right on Shichijo Dori, and then left. **Amenities:** Free Wi-Fi.

Matsubaya Ryokan ★★ The Hayashi family has managed this inn, just east of Higashi Honganji Temple, since the late Edo Period; it's now under ownership of the fifth Hayashi generation. It used to be an old wooden *ryokan* with character, but in 2008 it was torn down and enlarged, though some architectural details were salvaged. In any case, on the ground floor is a lounge that's a good place to connect with other travelers or to converse with the owners about sightseeing in Kyoto. Across the street is a company that rents bicycles. Rooms, all nonsmoking, are mostly Japanese style, with the best overlooking a garden. Also good bets are six Western-style rooms on the fifth floor with kitchenettes, tiny balconies, and free use of the washing machine. However, Wi-Fi reaches only the first three floors, so floors four and five have to make do with LAN cable or access Wi-Fi in the lounge.

Higashinotoin Nishi, Kamijuzuyamachi Dori, Shimogyo-ku. www.matsubayainn.com. ⓒ **075/351-3727.** 25 units (23 with bathroom). ¥4,400–¥4,700 single without bathroom, ¥6,800–¥9,400 single with bathroom; ¥8,100–¥8,600 double without bathroom, ¥12,800–¥14,000 double with bathroom. A 10-min. walk north of Kyoto Station's Central exit; walk north on Karasuma Dori and take the 3rd right after passing Shichijo Dori. **Amenities:** Free Internet or Wi-Fi.

Central Kyoto
EXPENSIVE

Hiiragiya Ryokan ★★★   This exquisite *ryokan* is as fine an example of a traditional inn as you'll find in Japan. Built in 1818 and nestled in the heart of old Kyoto, it has all the quintessential design characteristics of an old inn, making artful use of wood, bamboo, screens, and stones in its simple yet elegant *tatami* rooms, decorated with art and antiques and many with garden views and cypress baths. Even modern conveniences are cleverly hidden, like the remote controls for the lights and curtains, stored in gourd-shaped lacquered boxes designed by the present owner's great-grandfather. A 2006 wing added seven rooms, elegantly simple in that Zen-like Japanese sensibility of style. Dinners, served in your room in true *ryokan* fashion, are multi-course *kaiseki* feasts, and Western-style breakfasts are available on request. No wonder Hiiragiya has played host to writers, artists, politicians and even members of the imperial family over the decades. Its level of service and hospitality is intuitive and about as perfect as it gets, honed over the years and now under the watchful and caring eye of Ms. Nishimura, the inn's sixth-generation innkeeper.

277 Nakahakusancho, Fuyacho Anekoji-agaru, Nakagyo-ku. www.hiiragiya.co.jp. ⓒ **075/221-1136.** 28 units (23 with bathroom; 2 with toilet only). ¥32,000–¥90,000 per person, excluding tax. Rates include 2 meals. Located on the corner of Fuyacho and Oike sts. Subway: Kyoto Shiyakusho-mae (4 min.) or Karasuma-Oike (7 min.). Bus: 4, 17, or 205 to Kyoto Shiyakusho-mae (5 min.). **Amenities:** Free Wi-Fi.

Irori Machiya Stay ★★★   A *machiya* is a traditional Japanese home. There used to be many *machiya* in downtown Kyoto, but time and urban development have wrought the demise of many of them. Luckily, there's a push to preserve these traditional buildings before they disappear altogether. Irori Machiya Stay offers eleven traditional homes in central Kyoto, most built about a century ago and offering visitors the rare chance to experience living in one. Decorated with folding screens, *andon* floor lamps, *tansu* chests, hanging scrolls, ceramics, baths made of cypress, cedar, or stone, and other Japanese

Central Kyoto

HOTELS ■
APA Hotel Kyoto
  Gion Excellent **33**
First Cabin **27**
Hiiragiya Ryokan **7**
Hotel Gimmond **6**
Hotel Gran M's Kyoto **16**
Hotel Monterey Kyoto **20**
Hotel Mystays Kyoto Shijo **26**
Irori Machiya Stay **28**
Kyoto Okura Hotel **8**
Nishiyama Ryokan **4**
The Palace Side Hotel **1**
Royal Park Hotel The Kyoto **14**
The Screen **2**
Sumiya **18**

NIGHTLIFE ◆
Ace Café **12**
Gion Corner **34**
Hello Dolly **23**
Le Club Jazz **17**
Live Spot RAG **12**
Pig & Whistle **10**
Tadg's Gastro Pub **9**
Yoramu **3**

RESTAURANTS ◆
Ashoka **30**
Bio-Tei **19**
Ganko Sushi **11**
Gontaro **29**
Ichiba Coji **24**
Ippudo **25**
Kushi Kura **5**
Misoguigawa **22**
Musashi **15**
Orizzonte (Okura hotel) **8**
Pizza Salvatore Cuomo
  & Grill **13**
Second House **21**
Tagoto **31**
Tohkasaikan **32**

details, they also offer such modern conveniences as a fridge, microwave, and organic coffee and tea but do not have a TV, phone, or full kitchen (because of fire hazards). Houses vary in size, with the smallest good for two people and the largest accommodating up to 10. Ishifudono-cho, the smallest house, is located on a quiet alleyway and overlooks a tiny garden, but because the bedroom is up a steep flight of stairs (and the bathroom is downstairs), it's best for nimble travelers. Especially nice is Izumiya-cho sleeping six persons, as it's located on Kiyamachi Dori and has a view of the Kamo River from rooms and its own deck, as does the larger Minoya-cho, which sleeps eight. Check in is at the company's office, after which staff will escort you to your abode to show you around and how things work (the office is a bit difficult to find, so it's best to print out the website's map and show it to the taxi driver). This is a great choice for travelers who do not need the constant services of an on-site concierge (although staff is always available if you need them) and want more privacy than that afforded by a *ryokan.* For those interested in cultural enrichment, the company offers an Origin Arts Program that provides hands-on workshops in the tea ceremony, *Noh,* calligraphy, flower arranging, and other traditional activities; check the website for information and prices.

Irori Corporation (office), 144–6 Sujiya-cho, Tominokoji Takatsuji Agaru, Shimogyo-ku. www.kyoto-machiya.com. © **075/352-0211.** 11 houses. ¥28,000–¥52,000 double, depending on the season. Subway: Shijo Karasuma (10 min.). Bus: 5 or 26 to Karasuma Matsubara, or 4, 17, or 205 to Kawaramachi Matsubara (6 min.). **Amenities:** Concierge; free Wi-Fi.

Kyoto Okura Hotel ★★

This is one of Kyoto's oldest hotels, with a history dating back to 1888. You can't tell that by looking at it, however, as it underwent a complete reconstruction in 1994 that turned it into a 17-story hotel. In a nod to its earlier life, the hotel designed its lobby after the original 1920s ballroom, but rooms, which wrap around a central atrium, are thoroughly modern. The city's tallest building, it offers great views from top-floor restaurants and from more expensive rooms on upper floors, with panoramas of the Kamo River and the hills of Higashiyama rising beyond the city. In addition to restaurants located inside the hotel, there are two others managed by the hotel that are worth the journey: Awata Sanso, located in a traditional Japanese house and offering *kaiseki,* and The Garden Okazaki, a French restaurant with a garden and free shuttle service from the hotel. Unfortunately, its fitness facility is a members' club, so access is limited and it's off limits to those younger than 18. Note, too, that the cheapest double is actually a single room with a semi-double-size bed (bigger than a twin bed but not quite full-size), but it's an option for people who want to stay in this great central location for a cheaper price. Otherwise, standard rooms are on lower floors, while the best views are from superior rooms facing east.

537-4 Ichinofunairi-cho, Kawaramachi-Oike, Nakagyo-ku. http://okura.kyotohotel.co.jp. © **075/211-5111,** or 223-2333 for reservations. 323 units. ¥23,760–¥26,136 single (from ¥13,400 in off season); ¥27,324–¥59,400 double (from ¥16,000 in off season); from ¥53,460 executive double. Subway: Kyoto Shiyakusho-mae (1 min., below the hotel). Bus: 4, 17, or 205 to Shiyakusho-mae (2 min.). **Amenities:** 11 restaurants; bar; lounge;

children's day-care center (¥5,100 for 2 hr.); concierge; executive-level rooms; indoor pool w/Jacuzzi and sauna (fee: ¥2,160 7–10am, ¥3,250 other times, including use of gym); room service; free Wi-Fi.

Sumiya ★★★ Like the other traditional Japanese inns listed here, the 100-year-old Sumiya has a great location in a typical Kyoto neighborhood just a few minutes' walk from bustling downtown. Offering excellent service amid simple yet elegant surroundings, including wooden corridors that wrap around courtyard gardens and several tearooms (a tea ceremony is performed after dinner on the 7th and 17th of each month), it has a variety of rooms, most with wooden tubs and some with wonderful views of tiny private gardens with outdoor benches and platforms for sitting. The oldest rooms employ a striking variety of different woods in their design (be sure to notice the Edo-Era designs on the sliding doors), while rooms in a 1968 addition may have sliding screen doors that open onto a private garden. Elaborate meals feature Kyoto *kaiseki* cuisine that can last 2 hours or more (request ahead for special dietary needs); Western breakfasts are also available.

433 Shirakabecho, Sanjo-sagaru, Fuyacho, Nakagyo-ku. www2.odn.ne.jp/sumiya. (C) **075/221-2188.** 20 units. ¥35,000–¥63,000 per person, including 2 meals. On Fuyacho Dori just south of Sanjo St. Subway: Kyoto Shiyakusho-mae (6 min.) or Karasuma-Oike (10 min.). Bus: 4, 5, 17, or 205 to Kawaramachi Sanjo (3 min.). Taxi: 10 min. **Amenities:** Free Wi-Fi.

The Screen ★★ If you prefer small hotels and contemporary design, consider staying at this strikingly modern yet inviting hotel, complete with traditional touches that make it seem like a hybrid between a traditional *ryokan* and a boutique hotel. At check in, guests are treated to Ippodo tea (its shop is just down the street; see p. 256) and a local sweet. Each of its 13 rooms, by 13 different international designers, has its own style, but all have Jacuzzi tubs and a separate shower cabin. Two Japanese-style rooms, for example, have futon on raised *tatami* platforms along with black lacquered furniture, while another has a playful forest motif and another yet is lined with sheer white curtains. Its location between the Imperial Palace and downtown, on a street lined with craft and antiques stores, is another plus, and I also like the 5th-floor Sky Lounge with its outdoor seating. There aren't many cool hotels like this one in Japan, and after staying in unimaginative rooms, you might consider this a worthy splurge.

640–1 Shimogoryomae-cho, Nakagyo-ku. www.screen-hotel.jp. (C) **075/252-1113.** 13 units. ¥32,000–¥45,000 single or double (rates ¥10,000 higher on weekends and peak periods; from ¥21,000 off season). Subway: Karasuma Marutamachi (7 min.). Bus: 4, 17, or 205 to Kawaramachi Marutamachi (7 min.). Just south of Marutamachi Dori, on Teramachi Dori. **Amenities:** Restaurant; lounge; spa; free Wi-Fi.

MODERATE

Hotel Gimmond ★ This small hotel on Oike Dori was built almost 40 years ago, but it achieves an even older ambience in its lobby with antique-looking lighting and decor. Though the hotel calls itself a tourist hotel and offers mainly twins, its accommodations and lack of services and facilities place it squarely in the category of business hotel. Simple rooms, all nonsmoking, are soundproof and have sliding blackout panels behind the curtains, but I still think those that face away from Oike Dori are quieter. All doubles and some twins face the back; ask for one on a higher floor. Deluxe twin rooms, with a sofa, are decent sized for the price, while the cheapest rooms are quite small. The rates below, like many moderately priced hotels in Kyoto, show the wild swing from low to high season.

Takakura, Oike Dori, Nakagyo-ku. www.gimmond.co.jp. ✆ **075/221-4111.** 140 units. ¥5,100–¥11,048 single; ¥7,600–¥23,760 double. Subway: Karasuma-Oike (2 min.). On Oike Dori west of Takakura Dori. **Amenities:** 2 restaurants; free Wi-Fi.

Hotel Gran M's Kyoto ★   This new hotel occupies a former hotel's older brick building, but it's been completely renovated and updated. The lobby, bathed in white with splashes of fun colors and lots of space, has a hidden entrance near the Kawaramachi-Shijo Dori intersection, very centrally located. All rooms are nonsmoking. Because the cheapest singles face an inner courtyard and are fairly dark, it may be worthwhile to dish out extra yen for a brighter room. My favorite rooms overlook a quiet temple and Buddhist cemetery—a fitting view in a town that boasts so many religious structures. There are also three Japanese-style rooms with cedar tubs. In short, this is a good choice if you like to be in the thick of things and are willing to sacrifice space and facilities to be there.

Kawaramachi, Sango-agaru, Nakagyo-ku. www.alphakyoto.com. ✆ **075/241-2000.** 119 units. ¥5,300–¥11,800 single; ¥10,100–¥29,600 double. Subway: Kyoto Shiyakusho-mae (2 min.). Bus: 4, 5, 17, or 205 to Kawaramachi Sanjo (1 min.). Just off Kawaramachi Dori not far from Sanjo Dori; entrance is on a side street called Aneyakoji Dori. **Amenities:** Free Wi-Fi.

Hotel Monterey Kyoto ★★   The Monterey hotel chain is known for its Old-World designs, but always with some connection to the city they're located in. In this case, Monterey Kyoto, occupying a former bank, centers on the Arts & Crafts style of Edinburgh because Kyoto and the Scottish capital are sister cities. Its dark and subdued lobby plays up its part with marbled flooring, bookcases, and period European artwork. Rooms, on the other hand, are remarkably bold, with striped wallpaper in navy blue or crimson red, all with an eye to the largely Japanese female travelers this chain attracts. Its top-floor spa with great views across the city is worth the entrance fee for its sauna and indoor-outdoor hot-spring baths utilizing thermal waters obtained by drilling more than 1,000m (3,300 ft.) below ground. By paying an extra ¥1,575 fee, women also have access to the ladies-only Bedrock Bath, with hot stones that are thought to help draw out impurities when you lie on them.

604 Manjuya-cho, Karasuma Dori, Sanjo-sagaru, Nakagyo-ku. www.hotelmonterey.co.jp/kyoto. ✆ **075/251-7111.** 327 units. ¥11,500–¥22,000 single; ¥15,000–¥54,000 double. Subway: Karasuma Oike (exit 6, 3 min.). Just south of Sanjo Dori on Karasuma Dori. **Amenities:** 2 restaurants; spa (fee: ¥1,725); free Internet.

Hotel Mystays Kyoto Shijo ★   This tourist/business hotel is a step ahead of older competitors, offering a contemporary lobby (up on the second floor) decorated with traditional crafts and serving coffee and tea from a

machine, plus stylish rooms with modern furnishings (like red lounge chairs in its single and double rooms) and black-and-white photos of Kyoto on the walls. Nagomi rooms, with their bamboo floors and low bed, have a traditional Japanese atmosphere, while rooms on the top floors have good city views. Rates here fluctuate wildly depending on the season, but usually you can get a good deal. On the down side, it's a bit of a walk, about 15 minutes, from the downtown action.

52 Kasaboko-cho, Aburanokoji Higashi-iru, Shijo Dori, Shimogyo-ku. www.mystays. com/e/location/kyotoshijo. © **075/283-3939.** 224 units. ¥6,800–¥39,000 single or double. Subway: Shijo (6 min.). Bus: 26 to Shijo Nishinotoin (2 min.). On the north side of Shijo Dori, just west of Nishitoin and across from Oaks Hotel. **Amenities:** Restaurant; room service; free Wi-Fi.

Royal Park Hotel The Kyoto ★★★   I question the placement of "The" in this hotel's name, but everything else is pretty much on target. Close to sightseeing, shopping, nightlife and transportation, it's stylish, comfy and up to date, with a hidden (some might say too hidden) entryway down a dramatic, darkened corridor leading to a similarly subdued lobby, with spotlights trained on artwork behind the desk and statues arranged on shelves. Rooms are fairly standard and small, though deluxe rooms provide more space and have bathrooms with separate showers and soaking tubs. There's also a ladies' floor (accessible only by special key) with female-oriented toiletries. All have custom-designed mattresses and playful artwork of rabbits jumping over the moon or other motifs that add a dash of color. *And* the public spaces are non-smoking, including the bar (a rarity in Japan).

Kawaramachi Higashi-iru, Sango Dori, Nakagyo-ku. www.rph-the.co.jp/kyoto. © **075/ 241-1111.** 172 units. ¥10,800–¥31,985 single; ¥16,000–¥39,270 double. Subway: Kyoto Shiyakusho-mae (3 min.). On Sanjo Dori just east of Kawaramachi, on the north side. **Amenities:** Restaurant; bar; concierge; free Wi-Fi.

INEXPENSIVE

First Cabin ★   I can't imagine anyone who enjoys sleeping on a plane, but those who do might want to check in for a similar experience here. A step up from capsule hotels, it offers 77 cabins for men and 44 for women, all non-smoking and designed for single use (no doubles here) and available in two sizes. A Business Class Cabin is just a smidgen larger than the bed, with the rest of the space taken up by a nightstand with a small locker for valuables. That translates into absolutely no floor space; smaller people might be able to dress standing on the bed, but taller people will have to get creative. There's also no space for luggage, so you might find yourself sleeping with that as well. If that's too cozy for comfort, spring for a First Class Cabin, which offers a bit of floor space. All cabins have wall-mounted TVs and screens that close for privacy (there's no lock). I recommend picking up a free pair of earplugs from the front desk, because you're going to need them. Breakfast, beer, and other drinks and snacks are available in the lounge; there's another women's lounge on the dedicated ladies' floor. In short, these rooms are the smallest I've ever seen, but I'd kill to get one on a real plane.

Takanoha Square Building, 4th floor, 331 Kamiyanagimachi, Bokkuji Dori, Karasuma Higashi-iru. www.first-cabin.jp. © **075/361-1113.** 121 units (none with private bathroom). ¥4,600 business-class single, ¥5,600 first-class single. East of Karasuma Dori, across from Bokkuji Temple. Subway: Shijo (2 min.). **Amenities:** Lounge; free Wi-Fi.

Nishiyama Ryokan ★★★   This family-owned inn, now in its third generation of innkeepers and in the able hands of English-speaking Mr. Nishiyama, has a great location just a few minutes' walk from downtown. Although the building itself is nondescript, inside it strives for a traditional atmosphere, with a small courtyard garden visible just beyond the lobby, a public bath with a view of the garden's waterfall, and mostly Japanese-style *tatami* rooms (there are also three Western-style twins), all nonsmoking. *Kaiseki* dinners costing ¥8,000 are available with reservations made at least 3 days in advance; breakfasts cost ¥2,000. It even presents a free tea ceremony in the lobby most mornings, with other cultural events like calligraphy, origami, or koto performances offered once a week. The only downside, perhaps, is that its moderate rates attract school groups, but a youthful clientele seems hardly a deterrent for Japanese-style accommodations in this price range in the heart of Kyoto. The prices below reflect the seasons.

Gokomachi, Nijo-sagaru, Nakagyo-ku. www.ryokan-kyoto.com. © **075/222-1166.** 30 units (26 with bathroom, 4 with toilet only). ¥7,000–¥12,000 single; ¥10,000–¥30,000 double. Subway: Shiyakusho-mae (3 min.). Bus: 4, 17, or 205 to Shiyakusho-mae (3 min.). 2 blocks northwest of City Hall. **Amenities:** Free Wi-Fi.

The Palace Side Hotel ★★   Savvy, budget-conscious travelers have been flocking to this modest hotel with its contemporary lobby and cafe for more than 45 years. Although its location just west of the Imperial Palace is not as convenient as my other inexpensive recommendations in central Kyoto, it's near a subway line and the palace's expansive parklike grounds are popular with joggers. It keeps rates down by offering bare-boned small rooms (all nonsmoking) with the basics of fridge, desks too small for any serious work, and aging tiled bathrooms. The most expensive twins and doubles have kitchenettes with a hotplate and microwave, making them good for longer stays, but there's also a communal kitchen. Some rooms face the greenery of the palace, but they're also noisier due to busy Karasuma Dori. Probably the most impressive things about the hotel are the artwork in most rooms created over the years by artists who have stayed in the hotel, free Japanese lessons offered once or twice a week, and occasional mini-concerts held in the lobby.

Karasuma Shimodachiuri-agaru, Kamigyo-ku. www.palacesidehotel.co.jp. © **075/415-8887.** 120 units. ¥6,300–¥7,300 single; ¥10,200–¥12,000 double. Discounts for stays longer than 2 nights. Subway: Marutamachi (exit 2, 3 min.). **Amenities:** Restaurant; bar; Thai massage room; rental bikes (free 1st hour, then ¥800 for 12 hr.); free Internet.

Eastern Kyoto
EXPENSIVE

Hyatt Regency Kyoto ★★★   I love this hotel for its location (across the street from the Kyoto National Museum, next to Sanjusangendo Hall, and within walking distance of Kiyomizu Temple), its 850-year-old garden that was once part of Emperor Goshirakawa's residence, and its spa, which boasts more Asian treatments than any other hotel spa in Japan, including acupuncture, moxibustion, and shiatsu. Its lobby is stunning, with a modern take on traditional latticework that covers its walls and ceiling. Rooms, too, are top-notch, combining Japanese aesthetics such as kimono-fabric-covered headboards and elegant teaware with modern conveniences like large safes with electric hookups for laptops (so you can charge your computer while it's in storage) and DVD players (the hotel has a free DVD library). For travelers looking for a splurge, eight deluxe rooms have *tatami* areas plus Japanese-style tubs placed next to balconies, with views of the garden or National Museum. I also like the hotel's restaurants (including Touzan for Japanese and Sette for Italian), which use organic vegetables from the hotel's own garden, maintained by hotel staff. In short, this hotel is a great choice for many reasons, but note that its rates reflect the seasons, making it a bargain in the off season but pricey much of the year.

644–2 Sanjusangendo-mawari, Higashiyama-ku. http://kyoto.regency.hyatt.com. © **800/ 233-1234** in the U.S. and Canada, or 075/541-1234. 189 units. ¥23,000–¥43,000 single or double; ¥46,000–¥84,000 deluxe rooms. Rates exclude tax and service charge. Bus: 100, 206, or 208 to Hakubutsukan Sanjusangendo (1 min.). **Amenities:** 3 restaurants; bar; babysitting; concierge; gym (free for hotel guests); room service; spa (fee: ¥1,600); free Wi-Fi.

The Westin Miyako Kyoto ★★★

The Miyako opened in 1890 but has gone through many changes since Douglas Fairbanks, Queen Elizabeth II, and many other well-known travelers stayed here (the present hotel dates from 1992). What I like most about the Miyako is its hilltop setting, sprawling over more than 6.4 hectares (16 acres) and boasting a Japanese garden and a wild-bird sanctuary (and even a bird-watching trail). It also has a satellite office at Kyoto Station, where you can drop off luggage for delivery to the hotel (¥300 per bag) while you go off sightseeing, but there's also a free shuttle bus that can take you directly to the hotel. For families, there's a playroom equipped with a slide and toys for young children and both indoor and outdoor pools. A city zoo, Heian Shrine, and Nanzenji Temple are within walking distance. A variety of Western-style rooms are available, with the least expensive occupying the oldest wing and the best on the fifth floor with huge terraces overlooking the valley. For a *ryokan* experience, the Kasui-en annex, built in 1959 next to the hotel, offers 20 Japanese-style rooms complete with cypress baths and views of the garden. In any case, this is one of Japan's best-known hotels; you can't go wrong staying here.

1 Awadaguchi Kacho-cho, Keage, Sanjo, Higashiyama-ku. www.miyakohotels.ne.jp/ westinkyoto. © **075/771-7111.** 499 units. ¥30,240–¥59,400 single or double (from ¥12,150 off season); from ¥65,800 Executive Club floor; ¥45,360 double in Kasui-en. Free shuttle every 30 min. from Kyoto Station's Hachijo exit (9am–9pm). Subway: Keage (2 min.). **Amenities:** 5 restaurants; bar; babysitting; concierge; executive-level rooms; fitness center w/gym, 20m (66-ft.) indoor pool, and shallow outdoor pool (fee: ¥500; free for executive-level guests); room service; rooftop jogging path; sauna; sun decks (available also for viewing the full moon); grass tennis courts; wild-bird sanctuary and bird-watching trail; jogging trail; free Wi-Fi.

MODERATE

APA Hotel Kyoto Gion Excellent ★   The overwhelming reason to stay at this 40-some-year-old property is its superb location in Gion, within easy walking distance to downtown, the Pontocho and Kiyamachi nightlife districts, and Higashiyama-ku's many temples and sights. Other perks are the Starbucks on the ground floor and a rooftop beer garden open in summer. Otherwise, rooms are updated but tiny. The single rooms are among the smallest I've ever seen, and yet couples on a budget can attempt to squeeze into one, though with no room to unpack and no closet, they'll probably have to store luggage in the shower. There are also twins (no doubles), but they, too, are rather small. There are no views, but my recommendation is to ask for a room on a higher floor facing west, with floor-to-ceiling windows overlooking the tiled roofs of Gion. If off-season rates are on par with the lower spectrum given below, I'd consider this place a bargain. Otherwise, there are three other APA properties, all within walking distance of Kyoto Station, that are cheaper.

555 Gionmachi-minamigawa, Gion, Higashiyama-ku. www.apahotel.com. ℂ **075/551-2111.** 154 units. ¥6,400–¥17,400 single; ¥10,000–¥34,900 double. Bus: 100 or 206 to Gion (2 min.). On Shijo Dori, west of Yasaka Shrine. **Amenities:** Restaurant; bar; summer beer garden; Starbucks; free Wi-Fi.

Seikoro Inn ★★★   This *ryokan* just east of the Kamo River was established in 1831, with the present building dating from about 115 years ago. After passing through a traditional front gate and small courtyard, you'll find yourself in one of the most charming entryways I've seen in Kyoto, which adjoins a cozy parlor replete with an eclectic mix of Japanese and Western antiques. Rooms, occupying the older main building and an annex built just before the 1964 Olympics, are comfortable and decorated with antiques. Rooms in the main building consist of old and renovated *tatami* rooms, most of them with sliding doors and *shoji* screens that open onto the garden. Those in the annex only provide views over the surrounding rooftops. The nice public bath boasts a tub made of 400-year-old hinoki cypress, making it one of the inn's most treasured possessions. The English-speaking, seventh-generation innkeeper doesn't mind if you take your meals elsewhere in the off season, especially if you're here for a while. The staff is warm and welcoming and will prepare Western breakfasts on request. If you wish, you can dress up in an elaborate kimono (a 30-min. process) for ¥3,000 so you can take pictures.

Tonyamachi Dori, Gojo-sagaru, Higashiyama-ku. www.seikoro.com. ℂ **075/561-0771.** 22 units. ¥25,000–¥30,875 double room without meals; ¥28,875–¥57,750 per person including 2 meals. Bus: 4, 17, or 205 to Kawaramachi Gojo and then a 5-min. walk; cross the bridge over the Kamo River and after Kawabata Dori take the 1st right. Keihan Electric Railway: Gojo Station (2 min.). **Amenities:** Free Wi-Fi.

Northern & Western Kyoto

INEXPENSIVE

Kyoto Utano Youth Hostel ★★★   This could well be the most attractive youth hostel I've ever seen, located amidst greenery in northwest Kyoto and with an airy, lodgelike atmosphere that makes it seem more like a family resort. It stages free events most nights, from flute or guitar concerts to learning how to make Japanese sweets, plus traditional experiences that cost extra, such as trying on a Japanese kimono for ¥3,500. Rackets and balls are provided free for use on the tennis court. Otherwise, there's no denying that this is a youth hostel with its 11:30pm curfew, public baths and shower rooms, free Wi-Fi available only in the lobby and lounge, and simple rooms that include four twin rooms, eight triples, and dormitory rooms with bunk beds sleeping four to six people. There are also Japanese-style *tatami* rooms that sleep five or six people. There's a communal kitchen if you don't opt for breakfast or dinner, and rates are the same whether you're a hostel member or not.

29 Nakayama-cho, Uzumasa Ukyo-ku. www.yh-kyoto.or.jp/utano. © **075/462-2288.** 40 units (none with private bathroom). ¥8,220 double; ¥3,390 dormitory bed. Bus: Take bus 26 40 min. to Youth Hostel Mae (1 min.). **Amenities:** Bicycles (1 hr. free; ¥500 all day); tennis court.

Rakucho ★★★ This accommodation isn't as conveniently situated as most of the other inns listed above, but that shouldn't stop anyone from staying in this well-kept 80-year-old *ryokan,* managed by English-speaking Kimiko Urade and her son Katsunori, both very kind. All but one of the spotless *tatami* rooms, decorated with such traditional touches as scrolls, have views of a small peaceful garden. Entrance to the *ryokan* is through a well-tended tiny courtyard filled with plants. There's a kitchenette with two communal refrigerators, a toaster, microwave, and free instant coffee and tea, as well as laundry facilities.

67 Higashihangi-cho, Shimogamo, Sakyo-ku. www.rakucho-ryokan.com. © **075/721-2174.** 11 units (none with private bathroom). ¥5,300 single; ¥9,240 double; ¥12,600 triple. Subway: Kitaoji Station (10 min.); walk east on Kitaoji Dori and turn left at the 5th traffic light. Bus: 205 to Furitsudaigaku-mae (2 min. to the north). **Amenities:** Free Wi-Fi.

Shunko-In Temple and Guesthouse ★★★ For a different kind of experience, consider staying at this Buddhist temple in west Kyoto, established in 1590 and serving as a sub-temple of Myoshinji Temple with its expansive grounds. Although the Japanese-style rooms are rather basic and are located in a nondescript building (with the great name of "Cave of Enlightened Dragon"), perks include a communal kitchen offering free coffee and tea, free use of bicycles, and, best of all, the chance to join 90-minute Zen meditation classes offered most mornings. Costing ¥2,200, they're led by head priest Rev. Taka Kawakami, who speaks flawless English and is the fifth generation of his family to have presided over the temple the past 150 years. After making suggestions on how to incorporate Zen Buddhism into daily life, he leads two 15-minute meditation sessions and then gives a tour of the strikingly beautiful 18th-century temple, gardens and art treasures. No meals are served, but guests are given a hand-drawn map showing nearby restaurants. And in case you're interested, the temple also offers Buddhist weddings in English, regardless of sexual orientation. No credit cards are accepted.

42 Myoshinji-Cho, Hanazono, Ukyo-ku. www.shunkoin.com. © **075/462-5488.** 8 units. ¥6,500 single; ¥11,000 double. Station: Hanazono on the JR Sagano Line (6 min.). Bus:

26 to Myoshim-ji Kitamon stop (3 min.). **Amenities:** Bicycles (free); free guest computer; free Wi-Fi.

WHERE TO EAT

Kyoto cuisine, known as ***Kyo-ryori,*** is linked to Kyoto's long history and to seasonal foods produced in the surrounding region. Among the various types of Kyo-ryori available, most famous are the vegetarian dishes, which were created to serve the needs of Zen Buddhist priests and pilgrims making the rounds of Kyoto's many temples. Called *shojin ryori,* these vegetarian set meals may include *yudofu* (blocks of tofu simmered in a pot at your table and served with dipping sauce), filmy sheets of *yuba* (soy milk curd), and an array of local vegetables. Kyoto is also renowned for its own style of *kaiseki* called *Kyo-kaiseki,* originally conceived as a meal to be taken before the tea ceremony but eventually becoming an elaborate feast enjoyed by the capital's nobility with a blend of ceremonial court cuisine, Zen vegetarian food, and simple tea-ceremony dishes. You'll typically need a reservation for *kaiseki* (Kyoto's better *ryokan* also serve *kaiseki* as the evening meal). Simpler restaurants specialize in *obanzai,* home-style Kyoto cooking using traditional seasonal ingredients. For more on *kaiseki* and other Japanese cuisines, see "Tips on Dining in Japan," beginning on p. 27 in chapter 2.

Remember: Last orders are taken 30 to 60 minutes before the restaurant's actual closing time, even earlier for *kaiseki* restaurants. Bus information to each restaurant is from Kyoto Station.

Around Kyoto Station

In addition to the restaurants listed here, a good place to browse for dining is **Kyoto Station,** which houses dozens of restaurants in underground arcades, at major exits, and in Isetan department store, where there are more than 20 outlets alone, mostly on the 10th and 11th floors, including **The Kitchen Salvatore Cuomo.** A cheap stand-out is **Ramen Koji** (拉麺小路), where eight of the best ramen shops from around the country are assembled on the 10th floor of Isetan (© **075/361-4401**). Dishes, most priced less than ¥1,000, run from miso ramen (ramen in miso broth) from Sapporo to so-thick-it's-almost-creamy *tonkotsu* (pork broth) from Hakata (Fukuoka). After choosing what you want, buy a ticket from vending machines outside each shop (English-speaking staff is usually on hand to help) and then line up in that restaurant's queue. Ramen Koji is open daily from 11am to 10pm. Another inexpensive option is the conveyor-belt sushi shop **Musashi** (p. 231), located in Kyoto Station in the Asty Road concourse on the station's south side.

INEXPENSIVE

Donguri (どんぐり) ★★ OKONOMIYAKI/YAKISOBA   I don't care for pancakes, but I'll eat the Japanese version even for dinner. Called *okonomiyaki* and filled with your choice of meat and vegetables, it's the number-one choice in this lively basement restaurant with a young staff decked out like hip ninjas with their black outfits and black kerchiefs on their heads. The

English-language menu presents about 20 possibilities, from the "standard" with ground beef, pork, and squid to the "Italian" with bacon, cheese, and corn, flavored with your choice of sweet or spicy sauce and served on a *teppan* (steel plate) built into your table. *Yakisoba* (fried noodles) are also available, along with choices of side dishes like *gyoza* and tofu steak. Because it's open mostly for dinner, it's a popular drinking place as well, with beer, sake, *shochu,* and other drinks livening things up as the evening wears on, especially if you choose the all-you-can-drink option, costing ¥2,160 for 2 hours and ¥3,240 for 3.

Karasuma Shichijo-sagaru, Nishigawa. www.kyoto-donguri.co.jp. ℂ **075/361-5777.** Dishes ¥630–¥1,080. Mon–Sat 5pm–2am; Sun 11am–11:30am. Station: Kyoto (5 min.). On Karasuma Dori's west side, a 1/2 block north of Yodobashi and just south of Shichijo Dori.

Ichiba Coji (市場小路) ★ VARIED JAPANESE/INTERNATIONAL Isetan department store is connected to Kyoto Station, making it convenient for meals near the station. On the ninth floor, with views north over the city from window-side seats (make reservations for these), is this combination restaurant/beer hall offering food that pairs well with its extensive list of locally brewed beer and sake, with many dishes listed on an English-language menu and rendered in plastic for the food display case. The dinner menu includes the likes of salads (like the tofu avocado salad) and lots of charcoal-grilled skewered foods, including chicken thigh, meatballs, quail egg, pork-wrapped asparagus, potato, and green pepper, but there are also set dinners described only in Japanese and that give the option of all the beer, wine, sake, and other drinks you care to drink within 90 minutes for an extra ¥1,575. The set lunches provide several options for the main dish, such as grilled chicken or rice bowl with egg omelet. There's a downtown branch, in the Teramachi covered shopping arcade in the basement of the Withyou Building (ℂ **075/252-2008**).

10th floor, Isetan department store, Kyoto Station. ℂ **075/365-3388.** Grilled skewers ¥281–¥432; set lunches ¥972–¥1,994; set dinners ¥1,620–¥3,780. Daily 11am–10pm (last order). Above Kyoto Station.

Katsukura ★ TONKATSU *Tonkatsu* (breaded pork cutlet) is inexpensive comfort food in Japan. This restaurant, on the top floor of Isetan department store at Kyoto Station, has both a display case of popular dishes and an English-language menu to help you choose your meal. Set meals are the way to go, with combinations that might give you tonkatsu plus crab cream croquette or prawn cutlet, plus barley rice, miso soup, cabbage, and pickled vegetables (like most tonkatsu restaurants, you get free refills of rice, cabbage, soup, and vegetables). At your table will be a mortar and pestle for sesame seeds that you can grind up and add to your tonkatsu sauce. But what really sets this place apart from tonkatsu restaurants across Japan is that because it's in Kyoto, it also offers *yuba* (thin sheets of soy bean curd), such as the *yuba*-rolled seasonal vegetable cutlet, making it good also for vegetarians.

Isetan department store, The Cube, 11th floor, JR Kyoto Station. ℂ **075/365-8666.** Set meals ¥1,180–¥1,950; set lunch ¥1,480. Daily 11am–9:15pm (last order).

Central Kyoto

The heart of Kyoto's shopping, dining, and nightlife district is in Nakagyo-ku, especially on Kawaramachi and Shijo Dori and along the many side streets. In summer, restaurants on the west bank of the Kamo River erect large wooden outdoor platforms that extend over the water and offer open-air dining.

EXPENSIVE

Misoguigawa (禊川) ★★★ FRENCH KAISEKI This is one of my favorite restaurants of all time due to its idyllic location on the Kamo River, its historic ambience, its innovative cuisine, and the welcoming personality of master-chef/owner Teruo Inoue, who has been creating his own take on fusion cuisine long before it became fashionable. Trained by a three-star Michelin chef, Inoue is a genius at blending classic French cuisine with Japanese ingredients, creating a style best described as French *kaiseki*. Served on Kyoto tableware, his dishes are like works of art, beautifully arranged to please both the eye and the palate. The restaurant, open since 1981, occupies a century-old former teahouse on Pontocho that once belonged to a geisha. It offers several options for dining: an L-shaped counter with *tatami* seating and leg wells; private *tatami* rooms; a casual counter offering a-la-carte dishes and the opportunity to watch the chef at work; and, my favorite, an outdoor summer veranda extending over the Kamo River.

Three dinners and four lunch sets are available, but chef Inoue always asks about allergies and preferences and makes changes accordingly. One of the delights of dining here is the English-speaking staff, with explanations of each dish as it's presented. Mr. Inoue travels to France every year to buy wine directly from the Bourgogne region and to commission chocolate from a Parisian chocolatier. Note that a 10% service charge is added to meals taken at the L-shaped counter and on the veranda, while a 15% service charge is added to meals in private *tatami* rooms (the casual a-la-carte counter, where dishes cost ¥1,500–¥2,500, doesn't add a service charge). Reservations are required; for lunch, you're asked to make reservations not less than a day before your intended visit. In any case, dining here could well be the culinary highlight of your trip.

Sanjo-sagaru, Pontocho. www.misogui.jp. ℂ **075/221-2270.** Set lunches ¥4,500–¥13,000; set dinners ¥15,000–¥30,000 (prices exclude tax and service charge). Tues–Sun 11:30am–1:30pm and 5:30–8:30pm (last order). Bus: 4, 5, 17, or 205 to Kawaramachi Sanjo (5 min.); on Pontocho, north of the playground.

MODERATE

Ashoka ★ INDIAN One of Kyoto's most popular and longest-running Indian restaurants, in business more than 35 years, this pleasant venue serves vegetarian and meat curries prepared by Indian chefs, including mutton, chicken, fish, vegetable, and shrimp selections, as well as tandoori and Halal dishes. On weekdays, it offers an even cheaper vegetable set lunch than given below, only ¥900.

Kikusui Building, 3rd floor, Teramachi Dori. www.ashoka-jp.com. (C) **075/241-1318.** Main dishes ¥1,500–¥2,400; set lunches ¥1,200–¥1,800; set dinners ¥2,800–¥6,000. Daily 11am–3pm and 5–9pm (last order). Bus: 4, 5, 17, or 205 to Shijo Kawaramachi (1 min.). On the north side of Shijo Dori, to the right at the entrance of the Teramachi covered shopping arcade.

Ganko Sushi (がんこ寿司) ★ SUSHI/VARIED JAPANESE   This popular, lively sushi chain got its start in 1963 in Osaka but can now be found throughout the Kansai area and Tokyo. Although its specialty is sushi, with seafood sourced directly from fishermen, it also offers plenty of a-la-carte alternatives for people who don't like fish, including baked chicken, *yakitori*, tempura, french fries, tofu, and crab dishes on an English-language menu. This branch has several floors for dining, with the ground floor offering a long sushi counter (sit here if you want to order sushi a la carte) and tables divided by screens to make them more private.

Kawaramachi-Sanjo, Higashi-iru. www.gankofood.co.jp/en. (C) **075/255-1128.** Set meals ¥1,296–¥3,650. Daily 11am–11pm. Subway: Kyoto Shiyakusho-mae (4 min.). Bus: 4, 5, 17, or 205 to Kawaramachi Sanjo (2 min.). On Sanjo Dori, just west of the Kamo River (look for its logo of a face with glasses and a bandanna).

Kushi Kura (串くら) ★★ YAKITORI   This restaurant has a great atmosphere, in a century-old warehouse with heavy beams and dark-polished wood contrasting with whitewashed walls. Seating is at the counter where you can watch the chefs, or at tables or on *tatami*. It specializes in grilled chicken using top-grade charcoal, served *yakitori*-style on skewers. The English-language menu, with photos, lists other possibilities as well, along with set meals and a variety of meat and vegetable individual skewers you can order a la carte. The least expensive set dinner includes an appetizer, raw veggies with a dipping sauce, and five skewers consisting of chicken breast, Kyoto-style wheat gluten, chicken and leeks, ground chicken, and small sweet green peppers, although most diners prefer to select their own meal so they can get exactly what they want. For liquids, you might wish to try the locally made Fushimi sake. On weekdays, there's a set lunch for ¥880 along with more expensive meals.

Takakura Dori, Oike-agaru. (C) **075/213-2211.** Set lunches ¥880 (weekdays only) to ¥3,100; set dinners ¥2,100–¥5,000. Daily 11:30am–2pm and 5–9:40pm (last order). Subway: Karasuma-Oike (2 min.). Just north of Oike Dori on Takakura Dori.

Orizzonte ★★ INTERNATIONAL   A buffet restaurant by day and a cocktail lounge at night, this 17th-floor venue offers expansive views of eastern Kyoto and the Higashiyama mountain range. Its mostly Western fare ranges from salads and seafood to casseroles and dim sum (dumplings). If you come for drinks, be aware that there's a ¥324 cover charge from 8:30pm.

Kyoto Hotel Okura, 537-4 Ichinofunairi-cho, Kawaramachi-Oike. http://okura.kyoto hotel.co.jp. (C) **075/254-2534.** Buffet lunch ¥3,654; buffet dinner ¥5,108. Daily

11:30am–2:30pm and 5:30–8pm. Subway: Kyoto Shiyakusho-mae (1 min., below the hotel). Bus: 4, 17, or 205 to Shiyakusho-mae (2 min.).

Tagoto (田ごと) ★★ KYO-RYORI/KAISEKI/BENTO/SOBA   Open since 1868 and nestled just off bustling Shijo Dori in an inner courtyard complete with a koi pond, this modestly decorated restaurant offers a variety of Japanese dishes. Its English-language menu offers many choices, including *soba* noodles starting at ¥850 and Kyoto specialties like *yuba* set meals for ¥3,900. For a splurge there are seasonal *kaiseki* meals. With its convenient yet buffered location, in the heart of downtown, this is a good choice for high-quality meals at reasonable prices.

Shijo-Kawaramachi, Nishi-iru, Kitagawa. www.kyoto-tagoto.co.jp. ℂ **075/221-1811.** Set lunches ¥2,000–¥4,000; set meals ¥3,850–¥10,800. Daily 11am–3pm and 4:30–8:30pm. Bus: 4, 5, 17, or 205 to Shijo Kawaramachi (1 min.). The entrance is on the north side of Shijo Dori just west of Kawaramachi (look for a narrow passageway to the back courtyard).

INEXPENSIVE

In addition to the choices here, there's a branch of **Ichiba Coji** (p. 227) in the Teramachi covered shopping arcade (on the west side about halfway down), with modern, hip decor and pub food that goes well with beer, sake, and spirits.

Bio-Tei (びお亭) ★★★ VEGETARIAN/HEALTH FOOD   An army of capable women slicing and dicing and cooking up aromatic dishes in the open kitchen make a meal here seem like you've been invited right into their home. The dining room is very casual, with seating at heavy wooden tables made from Japanese cypress that you'll likely share with other diners during peak times and food served on tableware from local kilns. Using organic, preservative-free ingredients, it offers only one thing for lunch: a tasty *teishoku* (daily fixed-price meal) that comes with *genmae* (brown rice), miso soup, pickles, and a choice of a main dish that's different every day and includes vegan and vegetarian options (on the day I tried it, it was curry-based tofu stew with potatoes and carrots). Dinner offers set meals and a-la-carte selections from an English-language menu that might include tea-simmered chicken with mustard and fresh greens, salmon salad, and deep-fried tofu. In short, for a vegetarian or health-food fix, this unassuming and cozy place hits the spot, but be sure to bring cash because no credit cards are accepted. As befits a health-food restaurant, smoking is not allowed.

Sanjo Dori Higashinotoin. ℂ **075/255-0086.** Lunch *teishoku* ¥860; set dinner ¥1,290; dinner main courses ¥750–¥1,200. Tues–Fri 11:30am–2pm; Tues–Wed and Fri–Sat 5–8:30pm (last order). Closed holidays. Subway: Karasuma-Oike (exit 5, 3 min.). On the southwest corner of Sanjo-Higashinotoin intersection (cattycorner from the post office), on the 2nd floor up a tightly wound spiral staircase.

Gontaro (権太呂) ★★ NOODLES   This shop has been serving its own handmade noodles for a mere 100-some years. A small place with a modern yet traditional interior and an English-language menu, it offers various noodle dishes of either *soba* (buckwheat) or *udon* (a thicker wheat noodle) with such toppings as tempura, as well as *donburi* (a rice casserole with tempura, *yakitori,* or other topping) and *nabe* (udon boiled in broth with seafood, chicken, and vegetables). Those with insatiable appetites can have it all with the Okimari set meal for ¥6,000, which comes with *nabe,* tempura, barbecue chicken, and noodles. There's a branch in northern Kyoto (© **075/463-1039**), between Ryoanji and Kinkakuji temples.

Fuyacho Dori, Shijo-agaru. http://gontaro.co.jp. © **075/221-5810.** Noodles ¥1,000–¥2,000; *donburi* ¥1,000–¥1,500; *nabe* ¥4,300 per person. Thurs–Tues 11am–9pm. Bus: 4, 5, 17, or 205 to Shijo Kawaramachi (5 min.). On the west side of Fuyacho Dori just north of Shijo Dori; look for lacquered lanterns, a tiny shrine out front, and a lone pine tree.

Ippudo (一風堂) ★ RAMEN This chain opened its first restaurant in Fukuoka in 1985 and has since spread to hundreds of locations in Japan and abroad. But while ramen might be eaten around the world, no one eats it with as much gusto as the Japanese. To fully enjoy the full flavors of ramen, which at Ippudo means a broth made from three types of pork bones simmered for 18 hours, it's imperative to slurp the noodles, which also helps cool the hot temperature so you don't burn yourself (waiting until the ramen cooled would totally diminish the aroma and flavor). In any case, ramen noodles served here are thin and offer a variety of choices, like the Ippudo Karaka with a spicy miso topping (you get to choose the level of spiciness), but you can also add extra toppings like scallions or pork for ¥80 to ¥200. On your table is also pickled ginger, spicy sprouts, and do-it-yourself sesame grinders and garlic presses. I also can't resist the *gyoza* (fried pork dumplings), so my favorite time to come is for the weekday lunch that comes with ramen, *gyoza,* and rice. It has a contemporary setting, with both tables and counters where you can watch the cooks in action in the open kitchen.

653-1 Higashitoin Bandoyacho. www.ippudo.com. © **075/213-8800.** Ramen ¥780–¥1,100; set lunch (weekdays only) ¥780–¥880. Mon–Sat 11am–3am, Sun and holidays 11am–2am. Subway: Shijo (3 min.). On Nishiki-Koji Dori, west of the food market and Higashitoin Dori.

Musashi (むさし) ★ SUSHI Purists might think it's sacrilege to eat sushi from a conveyor belt, but for the rest of us it's one of the cheapest ways to eat sushi. Besides, sushi in Japan is almost always better than what passes for sushi in many other places in the world, even in conveyor-belt restaurants, because the standard is so high. In any case, plates of sushi slowly swing by via a conveyor on the counter, so all you have to do is reach out and take whatever you wish. It's quick, there's no menu or ordering to deal with, and all plates are priced at ¥130 plus tax, with usually two pieces of sushi per plate. But if you're really in a hurry, takeout sushi is sold from the restaurant's sidewalk kiosk. And in case you want some takeout when departing Kyoto, there's a branch in Kyoto Station.

440 Ebisucho. www.sushinomusashi.com. © **075/222-0634.** ¥130 per plate. Daily 11am–10pm. Bus: 4, 5, 17, or 205 to Kawaramachi Sanjo (1 min.). On the northwest corner of the Kawaramachi-Sanjo intersection.

Pizza Salvatore Cuomo & Grill ★★ ITALIAN   Instead of the usual Japanese greeting of *irashaimase!* when you walk into this restaurant, here you'll get a *buonasera!* And if it is indeed a fine evening and you're dying for pizza, there's no better place to be than here with its very cool setting alongside the Kiyamachi canal. Seating is either outdoors or indoors where a wall of glass faces the canal. In any case, the emphasis here is clearly on pizza, with more than a dozen varieties available in two different sizes (hearty appetites will find even the small one ample, but daintier diners might want to share). Salads, pasta, and a few meat entrees like grilled fish or spareribs round out the menu, along with the requisite Italian desserts and wines, but the real bargain is the lunch buffet with appetizers, salads, pizzas, pastas and desserts on offer.

90 Nakajima-cho, Kawaramachi Sanjo-Higashiiru. ℂ **075/212-4965.** Small pizzas ¥1,470–¥2,200; lunch buffet ¥1,000 Mon–Fri, ¥1,200 Sat–Sun. Daily 11am–3pm and 5–11pm. Subway: Kyoto Shiyakushomae (3 min.). Bus: 4, 5, 17, or 205 to Kawaramachi Sanjo (2 min.). On the west side of Kiyamachi canal, north of Sanjo Dori.

Second House ★ PASTA   Occupying a former *machiya* (merchant's house) with tall ceilings, a large nonsmoking section, and a young staff, this casual restaurant (no credit cards accepted) is part of a local chain offering a variety of Western and Asian pasta dishes, such as spaghetti with eggplant, tomato, and bacon or pasta with pork and *kimchi* (Korean-style spicy cabbage). Its English-language menu also offers homemade cakes and pastries. The restaurant is up on the second floor, with rustic furnishings and a view of a park, while on the ground floor is a cake shop.

Higashinotoin Takoyakushi-agaru. ℂ **075/241-2323.** Pasta ¥880–¥1,167; pasta set lunch ¥1,000. Daily 11am–10pm (last order). Subway: Shijo (3 min.). Bus: 5 or 101 to Shijo Karasuma (3 min.). Head north on Karasuma Dori and turn right on Takoyakushi Dori, and left again at the little park. The restaurant is on the left, across from the park.

Tohkasaikan ★ BEIJING CHINESE   This Beijing-style Chinese restaurant popular with families started life as a Western restaurant. The old building features an ancient, manually operated elevator (Japan's oldest, installed in 1924), lots of wood paneling, high ceilings, old-fashioned decor, and a friendly staff. From May to mid-September, you can sit outside on a wooden veranda over the Kamo River, one of the cheapest places along the river to do so. If it's winter or raining, consider sitting in the fourth- or fifth-floor dining rooms, which have nice views of the city. The best views, however, are from the rooftop garden (open weekends in summer only), where you can order mugs of beer and dine on dishes from the English-language menu listing sweet-and-sour pork, fried shrimp with chili sauce, and chicken with red pepper. I've had better Chinese food, but the atmosphere is great and is reminiscent of another era.

Nishizume, Shijo Ohashi. ℂ **075/221-1147.** Main dishes ¥1,400–¥2,500; set meals from ¥5,000 (2-person minimum). Daily 11:30am–9pm (last order). Bus: 4, 5, 17, or 205 to Shijo Kawaramachi (2 min.). A large stone building on Shijo Dori, on the west end of the bridge spanning the Kamo River.

Eastern Kyoto
EXPENSIVE

Hyotei (瓢亭) ★★★ KAISEKI/BENTO   This is one of Kyoto's oldest and most famous restaurants, opened around 400 years ago as a teahouse to serve pilgrims on their way to Nanzenji Temple. It specializes in *kyo-kaiseki,* a multi-course meal that originated with the tea ceremony but has evolved into Kyoto's special cuisine. The setting is rustic and lovely, with individual teahouses, the oldest of which is 300 years old, spread around a beautiful garden with a pond. Kimono-clad women deliver your *kaiseki* meal to your private *tatami* room, much as they have been doing for centuries. The cuisine, the dishes they're served on, the outdoor scenery, and the gracious service all conspire to create the ultimate traditional Japanese experience.

For travelers who find the prices of *kaiseki* prohibitive, adjoining the main *kaiseki* restaurant is an annex *(bekkan)* to the left with its own separate entrance. It specializes in *shokado bento* (lunch boxes), which also change with the seasons and are served in a communal *tatami* room with views of a garden.

There are also seasonal options. In July and August, a special breakfast called *asagayu* is available in the main restaurant from 8 to 10am for ¥6,000; in the annex it's available from mid-March through November from 8 to 11am for ¥4,500. From December to mid-March, the main restaurant offers the seasonal *uzuragayu* meal from 11am to 2pm for ¥12,100, while the annex offers it from 8 to 11am for ¥4,500. No matter where or when you dine, boiled eggs, served to Hyotei's guests since its founding and one of its specialties, will be part of your meal. Note that reservations are required for *kaiseki,* but it's also recommended for the annex. Note, too, that you should dress respectfully (no T-shirts, shorts, or sandals), and only children older than 10 are allowed. If you want a time machine to old Kyoto, you can't get any closer than this.

35 Kusakawa-cho, Nanzenji. http://hyotei.co.jp. ℂ **075/771-4116.** *Kaiseki* lunches from ¥23,000, dinners from ¥27,000; *shokado bento* ¥5,400. *Kaiseki* daily 11am–7:30pm (closed 2nd and 4th Tues of each month); *shokado bento* daily noon–4pm. Subway: Keage (5 min.). Bus: 5 or 100 to Dobutsuen-mae (7 min.). West of Shirakawa Dori Murin-an; look for a plain facade hidden behind a bamboo fence with a sign shaped like a gourd.

Minoko (美濃幸) ★★★ KAISEKI/BENTO   This former villa is an enclave of traditional Japan with a simple, austere exterior and an interior of wooden corridors that gently creak underfoot, *tatami* rooms, and a garden. Opened nearly a century ago, Minoko retains the spirit of the tea ceremony with *kaiseki* utilizing seasonal ingredients beautifully arranged to please both the palate and the eye and served in a private *tatami* rooms. Lunch, which is served communally in a large *tatami* room with a view of a beautiful garden, is more economical and less formal but still draws on the tea ceremony for inspiration. The *chabako-bento* lunch box, for example, is named after the lacquered box it's served in, traditionally used to carry tea utensils. A *hiru-kaiseki*, or mini-*kaiseki* set meal, is also available at lunch. Reservations are required for dinner and recommended for lunch. Its entry is through a courtyard, whereupon you'll be whisked away by kimono-clad staff to begin your culinary adventure.

480 Kiyoi-cho, Shimogawara-dori, Gion. www.minoko.co.jp. © **075/561-0328.** Dinner *kaiseki* from ¥16,150; *hiru-kaiseki* lunch from ¥10,000; *bento* ¥3,500–¥6,930. Daily 11:30am–2:30pm and 5–8pm (last order). Closed irregularly 3 days a month. Bus: 100 or 206 to Gion (3 min.). A short walk south of Yasaka Shrine.

MODERATE

Junsei (順正) ★★ TOFU/KAISEKI/BENTO   This well-known tofu restaurant near Nanzenji has been open since 1961, but its extensive garden and main building with a thatched roof are remnants from the days when this location served as a medical school established in 1839 during the shogun era. It attracts tourists and tour groups, but everything runs smoothly with Japanese efficiency. As soon as you arrive you'll be given an English-language menu and asked what you'd like to eat, because that determines where you'll be seated in the restaurant's various buildings. If you order the house specialty—one of the *yudofu* set meals that includes tofu simmered in an earthen pot, vegetable tempura, skewered and grilled tofu, and an assortment of other dishes—you'll probably be led to an older building near the front of the property filled with antiques and overlooking the garden. Other set meals offer *yuba* (like the *yuba kaiseki* for ¥6,000) and other possibilities. If you want *kaiseki* (served in your own *tatami* room with a view of the garden), shabu-shabu, or sukiyaki, you need a reservation.

There's a branch, Kiyomizu Junsei Okabeya (© **075/541-7111**), located just off Kiyomizu-zaka, the main slope leading to Kiyomizu Temple. Housed in a grand, 1914 former villa with high ceilings, wainscoting, and stained-glass windows, it offers just three set tofu meals priced ¥2,160 to ¥5,400 and is open daily 10:30am to 5pm (last order), closed irregularly.

Nanzenjimon-mae, Sakyo-ku. www.to-fu.co.jp. © **075/761-2311.** Yudofu meals ¥3,090–¥4,110; shabu-shabu or sukiyaki ¥8,230; *kaiseki* ¥8,000–¥15,000; *kaiseki* set lunches ¥5,000–¥8,000; shabu-shabu or sukiyaki ¥8,000. Daily 11am–8pm (last order). Subway: Keage (5 min.). Bus: 5 to Nanzenji-Eikando-michi (7 min.). East of Shirakawa Dori on the road to Nanzenji Temple, north side.

Okutan (奥丹) ★★★ TOFU/VEGETARIAN   If you love tofu or simply want to have a quintessential Kyoto meal in a wonderful setting, this 370-year-old restaurant should be high on your list. Located near Nanzenji Temple and originally serving Buddhist monks, today the rustic, thatched-roof restaurant offers just one thing, making ordering easy: *yudofu* (a tofu set meal). Although it changes slightly with the seasons, it comes with a pot of tofu boiled at your table, *dengaku* (baked tofu on a stick), vegetable tempura, *goma-dofu* (a sesame dish), grated yam soup, and pickled vegetables. But in my opinion, it's the atmosphere that makes a meal here extra special. The restaurant has a pond and garden, and in fine weather you can sit outside on cushioned platforms. Otherwise you'll sit in rustic *tatami* rooms. Women wearing traditional rural clothing bring your food, making the atmosphere seem like you're dining somewhere in the countryside a long time ago. Note that reservations are accepted only for groups of six people or more, so you might have to stand in line during peak season. In any case, it requires cash only to dine here.

86–30 Fukuchi-cho, Nanzenji. ℂ **075/771-8709.** Yudofu set meal ¥3,240. Fri and Mon–Wed 11am–4pm; Sat–Sun and holidays 11am–4:30pm (last order, but they close earlier if they run out). Bus: 5 to Nanzenji-Eikando-michi (6 min.). Just north of Nanzenji Temple's main gate (the Sanmon Gate).

The Sodoh ★★★ ITALIAN   Temples, Japanese restaurants, and boutiques have long been the draws of Higashiyama-ku, so it comes as somewhat of a pleasant surprise to find an Italian restaurant—especially one of this caliber and in this setting—amongst their midst. It occupies a 1929 villa that once served as residence, studio, and garden of Seiho Takeuchi, whose family owned a restaurant in nearby Arashiyama and who was a well-known master of the sparse *nihonga* style of painting. With a somewhat rustic yet refined atmosphere and with dining rooms overlooking the dense garden, the restaurant serves reasonably priced weekday lunches that change according to what's fresh and in season. My ¥2,800 lunch, which came with an appetizer, sweet-potato soup, carbonara pasta with bacon and spinach, a choice of six main dishes (I had the grilled chicken cacciatore), dessert, and coffee, was plenty enough for me. Dinner offers set meals and a-la-carte choices like spaghettini with sea urchins and clams or char-grilled lamb with salsa verde. Be sure to take a look around the garden after your meal, and because this is understandably a popular venue for weddings and private parties, be sure to call for reservations to make sure they›re open.

366 Yasaka Kami-machi, Yasakadori Shimokawara Higashi-iru. www.thesodoh.com. ℂ **075/541-3331.** Main dishes ¥1,800–¥3,200; set lunches ¥1,500–¥5,500; set dinners ¥4,000–¥10,000. Bus: 206 to Higashiyama Yasui (3 min.). Cattycorner from Ryozen Kannon Temple.

Western Kyoto

There's a branch of **Gontaro,** serving noodles, at Hinomiyashiki-cho 26 (ℂ **075/463-1039**), with the same English-language menu as its main shop (p. 230). It's located about halfway down the street that runs between Ryoanji and Kinkakuji, on the west side; look for the red paper lantern. Closed Wednesday.

INEXPENSIVE

Seigenin-in ★★ TOFU/VEGETARIAN   If you're visiting Ryoanji Temple in northeastern Kyoto, there's no lovelier setting for a meal than this traditional restaurant, which calls itself the Ryoanji Seven Herb Tofu Restaurant in honor of its signature dish, *yudofu,* boiled tofu and vegetables topped with seven herbs. You can order it by itself, or as a set meal of *shojin ryori* (Buddhist vegetarian) with side dishes (no credit cards accepted; there's an English menu). Entrance to the restaurant, situated beside the Kyoyoike Pond on temple grounds, is along a small path that takes you past a stream, a small pond, a grove of maple and pine, and moss-covered grounds, which are also what you see as you dine seated on *tatami*. You'll know you're getting close to the restaurant when you hear the *thonk* of a bamboo trough fed by a stream, which fills and hits against stone as it empties.

Home-Style Cooking Class

So you've eaten your way around town and would now like to cook your own Japanese food. Taro Saeki, who once cooked the meals at a *minshuku* (family-style inn), now teaches home-style cooking at his **Haru Cooking Class** (www.kyoto-cooking-class.com; ℂ **090/4284-7176**). Classes take place in his home in English (he used to live in the United States), and often his wife and young daughter are on hand to help. After instruction in the basics of soy sauce, miso and other common ingredients, you'll have hands-on kitchen time, and within a few hours you'll be eating your creations from the beef, chicken or vegetarian menu. There's a minimum of three persons, so you may be paired with others. Classes cost ¥5,900 for a vegetarian meal and ¥7,900 to ¥10,900 per person for the Kobe beef meal. Take bus No. 4 or 205 to Shin-Aoibashi bus stop in northeast Kyoto, and Taro will meet you. Some participants say this experience is the highlight of their trip. Also offering cooking lessons is **Cooking Sun** (www.cooking-sun.com; ℂ **075/746-5094**), with classes on everything from making your own bento box ingredients to sushi classes, held in a converted *machiya* (traditional town-house).

Ryoanji Temple. ℂ **075/462-4742.** Yudofu ¥1,500; yudofu vegetarian set meal ¥3,300. Daily 10am–4:30pm (last order). Bus: 59 from Shijo Kawaramachi to Ryoanji-mae (2 min.), or 50 to Ritsumeikan Daigaku-mae (4 min.).

EXPLORING KYOTO

As Japan's seventh-largest city with a population of more than 1.4 million people, Kyoto hasn't escaped the afflictions of the modern age. In fact, if you arrive in Kyoto by train, your first reaction is likely to be great disappointment. There's Kyoto Tower looming in the foreground like some misplaced spaceship. Kyoto Station itself is strikingly modern and unabashedly high tech, looking as though it was airlifted straight from Tokyo. Modern buildings and hotels surround the station on all sides, making Kyoto look like any other Japanese town.

Once you escape to Kyoto's old neighborhoods, however, you'll find yourself in an entirely different place. Kyoto boasts an astonishing 2,000 temples and shrines and 20% of Japan's National Treasures. Because there are so many worthwhile sights, you must plan your itinerary carefully. Even the most avid sightseer can become jaded after days of visiting yet another temple or shrine, no matter how beautiful or peaceful, so be sure to temper your visits to cultural and historical sites with time spent simply walking around. Kyoto is a city best seen on foot; take time to explore small alleyways and artisan shops, pausing from time to time to soak in the beauty and atmosphere. If you spend your days in Kyoto racing around in a taxi or a bus from one temple to another, the essence of this ancient capital and its charm may literally pass you by.

Before setting out, be sure to stop by **Kyoto City Tourist Information** at Kyoto Station to get a detailed map of the city, a bus map, and the *Kyoto's Visitor's Guide* (which also contains maps).

Keep in mind, too, that you must enter Kyoto's museums, shrines, and temples at least a half-hour before closing time. Listings in this section and those that follow give numbers not only for buses departing from Kyoto Station but from elsewhere as well.

Central Kyoto

Although much of downtown Kyoto has been taken over by the 21st century, it still has wonderful old neighborhoods with *machiya* (traditional townhouses) and historic treasures. My favorite thing to do is to simply explore the backstreets, especially those contained within the square of Shijo, Kawaramachi, Oike and Karasuma streets. If you've never been to a street market in Japan, for example, take a stroll down Nishiki-Koji Dori for a fascinating look at the fish-and-produce Nishiki Food Market right in the heart of town.

> ### Kyoto Illuminated
>
> When the cherry blossoms spring forth or leaves change color, many Kyoto temples (like Kiyomizu) are open at night, their buildings and gardens dramatically lit. It's a great way to see these wondrous spaces, literally in a different light. Ask the tourist office or concierge at your hotel for a list of temples offering "light up."

Kyoto Imperial Palace (Kyoto Gosho) ★★ PALACE   This is where the imperial family lived from 1331 until 1868 when they moved to Tokyo. The palace was destroyed several times by fire but was always rebuilt in its original style; the present buildings date from 1855. Modestly furnished with delicate decorations, the palace shows the restful designs of the peaceful Heian Period, and the emperor's private garden is graceful. You can visit the palace only on a free, 1-hour guided tour in English, but fair warning: Tours are conducted quickly, leaving little time for dawdling or taking pictures. In addition, tours view buildings only from the outside, though they do impart interesting information on court life and palace architecture.

Kyotogyoen-nai, Karasuma-Imadegawa. http://sankan.kunaicho.go.jp/english. ℂ **075/ 211-1215.** Free admission. Tours in English Mon–Fri at 10am and 2pm (tours also some Sat but only in Japanese). Closed national holidays. Permission must be obtained from the Imperial Household Agency Office, either online at least 4 days in advance or in person at palace grounds near the northeast corner, Mon–Fri 8:45am–noon and 1–5pm. Foreign visitors can apply in person in advance or on the day of the tour 20 min. before the tour starts (1-day advance application required for Sat tours), but tours can fill up (especially in spring and fall). You must be 18 or older (or accompanied by an adult) and you must present your passport. Subway: Imadegawa (exit 3, 5 min.). Bus: 59, 102, 201, or 203 to Karasuma Imadegawa (5 min.). On Karasuma Dori, south of Imadegawa Dori.

Kyoto International Manga Museum ★ MUSEUM   If you think *manga* (Japanese comics, or graphic novels) are just for kids, you'll come away with a whole different perspective after touring the largest *manga* museum in the world. With more than 300,000 items in its collection, it not only serves as a research facility for the study of *manga*'s history and cultural influence but also strives to preserve *manga* in all its forms, including early

What to See in Kyoto

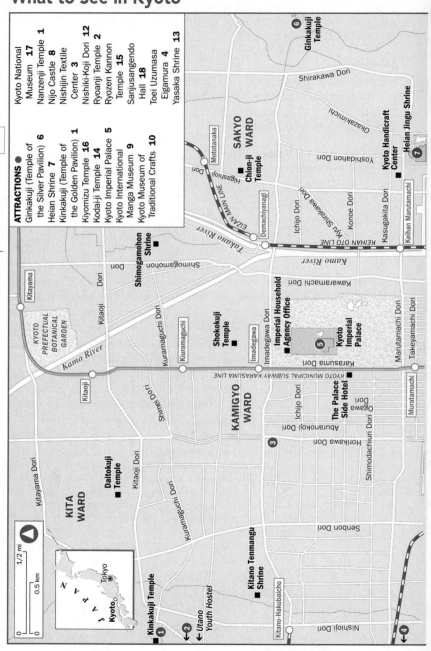

ATTRACTIONS ●

Ginkakuji (Temple of the Silver Pavilion) **6**
Heian Shrine **7**
Kinkakuji (Temple of the Golden Pavilion) **1**
Kiyomizu Temple **16**
Kodai-ji Temple **14**
Kyoto Imperial Palace **5**
Kyoto International Manga Museum **9**
Kyoto Museum of Traditional Crafts **10**
Kyoto National Museum **17**
Nanzenji Temple **1**
Nijo Castle **8**
Nishijin Textile Center **3**
Nishiki-Koji Dori **12**
Ryoanji Temple **2**
Ryozen Kannon Temple **15**
Sanjusangendo Hall **18**
Toei Uzumasa Eigamura **4**
Yasaka Shrine **13**

Railway
Subway
⊠ **Post Office**
ⓘ **Tourist Info**

Elkando Temple ■
Nanzenji Temple ⑪
Keage
KYOTO CITY SUBWAY TZAI LINE
The Westin Miyako Hotel ■
Higashiyama-Sanjo
Shoren-in Temple ■
Canal
⑩
MARUYAMA PARK
Yasaka Shrine ■
⑬
Furomonzen Dori
Shinmonzen Dori
Niomon Dori
Njio Dori
Kyoto Shiyakusho-mae
Kyoto Antiques Center ■
Kyoto City Hall ■
Sanjo
Nawate Dori
Pontocho Dori
⑭ ⑮
Sannenzaka
HIGASHIYAMA WARD
Otani Mausoleum ⑯
Kiyomizuzaka
Gojozaka
Kawai Kanjiro Memorial House ⑰
National Route no. 1
JR TOKAIDO MAIN LINE (JR KYOTO LINE)

Higashioji Dori
Hanamikoji Dori
Yamatooji Dori
Honmachi Dori
Kawaramachi Dori
Shijo
Kiyamachi Dori
KEIHAN MAIN LINE
Tominokoji Dori
Sakaimachi Dori
Ainomachi Dori
Kurumayacho Dori
Teramachi Dori
Kawaramachi
Yanaginobanba Dori
Fuyacho Dori
Gokomachi Dori
Shichijo
Shosei-en Garden
Kamo River
⑱
JR NARA LINE
Tofukuji

Muromachi Dori
Shinmachi Dori
Wakamiya Dori
Oshikoji Dori
Njio Dori
Ebisugawa Dori
Oike Dori
Karasuma-Oike
⑨
Higashinotoin Dori
Takakura Dori
Koromonodana Dori
Ryogaemachi Dori
KYOTO MUNICIPAL SUBWAY KARASUMA LINE
Karasuma
Hinomoto
Kawaramachi Dori
Higashi-Honganji Temple ■
Karasuma Dori
Shiokoji Dori
Shichijo Dori
⊠
Kyoto
Kyoto Station
ⓘ

TOZAI LINE
Nijojo-mae
Nijo Castle ⑧
NAKAGYO WARD
Sanjo
Aneyakoji Dori
Takoyakushi
Rokkaku
Nishikikoji
Nishinotoin Dori
Shijo Dori
Ayanokoji Dori
Bukkoji Dori
Shijo
Takatsuji Dori
Matsubara Dori
Manjuji Dori
Gojo Dori
Gojo
Horikawa Dori
Shioji Dori
Hachijo Dori
Kujo Dori
Kujo
KINTETSU KYOTO LINE
Toji

Nijo
JR SAN-IN MAIN LINE (JR SAGANO LINE)
Nishioji Sanjo
Omiya
Shijomiya
Nishi-Honganji Temple ■
Omiya Dori
SHIMOGYO WARD
Tanbaguchi
Toji Temple ■
Saiin
Nishioji Dori
Nishioji

UKYO WARD

239

A Look at the Past

Kyoto served as Japan's capital for more than 1,000 years, from 794 to the Meiji Restoration in 1868. Originally known as Heian-kyo, it was laid out in a grid pattern borrowed from the Chinese with streets running north, south, east, and west. Its first few hundred years—from about A.D. 800 to the 12th century— were perhaps its grandest, a time when culture blossomed and court nobility led luxurious and splendid lives dotted with poetry-composing parties and moon-gazing events. Buddhism flourished and temples were built. A number of learning institutions were set up for the sons and daughters of aristocratic families, and scholars were versed in both Japanese and Chinese.

Toward the end of the Heian Period, military clans began clashing for power as the samurai class grew more powerful, resulting in a series of civil wars that eventually pushed Japan into the Feudal Era of military government that lasted nearly 680 years—until 1868. The first shogun to rise to power was Minamoto Yoritomo, who set up his shogunate government in Kamakura. With the downfall of the Kamakura government in 1336, however, Kyoto once again

became the seat of power, home to both the imperial family and the shogun. The beginning of this era, known as the Muromachi and Azuchi-Momoyama periods, was marked by extravagant prosperity and luxury, expressed in such splendid shogun villas as Kyoto's Gold Pavilion and Silver Pavilion. Lacquerware, landscape paintings, and the art of metal engraving came into their own. Zen Buddhism was the rage, giving rise to such temples as the Ryoanji rock garden. And, despite civil wars that rocked the nation in the 15th and 16th centuries and destroyed much of Kyoto, culture flourished. During these turbulent times, *Noh* drama, the tea ceremony, flower arranging, and landscape gardening gradually took form.

Emerging as the victor in the civil wars, Tokugawa Ieyasu established himself as shogun and set up his military rule in Edo (presently Tokyo) far to the east. For the next 250 years, Kyoto remained the capital in name only, and in 1868 (which marked the downfall of the shogunate and the restoration of the emperor to power), the capital was officially moved from Kyoto to Tokyo.

and contemporary Japanese works, foreign *manga,* animation, and other related images. Most visitors, however, come because of its changing exhibitions, with about 50,000 items on display at any one time. Occupying a former primary school built in 1869, its various rooms include a children's library with *manga* and picture books, an archive illustrating the long history of Japanese *manga,* a display describing the process of making *manga,* an exhibit dedicated to the building's former life as an elementary school, and, perhaps most amazing of all, a Wall of Manga with shelves containing thousands of *manga* you can look through at leisure. On weekends, you can even see *manga* artists at work. Of course, while display descriptions are in English, unless you can read Japanese you'll mostly be looking at pictures rather than taking full advantage of what this place offers. But that shouldn't be a deterrent for enjoying this unique art form. In addition to cafe, there's also a museum shop selling *manga* (including *manga* translated into English), figurines, notepads, and other items.

452 Kinbuki-cho, Karasuma Oike. www.kyotomm.jp. © **075/254-7414.** Admission ¥800 adults, ¥300 junior-high and high-school students, ¥100 children. Thurs–Tues 10am–6pm. Subway: Karasuma-Oike (1 min.). On Karasuma Dori, north of Oike.

Nijo Castle (Nijojo) ★★★ CASTLE   The Tokugawa shogun's Kyoto home stands in stark contrast to most of Japan's other remaining castles, which were constructed purely for defense. Built by the first Tokugawa shogun, Ieyasu, in 1603, Nijo Castle, a UNESCO World Heritage Site, is considered the quintessence of Momoyama architecture, built almost entirely of Japanese cypress and boasting delicate transom woodcarvings and paintings by the Kano School on sliding doors. Unfortunately, no interior photos are allowed.

I prefer Nijo Castle to the Imperial Palace because you can explore its interior on your own. The main building, **Ninomaru Palace,** has 33 rooms, some 800 *tatami* mats, and an understated elegance, especially compared with castles being built in Europe at the same time. All the sliding doors on the outside walls of the castle can be removed in summer, permitting breezes to sweep through the building. Typical for Japan at the time, rooms were unfurnished, with futon stored in closets during the day.

One of the castle's most intriguing features is its so-called **nightingale floors.** To protect the shogun from real or imagined enemies, the castle was protected by a moat, stone walls, and these special floorboards in the castle corridors, which creaked when trod upon. The nightingale floors were supplemented by hidden alcoves for bodyguards. Furthermore, only female attendants were allowed in the shogun's private living quarters. Ironically, it was from Nijo Castle that Emperor Meiji issued his 1868 decree abolishing the shogunate form of government.

Outside the castle is an extensive **garden,** designed by the renowned gardener Kobori Enshu and famous in its own right. The original grounds of the castle, however, were without trees—supposedly because the falling of leaves in autumn reminded the shogun and his tough samurai of life's transitory nature, making them terribly sad. Plan on spending 1½ hours here, especially if you pay ¥500 extra for an audio guide, recommended because it describes the significance of what you're seeing.

Corner of Horikawa Dori and Nijo Dori. www.city.kyoto.jp/bunshi/nijojo/english/index. html. © **075/841-0096.** Admission ¥600 adults, ¥350 junior-high and high-school students, ¥200 children. Daily 8:45am–6pm (last entry 4pm; Ninomaru closes at 4pm).

Cultural Immersion

If you're interested in learning firsthand about the tea ceremony, flower arranging, origami, Japanese calligraphy, Japanese cooking, and other cultural pursuits, you can do so with the help of the members of the **Women's Association of Kyoto (WAK Japan;** www.wakjapan. com; © **075/212-9993).** Courses, conducted in their downtown facility and in members' homes, run 55 minutes to 1½ hours and range from ¥3,800 for the tea ceremony to ¥13,500 for flower arranging including pickup from your hotel (it's cheaper if there are two or more people). Reservations should be made up to 2 weeks in advance, if possible.

Walk in Kyoto Talk in English

For a personalized English-language tour that takes in temples and shrines, a former Geisha area, workshops, and Kyoto backstreets before ending near Kiyomizu Temple, join **Walk in Kyoto Talk in English** (www.waraido.com/walking/index.html), conducted rain or shine every Monday, Wednesday, and Friday from 10am to 3pm March through November. Tours start from in front of Kyoto Station and cost ¥2,000 for adults, ¥1,000 for 13- to 15-year-olds, and free for children. No reservations are required; pick up the brochure at the tourist office or look online for information. The same company also conducts night tours of **Gion** (p. 261).

Closed Tues Dec–Jan and July–Aug. Subway: Nijojo-mae Station (1 min.). Bus: 9, 12, 50, or 101 to Nijojo-mae (1 min.).

Nishijin Textile Center (Nishijin-Ori Kaikan) ★★ MUSEUM   Kyoto's Nishijin weavers, whose history can be traced back to Kyoto's earliest years, were famous for richly decorative textiles, made into clothing worn by the Imperial family, Buddhist monks, and Shinto priests. During the Edo Period (1603–1867), there were an estimated 7,000 looms crammed into 160 city blocks comprising the Nishijin District. Unsurprisingly, the district suffered a terrible blow when the capital was moved to Tokyo, but the industry bounced back by adopting Western weaving technology and equipment, which allowed them to produce machine-woven inexpensive clothing alongside luxurious hand-woven fabrics. Today, Nishijin remains one of the country's largest districts for hand weaving, with this commemorative museum located on the very spot where merchants once gathered to bid for elegant textiles sold at auction.

On display are silkworms and descriptions of how they produce silk, old and modern Nishijin fabrics, and looms, with frequent demonstrations of handlooms using the Jacquard system of perforated cards for weaving. A shop sells Nishijin products and fabrics, including kimono, sashes, purses, and more. But my favorite thing to do here is to attend one of the museum's free 15-minute kimono fashion shows held seven times daily (the first show is at 10am and the last at 4pm), showcasing kimono that change with the seasons. If you have 3 hours and make reservations, you can also weave your own table mat for ¥1,800 or scarf for ¥5,000. Reservations are also required if you'd like to dress up as a *maiko* (geisha apprentice), *geiko* (professional entertainer), or lady of the Imperial court in a 12-layer kimono. These, along with an ancient ceremonial court dress for men, cost ¥10,000, including hair styling, makeup, and photo, but there are also simpler everyday kimono you can put on for ¥3,600. If you're so inclined, you can even wander around Kyoto in full garb from 9am to 4pm for an extra fee; I'm surprised by how popular this has become in the past couple of years, especially among young visitors from other Asian countries.

Horikawa-Imadegawa, Minami-iru. www.nishijin.or.jp. ℂ **075/451-9231.** Free admission. Daily 9am–5pm. Subway: Imadegawa (8 min.). Bus: 9, 12, 59, 101, 102, 201, or 203 to Horikawa Imadegawa (2 min.). On Horikawa Dori just south of Imadegawa Dori.

Eastern Kyoto

The eastern part of Kyoto, embracing the area of Higashiyama-ku with its Kiyomizu Temple and stretching up all the way to the Temple of the Silver Pavilion (Ginkakuji Temple), is probably the richest in terms of culture and charm. Although temples and gardens are the primary attractions, Higashi-yama-ku also boasts several fine museums, forested hills and running streams, great shopping opportunities, and some of Kyoto's oldest and finest restaurants. To make the most of your visit, follow my recommended stroll later in this chapter that will lead you to the region's best attractions, as well as to some lesser-known sights that are worth seeing if you have the time.

Ginkakuji (Temple of the Silver Pavilion) ★★ TEMPLE   Ginkakuji, considered one of the more beautiful structures in Kyoto, was built in 1482 as a retirement villa for Shogun Ashikaga Yoshimasa, who intended to coat the structure with silver in imitation of the Golden Pavilion built by his grandfather. He died before this could be accomplished, however, so the Silver Pavilion is not silver at all but remains a simple, two-story wood structure enshrining the goddess of mercy and Jizo, the guardian god of children. The entire complex is designed for enjoyment of the tea ceremony, moon viewing and other aesthetic pursuits. Note the sand mound in the garden, shaped to resemble Mount Fuji, and the sand raked in the shape of waves, created to enhance the views during a full moon. It's easy to imagine the splendor, formality, and grandeur of the life of Japan's upper class as you wander the grounds and climb the hillside pathway to its lookout point.

Ginkakuji-cho. © **075/771-5725.** Admission ¥500 adults, ¥300 junior-high and elementary students, younger children free. Mar–Nov daily 8:30am–5pm; Dec–Feb daily 9am–4:30pm. Bus: 5, 17, 102, 203, or 204 to Ginkakuji-michi (10 min.); or 32 or 100 to Ginkakuji-mae (5 min.).

Heian Shrine ★★★ SHRINE   Although it dates only from 1895, Kyoto's most famous Shinto shrine was built in commemoration of the 1,100th anniversary of the founding of Kyoto and is a replica of the first Imperial Palace, though on a less grand scale. It deifies two of Japan's emperors: Emperor Kammu, 50th emperor of Japan, who founded Heian-kyo in 794; and Emperor Komei, the 121st ruler of Japan, who ruled from 1831 to 1866. Although the orange, green, and white structure is interesting for its Heian-Era architectural style, the most important thing to see here is the 33,000-sq.-m (8-acre) **Shinen Garden,** the entrance to which is on your left as you face the main hall. Typical of gardens constructed during the Meiji Era, it's famous for its weeping cherry trees in spring, its irises and water lilies in summer, and its changing maple leaves in the fall, all beautifully arranged around a central pond. Don't miss it.

Nishi Tennocho, Okazaki. www.heianjingu.or.jp. © **075/761-0221.** Free admission to grounds; Shinen Garden ¥600 adults, ¥300 children. Garden mid-Mar to Sept daily 8:30am–5:30pm (to 4:30pm Nov–Feb; to 5pm Mar 1–14 and Oct). Subway: Higashi-yama (10 min.). Bus: 5, 32, 46, or 100 to Kyoto Kaikan Bijutsukan-mae (2 min.). Look for the shrine's large orange *torii*.

Kiyomizu Temple (Kiyomizudera) ★★★ TEMPLE This is Higashi-yama-ku's most famous temple, known throughout Japan for the grand views afforded from its main hall. Founded in 778 and rebuilt in 1633 by the third Tokugawa shogun, Iemitsu, the temple occupies an exalted spot on Mount Otowa, with its main hall constructed over a cliff and featuring a large wooden veranda supported by 139 massive pillars, each 15m (49 ft.) high. The main hall (undergoing renovation until spring 2016) is dedicated to the goddess of mercy and compassion, but most visitors come for the magnificence of its height and view, which are so well known to Japanese that the idiom "jumping from the veranda of Kiyomizu Temple" means that they're about to undertake some particularly bold or daring adventure. Kiyomizu's grounds are particularly spectacular (and crowded) in spring during cherry-blossom season and in fall during the turning of the maple leaves.

Also worth checking out are the three-story pagoda and Otowa Falls (known for the purity of its water; *kiyomizu* translates as "pure water"), but be sure not to spite the gods by neglecting to visit **Jishu Shrine** (✆ 075/541-2097), a vermilion-colored Shinto shrine behind Kiyomizu's main hall that has long been considered the dwelling place of the god of love and matchmaking. Be sure to take the ultimate test: On the shrine's grounds are two "love-fortune telling" stones placed 9m (30 ft.) apart; if you're able to walk from one to the other with your eyes closed, your desires for love will be granted.

1–294 Kiyomizu. www.kiyomizudera.or.jp. ✆ **075/551-1234.** Admission ¥300 adults, ¥200 children 7–15, children 6 and under free. Daily 6am–6pm (until 6:30pm in summer; special evening hours several times a year). Jishu Shrine daily 9am–5pm. Bus: 100, 202, 206, or 207 to Gojo-zaka (10 min.).

Kodai-ji Temple ★★ TEMPLE Located between Kiyomizu Temple and Yasaka Shrine, this temple was founded in 1605 by Toyotomi Hideyoshi's widow, popularly referred to as Nene, to commemorate her husband and to pacify his spirit. Shogun Tokugawa Ieyasu, who served under Toyotomi before becoming shogun, financed its construction. It contains lovely gardens laid out by Kobori Enshu and Nene's grave (the Otama-ya), as well as teahouses designed by Sen no Rikyu, a famous 16th-century tea master. A memorial hall enshrines wooden images of Hideyoshi and Nene. Nene, by the way, became a Buddhist nun after her husband's death, as was the custom of noblewomen at the time. The one-room Kodaiji Sho Museum, across the street from the temple and included in the admission price, contains artifacts relating to Nene and the temple, but skip it if your time is limited.

526 Shimogawara-cho. www.kodaiji.com. ✆ **075/561-9966.** Admission ¥600 adults, ¥250 children 17 and under. Daily 9am–5:30pm. Bus: 100, 202, 206, or 207 to Higashi-yama Yasui (5 min.).

Kyoto Museum of Traditional Crafts (Fureaikan) ★★★ MUSEUM Near Heian Shrine is this excellent museum dedicated to the many crafts that flourished during Kyoto's long reign as the imperial capital. Various displays and videos demonstrate the step-by-step production of crafts ranging from stone lanterns and fishing rods to textiles, paper fans, umbrellas, boxwood combs, lacquerware, Buddhist altars, *Noh* masks, and much more. The displays are fascinating, the crafts beautiful, and explanations are in English, making even a 30-minute stop here well worth the effort. Artisans demonstrate their skills most days except Mondays and Thursdays, while *maiko* (geisha apprentices) perform traditional dance on Sundays (check the website for times). Be sure, too, to browse the museum's crafts store.

In the basement of the Miyako Messe (International Exhibition Hall; look for the bright orange installation outside), 9–1 Seishoji-cho, Okazaki. www.miyakomesse.jp/fureaika. (C) **075/762-2670.** Free admission. Daily 9am–5pm. Subway: Higashiyama (7 min.). Bus: 5, 32, 46, or 100 to Kyoto Kaikan Bijutsukan-mae (2 min.), or 32, 201, 202, 203, or 206 to Higashiyama-Nijo.

Kyoto National Museum (Kokuritsu Hakubutsukan) ★★ MUSEUM
Housed in an imposing French baroque-style building constructed in 1897 expressly for the museum's collection, as well as in a new wing completed in 2014, this museum displays stone and bronze Buddhist and Shinto sculpture, paintings, ceramics from the Nara through Edo periods, textiles and clothing, lacquerware, swords and other metal works, archaeological relics (like 6th-c. *Haniwa* clay figures excavated from burial mounds) and much more, displayed on a rotating basis from the museum's vast collection. The museum is especially famous for its artifacts from the Heian Period (794–1192) and ancient sutras. Many of the treasures were once in Kyoto's many temples, shrines, and imperial palaces, while others—like Chinese sculpture or paintings—were imported into Japan at different times during its history. Plan on staying about an hour, more if you pay ¥500 extra for the audio guide, which describes about 30 items in more detail. If you've seen the larger Tokyo National Museum, you may want to skip this one if your time in Kyoto is short, though special exhibitions concentrating on a specific period or genre draw huge crowds.

527 Chaya-machi (across the street from Sanjusangendo Hall). www.kyohaku.go.jp. (C) **075/525-2473.** Admission ¥520 adults, ¥260 university students, free for children. Special exhibitions cost more. Tues–Sun 9:30am–5pm (open to 6 or 8pm during special exhibits). Bus: 100, 206, or 208 to Hakubutsukan Sanjusangendo-mae (1 min.).

Nanzenji Temple ★★ TEMPLE
This Rinzai Zen temple with its massive front gate is set amid a grove of spruce and maple. One of Kyoto's best-known Zen temples, it was founded in 1293, though its present buildings date from the latter part of the 16th century during the Momoyama Period. Attached to the main hall is a Zen rock garden attributed to Kobori Enshu; it's sometimes called "Young Tigers Crossing the Water" because of the shape of one of the rocks, but the association is a bit of a stretch for me. In the building behind the main hall is a sliding door with a famous painting by Kano Tanyu of a tiger drinking water in a bamboo grove. Spread throughout the temple precincts are a dozen other lesser temples and buildings worth exploring if you have the time, including Nanzen-in with its moss and rock garden, which was built about the same time as Nanzenji Temple and served as the emperor's vacation house whenever he visited the temple grounds.

Nanzenji-Fukuchi-cho. www.nanzenji.com. ℂ **075/771-0365.** Admission ¥500 adults, ¥400 high-school students, ¥250 children; Nanzen-in ¥300, ¥250, and ¥150 extra, respectively. Daily 8:40am–5pm (to 4:30pm Dec–Feb). Bus: 5 to Nanzenji, Eikando-michi (3 min.).

Sanjusangendo Hall ★★★ TEMPLE   Originally founded as Rengeoin Temple in 1164 and rebuilt in 1266, Sanjusangendo Hall has one of the most visually stunning sights I've seen in a Japanese temple: 1,001 wooden statues of the thousand-handed Kannon. Row upon row, these life-size figures, carved from Japanese cypress in the 12th and 13th centuries, make an impressive sight; in the middle is a large seated Kannon carved in 1254 by Tankei, a famous sculptor from the Kamakura Period. Don't expect to actually see a thousand arms on each statue; there are only 40, the idea being that each hand has the power to save 25 worlds. In front of the 1,001 Kannon are a row of 28 guardian deities; not only are they all National Treasures, but it's rare to find a whole set like this one still intact. In any case, to accommodate all these statues, the hall stretches almost 120m (400 ft.), making it the longest wooden building in Japan (no photography or videos are allowed in the building). Its length was too hard to ignore—in the corridor behind the statues, archery competitions have been held for centuries; standing here, you can easily imagine how hard it must be to hit a piece of sacred cloth attached to the wall at the opposite end.

Shichijo Dori. ℂ **075/525-0033.** Admission ¥600 adults, ¥400 junior-high and high-school students, ¥300 children. Apr to mid-Nov daily 8am–5pm; mid-Nov to Mar daily 9am–4:30pm. Bus: 100, 206, or 208 to Hakubutsukan Sanjusangendo-mae (1 min.).

Western Kyoto

Two of Kyoto's most famous sights are to the west of downtown Kyoto.

Kinkakuji (Temple of the Golden Pavilion) ★★★ TEMPLE   One of Kyoto's best-known attractions—and the inspiration for the Temple of the Silver Pavilion (see above)—Kinkakuji was constructed in the 1390s as a retirement villa for Shogun Ashikaga Yoshimitsu and features a three-story pavilion covered in gold leaf with a roof topped by a bronze phoenix. Apparently, the retired shogun lived in shameless luxury while the rest of the nation suffered from famine, earthquakes, and plague. If you come here on a clear day (best is late afternoon), the Golden Pavilion shimmers against a blue sky, its reflection captured in the waters of a calm pond. However, this pavilion is not the original; in 1950, a disturbed student monk burned Kinkakuji to the ground (the story is told by author Mishima Yukio in his famous novel *The Temple of the Golden Pavilion*). The temple was rebuilt in 1955 and in 1987 was recovered in gold leaf, five times thicker than the original coating: You almost need sunglasses. Be sure to explore the surrounding **park** with its moss-covered grounds and teahouses.

1 Kinkakuji-cho. ℂ **075/461-0013.** Admission ¥400 adults, ¥300 children. Daily 9am–5pm. Bus: 12 or 59 to Kinkakuji-mae (1 min.) or 101, 102, 204, or 205 to Kinkakuji-michi (3 min.).

Ryoanji Temple ★★★ TEMPLE About a 20-minute walk (or short ride on bus no. 59) southwest of the Golden Pavilion is Ryoanji—home to what is probably the most famous **Zen rock garden** in all of Japan—laid out at the end of the 15th century during the Muromachi Period. Fifteen rocks set in waves of raked white pebbles are surrounded on three sides by a clay wall and on the fourth by a wooden veranda, in an area that measures about 25m (80 ft.) long and 10m (30 ft.) wide. Sit down and contemplate what the artist was trying to communicate. The interpretation of the rocks is up to the individual. (Mountains above the clouds? Islands in the ocean?) My only objection to this peaceful place is that, unfortunately, it's not always peaceful—a loudspeaker on occasion extols the virtue of the garden, destroying any chance for peaceful meditation. If you get here early enough, you may be able to escape both the crowds and the noise.

After visiting the rock garden, be sure to take a walk around the temple grounds. There's a 1,000-year-old **pond,** on the rim of which sits a beautiful little restaurant, **Seigenin-in** (p. 235), with *tatami* rooms and screens, where you can eat *yudofu* and enjoy the view. There's also a nice landscape garden, with moss so inviting you'll wish you could lie down and take a nap.

13 Ryoanji-Goryo-shita-machi. www.ryoanji.jp. ⓒ **075/463-2216.** Admission ¥500 adults, ¥300 children 14 and under. Mar–Nov daily 8am–5pm; Dec–Feb daily 8:30am–4:30pm. Bus: 59 to Ryoanji-mae (2 min.); or 12 or 50 to Ritsumeikan Daigaku-mae (6 min.).

Toei Kyoto Studio Park (Toei Uzumasa Eigamura) ★★ AMUSE-MENT PARK If your kids are ready to mutiny because of yet another temple, get on their good side by coming to this studio park, owned by one of Japan's three major film companies and where many samurai flicks and TV shows are made. Don't expect the high-tech, polished glitz of American theme parks—rather, this is a working studio where more than 100 TV and movie productions are filmed each year. Indoor and outdoor movie sets re-create the mood, setting, and atmosphere of feudal and turn-of-the-20th-century Japan, complete with photogenic period "villages" lined with samurai houses and old-time shops. Stagehands carry around props, hammers, and saws, and rework sets. You may even see a famous star walking around dressed in samurai garb, or come upon a scene being filmed.

Otherwise, there are many tourist-oriented attractions, including a 20-minute ninja show three times daily (it's in Japanese, but the action is easy to grasp), street performers, an exhibition hall of *ukiyo-e* (woodblock prints) with useful explanations in English, an anime museum featuring objects from Toei's films, an indoor playground, and a games arcade. Unfortunately, you have to pay extra (usually ¥500 each) to enjoy some of the attractions most likely to appeal to older children, including the mazelike Ninja Mystery House that requires figuring out trap doors and other tricks in order to "escape"; a Ninja training house where participants can climb a wall, throw *shuriken* (round darts used by ninja), and partake in other challenges; a haunted house; and a Trick Art Museum that contains optical illusions and murals that encourage visitors to ham it up and become part of the action (like fighting serpents or bullfighting). You can also pay extra to dress up like a geisha, ninja, or samurai at the Costume Photo Shop for that lasting momento, or, for ¥8,500, to spend about 40 minutes getting the full treatment of wigs, makeup and costumes, after which you can stroll around the studio park for an hour (in fine weather only). Come here only if you have a lot of time (you'll probably spend a minimum of 2 hr. here), are a cinema buff, or have youngsters in tow.

10 Higashi-Hachigaokacho, Uzumasa, Ukyo-ku. www.toei-eigamura.com. © **075/864-7716.** Admission ¥2,200 adults, ¥1,300 junior-high and high-school students, ¥1,100 children. Daily 9am–5pm (9:30am–4:30pm weekdays Dec–Feb; 9:30am–5pm weekends Dec–Feb; 9am–6pm weekends Mar–Sept and daily Aug). Closed periodically for maintenance. Train: JR line to Uzumasa (5 min.) or Hanazono (13 min.) or Keifuku Line to Uzumasa (5 min.). Bus: 91 or 93 to Uzumasa Eigamuramae or 75 to Eigamura-michi.

IMPERIAL VILLAS & TEMPLES WITHIN EASY REACH OF KYOTO

If this is your first visit to Kyoto and you're here for only a couple days, you should concentrate on seeing sights in Kyoto itself. If, however, this is your second trip to Kyoto, you're here for an extended period of time, or you have a passion for traditional Japanese architecture or gardens, there are a number of worthwhile attractions in the immediate region surrounding Kyoto. Foremost on my list is **Katsura Imperial Villa.**

Note: The Katsura Imperial Villa and **Shugakuin Imperial Villa** require advance permission to visit. To see the Katsura Imperial Villa or Shugakuin Imperial Villa, which are free, you must apply for permission either online in English at **http://sankan.kunaicho.go.jp** at least 4 days before your intended visit; or go in person to the **Imperial Household Agency Office** (© 075/211-1215; no English is spoken and no reservations are accepted by phone, but you can have a Japanese speaker call to see whether space is available), located on the northwest grounds of the **Kyoto Imperial Palace** near Inui Gomon Gate, a 5-minute walk from Imadegawa subway station. It's open Monday through Friday from 8:45am to noon and 1 to 5pm. In the off season, you may be able to make a reservation for a tour on the same day, though keep in mind that it takes an hour to reach Katsura Imperial Villa and 30 minutes to reach Shugakuin by taxi from the Imperial Household Agency Office. It's always better, therefore, to make a reservation a day or two in advance if applying in person; in spring and fall, try to make a reservation up to 3 months in advance. The time of your tour will be designated when you apply. Parties are limited to four persons, everyone must present their passports, and **participants must be at least 18 years old.** Tours are conducted in Japanese only, but there are videos and a free handheld audio guide in English.

Tours, which take place weekdays (except holidays) and the third Saturday of every month year-round, as well as on Saturdays in March, April, May, October, and November (even if they are national holidays), are given at

Katsura Imperial Villa at 9am, 10am, 11am, 1:30pm, 2:30pm, and 3:30pm and at Shugakuin Imperial Villa at 9am, 10am, 11am, 1:30pm, and 3pm.

KATSURA IMPERIAL VILLA ★★★   About a 20-minute walk from Katsura Station on the Hankyu railway line, or a 30-minute bus ride from Kyoto Station (take bus no. 33 to the Katsura Rikyu-mae stop) and then an 8-minute walk, this villa is considered the jewel of traditional Japanese architecture and landscape gardening. It was built between 1620 and 1624 by Prince Toshihito, brother of the emperor, with construction continued by Toshihito's son. The garden, markedly influenced by Kobori Enshu, Japan's most famous garden designer, is a "stroll garden" in which each turn of the path brings an entirely new view.

The first thing you notice upon entering Katsura is its simplicity—the buildings were all made of natural materials, and careful attention was paid to the slopes of the roofs and to the grain, texture, and color of the various woods used. In addition, every garden detail was carefully planned, down to the stones used in the path, the way the trees twist, and how scenes are reflected in the water. A pavilion for moon viewing, a hall for imperial visits, a teahouse, and other buildings are situated around a pond; as you walk along the pathway, you're treated to views that literally change with each step you take. Islets; stone lanterns; various scenes representing seashores, mountains, and hamlets; manicured trees; and bridges of stone, earth, or wood that arch gracefully over the water—everything is perfectly balanced. No matter where you stand, the view is complete and in harmony. Little wonder the Katsura Imperial Villa has influenced architecture not only in Japan but around the world. Sadly, tours are much too hurried (they last only 1 hr.).

SHUGAKUIN IMPERIAL VILLA ★★   Northeast of Kyoto, about a 40-minute bus ride from Kyoto Station (take bus no. 5 from Kyoto Station to the Shugakuin Rikyu-michi bus stop) and then a 15-minute walk, this villa was built in the mid-1600s as a retirement retreat for Emperor Go-Mizunoo, who came to the throne at age 15 and suddenly abdicated 18 years later to become a monk, passing the throne to his daughter in 1629. Amazingly, though the villa was only 2 hours from the Imperial Palace, the emperor came here only on day trips; he never once spent the night. The 53-hectare (133-acre) grounds, among Kyoto's largest, are situated at the foot of Mount Hiei and are famous for the principle known as "borrowed landscape" in which the surrounding landscape is incorporated in the overall garden design. Grounds are divided into three levels (only two of which have compelling features): The **upper garden,** with its lake, islands, and waterfalls, is the most extensive of the three and offers grand views of the surrounding countryside from its hillside pavilion. The **middle garden,** built as a residence for the emperor's daughter, contains a villa with the famous "Shelves of Mist"; in keeping with the Japanese penchant for ranking the best three of everything, this is considered one of the three most beautiful shelves in Japan. The gardens are more spacious and natural than most Japanese-style gardens, which are often small and contrived. Tours, which take 1 hour and 15 minutes and cover about 3km (2 miles) of hilly grounds, allow ample time for photography.

FUSHIMI–INARI SHRINE ★★★   Just a 2-minute walk from the JR Inari Station (which is just two stops by local commuter train from Kyoto Station), Fushimi-Inari Shrine (© **075/641-7331**) is one of Japan's most celebrated Shinto shrines and one of Kyoto's most visually memorable sights. Founded in 711, it's dedicated to the goddess of rice (rice was collected as taxes during the shogun era) and has therefore long been popular with merchants, who come here to pray for success and prosperity. The 4km (2½-mile) pathway behind the shrine is lined with more than 10,000 red *torii,* presented by worshipers throughout the ages and by Japanese businesses. There are also stone foxes, which are considered messengers of the gods, usually with a key to the rice granary hanging from their mouths. It's a glorious, almost surreal, walk as you wind through the woods and the tunnel of vermilion-colored *torii* gates and then gradually climb a hill, where you'll have a good view of Kyoto. At several places along the path are small shops where you can sit down for a bowl of noodles or other refreshments. Admission is free, and the expansive grounds never close. The most popular times to visit are the first day of each month and New Year's, but I prefer weekdays when almost no one is there.

Note: Fushimi-Inari Shrine is on the same JR line that continues to Nara. If you plan on spending the night in Nara, you could easily take in these two attractions on the way. Note, however, that the express train to Nara does not stop at JR Inari Station; for that you'll have to take a local train.

A STROLL THROUGH HIGASHIYAMA-KU

START:	**Sanjusangendo Hall on Shichijo Dori a couple of blocks east of the Kamo River; to get there, walk 20 minutes from Kyoto Station or take bus no. 100, 206, or 208 to Hakubutsukan Sanjusangendo-mae.**
FINISH:	**Gion.**
TIME:	**Allow approximately 5 hours, including stops for shopping and museums.**
BEST TIMES:	**Weekdays, when temples and shops aren't as crowded.**
WORST TIMES:	**Monday, when museums are closed.**

A stroll through Higashiyama-ku will take you to Kiyomizu Temple, one of Kyoto's most famous sights, and other worthwhile attractions like Sanjusangendo Hall. It will also take you through some of Kyoto's most charming neighborhoods, with plenty of shopping opportunities en route.

Start your stroll at:

1 Sanjusangendo Hall
This hall dates from 1266 and is only about 15m (50 ft.) wide, but stretches almost 120m (400 ft.), making it the longest wooden building in Japan.

Walking Tour: Higashiyama-ku

1 Sanjusangendo Hall (Rengeoin Temple)
2 Kyoto National Museum
3 Kawai Kanjiro Memorial House
4 Otani Mausoleum
5 Toribeyama
6 Kiyomizu Temple
7a Taki-no-ya ☕
7b Kiyomizudera Junsei ☕
7c Inoda's Coffee ☕
8 Jishu Shrine
9 Sannenzaka
10 Ryozen Kannon Temple
11 Kodaiji Temple
12a The Sodoh ☕
12b Kodaiji Rakusho Tea Room ☕
12c Chorakukan ☕
13 Maruyama Park
14 Yasaka Shrine (Gion Shrine)
15 Gion

However, it's not the building itself that impresses but what it contains—1,001 life-size images of the thousand-handed Kannon. Seeing so many of them—row upon row of gold figures, glowing in the dark hall—is stunning (unfortunately, no photographs or videos allowed). In the middle is a 3.3m-tall (11-ft.) seated figure of Kannon carved in 1254. At the back of the hall is a 117m (384-ft.) archery range where a competition is held every January 15. (See "Exploring Kyoto," earlier in this chapter, for more information on this and other major sights described in this stroll.)

Across the street is the:

2 Kyoto National Museum (Kokuritsu Hakubutsukan)

In 1889, the Meiji government, fearful that Japan's cultural objects were going the way of the samurai with the increasing import of Western ways and products, established three national museums—one in Tokyo, one in Nara, and this one in Kyoto, which serves as a repository for art objects and treasures that once belonged to Kyoto's temples and royal court. In addition, special exhibitions are mounted three to four times a year.

East of the Kyoto National Museum (toward the wooded hills) are Higashioji Dori and a stoplight; take a left here and walk about 5 minutes until you come to the second stoplight, at a small intersection with a Lawson convenience store. Turn left here, take the first right down a narrow street, and to your right you'll soon see:

3 Kawai Kanjiro Memorial House

Kawai Kanjiro Memorial House, Gojo-zaka (© **075/561-3585**), is the former home and studio of one of Japan's most well-known potters, Kawai Kanjiro (1890–1966). Inspired at a young age by Bernard Leach and one of the cofounders of the Japan Folk Crafts Museum in Tokyo, this versatile man handmade much of the furniture in this lovely home, which is a traditional Japanese house with an indoor open-pit fireplace and gleaming woodwork. Pottery, folkcraft, personal effects, and his outdoor clay kiln, built on a slope in the traditional Japanese method, are on display, but this museum is worth seeing for the 1930s house alone, especially if you haven't had much opportunity to see the interiors of traditional Japanese homes. Admission is ¥900 for adults, ¥500 for students, and ¥300 for children. It's open Tuesday to Sunday from 10am to 5pm.

Take a right out of the museum, walk to the busy road with the overpass, and turn right. When you get to the big intersection, look catty-corner across the intersection to the left and you'll see a slope leading uphill between two big stone lanterns. This marks the entrance to the:

4 Otani Mausoleum

It serves as a major mausoleum for members of Shin Buddhism (a Japanese religious sect). In addition to a memorial hall dedicated to victims of World War II, it holds many memorial services for deceased Shin Buddhists from throughout Japan. After passing the second two-story wooden gate, you should turn left and then right for:

5 Toribeyama

Since ancient times it has served as a cremation site and burial ground, with more than 15,000 tombs spread along the slopes.

Follow the pathway uphill through the cemetery for about 10 minutes to the top, where you should then turn left and follow the painted white arrow with a wheelchair symbol in the street to the vermilion-colored tower gate, which marks the entrance to:

6 Kiyomizu Temple

This temple is the star attraction of this stroll. First founded in 798 and rebuilt in 1633 by the third Tokugawa shogun, Iemitsu, the temple occupies an exalted spot. The main hall is built over a cliff and features a large wooden veranda supported by 139 pillars, each 15m (50 ft.) high. Take in the view of Kyoto from its deck, but to fully appreciate the grandeur of the main hall with its pillars and dark wood, be sure to walk to the three-story pagoda, which offers the best view of the main hall, built without the use of a single nail. From the pagoda, descend the stone steps to Otowa Falls, where you'll see Japanese lined up to drink from the refreshing spring water. Kiyomizu's name, in fact, translates as "pure water" and it's supposedly good for health. From here you'll also have the best view of the temple's impressive pillars.

7 Temple Dining ☕

On the grounds of Kiyomizu Temple, just beside Otowa Falls, is **Taki-no-ya** (© **075/561-5117**), an open-air pavilion where you can sit on *tatami* and enjoy *yudofu*, noodles, a beer, or flavored shaved ice from the English-language menu. This is a great place to stop; if you're lucky to be here in autumn, the fiery reds of the maple trees will set the countryside around you aflame. Open Friday through Wednesday from 10am to 5pm. For something more substantial, wait until after your temple visit to dine on tofu at **Kiyomizudera Junsei,** located off Kiyomizu-zaka (p. 234). On Sannenzaka (see below), keep your eyes peeled for **Inoda's Coffee** (© **075/532-5700**), where you'll have views of a Japanese-style garden along with pastries, sandwiches, and coffee. It's open daily 9am to 5pm.

Before departing Kiyomizu Temple, be sure to make a stop at the vermilion-colored Shinto shrine located behind the temple's main hall:

8 Jishu Shrine

This shrine is regarded as a dwelling place of the deity of love and match-making. Throughout the grounds are English-language signs and descriptions telling about its various good-luck stations; for once, you're not left in the dark about the purpose of the various statues and memorials and what Japanese are doing as they make their rounds. It's very enriching. You can buy good-luck charms for everything from a happy marriage to easy delivery of a child to success in passing an examination. On the shrine's grounds are two stones placed about 9m (30 ft.) apart—if you're able to walk from one stone to the other with your eyes closed, you're supposedly guaranteed success in your love life. It sure doesn't hurt to try. There's also a place where you can write down your troubles on a piece of paper and then submerge it in a bucket of water for ¥200, which supposedly will cause both the paper and your troubles to dissolve. If you failed the rock test, you might make a point of stopping here.

From Kiyomizu Temple, retrace your steps to the vermilion-colored entry tower gate you passed earlier. From here, on a downhill slope called Kiyomizu-zaka, you'll pass shop after shop selling sweets, tea, pottery, fans, ties, hats, souvenirs and curios. If you go crazy shopping here, remember that you're going to have to carry whatever you buy. After a couple of small shrines nestled in among the shops, you'll come to a split in the road and a small shrine on the right shaded by trees. Just beside this shrine are stone steps leading downhill (north) to a stone-cobbled street called:

9 Sannenzaka

The slope leads past lovely antiques stores, upscale craft shops, and restaurants and winds through neighborhoods of wooden buildings reminiscent of old Kyoto. Keep your eyes peeled for downhill stairs to the right leading to Kodaiji and Maruyama Park; after you take these, the street will wind a bit as it goes downhill and eventually end at a T intersection. (The Sodoh restaurant, described below, is here to the left.) Take the stairs opposite the road and look to the right for:

10 Ryozen Kannon Temple

This temple (© **075/561-2205**) has a 24m-high (80-ft.) white statue dedicated to unknown soldiers who died in World War II. Memorial services are conducted four times daily at a shrine that contains memorial tablets of the two million Japanese who perished during the war. There's also a Memorial Hall commemorating the more than 48,000 foreign soldiers who died on Japanese territory. Open daily from 8:45am to 4:20pm; because admission is ¥200, you may only want to take a peek at the statue. Just past Ryozen Kannon Temple, across the parking lot, is:

11 Kodaiji Temple

This temple was founded by the widow Nene in commemoration of her husband, Toyotomi Hideyoshi, who succeeded in unifying Japan at the end of the 16th century. In addition to teahouses and a memorial hall containing wooden images of the couple, there's a beautiful garden designed by master gardener Kobori Enshu. Don't miss it (a one-room museum is included in admission, but skip it if time is of the essence).

Exit Kodai-ji Temple via the main steps leading downhill and turn right, continuing north.

12 Temple Dining ☕

At the end of Sannenzaka, to the left, is the **Sodoh,** an Italian restaurant located in a rustic 1929 villa (p. 235). Past Kodai-ji Temple and just before the street ends at a pagoda with a crane on top, keep your eyes peeled for a teahouse on your right with a garden, which you can glimpse from the street through a gate. The **Kodaiji Rakusho Tea Room** (洛匠), 516 Washiochiyo (© **075/561-6892**), is a lovely place and one of my favorite tearooms in Kyoto. It has a 100-year-old miniature garden with a pond that's home to some of the largest and most colorful carp I've ever seen, some of which are 20 years old and winners of the many medals displayed in the back room. Sit at one of the tables or in the ba... matcha (frothed, powdered green tea), warabi mochi (cub... coated in toasted soy flour), and, in summer, somen (finely s... If you're a gardener, you'll probably want to give up the hobby a... what's possible—but rarely achieved. Open from 9:30am to 6pm; ... a week but, unfortunately, not a fixed day. For coffee, sandwiches, or a... tea, just inside Maruyama Park to the left, there's an ornate cafe in **Chorak...** a brick-and-stone Meiji-Era building; it's open daily from 10am to 9:30pm.

Continuing on your stroll north, turn right at the pagoda with the crane and then take an immediate left, which marks the beginning of:

13 Maruyama Park

An unkempt field of shrubs and weeds until designated a public park in 1886, this is one of Kyoto's most popular outdoor respites, filled with ponds, pigeons, and gardens. In spring, it's one of the most popular spots for viewing cherry blossoms; to the left after you enter the park is one of the oldest, most famous cherry trees in Kyoto. Also farther west is:

14 Yasaka Shrine

Yasaka Shrine is also known as Gion Shrine because of its proximity to the Gion District. Its present buildings date from 1654; the stone *torii* (gates) on the south side are considered among the largest in Japan. But the reason most people come here is one of practicality—the shrine is dedicated to the gods of health and prosperity, two universal concerns. This shrine, free to the public and open 24 hours, is packed during the Gion Festival and on New Year's Eve.

Exit Yasaka Shrine to the west; this brings you to a busy street called Higashioji. Cross it and continue walking west on busy Shijo Dori, until you reach Hanamikoji Dori on your left. This is:

15 Gion

Gion is one of Japan's most famous nightlife districts. It's centered primarily on Hanamikoji Dori, which translates as "Narrow Street for Flower Viewing." This is one of Kyoto's long-standing geisha districts, an enclave of discreet, traditional, and almost solemn-looking wooden homes that reveal nothing of the gaiety that goes on inside—drinking, conversation, and business dealings with dancing, singing, and music provided by geisha and their apprentices, called *maiko*. If it's early evening, you might glimpse one of these women as she small-steps her way in *geta* (a traditional wooden shoe) to an evening appointment, elaborately made up and wearing a beautiful kimono. You might also wish to visit **Gion Corner** on Hanamikoji Dori, which offers performances of dance, puppetry, and other traditional arts nightly, or join a guided night tour of Gion; see "Kyoto After Dark," later in this chapter, for details.

Winding Down

If all this sightseeing and shopping have made you thirsty, there are many restaurants and bars to the west across the Kamo River, on Pontocho, and near

See "Where to Dine in Kyoto" and "Kyoto After
uggestions in this area.

han 1,000 years, Kyoto spawned a number
that catered to the elaborate tastes of the
sses. Kyoto today is still renowned for its
s, Yuzen-dyed fabrics, Kyo pottery (pottery
y, gold-leaf work, umbrellas, paper lanterns,
s, cloisonné, and lacquerware.

k tatami room and enjoy
s of a jellylike dessert
un cold noodles).
er you've seen
osed 1 day
fternoon
kan,

GREAT SHOPPING AREAS   The majority of Kyoto's tiny specialty shops
are in central Kyoto's downtown. The rectangular grid formed by **Kawaramachi Dori, Shijo Dori, Nijo Dori,** and **Teramachi Dori** includes two covered
shopping arcades and specialized shops selling lacquerware, combs and hairpins, knives and swords, tea and tea-ceremony implements, and more—
including, of course, clothing and accessories for customers of all ages.

For antiques, woodblock prints, and art galleries, head toward the high-end
Shinmonzen Dori and **Furumonzen Dori** in Gion, which parallel Shijo Dori
to the north on the eastern side of the Kamo River, as well as **Teramachi Dori**
north of Oike, home also of Kyoto Antiques Center. You'll find pottery and
souvenir shops in abundance on the roads leading to Kiyomizu Temple, particularly the hill known as **Chawan-zaka** (Teacup Slope).

For clothing, accessories, and modern goods, **department stores** are good
bets. They're conveniently located in central Kyoto near the Shijo-Kawaramachi intersection and Kyoto Station. Near Kyoto Station are also two large
shopping malls selling everything from clothing and shoes to stationery and
local souvenirs: an underground mall beneath the station and **Aeon** southwest
of the station across Hachijo Dori. **Kyoto-Yodobashi,** on Karasuma Dori a
block north of Kyoto Tower, contains the Yodobashi Camera electronics store,
fashion boutiques, and restaurants.

Crafts & Specialty Shops

Aritsugu (有次) ★★   The fact that this family-owned business is located at
the Nishiki Food Market is appropriate, as it sells hand-wrought knives and
other handmade cooking implements, including sushi knives, bamboo steamers,
pots, pans, and cookware used in the preparation of traditional Kyoto cuisine, as
well as *ikebana* scissors. In business for 450 years, the shop counts the city's top
chefs among its customers despite its diminutive size; look for its display cases
of knives. Open daily 9am to 5:30pm. Nishiki-Koji Dori, Gokomachi Nishi-iru, Nakagyo-
ku. ℂ **075/221-1091.** Bus: 4, 5, 10, 11, 12, 17, 32, 46, 59, 201, 203, 207, or 205 to Shijo Kawaramachi
(5 min.). 1 block north of Shijo Dori on the north side of Nishiki-Koji Dori, west of Gokomachi.

Ippodo (一保堂) ★★   In business since 1717, this famous shop is a good
place not only to buy high-quality Japanese green teas but to learn more about
them. Pick up the shop's English-language brochure that explains the different

Shopping for Second-Hand Kimono

Flea markets, especially the one at Toji Temple (see "Markets," below), are good stomping grounds for inexpensive used kimono. I also like **Kikuya,** tucked away in a residential neighborhood on Manjuji Dori, east of Sakaimachi (ⓒ **075/351-0033;** Mon–Sat 9am–7pm), on the second floor of a nondescript building. Its three rooms are packed to the ceiling with used kimono (both antique and modern), *haori* (short kimono-like jackets, traditionally worn by men), *obi*

(kimono sashes often worn today as scarves), and other kimono accessories for both adults and children. Another good place to look is **Chicago,** a thrift store about halfway down the Teramachi covered shopping arcade (ⓒ **075/212-5391;** daily 11am–8pm). Its entire second floor is devoted to used kimono (including wedding kimono), *obi, jinbei* (men's pajamas), and *yukata* (cotton sleeping kimono).

varieties, from *matcha* to *sencha* to *genmaicha,* or sample them at the shop's hands-on tearoom, Kaboku, where you can experience brewing techniques for the different types of tea. In a nod to modern times, Ippodo also sells teabags. Open Monday to Saturday 9am to 7; Saturday and holidays 9am to 6pm (Kaboku open daily 11am–5:30pm). Teramachi Dori, north of Nijo, Nakagyo-ku. www.ippodo-tea.co.jp. ⓒ **075/211-3421.**

Kyoto Aburatorishi Senmontenzo (きょうとあぶらとり紙) ★ I realize this is a bit odd, but this shop is dedicated to one of my favorite Japanese cosmetic products: face paper. Kyoto is famous for its face paper, long used by geisha and *maiko,* and this shop sells a bewildering choice of varieties, for everything from dry to troubled skin. I like it for blotting oily skin on hot, humid days. There are other beauty products also for sale, including scented creams. Daily 11am to 8pm. Kawaramachi, Shijo-agaru, Nakagyo-ku.ⓒ **075/213-3322.** Bus: 4, 5, 10, 11, 12, 17, 32, 46, 201, 203, 207, or 205 to Shijo Kawaramachi. On the east side of Kawaramachi Dori, north of Shijo Dori; look for its sign with an elephant.

Kyoto Antiques Center ★ Teramachi is known for its antique and specialty shops, but this store, with about 20 vendors, is the largest. Offering both Western and Japanese antiques and curios, it's a fun place to browse for jewelry, lacquerware, pottery, dolls, glassware, and more. Wednesday to Monday 10:30am to 7pm; closed the third Monday of every month. East side of Teramachi, north of Nijo Dori, Nakagyo-ku. ⓒ **075/222-0793.** Bus: 4, 10, 17, 32, 59, and 205 to Kyoto Shiyakushomae (10 min.).

Kyoto Handicraft Center ★★★ For one-stop shopping for Japanese souvenirs and crafts, your best bet is the city's largest craft, gift, and souvenir center, in business for more than 80 years (but recently renovated and expanded) and founded by the present owner's grandfather. Its two buildings offer pearls, woodblock prints, lacquerware, pottery, dolls, kimono, paper products, ornamental swords, samurai armor and helmets, iron teapots, fans, wind chimes, chopsticks, cloisonné, lunch boxes, incense, Nishijin textile goods, sake and sake cup sets, green tea, *furoshiki* (cloth used for wrapping gifts), T-shirts, and refrigerator magnets—and that's just for starters. In addition to a tourist office (where you can also exchange money), it provides workspace for artisans producing their various crafts, including woodblock printing and the production of damascene. You can also try your own hand at 9 different craft activities, including woodblock prints, cloisonné, damascene, and more, with English instruction provided. No reservations are necessary, but plan on at least an hour. Lessons run ¥1,950 to ¥4,100 and are a great way for older children to get creative while you shop. Open daily from 10am to 7pm. 21 Entomi-cho, Shogoin, Sakyo-ku. www.kyotohandicraftcenter.com. ℂ **075/761-7000.** Bus: 93, 201, 202, 203, 204, or 206 to Kumano-jinja-mae (1 min.). On Marutamachi Dori, north of Heian Shrine.

Robert Yellin Yakimono Gallery ★★ Robert Yellin may be American-born, but after decades in Japan he's become one of the world's foremost experts on Japanese pottery, published regularly in the *Japan Times* and leading arts journals and selling both contemporary and traditional works by some of Japan's top contemporary ceramic artists, shown in changing exhibits. In 2011, he moved his gallery from a remote town in the Kanto region to this gorgeous Taisho-Era house near Ginkakuji Temple, making it easier for visitors to see and learn about the various wares and the artists who created them. Open Tuesday to Friday from 10:30am to 5pm or by appointment (it's best to call beforehand if you want to meet Yellin personally). 39 Ginkakuji-mae-cho, Sakyo-ku. www.japanesepottery.com. ℂ **075/708-5581.** Bus: 5, 17, 102, 203, or 204 to Ginkakuji-michi (5 min.); or 32 or 100 to Ginkakuji-mae (5 min.). Facing Ginkakuji, turn left at the police box to cross the stream, walk right along the stream and make your first left. The gallery is about 100 yards ahead on the left up on a hill, before the stone stairs straight ahead.

Department Stores

Department stores are good places to shop for Japanese items and souvenirs, including pottery, lacquerware, and kimono as well as clothing, foodstuff, and everyday items.

JR Kyoto Isetan, located in Kyoto Station (http://kyoto.wjr-isetan.co.jp; ℂ **075/352-1111;** daily 10am–8pm), is Kyoto's most fashionable department store, specializing in women's imported and domestic clothing.

In central Kyoto, **Daimaru,** on Shijo Dori west of Takakura (www.daimaru.co.jp/kyoto; ℂ **075/211-8111;** daily 10am–8pm), is Kyoto's largest department store, with everything from clothing to food to electronic goods spread on nine floors (and branches of well-known restaurants on the 8th floor). Nearby are **Marui,** on the southeast corner of Shijo-Kawaramachi intersection (ℂ **075/257-0101;** daily 10:30am–8:30pm), with nine floors of fashion, housewares, food, and restaurants; and **Takashimaya,** across the street at the southwest corner of the Shijo-Kawaramachi intersection (www.takashimaya.co.jp/kyoto; ℂ **075/221-8811;** daily 10am–8pm), one of Japan's oldest and most respected department stores with a good selection of traditional crafts. **Tokyu Hands** (http://kyoto.tokyu-hands.co.jp/en/index.html; ℂ **075/254-3109;** daily

10am–8:30pm), on Shijo Dori east of Karasuma Dori, sells tools and gadgets for hobbyists, as well as kitchenware, luggage, beauty goods, and many other items for the home.

Markets

On the 21st of each month, a flea market is held at **Toji Temple** (✆ **075/691-3325**), about a 15-minute walk southwest of Kyoto Station. Japan's largest flea market, it's also one of the oldest; its history stretches back more than 700 years, when pilgrims began flocking to Toji Temple to pay their respects to Kobo Daishi, who founded the Shingon sect of Buddhism. Today, Toji Temple, a World Heritage Site, is still a center for the Shingon sect, and its market (popularly known as Kobo-san) is a colorful affair with booths selling Japanese antiques, old kimono, ethnic goods, flowers, bonsai, dried foods, fish, vegetables, crafts, odds and ends, and many other items. Worshipers come to pray before a statue of Kobo Daishi and to have their wishes written on wooden slats by temple calligraphers. Even if you don't buy anything, the festive atmosphere of the market and booths makes a trip memorable. The largest Kobo-san markets take place in December and January. All markets at Toji are held from about 8am to 4pm. A smaller market, devoted entirely to Japanese antiques, is held at Toji Temple on the first Sunday of each month.

Commemorating the scholar and poet Sugawara Michizane, the **Tenjin-san market** held at **Kitano Tenmangu Shrine** (✆ **075/461-0005**) the 25th of every month is a large market offering a little bit of everything—antiques, used clothing, ceramics, food—in a beautiful setting. It's open from about 8am to dusk, but go as early as you can. Kitano Shrine is on Imadegawa Dori between Nishi-oji and Senbon; take bus no. 10, 101, 102, and 203 to the Kitano Tenmangu-mae stop.

Unlike the other temple markets, the **Chion-ji market** (✆ **075/691-3325**), held the 15th of each month from 9am to 4pm, is devoted to handmade goods and crafts, including pottery and clothing. To reach it, take bus no. 17, 102, 201, 203, or 206 to Hyakumanben at the Higashioji and Imadegawa intersection; **Chion-ji Temple** is just to the northeast.

Once a month on Sunday (the date is irregular), a flea market is held in front of **City Hall** from 10am to 4pm, with local citizens selling unwanted stuff, mostly clothing. Although you may not buy anything to take home with you, a stroll through the **Nishiki Food Market** is worthwhile just for the atmosphere. With a 400-plus-year history, this covered shopping arcade in the heart of downtown Kyoto on Nishiki-Koji Dori (1 block north of Shijo Dori) has approximately 135 open-fronted shops and stalls selling fish, seasonal produce (like chestnuts in autumn), flowers, eggs, pickled vegetables, fruit, take-out foods, kitchenware, and—to cash in on an increasing number of foreign visitors—crafts and souvenirs. This is where locals, as well as the city's finest restaurants and inns, buy their food. It's open from the early hours to about 6pm; some shops close on either Wednesday or Sunday.

ENTERTAINMENT & NIGHTLIFE

Nothing beats a fine summer evening spent strolling the streets of Kyoto. From the geisha district of Gion to the bars and restaurants lining Pontocho, Kyoto is utterly charming and romantic at night. Begin with a walk along the banks of the Kamo River—it's a favorite place for young couples in love. In summer, restaurants stretching north and south of Shijo Dori along the river erect outdoor wooden platforms on stilts over the water.

There are many annual events and dances, including the very popular geisha dances held in June, the only time of year you can see traditional dances performed by all five of Kyoto's traditional geisha districts; Miyako Odori dances in April and Gion Odori dances in October or November feature *geiko* and *maiko* (geisha and apprentice geisha) dressed in elaborate costume; and *kabuki* at the Minamiza Theater in December.

To find out what's happening during your stay, ask the tourist office for the **Kyoto Visitor's Guide** or check online at www.kyotoguide.com, www.kansai scene.com, and http://kyoto.travel/enplanyourvisit/events.

The Major Nightlife Districts

GION

Of Kyoto's five geisha districts, Gion is the most famous. A small neighborhood of plain wooden buildings in Higashiyama-ku on the eastern side of the Kamo River, Gion doesn't look anything like what you've probably come to expect from an urban Japanese nightlife district. There's little neon in sight, and the atmosphere is almost austere and solemn, as though its raison d'être were infinitely more important and sacred than mere entertainment. Gion is a shrine to Kyoto's past, an era when geisha numbered in the thousands.

Contrary to popular Western misconceptions, geisha are not prostitutes. Rather, they're trained experts in conversation and the traditional arts of music and dance (*geiko,* as they're usually referred to in Kyoto, translates as "art professional"), and their primary role is to make men feel like kings when they're in the soothing enclave of the geisha house. There are now a mere 250 geisha in Kyoto and fewer than 70 in Gion; after all, in today's high-tech world, few women are willing to undergo the years of rigorous training to learn how to conduct the tea ceremony, to play the *shamisen* (a three-stringed instrument), and perform ancient court dances. *Maiko* are not allowed to have cellphones.

Gion is about a 5-minute walk from the Shijo-Kawaramachi intersection; to reach it, walk east on Shijo Dori and then take a right on Hanamikoji Dori. Its narrow streets are great for strolling; a good time to take a walk through the neighborhood is around dusk when geisha are on their way to their evening appointments. Perhaps you'll see one—or a *maiko* (a young woman training to be a geisha)—clattering in her high *geta* (wooden shoes). She'll be dressed in a brilliant kimono, her face a chalky white, and her hair adorned with hairpins and ornaments. From geisha houses, music and laughter lilt from behind paper screens, sounding all the more inviting because you can't enter. Don't take it personally; not even Japanese will venture inside without the proper introductions. There are, however, an increasing number of bars and restaurants in Gion that are open to outsiders; it's not hard to imagine that in another 100 years, Gion will look no different from many other nightlife districts.

If you want to find out more about geisha and *maiko,* consider joining a guided **Gion Night Tour** lasting 1 hour and 40 minutes and offered Monday, Wednesday, and Friday at 6pm March to November and at 5pm December to February. Costing ¥1,000, the walking tour leads past entertainment and boarding houses and describes what life is like for *maiko* as she prepares to become a *geiko.* The day after I took this tour, I saw three young women at Yasaka Shrine and was able to identify right away by the way they dressed that they were *maiko* rather than geisha. Reservations are not required. For more information on this tour, pick up a brochure at the tourist office or go to www.waraido.com/walking/gion.html.

Gion Corner ★★   After strolling around Gion, you might also want to visit Gion Corner, which introduces Japan's ancient cultural arts. Short demonstrations and performances of the tea ceremony, Japanese flower arranging, *koto* (Japanese harp) music, *gagaku* (ancient court music and dance), *kyogen* (*Noh* comic plays), *kyomai* (Kyoto-style dance) performed by *maiko,* and *bunraku* (puppetry) follow each other in quick succession and are described in detail in an English-language program. The shows caters to tourists, and none of the individual performances can match a full-scale production of the real thing, but this is a quick and convenient introduction. Before or after the show, take a look at the Maiko Gallery with its small display of *maiko* hairstyles and accessories. Note that no credit cards are accepted. Performances are nightly at 6pm and 7pm mid-March through November (no performances July 16 and Aug 16); December through early March performances are only on Friday, Saturday, Sunday, and holidays. Reservations are not necessary, but arrive early or purchase in advance at most hotels or Gion Corner box office. Yasaka Hall, 570–2 Minamigawa, Gion. www.kyoto-gioncorner.com. ✆ **075/561-1119.** Tickets ¥3,150 adults, ¥2,200 high-school and university students, ¥1,900 children. Bus: 12, 46, 100, 102, 201, 202, 203, 206, or 207 to Gion (6 min.). Located on Hanamikoji Dori south of Shijo Dori.

PONTOCHO & KIYAMACHI

Pontocho is a narrow alley that parallels the Kamo River's western bank, stretching from Shijo Dori north to Sanjo Dori. Once riddled with geisha houses and other members-only establishments, it is now lined with bars, clubs, restaurants, and hostess bars that fill every nook and cranny. Pontocho makes for a fascinating walk as you watch groups of Japanese enjoying themselves.

Kyoto's liveliest nightlife district, with bar after bar, is along **Kiyamachi,** another small street that parallels Pontocho just to the west and runs beside a small canal.

The Live Music Scene

Hello Dolly ★★   Amongst the bars and restaurants on Pontocho is this dark and narrow jazz club overlooking the Kamo River. Open since 1939 but with a retro look more reminiscent of the 1950s, with velvet-upholstered chairs and an album cover of Doris Day in the front window, it offers live jazz Fridays and Saturdays by Japanese musicians, with three sets at 8, 9:30, and 11pm. During the rest of the week it plays classic jazz recordings. In any case, this is a very civilized and old-school place in fast-changing Pontocho. Open daily 6pm (7pm Mon) to 1:30am (to 12:20am Sun). Pontocho. http://hellodolly. hannnari.com. ℭ **075/241-1728.** Cover Fri–Sat ¥900–¥1,000 1st hr., half price subsequent hours, plus ¥900 per person table charge. No charge Sun–Thurs. Bus: 4, 5, 17, or 205 to Shijo Kawaramachi (4 min.). East (river) side of Pontocho, south of the playground.

Le Club Jazz ★★ For serious jazz fans, this has been the real deal for more than 20 years, with musicians from around Japan performing on a simple stage 6 nights a week. It's in a contemporary concrete building on Sanjo Dori, but its upstairs entrance can be hard to find. Its website is in Japanese only, but you can at least get an idea of what you'll pay. Open Tuesday to Sunday 7pm to 1am. Arimoto Building, 2nd floor, Sanjo Dori Gokomachi. http://web.kyoto-inet.or.jp/people/ktsin. ℭ **075/211-5800.** Live music cover ¥2,000–¥3,000, including 1 or 2 drinks. Subway: Kyoto Shiyakusho-mae (3 min.). On the northwest corner of Sanjo Dori and Gokomachi.

Live Spot RAG ★★★ This is one of Kyoto's oldest live clubs, established in 1981 and still pulling in the college-age crowd with its mostly Japanese bands that play rock, jazz, acoustic, and fusion. It's a small and popular place and can fill up fast, so get tickets in advance to avoid disappointment (you also get a slight discount with advance purchases); students also often get discounts. Live music is from 7:30 to 10:30, after which it winds down to become a mellow bar, so you might also just want to drop in for a drink. Open nightly from 6pm to 2am (to 4:30am on weekends). Empire Building, 5th floor, Kiyamachi Dori, Sanjo Agaru. www.ragnet.co.jp. ℭ **075/241-0446.** Live music cover ¥1,800–¥3,000 for most performances, plus a 1-drink, 1-dish minimum. Subway: Kyoto Shiyakusho-mae (3 min.). Bus: 4, 5, 10, 11, 17, 32, 59, or 205 to Kawaramachi Sanjo (2 min.). On the east side of Kiyamachi with its narrow canal, north of Sanjo Dori.

The Bar Scene

Ace Cafe ★★ In the same building as RAG (above), this 10th-floor bar has a concrete floor and ceiling, giving it a slight industrial look. But with windows on three sides, it's the view that's the draw, along with reasonable prices for cocktails (all priced at ¥700), snacks, and more. Open daily 6pm to 2am (to 3am Fri–Sat). Empire Building, 10th floor, Kiyamachi Dori, Sanjo Agaru. www.ace cafe.com. ℭ **075/241-0009.** Kyoto Shiyakusho-mae (3 min.). Bus: 4, 5, 10, 11, 17, 32, 59, or 205 to Kawaramachi Sanjo (2 min.). On the east side of Kiyamachi with its narrow canal, north of Sanjo Dori.

Pig & Whistle ★★★ Several generations of Japanese locals, expats, and foreign travelers have visited this English-style pub, a Kyoto mainstay since 1985 where you can play darts, stand at the bar, or sit at a table with your mum. It attracts a mostly older crowd early in the evening followed by younger patrons later in the night, who come for its 9 different beers on tap, 60 single-malt whiskies, free Wi-Fi, foosball table, TVs showing sports from around the world, bar food ranging from fish and chips to minced meat pie, and happy hour weekdays to 8pm and weekends to 7pm. There are also weekly specials, like discounts for foreigners on Tuesdays and for ladies on Wednesday. Open daily 5pm to 2am. Shobi Building, 2nd floor, 115 Ohashi-cho, Ohashi, Higashi Iru, Sanjo Dori. www.pigandwhistle.org.uk. ℰ **075/761-6022.** Subway: Sanjo Keihan (2 min.). Bus: 5, 10, 11, 12, or 59 to Sanjo Keihan-mae (2 min.). East of the Kamo River, on the north side of Sanjo Dori.

Tadg's Gastro Pub ★★★   There's no better place to explore the world of Japanese craft beers than this home-away-from-home for owner Tadg, a professional chef. In addition to Japanese beers offered on tap and in bottles, it is also worth visiting for its signature lamb chop, slow-cooked for 48 hours, cut into thin chops, and then roasted and served with creamed potatoes and mushy peas and smothered in a red-wine sauce, but you also can't go wrong with one of the pizzas made from scratch. Long and narrow but open to the street, it's also worth checking out for lunch specials. This is a friendly and welcoming place, so even solo female travelers should feel at home here. Open daily 11:30am to 11pm. 498 Kamikoriki-cho. www.tadgs.com. ℰ **075/213-0214.** Subway: Kyoto Shiyakusho-mae (3 min.). Bus: 4, 10, 17, 32, 59, or 205 to Kyoto Shiyakushomae (2 min.). On the east side of Kiyamachi with its narrow canal, north of Oike Dori.

Yoramu ★★   If you're simply out to have a good time, don't come here. If you're serious about sake, however, join novices and experts alike and claim one of the nine counter seats for tastings of what owner Yoram, who hails Israel, calls the very best he can find, from unpasteurized to vintage sake, all offered by the glass. Ask for recommendations or go with the three-glass sampler for ¥1,200. It has a discreet and rather hidden entrance, with lit lanterns; by day the same space operates as a *soba* shop. Open Wednesday to Saturday from 6pm to midnight. Nijo Dori Higashinotoin. www.sakebar-yoramu.com. ℰ **085/213-1512.** Subway: Karasuma-Oike (5 min.). Nijo Dori east of Higashinotoin. From Oike Dori, head north on Higashinotoin Dori 2 blocks and turn right; it's immediately on the right in the 3rd building, next to a flower shop.

OSAKA

Although its history stretches back almost 1,500 years, Osaka first gained prominence when Hideyoshi Toyotomi, the most powerful lord in the land, built Japan's most magnificent castle here in the 16th century. To develop resources for his castle town, he persuaded merchants from other parts of the nation to resettle in Osaka. During the Edo Period, the city became an important distribution center as feudal lords from the surrounding region sent their rice to merchants in Osaka, who in turn sent the rice onward to Edo (present-day Tokyo) and other cities. As the merchants prospered, the town grew and such arts as *kabuki* and *bunraku* flourished. With money and leisure to spare, the merchants also developed a refined taste for food.

Today, with the legacy of the city's commercial beginnings still present, Osaka is the mover and shaker of the Kansai region, known for its international and progressive business and high-tech industries. Capital of Osaka Prefecture and with a population of about 2.6 million, it's the third-most populated city in Japan (after Tokyo and Yokohama). Osakans are usually characterized as being outgoing and clever at money affairs. (One Osakan greeting is "Are you making any money?") It's also known for its food, castle, port, underground shopping arcades, and *bunraku* puppet theater. It boasts Japan's oldest state temple and tallest skyscraper, one of the nation's best aquariums, and the only Universal Studios outside the United States. Because of its international airport, it also serves as a gateway to the rest of Japan. Indeed, some travelers base themselves in Osaka, taking side trips to Kyoto, Nara, Kobe, Himeji, and Mount Koya.

ESSENTIALS

Getting There

BY PLANE Constructed on a huge man-made island 5km (3 miles) off the mainland in Osaka Bay and almost 50km (30 miles) from the center of Osaka, **Kansai International Airport** (**KIX;** www.kansai-airport.or.jp; © **072/455-2500**) receives both international and domestic flights, and, like the city itself, is traveler-friendly. Signs are clear and abundant, and facilities and services—which range from restaurants and shops to a **tourist information center** (see below), **post office, ATMs** that accept foreign credit cards, a children's **playroom** in the international departure area (free of charge), **cell-phone** rental counters, computer stations providing Internet access (¥100 for 10 min.), and free **Wi-Fi**—are seemingly endless.

Getting from KIX to Osaka   Taxis are prohibitively expensive: Expect to spend ¥14,000 to ¥17,000 for an hour's cab ride to the city center. Easiest if you have luggage, is the **Kansai Airport Transportation Enterprise** (www.kate.co.jp; ℭ 072/461-1374), which provides bus service to major stations and some hotels in Osaka, as well as to Kyoto, Kobe, Nara, and Himeji. Fares to Osaka average ¥1,550; purchase tickets at counters in the arrival lobby. Another bus service, the **OCAT Shuttle** (www.ocat.co.jp; ℭ 06/6635-3000), travels from KIX to the Osaka City Air Terminal, located in the heart of Osaka next to JR Namba Station and serving as a major bus terminal for express buses to cities throughout Japan; buses depart KIX every 30 minutes for the 48-minute ride and cost ¥1,050.

You can also take the **train** into Osaka. The **JR Airport Express Haruka** (www.westjr.co.jp; ℭ 0570/00-2486), which travels to Tennoji and Shin-Osaka stations (but not Osaka Station) before continuing to Kyoto, departs about twice an hour; the fare to Shin-Osaka is ¥2,330 for the 50-minute trip. Slower is the **JR Rapid Service (JR Kanku Kaisoku),** which travels from the airport to Tennoji and Osaka stations, with the 70-minute trip to Osaka Station costing ¥1,190. If you a have a **Japan Rail Pass,** you can ride these trains for free after exchanging your voucher at the Kansai Airport (rail) Station on the third floor, open daily 5:30am to 11pm.

Across from the JR trains in the same station at the airport is the private **Nankai Line** (www.howto-osaka.com; ℭ 06/6643-1005), whose sleek **rapi:t** (pronounced "rapito") train reaches Namba Nankai Station in 38 minutes. There are usually two trains an hour, and ordinary reserved seats cost ¥1,430, though discounts are often available if purchased in advance online, including tickets that bundle airport transfer with local transportation. If you're on a budget, you can also take an ordinary **Nankai Express Line** for ¥920 and reach Namba in 47 minutes.

BY TRAIN   Osaka is 2½ to 3 hours from Tokyo and about 80 minutes to almost 3 hours from Hiroshima, depending on the Shinkansen bullet train, with the fare from Tokyo costing ¥13,620 for an unreserved seat. All Shinkansen bullet trains arrive at **Shin-Osaka Station** at the city's northern edge. Take the **Midosuji** subway line from Shin-Osaka Station to Osaka Station (the subway station here is called **Umeda Station**), Namba, Tennoji, and other points south.

JR trains also make runs between Shin-Osaka and Osaka stations. If you haven't turned in your voucher for your **Japan Rail Pass** yet, you can do so at either Osaka Stations or Shin-Osaka Station daily from 5:30am to 11pm.

If you're arriving in Osaka from Kobe or Kyoto, the commuter lines, which will deliver you directly to Osaka Station in the heart of the city, are more convenient than the Shinkansen, which will deposit you at out-of-the-way Shin-Osaka Station.

Osaka

ATTRACTIONS ●
Harukas 300 **24**
Museum of Oriental Ceramics **6**
Osaka Castle **7**
Osaka International Peace Center **8**
Shitennoji Temple **9**
Spa World **23**

NIGHTLIFE ◆
Cinquecento **17**
Dig Me Out Art & Diner **14**
Murphy's **16**
National Bunraku Theater **10**
Rug Time Osaka **15**

9

OSAKA | Essentials

KITA-KU
(NORTH WARD)

HIGASHI (EAST)

NISHI (WEST)

Osakajo-Koen

OSAKA CASTLE PARK

■ Remains of Naniwa Palace

NISHINOMARU GARDEN

Katamachi

Kyobashi

Morinomiya

Tanimachi-4-Chome

Temmabashi

TANIMACHI LINE

MINAMI-TEMMA PARK

Macchamachisuji Dori

Hanshin Expressway Loop Route

Chuo Odori

CHUO LINE

Neya River

Sakuranomiya

O-Kawa River

Aqua Bus Port ■

Temma

Ogimachi

OGIMACHI PARK

Nakazakicho

Minamimorimachi

Naniwabashi

Oimatsucho Dori

NAKANOSHIMA PARK

Sakai Suji

SAKAISUJI LINE

Sakaisuji Hommachi

Hommachi Dori

Kitahama

Osaka Visitors' Information Center Umeda

Yodobashi Camera ■

Umeda

Higashiumeda

Nishi-Umeda

Kusuri-Tokyagai (wholesale street)

Midosuji Dori

MIDOSUJI LINE

Aqua Bus Port ■

Oebashi

Yodoya-bashi

Hommachi

Grand Front Osaka

Umeda

Osaka

JR Osaka Station

Yotsubashisuji Dori

YOTSUBASHI LINE

Hommachi

UTSUBO PARK

Umeda Sky Building ■

YODOGAWA RIVERSIDE PARK

Watanabebashi

Higobashi

Nakanoshima

Awaza

Naniwa Suji

Chuo Odori

KEIHAN NAKANOSHIMA LINE

Dojima River

Tosabori Dori

Tosabori River

Fukushima

HANSHIN RWY. MAIN LINE

JR LOOP LINE

0 — 1/4 mi
0 — 0.25 km

——— Railway
——— Subway
ⓘ Tourist Info

BY BUS JR "Dream" night buses depart from both Tokyo Station's Yaesu exit and Shinjuku Station's New South exit several times nightly (including buses just for women), arriving at Osaka Station about 8 or 9 hours later and costing ¥5,000 to ¥9,600, depending on the bus and seat. There are also **JR day buses** from Tokyo and Shinjuku stations to Osaka Station. Tickets for most buses can be bought at any major JR station, JR bus terminal, or travel agency; for inquiries, call ✆ **03/3844-1950** (✆ **03/3844-0489** for reservations; the website www.jrbuskanto.co.jp is in Japanese only). In addition, **Willer Express** (http://willerexpress.com; ✆ **050/5805-0383**) operates buses departing Tokyo and Shinjuku stations several times nightly, arriving at Osaka Station the next morning. The cost of these range from ¥4,000 to ¥11,100, depending on the date and type of seat (reclining seats cost more); student and senior discounts are available.

Visitor Information

At KIX Airport, the **Kansai Tourist Information Center** (✆ **072/456-6025;** daily 7am–8:30pm) is in the International Arrivals Lobby of Terminal 1. The multilingual staff dispenses general travel information about Japan and maps and brochures of the Kansai area, including Kyoto and Kobe, and can make hotel reservations.

In Osaka, there's a **Visitors Information Center Umeda** (✆ **06/6345-2189;** daily 8am–8pm) at Osaka Station, in the Central Concourse's north end near the Mitsukoshi Isetan department store. There's also the downtown **Visitors Information Center Namba** (✆ **06/6631-9100;** daily 9am–8pm), in Nankai Namba Station across from Takashimaya Department Store.

To find out what's going on in Osaka, *Kansai Scene* (www.kansaiscene.com) is a free bilingual monthly magazine with articles, reviews, listings, and information on the Kansai area. Information on Osaka city is also available on the Web at **www.osaka-info.jp**, while **www.kansai.gr.jp** gives information on the Kansai region.

City Layout

Osaka is divided into various wards, or *ku,* the most important of which for visitors are Kita-ku (North Ward), which encompasses the area around Osaka and Umeda stations; and Chuo-ku (Central Ward), where you'll find Osaka Castle and Namba, the heart of the city. Some city maps divide Osaka by location, with Kita (North) around Osaka Station and Minami (South) encompassing Namba and Shinsaibashi. Shin-Osaka Station, three subway stations north of Osaka (Umeda) Station, is a tourist wasteland with only a few hotels.

AROUND OSAKA STATION Kita embraces the area around Osaka and Umeda stations and includes many of the city's top hotels, office and entertainment complexes (like Grand Front Osaka), lots of restaurants, Nakanoshima with its park and museums, and several shopping complexes, mostly underground. Its maze of buildings and streets, however, make it frustrating to navigate, even for Japanese.

AROUND OSAKA CASTLE   Osaka Castle, which lies to the east, is the historic center of the city and is surrounded by a huge park.

MINAMI/NAMBA   Four subway stops south of Umeda Station is Namba (also referred to as **Minami,** or South Osaka), with a cluster of stations serving subways, JR trains, and Kintetsu and Nankai lines, all of which are connected to one another via underground passageways. This is the heart of the city, bustling with the spirit of old Osaka, where you'll find more hotels, Osaka's liveliest eating and entertainment district centered on a narrow street called **Dotombori** (also written Dotonbori), the **National Bunraku Theatre,** and major shopping areas such as the enclosed pedestrian street **Shinsaibashi-Suji,** underground arcades, and **America-Mura** (check out the unique street lamps!) with imported goods from America. Farther south is **Dogayasuji,** famous for cooking supplies; and **Den Den Town,** Osaka's electronics and *anime* district. Connecting Kita-ku with Namba is Osaka's main street, **Midosuji Dori,** a wide boulevard lined with gingko trees and international name-brand shops.

AROUND TENNOJI/ABENO   At the south end of the JR Loop Line is **Tennoji-ku,** which was once a thriving temple town with **Shitennoji Temple** at its center. In addition to a park with a zoo, it boasts **Spa World,** one of Japan's biggest and most luxurious public bathhouses. In neighboring **Abeno-ku** is **Abeno Harukas,** which opened in 2013 as Japan's tallest building, with an observatory, Japan's largest department store, a luxury hotel, shops, and restaurants.

OSAKA BAY & PORT   West of the city, Osaka's well-developed waterfront offers a quick getaway for Osakans wishing to escape urban life. In addition to its domestic and international ferry terminals, Osaka Bay is where you will find **Universal Studios Japan,** one of Japan's major draws, and the excellent **Osaka Aquarium.**

Getting Around

Despite its size, I find Osaka easy to navigate due to lots of English-language signs and information. The exception is Osaka Station, used for JR trains, and its adjoining Umeda Station, used by subway lines and private railway lines Hankyu and Hanshin. Underground passages and shopping arcades complicate navigation; there's no escaping—you will get lost.

When exploring by foot, it helps to know that most roads running east and west end in *"dori"* (street), while roads running north and south end in *"suji,"* meaning "avenue."

BY SUBWAY & PRIVATE RAILWAY   The **Osaka Municipal Transportation Bureau** (www.kotsu.city.osaka.lg.jp; ✆ **06/6582-1400**) operates Osaka's user-friendly subway network. All lines are color-coded and identified with a letter ("M" for the Midosuji line); stations are assigned a number in addition to English signage (M20 for Namba Station's Midosuji's stop); and in-car announcements are in English. Lines run from about 5am to midnight. Of the eight lines, the red **Midosuji Line** is the most important one for visitors; it passes through Shin-Osaka Station and on to Umeda (the subway station next to Osaka Station), Shinsaibashi, Namba, and Tennoji. Fares begin at ¥180 and increase according to the distance traveled. The prepaid **Rainbow Card,** which you can purchase in values of ¥500 to ¥3,000, prevents having to buy an individual ticket each time. Although there are also city buses, I find it more convenient to travel by subway.

Transportation Passes   If you think you'll be traveling a lot by subway on a given day, consider purchasing a **1-Day Enjoy Eco Card** for ¥800 (¥600 weekends and holidays), which allows unlimited rides on subways and buses all day and offers slight discounts to several attractions. There's also the **Osaka Amazing Pass,** which costs ¥2,300 for 1 day and allows unlimited rides on subways, city buses, and private railways in Osaka plus free entrance to 20-some attractions, including Osaka Castle, Shitennoji Temple, Museum of Oriental Ceramics, and Osaka International Peace Center. A 2-day Osaka Amazing Pass costs ¥3,000 (you need to show your passport for this one) but doesn't include private railways. Note that JR trains are not included in any of these passes, and you'd have to be fairly manic to get your money's worth. For information on the Amazing Pass, go to www.osaka-info.jp/osp/en.

For trips outside Osaka, the **Kansai Thru Pass** (**Surutto Kansai;** www. surutto.com) allows foreigners (you must show your passport) to ride subways, private railways (no JR trains), and buses throughout Kansai, including Osaka, Kyoto, Kobe, Nara, Himeji, and Mount Koya, for 2 or 3 days plus slight discounts to tourist sights. There are also JR West Passes that allow travel on JR trains that cover a wider area. For more information on regional passes, see p. 328 in chapter 12.

BY JR TRAIN   A Japan Railways train called the **JR Loop Line** passes through Osaka Station and makes a loop around the central part of the city (similar to the Yamanote Line in Tokyo); take it to visit Osaka Castle. Fares begin at ¥120, but you can ride free with a valid Japan Rail Pass. For trips outside Osaka, JR-West offers several passes, with a **1-day Kansai Area Pass** giving unlimited rides to and around Osaka, Kyoto, Himeji, and Kobe for ¥2,060.

[FastFACTS] OSAKA

ATMS/Banks   In addition to banks, **Travelex** counters exchange money in Grand Front Osaka near Osaka Station (📞 **06/6359-1990;** daily 11am–7:30pm) and Namba Walk downtown (📞 **06/6214-5580;** daily 10am–9pm). The Central Post Office (see below) offers ATM service for inter-national credit cards from 12:05am to 11:55pm

Monday to Saturday and from 12:05am to 9 Sunday.

Internet & Wi-Fi Access   Osaka Free Wi-Fi offers 30 minutes of free Wi-Fi connection at subway stations, Visitors Information Centers, and sightseeing facilities. If you need to use a computer, in Namba there's a **Gran Cyber Cafe** at 1–7–19 Dotombori

(📞 **06/6484-2660**), open 24 hours and charging ¥100 for 30 minutes.

Mail   The Central Post Office (Osaka Chuo Yubin-kyoku), is in the Osaka Eki-mae No. 1 Building, 1–3–1 Umeda, Kita-ku (📞 **06/6347-8112**), a 5-minute walk south of Osaka Station. It's open for mail daily 9am to 7pm.

A NOTE ON directions

For all the attractions, accommodations, and restaurants listed below, I've included the nearest subway or JR station followed by the walking time (in parentheses) to the establishment once you reach the indicated station.

WHERE TO STAY

Many hotels are clustered around Osaka Station, but Namba in the city's downtown offers more interesting surroundings. The Tennoji/Abeno area is also emerging as a vibrant place to stay. The prices below reflect the seasons and can vary markedly; note too, that many hotels charge more on Saturday and nights before a holiday.

Around Osaka & Shin-Osaka Stations

MODERATE

Hotel Granvia Osaka ★★ You can't get any closer to Osaka Station than this hotel, with discounts for holders of Japan Rail Passes making it even more attractive for train travelers. But there are prices to pay: a ground-floor lobby that's hard to find in the maze that is Osaka Station, and elevators that are crowded with hungry masses on their way to the hotel's many 19th-floor restaurants. Rooms, recently redone in shades of beige and brown and offering many choices, are on floors 21 to 27, with the top floor newly added to accommodate Granvia Floor club rooms, where large windows offer the best views. I also like the Superior doubles for their massage chair and layout, with the bed either in a dark corner or facing window views. Families might like one of the 20 huge "Corner Family" rooms (although they're a steep ¥47,520 or more) with their two sinks and toilet separate from the bathroom. Those in search of R & R might find relaxation in the 24th-floor Freja rooms, designed with unique Scandinavian furnishings and aromatherapy amenities. Note, however, that standard rooms are tiny, face an inner courtyard, and are dark.

3-1-1 Umeda, Kita-ku. www.granvia-osaka.jp. ☏ **06/6344-1235.** 716 units. ¥13,500–¥24,948 single; ¥16,625–¥53,460 double. Granvia Floor ¥27,324–¥65,340 single or double. Discounts available for holders of Japan Rail Pass. Station: Osaka or Umeda (1 min.; above the station). **Amenities:** 7 restaurants; bar; 2 lounges; executive-level rooms; room service; free Wi-Fi.

INEXPENSIVE

There are 18 **Toyoko Inn** hotels in Osaka, including those near Osaka and Shin-Osaka stations and in Namba and Tennoji. See www.toyoko-inn.com.

Family Inn Fifty's Osaka ★ This motel-like facility, south of Nakanoshima island, offers low prices and no-nonsense small but clean rooms, identically outfitted with double bed, sofa bed, retro photo in keeping with its 1950s theme, wall-mounted TV, and tiled bathroom (but no closet). Check-in is automated, but humans behind the front desk can help with the process. You'll pay extra for rooms reserved by phone (rates below are those made online), as well as on weekends and holidays. The catch is that it's a bit of a chore to reach from Osaka Station (because it's across a footbridge south of the Rihga Royal Hotel's back parking lot, some travelers have been known to use the luxury hotel's shuttle bus). Once you're settled in, you'll find its location fine.

2–6-18 Edobori, Nishi-ku. www.fiftys.com. ☏ **06/6225-2636.** 85 units. ¥5,250–¥9,700 single; ¥7,800–¥10,800 double; ¥9,450 triple. Rates include continental breakfast. Station: Nakanoshima (exit 2, 5 min.); walk around the conference center Grand Cube, cross Tosabori-bashi bridge and busy Tosabori Dori, and then take the next left. **Amenities:** Free Wi-Fi.

2nd Inn Umeda ★ This bare-bones business hotel, next to the Ritz-Carlton, is convenient to the station and offers a coin-operated laundry room (visible from the lobby) and sparse rooms that meet all basic needs, with showers instead of tubs. Note, however, that rooms do not have telephones and Internet connection is via LAN cable. Determined couples can save money by sharing a semi-double-size bed for ¥7,200. Some rooms face a highway; those facing south are probably best.

2–5-16 Umeda, Kita-ku. ☏ **06/6346-1177.** 128 units. ¥5,800–¥6,200 single; ¥8,400–¥9,000 double. Station: Osaka (7 min.) or Nishi-Umeda (exit 10, 4 min.). **Amenities:** Free Internet.

Namba & Shinsaibashi

EXPENSIVE

Hotel Nikko Osaka ★★ A white monolith soaring 32 stories above ground, the Nikko has a great location atop a subway station right on Osaka's most fashionable boulevard, Midosuji Dori, making its lobby lounge a popular spot for locals meeting friends. In fact, location is mainly what you're paying for here: There is no health club, and guests are overwhelmingly business travelers. Rooms, on the 10th to 30th floors, have a pleasing, clean modern design, especially superior and premium rooms with their contemporary flair, the latter also with DVD players. However, because there are no high buildings to obstruct views, city panoramas are a plus from most floors; the best deal is an Upper View Standard room (ask for one on the 30th floor). In short, this is a good choice if you want to be in the midst of Osaka's shopping and nightlife.

1–3-3 Nishi-Shinsaibashi, Chuo-ku. www.hno.co.jp. ☏ **06/6244-1111.** 635 units. ¥15,000–¥30,000 single; ¥16,500–¥54,000 double; Nikko Deluxe executive floors from ¥53,000 double. Station: Shinsaibashi (exit 8 underneath the hotel, 1 min.). **Amenities:** 6 restaurants; 2 bars; 2 lounges; executive-level rooms; access to 2 health clubs (fee: ¥1,080); room service; free Wi-Fi.

MODERATE

Hotel Vista Grande Osaka ★★★ This hotel has a great location for night owls, just a few minutes' walk from Dotombori, Osaka's main nightlife district. It has other notable features, too, including the fact that it's independent (not part of a chain), doesn't target tour groups, and offers mostly double rooms for one or two persons in addition to twins. Sleek and contemporary, rooms sport a somber brown or bright red color scheme and are spacious for their price, with a glass wall partitioning the bathroom from sleeping quarters. For convenience, there's a 7-Eleven off the lobby.

5–15 Soemon-cho, Chuo-ku. www.vistagrande.jp. ℂ **06/6212-7999.** 314 units. ¥11,000–¥15,000 single; ¥15,000–¥20,000 double. Station: Nipponbashi (exit 2, 5 min.); cross Dotombori canal and turn left. Or Namba (exit 14, 10 min.); cross Dotombori Canal and turn right. **Amenities:** Restaurant; free Wi-Fi.

Around Tennoji/Abeno

EXPENSIVE

Osaka Marriott Miyako Hotel ★★★   Located in Japan's tallest building, this hotel is so strikingly different from any other I've seen in Japan, I thought I'd landed at the wrong place when I walked into the 19th-floor lobby soon after its 2014 opening. With a soaring 7m-high (23-ft.) ceiling and floor-to-ceiling windows on three sides revealing sweeping views of Osaka, and with the front desk tucked discretely in a far corner, it seems more like a continuum of the 58th-floor Harukas 300 observatory (p. 278) than a hotel. Yet it's also a world apart, with a chic lounge and popular buffet restaurant off to one side of the lobby, far from the madding crowds. For even more eye-popping panoramas, there's Restaurant ZK on the 57th floor, serving *teppan-yaki* and a variety of food. Rooms, on the 38th to 55th floors, offer many possibilities, though all have a wall of glass providing outstanding views of the city and some even of the harbor. Deluxe rooms have views even from the bathroom, but probably best are corner kings, offering views in two directions and from windowside tubs. Clearly, vast views are the emphasis here, though the hotel's exuberantly contemporary decor ensures guests stay rooted also to earth.

1–1–32 Abeno-suji, Abeno-ku. www.miyakohotels.ne.jp. ℂ **06/6628-6111.** 360 units. ¥40,425–¥65,000 single or double. Club room from ¥48,000. Station: Tennoji or Osaka Abenobashi (1 min.). **Amenities:** 2 restaurants; bar; lounge; concierge; gym; room service; free Wi-Fi.

INEXPENSIVE

Tabinoyado Hokousou (旅‡の宿葆晃荘) ★★★   This family-owned ryokan (now in its fourth generation of innkeepers) is a gem. The 120-some-year-old traditional Japanese home has many charming features, including a breakfast room with a soaring ceiling and heavy wooden beams; even the big bouquet of fake flowers by the front door has class. Rooms, with both Japanese- and Western-style available, vary in style and size, with the best, 10-tatami-mat room sleeping up to five people and overlooking a small garden. It has a great location, within walking distance of Shitennoji Temple and Spa World and with direct access to Kansai airport, Osaka and Shin-Osaka Stations, Osaka Castle, and Nara. Finally, the family that's been running the inn for 60 years is warm and welcoming. No credit cards are accepted.

14–16 Horikoshi-cho, Tennoji-ku. www.hokousou.com. ℂ **06/6771-7242.** 14 units (none with private bathroom). ¥5,250–¥6,300 single; ¥8,900–¥12,600 double. Station: Tennoji (north exit, 1 min.). Walk north from Tennoji JR Station on Tanimachi-suji Street and after passing FamilyMart, turn right at the tiny side street (there's a sign with the inn's phone number here); it's immediately on the right, down a small pathway (look for the big stone lantern at the front door).

WHERE TO EAT

There's a saying among Japanese that whereas a Kyotoite will spend his last yen on a fine kimono, an Osakan will spend it on food, not surprising given Osaka's historic role as a distribution center for rice and produce, earning it the nickname of the "nation's kitchen." You don't have to spend a lot of money, however, to enjoy good food. Local specialties include *Oshi-zushi* (pressed square-shaped sushi), *udon* noodles with white soy sauce, *omurice* (a rice omelet topped with ketchup), and *takoyaki* (wheat-flour dumplings with octopus).

Osaka is probably best known, however, for *okonomiyaki,* which literally means "as you like it." Its origins date from about 1700, when a type of thin flour pancake cooked on a hot plate and filled with miso paste was served during Buddhist ceremonies. It wasn't until the 20th century that it became popular, primarily during food shortages, and gradually, other ingredients such as pork, egg, and cabbage were added. Today, Osaka is riddled with inexpensive *okonomiyaki* restaurants—more than 4,000 of them.

Around Osaka Station
INEXPENSIVE

In addition to the choices here, there are a multitude of possibilities in and around Osaka Station, including the 8th floor of Yodobashi-Umeda on the station's north side, where more than 30 restaurants offer pizza, pasta, sushi, dim sum, *udon,* ramen, *shabu-shabu, omurice, tonkatsu,* and more.

Aux Bacchanales ★★ FRENCH   This casual brasserie offers sidewalk seating and specials written in French and Japanese on a blackboard. My set lunch of coq au vin, served with crusty French bread to sop up the very good sauce, mashed potatoes, green beans, and salad, was enough to qualify as my main meal of the day, but equally satisfying selections include quiche, fish of the day, and croque monsieur. Dinner is more substantial, with choices ranging from terrine de canard to roast lamb. Posters of Francois Truffaut French and radio playing in the bathrooms are a nice touch.

Grand Front Osaka (south building), Ofukacho. ⓒ **06/6359-2722.** Main dishes ¥650–¥2,580; set lunches ¥1,550–¥2,380; set dinner ¥2,980. Daily 9am–11pm. Station: JR Osaka or Umeda (1 min.). Just north of JR Station, on the ground floor of the south building, facing the north building.

Okonomiyaki Kiji (お好み焼きじ) ★ OKONOMIYAKI   Takimikoji Village is a fun place for a meal. It's a re-created Showa-Era 1920s and 1930s Japanese village, filled with period relics ranging from a barbershop and a post office to a police box and a miniature shrine, complete with music of the era. There are also about a dozen small restaurants here, including those serving ramen, *soba, shabu-shabu,* tempura, and this one, offering what some Osakans swear is the best *okonomiyaki* in town. Customer photos and *meishi* (business cards) that paper the walls and ceiling are testimony of customer appreciation. No credit cards are accepted.

Umeda Sky Building basement, 1–1–90 Oyodo-naka. www.takimikoji.jp/shop/kiji. ⓒ **06/ 6440-5970.** *Okonomiyaki* ¥600–¥950. Fri–Wed 11:30am–9:30pm. Station: JR Osaka or Umeda (Central North exit of JR Osaka Station, 8 min.). Keep left of Grand Front Osaka (south building) to the first intersection, turn left, and take the underpass.

Namba

Dotombori (or Dotonbori), a narrow pedestrian lane just off Midosuji Dori that flanks the south bank of the Dotombori River Walk, is the center of Osaka's most famous nightlife district; you'll find lots of restaurants and bars in this area.

EXPENSIVE

Kani Doraku (かに道楽) ★★ CRAB   Specializing in *kani* (crab), this restaurant is difficult to miss: It has a huge model crab on its facade, waving its legs and claws. Part of a chain originating in Osaka 55 years ago, this is the main shop of dozens of branches in Japan, including two others just down the street. There's an English-language menu listing crab sukiyaki and other dishes, but it's easiest to simply order a set meal. My ¥2,160 lunch came with boiled crab with sweet vinegar, steamed egg custard with crab, crab croquette, crab sushi, and clear soup. There are several floors for dining, all with kimono-clad waitresses and some with tables offering a view of the canal. Note that this place is very popular. But instead of forcing customers to wait in line, they're assigned a specific dining time when they can come back. Otherwise, avoid peak times if you can (lunch is served until 4pm).

1–6–18 Dotonbori. www.douraku.co.jp. ⓒ **06/6211-8975.** Set lunches ¥2,160–¥4,320; set dinners ¥4,968–¥8,748. Daily 11am–10pm (last order). Station: Namba (exit 14, 2 min.). On Dotombori beside the Ebisu-bashi Bridge.

MODERATE

Yume-Hachi ★★ VARIED JAPANESE   I was sad to see the Cuidaore restaurant, a Dotonbori landmark for more than 50 years, close its doors, but the restaurant's famous clown model, beating a drum and wiggling its eyebrows, still stands at the building's entrance, making it easy to find this hip restaurant/bar. What I like most is the venue's open-air patio (although its view of the statue above Don Quijote is jarring), but it also offers all-you-can-eat-in-2-hours dining options for big appetites: From 5 to 8:30pm, it offers a 2-hour buffet for ¥2,980, including drinks like wine and beer (¥3,480 if you prefer whiskey and other drinks); from 8:30pm to 6am, set meals allow you to order as much as you want from a food and drink menu within 2 hours. Or, simply order a drink or snack (like pasta, salad, pizza, curry rice, desserts), most priced at ¥330, plus a ¥346 table charge for people ordering a la carte.

Cuidaore Building, 5th floor, 1–7–21 Dotonbori. ⓒ **06/6211-0033.** Main dishes ¥330; dinner buffets ¥2,980–¥3,480; all-you-can-eat set courses ¥3,000–¥3,500. Open daily 24 hrs. Station: Namba (exit 14, 3 min.). On Dotombori.

INEXPENSIVE

Bar Tachibana (たちばな) ★★ TOFU/VARIED JAPANESE   Whether you're sightseeing in Dotombori or here for *kabuki*, this restaurant, in a lovely, typical Japanese setting in the basement of the Shochikuza Theater, is a good pick. A microbrewery that makes its own Doutonbori brand beer on site (¥450 for a glass of light or dark beer; you can see the tanks from the dining hall), Tachibana also specializes in tofu (only in Japan!), with tofu included in most of the set meals. In winter it also offers *fugu* (blowfish). There's no English-language menu, but a changing daily lunch and the *tofu teishoku* (¥2,600) are affordable and delicious. You can see famous *kabuki* actors dining here, but how could you recognize them without their makeup?

Osaka Shochikuza Theater, 2nd basement, 1–9–19 Dotonbori. ✆ **06/6212-6074.** Main dishes ¥680–¥1,700; set lunches ¥850–¥2,700; set dinners ¥2,600–¥5,800. Daily 11:30am–10pm (last order). Station: Namba (exit 14, 2 min.). On Dotombori near the bridge; look for its improbable side entrance to the left and then take 2 escalators to the second basement.

Fugetsu (風月) ★ OKONOMIYAKI   Big Step is the biggest shopping complex in America-Mura, young Osakans' favorite place to shop for American clothing. As such, there are several restaurants here that appeal to young diners, including Mexican and Korean eateries and this branch of a famous *okonomiyaki* chain, with a hip, modern interior. The English-language menu gives various options, from *yakisoba* to *okonomiyaki* with pork and egg or even pork and kimchee, prepared at your table by staff. There are more than 20 Fugetsu restaurants in Osaka; check the website for locations.

Big Step, 3rd floor, 1–6–14 Nishi-Shinsaibashi. www.ideaosaka.co.jp/web/english. ✆ **06/6258-5189.** *Okonomiyaki* and *yakisoba* ¥760–¥1,310. Daily 11am–10:30pm. Station: Shinsaibashi (2 min.).

Honfukuzushi (本福寿司) ★★★ SUSHI   More than just a place to dine, this sushi shop, in operation since 1829, is part of the Osaka experience. Back in the old days, sushi shops were strictly takeout operations, with customers bringing in their own dishes, placing their orders, and then returning home to wait for *geta*-clad deliverers. While there's still a takeout counter, you can also eat your sushi here; best are the counter seats, where you can watch sushi being pressed in wooden molds, Osaka style. There's an English-language menu with photos on an iPad, but if you want to try *oshi-zushi* (Osakan sushi), order the *hakozushi,* which comes with six pieces for ¥1,050. Tokyo-style *nigiri* and *maki*-sushi are also available.

1–4–19 Nishi-Shinsaibashi-suji. ✆ **06/6271-3344.** Sushi sets ¥1,080–¥3,500; set lunches ¥800–¥1,300. Daily 11am–8pm (last order). Station: Shinsaibashi (2 min.). Inside the Shinsaibashi covered shopping arcade, behind the main (oldest) Daimaru department store; look for the old-fashioned facade and takeout counter.

EXPLORING OSAKA

Near Osaka Station

Museum of Oriental Ceramics (Toyotoji Bijutsukan) ★★★
MUSEUM   About a 15-minute walk south of Osaka Station, on Nakanoshima Island between the Dojima and Tosabori rivers, this is my favorite museum in

Osaka. Indeed, its 6,000-piece collection of Chinese, Korean, and Japanese ceramics—of which 400 are on display at any one time on a rotating basis—ranks as one of the finest in the world. Built specifically for the collection and featuring shock-absorbent platforms to protect its fragile wares, the museum does a superb job showcasing the exquisite pieces as the masterpieces they truly are, in darkened rooms that utilize natural light and computerized natural-light simulation. Korean celadon, Chinese ceramics from the Eastern Han, Song and Ming dynasties, Chinese snuff bottles, Aritaware from the Edo Period, Imari ware that once graced European palaces, and works by Hamada Shoji are just some of the items that might be on display. Even if you've never given ceramics more than a passing glance, you're likely to come away with a heightened sense of appreciation. You'll want to spend up to an hour here.

1-1-26 Nakanoshima. www.moco.or.jp. © **06/6223-0055.** Admission ¥500–¥600 adults, ¥300–¥400 high-school and university students, free for children. Tues–Sun 9:30am–5pm. Closed during exhibition changes. Station: Naniwabashi on the Keihan Nakanoshima Line (exit 1, 1 min.) or Yodoyabashi (exit 1, 5 min.).

Around Osaka Castle

Osaka Castle (Osaka-jo) ★★★ CASTLE   First built in the 1580s on the order of Toyotomi Hideyoshi, Osaka Castle was the largest castle in Japan, a magnificent structure used by Toyotomi as a military stronghold from which to wage war against rebellious feudal lords in far-flung provinces. By the time he died in 1598, Toyotomi had accomplished what no man had done before: crushed his enemies and unified all of Japan under his command. After Toyotomi's death, Tokugawa Ieyasu seized power and established his shogunate government in Edo. But Toyotomi's heirs had ideas of their own: Considering Osaka Castle impregnable, they plotted to overthrow Tokugawa. In 1615, Tokugawa sent 155,000 soldiers to Osaka where they not only annihilated the 55,000 Toyotomi insurrectionists but also destroyed Osaka Castle. The Tokugawas rebuilt the castle in 1629, but the main tower was destroyed by lightning 36 years later, and the rest burned in 1868 as the shogunate made their last stand against imperial forces in what later became known as the Meiji Restoration.

The present Osaka Castle, surrounded by an expansive park famous for its cherry trees and stone-walled moats, dates from 1931 and was extensively renovated in 1997. Built of ferroconcrete, it's not as massive as the original but is still one of Japan's most famous castles and is impressive with its massive stone walls, black and gold-leaf trim, and copper roof. Its eight-story *donjon* (keep) rises 39m (130 ft.), with a top-floor observatory offering bird's-eye views of the city. The rest of the *donjon* houses a high-tech museum that uses videos, holograms, models, replicas, and artifacts to describe the life and times of Toyotomi Hideyoshi and history of the castle. Be sure to pick up the free audio guide, as some explanations are in Japanese only, but there's plenty to see as well, including a magnificent folding screen with meticulously painted scenes of the intense fighting that took place between Toyotomi and Tokugawa forces, samurai armor and gear, a full-scale reproduction of

Toyotomi's Gold Tea Room, and a model of Osaka Castle during the Toyotomi Era. For ¥300 you can dress up in period clothing, including some awe-inspiring samurai helmets. Plan on 45 minutes here.

1–1 Osakajo, Chuo-ku. www.osakacastle.net. ℂ **06/6941-3044.** Admission ¥600 adults, free for children 15 and under. Daily 9am–5pm. Station: Osakajo-Koen on the JR Loop Line or Morinomiya (15 min.); or Temmabashi or Osaka Business Park (10 min.).

Osaka International Peace Center (Peace Osaka) ★★ MUSEUM
On the southern edge of Osaka Castle Park under a canopy of trees, this museum strives for global peace by educating present and future generations about the horrors of war, related by those who survived it. Unlike other museums in Japan dedicated to peace—including those in Hiroshima and Nagasaki—this one does not shy away from Japan's role in the Asian conflict, including its war campaign in China, the abduction of Koreans to work in dangerous areas, and massacres committed by Japanese in Singapore, Malaysia, and elsewhere. But its main focus is on wartime death and destruction, with personal testimonies of air raid survivors (15,000 people died during World War II air raids on Osaka), displays centering on suicide attacks by *kamikaze* pilots at the end of the war, graphic photographs of atomic destruction in Hiroshima and Nagasaki, and more. You'll probably spend 30 sobering minutes here.

2–1 Osakajo, Chuo-ku. www.peace-osaka.or.jp. ℂ **06/6947-7208.** Admission ¥250 adults, ¥150 high-school students, free for children and seniors. Tues–Sun 9:30am–5pm. Closed on days following national holidays and last day of each month. Station: Morinomiya (3 min.) or Osakajo-Koen (8 min.).

Around Tennoji/Abeno

Harukas 300 ★ OBSERVATION DECK   Sunlight bathes this 300-m.-high (990 ft.) glass-walled observatory in Japan's tallest building (if it's raining or foggy, spend your time elsewhere). Not as memorable as Tokyo SkyTree (p. 130) but also not as expensive, it's a good place to get some perspective on sprawling Osaka. If you squint you may be able to pick out Osaka Castle or the bay, and on clear days you can see even farther. Because there isn't much to do here besides gawk at the 360-degree views, stop for a snack at the observatory's cafe. There's also a free public outdoor terrace down on the building's 16th floor, with views north toward to the city, but it doesn't compare to those from the observatory. Other diversions in Abeno Harukas include restaurants, shops, and Japan's largest department store.

Abeno Harukas (ticket counter on 2nd floor), 1–1–43 Abeno-suji. ℂ **06/6621-0300.** Admission ¥1,500 adults, ¥1,200 children 12–17, ¥700 children 6–11, ¥500 children 4–5. Daily 10am–10pm. Tennoji or Osaka Abenobashi (1 min.).

Shitennoji Temple ★ TEMPLE   Founded over 1,400 years ago as the first—and therefore oldest—officially established temple in Japan, Shitennoji Temple is the spiritual heart of Osaka. It was constructed in 593 by Prince Shotoku, who is credited with introducing Buddhism to Japan and remains a revered, popular figure even today. However, like most wooden structures in Japan, the temple's buildings have been destroyed repeatedly through the centuries by fire and war, including the 1615 Tokugawa raid on Osaka Castle and World War II. And through the centuries, the buildings have been faithfully reconstructed exactly as they were in the 6th century, with the Central Precinct *(Garan)* consisting of the Inner Gate, the five-story Buddhist Pagoda, the Main Hall with its statue of Prince Shotoku as the Buddha of Infinite Mercy, and the Lecture Hall all on a north-south axis. Be sure, too, to wander the temple's Gokuraku-Jodo Teien, a restored Japanese landscape garden first laid out during the Tokugawa regime. Buddhists believe that if you follow the path between the two streams representing greed and anger, you will symbolically reach Paradise, a place of sublime beauty, tranquility, and peace. A flea market is held on the temple's grounds on the 21st and 22nd of each month

1–11–18 Shitennoji, Tennoji-ku. © **06/6771-0066.** Admission to either Garan or garden, ¥300 adults, ¥200 students and children. Daily 8:30am–4:30pm Apr–Sept, 8:30–4pm Oct–Mar. Station: Shitennoji-mae Yuhigaoka (exit 4, 5 min.); or JR Tennoji (north exit, 10 min.).

Spa World ★★ SPA   This is one of the most luxurious and ambitious bathhouses I've seen. Accommodating up to 5,000 people, it draws upon hot springs 890m (2,970 ft.) below the earth's surface. On its roof, in a large hangarlike room, is a covered swimming complex that includes a pool, various water slides (¥300 extra for some rides), a kids' pool with aquatic activities, and a sunning terrace with Jacuzzi. You wear your swimming suits here (rental suits available). For a more grown-up experience, there's an *onsen* divided into themed, geographical bathing zones, which are rotated between the sexes (no suits allowed) and include luxurious locker rooms. At the Asian Zone, for example, Middle Eastern music and tiled mosaics set the tone for the Turkish bath, while the Japan zone features outdoor baths. There's also a gym (included in admission price), plus treatment rooms that cost extra. If you're timid about visiting a public bath, this one will convert you. But sorry, people with tattoos—associated with the Japanese mafia—aren't allowed.

3–2–24 Ebisu-higashi, Naniwa-ku. www.spaworld.co.jp/english. © **06/6631-0001.** Admission weekdays: ¥2,400 adults, ¥1,300 children for 3 hr.; ¥2,700 adults, ¥1,500 children for all day. Weekends: ¥2,700 adults, ¥1,500 children for 3 hr.; ¥3,000 adults, ¥1,700 children for all day. Swimming zone Mon–Fri 10am–7pm, Sat–Sun 10am–10pm; *onsen* daily 10am–8:45am the next morning. Station: Shin-Imamiya or Dobutsuenmae (2 min.).

Osaka Bay Area

Osaka Aquarium (Kaiyukan) ★★★ AQUARIUM   Of Japan's many aquariums, this one is among the best. It's constructed around the theme "Ring of Fire," which refers to the volcanic perimeter encircling the Pacific Ocean. Visits begin through a tunnel filled with reef fish and small sharks, followed by an escalator ride to the eighth floor. From there you'll pass through 15 different habitats ranging from arctic to tropical as you follow a spiraling corridor back to the ground floor, starting with the daylight world—a Japanese forest—above the ocean's surface and proceeding past the Aleutian Islands, Monterey Bay, South American rainforests, Antarctica, the Great Barrier Reef, and other ecosystems as you travel to the depths of the ocean floor.

The walls of the aquarium tank are constructed of huge acrylic glass sheets, making you feel as if you're immersed in the ocean; piped-in classical music transforms swimming fish into performances of aquatic choreography. You'll see 30,000 specimens representing 580 species; stars of the show include whale sharks (the largest fish in captivity), Antarctic penguins, the odd-looking ocean sunfish (with the circumference of a truck tire but as flat as a pancake), and the Japan giant spider crab with its incredible 3m (9¾-ft.) span. English-spoken audio/visual guides are ¥500 extra. Allow about 1½ hours to tour the aquarium, avoiding weekends.

1–1–10 Kaigan-dori, Minato-ku. www.kaiyukan.com. © **06/6576-5501.** Admission ¥2,300 adults, ¥2,000 seniors, ¥1,200 children 7–15, ¥600 children 4–6. Daily 10am–8pm. Closed 4 days a year in winter for maintenance. Station: Osakako (5 min.).

Universal Studios Japan ★★★ THEME PARK   Following the tradition of Universal's Hollywood and Orlando theme parks, this park takes guests on a fantasy trip through the world of American blockbuster movies, with thrill rides, live entertainment, shows, back-lot streets, restaurants, shops, and other attractions based on actual movies. Board a boat for a harrowing encounter with a great white straight out of JAWS®, escape a T-Rex as you roller-coaster your way through Jurassic Park—The Ride®, dream your way through the mega-coaster Hollywood Dream—The Ride, fly and leap at high speed among skyscrapers in The Amazing Adventures of SpiderMan—The Ride 4K3D, and see, feel, and smell Shrek's 4D Adventure™ (4-D in movie lingo means there are smells and other sensations). Universal Wonderland features rides and attractions (think Snoopy, Sesame Street, and Hello Kitty) for the wee ones. The newest attraction is The Wizarding World of Harry Potter™, which recreates Hogsmeade village. Inside Hogwarts castle is the ride, Harry Potter and the Forbidden Journey, which is so convincing I felt like I was flying with Harry and participating in a Quidditch game, making it hands down the best ride I've ever experienced (height restrictions apply). Plan for an entire day here, but note that it is immensely popular: Avoid weekends, arrive early, and splurge on one of three Universal Express Passes, which allow priority entry into designated rides. Alternatively, choose the "single" line for lone riders, which you may get you inside attractions up to three times quicker than regular lines.

2–1–33 Sakurajima, Konohana. www.usj.co.jp/e. © **06/6465-4005.** Studio Pass to all attractions ¥7,200 adults, ¥6,470 seniors, ¥4,980 children 4–11. Hours vary according to the season; generally daily 10am–6pm in winter, 9am–9pm in summer. Station: JR Universal City (5 min.).

SHOPPING

Osaka is famous in Japan for shopping, in no small part because of the discerning nature of the Osakans themselves. Osaka, after all, developed as a commercial town of merchants—and who knows merchandise better than the merchants themselves?

Osaka ranks as one of the world's leading cities in underground shopping arcades. Enter the vast underground arcades in Umeda (where the JR, Hanshin, subway, and Hankyu train lines intersect), with names like **Whity Umeda** and **Diamor Osaka,** and you may never emerge in this lifetime. Downtown, **Crysta Nagahori** is one of the prettiest underground malls in Japan, with a glass atrium ceiling, flowing streams of water, and 100 shops.

There are plenty of aboveground options as well. **Midosuji Dori,** a wide boulevard lined with gingko trees running north and south in the heart of the city, is Osaka's calling card for name-brand international boutiques, but here, too, is the lovely old **Daimaru** department store, with newer annexes on both sides. Just to the east is **Shinsaibashi-suji,** a covered promenade with many long-established shops, some dating back to the Edo Period, others new like the **Daiso** ¥100 shop. On the other side of Midosuji Dori is **America-Mura,** a popular spot for young Japanese shopping for American second-hand clothing and other fashions at inflated prices. Teens also flock to **Marui 0101,** a seven-story department store on the corner of Shinsaibashi-suji and Nankai Dori, and to **HEP FIVE,** a huge shopping complex near Umeda Station with a Joypolis amusement arcade and a Ferris wheel on top. At JR Osaka Station are the 10-story **Isetan Mitsukoshi** and flagship **Hankyu** department stores, plus **Yodobashi Camera** with computers, bikes, luggage, and more in addition to cameras. But the granddaddy department store of them all is **Kintetsu Abeno Harukas** near Tennoji Station, boasting more floor space than any other department store in Japan.

One of the most fun places to shop—or simply browse—is at one of many famous shopping areas specializing in specific goods. In the heart of the city, just east of Sakaisuji Avenue near Nipponbashi Station, is **Kuromon Ichiba,** a covered street where professional chefs shop for seafood, fruit, vegetables, pickles, and other edibles. To the south, a few blocks east of Nankai Namba Station, is **Sennichimae Doguya-suji,** a covered shopping lane with about 45 open-fronted shops selling pots, pans, dishes, chopsticks, kitchen knives, aprons, plastic food, and all the other implements you'd ever need to prepare and serve Japanese food, at very inexpensive prices.

Just south of that is Nipponbashi's **Den Den Town,** stretching along Sakaisuji Avenue and its side streets (station: Ebisucho). This is Osaka's electronics shopping mecca (*Den* is short for "electric"), similar to Tokyo's Akihabara but not as big. Some 200 open-fronted shops deal in electrical and electronic equipment, from rice cookers and refrigerators to calculators, cameras, and computers. As in Tokyo, shops specializing in *manga, anime,* and costumes have also moved in, especially on Sakaisuji. Stop by the **Nipponbashi Information Center,** just north of Ebisucho Station on Sakaisuji

(*©* **06/6655-1717;** daily 11–7pm) for an English map of the area. Another fun neighborhood is **Matsuyamachi-suji** (station: Matsuyamachi), a shop-lined street offering toys, dolls, *anime* figures, and seasonal party decorations.

Of Osaka's many shopping complexes, worth noting is **Rinkan Premium Outlets** near KIX airport (station: Rinku Town), one of the largest outlet malls in Japan and offering some 150 shops and even shuttle bus service from the airport (fare: ¥200).

ENTERTAINMENT & NIGHTLIFE
Performing Arts

BUNRAKU The **National Bunraku Theater,** 1–12–10 Nipponbashi, Chuo-ku (www.ntj.jac.go.jp; *©* **06/6212-2531** for information, or 0570/07-9900 for reservations), was completed in 1984 as the only theater in Japan dedicated to Japanese traditional puppet theater. Productions are staged five times a year, with most productions running for about 3 weeks and held daily at 11am for Part 1 and at 4pm for Part 2; each part requires a separate ticket, with prices ranging from ¥2,400 to ¥6,000. English-language programs are available. The theater is located just east of Namba and Dotombori, a 1-minute walk from exit 7 of Nipponbashi Station.

LIVE MUSIC **Rug Time Osaka,** on Midosuji Dori on the fourth floor of the Across Building, 2–6–14 Shinsaibashi Suji, Minami-ku (*©* **06/6214-5306;** station: Namba or Shinsaibashi), is an intimate venue offering a wide range of live jazz bands in three nightly sets, with cover charge averaging ¥2,500 to ¥3,000. It's open Monday to Saturday 5pm to 2am, Sunday and holidays from 5pm to midnight.

THE BAR SCENE

Osaka's liveliest—and most economical—nightlife district radiates from a narrow pedestrian lane called **Dotombori** (or Dotonbori), which flanks the south bank of the Dotombori Canal. It's lined with restaurants and drinking establishments, making it good for a lively evening stroll even if you don't wish to stop anywhere.

Cinquecento ★★ This bar with a U-shaped counter is a cut above the rest with its welcoming staff and decent Western fare (including burgers, pasta, pizza, and fish and chips), not to mention that all food and drink are priced at only ¥500. Of note is the red Wall of Shame, where gold plaques identify those crazy enough to have consumed 100 shots in one sitting. Monday to Saturday 8am to 5am, Sunday and holidays 8pm to 3am. Matsumiya Building, 2–1–10 Higashi-Shinsaibashi. *©* **06/6213-6788.** Station: Nigahoribashi or Nipponbashi (5 min.). Just off Sakaisuji Ave., 1 block south of Suomachi/Europa Dori.

Dig Me Out Art & Diner ★★ In the heart of America-Mura, this casual, friendly bar offers occasional live music, changing art exhibitions, free Wi-Fi, and inexpensive snacks (and a good set lunch for ¥980), making it a good place to relax and hang out. It opens at 11:30am daily, closing at midnight

Sunday to Thursday and 1am Friday and Saturday. 2–9–32 Nishi-shinsaibashi. http://digmeoutcafe.com. ℭ **06/6213-1007.** Station: Yotsubashi (5 min.) or Shinsaibashi (7 min.). Below the Arrow Hotel.

Murphy's ★★   Of Osaka's several Irish pubs, this is probably the most popular (and my favorite), open 25 years and drawing a mixed crowd of both Japanese and foreigners. It offers a room for nonsmokers, live music Saturday nights, free Wi-Fi, and TVs broadcasting major sporting events. Fish and chips or shepherd's pie are reasonable and surprisingly good, but you can also make a meal of the Guinness or Kilkenny Ale. Sunday through Thursday 5pm to 1am; Friday to Saturday 5pm to about 4am. Lead Plaza Building, 6th floor, 1–6–31 Higashi Shinsaibashi. www.murphysosaka.com. ℭ **06/6282-0677.** Station: Nagahoribashi (1 min.) or Shinsaibashi (4 min.). Several blocks east of Shinsaibashi-suji covered arcade, 1 block north of Suomachi/Europa Dori, on the road running south along Daimaru just before the Minami Police Station. Keep your eye out for the sign, as it's easy to miss.

SIDE TRIPS FROM KYOTO & OSAKA

Using Kyoto or Osaka as a base, there are several destinations worth a day's trip or more. Foremost is **Nara,** which predates even Kyoto as the nation's capital and is full of gems that comprise the Historic Monuments of Ancient Nara World Heritage Site. Other World Heritage Sites are **Mount Koya,** a Buddhist mountain retreat offering temple accommodations, and Japan's most beautiful castle in **Himeji.** At the other end of the spectrum is the cosmopolitan city of **Kobe,** with a vibrant nightlife and neighborhoods that harken back to its beginnings as one of Japan's first international ports. For information on regional rail passes, see p. 238 in chapter 12.

10

NARA, ANCIENT CAPITAL ★★★

42km (26 miles) S of Kyoto; 48km (30 miles) east of Osaka

In early Japanese history, the nation's capital was moved to a new site each time a new emperor came to the throne. In 710, however, the first permanent Japanese capital was set up at **Nara.** Not that it turned out to be so permanent: After only 74 years, the capital was moved first to Nagaoka and shortly thereafter to Kyoto, where it remained for more than 1,000 years. What's important about those 74 years, however, is that they witnessed the birth of Japan's arts, crafts, and literature, as Nara imported everything from religion to art and architecture from China. Even the city was laid out in a rectangular grid pattern, modeled after Chinese concepts. It was during the Nara Period that Japan's first historical account, first mythological chronicle, and first poetry anthology (with 4,173 poems) were written. Buddhism flourished, and Nara grew as the political and cultural center of the land with temples, shrines, pagodas, and palaces.

Japanese flock to Nara because it gives them the feeling that they're communing with ancestors. Foreigners come here because Nara offers a glimpse of Japan's past. Remarkably enough, many of

Nara's historic buildings and temples remain intact, and long ago someone had enough foresight to enclose many of these historical structures in the quiet and peaceful confines of a large and spacious park, which has the added attraction of free-roaming deer. Farther afield is Horyuji, home to some of Japan's most historically significant religious architecture and the world's oldest buildings.

Although you can see Nara's highlights in a day's trip, I've included a couple of lodging recommendations in case you wish to also explore more leisurely. An extra incentive: From mid-July through September, many of Nara's most important historic buildings, like Todaiji Temple, are lit at night, making for a romantic nighttime stroll.

Essentials

GETTING THERE From Kyoto Station, Nara is easily reached on two lines: the JR Nara Line and the Kintetsu Limited Express. If you have a Japan Rail Pass, you'll probably want to take the commuter **JR Nara Rapid (Kaisoku) Line,** which departs about four times an hour and takes 43 to 57 minutes depending on the train; if you don't have a pass, the trip costs ¥710 one-way. If speed or luxury is of the utmost importance, the deluxe **Kintetsu Special Limited Express** whisks you to Nara in 35 minutes, guarantees you a seat (all seats are reserved), costs ¥1,130 and departs every 30 minutes (advance purchase suggested in peak season). A slower **Kintetsu ordinary express** takes 50 minutes and costs ¥620.

From Osaka, it takes 30 to 50 minutes, depending on the train and station. The **Kintetsu Nara Line,** from Namba Station, takes 40 minutes and costs ¥560. The **JR Yamatoji Rapid Line** from Osaka Station takes 50 minutes and costs ¥800.

VISITOR INFORMATION Tourist information offices at **JR Nara Station** (✆ 0742/22-9821) and **Kintetsu Nara Station** (✆ 0742/24-4858), both open daily 9am to 5pm, dispense brochures and maps with useful information on how to get around by foot and bus. Just outside the JR Station to the left is the attractive former JR station, with a **Nara City Tourist Information Center** (✆ 0742/27-2223; daily 9am–7pm) offering luggage storage (¥410 a bag) and free Wi-Fi. In between both JR and Kintetsu stations, on Sanjo Dori about

---

Your Own Personal Guide

Nara has many volunteer guides (from students and housewives to retirees), who will happily show you the town's sights in exchange for the chance to practice their English. There's no charge, but you pay your own admission and are requested to cover the guide's transportation expenses to meet you (guides do not have to pay admission to attractions);

I suggest you also pay for the guide's lunch. Although guides are sometimes waiting at tourist offices, 3-day advance reservations are advised at one of the following organizations: **YMCA Goodwill Guides** (✆ 0742/45-5920), **Nara Guide Club** (✆ 0742/43-2938), or **Nara SGG Club** (✆ 0742/22-5595).

a 5-minute walk from either, is the main **Nara City Tourist Information Center** (☏ **0742/22-3900;** daily 9am–9pm). Check information online at **www.naraexplorer.jp** and **www.pref.nara.jp.**

GETTING AROUND   If you take the Kintetsu Line, you'll arrive at **Kintetsu Nara Station;** if you take the JR train, you'll arrive at **JR Nara Station.** Both stations are in Nara's small downtown, with Sanjo Dori serving as the main shopping street and running from JR Nara Station to Nara Park and its attractions. Kintetsu Station is slightly closer, about a 5-minute walk to the entrance of the park, while the JR Station is about a 10-minute walk to the park. Keep in mind, however, that Nara Park is quite large and its attractions are far-flung; it takes about 20 minutes to walk from Kintetsu Nara Station to Todaiji Temple and another 20 minutes to Kasuga Taisha Shrine. Otherwise, buses no. 70 and 97 travel from both stations all the way to Kasuga Shrine

IF YOU'RE HEADING TO HORYUJI   To visit the Horyuji Temple area (see below), the cheapest and fastest way is on the JR Yamatoji Rapid Line, which travels between Osaka Station and JR Nara Station. Departures from either station are every 10 to 15 minutes, taking 38 minutes from Osaka (fare: ¥640) or 13 from Nara (fare: ¥220). From there, you can either walk to the temple area in about 20 minutes or take a bus. Alternatively, bus no. 97 is an excursion line that runs between Kasuga Taisha Shrine and Horyuji, passing Todaiji Temple and both train stations on the way, but it takes about an hour and costs ¥760 one-way (a day pass costs ¥1,000), with departures once an hour. If you're coming from Osaka, it makes sense to stop by Horyuji on the way to Nara. Otherwise, consider spending the night.

Exploring Nara

The best way to enjoy Nara is to arrive early in the morning before the first tour buses start pulling in. If you don't have much time, the most important attractions to see are **Todaiji Temple, Kasuga Taisha Shrine,** and **Kofukuji Temple,** all part of the World Heritage Site and which you can view in about 3 or 4 hours. If you have more time, add **Horyuji Temple.** Or, take a stroll south of downtown and Nara Park through **Naramachi,** the historic part of town boasting many *machiya* (traditional wooden residences). Although a reproduction, the free **Koshi-no-ie** (☏ **0742/23-4820;** Tues–Sun 9am–5pm) displays common *machiya* features, such as high windows operated by pulleys and an ingenious front entrance; ask the tourist office for a Naramachi map.

AROUND NARA PARK

With its ponds, grassy lawns, trees, and temples, Nara Park covers about 520 hectares (1,300 acres) and is home to more than 1,200 deer, which are considered divine messengers and are therefore allowed to roam freely through the park. The deer are generally quite friendly; throughout the park you can buy "deer crackers," which all but the shyest fawns will usually snatch right out of your hand. All of the below listings are within Nara Park, in the order you'll reach them walking east from the stations.

Kofukuji Temple ★★ Established in 710, this was the family temple of the Fujiwaras, the second-most powerful clan after the imperial family from the 8th to 12th centuries. There were once as many as 175 buildings on the Kofukuji Temple grounds, giving it significant religious and political power up until the 16th century; through centuries of civil wars and fires, however, most of the structures were destroyed. Only a handful of buildings remain, but even these were rebuilt after the 13th century.

The **five-story pagoda,** first erected in 730, burned down five times. The present pagoda dates from 1426 and is an exact replica of the original; at 50m (164 ft.) tall, it's the second-tallest pagoda in Japan (the tallest is at Toji Temple in Kyoto). The **Eastern Golden Hall (Tokondo)** was originally constructed in 726 by Emperor Shomu to speed the recovery of the ailing Empress Gensho. Rebuilt in 1415, it houses several priceless images, including a bronze statue of Yakushi Nyorai (the healing Buddha) installed by Emperor Shomu on behalf of his sick wife; a 12th-century wooden bodhisattva of wisdom, long worshiped by scholar monks and today by pupils hoping to pass university entrance exams; and the 12 Heavenly Guards, wooden reliefs carved in the 12th century (the hall is under renovation until 2018, but you can still enter).

But the best thing to see is the temple's **Treasure House (Kokuhokan),** which displays statues and works of art originally contained in the temple's buildings, many of them National Treasures. Most famous are the standing Ashura statue carved in the 8th century and a bronze head of Yakushi Nyorai, but my favorites are the six 12th-century carved wooden statues representing priests of the Kamakura Period with fascinating facial features that render them strikingly human. Nara Park. www.kohfukuji.com. ✆ **0742/22-7755.** Admission to Treasure House ¥600 adults, ¥500 junior-high and high-school students, ¥200 elementary-school students; Eastern Golden Hall ¥300 adults, ¥200 junior-high and high-school students, ¥100 elementary-school student. Combination ticket ¥800, ¥600, and ¥250, respectively. Daily 9am–5pm.

Todaiji Temple ★★★ Nara's premier attraction is Todaiji Temple and its **Great Buddha (Daibutsu),** Japan's second-largest bronze Buddha. When Emperor Shomu ordered construction of both the temple and Daibutsu in the mid-700s, he intended to make Todaiji the headquarters of all Buddhist temples in the land. As part of his plans for a Buddhist utopia, he commissioned work for this Daibutsu, a remarkable work of art that took eight castings. At a height of more than 15m (50 ft.), the Daibutsu is made of 437 tons of bronze, 286 pounds of pure gold, 165 pounds of mercury, and 7 tons of vegetable wax. However, thanks to Japan's frequent natural calamities, the Buddha of today isn't quite what it used to be. In 855, in what must have been a whopper of an earthquake, the statue lost its head. It was repaired in 861, but alas, the huge wooden building housing the Buddha, the **Daibutsuden,** was burned twice during wars, melting the Buddha's head. The present head dates from 1692. As for the Daibutsuden, it was also destroyed several times through the centuries; the present structure dates from 1709. Measuring 48m (160 ft.) tall, 57m (187 ft.) long, and 50m (165 ft.) wide, it's the largest wooden structure in the world—but is only two-thirds its original size. My architect sister, just completing a year's trip around the world with her family, declared the Daibutsuden among the most magnificent buildings she had ever seen.

Be sure to walk in a circle around the Great Buddha to see it from all angles. Behind the statue is a model of how the Daibutsuden used to look, flanked by two massive pagodas. Behind the Great Buddha to the right is a huge wooden column with a small hole in it near the ground. According to popular belief, if you can manage to crawl through this opening, you'll be sure to reach enlightenment (seemingly a snap for children). You can also get your English-language fortune for ¥300 by shaking a bamboo canister until a wooden stick with a number comes out; the number corresponds to a piece of paper. Mine told me that though I will win, it will be of no use, an illness will be serious, and the person for whom I am waiting will not come. And the monk who gave me the fortune said mine was a good one!

Nara Park. Ⓒ **0742/22-5511.** Admission ¥500 adults, ¥300 children. Mar daily 8am–5pm; Apr–Sept daily 7:30am–5:30pm; Oct daily 7:30am–5pm; Nov–Feb daily 8am–4:30pm.

Kasuga Taisha Shrine ★★   A stroll through the park will bring you to one of my favorite Shinto shrines in the Kyoto area. Originally the tutelary shrine of the powerful Fujiwara family, it was founded in 768 and, according to Shinto concepts of purity, was torn down and rebuilt every 20 years in its original form until 1863 (in 2015–16 it will be torn down and rebuilt again, a momentous occasion sure to attract many visitors). As virtually all empresses hailed from the Fujiwara family, the shrine enjoyed a privileged status with the imperial family. Nestled in the midst of verdant woods (the Kasugayama Primeval Forest rising behind it has been protected since the 9th c.), it's a shrine of vermilion-colored pillars and an astounding 3,000 stone and bronze lanterns. The most spectacular time to visit is mid-August or the beginning of February, when all 3,000 lanterns are lit. Although admission to the grounds is free, admission is charged for the garden of Kasuga Grand Shrine, **Shin-en,** a botanical garden preserving about 300 varieties of native Japanese plants and famous for its wisteria (it's located to the left on the approach to the shrine), and to the **Homotsuden,** a treasure house displaying costumes, swords, and armor in exhibitions that change four times a year. Fork out the extra yen only if you have time and the interest.

Nara Park. www.kasugataisha.or.jp. Ⓒ **0742/22-7788.** Free admission to grounds; Shin-en ¥500 adults, ¥250 children; Homotsuden ¥400 adults, ¥300 junior- and senior-high students, ¥200 children. Grounds daily 6am–6pm Apr–Sept, 6:30am–5pm Oct–Mar; Homotsuden and Shin-en daily 9am–4pm.

The Horyuji Temple Area ★★★

Founded in 607 by Prince Shotoku as the center for Buddhism in Japan, **Horyuji Temple** (www.horyuji.or.jp; Ⓒ **0745/75-2555**) is one of Japan's most significant gems for historic architecture, art, and religion. It was from here that Buddhism blossomed and spread throughout the land. Today about 45 buildings remain in the complex, some dating from the end of the 7th century and comprising what are thought to be the oldest wooden structures in the world. Although they are the main reason to come here, it's the atmosphere of the compound itself that I love—serene, ancient, and a fitting tribute to Prince Shotoku, founder of Buddhism in Japan and much revered still today. Little wonder Horyuji was selected as one of Japan's first UNESCO World Heritage Sites, in 1993 (for details on reaching Horyuji, see "Essentials," above).

At the western end of the grounds is the two-story, 17m-high (58-ft.) *kondo,* or main hall, which is considered the oldest building at Horyuji Temple, erected sometime between the 6th and 8th centuries. It contains Buddhas commemorating Prince Shotoku's parents, protected by Japan's oldest set of four heavenly guardians (from the late 7th or early 8th c.). Next to the main hall is Japan's oldest **five-story pagoda,** dating from the foundation of the temple and cleverly built to withstand earthquakes; it contains four scenes from the life of Buddha around its base. The **Gallery of Temple Treasures** contains statues, tabernacles, and other works of art from the 7th and 8th centuries, many of them National Treasures. On the eastern precincts of Horyuji Temple is an octagonal building called **Yumedono Hall,** or the Hall of Visions, built in 739 as a sanctuary to pray for the repose of Prince Shotoku.

Admission to these Horyuji treasures is ¥1,500 for adults and ¥750 for children. The grounds are open daily from 8am to 5pm (to 4pm Nov 4–Feb 21).

Just behind Yumedono is **Chuguji Temple** (中宮寺; ☎ **0745/75-2106**), once part of a large nunnery built for members of the imperial family. It contains two outstanding National Treasures: The wooden statue of **Nyoirin Kannon Bosatsu,** dating from the 7th century, is noted for its serene and compassionate expression. The **Tenjukoku Mandala,** the oldest piece of embroidery in Japan, was originally about 5m (16 ft.) long and was created by Shotoku's consort and her female companions after Shotoku's death at the age of 48. It shows scenes from the Land of Heavenly Longevity, where only those with good karma are invited by the Buddha in the afterlife and where Shotoku surely resides. Only a replica of the fragile embroidery is now on display. Open daily from 9am to 4:30pm (to 4pm Oct–Mar 20); admission is ¥500 for adults, ¥250 for children.

Where to Stay & Eat

Harishin (はり新) ★★★ BENTO Many tourists never see Naramachi, a lovely area of old Nara with narrow lanes and traditional wooden homes and shops. This restaurant, with a wood-slat facade and an entrance through a tiny courtyard, occupies a 200-some-year-old house of ocher-colored walls, with dining on *tatami* with a view of a garden. For lunch, only one seasonal bento is served, the creation of chef-owner Nakagawa-san. My recent bento included an aperitif wine, light tofu flavored with sesame, soup, rice, pickled vegetables, tempura, and various exquisitely prepared bite-size morsels of shrimp, chicken, potatoes wrapped in bacon, and scallops. Kaiseki is available for dinner (make reservations at least 1 day in advance).

15 Nakashinya-cho. ☎ **0742/22-2669.** Bento ¥2,980; kaiseki from ¥4,320. Tues–Sun 11:30am–2:30pm and 6–8pm (last order); closed Tues if Mon is a national holiday. A 5-min. walk south of Sarusawa-ike Pond, on the road that leads south from the west edge of the pond, on the right.

Nara Hotel ★★★   This historic hotel, with a staff eager to please, is reason enough to spend the night in Nara. Spreading like a palace atop a hill on the south edge of Nara Park, it was built in 1909 as a Western-style hotel to accommodate foreigners pouring into the country, but it has many Japanese features in the Momoyama Period style of architecture. Accommodations in the old part of the hotel feature wide corridors, high ceilings, antique light fixtures, bamboo blinds, fireplaces (no longer in use), and comfortable old-fashioned decor, while a 1984 addition offers larger, modern rooms and verandas overlooking woods or the old town (*note:* Only the newer wing has an elevator). It's also worth dropping by just for a meal, either in the graceful Tea Lounge with a view of a pond and serving sandwiches for lunch, or in the elegant Mikasa French restaurant with its soaring ceiling and original fixtures.

Nara-Koennai. www.narahotel.co.jp. ✆ **0742/26-3300.** 127 units. ¥13,000–¥19,000 single; ¥23,000–¥59,400 double. 25% discount for holders of Japan Rail Pass. From either station, an 8-min. taxi ride or by bus to the Nara Hotel stop. **Amenities:** 2 restaurants; bar; lounge; room service (not available in all rooms); free Wi-Fi.

Seikan-so ★★   A lovely choice in inexpensive Japanese-style accommodations, this former geisha house boasts a beautiful garden, complete with azalea bushes and manicured trees—the kind of garden usually found only at *ryokan* costing twice as much. Located in quaint Naramachi about a 10-minute walk south of Nara Park, the traditional Japanese building dates from 1916 and wraps around the inner garden. Although the simple *tatami* rooms are showing their age, all is forgiven if you can reserve one of the five rooms facing the garden (those facing streetside are usually for single use). Note that there's an 11pm curfew.

29 Higashi-Kitsuji-cho. www.nara-ryokanseikanso.com. ✆ **0742/22-2670.** 8 units (none with bathroom). ¥4,320 per person. Station: Kintetsu Nara (12 min.) or JR Nara (25 min.). Bus: Loop bus 1 to Kitakyobate stop (1 min.). **Amenities:** Free Wi-Fi.

Shizuka (志津香) ★ KAMAMESHI   This much loved, low-key local shop across from Nara Park and near Todaiji Temple is best known for its *kamameshi,* rice in a small metal pot and topped with other ingredients. Order from the English menu for *kamameshi* like the simple *wakadori* (chicken with vegetables) or the *Nara nanashu* (seven flavors of Nara), but don't stir the *kamameshi* right away until an *okoge* (crispy rice crust) can form where the rice meets the metal of the pot. The Tempura Gozen includes tempura and Nara-nanashu. No credit cards are accepted.

59 Noborioji-cho. www.kamameshi-shizuka.jp. ✆ **0742/27-8030.** Set meals ¥1,700–¥2,610. Wed–Mon 11am–8pm. On the main road between Kintetsu Station and Todaiji, across from the Nara National Museum (look for the white curtains).

TEMPLES OF KOYASAN ★★★

748km (465 miles) W of Tokyo; 199km (124 miles) S of Osaka

If you've harbored visions of wooden temples nestled in among trees whenever you've thought of Japan, the sacred mountain of **Mount Koya** is the place to go. It's all here—head-shaven monks, religious chanting at the crack of dawn, the wafting of incense, towering cypress trees, tombs, and early morning mist rising above the treetops. Mount Koya—called Koyasan by Japanese—is one of Japan's most sacred places and the mecca of the Shingon Esoteric sect of Buddhism. Standing almost 900m (3,000 ft.) above the world, the top of Mount Koya is home to 117 Shingon Buddhist temples scattered through the mountain forests and to Japan's most magnificent graveyard. Fifty-two temples offer accommodations, making this one of the top places in Japan to observe temple life firsthand. Koyasan is one of my favorite destinations.

A World Heritage Site since 2004, Koyasan, located in the Kii Mountain Range, first became a place of meditation and religious learning 1,200 ago when Kukai, known posthumously as Kobo Daishi, was granted the mountaintop by the imperial court in 816 as a place to establish his Shingon sect of Buddhism. Kobo Daishi was a charismatic priest who had spent 2 years in China studying esoteric Buddhism before returning to his native land to spread his teachings among Japanese. Admired for his excellent calligraphy, his humanitarianism, and his teachings, Kobo Daishi remains one of the most beloved figures in Japanese Buddhist history. When he died in the 9th century, he was laid to rest in a mausoleum on Mount Koya. His followers believe Kobo Daishi is not dead but simply in a deep state of meditation, awaiting the arrival of the last bodhisattva (Buddha messiah). According to popular belief, priests opening his mausoleum decades after his death found his body still warm.

Through the centuries, many of Kobo Daishi's followers, wishing to be close at hand when the great priest awakens, have had huge tombs or tablets constructed close to Kobo Daishi's mausoleum, and many have had their ashes interred here. Pilgrims over the last thousand years have included emperors, feudal lords, samurai, and common people, all climbing to the top of the mountain to pay their respects. Women, however, were barred from entering the sacred grounds of Koyasan until 1872.

Essentials

GETTING THERE Osaka is the gateway to Koyasan. **Nankai Railway's** rapid express **Koya Line** departs from Osaka's Namba Station (with a stop at Shin-Imamiya, on the Osaka Loop Line) every half-hour or hour bound for Gokurakubashi, with the trip taking about 1 hour and 30 minutes. If you want to ride in luxury, Nankai limited-express (also called super express) trains with reserved seating depart less frequently (three times in the morning) and arrive in Gokurakubashi about 1 hour and 10 minutes later (the last stretch through the mountains is beautiful). After arriving at the last stop, Gokurakubashi, you continue your trip to the top of Mount Koya via a 5-minute ride in a cable car. The entire journey from Namba Station to Mount Koya costs ¥1,380 one-way, including the cable car; if you take the faster express, it'll cost ¥780 extra. You'll save money, however, with Nankai's **Koyasan World Heritage Ticket** (available at Namba Station), which includes round-trip travel from Namba Station and the cable car, plus unlimited rides on Koya's buses for 2 days and a 20% discount to the attractions listed below. The cost is ¥2,860 if you travel by rapid express and ¥3,400 by limited-express (the return trip is by rapid express). Children pay half fare. For information on travel to and around Koyasan, go to **www.nankaikoya.jp**.

VISITOR INFORMATION   The **Koyasan Tourism Association** (www. koya.org; ✆ **0736/56-2616**) is located approximately in the center of Koyasan village, on Odawara street near Kongobuji Temple, where you can pick up a map and a bus schedule. It also offers a computer with Internet access you can use for free, a few lockers for luggage, and a 90-minute rental audio guide for ¥500 that's highly useful for learning more about what you're seeing throughout Koyasan, including the location of famous mausoleums and tombstones in Okunoin cemetery. You can also book temple lodgings here, but it's better if you reserve a minimum of 7 business days in advance (check http://eng.shukubo. net for details). It's open daily 8:30am to 7pm (9am–5pm Dec–Feb).

GETTING AROUND   Upon reaching Koyasan via cable-car, you must board a **bus** that travels 2km (1¼ miles) on a narrow, winding road (no pedestrians allowed) before winding through the village of Koyasan along the main street all the way to the Okunoin-guchi and Okunoin-mae bus stops, the location of Kobo Daishi's mausoleum. The bus passes most sights along the way, as well as temples accommodating visitors and the Koyasan Tourist Association office. Buses depart about 5 minutes after the arrival of every cable car; the trip to Okunoin-mae takes 20 minutes and costs ¥410. Otherwise, once you've dropped off your luggage or settled into your temple lodging, you can walk to Okunoin and other locations mentioned below. Or, rental bicycles are available at the tourist office for ¥400 for 1 hour, plus ¥100 for every 30 minutes after that (because the number of bikes is limited, you might want to reserve one in advance by calling the tourist office).

Exploring Mount Koya

THE TOP ATTRACTION   The most awe-inspiring and magnificent of Koyasan's many sights, **Okunoin ★★★** is the cemetery containing the mausoleum of Kobo Daishi. The most dramatic approach to Okunoin is from the Okunoin-guchi bus stop, where the Sando pathway leads 2km (1.2 miles) to the mausoleum. Swathed in a respectful darkness of huge cypress trees forming a canopy overhead are monument after monument, tomb after tomb—approximately 200,000 of them, all belonging to faithful followers from past centuries. The audio guide from the tourist office (see "Visitor Information," above) will guide you to the most famous tombstones, including those of the Toyotomi, Shimadzu, Maeda, Asano, and Matsudaira clans.

I don't know whether being here will affect you the same way, but I am always awestruck by the sheer density of tombstones, the iridescent green moss, the shafts of light streaking through the treetops, the stone lanterns, and the gnarled bark of the old cypress trees. There are also many small *Jizo* statues, believed to protect children in the afterlife, wearing red bibs donated by parents who have lost a child. Altogether, the dramatic scene represents more than a thousand years of Japanese Buddhist history. If you're lucky, you won't meet many people along the way. Tour buses park at a newer entrance to the mausoleum at the bus stop called Okunoin-mae. I absolutely forbid you to take this shorter route; its crowds lessen the impact of this place considerably. Rather, take the longer Sando path from the Okunoin-guchi/Ichinohashi bus stops. Much less traveled, it's also much more impressive and is one of the main reasons for coming to Koyasan in the first place. And be sure to return to the mausoleum at night; the stone lanterns (now lit electrically) create a mysterious and powerful effect.

At the end of the pathway, about a 30-minute walk away, is the **Lantern Temple,** or Torodo, which houses about 10,000 lanterns, donated by prime ministers, emperors, and even commoners. Two sacred fires, which reportedly have been burning since the 11th century, are kept safely inside. The mausoleum itself, the Okunoin Gyobo, is behind the Lantern Hall to the left. Buy a white candle, light it, and wish for anything you want. Then sit back and watch respectfully as Buddhists come to chant and pay respects to one of Japan's greatest Buddhist leaders. Many who have successfully completed the pilgrimage to Shikoku Island's 88 Buddhist temples, often dressed in white and carrying a staff, conclude their journey here. Twice a day, at 6am and 10:30am, monks ritually offer meals to Kobo Daishi.

MORE TO SEE & DO **Kongobuji Temple** (金剛峯寺) ★★, located near the Koyasan Tourist Association in the center of town (⌀ **0736/56-2011**), is the central monastery headquarters of the Shingon sect in Japan. Although Kongobuji was originally built in the 16th century by Toyotomi Hideyoshi to commemorate his mother's death, the present building dates from 1869. Pictures by famous artists from long ago decorate sliding screens and depict Kobo Daishi's trip to China. The huge kitchen, big enough to feed multitudes of monks, is also on view. The most important thing to see, however, is the temple's magnificent rock garden, the largest in Japan and said to represent a pair of dragons in a sea of clouds. If it's raining, consider yourself lucky—the wetness adds sheen and color to the rocks. Admission is ¥500 for adults, ¥200 for children.

A short walk farther west is the **Garan ★** (⌀ **0736/56-3215**), the first buildings constructed on Koyasan and still considered the center of religious life in the community. It's an impressive sight with a huge *kondo* (main hall), first built in 819 by Kobo Daishi; a large vermilion-colored *daito* (pagoda), which many consider to be Koyasan's most magnificent structure and which is very much worth entering for its brightly colored murals and statues (¥200 each for the *kondo* and *daito*); and the oldest remaining building on Mount Koya, the Fudodo, which was built in 1198.

All of the sites above are open daily 8:30am to 5pm (you must enter by 4:30pm).

Where to Stay & Eat

Although this community of 4,000 residents has the usual stores, schools, and offices of any small town, temple lodgings are where most visitors stay and I strongly urge you to do so, too, traveling only with an overnight bag if possible. Japanese almost always make reservations beforehand, and though you can do so in person upon arrival at the Tourist Association office, it's better to make reservations a minimum of 7 days in advance, especially in peak season. See "Visitor Information," above, for details.

WHAT IT'S LIKE TO STAY AT A KOYASAN TEMPLE   Prices for an overnight stay in one of the temples, including two vegetarian meals, range from ¥9,800 to ¥16,000 per person, depending on the temple, room, and meal. Check-in is around 2 or 3pm (5pm at the latest) and checkout is at 9 or 10am (you can leave your luggage at the temple while sightseeing).

Your room will be *tatami* and may include a nice view of a garden. Both baths and toilets are communal (you may need to supply your own towel and toiletries). College students studying at Koyasan's Buddhist university and living at the temple might attend you, bringing your meals to your room, making up your futon, and cleaning your room. The *shojin ryori* (Buddhist vegetarian meals) are generally quite good, and because Buddhist monks are vegetarians but not teetotalers (beer and sake are made of rice and grain), alcoholic drinks are readily available at the temples for an extra charge. Meals are at set times. Dinner is at 5:30pm, and because the students must leave for school, breakfast is usually served by 7:30am. The morning religious service is at 6 or 6:30am; you don't have to attend, but I strongly recommend that you do. There's something uplifting about early morning meditative chanting, even for non-believers; some temples include sacred fire ceremonies as well.

> ### A Guest House for Budget Travelers
>
> **Koyasan Guest House Kokuu** (http://koyasanguesthouse.com; ✆ **0736/26-7216**) is a compact A-frame inn that squeezes in 8 capsule beds for ¥3,500 and 3 private rooms (¥9,000 for a double), plus a cozy bar offering food and drink. Owner Ryochi Takai, a Mt. Koya native, is happy to give tips on sightseeing.

Unfortunately, a flood of tourists since Koyasan became a World Heritage Site has taken its toll, with some temples seemingly more interested in cashing in than in helping souls and some guests showing little respect for their surroundings; don't be one of them. In any case, below are just a few of the dozens of area temples open to overnight guests. Rates are based on two people to a room.

Bon On Shya ★   A Japanese and French couple, Takeshi and Veronique, run this small, casual cafe on Koyasan's main street. Simply outfitted with wooden tables and a play corner for children, it offers coffees, cakes, and a daily set meal from 11:30am until they run out, which can include rice and beans, potato salad, cake and a drink (vegan and vegetarian options available; gluten-free, too, with 24-hr. notice). Credit cards aren't accepted and there are no set hours. It's that kind of place.

730 Koyasan. ✆ **0736/56-5535.** Set meal ¥1,200. Wed–Sun around 7am–afternoon. Bus: Odawaradori. It's identified as Bononsha on the tourist map.

Ekoin (恵光院) ★★   This 100-year-old temple, with origins stretching back almost 1,100 years when Kukai was said to have erected a stupa on this site, has nice grounds and is nestled in a wooded slope an easy walk from Okunoin. For centuries it enjoyed support of the Shimadzu clan of southern Kyushu. It's known for its excellent Buddhist cuisine and free meditation lessons at 4:30pm, usually in English. Every morning there's also both a chanting service and a fire ceremony. All rooms have views of the garden (and some even have balcony) and contain information on how to wear a *yukata* (cotton kimono) and take a bath and about the morning service. The temple also recently added a room with computers for guests to use.

497 Koyasan. www.ekoin.jp. ✆ **0736/56-2514.** 37 units (36 without bathroom). ¥10,500–¥15,800 per person. Rates include 2 meals. Bus: Karukayado-mae. **Amenities:** Hot-spring bath; free Wi-Fi.

Rengejoin Temple (蓮華定院) ★★   This temple's head priest speaks English, so a lot of foreigners are directed here. It's a good place to find out about Buddhism and the significance of Koyasan. Established 900 years ago, it was rebuilt 150 years ago after a fire. Lodging, up the hill in a newer annex, ranges from simple *tatami* rooms to those nicely decorated with painted screens and antiques, the best with views of a garden with a pond. Pluses include a lounge with TV and free Wi-Fi, as well as both evening and morning services conducted in both Japanese and English. Too bad it's on the opposite end of town from Okunoin, about a 40-minute walk away. Note that unlike the other temples listed here, no credit cards are accepted.

700 Koyasan. ✆ **0736/56-2233.** 46 units (none with bathroom). ¥9,000–¥15,000. Rates include 2 meals and exclude tax. Bus: Ishinguchi stop.

Shojoshinin (清浄心院) ★★★   Of all Koyasan's temples, this one has the most curbside appeal. Best of all, it has a great location at the beginning of the tomb-lined pathway to Okunoin, making it convenient for your late-night stroll to the mausoleum. Originating as a thatched hut built by Kobo Daishi almost 1,200 years ago and once the second-largest temple in Koyasan after Kongobuji, today it boasts attractive 150-some-year-old buildings against a wooded backdrop, including a large wooden structure with rooms overlooking a small garden and pond. It's usually full in August and peak seasons, so make reservations early.

566 Koyasan. ✆ **0736/56-2006.** 30 units (29 without bathroom). ¥9,720–¥15,100 per person. Rates include 2 meals. Bus: Okunoin-guchi. **Amenities:** Free Wi-Fi.

HIMEJI, A CASTLE TOWN ★★

640km (400 miles) W of Tokyo; 130km (81 miles) W of Kyoto; 250km (155 miles) E of Hiroshima

The main reason tourists come to Himeji, in Hyogo Prefecture, is to see its 400-year-old magnificent **castle,** which embodies the best in Japan's military architecture. If you were to see only one castle in Japan, this World Heritage Site would be my top pick. If time permits, I also recommend strolling the delightful nearby garden, Koko-en.

Essentials

GETTING THERE   A stop on the **Tokaido/Sanyo Shinkansen** bullet train, which runs between Tokyo and Kyushu, Himeji is about 3½ hours from Tokyo, 1 hour from Kyoto, and 2 hours from Hiroshima. The fare from Tokyo is ¥15,120 for a nonreserved seat. From Osaka Station, the JR commuter Tokaido line arrives in Himeji 1 hour later; from Kobe's Sannomiya Station, 39 minutes later. From Kansai International Airport outside Osaka, there are 10 Airport Limousine Buses daily to Himeji Station; the trip takes over 2 hours and costs ¥3,300.

VISITOR INFORMATION   The **Himeji Tourist Information Center** (officially called the Himeji Kanko Navi Port; _C_ **079/287-0003;** daily 9am–7pm) is located at the north exit of Himeji Station. It offers maps, free Wi-Fi, and even rents bikes free of charge (see below). For online information, see **www.himeji-kanko.jp/en**. The station has coin lockers for those stopping only for a few hours.

GETTING AROUND   You can **walk** to Himeji's attractions. The main road in town is Otemae Dori, a wide boulevard stretching from Himeji Station north to Himeji Castle (you can walk the distance in about 15 min.). To the east (right) of Otemae Dori are two parallel streets, Miyukidori and Omizo-suji, both covered shopping arcades. If you want, you can use a **bicycle** free of charge from 9am to 5:30pm by filling out an application form before 4pm at the tourist information office, where you'll be given a ticket and told where to pick up the bike. Finally, the retro-looking **Himeji Castle Loop Bus** makes runs daily from 9am to 5pm every half-hour (every 15 min. weekends and holidays) from the station to the castle, Koko-en, and beyond. It costs ¥100 per ride; an all-day ticket for ¥300 includes discounts to Himeji Castle and Koko-en, but frankly, you can just as easily walk and save money by buying a combination ticket to the castle and garden.

Exploring Himeji

Himeji Castle ★★★ CASTLE   As soon as you exit from Himeji Station's north exit, you'll see Himeji Castle straight ahead at the end of Otemae Dori. Probably the most beautiful castle in all of Japan, Himeji Castle is nicknamed "White Heron Castle" in reference to its white walls, which stretch out on either side of the main _donjon_ (castle keep) and resemble a white heron poised in flight over the plain. Whether it looks to you like a heron or a castle, the view of the white five-story _donjon_ under a blue sky is striking, especially when the area's 1,000-some cherry trees are in bloom. This is also one of the few castles in Japan that has remained virtually as it was since its completion in 1609, surviving even World War II bombings that left Himeji in ruins. In 1993, the castle, along with Horyuji Temple in Nara, became Japan's first UNESCO's World Heritage Sites. In March 2015, the castle keep reopened after a massive 5-year renovation.

Originating as a fort in the 14th century, Himeji Castle took a more majestic form in 1581 when a three-story _donjon_ was built by Toyotomi Hideyoshi during one of his military campaigns in the district. In the early 1600s, the castle became the residence of Ikeda Terumasa, one of Hideyoshi's generals and a son-in-law of Tokugawa Ieyasu. He remodeled the castle into its present five-story structure. With its extensive gates, three moats, turrets, and a secret entrance, it had one of the most sophisticated defense systems in Japan. The maze of passageways leading to the *donjon* was so complicated that intruders would find themselves trapped in dead ends. The castle walls, made of fire-proof white plaster, were constructed with square or circular holes through which gun muzzles could poke; the rectangular holes were for archers. There were also drop chutes where stones or boiling water could be dumped on enemies trying to scale the walls. Roof eaves were designed to collect rainwater, a bonus if the castle were ever under siege.

On weekends (and sometimes weekdays), volunteers hanging around the castle ticket office offer guided tours of the castle for free. It gives them an opportunity to practice their English while you learn about the history of the castle and even old castle gossip. But even if you go on your own, you won't have any problems learning about the history of the castle, as there are good English-language explanations throughout the castle grounds. With or without a guide, you'll spend at least 2 hours here. But beware, there are lots of stairs. *Tip:* A combination ticket, allowing discounted admission to both the castle and Koko-en (see below), is available at either entrance.

68 Honmachi. www.himeji-castle.gr.jp. ℂ **079/285-1146.** Admission ¥1,000 adults, ¥300 children. Combination ticket to both Himeji Castle and Koko-en ¥1,040 adults, ¥300 children. May–Aug daily 9am–6pm; Sept–Apr daily 9am–5pm. You must enter 1 hr. before closing time. A 15-min. walk straight north of Himeji Station via Otemae Dori.

Koko-en (好古園) ★★★ PARK/GARDEN   Although laid out only in 1992, this is one of my favorite gardens, occupying land where samurai mansions once stood at the base of Himeji Castle, about a 5-minute walk away. Actually it's composed of nine separate small gardens, each one different and enclosed by traditional walls, with lots of rest areas to soak in the wonderful views. The gardens, typical of those in the Edo Period, include an area of deciduous trees, a garden of pine trees, a bamboo grove, a garden of flowers popular during the Edo Period, tea-ceremony gardens, and traditional Japanese gardens with ponds, waterfalls, and running streams. If you wish, relax at the Souju-an teahouse in the Cha-no-niwa (tea-ceremony garden) with tea and a sweet (¥500; daily 10am–4pm) or dine at a restaurant overlooking a carp pond (see below). In any case, I wouldn't miss this special place. If you don't stop (but how could you resist?), you can stroll through all the gardens in about 45 minutes.

68 Honmachi. ℂ **079/289-4120.** Admission ¥300 adults, ¥150 children. Combination ticket to Himeji Castle and Koko-en ¥1,040 adults, ¥360 children. Daily 9am–5pm (to 6pm May–Aug). A 15-min. walk north of Himeji Station; turn left in front of Himeji Castle (the entrance will be on your right).

Where to Eat

In addition to the choices below, consider stopping by **Kassui-ken** (活水軒; ℂ **079/289-4131**) in Koko-en garden. To be honest, this restaurant would not have much to recommend it except for one overwhelming feature: It overlooks a koi pond and waterfall and is certainly the most picturesque place in town to try Himeji's specialty, conger eel. If that's too exotic, it also serves a few noodle dishes and beef curry, as well set meals ranging from ¥1,350 to ¥2,570 (no credit cards accepted). Or you can stop just for dessert or a refreshing drink of beer, soda, or coffee if you avoid the busy lunchtime crowd. Last order is an hour before Koko-en closes (see above).

In the listings below, directions are from Himeji Station.

Menme (めんめ) ★★ UDON NOODLES   The friendly husband-and-wife team here has been dishing out udon noodles at this same spot for more than 30 years, with tempura udon, curry udon, and other various udon listed on the English menu. Tanimoto-san makes all of his udon on the spot, so though you might have to wait, it's interesting to watch the process, which he accomplishes practically at the speed of light. Though the restaurant's location draws in many passing tourists, it's also popular with locals. You'll feel very welcomed here, but note that no credit cards are accepted.

68 Honmachi. ℂ **079/225-0118.** Udon ¥650–¥1,000; set meal (Mon–Fri only) ¥730. Thurs–Tues noon–6pm. On Otemae Dori, on the left a couple blocks before reaching Himeji Castle; look for the sign board showing plates of noodles.

Mille ★★★ VARIED JAPANESE/WESTERN   Great views of Himeji Castle, which is lit at night, are the trademark of this fancy but reasonably priced restaurant, with seating along a window-side counter or at tables. Set meals are the way to go, with the cheapest lunch including an appetizer, sashimi, conger eel on steamed rice, noodles cooked with red snapper, pickled vegetables and dessert. Or, you might wish to go with the Egret lunch of Western fare that offers an hors d'oeuvre, soup, main dish like fish, rice or bread, and tea or coffee.

Egret Himeji Building, 4th floor, 68 Honmachi. ℂ **079/225-0030.** Set lunches ¥1,620–¥4,320; set dinners ¥3,240–¥6,480. Mon–Fri 11:30am–2:30pm; Sat–Sun & holidays 11am–2:30pm; daily 5–9pm (last order). Walking north on Otemae Dori, turn right at the next-to-last streetlight before Himeji Castle; it's the soaring glass building on the right.

Sainte Vierge ★★ FRENCH   This is Himeji's swankiest place for French cuisine, with an elegant drawing-room ambience, white table-clothed tables spaced far apart for privacy, a well-trained staff, and classical music. Only set meals are served, giving choices of fish, meat, or both as main courses, along with side dishes. The ¥2,500 set lunch, for example, may consist of bread, an appetizer of homemade ham with organic vegetables, sweet potato soup, and sea bass. Because this is a popular wedding venue, especially on weekends, be sure to call first to see whether it's open to the public.

Konyamachi 23. ℂ **079/223-1122.** Set lunches ¥2,500–¥5,000; set dinners ¥3,500–¥10,000. Wed–Mon 11:30am–2pm and 6–8pm (last order). Walk north on Otemae Dori toward the castle and after the Shirogane intersection take the 2nd right (Mizuho and Tokyo-Mitsubishi UFJ banks are on the corner here); it's past the 2 covered shopping arcades, on the right, with faded red curtains.

HIGHLIGHTS OF CHUGOKU

The western-most end of Honshu, known as the Chugoku region, has long been a destination for international tourists because of **Hiroshima,** the first city ever destroyed by an atomic bomb and home to the thought-provoking Peace Memorial Park with its museum. Near Hiroshima is **Miyajima,** a jewel of an island considered to be one of Japan's most scenic spots and home to a shrine that's a World Heritage Site. Another worthwhile destination is **Kurashiki,** famous for its willow-fringed canal and black-and-white granaries that make this old merchant's town a photographer's dream.

KURASHIKI, MARKET TOWN OF MANY CHARMS ★★★

750km (465 miles) W of Tokyo, 235km (380 miles) W of Kyoto, 177km (110 miles) E of Hiroshima

If I were to select the most picturesque town in Japan, **Kurashiki** would certainly be a top contender. Here, in the heart of the city, clustered around a willow-fringed canal and surrounding lanes, is a delightful historic district perfect for camera buffs.

As an administrative center of the shogunate in the 17th century, Kurashiki blossomed into a prosperous market town where rice, sake, and cotton were collected from the surrounding region and shipped off to Osaka and beyond. Back in those days, wealth was measured in rice; large granaries were built to store the mountains of granules passing through the town, and canals were dug so that barges laden with grain could work their way to ships anchored in the Seto Inland Sea. Kurashiki, in fact, means "Warehouse Village."

It's these warehouses, still standing and now converted into restaurants, shops, and *ryokan,* that give Kurashiki its distinctive charm. Kurashiki is also known for its museums, especially the prestigious Ohara Museum of Art with its collection of European and Japanese art. For these reasons, Kurashiki, located in Okayama Prefecture, is hardly undiscovered, and Japanese flock here in droves, especially in summer months. Yet despite its overcrowdedness (try to avoid coming on a weekend), Kurashiki still rates high on my list of places to see in Japan.

Essentials

GETTING THERE   By Train   Although Kurashiki has a Shinkansen station **(Shin-Kurashiki),** most Shinkansen trains do not stop there, and the station is inconveniently located about 9.5km (6 miles) west of the city center (a local train runs between Shin-Kurashiki and Kurashiki stations about every 15 min. and takes 9 min.). From most destinations, you're better off disembarking the Shinkansen in Okayama and then transferring to the **JR Sanyo Line** to **Kurashiki Station,** in the heart of the city; trains depart frequently and take about 15 minutes (fare: ¥320). From Tokyo, an unreserved seat on the Shinkansen to Okayama followed by the JR Sanyo Line to Kurashiki Station takes about 4 hours and costs ¥16,300.

By Bus   A Ryobi Bus (© 03/3928-6011) departs Tokyo's Shinjuku Station nightly at 9:45pm, arriving in Kurashiki at 8:45am and costing ¥10,000 one-way.

VISITOR INFORMATION   There's a **tourist information office** outside Kurashiki Station to the right (© 086/424-1220), open daily 9am to 7pm (to 6pm Oct–Mar). Another tourist information office, called the **Kurashiki-Kan** (© 086/422-0542), is right on the canal in the historic district and has a rest area with tables and vending machines; open daily 9am to 6pm, it was built in 1916 and is ironically the only Western-looking wooden building in the area. Both offices distribute maps and brochures. For more information, go to **www. kurashiki-tabi.jp**.

ORIENTATION   Kurashiki's warehouse district, called the **Bikan Historical Quarter,** is only an 8-minute walk from Kurashiki Station; take the south exit and walk south on Chuo Dori, turning left just before the Kurashiki Kokusai Hotel. In fact, you can walk virtually everywhere of interest in Kurashiki; the Bikan Historical Quarter is zoned mostly for pedestrians.

[FastFACTS] KURASHIKI

ATM/Mail   There's a post office around the corner from the tourist office, with an ATM open Monday to Friday from 9am to 7pm and weekends and holidays from 9am to 5pm.

Wi-Fi   Both tourist offices provide 10 minutes of free Wi-Fi; ask for details.

Where to Stay

EXPENSIVE

Ryokan Kurashiki (旅館くらしき) ★★★   The best lodgings to get a feeling for old Kurashiki is right in the heart of it—in one of the old warehouses on Kurashiki's picturesque willow-lined canal. This venerable *ryokan* consists of an old mansion and three converted rice-and-sugar warehouses more than 260 years old, all in its own little compound connected by a corridor of black marble polished to a sheen. Filled with antiques and curios, it has long, narrow corridors, nooks and crannies, and the peaceful sanctuary of an inner garden. There's no other *ryokan* in Japan quite like this one. Its five rooms, which are actually two- and three-room suites consisting of a *tatami* living room and sleeping quarters with Western-style beds, are simply elegant, with antiques placed here and there, two TVs, and Jacuzzi tubs. Two are big enough for up to six people (although no children younger than 13 are allowed). Meals are served in your room (Western-style breakfasts are available). There's also a delightful terrace tea lounge overlooking a small garden, open daily except Monday for lunch and tea time and the only place in the *ryokan* with (free) Wi-Fi.

4–1 Honmachi. www.ryokan-kurashiki.jp. © **086/422-0730.** 5 units. ¥29,000–¥49,500 per person. Rates include 2 meals but exclude service charge. Rates ¥1,000 higher Fri, Sat, and in peak season. In the Bikan Historical Quarter. **Amenities:** Restaurant.

Tsurugata (鶴形) ★★ Rustic furniture, aged wood and memorable meals of seasonal specialties are trademarks of this *ryokan*, on the canal in the Bikan Historical Quarter's oldest building, constructed in 1744. It was once a merchant's house and shop selling rice, cotton, seafood, and cooking oil. The most expensive two rooms have a view of the garden with its 400-year-old pine trees and stone lanterns even from their cypress tubs, while the least expensive, rather ordinary six-mat *tatami* rooms are on the second floor with views over the Bikan historic district. There is, however, one six-mat *tatami* room with both a garden view and a tub that costs slightly more. Otherwise, all rooms have private toilets, but except for the three rooms mentioned here you'll be using the common baths. Wi-Fi is available only in the lobby.

1–3–15 Chuo. © **086/424-1635.** 11 units (all with toilet, 3 with bathroom). ¥15,220–¥34,560 per person. Rates include 2 meals. In the Bikan Historical Quarter, on the canal. **Amenities:** Restaurant.

MODERATE

Kurashiki Ivy Square Hotel ★★ When this 1882 brick cotton mill was converted to a hotel in 1974, much of the old architectural style was left intact, making for an interesting setting. Rooms are simple and spotlessly clean (and could do with some updating), with some facing a tiny expanse of green grass and an ivy-covered wall or a koi-filled canal. Rooms range from inexpensive small economy rooms with very narrow beds and no private bath (although guests can don the hotel's cotton *yukata* robes and use the common baths) to deluxe two-room suites with a sofa that doubles as an extra bed. The Bikan Historical Quarter is just a minute's walk away, but the train station is a 15-minute hike away. Free Wi-Fi is available only in the lobby.

7–2 Honmachi. www.ivysquare.co.jp. © **086/422-0011.** 161 units (all with toilet, 67 with bathroom). ¥7,500–¥8,500 single with toilet, ¥10,000–¥1,000 single with bathroom; ¥12,500–¥14,500 twin with toilet; ¥16,000–¥29,000 twin/double with bathroom. A minute's walk south of the Bikan Historical Quarter. **Amenities:** Restaurant; bar; summer beer garden; access to nearby sports club w/gym and pool (fee: ¥800).

Kurashiki Kokusai Hotel ★★★ This has long been Kurashiki's most popular Western-style hotel—and it's easy to see why. Built in 1963, it blends into its surroundings with black-tile walls set in white mortar, while the interior pays tribute to the mid-20th-century Japanese modernist style with an old-fashioned charm, retro furnishings, and huge woodblock murals in the lobby by *mingei* artist Munakata Shiko (you can see more of his work at the Ohara Museum). The lobby also offers free Wi-Fi. Rooms, recently renovated, have nice touches of locally made crafts that lift them out of the ordinary, including Kurashiki glass lampshades and woodblock prints by a local artist. A newer annex offers slightly larger (mostly) twin rooms with larger bathrooms, but I prefer the smaller, and cheaper rooms in the old building facing the back with a pleasant view of the Ohara Museum, garden greenery, and the black-tile roofs of the old granaries.

1–1–44 Chuo. www.kurashiki-kokusai-hotel.co.jp. © **086/422-5141.** 106 units. ¥10,800 single; ¥16,200–¥24,840 double. Rates exclude service charge. Add ¥1,080 per person in peak season. An 8-min. walk south of Kurashiki Station, on Chuo Dori adjacent to the Bikan Historical Quarter. **Amenities:** Restaurant; bar; lounge; summer barbecue garden; free Internet.

INEXPENSIVE

Toyoko Inn Kurashiki-eki Minami-guchi ★   This inexpensive business hotel has a good location between Kurashiki Station and the Bikan Historical Quarter, above a convenience store. It also tries harder than most business hotels to draw in customers, offering free Internet access from two computers in the lobby, free domestic calls from lobby phones, free Wi-Fi in the lobby, and free breakfast. Rooms are tiny, with most of the room taken up by double- or queen-size beds, but the price is right. Ask for a room on a top floor for unobstructed city views and be sure to pick up your sleepwear in the lobby.

2–10–20 Achi. www.toyoko-inn.com. © **086/430-1045.** 154 units. ¥5,184–¥6,264 single; ¥6,480–¥8,640 double. Rates include continental breakfast. A 3-min. walk south of Kurashiki Station, on Chuo Dori on the left side. Amenities: Free Wi-Fi.

Cuore Kurashiki ★★★   This is a very cool hostel hidden in the Bikan Historical Quarter. Check-in is downstairs in the super comfy cafe/bar, at the reception desk cleverly constructed out of stacked old suitcases. It's the kind of place you wouldn't mind hanging out in—quite literally, as it even has a small separate room strung with four hammocks—with its free Wi-Fi, sofas, an alcove library, bar food like pizza, and a full-service bar. A central glass ceiling hints at the rooms above, lined along an atrium corridor on the second and third floors (there's no elevator). In addition to three dormitory rooms, two with four bunkbeds sleeping eight women and one with three bunks for both genders, there are single, twin, and double rooms, small but with individuality like colored walls and funky decor making each one different. The two most expensive rooms, for one or two persons, have shower, but none have toilet. Opened in 2014, this hostel seems destined to be a winner for budget travelers.

1–9–4 Chuo. www.bs-cuore.com. © **086/486-3443.** 17 units (2 with toilet, none with bathroom). ¥4,500–¥7,000 single; ¥7,500–¥10,000 double. A 10-min walk south of Kurashiki Station. Walk past the Bikan Historical Quarter on Chuo Dori, turn left at Shirakabe Dori and then the first left; it's across from a children's day-care center. **Amenities:** Cafe/bar.

Where to Eat

In addition to options below, **Ryokan Kurashiki** serves elegant, seasonal set lunches (¥1,850–¥2,500) with views of its garden, while evening summer beer gardens are located in the courtyard of **Ivy Square** and on the lawn of the **Kokusai Hotel.**

MODERATE

Hachikengura ★★★ FRENCH   Occupying a converted rice granary that once belonged to the Ohashi family (described below in the Ohashi House review), this is my top pick for an atmospheric meal, boasting a soaring wood-beamed ceiling, tiled walls, a worn wooden floor, and tables widely spaced for privacy. Traditional French cuisine, such as sautéed scallop and eggplant, lobster or steak, is served in nouvelle style and listed on the English-language menu. You can eat here more economically if you come for lunch; my ¥1,500 set meal came with an amuse-bouche, one of the best mushroom soups I've ever had, salmon and crab wrapped in cabbage with a shrimp sauce, a tiny salad, green-tea cake, and coffee. Reservations recommended.

Kurashiki Royal Art Hotel, 3–21–19 Achi. www.royal-art-hotel.co.jp. ℂ **086/423-2122** (423-2400 after 7pm). Main dishes ¥2,000–¥7,000; set lunches ¥1,500–¥3,700; set dinners ¥4,104–¥10,800. Daily 11:30am–3pm and 5:30–10pm. Across Chuo Dori from the Bikan Historical Quarter.

INEXPENSIVE

For a drink or snack, the one-room **El Greco Coffeehouse** (ℂ **086/422-0297;** Tues–Sun 10am–5pm) is Kurashiki's most famous coffee shop, open since 1959 and located next to the Ohara Museum. With an ivy-covered stone facade and simply decorated with a wooden floor, wooden tables, vases of fresh flowers, and El Greco photos, it serves coffee, green tea, fruit juice, milkshakes, ice cream, and cake (cash only).

Kamoi (カモ井) ★★ VARIED JAPANESE   This restaurant, occupying a 200-year-old rice granary on Kurashiki's willow-fringed canal, is sparingly decorated with stark-white walls, dark wooden beams, and hanging white paper lamps. An English-language menu has photos of sushi set meals, noodle dishes, a *tempura teishoku*, the *Kamoi teishoku* (featuring sashimi and *chirashi-zushi*—seafood rice bowl), and—my favorite—the *Kurashiki bento* with tempura, vegetables, and seasonable goodies. But what I love most is gazing out the window, watching people strolling along the canal.

1–3–17 Chuo. ℂ **086/422-0606.** Set meals ¥1,300–¥2,600. Thurs–Tues 10am–6pm (closed 2nd Mon of each month). Catty-corner across the canal from the Ohara Museum of Art.

Kiyutei (亀遊亭) ★ STEAK   Enter through the front gate just off the canal, pass through the small courtyard, and dine in a room dominated by a counter with cooks grilling steaks, the specialty of the house, served with grated *daikon* (Japanese radish) or Madeira sauce. There's an English-language menu, but best is probably one of the set meals, which in addition to steaks also offer fried prawns and scallops or stewed beef for dinner, or beef curry, grilled chicken, and a hamburger steak for lunch.

1–2–20 Chuo. ✆ **086/422-5140.** Set lunches ¥1,100–¥4,700; set dinners ¥1,650–¥5,500. Tues–Sun 11am–9pm (to 8:30pm Dec–Feb). Opposite the canal from Ohara Museum.

Ristorante Rentenchi ★ PIZZA/PASTA   This cozy, tiny restaurant, run by a husband-and-wife team, is a good choice for inexpensive dining near the Bikan Historical Quarter. Neapolitan-style, thick-crusted pizza from a wood-burning oven is the specialty, and the sommelier can make suggestions from a list of some 200 Italian wines. Not on the English menu are fixed-price dinners, the cheapest of which gives a choice of pizza or pasta of the day, salad, bread, dessert, and coffee or espresso. Reservations recommended.

2–19–18 Achi. ✆ **086/421-7858.** Pizza and pasta ¥1,100–¥2,500; set lunches ¥1,000–¥2,800; set dinners ¥3,000–¥4,500. Wed–Mon 11:30am–2pm and 6–10pm. On the left side of Chuo Dori when walking from Kurashiki Station, just before the historic district.

Exploring Kurashiki's Bikan Historical Quarter

Kurashiki's **historic old town** is centered on a canal lined with graceful willows and 200-year-old granaries made of black-tile walls topped with white mortar. Many of the granaries have been turned into museums, *ryokan,* restaurants, and boutiques selling hand-blown glass, Bizen pottery, papier-mâché toys, women's ethnic clothing imported from Bali and India, and mats and handbags made of *igusa* (rush grass), a local specialty. Street vendors sell jewelry, their wares laid out beside the canal, and healthy young men stand ready to give visitors rides in rickshaws.

A resident advised me that because of the crowds that descend upon Kurashiki, I should awaken early before shops and museums open and explore this tiny area while it's still under the magic spell of the early morning glow; even rain only enhances the contrasting black and white of the buildings. "Real lovers of Kurashiki come on Monday," he added. "Because that's when most everything is closed, and there are fewer people." (If Mon is a holiday, however, most museums stay open and close on Tues instead.) Don't neglect the side streets between the canal and Achi Shrine on Tsurugatayama Park, especially the neighborhoods of Honmachi and Higashimachi. I've found that early evening is also a magical time to walk the streets, especially after sunset, when many buildings along the canal are illuminated.

Ohara Museum of Art (Ohara Bijutsukan) ★★★ ART MUSEUM This is by far Kurashiki's most impressive museum, a must-see even on a short list of sightseeing. Industrialist Ohara Magosaburo, who believed that people even in remote Kurashiki should have the opportunity to view great works of art (that's his stately mansion across the canal from the museum), founded it in 1930 as Japan's first museum of Western art. The main building, a two-story stone structure resembling a Greek temple, is small but manages to contain the works of Picasso, Matisse, Vlaminck, Courbet, Monet, Pissarro, Sisley, Utrillo, Toulouse-Lautrec, Gauguin, Cézanne, El Greco, Modigliani, Renoir, Miró, Kandinsky, Pollack, Jasper Johns, De Kooning, Warhol, and many more. The museum has expanded so much over the years that several annexes have been added. A *mingei* (Japan's 20th-c folkcrafts) gallery housed in a renovated Edo-era granary contains works by some of my favorites, including ceramics by Hamada Shoji, Bernard Leach, and Kawai Kanjiro; and woodblock prints by Munakata Shiko, who lived in Kurashiki 3 years. An annex is devoted to Japanese artists painting in the Western style and to contemporary Japanese artists like Shigeru Aoki, Ryusei Kishida, and Ryuzaburo Umehara. Yet another building displays ancient Chinese art, primarily from prehistoric times to the Tang Dynasty (A.D. 618–907); your ticket also includes entry to the Kojima Torajiro Memorial Hall, commemorating the Japanese artist who selected many of the museum's early works. Allow up to 2 hours to see everything, but your ticket is good all day so you don't have to see it all at once, taking a break, perhaps, in the museum's Shikeien Garden. An audioguide (¥500) covers works in the main gallery.

1-1–15 Chuo. www.ohara.or.jp. ✆ **086/422-0005.** Admission ¥1,300 adults, ¥800 university and senior-high students, ¥500 children. Tues–Sun 9am–5pm. On the canal.

The Ohashi's House (Ohashi-ke; 大橋家住宅) ★ HISTORIC BUILDING   Built in 1796 by a wealthy salt and rice merchant, this traditional mansion is typical of the era, with front rooms used for entertaining guests and for business (the doorsill leading to the warehouse can be removed for easy transport), and the rear used as family living quarters. An imposing front gate, usually allowed only in homes belonging to the samurai class, is proof how important the Ohashi family was (remarkably, the Ohashi family still owns the house). Once much larger (sadly, a hotel occupies the former garden), the home's 20 remaining rooms contain some family heirlooms. Listen to short audio introduction in English and take a 15-minute spin through if you've never seen the inside of a traditional Japanese home.

3-21–31 Achi. www.ohashi-ke.com. ✆ **086/422-0007.** Admission ¥500 adults, ¥300 seniors and children. Daily 9am–5pm (Sat to 6pm Apr–Oct). Closed on Fri Dec–Feb. Across Chuo Dori from the Bikan Historical Quarter, behind the Royal Art Hotel.,

A Cycling Excursion

For some rural R & R, head north to the historic Kibiji District, once home to the ancient Kibi kingdom and known today for its huge *kofun* (burial mounds), temples, shrines, and five-story pagoda, all connected via a marked biking path that traverses this pastoral landscape. It's fun to cycle from one historic destination to the next, but what I like most about this ride is its rural setting, through villages, past peach groves, and along paddies (much of the bike path is actually on the same raised walkways farmers use to separate and dam their paddies and to get to their fields).

Rental bikes (✆ **0866/92-0233**) are available daily 9am to 6pm outside Soja Station, which you can reach in 11 minutes from Kurashiki Station on the JR Hakubi Line (fare: ¥240). Bikes rent for ¥400 for 2 hours, but I suggest you fork out ¥1,000 for the whole day and cycle the entire 15km (10 miles) to Bizen-Ichinomiya Station, where you can ditch the bike and hop on the JR Kibi Linea train for an 11-minute ride to Okayama Station (fare: ¥210) and transfer there for the train back to Kurashiki. It takes 3 to 4 hours to bike the entire path and stop at sights along the way. *Caveat:* Although the bike path is well marked in English most of the way, I got lost trying to find Bizen-Ichinomiya Station. Villagers are apparently used to lost cyclers and soon had me merrily on my way. You'll get a cycling map when you rent your bike; the Kurashiki tourist office also has information on the Kibiji District.

HIROSHIMA, THEN & NOW ★★

894km (554 miles) W of Tokyo; 376km (235 miles) W of Kyoto

With a population of 1.18 million, Hiroshima, capital of Hiroshima Prefecture and the largest metropolis in the Chugoku region, looks just like any other city in Japan. With modern buildings and an industry that includes the manufacture of cars and ships, it's a town full of vitality and purpose with a steady flow of both Japanese and foreign business executives in and out. But unlike other cities, Hiroshima's past is clouded: It has the unfortunate distinction of being the first city ever destroyed by an atomic bomb. (The second city—and it is hoped the last—was Nagasaki, on Kyushu island.)

It happened one clear summer morning, August 6, 1945, at 8:15am, when a B-29 approached Hiroshima from the northeast, passed over the central part of the city, dropped the bomb, and then took off at full speed. The bomb exploded 43 seconds later at an altitude of 600m (1,980 ft.) in a huge fireball, followed by a mushroom cloud of smoke that rose 8,910m (29,700 ft.) in the air.

There were approximately 350,000 people living in Hiroshima at the time of the bombing, and almost a third lost their lives on that day. The heat from the blast was so intense that it seared people's skin, while the pressure caused by the explosion tore clothes off bodies and caused the rupture and explosion of internal organs. Flying glass tore through flesh like bullets, and fires broke out all over the city. But that wasn't the end of it: Victims who survived the blast were subsequently exposed to huge doses of radioactive particles. Even people who showed no outward signs of sickness suddenly died, creating panic and helplessness among the survivors. In the years that followed, blast survivors continued to suffer from the effects of the bomb, with a high incidence of cancer, disfigurement, scars, and keloid skin tissue.

Ironically, Hiroshima's tragedy is now the city's largest tourist draw, and visitors from around the world come to see Peace Memorial Park with its haunting museum and memorials. But Hiroshima, laced with rivers and wide, tree-lined boulevards, boasts a few other worthwhile attractions as well and is the most popular gateway for trips to nearby Miyajima, a small island renowned for its shrine and nature (p. 317).

Essentials

GETTING THERE   By Train   Hiroshima is about 5 hours from Tokyo by **Shinkansen** bullet train (you have to change trains in Shin-Osaka if you have a Japan Rail Pass, because only the Nozomi, which is not covered by the pass, covers the entire distance in 4 hr.), and a little more than 2 hours from Kyoto. The fare for an unreserved seat is ¥18,040 from Tokyo and ¥10,890 from

Yokogawa

Yokogawa

Ota River

River

Nishi-
Hongan-ji
Temple

Johoku

Johoku Dori

Hakushima

Kateisaibanshomae

JAPAN

Tokyo
●Hiroshima

Toshogu
Shrine

3

Chuo
(Central)
Park

① Gokoku
Shrine

Shukkeienmae

② 4

Hiroshima

i

8

Hiroshima
Baseball
Stadium

Jonan Dori

Jogakuinmae

Hiroshima

Honkawacho

9 Kenchomae

Genbaku
Dome-Mae

10

Kamiyachonishi

7

6

i

5

13

Ota River

12

11

Aioi Dori

14

i

Peace
Memorial
Park

15

Hondori

Tatemachi

16

Hatchobori

19

Inarimachi

Rijo Dori

Hondori Shopping Arcade

Ebisucho

Kanayamacho

23

River

17

Chuo Dori

18

Fukuromachi

20

i Information
⊠ Post Office
┼─┼ Tram
═══ Railway

Kokutai-ji
Temple

Motoyasu

22 22

Heiwa Odori

21

Hijiyama
Shrine

To Hiroshima
Airport

Chudenmae

City
Hall

Eki-mae Odori

Kyobashi River

Hijiyama
Park

HOTELS ■
Hana Hostel **5**
Hotel Flex **6**
Hotel Granvia Hiroshima **4**
Hotel Sunroute **22**
Regalo **19**
Rihga Royal Hiroshima **9**
Sansui Ryokan **13**
Toyoko Inn Hiroshima-Eki
    Minamiguchi-Migi **7**
Toyoko Inn Hiroshima-Eki
    Shinkansen-Guchi **3**
Toyoko Inn Hiroshima
    Heiwa-Odori **21**

RESTAURANTS ◆
Anderson Kitchen **16**
Caffe Ponte **15**
Kissui **22**
Kushinobo **17**
Molly Malone's **18**
No-no-Budou **10**
Okonomi-Mura **20**
Sushi Tei **11**

ATTRACTIONS ●
A-Bomb Dome **12**
Hiroshima Castle **1**
Hiroshima Museum of Art **8**
Peace Memorial Museum **23**
Peace Memorial Park **14**
Shukkei-en Garden **2**

...ation is undergoing massive renovation until ...navigate.

...n Tokyo Station nightly at 8pm (with a stop in ...a Station the next morning at 7:50am for ... (www.willerexpress.com), departing nightly ...ing at Hiroshima Station at 9am, costs ¥8,900 ... From Kyoto (with a stop in Osaka), Willer ...taking more than 7 hours to reach Hiroshima

There are two Hiroshima City Tourist Information counters at **Hiroshima Station,** a small one at the north exit where Shinkansen bullet trains arrive and the main one at the station's south exit, where the streetcars are (© **082/261-1877**). Both are open from 9 to 5:30pm daily (the small one is closed 12:30–1:30pm). A third tourist office is located in **Peace Memorial Park** in the Rest House (© **082/247-6738**). It's open daily from 8:30am to 6pm March to November (to 7pm Aug) and to 5pm the rest of the year. All three facilities have English-language maps of Hiroshima and Miyajima, including transportation maps. Online information on Hiroshima is also available at **www.hiroshima-navi.or.jp.**

GETTING AROUND   One legacy of Hiroshima's total destruction was its rebirth into one of Japan's most navigable cities, with wide, open boulevards instead of the usual cramped streets. Hiroshima's main attractions, including Peace Memorial Park, Hiroshima Castle, Shukkei-en Garden, and Hiroshima Museum of Art, lie to the west and southwest of Hiroshima Station. I find it easiest to make the circuit to Hiroshima's centrally located attractions **on foot.** From Hiroshima Station, you can walk to Shukkei-en Garden in about 15 minutes, from which it's another 10-minute walk to Hiroshima Castle. You can walk onward to Peace Memorial Park in about 15 minutes, passing the Hiroshima Museum of Art and the A-Bomb Dome on the way. Just east of Peace Park is the **Hondori** covered shopping arcade and its neighboring streets, considered the heart of the city with its many department stores, shops, and restaurants.

Otherwise, the most convenient mode of transportation is **streetcar,** which costs only ¥160 one-way (children pay half fare). If you need to transfer to another line, ask the driver for a *norikae* (transfer) card, which you then pass through the card machine upon alighting from the first streetcar ... again when boarding the second streetcar. When you arrive at your destination, return the card to the streetcar driver. A 1-day pass, which you can buy from the conductor, costs ¥600. Be sure to pick up a streetcar map from the tourist office.

There's also a sightseeing loop bus, the "Hiroshima Meipuru-pu," with two routes departing from the backside of Hiroshima Station from about 9am to 5:30pm daily and traveling to Peace Memorial Park among other attractions. The fare is ¥200 for one ride or ¥400 all day; holders of the Japan Rail Pass ride for free. Ask the tourist office for a bus map.

[Fast FACTS] HIROSHIMA

ATM/Mail   Hiroshima's main post office, 2–62 Matsubara-cho (℃ **082/261-6401**), is located to the right after exiting from Hiroshima Station's south side and is open 24 hours for mail. Its ATM services are available Monday to Saturday 12:05am to 11:55pm and Sunday and holidays 12:05am to 9pm.

Internet & Wi-Fi Access   Free Wi-Fi is available at the tourist office in Peace Memorial Park. For use of a computer, **Media Café Popeye,** located in the Hondori covered shopping arcade (℃ **082/545-0369**) above a shop called Beams, is open 24 hours and charges ¥108 for the first 30 minutes, and then ¥64 for each subsequent 10 minutes.

Where to Stay

Directions are from Hiroshima Station. The rates reflect the seasons.

EXPENSIVE

Hotel Granvia Hiroshima ★   Owned by JR West (and offering discounts to holders of the Japan Rail Pass), this hotel is convenient for short stays because it's connected to the Shinkansen (north) side of the station. Inconvenient, however, is that to get to Hiroshima's sights and streetcars, which are on the other side of the station, you have to navigate a confusing underground passage, made even worse by station renovations lasting until 2018 (if you have a rail pass, you can pass through the station, which is much quicker). Rooms consist of rather small standard rooms from the 6th to 18th floors, superior rooms on the 19th floor that are larger and more chic, and Granvia rooms on the 20th floor, the best of which are huge deluxe twins with spacious bathrooms. Still, none have great views, unless you count views of the Shinkansen pulling into the station.

1–5 Matsubara-cho. www.hgh.co.jp. ℃ **082/262-1111.** 403 units. ¥5,100–¥16,747 single; ¥12,457–¥31,185 double. 20% discount for holders of Japan Rail Pass. Attached to Hiroshima Station. **Amenities:** 9 restaurants; 2 bars; lounge; outdoor beer terrace (summer only); access to health club in Hiroshima Station w/gym, indoor pool, and sauna (discount ticket at concierge desk ¥1,000); room service; free Wi-Fi.

Rihga Royal Hotel Hiroshima ★★★   The 33-story Rihga Royal stands out as Hiroshima's tallest hotel, has a convenient location in the heart of the city between Hiroshima Castle and Peace Park, and is connected to a large complex that includes the Pacela shopping mall and Sogo department store. Large rooms with luxurious furnishings come with plenty of features, including magnifying mirrors and lots of counter space in the bathrooms. Rates are based on floor height and room size, but even some of the cheapest twins have views of a park across the street and the castle. The best views, however, are from top floors with panoramas of the Seto Inland Sea (you can even see Miyajima). A nice touch are the pictorial maps in each room describing the view, but the best view of all is afforded from the 33rd-floor Rihga Top lounge (no cover charge if you sit at the bar). Unfortunately, the lobby lounge I used to love has been converted into a chapel for weddings, a trend I've noticed at several Hiroshima hotels.

6–78 Motomachi. www.rihga-hiroshima.co.jp. ℃ **082/502-1121.** 486 units. ¥11,500–¥19,008 single; ¥14,300–¥46,332 double; from ¥35,000 executive double. Streetcar: 1,

2, or 6 to Kamiya-cho-nishi (1 min.). **Amenities:** 6 restaurants; 2 bars; lounge; concierge; executive-level rooms; health club w/gym, atrium-style 25m (82-ft.) 5-lane pool, Jacuzzi, and sauna (fee: ¥3,250 for pool and sauna; ¥6,480 for everything); health and dental clinic; room service; free Wi-Fi.

MODERATE

Hotel Flex ★★★   This is Hiroshima's most unconventional hotel, apparent the moment you walk in and find yourself in a cafe that doubles as the front desk and opens out onto a terrace overlooking the tree-lined Kyobashi-gawa river, with jazz playing in the background. A modern concrete structure, it, offers tiny but fashionable rooms, some with relaxing river views and/or floor-to-ceiling windows and all crisply decorated with blue-and-green pillows and bed runners, stark with white walls, and wooden floors. The best and most expensive are three top-floor rooms that are almost like mini-apartments without the kitchen (one even has an outdoor terrace).

7–1 Kaminobori-cho. www.hotel-flex.co.jp. © **082/223-1000.** 65 units. ¥7,150–¥8,800 single; ¥12,100–¥24,200 double. Hiroshima Station (7 min.). From the station's south exit, turn right and then left after the post office; after crossing the pedestrian Ekinishi-koka-bashi bridge and turning right to cross another bridge, it will be immediately on your right. **Amenities:** Cafe/restaurant; free Wi-Fi.

Hotel Sunroute ★★★   Although most hotels in this chain are strictly business hotels, this property's excellent location, next to the river and catty-corner from the museum in Peace Memorial Park, plus two very good restaurants with great views, makes it a popular choice for tourists as well. The highest-priced rooms have the additional advantage of views of the park and river (only one of the 11 double rooms faces the park, however), and the cheapest rooms are on low floors and have no views whatsoever. Room were recently renovated and are now all no-smoking.

3–3–1 Otemachi. www.sunroutehotel.jp/hiroshima. © **082/249-3600.** 283 units. ¥9,450–¥11,550 single; ¥7,400–¥26,250 double. Streetcar: 1 to Chuden-mae (3 min.). Backtrack north to Heiwa Odori and turn left; it's on your left before the river. **Amenities:** 2 restaurants, free Wi-Fi.

INEXPENSIVE

There are four inexpensive Toyoko Inns in Hiroshima. Check www.toyoko-inn.com for locations.

Hana Hostel ★★   This former business hotel turned backpacker's hostel offers 13 small private rooms, four Western-style with private shower and toilet and the rest *tatami* rooms with either wash basin and toilet or bathroom. There are also dormitory rooms, including one with two bunk beds (and a toilet) and two for women only, making this a good choice for both families and females on a budget. Pluses include its location near Hiroshima Station, communal kitchen with free tea and coffee, a fifth-floor lounge with TV and DVDs (there's an elevator), and a rooftop terrace where you can hang out and hang laundry. If I were you, I'd ask for a room facing the front of the building, away from the train tracks.

1–15 Kojin-machi. http://hiroshima.hanahostel.com. ☏ **082/263-2980.** 16 units (4 with toilet only, 9 with bathroom). ¥3,700 single with toilet only, ¥3,900 with bathroom; ¥6,400 double with toilet only, ¥6,800 double with bathroom; ¥2,500 dormitory bed. Rates ¥300 more per person in high season. Hiroshima Station (4 min.). Turn left out of the station's south exit and follow the road that hugs the tracks; after passing by the road that crosses the tracks (don't cross the tracks), take the 1st right and then 1st left at the small parking lot. **Amenities:** Rental bikes (¥500 per day); free Wi-Fi.

Regalo ★ Located on one of Hiroshima's many rivers, about halfway between Hiroshima Station and downtown, this nine-story hotel capitalizes on its river views with an atmospheric Italian restaurant and, across the street beside the river, an open-air pavilion cafe. While the cheapest rooms have glazed windows facing the back and are dark, rooms only slightly more expensive have refreshing views of the river and are larger. Bedspreads instead of covered duvets, however, give the hotel an outdated appearance. Still, this establishment is a pleasant alternative to most inexpensive lodgings, with more personality than the cookie-cutter Toyoko Inn chain.

9–2 Hashimoto-cho. www.regalo-h.com/hiroshima/index.html. ☏ **082/224-6300.** 63 units. ¥4,907–¥7,000 single; ¥7,500–¥10,000 double. Streetcar: 1, 2, or 6 to Kanayama-cho (2 min.). Walk back toward the bridge (but don't cross it) and turn left at the river. Or a 13-min. walk from Hiroshima Station. **Amenities:** Restaurant; cafe; free Wi-Fi.

Sansui Ryokan ★★★ This is a good choice for travelers who like meeting locals rather than staying in impersonal hotels. It's run by the motherly and very hospitable Kato-san, who cheerfully oversees operations and hands out maps and sightseeing brochures, has kimono you can try on for free, and can even arrange 1-hour lessons in calligraphy or the tea ceremony (¥1,500 each) if you make reservations 3 weeks in advance. It has a cozy communal room offering free coffee and tea; three showers for its only six *tatami* rooms; and walls covered with photos showing past happy guests. Note, however, that rooms on the second floor are reached by steep stairs. It has a good location, only a 7-minute walk west of Peace Memorial Park.

4–16 Koami-cho. www.sansui-ryokan.com. ☏ **082/293-9051.** 6 units, none with bathroom. ¥4,500 single; ¥9,500 double; ¥12,000 triple. Streetcar: 2 to Koami-cho (1 min.). Walk toward and turn left at the river and then the 1st left. **Amenities:** Rental bikes (¥300 per day); free Wi-Fi.

Where to Eat

Although the people of Osaka claim to have made *okonomiyaki* popular among the masses, the people of Hiroshima claim to have made it an art. *Okonomiyaki* is a kind of Japanese pancake (or perhaps pizza) filled with cabbage, meat, and other fillings. Whereas in Osaka the ingredients are mixed together, in Hiroshima each layer is prepared separately, which means the chefs have to be quite skilled at keeping the whole thing together. Hiroshima is also famous for oysters (among the largest I've ever seen), with thousands of rafts cultivating oysters in Hiroshima Bay and producing 20,000 tons of shelled oysters yearly.

MODERATE

Caffé Ponte ★ ITALIAN   What I like most about this smoke-free restaurant is that it's easy to find (just across the river from the Rest House tourist office in Peace Park) and offers outdoor seating under white umbrellas even in winter due to heaters, making a meal here seem like a mini-vacation. Its English-language menu with photos offers lots of choices, including Hiroshima oysters, pasta, pizza, fish, and meat dishes, as well as cocktails and other alcoholic drinks.

1–9–21 Otemachi. www.caffeponte.com. ✆ **082/247-7471.** Main dishes ¥1,200–¥1,500; set lunches ¥1,180–¥1,850; set dinners ¥3,800–¥5,800. Mon–Fri 10am–10pm, Sat–Sun and holidays 8am–10pm (7:30am–10pm daily in Aug). Streetcar: Hondori (3 min., through the covered shopping arcade) or Genbaku Dome-mae (2 min.). East of Peace Park, on the bank of Motoyasu-gawa river at the Motoyasu-bashi bridge.

Kissui ★★★ KAISEKI   Convenient to Peace Memorial Park, great 15th-floor views, an English-language menu, and beautifully prepared *kaiseki* meals make this an optimal restaurant for tourists. For lunch, the Kissui Set for ¥2,600 is a great choice, but no matter what you choose, you can't go wrong here unless you forget to make reservations, as this place is popular. Alternatively, Viale, also on the 15th floor with the same open hours, offers Italian fare with the same great views.

Hotel Sunroute, 15th floor, 3–3–1 Otemachi. ✆ **082/249-5657.** Set lunches ¥2,600–¥6,200; *kaiseki* set dinners ¥5,500–¥9,900. Daily 11:30am–2pm and 5–8pm (last order). Streetcar: Chuden-mae (see directions to hotel in review of Hotel Sunroute, above).

INEXPENSIVE

Anderson Kitchen ★★ INTERNATIONAL   Occupying a former bank building in the Hondori covered shopping arcade, this popular place not far from Peace Memorial Park has a gourmet food department on its ground floor offering baked goods, wine, and imported delicacies, while the second floor has a cafeteria with five counters specializing in different types of food—salads, sandwiches, pizza, pasta, steaks, Chinese dishes, desserts, or drinks, including wine and beer. After first taking a seat, a waitress will bring you a ticket, which you use when selecting the items you want. You pay when you leave. From 6pm, it's an all-you-can-eat buffet.

7–1 Hondori. ✆ **082/247-4800.** Main dishes ¥1,080–¥1,671; set meals ¥1,728–¥2,238. Dinner buffet ¥3,980 (¥4,720 including alcohol). Daily 11am–9pm (last order). Streetcar: Hondori (1 min.); in the Hondori covered shopping arcade 1 block to the east.

Kushinobo (串の坊) ★★★ KUSHIYAKI   This is a friendly, rub-elbows-with-the-locals kind of place, lively and crowded and decorated with Japanese knickknacks. Although kushiyaki connoisseurs like ordering skewers à la carte, you'll probably be better off ordering from the English-language menu listing only set meals. I always order the Kushinobo-gozen with 10 skewers of vegetables, meat, and seafood plus pickled vegetables and soup. For dipping, there's soy sauce, mustard, and coarse salt, while a ceramic fish with an open mouth serves as the receptacle for your empty skewers. In addition to the food, what I enjoy most about dining here is watching skewers being prepared

behind the counter and the friendly interactio[...]
is a serious fellow, but he speaks English and s[...]
the orders straight. It's located off the east end of th[...]
behind Parco department store.

Parco-mae, 7–4 Horikawa-cho. ℂ **082/245-9300.** Set lunches ¥[...]
ners ¥2,450–¥4,000. Daily 11:30am–1:30pm and 5–9:30pm (last [...]
Hatchobori (2 min.). Walk south on Chuo Dori 2 blocks to Parco depar[...]
turn right into a covered shopping arcade; take the 1st left and then the 1s[...]
for its old-fashioned red facade.

Molly Malone's ★ VARIED WESTERN An Irish pub with good foo[...]
what more do you need? In addition to 8 beers on tap (a sampler of three costs[...]
¥1,100), it offers soups, salads (like a poached salmon salad), pastas (including vegetarian choices), burgers, steak, and classic pub fare ranging from fish
and chips and bangers and mash to cottage pie and Irish stew. Tuesdays offer
cheaper-priced cocktails for ladies, while Thursdays are Dice Night (you roll
for the price of your drink, making it anywhere from ¥200 to ¥1,200). Add
happy hour Monday to Saturday from 5 to 7pm, screens showing international
soccer and rugby games, and free Wi-Fi, and this could be your new favorite
hot spot.

Teigeki Building, 4th floor, 1–20 Shintenchi. www.mollymalones.jp. ℂ **082/244-2554.**
Main dishes ¥950–¥2,100. Mon–Fri 5pm–1am, Sat–Sun and holidays 11:30am–
midnight. Streetcar: Hatchobori (1 min.). Walk south on Chuo Dori Ave.; it's on the left
(across from Parco) and is easy to miss. Look for the Guinness sign.

No-no-Budou (野の葡萄) ★★ JAPANESE BUFFET With an open
kitchen and jazz as background music, this popular buffet restaurant in the
Pacela shopping complex (next to Righa Royal Hotel) specializes in healthy,
organic foods, with some 50 choices that change daily but always include
choices of Chinese and Japanese dishes, from noodles and tempura to soups
and salads. Some seats beside windows provide city views, but avoid the
lunchtime rush.

Motomachi CRED complex, 7th floor of Pacela, 78–6 Motomachi. ℂ **082/502-3340.**
Buffet lunch ¥1,740; buffet dinner ¥2,160. Daily 11am–3pm and 5–9pm (last order).
Streetcar: Kamiya-cho-nishi (1 min.); follow the underground signs for the Astram Line
and take the exit on your left.

Okonomi-Mura (お好み村) ★★ OKONOMIYAKI Open for 50 years
one of Hiroshima's most beloved establishments, this is the best place in town
to witness *okonomiyaki* short-order cooks at their trade. Although the shabby
building doesn't look like it contains restaurants, its name means "*okonomiyaki* village," and that's what it is—three floors of some 20 individual stalls
dishing out *okonomiyaki*. All offer basically the same menu—sit down at one
of the counters and watch how the chef first spreads pancake mix on a hot
griddle; follows it with a layer of cabbage, bean sprouts, and bacon; and then
adds an egg on top. If you want, you can have yours with Chinese noodles.
Portions are huge (no credit cards accepted). I suggest wandering through and
choosing one that catches your fancy, but for a specific recommendation, try

on the second floor, with a female
until midnight (closed Tues).

2/241-2210. Set meals ¥800–¥1,400.
er. Streetcar: Hatchobori (2 min.). Walk
on Quijote.

ent sushi at reasonable prices is the
After being seated at the counter,
ge menu and an order form you fill
your plate for rolled sushi (like the
here are many Sushi Tei restaurants
r the A-Bomb Dome.

–¥432; sushi sets ¥864–¥2,160. Mon–Sat
m. Streetcar: Kamiya-cho-nishi (1 min.).
ngs and turn right; it's on the left.

Take the small street between the

Exploring Hiroshima

As you walk around Hiroshima today, you'll find it hard to imagine that the
city was the scene of such widespread horror and destruction just 70 years
ago. On the other hand, Hiroshima doesn't have the old buildings, temples,
and historic structures that other cities have, yet it draws a steady flow of
travelers, including Japanese school groups, who come to see Peace Memorial
Park, the city's best-known landmark. Dedicated to peace, the city also seems
committed to art: In addition to art museums, you'll find statues, stone lanterns, memorials, and sculptures lining the streets.

PEACE MEMORIAL PARK

Peace Memorial Park (Heiwa Koen) ★★★ lies in the center of the city.
English-language signs all over the city indicate how to reach it. From Hiroshima Station's south side, take streetcar No. 2 or 6 to the Genbaku-Domu-
mae stop, which is just north of the park. The first structure you'll see as you
alight from the streetcar is the **A-Bomb Dome (Genbaku Domu),** the skeletal
ruins of the former Industrial Promotion Hall, left as a visual reminder of the
death and destruction caused by the atomic bomb and now on the World Heritage List. Across the river is the park; it takes about 10 minutes to walk from
its northern end to the museum.

Along the way you'll see the many of the park's 50-some statues and memorials. Most touching is the **Children's Peace Monument,** dedicated to the
war's most innocent victims, not only those who died instantly in the blast but
also those who died afterward from the effects of radiation. It's a statue of a
girl with outstretched arms, and rising above her is a crane, a symbol of happiness and longevity in Japan. The statue is based on the true story of a young
girl, Sadako, who suffered from the effects of radiation. She believed that if she
could fold 1,000 paper cranes she would become well again. However, even
though she folded more than 1,000 cranes, she still died of leukemia. Today, all
Japanese children are familiar with her story, and around the memorial are
streamers of paper cranes donated by schoolchildren from all over Japan. To

the east of the statue is a former kimono shop now serving as the **Rest House,** where you'll find a branch of the Hiroshima Tourist Office. To the west is a **Cenotaph for Korean Victims.** It's a little-publicized fact that some 20,000 Koreans were killed that fateful summer day, most of them brought to Japan as forced laborers. It's significant to note that for 29 years, the cenotaph remained outside the park. In 1999, Hiroshima's mayor, calling for an end to prejudice against Korean residents in Japan, gave the memorial a new home here.

Between the Children's Peace Monument and the museum is the **Cenotaph for the A-bomb Victims,** designed by Japan's famous architect Kenzo Tange (who also designed the Tokyo Metropolitan Government offices in Shinjuku; see p. 122). Shaped like a figurine clay saddle found in ancient tombs, it shelters a stone chest, which in turn holds the names of all of those killed by the bomb and its aftereffects (more than 280,000 names have been registered so far). An epitaph, written in Japanese, carries the hopeful phrase, "Let all the souls here rest in peace, for we shall not repeat the evil." If you stand in front of the cenotaph, you'll have a view through the hollow arch of the Flame of Peace and the A-Bomb Dome. It is said that the **Flame of Peace** will continue to burn until all atomic weapons vanish from the face of the earth and nuclear war is no longer a threat to humanity.

East of the Peace Flame is the **Hiroshima National Peace Memorial Hall for the Atomic Bomb Victims** (www.hiro-tsuitokinenkan.go.jp; © **082/543-6271**). Its Hall of Remembrance, a 360-degree panorama re-creating the bombed city as seen from the hypocenter, is made of 140,000 tiles, the number of people estimated to have died by the end of 1945. The rest of the memorial serves as a computerized audiovisual library with information on victims, their histories, and photos. Admission is free and it's open the same hours as the Peace Memorial Museum.

Peace Memorial Museum (Heiwa Kinen Shiryokan) ★★★ At the south end of Peace Park, this museum is the main destination in the park. It comprises two buildings, the East Building and the Main Building, which tell the story of Hiroshima before, during and after the bomb was dropped. *Note, however, that the museum is undergoing a massive renovation.* Until spring of 2016, only the Main Building is open while the East Building is closed for renovation. Then the East Building will be open while the Main Building undergoes renovation until 2018.

In any case, the Main Building is the focus of the museum (the theme of its new exhibit will be "Truth of the Bombing") and concentrates on the inhumanity of atomic bombs, the A-bomb's enormous destruction (90% of Hiroshima's buildings were destroyed or burned), and the indescribable suffering of atomic bomb survivors and families on that awful day. Exhibits show in graphic detail the effects of the blast on bodies, buildings, and materials. There are photographs of scorched earth, charred remains of bodies, and people with open wounds, while displays explain the effects of radiation, including hair loss, keloid scars, leukemia, and cancer. There's a bronze Buddha that was half-melted in the blast. Tattered clothing and other personal effects are accompanied by short biographies of their owners, many of them children and teenagers and many of whom died in the blast. There are also survivor accounts, not only of what they suffered the day of the blast but in the many years that followed.

When reopened in 2016, the East Building will serve as an introduction to the museum and will contain exhibits on Hiroshima before the bombing, the progress it has made since then, and the danger of nuclear proliferation.

Needless to say, visiting Peace Memorial Park is a sobering and depressing experience but perhaps a necessary one. And to think that what was dropped on Hiroshima is small compared to the bombs of today; as early as 1961, the Soviet Union had tested a hydrogen bomb 3,300 times more powerful than the atomic bomb dropped on Hiroshima. You'll need at least 1 hour here to do the museum justice.

1–2 Nakajima-cho. www.pcf.city.hiroshima.jp. © **082/241-4004.** Admission ¥50 adults, ¥30 high-school students and seniors; free for children. Daily 8:30am–6pm Mar–Nov [until 7pm in Aug], daily 8:30am–5pm Dec–Feb. Streetcar: Fukuro-machi (3 min.). Hiroshima Meipuru-pu: Peace Memorial Park (1 min.).

More Sights & Attractions

Hiroshima Castle ★★★ CASTLE   Completed in 1591 but destroyed in the atomic blast, Hiroshima Castle was reconstructed in 1958. Its five-story wooden *donjon* is a faithful reproduction of the original, but the main reason to come here is the museum housed in the castle's modern interior, which can be toured in about 30 minutes and is devoted to Hiroshima's history as a flourishing castle town, with excellent English-language presentations. It also gives a good explanation on castles in Japan, including differences in architecture between those built on hills (for defense) and those built on plains (mainly administrative; Hiroshima's is an example of a flatland castle). Videos, with English translations via earphones, describe Hiroshima's founding and the construction of Hiroshima Castle to serve as a hub for transportation, while displays explain the differences in lifestyle between samurai and townspeople, the hierarchy of the feudal administration system, and other aspects of Edo life. There's also samurai gear, swords, models of old Hiroshima and the castle, as well as a kimono and helmet and breast plate you can try on for free. The top of the *donjon* provides a panoramic view of the city.

21–1 Moto-machi. www.rijo-castle.jp/rijo/main.html. © **082/221-7512.** Admission ¥370 adults, ¥180 high-school students and seniors, free for children. Daily 9am–6pm (to 5pm Dec–Feb). A 15-min. walk north of Peace Memorial Park. Streetcar: Kamiya-cho-higashi (10 min.). Hiroshima Meipuru-pu: Hiroshima Museum of Art (5 min.).

Hiroshima Museum of Art (Hiroshima Bijutsukan) ★★ MUSEUM This gem of a private museum, housed in a modern one-story round building surrounded by trees, is located in a park in the heart of the city. Its permanent collection of some 300 paintings, half by French painters from Romanticism to Ecole de Paris, is presented in chronological order in four rooms, with about 100 on display at any one time. Though small, virtually every piece is by a well-known artist, including Delacroix, Courbet, Manet, Monet, Renoir, Sisley, Degas, Toulouse-Lautrec, Rousseau, Cézanne, Gauguin, van Gogh, Matisse, Picasso, Braque, Utrillo, Chagall, and Modigliani. The museum also shows Japanese art in the Western style from the Meiji Era to the present, with works by Kuroda Seiki, Yokoyama Taikan, and Kishida Ryusei. Plan on an hour here.

3–2 Motomachi. www.hiroshima-museum.jp. ⓒ **082/223-2530.** Admission ¥1,000 adults, ¥500 university and high-school students, ¥200 junior-high and elementary students. Prices may change due to special exhibits. Tues–Sun 9am–5pm. Streetcar: Kamiya-cho-higashi (3 min.). Hiroshima Meipuru-pu: Hiroshima Museum of Art (5 min.). In Chuo Park, across from the Rihga Royal Hotel (Hiroshima's tallest building).

Shukkei-en Garden ★ PARK/GARDEN Shukkei-en Garden, which means "landscape garden in miniature," was first laid out in 1620 by a master of the tea ceremony, with a pond constructed in imitation of famous Lake Xi Hu in Hangzhou, China. Using streams, ponds, islets, and bridges, the feudal lord's garden was designed to appear much larger than it actually is and is best viewed on a 30-minute circular stroll. Like everything else in Hiroshima, it was destroyed in 1945, but amazingly, it looks like it's been here forever. Unfortunately, like most gardens in Japan, tall neighboring buildings detract from the garden's beauty (there ought to be a law), but there are vantage points for photos where you can't see any buildings and there are lots of places to sit and relax.

2–11 Kaminobori-cho. http://shukkeien.jp. ⓒ **082/221-3620.** Admission ¥260 adults, ¥150 university and high-school students, ¥100 children. Daily 9am–6pm (to 5pm Oct–Mar). Streetcar: Shukkeien-mae (1 min.). Hiroshima Meipuru-pu: (Hiroshima Prefectural Art Museum). A 15-min. walk from Hiroshima Station.

MIYAJIMA, SCENIC ISLAND IN THE SETO SEA ★★★

13km (8 miles) SW of Hiroshima

Easily reached in about 40 minutes from Hiroshima, **Miyajima** is a treasure of an island only 2km (1¼ miles) off the mainland in the Seto Inland Sea. No doubt you've seen pictures of its most famous landmark: a huge red *torii,* or shrine gate, rising out of the water. Erected in 1875 and made of camphor wood, it's one of the largest *torii* in Japan, measuring more than 16m (53 ft.) tall. It guards Miyajima's main attraction, Itsukushima Shrine, designated a World Heritage Site in 1996.

With the Japanese penchant for categorizing the "three best" of virtually everything in their country—the three best gardens, the three best waterfalls, and so on—it's no surprise that Miyajima is ranked as one of the three most scenic spots in Japan (the other two are Matsushima in Tohoku; and Amanohashidate, a remote sand spit, on the Japan Sea coast). Only 31 sq. km (12 sq. miles) in area and consisting mostly of steep, wooded hills, it's an exceptionally beautiful island, part of the Seto-Naikai (Inland Sea) National Park that is mostly water, islands, and islets. Of course, this distinction means it can be extremely crowded with visitors, particularly in summer and autumn.

Miyajima has been held sacred since ancient times. In the olden days, no one was allowed to do anything so human as to give birth or die on the island, so both the pregnant and the ill were quickly ferried across to the mainland. Even today there's no cemetery on Miyajima. Covered with cherry trees that illuminate the island with snowy petals in spring, and with maple trees that emblazon it in reds and golds in autumn, Miyajima is home to tame deer that roam freely through the village.

Although you can see Miyajima in a day's trip from Hiroshima, it's such a delightful island for strolls and hikes and is such a beautiful respite from city life, you'll enjoy the island much more if you stay behind after the hordes of day-trippers have left. An added benefit of a longer stay: Itsukushima Shrine is illuminated at night, a gorgeous sight overnighters should not miss (although I'm horrified by night cruises offered around the *torii*). I've therefore included a few recommendations on where to stay, but avoid Golden Week and weekends in July, August, October, and November (when maple leaves are in full color), because accommodations are usually full. In fact, if you can, avoid coming on a weekend even if you don't spend the night.

Essentials

GETTING THERE   The easiest way to reach Miyajima is from Hiroshima, via JR train, streetcar, or boat. The fastest and most reliable method is the **train,** which departs from Hiroshima Station approximately every 15 minutes or less and costs ¥410 (free for JR Rail Pass holders) for the 26-minute ride to Miyajimaguchi (if you're downtown or in Peace Memorial Park, you'll find it easier to catch the train at Nishi-Hiroshima Station). Otherwise, **streetcar no. 2** takes about an hour from Hiroshima Station to Hiroden Miyajimaguchi, the last stop, and costs ¥260. Both the train and streetcar deposit you at Miyajimaguchi, from which it's just a 2-minute walk to the **ferry** bound for Miyajima. There are two ferry companies (JR and Matsudai) offering the 10-minute ride to Miyajima for ¥180, but if you have a **Japan Rail Pass** you can ride on the JR ferry for free.

Alternatively, boats travel from downtown Hiroshima directly to Miyajima in about 45 minutes. Operated by **Aqua Net Hiroshima** (www.aqua-net-h. co.jp; © **082/240-5955**), boats depart from Motoyasu-bashi bridge, south of the A-Bomb Dome, 8 to 14 times daily depending on the season. Fare is ¥2,000 one-way; children pay half fare. Note that service is suspended during inclement weather and when the tide is low.

VISITOR INFORMATION   On Miyajima island, stop off at the **Tourist Information Office** (www.miyajima.or.jp; © **0829/44-2011**), located in the Miyajima ferry terminal and open daily 9am to 6pm. It has an English-language brochure and a map. For more information, see **www.visit-miyajima-japan.com**.

GETTING AROUND   You can **walk** to all the sights, accommodations, and restaurants listed below. Omotesando Dori, the main street leading to the shrine, is lined with shops and restaurants. If you wish to visit the island's beaches, shuttle **buses** travel to the beaches year-round and twice an hour from mid-July through August for ¥300. Ask the Tourist Information Office for a schedule.

Where to Stay

EXPENSIVE

Kurayado Iroha ★★★   Located on the main Omotesando Dori pedestrian shopping street, this is modern Japanese elegance at its finest, with service so flawless you feel like staff has been waiting just for you. Before arrival you'll be asked your food preferences and allergies, and with good reason since dinners (served in a dining room) are a feast of organic vegetables, seafood from the Seto Inland, and other local dishes; the meal typically lasts 2 hours and is a highlight of staying here. Several types of rooms, all no-smoking, are available, with the cheapest on the second floor offering only inner courtyard views and the best offering both beds and *tatami* with sweeping views of the sea or mountains. In any case, don't miss the top-floor baths. Off the lobby is a high-end folkcraft store, chosen directly from artisans by the hotel.

589–4 Miyajima-cho. www.visit-miyajima.jp. ✆ **0829/44-0168.** 18 units. ¥32,000–¥39,960 per person. Rates higher in peak season. Rates include 2 meals. A 5-min. walk from the ferry pier. **Amenities:** Restaurant; free Wi-Fi (on request).

MODERATE

Momiji-so ★★   This small, Japanese-style inn, in business for 100 years, has a great location in Momijidani Park, about halfway to the ropeway to Mount Misen. *Tatami* rooms vary in size, though all have artwork, flowers, and views of the surrounding park; the best looks out over a koi pond. A plus is the outdoor Japanese restaurant serving noodles, barbecued conger eel on rice, and other dishes—weather permitting, you'll dine outside. Not much English is spoken, but they're used to foreigners and are very kind. No credit cards are accepted, and Wi-Fi is available only in the lobby.

Momijidani-koennai. www.gambo-ad.com. ✆ **0829/44-0077.** 7 units. ¥8,640 per person without meals (not available peak season); ¥17,280 per person with 2 meals. A 25-min. walk from the ferry pier in Momijidani Park. Pickup service available.

Ryoso Kawaguchi (旅荘かわぐち) ★★★   This 300-year-old home, with whitewashed walls, wood floors, exposed beams, and nice touches like bamboo containers holding flowers, has a traditional atmosphere. *Tatami* accommodations include two airy rooms with lofts for sleeping and a two-room suite good for families. The dining room and bar overlook a garden courtyard, while the third-floor lounge has a view of the nearby five-story pagoda. The ninth-generation innkeepers speak English and are gracious and welcoming. No credit cards are accepted.

469 Miyajima-cho. http://ryoso-kawaguchi.jp. ✆ **0829/44-0018.** 7 units (all with toilet, none with bathroom). ¥7,560 single; ¥14,040–¥15,120 double. Breakfast ¥1,080 extra; dinner ¥4,860 extra. A 10-min. walk from the ferry pier, on Machiya Dori. **Amenities:** Bar; free Wi-Fi.

INEXPENSIVE

Miyajima Morinoyado (みやじま杜の宿) ★★ You're forgiven if you pass this place by, thinking it must be an exclusive *ryokan*. Indeed, if it weren't a municipally owned People's Lodge (Kokumin Shukusha), rates here could easily be three times as much as they are. Though modern, with a pale lime-green exterior, it has a lovely Japanese design with a lobby overlooking a carp pond. On the other hand, the many school groups and families staying here leave no doubt that it's a public lodge, and it's quite a hike from the ferry pier, on the edge of town beside a park. Both *tatami* rooms and Western-style twins—simple but spacious and spotless—are available, some with views of the bay. The public baths look onto rock gardens. Reservations should be made 11 months in advance, but sometimes there are cancellations; when I once dropped by on a weekday in June, rooms were available. Meals are served in the restaurant. No credit cards accepted.

Miyajima-cho. www.morinoyado.jp. ☏ **0829/44-0430.** 30 units (26 with bathroom, 4 with toilet only). ¥5,184–¥5,940 per person room only; ¥12,204–¥12,960 per person with 2 meals. A 25-min. walk from the ferry pier, across from the aquarium and just before the tunnel (follow signs to OHMOTO PARK). **Amenities:** Restaurant.

Nakaya Bed & Breakfast ★★★ Hiroshima transplant Rie Nakaya, who speaks fluent English, lives in the front house and offers three rooms in another house out back: a Japanese-style two-room suite for three people or more, with a carved transom, a view of the pagoda over rooftops, and a toilet; a room with twin beds for one or two people; and two connecting rooms with four single beds. Only breakfast is available, but Nakaya-san is happy to provide recommendations for dinner, and while there's Wi-Fi, the signal is strong only in the front house's lounge. No credit cards.

511 Miyajima-cho. www.nakaya-bandb.com. ☏ **0829/44-0725.** 3 units (1 with toilet, none with bathroom). ¥6,000 single; ¥11,000–¥13,000 double. Breakfast ¥500 extra. A 7-min. walk from the ferry pier, on Machiya Dori (a block inland from Omotesando Dori).

Where to Eat

Grilled conger eel and oysters (available fresh Nov–Mar) are two of Miyajima's specialties; it even celebrates an oyster festival in early February. There are also stalls along Omotesando Dori, the main street, selling oysters on the half shell, ice cream, and snacks. Note that there are no addresses in this and the sightseeing dining sections because the village is small, and the address would only be meaningful to the postman.

Kakiya (牡蠣屋) ★★ OYSTERS Located on Miyajima's main street, this open-fronted and very narrow shop with the motto "We're so shuckin' good," is one of several selling humongous oysters cooked over a grill, along with products like oyster pesto or truffle and oyster shavings you might want to take home. An English-language menu offers oysters prepared a half-dozen ways, including raw when in season (¥470 for one), barbecued in the shell (¥1,150 for four), and breaded and fried (¥1,620 for three), but note no credit cards are accepted. It even offers wine, beer, shochu, and sake to wash it all down. How civilized!

© **0829/44-2747.** Oyster dishes ¥1,150–¥1,620. Daily 10am–6pm. On Omotesando Dori, about a 6-min. walk from the ferry pier.

Koumitei (好味亭) ★ OKONOMIYAKI   Convenient to the ferry pier, this simple restaurant, run by the same family for more than 20 years, seems like an extension of their home and stays open later than most restaurants on the island, attracting locals as well as tourists. Hiroshima-style *okonomiyaki*, which is prepared for you with a choice of udon or soba noodles and toppings of pork, seafood, cheese, fried garlic or fried squid, is available from the English-language menu. No credit cards accepted.

© **0829/44-0177.** *Okonomiyaki* ¥810–¥1,080; set meals ¥1,150–¥1,350. Thurs–Tues 11am–2:30pm and 5–8pm. A 1-min. walk from the ferry pier, catty-corner to the right, in a wood building.

Mizuha (水羽) ★ VARIED JAPANESE   Occupying an old rice granary, this bustling restaurant offers local specialties like conger eel and oysters, as well as more ordinary choices like tempura and *kamameshi* (rice casserole with toppings) from an English-language menu, with a choice of table and *tatami* seating.

© **0829/44-1570.** Set meals ¥1,470–¥2,100. Daily 9am–5pm. A 10-min. walk from the ferry pier, behind Itsukushima Shrine and near the five-story pagoda.

Exploring Miyajima Island
SEEING THE SIGHTS

Miyajima's major attraction, **Itsukushima Shrine ★★★** (*©* **0829/44-2020**), is about a 10-minute walk from the ferry pier (turn right from the terminal), at the end of a long narrow pedestrian street called Omotesando Dori that is lined with souvenir shops and restaurants. Founded in 593 to honor three female deities, the wooden shrine is built over the water so that, when the tide is in, it appears as though the shrine is floating. A brilliant vermilion, it contrasts starkly with the wooded hills in the background and the blue of the sky above, casting its reflection in the waters below. If you do happen to see Itsukushima Shrine when the tide is in and it's seemingly floating on water, you should consider yourself very lucky indeed—most of the time the lovely shrine floats above a surface that's only a little more glamorous than mud. That's when imagination comes in handy (the Hiroshima tourist offices may have a tide calendar).

The majority of the shrine buildings are thought to date from the 16th century, preserving the original Shinden style of 12th-century architecture, but they have been repaired repeatedly through the centuries. Most of the shrine buildings are closed, but from 6:30am to sunset daily (usually 6pm in summer, to 5 or 5:30pm in winter), you can walk along the 230m (770-ft.) covered **dock,** which threads its way past the outer part of the main shrine and one of the oldest *Noh* stages in Japan. From the shrine, you'll have a good view of the red *torii* standing in the water. **Bugaku,** an ancient court dance performed to the accompaniment of court music that was introduced to Japan centuries ago from India through China and Korea, is staged here 10 times a year (expect those days to be crowded with tour groups). Admission to the shrine is ¥300 for adults, ¥200 for high-school students, ¥100 for children.

Another sight worth exploring is **Daisho-in Temple ★★**, on the slope of Mount Misen (© **0829/44-0111;** daily 8am–5pm). One of the most famous Shingon Buddhist temples in western Japan, it has numerous worthwhile sights spread on its leafy grounds, including a mandala made of colored sand that was created by Tibetan priests, a main hall where worshipers pray for health and contentment, and a hall dedicated to Kobo Daishi, founder of the Shingon sect (his remains are interred on Mount Koya). In Henshokutsu Cave are Buddhist icons and sand gathered from all 88 pilgrimage temples on Shikoku; making a round here is considered as auspicious as visiting the temples themselves. Other halls contain deities thought to bring good health and to save humans from earthly sexual desires. Every April 15 and November 15 there are fire-walking festivals here, in which worshipers walk over hot coals; in March there's a ceremony to give thanks to retired old kitchen knives. An excellent brochure at the entrance describes the various sights, free to the public. From Daisho-in, there's a path leading to Mount Misen, which you can hike in about 90 minutes.

ENJOYING MIYAJIMA'S NATURAL WORLD

The other popular thing to do on Miyajima is to visit its highest peak, 535m (1,755-ft.) **Mount Misen ★★**, which seems light years away from the crowds down below. Signs direct you to Momijidani Park, a pleasant hillside park covered with maple trees (spectacular in autumn) and cherry trees (heavenly in spring) and marked by a picturesque stream. A 10-minute walk through the park brings you to the **Miyajima Ropeway** (www.miyajima-ropeway.info; © **0829/44-0316**) to Mount Misen; round-trip tickets cost ¥1,800 for adults (half fare for children). However, you might wish to buy only a one-way ticket for ¥1,000 and enjoy more scenery by walking back down; it takes about 60 to 90 minutes, down one of three different pathways. In any case, the actual summit of Mount Misen, a 30-minute walk from the cable car terminus over a strenuous up-and-down pathway, offers splendid 360-degree views of the Seto-Naikai (Inland Sea) National Park. Mount Misen is best known for Kobo Daishi's visit in 806, when he spent a 100-day retreat here and is said to have lit the Eternal Fire (located in the Kiezu-no Reikado Hall), which has reputedly been burning for more than 1,200 years and was used to light the Peace Flame in Hiroshima's Peace Memorial Park; in recent years, the Eternal Fire has come to symbolize the eternal fire of love, making it popular also with couples. Plan on at least 2 hours roundtrip for the ropeway and hike to the summit, noting the last ropeway departure from Mount Misen (5 or 5:30pm most of the year). If you're hiking back down, plan on a total of 3 to 4 hours.

Miyajima is also known for its beaches. If you're looking to swim, there are two beaches west of the town and shrine: **Suginoura** and **Tsutsumigaura Natural Park** (you can also camp here). Ask the tourist office for a schedule of shuttle buses that will bring you to the beaches.

PLANNING YOUR TRIP TO JAPAN

P robably two worries many first-time visitors have about a trip to Japan concern the language barrier and the high cost of living. To help alleviate fears about the first, I've provided the Japanese characters for establishments listed in this book that do not have English-language signs so you can recognize their names, given brief instructions on how to reach most of the places I recommend, made suggestions for ordering in restaurants without English-language menus, and provided prices for everything from train rides to museums.

As for costs, probably everyone has heard horror stories about Japan's high prices. In various surveys of the most expensive cities around the world, Tokyo is always among the top 10, while Osaka and other major Japanese cities have also had their spot in the top 10. But after Japan's economic bubble burst in the early 1990s, something happened that would have been unthinkable during the heady spending days of the 1980s: Japanese became bargain conscious, ushering a new era of inexpensive French bistros, second-hand clothing stores, 100-yen shops, and budget hotels. Furthermore, as we go to press, the dollar/yen exchange rate is more favorable for visitors to Japan than it has been in years, making a trip now more affordable than ever.

The secret to seeing Japan on the cheap–or at least, to see it without breaking the bank–is to live and eat as Japanese do. This book will help you do exactly that, with descriptions of eateries and Japanese-style inns that are affordable and with tips on how to save money on everything from transportation to sightseeing. While you may never find Japan as inexpensive as many other Asian countries, you will find it richly rewarding for all the reasons you chose Japan as a destination in the first place.

Another major complaint of foreign visitors to Japan is lack of convenient Wi-Fi. Although most hotels provide free in-room access and many businesses such as restaurants and department stores also provide free access, it's hard to stay connected when traveling or you're out and about. In addition, Japan uses a different phone system than the rest of the world, which makes using your own mobile phone challenging. Luckily, improvements in these areas for overseas visitors is improving, outlined below under "Fast Facts."

Furthermore, Japan remains one of the safest countries in the world; in general, you don't have to worry about muggers, pickpockets, or crooks. In fact, I sometimes feel downright coddled in Japan. Everything runs like clockwork: Trains are on time, and the service—whether in hotels, restaurants, or department stores—ranks among the best in the world. I know if I get truly lost, someone will help me and will probably even go out of his or her way to do so. Japanese are honest and extremely helpful toward foreign visitors. Indeed, it's the people themselves who make traveling in Japan such a delight.

GETTING THERE

By Plane

Japan has four international airports. Outside Tokyo is **Narita International Airport** (**NRT;** www.narita-airport.jp; ℂ **0476/34-8000**), where you'll want to land if your main business is in the capital or surrounding region. Much closer to central Tokyo is **Haneda Airport** (**HND;** www.tokyo-airport-bldg.co.jp; ℂ **03/5757-8111**), which has long served as Tokyo's domestic airport but began accepting international flights in 2010, mostly from Asia. International long-distance flights land mostly at Narita.

Outside Osaka, **Kansai International Airport** (**KIX;** www.kansai-airport.or.jp; ℂ **072/455-2500**) is convenient if your destination is Osaka, Kyoto, or cities farther west. In between Narita and Kansai airports, outside Nagoya, is the **Central Japan International Airport** (**NGO;** www.centrair.jp/en; ℂ **0569/38-1195**), nicknamed Centrair, which serves international flights mostly from Asia.

GETTING AROUND

Japan has an extensive transport system, the most convenient segment of which is the nation's excellent rail service. Buses are useful for reaching places that trains don't go, like Shirakawa-go in the Japan Alps. There are also long-distance buses connecting major cities in western Honshu that are cheaper alternatives than train.

By Train

The most efficient way to travel around most of Japan is by train. Whether you're being whisked through the countryside aboard the famous Shinkansen bullet train or are winding your way up a wooded mountainside in an electric tram, trains in Japan are punctual, comfortable, safe, and clean. And because train stations are usually located in the heart of the city next to the city bus terminal or a subway station, arriving in a city by train is usually the most convenient method. Major train stations also have tourist offices, where you can pick up brochures and maps in English and often even make reservations for local hotels free of charge. Most of Japan's passenger trains are run by the

Japan Railways (JR) Group, which is made up of six regional companies (such as JR East) that together cover 20,000km (12,400 miles) and operate about 20,000 departures daily, including those of the Shinkansen. There are also private regional companies, like **Kintetsu (Kinki Nippon Railway)** operating around Osaka and Kyoto and **Odakyu Electric Railway** operating from Tokyo to Hakone.

SHINKANSEN (BULLET TRAIN)   The Shinkansen is probably Japan's best-known train. With a front car that resembles a space rocket, the Shinkansen hurtles along at a maximum speed of 300kmph (187 mph) through the countryside on its own special tracks.

> **Travel Tip**
>
> To help you reach the hotels, restaurants, and sights recommended in this book, I've included the nearest train or subway station or bus or streetcar stop, followed in parentheses by the approximate number of minutes it takes to walk from the station or bus stop to your destination.

In western Honshu, the most widely used Shinkansen route is the **Tokaido/Sanyo** line, which runs from Tokyo and Shinagawa stations west to Kyoto, Osaka, Kobe, Himeji, Kurashiki, Hiroshima and other cities before reaching its final destination on the island of Kyushu. Each stop is announced in English through a loudspeaker and on a digital signboard in each car. There are several types of Shinkansen traveling along this route. The *Nozomi* Shinkansen is the fastest and most frequent train and is the only one that covers the entire 1,179km (730 miles) between Tokyo and Hakata in Kyushu; the *Mizuho* Shinkansen travels from Nagoya farther into Kyushu. Frustratingly, neither the *Nozomi* nor the *Mizuho* are covered by the Japan Rail Pass (see "Japan Rail Pass," below). Instead, holders of the Japan Rail Pass must take the *Hikari,* which makes more stops than the *Nozomi,* or the *Kodama,* which stops at every station (if your destination is a smaller city on the Shinkansen line, make sure the train you take stops there). Rail-pass holders wishing to travel between Tokyo and Hiroshima must therefore take the *Hikari* or *Kodama* and transfer in Osaka or Okayama. On the other hand, if you're buying individual tickets, the price is the same whether you're traveling by *Nozomi* or a slower Shinkansen. In March 2015, the new *Hokuriku* **Shinkansen** began service between Tokyo and Kanazawa.

REGULAR SERVICE   In addition to bullet trains, there are also two types of long-distance trains that operate on regular tracks. The **limited-express trains,** or LEX *(Tokkyu),* branch off the Shinkansen system and are the fastest after the bullet trains, often traveling scenic routes, while the **express trains** *(Kyuko)* are slightly slower and make more stops. Slower still are **rapid express trains** *(Shin-Kaisoku)* and the even slower **rapid trains** *(Kaisoku).* To serve the everyday needs of Japan's commuting population, **local trains** *(Futsu)* stop at all stations.

INFORMATION   For information on routes, including transfers, fares, and timetables for trains and planes in Japan, there's the very useful **www. hyperdia.com.**

In Japan, information on JR trains, fares, schedules, and routes is available at **Travel Service Centers** at major stations. In Tokyo, the best place for personal consulting on routes and sightseeing is at the JR East Travel Service Center in Tokyo Station (p. 67), where you can also ask for the invaluable *Japan Railway Time Table,* published in English and providing train schedules for the Shinkansen and limited express JR lines throughout Japan. **Tourist Information Centers** in downtown Tokyo or at the international airports in Narita or Osaka also carry the timetable.

TRAIN FARES & RESERVATIONS Ticket prices are based on the type of train (Shinkansen bullet trains are the most expensive), the distance traveled, whether your seat is reserved, and the season, with slightly higher prices (usually a ¥200 surcharge) during peak seasons (Golden Week, July 21–Aug 31, Dec 25–Jan 10, and Mar 21–Apr 5) and a ¥200 discount during low season. Children (ages 6–11) pay half fare, while up to two children 5 and younger travel free if they do not require a separate seat. I've included train prices from Tokyo for many destinations covered in this book (see individual cities for more information). Unless stated otherwise, prices in this guide are for adults for **nonreserved seats** on the fastest train available during regular season. Note, however, that you can save money by purchasing a round-trip ticket for long distances. A round-trip ticket by train on distances exceeding 601km (373 miles) one-way costs 10% less than two one-way tickets. In any case, no matter which train you ride, be sure to hang onto your ticket—you'll be required to give it up at the end of your trip as you exit through the gate.

You can reserve seats for the Shinkansen, as well as for limited-express and express trains (but not for slower rapid or local trains, which are on a first-come, first-served basis) at any major JR station in Japan. Reserved seats cost slightly more than unreserved seats (¥300–¥510 for the Shinkansen and express trains). It's a good idea to reserve your seats for your entire trip through Japan as soon as you know your itinerary if you'll be traveling during peak times; however, you can only reserve 1 month in advance. If it's not peak season, you'll probably be okay using a more flexible approach to traveling— all trains also have nonreserved cars that fill up on a first-come, first-seated basis. You can also reserve seats on the day of travel up to departure time. I rarely reserve a seat when it's not peak season, preferring instead the flexibility of being able to hop on the next available train (or sometimes I reserve a seat just before boarding). In any case, nonreserved seats *(jiyuuseki)* are located in cars at the front or back of Shinkansen trains. To determine where you should stand to board the train, look for the platform display showing a diagram of the train cars and which ones are reserved and nonreserved. Then look for signs—either on digital boards overhead or written on the platform itself—that shows the location for each car.

SAVING MONEY WITH A RAIL PASS The Japan Rail Pass is without a doubt the most convenient way to travel around Japan. With the rail pass, you don't have to worry about buying individual tickets, you have unlimited travel on all JR trains throughout Japan including the Shinkansen (except

Advantages of a Japan Rail Pass

You can save quite a bit by purchasing a rail pass, even if you only plan to travel a little. How economical is a Japan Rail Pass? If you were to buy a round-trip reserved-seat ticket on the Shinkansen from Tokyo to Kyoto, it would cost approximately ¥27,820, which is almost as much as a week's ordinary rail pass. Thus, if you plan to see more than just Tokyo and Kyoto, it pays to use a rail pass, **which you must buy outside Japan** (some regional rail passes, however, described below, can be purchased in Japan if you're a tourist).

With a Rail Pass, you can make seat reservations for free, which otherwise costs up to ¥510 per ride on the Shinkansen. Another advantage to a rail pass is that it offers a 10% discount or more off room rates at more than 50 JR Hotel Group hotels, including the Hotel Granvia in Kyoto, Okayama, and Hiroshima and the Nara Hotel. A Japan Rail Pass booklet, which comes with your purchase of a rail pass, lists member hotels (or go to www.jrhotelgroup.com). Note that regional rail passes, however, do not qualify for the hotel discount.

regrettably, the *Mizuho* and *Nozomi*), and you can reserve your seats on all JR trains for free.

Several types of rail passes are available; make your decision based on your length of stay in Japan and the cities you intend to visit. You might even find it best to combine several passes to cover your travels in Japan, such as a 1-week pass to journey around Honshu, plus a regional pass just for Kansai (see below). Information on the Japan Rail Pass is available at **www.japan railpass.net**, which also provides links to the websites of all six JR companies with information on regional passes.

A Japan Rail Pass is available for ordinary coach class and for the first-class Green Car for travel lasting 7, 14, or 21 consecutive days. Rates for coach class are ¥29,110 for 7 days, ¥46,390 for 14 days, and ¥59,350 for 21 days. Rates for the Green Car are ¥38,880, ¥62,950, and ¥81,870 respectively. Children (ages 6–11) pay half fare. Personally, I have never traveled in the first-class Green Car in Japan and don't consider it necessary, especially since there are no green cars on *Hikari* and *Kodama* bullet trains between Osaka and Hiroshima.

The main thing to remember is that the Japan Rail Pass is available only to foreigners visiting Japan as tourists and *can be purchased only outside Japan.* It's available from most travel agents, including **Kintetsu International** (www.kintetsu.com) and **JTB USA** (www.jtbusa.com). A full list of authorized travel agents, plus their addresses and contact information, is available at **www.japanrailpass.net**.

Upon purchasing your pass, you'll be issued a voucher (called an **Exchange Order**), which you'll then exchange for the real pass after your arrival in Japan. Note that once you purchase your Exchange Order, you have 3 months until you must exchange it in Japan for the pass itself. When obtaining your actual pass in Japan, you must then specify the date you wish to start using the pass within a 1-month period.

In Japan, you can exchange your voucher for a Japan Rail Pass at more than 40 JR stations that have Japan Rail Pass exchange offices, at which time you must present your passport and specify the date you wish to begin using the pass. You'll find exchange offices at both Narita Airport (daily 6:30am–9:45pm) and Kansai International Airport (daily 5:30am–11pm). Other exchange offices, all located in JR train stations, include those at Tokyo, Ueno, Shinjuku, Ikebukuro, Shibuya, and Shinagawa stations in Tokyo; Kyoto Station; Shin-Osaka and Osaka stations; and Nara, Kanazawa, and Hiroshima stations. Stations and their open hours are listed in a pamphlet you'll receive with your voucher, as well as at www.japanrailpass.net.

REGIONAL PASSES FOR FOREIGN VISITORS In addition to the standard Japan Rail Pass above, there are regional JR rail passes available for ordinary coach class that are convenient for travel in western Honshu, among other places. These can be purchased before arriving in Japan from the same vendors that sell the standard pass, but they can also be reserved online or purchased inside Japan, usually only within the area covered by the pass but also at Narita airport for some passes. These regional passes are available only to foreign visitors and require that you present your passport to verify your status as a "temporary visitor"; you may also be asked to show your plane ticket. Only one pass per region per visit to Japan is allowed.

In the Tokyo area, the **JR Kanto Area Pass** (www.jreast.co.jp) is a 3-day pass for ¥8,300 that allows unlimited travel on JR trains, including Shinkansen bullet trains traveling north from Tokyo as far away as Utsunomiya (useful for trips to Nikko), Karuizawa, Mount Fuji, Izu Peninsula, Narita (including the airport), and other areas. As for non-JR passes, the **Hakone Free Pass,** offered by Odakyu railways (www.odakyu.jp/english), includes round-trip transportation from Tokyo and unlimited travel in Hakone for a specific number of days (p. 169).

If you're arriving by plane at the Kansai Airport outside Osaka and intend to remain in western Honshu, consider buying one of several different **JR-West Passes** (www.westjr.co.jp/english), available at Kansai Airport, Osaka JR station, Kyoto Station, and other locations, as well as online. The **Kansai Area Pass,** which can be used for travel between Osaka, Kyoto, Kobe, Nara, Himeji, and other destinations in the Kansai area, is available as a 1-day pass for ¥2,060, 2-day pass for ¥4,110, 3-day pass for ¥5,140, or 4-day pass for ¥6,170. Travel is restricted to JR rapid and local trains, as well as unreserved seating in the Kansai Airport Express Haruka operating between Kansai Airport, Shin-Osaka, and Kyoto (that is, Shinkansen are not included in the pass). Similar but covering a wider area, including all Shinkansen traveling between Shin-Osaka Station and Kurashiki stations (including *Nozomi* and *Mizuho*), is the **Kansai Wide Area Pass,** which costs ¥7,200 for 4 consecutive days. Finally, the **Sanyo Area Pass** covers a larger area still, including the Shinkansen from Shin-Osaka through Hiroshima all the way to Hakata (in the city of Fukuoka on Kyushu). This pass costs ¥20,570 for 4 days and ¥30,860 for 8 days. Children 6 to 11 years of age pay half-price for all passes; up to two children 5 years old and younger can travel free with a paying adult.

There are also a couple other non-JR passes available for Kansai. The **Kansai Thru Pass** (www.surutto.com) is valid on city subways, private railways (*not* JR trains), and buses throughout the Kansai area, including Kansai Airport, Osaka, Kyoto, Nara, Kobe, Himeji, and Mount Koya, and provides slight discounts to hundreds of tourist facilities (usually ¥100 or 10%). Available only to tourists, it costs ¥4,000 for a 2-day pass and ¥5,200 for 3 days and can be used on nonconsecutive days; it's sold at Kansai International Airport, Tourist Information Centers in Osaka and Nara, and the Kyoto Station Bus Information Center.

By Bus

Buses often go where trains don't and thus may be the only way for you to get to the more remote areas of Japan, such as Shirakawa-go in the Japan Alps. They are also low-cost alternatives to trains for long-distance travel.

Some intercity buses require you to make reservations or purchase your ticket in advance at the ticket counter at the bus terminal. For others (especially local buses), when you board a bus you'll generally find a ticket machine by the entry door. Take a ticket, which is number-coded with a digital board displayed at the front of the bus. The board shows the various fares, which increase with the distance traveled. You pay when you get off.

In addition to serving the remote areas of the country, **long-distance buses** (called *chokyori basu*) operate between major cities in Japan and offer the cheapest mode of transportation. Although **Japan Railways** (www.jrbuskanto. co.jp, but no English available) operates almost a dozen bus routes, the majority of buses are run by private companies (most of which do not have English-language websites). The **Nihon Bus Association** (www.bus.or.jp) is comprised of bus companies throughout Japan and has some information in English.

Otherwise, the company with the best English website is **Willer Express** (http://willerexpress.com), which offers service from Tokyo, Kanazawa, Kyoto, Osaka, Nara, Kobe, Himeji, Okayama, and Hiroshima. Some buses travel during the night and offer reclining seats and toilets, thus saving passengers the price of a night's lodging; double-decker buses may even have salons or bars on the first floor. Some buses are just for women, and many have a variety of seats to choose from. Long-distance buses running between Tokyo and Kyoto cost ¥3,900 to ¥9,800, depending on the seat selected (reclining seats cost more), time of day (weekdays are generally cheaper), and season. Willer Express also offers a bus pass for foreign tourists good for any 3 days of travel for ¥10,000 or 5 days for ¥15,000 within a 2-month period. See the website for more information and promotions.

By Car

Driving is not recommended for visitors wishing to tour Japan. Driving is British style (on the left side of the road), which may be hard for those not used to it; traffic can be horrendous; and driving isn't even economical. Not only is gas expensive, but all of Japan's expressways charge high tolls—the one-way toll from Tokyo to Kyoto is almost the same price as a ticket to

Kyoto on the Shinkansen. And whereas the Shinkansen takes only 3 hours to get to Kyoto, driving can take about 8 hours. Driving in cities is even worse: Streets are often hardly wide enough for a rickshaw, let alone a car, and many roads don't have sidewalks so you have to dodge people, bicycles, and telephone poles. Free parking is hard to find, and garages are expensive. Except in remote areas, it just doesn't make sense to drive.

If you're undeterred, major car-rental companies in Japan include **Toyota Rent-A-Car** (https://rent.toyota.co.jp; ℂ **0800/7000-815** toll-free); **Nippon Rent-A-Car Service** (www.nipponrentacar.co.jp; ℂ **03/3485-7196** for the English Service Desk), **Nissan Rent-A-Car** (https://nissan-rentacar.com; ℂ **0120/00-4123** toll-free), and **Avis** (www.avis-japan.com; ℂ **0120/31-1911** toll-free). You'll need either an **international** or a **Japanese driving license.** Signs on all major highways are written in both Japanese and English, though some rental companies offer GPS with English voice guidance as well. It is against the law to drink alcohol and drive, all passengers must wear seat belts, and it's prohibited to use a mobile phone while driving. Although anyone 18 and older can drive in Japan, some rental companies may require a driver to have held a driving license at least 3 years.

BREAKDOWNS & ASSISTANCE   The **Japan Automobile Federation** (**JAF;** www.jaf.or.jp) is one of several road service providers maintaining emergency telephone boxes along Japan's major arteries to assist drivers whose cars have broken down or drivers who need help. Calls from these telephones are free and will connect you to JAF's operation center at your request. English is spoken.

[Fast FACTS] JAPAN

Area Codes   The country code for Japan is 81. All telephone area codes for Japanese cities begin with a zero (03 for Tokyo, 06 for Osaka, 075 for Kyoto), but drop the first zero if calling Japan from abroad. If you're calling a Japanese cellphone from overseas, which generally starts with **090** (080 has been recently added), you should drop the first zero and just dial **09** after the country code.

Business Hours   Banks are open Monday through Friday 9am to 3pm (but usually will not exchange money until 10:30 or so,

after that day's currency exchange rates come in). Neighborhood post offices are open Monday through Friday 9am to 5pm. Major post offices, however (usually located near major train stations), have longer hours and may be open weekends as well. (Some central post offices, such as those in Tokyo and Kyoto, have counters open 24 hr. for mail.)

Keep in mind that museums, gardens, and attractions stop selling admission tickets at least 30 minutes before the actual closing time. Similarly, restaurants take their last orders at least

30 minutes before the posted closing time (even earlier for *kaiseki* restaurants). Most national, prefectural, and city museums are closed on Monday; if Monday is a national holiday, however, they'll remain open and close on the following day, Tuesday, instead. Privately owned museums, however, usually close on holidays.

Customs   Visitors entering Japan must fill out a "Customs Declaration" form (handed out on incoming flights). If you're 20 or older, you can bring duty-free into Japan up to 400 cigarettes or 500 grams of tobacco or 100 cigars; three bottles (760cc each) of alcohol; and 2 ounces of perfume. You can also bring in goods for personal use that were purchased abroad whose total market value is less than ¥200,000. For more information, check the website www.customs.go.jp.

Disabled Travelers
For those with disabilities, traveling can be a nightmare in Japan, especially in Tokyo and other large metropolises. City sidewalks can be so jam-packed that getting around on crutches or in a wheelchair is exceedingly difficult; some busy thoroughfares can be crossed only via pedestrian bridges.

Only half of Japan's train stations have barrier-free toilets, but Shinkansen and some limited express trains have spaces for wheelchairs and accessible toilets. Most major train and subway stations have elevators, but they can be difficult to locate. Otherwise, smaller stations, especially in rural areas, may be accessible only by stairs or escalators, though in recent years some have been equipped with powered seat lifts. While some buses are no-step conveyances for easy access, subway and train compartments are difficult for solo wheelchair travelers to navigate on their own due to a gap or slight height difference between the coaches and platforms. In theory you can ask a station attendant to help you board, though you might have to wait if he's busy;

you can also request an attendant at your destination to help you disembark. Although city trains and buses have seating for passengers with disabilities—called "Priority Seats" and located in the first and last compartments of the train—subways can be so crowded that there's barely room to move. Moreover, Priority Seats are almost always occupied by commuters, so unless you look visibly handicapped, no one is likely to offer you a seat.

As for accommodations, only 10% of the nation's hotels have barrier-free rooms (called a "universal" room in Japan and used primarily by seniors), mostly in the expensive category, and even then there are usually only one or two such rooms. Only a scant 1% of Japanese inns have such rooms. Lower-priced accommodations may also lack elevators.

Restaurants can also be difficult to navigate, with raised doorsills, crowded dining areas, and tiny bathrooms that cannot accommodate wheelchairs. Best bets for ramps and easily accessible bathrooms include restaurants in department stores and upper-end hotels. Even Japanese homes are not very accessible, since the main floor is always raised about a foot above the entrance-hall floor.

For information on traveling with a wheelchair, www. japan-accessible.com and www.tesco-premium.co.jp/ aj/index.htm provide valuable tips on accessibility for

sights, neighborhoods, hotels, and more.

When it comes to facilities for the blind, Japan has a very advanced system. At subway stations and on many major sidewalks in large cities, raised dots and lines on the ground guide blind people at intersections and to subway platforms. In some cities, streetlights chime a theme when the signal turns green east-west, and chime another for north-south. Even Japanese yen notes are identified by a slightly raised circle—the ¥1,000 note has one circle in a corner, while the ¥10,000 note has two. Many elevators have floors indicated in Braille, and some hotels identify rooms in Braille.

Doctors Many first-class hotels offer medical facilities, an in-house doctor, or a doctor on call. Otherwise, your embassy or the AMDA International Medical Information Center (http://eng. amda-imic.com; ✆ **03/ 5285-8088** in Tokyo daily 9am–8pm; ✆ **06/4395-0555** in Osaka Mon–Fri 9am–5pm) can refer you to medical professionals who speak English.

Drinking Laws The legal drinking age is 20. Beer, wine, and spirits are readily available in department stores, grocery stores, convenience stores, and liquor stores. Many bars, especially in nightlife districts such as Shinjuku and Roppongi, are open until dawn. If you intend to drive in Japan, you are not allowed even one drink.

Electricity The electricity throughout Japan is 100 volts AC, but there are two different cycles in use (which ended up playing havoc during electricity shortages after the Great East Japan Earthquake): In Tokyo and in regions northeast of the capital up through Hokkaido, it's 50 cycles, while in Nagoya, Kyoto, Osaka, and all points to the southwest, it's 60 cycles. In any case, it's close enough to the American system that I've never encountered any problems plugging in my American electronics, including laptops and camera rechargers. Leading hotels in Tokyo often have two outlets, one for 110 volts and one for 220 volts (with the appropriate plugs used in the U.S. and Europe), so you can use most American or European appliances (electric razors, travel irons, laptops, and so forth) during your stay. Note, too, that the flat, two-legged prongs used in Japan are the same size and fit as in North America, but three-pronged appliances are not accepted (for my laptop, I bring the small two-prong attachment so I can plug into a Japanese socket).

Embassies & Consulates The following embassies are located in Tokyo (visa or passport sections of most embassies are open only at certain times during the day, so it's best to call in advance). There are also Australian, British, and U.S. consulates in Osaka and a Canadian consulate in Nagoya.

Australian Embassy: 2–1–14 Mita, Minato-ku (www.australia.or.jp; ✆ 03/5232-4111; station: Azabu-Juban Station, exit 2).

British Embassy: 1 Ichibancho, Chiyoda-ku (www.gov.uk/government/world/organisations/british-embassy-tokyo; ✆ 03/5211-1100; station: Hanzomon).

Canadian Embassy: 7–3–38 Akasaka, Minato-ku (www.canadainternational.gc.ca/missions/japan-japon; ✆ 03/5412-6200; station: Aoyama-Itchome).

Embassy of Ireland: Ireland House, 2–10–7 Kojimachi, Chiyoda-ku (www.irishembassy.jp; ✆ 03/3263-0695; station: Hanzomon, exit 3).

New Zealand Embassy: 20–40 Kamiyama-cho, Shibuya-ku (www.nzembassy.com/japan; ✆ 03/3467-2271; station: Shibuya).

U.S. Embassy: 1–10–5 Akasaka, Minato-ku (http://japan.usembassy.gov; ✆ 03/3224-5000; station: Toranomon).

Emergencies The national emergency numbers are ✆ **110** for **police** and ✆ **119** for **ambulance** and **fire** (ambulances are free in Japan unless you request a specific hospital). You do not need to insert any money or a prepaid telephone card into public telephones to call these numbers. Be sure to speak slowly and precisely.

Health Foremost in most people's minds since the 2011 Great East Japan Earthquake and the subsequent struggle to contain the damaged Fukushima nuclear power plant is fear of radiation. After all, reports of contaminated food plagued the country after the disaster, including contaminated tea, beef, spinach, rice, mushrooms, milk, and even infant formula. That being said, measures are in place to protect food and water safety (Japan's standards for radioactive contamination are the same as in the U.S.), and in any case, Tokyo is 240km (150 miles) from the crippled Fukushima plant. My personal take on the radiation situation is that a month's stay will have no long-term effects on my longevity, and frankly, you're likely to get more radiation on the flight to Japan than being in west Honshu.

Otherwise, it's safe to drink tap water and eat to your heart's content everywhere in Japan (pregnant women, however, are advised to avoid eating raw fish and to avoid taking hot baths). To prevent the spread of avian and H1N1 flu, all incoming passengers are monitored upon arrival at Narita Airport for fever; those with a higher than normal temperature may be quarantined. To be on the safe side, therefore, you may opt for an influenza vaccine before departing from home.

You don't need any inoculations to enter Japan. **Prescriptions** can be filled at Japanese pharmacies *only if they're issued by a Japanese doctor.* To avoid hassle, bring more prescription medications than you think you'll need, clearly labeled in their original containers, and be sure to pack them in your carry-on. To be safe, bring copies of your prescriptions with you, including generic names of medicines in case a local pharmacist is unfamiliar with the brand name. Over-the-counter items are easy to obtain, though name brands are likely to be different from those back home, some ingredients allowed elsewhere may be forbidden in Japan, and prices may be higher.

Internet & Wi-Fi Narita International Airport, Haneda Airport, and Kansai International Airport all offer free **Wi-Fi** (wireless fidelity), as well as computer terminals (¥100 per 10 min.).

With the exception of lodging in remote areas and many *ryokan* or budget inns, most accommodations provide Internet access in their guest rooms. Most provide Wi-Fi, though older properties that have not upgraded services may provide only dataports. Although you might want to pack a phone cord and spare Ethernet network cable just to be safe if you're staying in cheap accommodations, you probably won't need them otherwise, as most hotels supply them to guests free of charge if Wi-Fi isn't available. Best of all, Wi-Fi and Internet access is usually free. Throughout this book, I've indicated for each hotel and inn whether Wi-Fi or Internet connection is available in guest rooms and whether it's free or at a cost.

Most accommodations also have computers for guest use, either for a fee (in the hotel business center, which can be exorbitant, or coin-operated, usually ¥100 for 15 min.) or—mostly in cheaper accommodations—for free. Note that accommodations that charge for Internet or don't have Wi-Fi in their rooms sometimes offer Wi-Fi in their lobby for free, so it always pays to ask.

Outside hotels, more and more restaurants, cafes, and bars offer free Wi-Fi; you'll probably have to ask for the password. I've also found that more and more cities, and even neighborhoods within cities, are beginning to offer free Wi-Fi hotspots to tourists, though time usage may be limited. I've included information on free Wi-Fi usage for many cities in this book, but since more and more cities seem to be jumping on the Internet bandwagon, ask the local tourist information office for updated information. Otherwise, you can also rent a mobile Wi-Fi router upon arrival at Narita, Haneda, and Kansai airports that provides Internet access virtually anywhere. See "Mobile Phones," below, for more information.

Cybercafes can be found in most cities, though they're often nonexistent in small towns. I've listed cybercafes for many destinations when I could find them (see individual chapters), but more may have opened by the time you travel. Ask local tourist offices for updated locations.

LGBT Travelers Japan has no laws forbidding homosexual activity and there is no ban against homosexuality by either Buddhism or Japan's indigenous religion, Shintoism. Indeed, same-sex relationships have been well documented through the ages in Japanese literature and woodblock prints. On the other hand, gays have no legal rights in Japan. Although there are many gay and lesbian establishments in Tokyo (concentrated mostly in Shinjuku's Ni-chome district; see chapter 5), the gay community in Japan is not a vocal one, and local information in English is hard to come by. A useful website for information on the gay scene in Japan, as well as gay and lesbian club listings in cities around the country, is **www.utopia-asia.com/tipsjapn.htm**. **Out Asia Travel** (www.outasiatravel.com) is a gay travel agency based in Tokyo that offers 2-hour guided tours of Ni-chome, individually oriented trips, and tours to other destinations in Japan and Asia.

Legal Aid Contact your embassy if you find yourself in legal trouble. The **Legal Counseling Center** (www.horitsu-sodan.jp) is operated by three bar associations that provide legal counseling in English. The fee is generally ¥5,000 for 30 minutes, plus ¥2,500 for each additional 15 minutes.

Luggage & Lockers Storage space on Shinkansen bullet trains is limited, so travel with the smallest bag you can get away with. Coin-operated lockers are located at major train stations throughout the country as well as at most subway stations, but lockers are generally not large enough to store huge pieces of luggage (and those that do are often taken). Lockers generally cost ¥300 to ¥800 depending on the size. Some major stations like Kyoto also have check-in rooms for luggage, though these are rare. If your bag becomes too much to handle, you can have it sent ahead via *takkyu-bin*, an efficient forwarding service available at upper- and mid-range hotels and all convenience stores in Japan. At Narita and Kansai international airports, service counters will send luggage to your hotel the next day (or vice versa) for about ¥2,000 per bag.

Mail & Postage   If your hotel cannot mail letters for you, ask the concierge for the location of the nearest post office, recognizable by the red logo of a capital T with a horizontal line over it. Mailboxes are bright orange-red. It costs ¥110 to airmail letters weighing up to 25 grams and ¥70 for postcards to Australia, North America, and Europe. Domestic mail costs ¥82 for letters up to 25 grams, and ¥52 for postcards. Post

offices throughout Japan are also convenient for their ATMs, which accept international credit cards for money exchange.

Although all **post offices** are open Monday through Friday from 9am to 5pm, international post offices (often located close to the central train station) have longer hours, often until 7pm or later on weekdays and with open hours also on weekends (in Tokyo and Kyoto, counters are open 24 hr.). If your hotel does not have a shipping service, it is only at these larger post offices that you can mail packages abroad. Conveniently, they sell cardboard boxes in several sizes with the necessary tape. Packages sent via surface mail cannot weigh more than 20 kilograms (about 44 lb.) and take about a month to reach North America, with a package weighing 10 kilograms (about 22 lb.) costing ¥6,750. Express EMS packages, which take 3 days to North America and can weigh up to 30 kilograms (66 lb.), cost ¥14,000 for 10 kilograms (22 lb.); the same package to Australia also costs ¥14,000 while to Europe it costs ¥16,200. For more information, visit **www.post.japanpost.jp**.

Measurements   Before the metric system came into use in Japan, the country

had its own standards for measuring length and weight. Rooms are still measured by the number of *tatami* straw mats that will fit in them. A six-*tatami* room, for example, is the size of six *tatami* mats, with a *tatami* roughly .9m (3 ft.) wide and 1.8m (6 ft.) long.

Mobile Phones   The three letters that define much of the world's wireless capabilities are GSM (Global System for Mobiles). Unfortunately, Japan uses a system that is incompatible with GSM, and foreigners are not allowed to buy cellphones in Japan. You can, however, **bring your own mobile phone** and rent a SIM card in the arrival lobbies of Narita, Haneda, and Kansai airports from **Softbank** (www.softbank-rental.jp), **NTT DoCoMo** (www.worldke-tai.com), **G-Call** (www.g-call.com/e), and many other companies (call your phone company to ensure that your phone SIM is unlocked and available for international roaming). Note that this works *only* if you rent a SIM at the airport (in-town Softbank and other phone outlets cannot handle this).

You can also simply rent a mobile phone. All three companies above, as well as many others, offer phone rentals with various packages available (check airport

Over & Out

If you're traveling with a buddy or family, consider bringing along walkie-talkies. They're cheaper than phones, could be a lifesaver if you get separated, and make it easier to rendezvous, especially in big cities.

websites for company listings, provided under "Getting There," earlier in this chapter). **PuPuRu** (www. pupuru.com/en) offers the extra convenience of delivering a rental phone to any address in Japan (such as your hotel), with its return via a prepaid, preaddressed envelope.

Finally, all these companies also rent mobile Wi-Fi routers that let you connect to the Internet virtually anywhere, allowing you to check mail and make phone calls via Skype and other Internet-based phone companies. None of these services are cheap, but they do allow you to stay in touch.

Money & Costs Frommer's lists exact prices in the local currency. The currency conversions quoted above were correct at press time. However, rates fluctuate, so before departing consult a currency exchange website such as **www.oanda.com/ currency/converter** to check up-to-the-minute rates.

The currency in Japan is called the *yen,* symbolized by ¥. Coins come in denominations of ¥1, ¥5, ¥10, ¥50, ¥100, and ¥500. Bills come in denominations of ¥1,000, ¥2,000, ¥5,000, and ¥10,000, though ¥2,000 notes are rarely seen. Keep plenty of change handy for riding local transportation such as buses or streetcars. Although change machines

are virtually everywhere, even on buses where you can change larger coins and ¥1,000 bills, you'll find it faster to have the exact amount on hand.

Some people like to arrive in a foreign country with that country's currency already on hand, but I do not find it necessary for Japan. **Narita, Haneda,** and **Kansai** have exchange counters for all incoming international flights that offer better exchange rates than what you'd get abroad, as well as ATMs. I usually change enough money to last several days.

Most Japanese pay with either credit cards or cash (personal checks are not used). The most readily accepted cards are **American Express, Diners Club, MasterCard** (also called Eurocard), **Visa,** as well as the Japanese credit card **JCB** (Japan Credit Bank) and those from other countries. The bulk of your expenses—hotels, train tickets, major purchases, meals in most restaurants—can be paid for with credit cards. Shops and restaurants accepting credit cards will usually post which cards they accept at the door or near the cash register. However, some establishments may be reluctant to accept cards for small purchases and inexpensive meals, so inquire beforehand. Note,

too, that the vast majority of Japan's smaller and least-expensive businesses, including many restaurants, noodle shops, fast-food joints, ma-and-pa establishments, and the cheapest accommodations, do not accept credit cards. For that reason, you'll want to have cash on hand, especially if you're traveling in rural areas where you might not have easy access to an ATM for cash withdrawals.

I also find traveler's checks still useful in Japan. Traveler's checks help you avoid annoying credit card fees and withdrawal limits, generally fetch a better exchange rate than cash, and offer protection in case of theft. *You may need your passport to exchange traveler's checks.* Note, however, that in some very remote areas, even banks won't cash them. Before taking off for small towns, be sure you have enough cash.

Exchanging Money All banks in Japan displaying an AUTHORIZED FOREIGN EXCHANGE sign can exchange currency and traveler's checks, with exchange rates usually displayed at the appropriate foreign-exchange counter. **Banks** are generally open Monday through Friday from 9am to 3pm, though business hours for exchanging foreign currency usually don't begin until 10:30 or 11am (be

THE VALUE OF THE YEN VS. OTHER POPULAR CURRENCIES

Yen	Aus$	Can$	Euro (€)	NZ$	UK£	US$
100	A$1.07	C$1.05	€0.75	NZ$1.14	£0.56	$0.85

prepared for a long wait; you'll be asked to sit down as your order is processed). More convenient—and quicker—are **Travelex** (www.travelex.com) foreign-exchange kiosks, with locations in several cities, including Tokyo, Kyoto, Kobe, and Osaka.

Other places to exchange money include your hotel and **department stores,** which are often open until 7:30 or 8pm. Note, however, that hotels and department stores may charge a handling fee, offer a slightly less favorable exchange rate, and require a passport for all transactions. In a welcome development, I've noticed some hotels and department stores with money-changing machines, like Isetan at Kyoto Station, though these are still rare.

ATMs The best way to get cash is from an ATM (automated teller machine). Because most bank ATMs in Japan accept only cards issued by Japanese banks, your best bet for obtaining cash is the ubiquitous **7-Eleven** convenience store (www.sevenbank.co.jp/intlcard), most of which are open 24 hours and have ATMs that accept foreign bank cards operating on the **Cirrus** (www.mastercard.com) and **PLUS** (www.visa.com) systems, as well as American Express. Note, however, that not all cards, even those issued through Visa or MasterCard, are accepted. For that reason, I suggest traveling with at least two cards from different issuers.

More user-friendly are the 26,000-some ATMS operated by the **Japan Post Bank,** most of them located in **post offices** all over Japan and with instructions in English. Although major post offices, usually located near central train stations, have long open hours for ATMs (generally 7am–11pm weekdays and 9am–7 or 9pm on weekends, though some are open almost 24 hours a day), small post offices may have only limited hours for ATMs (depending on the post office, that may be until 6 or 7pm weekdays and until 5pm on weekends). You might also find Japan Post Bank ATMs in train stations and shopping malls.

Newspapers & Magazines Two English-language newspapers are published daily in Japan: the *Japan Times* (www.japantimes.co.jp), which comes distributed also with the *International New York Times,* and the *Japan News* (www.the-japan-news.com), published by *Yomiuri Shimbun.* In addition, the *Asahi Shimbun* has an English website, http://ajw.asahi.com, with news on Japan. I also like reading http://newsonjapan.com, which gives a roundup of the daily news—business, politics, travel, society, and more—with excerpts drawn from Japanese news sources.

Packing Tips The first thing you'll want to do when you're packing is select the smallest bag you can get away with and **pack as lightly as you can.**

Storage space is limited on Japan's trains, including the Shinkansen bullet train, business hotels sometimes lack closets, and there are multitudes of stairs and overhead and underground passageways to navigate in virtually every train station in the country.

The most important item is **a good pair of walking shoes,** well broken in, as you will probably be walking more than you do at home. Because you have to remove shoes to enter Japanese homes, inns, shrines, temples, and even some restaurants, bring a pair that's easy to slip on and off. As for **clothes,** you'll need a coat in winter and very light clothing for the hot and humid summer months. Jackets are necessary for spring and autumn; I've seen it snow in March in Tokyo, and even May can be quite crisp. Japan's top French restaurants may require jackets for men. If you're a woman conducting business, you should know that most companies consider it inappropriate for women to wear dresses without hose, tops without sleeves, or sandals. Otherwise, for sightseeing, casual wear is okay, including jeans, shorts, and sandals, but be aware that Japanese put more stock in how you dress and look than maybe back home. Because the sun rises early in summer (as early as 4am), you might also want to pack a pair of eyeshades.

It's also good to carry a supply of pocket tissues, change for local buses (faster than trying to change ¥1,000 notes), a folding umbrella, and a compass for getting your bearings and following my directions using local maps.

Pharmacies Drugstores, called *yakkyoku,* are found readily in Japan. Note, however, that you cannot have a foreign prescription filled in Japan without first consulting a doctor in Japan, so it's best to bring an adequate supply of important medicines with you. No drugstores in Japan stay open 24 hours. However, ubiquitous convenience stores like 7-Eleven, Lawson, and FamilyMart, open day and night throughout Japan, carry such nonprescription items as aspirin.

Safety The tragic 2011 Great East Japan Earthquake brought world-wide attention to the fact that Japan is earthquake-prone, but in reality, most earthquakes are too small to detect (of the more than 100,000 earthquakes annually in Japan, only 1% are big enough to feel). In any case, Japan has the world's best early-warning systems for impending earthquakes and tsunamis (the death toll would have been much

higher without them) and has strict building codes (it's worth noting that not one skyscraper was felled by the 3/11 earthquake; the tsunami caused most of the damage). If you're around other people, you'll most likely hear everyone's phones going off at once for an earthquake alert, as most people are signed up for the warning that an earthquake may take place. In any case, in the event of a warning or an earthquake, there are a few precautions you should take. If you're indoors, the three rules of thumb are Drop, Cover, and Hold On. In other words, you should drop to the ground, take cover under a sturdy table, a piece of furniture or under a doorway, and then hold on until the shaking stops. Do not go outdoors, as the greatest danger is from falling debris, collapsing walls, and flying glass. Never use elevators during a quake.

If you're outdoors, stay away from trees, power lines, streetlights, and the sides of buildings; if you're surrounded by tall buildings, seek cover in a doorway. If you're in a coastal area, move away from the beach.

The authorities will issue a tsunami warning if dangerous waves seem imminent. And expect aftershocks. Although secondary shockwaves are generally not as severe as the first one, they can damage weakened structures and can occur in the first hours or days—and even months—after the first quake. In case of major emergencies, there are emergency shelters throughout Japan, mostly schoolyards and other public facilities. Other precautions include noting emergency exits wherever you stay; all hotels supply flashlights, usually found attached to your bedside table. For more information on earthquakes, tsunamis, volcanic information, the weather, and warnings and advisories, see the Japan Meteorological Agency's website at www.jma.go.jp/jma/index.html.

As for crime, Japan has long been recognized as one of the safest countries in the world. In all the years I've lived and worked in Japan, I've never had even one fearful encounter, and I never hesitate to walk anywhere any time of the night or day. After the 2011

Take a Load off Heavy Bags

If your bag becomes a burden but you don't want to mail items home, an alternative is to send a bag onward to your next or last stop by *takkyu-bin,* available at larger hotels, train stations, and convenience stores. Bags reach most destinations in 1 or 2 nights, with the delivery cost of an average-size bag weighing 10 kilograms (22 lb.) about ¥1,400. I love this amazingly efficient service—it's a lifesaver! For more information, see Yamato Transport's website at www.kuronekoyamato.co.jp.

tsunami, the possibility of looting occurring along the damaged coast never even crossed my mind; in fact, millions worth in yen and other valuables found in the rubble was turned over to authorities. When a friend of mine forgot her purse in a public restroom in Osaka, someone turned it in to the police station complete with money, digital camera, and passport. In other words, if you lose something, say on a subway or in a park, chances are good that you'll get it back (to find out how, go to the nearest police station or contact the local tourist office).

That being said, crime—especially pickpocketing—is on the increase, and there are precautions you should always take when traveling: Stay alert and be aware of your immediate surroundings. Be especially careful with cameras, purses, and wallets in congested areas like Narita airport, subways, department stores, or tourist attractions. Some Japanese caution women against walking through parks alone at night.

Smoking The legal age for purchasing tobacco products and smoking in Japan is 20. Smoking is banned in most public areas, including in trains and subways, train stations (although there is sometimes a smoking room), and office buildings. In most cities, ordinances also ban smoking on sidewalks but allow it in marked areas, usually near train stations. Many restaurants

have nonsmoking sections or prohibit smoking during lunch hour, though bars do not. Entirely smoke-free restaurants are on the rise, with your best bet of finding one in a hotel. Virtually all hotels have designated nonsmoking floors, though Japanese-style inns, because of their small size, usually do not; some business hotels also don't. On the other hand, some lodgings are entirely smoke-free.

Taxes The tax imposed on goods and services, including hotel rates and restaurant meals, is 8%. In April 2017 it will increase to 10%. Hotels and restaurants are inconsistent about including the tax in their published rates, but will generally state whether tax is included or will be added on their tariff sheets and menus. Tokyo hotels also levy a separate accommodations tax of ¥100 to ¥200 per person per night. In hot-spring resorts, a ¥150 onsen tax is added for every night of your stay.

In addition to these taxes, a 10% to 15% **service charge** will be added to your bill in lieu of tipping at most of the fancier restaurants and at moderately priced and upper-end hotels; in ryokan, service charge can be as high as 20%. Business hotels, minshuku, youth hostels, and inexpensive restaurants do not impose a service charge.

As for **shopping,** the 8% consumption tax is also included in the price of most goods. Travelers from abroad are eligible for an

exemption on goods taken out of the country within 6 months, although only department stores, designer boutiques, souvenir shops, and specialty stores seem equipped to deal with the procedures. In any case, stores will grant a refund on the consumption tax only when the total amount of purchases for the day at their store exceeds ¥10,001. You can obtain a refund immediately by having a sales clerk fill out a list of your purchases and then presenting the list to the tax-exemption counter of the department store; you must present your passport. You can also get a refund for consumables (cosmetics, food, drinks) that total between ¥5,001 to ¥500,000 from any one shop on any given day, but you cannot consume them in Japan and must take them abroad within 30 days of purchase (they will be placed in a sealed bag). In any case, note that stores are allowed to charge 1.1% commission on the 8%, so you will be refunded only 6.9%. A Tax-free Proof of Purchase receipt will be attached to your passport to show when departing Japan; make sure to pack your purchases in your carry-on luggage.

Telephones Despite the proliferation of mobile phones, you can still find public telephones in telephone booths on the sidewalk, in or near train stations, in hotel lobbies, restaurants and coffee shops, and even on the bullet train (the latter require a prepaid card, sold from vending machines beside the phone). A local call costs ¥10 for each minute; a warning chime will alert you to insert more coins or you'll be disconnected. It's best, therefore, to insert two or three coins so that you won't have to worry about being disconnected; ¥10 coins that aren't used are returned at the end of the call. Most public phones accept both ¥10 and ¥100 coins. The latter is convenient for long-distance calls, but no change is given for unused minutes. Numbers beginning with **0120** or **0088** are toll-free.

If you think you'll be making a lot of domestic calls from public phones and don't want to deal with coins, purchase a magnetic **prepaid telephone card.** In fact, some public phones often accept only prepaid cards, which are available in a value of ¥1,000 and are sold at vending machines (sometimes located right beside telephones), station kiosks, and convenience stores. Domestic long-distance calls are cheaper at night, on weekends, and on national holidays for calls of distances more than 60km (37 miles).

To make an international call from a public telephone, look for telephones displaying an INTERNATIONAL AND DOMESTIC CARD/COIN TELEPHONE sign. However, most of these do not accept the magnetic prepaid cards described above for direct

overseas calls due to illegal usage, though you can still find them in a few key facilities such as the airport and some hotels. Some hotels and other establishments also have special phones equipped to accept credit cards; you'll have to insert a 100-Yen coin that's returned when the call is over. Otherwise, you'll either have to use coins or purchase an international calling card that provides an access number, like the KDDI Super World Card (www.001.kddi.com/en/lineup/with-guidance/swc), which you can purchase online or at convenience stores.

If you're not using a prepaid card (which has its own set of instructions and access numbers), to make a direct-dial international call you must first dial one of the international access codes offered by the various telephone companies—**001** (KDDI), **0033** (NTT Communications), or **0061** (Softbank Telecom)—followed by **010** and then the country code. The country code for the United States and Canada is **1;** for the United Kingdom, it's **44;** for Australia, it's **61;** and for New Zealand, it's **64.** Next you dial the area code and number. For example, if you wanted to call the British Embassy in Washington, D.C., using KDDI you would dial 001-010-1-202-588-6500. If you're dialing from your hotel room, you must first dial for an outside line, usually 0. The cheapest time to call is between 11pm and 8am Japan time, while the

most expensive time is weekdays from 8am to 7pm. The most economical way to make international calls, of course, is through the Internet using Skype or another VoIP Internet-based service.

Time Japan is 9 hours ahead of Greenwich Mean Time, 14 hours ahead of New York, 15 hours ahead of Chicago, and 17 hours ahead of Los Angeles. Although there's been discussion of initiating daylight saving time to conserve energy in wake of the 2011 disaster, Japan currently does not use daylight saving time, so subtract 1 hour from the above times in the summer when calling from countries that have daylight saving time such as the United States.

Because Japan is on the other side of the international date line, you lose a day when traveling from the United States to Asia. (If you depart the United States on Tues, you'll arrive on Wed.) Returning to North America, however, you gain a day, which means that you arrive on the same day you left.

Tipping One of the delights of being in Japan is that there's no tipping—not even to waitresses, taxi drivers, or bellhops. If you try to tip them, they'll probably be confused or embarrassed. Instead, you'll have a 10% to 15% service charge added to your bill at higher-priced accommodations and restaurants. That being said, you might want to tip, say, your room attendant at a high-class *ryokan* if you're making special requests or meals are served in your room; in that case, place crisp, clean bills (¥3,000–¥5,000) in a white envelope on the table of your room at the beginning of your stay; but it's perfectly fine if you choose not to tip.

Toilets   If you need a restroom, your best bets are at train and subway stations (although these can be dirty), big hotels, department stores, and fast-food restaurants. Use of restrooms is free in Japan, and though public facilities supply toilet paper, it's a good idea to **carry a packet of tissues.** In parks and some restaurants in rural areas, don't be surprised if you go into a restroom and find men's urinals and private stalls in the same room. Women are supposed to walk past the urinals without noticing them.

Many toilets in Japan, especially those at train stations, are **Japanese-style toilets:** They're holes in the ground over which you squat facing forward toward the end with a raised hood. Men stand and aim for the hole. Although Japanese lavatories may seem uncomfortable at first, they're actually more sanitary because no part of your body touches anything.

Western-style toilets in Japan are usually very high-tech. Called **Washlets,** these combination bidet/toilets have heated toilet seats, buttons and knobs directing sprays of water of various intensities to various body parts, blow dryers, and even lids that raise when you open the stall. But alas, instructions are usually in Japanese only. Listen to the voice of experience: Don't stand up until you've figured out how to turn the darn spray off.

Visas   For most foreign tourists, including Americans, Canadians, Australians, New Zealanders, and citizens of the United Kingdom, visas are not required. Americans, Australians, Canadians, and New Zealanders can stay for 90 days without a visa. United Kingdom citizens can stay up to 6 months without a visa but must apply for an extension before the first 90 days are up.

Visitor Information
The **Japan National Tourism Organization (JNTO)** is the best source for travel information on Japan. You can reach JNTO via the Internet at **www.jnto.go.jp** (and at **www.japantravel info.com** for North American travelers; **www.see japan.co.uk** for British travelers; and **www.jnto.org.au** for Australian travelers), where you can read up on what's new, view maps, get the latest weather report, find links to online hotel reservation companies and tour companies, and browse through information ranging from hints on budget travel to regional events.

Water   The water is safe to drink anywhere in Japan, although some people claim it's too highly chlorinated. Bottled water is also readily available.

Index

See also Accommodations and Restaurant indexes, below.

General Index

A

The Access Narita, 55
Accommodations, 35–36
  best hotels and inns, 3
  business hotels, 36
  capsule hotels, 37
  Hiroshima, 309–311
  Japanese-style inns, 31–35
  Kanazawa, 180–182
  Koyasan, 293–295
  Kurashiki, 300–302
  Kyoto, 210–226
    Central Kyoto, 216–222
    Eastern Kyoto, 222–224
    around Kyoto Station, 211–216
    Northern and Western Kyoto, 224–226
    rates, 211
    taxes and service charges, 211
  love hotels, 37
  Miyajima, 319–320
  Nikko, 167–169
  Osaka, 271–273
  Takayama, 197–199
  tips on, 31–37
  Tokyo, 71–86
    Aoyama & Akasaka, 81–83
    Asakusa, 77–78
    double beds or twin beds, 74
    Ginza, 72–76
    prices, 72, 73
    Roppongi, 83–84
    Shibuya, 84
    Shinjuku, 80–81
    taxes and service charges, 72
    Tokyo Station, 76–77
    Ueno, 78–80
  Western-style, 35–37
Ace Cafe (Kyoto), 262
Addresses, 60
Advocates Café (Tokyo), 154
Airport Limousine Bus, 54, 55
Air travel, 52–56, 324
  Kyoto, 204
  Osaka, 264–265
Akasaka (Tokyo)
  accommodations, 81–83
  restaurant, 105
Akihabara (Tokyo), 62, 138
  shopping, 133–134
Albatross, 151
AMDA International Medical Information Center (Tokyo), 69
America-Mura (Osaka), 281

Ameya Yokocho (Ameyoko, Ameyokocho or Ameyacho), 141–142
Amida (Kamakura), 159
Amuse Museum (Tokyo), 113
Anime, shopping for (Tokyo), 133–134
AnimeJapan, 40
Antique Mall Ginza (Tokyo), 134–135
Antiques and curios, Tokyo, 134–135
Ant 'n Bee (Tokyo), 152
Aoi Matsuri (Hollyhock Festival; Kyoto), 40
Aoyama (Tokyo), 63
  accommodations, 81–83
  restaurants, 96–99
  shopping, 140
  sights and attractions, 122–124
Area codes, 330
Aritsugu (Kyoto), 256
Arts, traditional, 15–18
Arty Farty (Tokyo), 154
Asakura Choso Museum (Tokyo), 115–116
Asakusa (Tokyo), 7, 62
  accommodations, 77–78
  restaurants, 90–92
  sights and attractions, 113–115
Asian Gallery (Toyokan; Tokyo), 119
@home Cafés (Tokyo), 134
ATMs/banks, 335–336
  Hiroshima, 309
  Kanazawa, 180
  Kurashiki, 300
  Kyoto, 209
  Osaka, 270
  Tokyo, 69
Autumn, 38
Autumn Festival (Takayama Matsuri), 42

B

Bar Goldfinger (Tokyo), 154
Baseball, Tokyo, 129
Bathing, 20–21
Beer, 27
Benten-kutsu Cave (Kamakura), 159
Bic Camera (Tokyo), 139
Bikan Historical Quarter (Kurashiki), 7, 300, 304–305
Biking
  Himeji, 296
  Kurashiki, 305–306
  Kyoto, 208
  tours, 132
Boat trip on the Sumida River (Tokyo), 132
Bomb Dome (Genbaku Domu; Hiroshima), 314
Bowing, 19
Breakfast, buffet, 30
Buddha's Birthday, 40
Buddhism, 10, 11
Bunraku, 16
Business hotels, 36

Business hours, 330
Bus travel, 54–56, 329
  Hakone, 171
  Himeji, 296
  Hiroshima, 308
  Kanazawa, 179–180
  Koyasan, 292
  Kurashiki, 300
  Kyoto, 205, 207–208
  Ogimachi, 191
  Osaka, 268
  Takayama, 196–197
  Tokyo, 67–68

C

Calendar of events, 39–42
Capsule hotels, 37
Captain Line (Osaka), 280
Car travel, 329–330
Cellphones, 334–335
Cenotaph for Korean Victims (Hiroshima), 315
Cenotaph for the A-bomb Victims (Hiroshima), 315
Cherry blossoms, 6
Chicago (Kyoto), 257
Chicago (Tokyo), 140
Children's Day, 40
Children's Peace Monument (Hiroshima), 314–315
Children's Shrine-Visiting Day (Shichi-go-san), 42
Chion-ji market (Kyoto), 259
Chion-ji Temple (Kyoto), 259
Chokoku-no-Mori Bijutsukan (Hakone Open-Air Museum), 173
Chopsticks, 28
Chubu District (Tokyo), 45, 177
Chugoku region, 45, 299–322
Chuguji Temple (Nara), 289
Chuo Line (Tokyo), 66
Cinquecento (Osaka), 282
City Hall (Kyoto), 259
Coming-of-Age Day, 39
Comme des Garçons (Tokyo), 140
Cooking classes, Kyoto, 236
Crafts and traditional Japanese products, Tokyo, 135–136
Crocodile (Tokyo), 149
Currency and currency exchange, 69, 335
Customs regulations, 330–331

D

Daibutsuden (Nara), 287
Daimaru (Kyoto), 258
Daimonji Bonfire (Kyoto), 42
Daimyo, 12, 13, 32
Daimyo Gyoretsu (Feudal Lord Procession; Hakone), 42
Daisho-in Temple (Miyajima), 322
Daiso (Osaka), 281
Daiso (Tokyo), 142
Den Den Town (Osaka), 281
Dentists
  Kyoto, 209
  Tokyo, 69

Restaurants

347

New York Bar, Park Hyatt

3-7-1-2 Nishi Shinjuku,
Shinjuku-ku, Tokyo